ATLANTIS

THE COLLECTION

(4 BOOKS)

THE SUBMERGED CONTINENTS OF ATLANTIS AND LEMURIA, BY RUDOLF STEINER

THE STORY OF ATLANTIS & THE LOST LEMURIA, BY W. SCOTT-ELLIOT & CHARLES LEADBEATER

ATLANTIS: THE ANTEDILUVIAN WORLD, BY IGNATIUS DONNELLY.

THE NEW ATLANTIS , BY SIR FRANCIS BACON

CONTENTS

BOOK ONE. THE SUBMERGED CONTINENTS OF ATLANTIS AND LEMURIA

Rudolf Steiner

I. FROM THE ÂKÂSHIC RECORDS

It is but a small part of prehistoric human experience which can be learnt by the methods of ordinary history. Historic evidence throws light on only a few thousand years; and even what archaeology, palæontology, and geology can teach us is very limited. Added to this limitation is the untrustworthiness which attaches to everything based upon external evidence. We need only consider how the presentation of some event, even if comparatively recent, or connected with a nation, is totally transformed on the discovery of new historic evidence. We need but compare the descriptions given by different historians of one and the same thing in order to realise at once how insecure is the ground on which we stand. Everything belonging to the outer world of sense is subject to time, and time destroys what in time arises. Now, external history depends on what has been preserved to us in time; and no one, dependent only on external evidence, can even say whether that which has been preserved is true.

But everything which arises in time has its origin in the Eternal; and although the Eternal is not accessible to sense-perception, the paths that lead to a perception of the Eternal are available to man. He can so develop the forces that slumber within him as to be able to know this Eternal. In the articles on "How to Attain Knowledge of the Higher Worlds," which have appeared under the title *The Way of Initiation*, by Rudolf Steiner, Ph.D., with some Biographical Notes of the Author by Edouard Schuré and *Initiation and its Results*, [A sequel to the above.] the method of this training is indicated. In these two books it has been shown that at a certain high stage of knowledge man can even penetrate to the everlasting sources that underlie the passing things of time. (Let the reader here have patience; these matters can only be dealt with by degrees.) If a man in the way described has developed his power to know, then, as regards knowledge of the past, he is no longer restricted entirely to outer evidence. Then he can behold that which in the happening is imperceptible to the senses, that which no time can destroy. He presses on from evanescent history to that which does not pass away. It is true that this history is written in other than the ordinary characters, and in the Gnosis, in Theosophy, is called "The

Âkâshic Records." Only a feeble picture of these records can be given in our language, for it is adapted to the uses of the world of sense, and what we name with it receives at once the character of that world. Thus the narrator might give to the uninitiated, to one who cannot yet from his own experience convince himself of the actuality of a distinct spiritual world, the impression of being a mere visionary, if indeed not something worse.

He who has won for himself the power to observe in the spiritual world, there recognises bygone events in their eternal character. They stand before him, not as dead witnesses of history, but in the fullness of life. In a certain sense, the past events are played out before him. Those who have learnt to read such a living script can look back into a far more distant past than that which external history depicts; and they can also, by direct spiritual perception, describe those matters which history relates in a far more trustworthy manner than is possible by the latter. In order to avoid a possible error, let it here be at once understood that even mental vision is not infallible. Such perception may also be deceived; it may be inaccurate, crooked, topsy-turvy. Even in this domain nobody, however exalted, is necessarily free from error; therefore no one need take exception if communications that spring from such spiritual sources are not always in full accord. But the trustworthiness of such observations is certainly far greater here than in the outer world of sense; and those communications which, bearing on history and prehistoric times, can be given out by the various Initiates, agree in their essence. In all mystic schools there actually exists such history and pre-history, and such absolute agreement has reigned here for thousands of years that it is impossible to compare it with the agreement existing among ordinary historians even for a century. Initiates describe at all times and in all places essentially the same thing.

After these preliminary remarks, several chapters of the Âkâshic Records will be repeated here. At the outset those facts will be described which occurred during the existence of the so-called continent of Atlantis, which lay between America and Europe. This part of the surface of our earth was at one time land. To-day it is this land which forms the bottom of the Atlantic Ocean. Plato still told of the last remnant of this land — the Island of Poseidonis — lying to the west of Europe and Africa.

In the little book, *The Story of Atlantis*, by W. Scott-Elliot, the reader will learn that the bottom of the Atlantic Ocean was once a continent; that for about 1,000,000 years it was the scene of a civilisation certainly very different from ours of to-day; and that the last remnant of this continent was submerged nearly 10,000 years B.C. Details completing those given in that book, and bearing on this hoary civilisation, will be given here. While the outward events of the life of these our Atlantean forefathers are more conspicuously the subject of description in the above work, something will here be said of the soul-life, and of the inner nature of the conditions under which they lived. The reader must therefore go back in thought to a period lying more than 10,000 years behind us, and to a civilisation which had existed for many thousands of years. What is here related, however, took place not only on the continent submerged by the waters of the Atlantic Ocean, but also in the neighbouring regions that now form Asia, Africa, Europe, and America; and what subsequently happened in these regions was evolved out of that earlier civilisation. As to the sources of the information to be given here, I am for the present obliged to be silent. He who knows anything at all about such sources will understand why this must be so; but circumstances may arise which will make it possible to speak on this subject very shortly. How much of the knowledge lying hidden in the womb of the Theosophical movement may gradually be communicated, depends altogether on the attitude of our contemporaries. And now follows the first of the documents which are here to be reproduced.

II. OUR ATLANTEAN FOREFATHERS

OUR Atlantean ancestors differed more from the men of to-day than may be imagined by anyone who is wholly limited to the world of sense for his knowledge. This difference extends not only to the outward appearance, but also to mental capacities. Their science and also their technical arts, their whole civilisation, differed much from that of our day. If we go back to the early times of Atlantean humanity we shall find there a mental capacity altogether different from our own. Logical reasoning, the calculatory combinations upon which all that is produced at the present day is based, were entirely wanting in the early Atlanteans, but in place of these they possessed a highly-developed memory. This memory was one of their most prominent mental faculties. For example, they did not count as we do by the application of certain acquired rules. A multiplication table was something absolutely unknown in early Atlantean times. No one had impressed upon his understanding the fact that three times four were twelve. A person's ability to make such a calculation, when necessary, rested on the fact that he could remember cases of the same or a similar kind. He remembered how this was done on former occasions. Now it must be clearly understood that whenever a new faculty is developed in a being, an old one loses its force and precision. The man of the present day has the advantage over the Atlantean of possessing a logical understanding and an aptitude for combination; but on the other hand his memory power has waned. We now think in ideas, the Atlantean thought in pictures; and when a picture rose in his mind he remembered many other similar pictures which he had formerly seen, and then formed his judgment accordingly. Consequently all education then was quite different from that of later times. It was not intended to provide the child with rules or to sharpen his wits. Rather was life presented to him in comprehensive pictures, so that subsequently he could call to remembrance as much as possible, when dealing with this or that circumstance. When the child had grown up and had reached maturity, he could remember, no matter what he might have to do, that something similar had been shown to him in the days of his instruction. He saw clearly how to act when the new event resembled something already seen. When absolutely new conditions arose, the Atlantean found himself compelled to experiment; while the man of to-day is spared much in this direction, being furnished with a set of rules which he can easily apply in circumstances new to him. Such a system of education gave a strong uniformity to the entire life. Things were done again and again in exactly the same way during very long periods of time. The faithfulness of memory offered no scope for anything at all approaching the rapidity of our own progress. A man did what he had always seen done before; he did not think, he remembered. Not he who had learnt much was held as an authority, but he who had experienced a great deal and could therefore remember much. It would have been impossible in Atlantean times for anyone who had not reached a certain age to be called upon to decide on any affair of importance. Confidence was placed only in one who could look back on a long experience.

What is here said does not refer to Initiates and their schools, for *they* indeed are beyond the average development of their time. And for admission into such schools, *age* is not the deciding factor, but rather the consideration, whether the candidate in his former incarnations has acquired the ability to assimilate the higher wisdom. The confidence placed in Initiates and their agents in Atlantean times was not based on the extent of their personal experience, but on the age of their wisdom. For an Initiate, his own personality has ceased to have any importance; he is entirely at the service of the Eternal Wisdom, and therefore the characteristics of any period of time have no weight with him.

Thus, while the power of logical thinking was still wanting, especially in the earlier Atlanteans, they possessed in their highly developed power of memory something which gave a special character to their whole activity. But other powers are always bound up with the nature of one special human force. Memory is nearer to the deeper foundations laid by Nature in man than is the power of reason; and in connection with the former, other impulses were developed which bore greater resemblance to those lower nature forces than the motive forces of human action at the present day. Thus the Atlantean was master of what is called the Life-Force. Just as we now draw from coal the force of warmth, which is changed into the force of propulsion in our methods of traffic, so did the Atlanteans understand how to use the germinal force of living things in the service of their technical works. An illustration of this may be given as follows: Let us think of a grain of corn; in it slumbers a force; this force acts in such a way that out of the grain of corn the stalk sprouts forth. Nature can awaken this sleeping force in the grain, but the man of to-day cannot do so at will. He must bury the grain in the earth, and leave its awakening to the forces of Nature. The Atlantean could do something more. He knew what to do in order to transform the force in a heap of corn into mechanical power, just as the man of our day can transform into a like power the force of warmth in a heap of coal. In Atlantean times plants were not cultivated merely for use as food, but also in order that the slumbering force in them might be rendered serviceable to their commerce and industry. Just as we have contrivances for transforming the latent force of coal into the power to propel our engines, so had the Atlanteans devices for heating by the use of plant-seeds in which the life-force was changed into a power applicable to technical purposes. In this way were propelled the air-ships of the Atlanteans, which soared a little above the earth. These air-ships sailed at a height rather below that of the mountains of Atlantean times, and they had steering appliances, by means of which they could be raised above these mountains.

We must picture to ourselves that with the advance of time all the conditions of our earth have greatly changed. These air-ships of the Atlanteans would be quite useless in our days. Their utility lay in the fact that at that time the atmosphere enveloping our earth was much denser than now. Whether, according to the scientific conceptions of the present day, such an increased density of the air can be easily conceived, need not concern us here. Science and logical thought can never, from their very nature, determine what is possible and what impossible. Their task is only to explain what has been proved by experience and observation. And the density of the air here spoken of is, in occult experience, as much a certainty as any given fact of the world of sense can be to-day. And just as firmly established is the fact — perhaps even more inexplicable to the physics and chemistry of our time — that in those days the *water* over the whole earth was much more *fluid* than it is now. And owing to its fluidity, water (being driven by means of the life-force in seeds) could be used by the Atlanteans

9

for technical purposes impossible to-day. On account of the densification of water, it has become impossible to set it in motion and to guide it in the same premeditated manner as was once possible. From this it is sufficiently evident that the civilisation of Atlantean times differed fundamentally from our own, and it will also be readily conceivable that the physical nature of an Atlantean was quite different from that of the contemporary man. Water when drunk by the Atlantean could be worked upon by the life-force within his own body in quite another way than is possible in the physical body of to-day. And thus it arose that the Atlantean could use his physical strength at will, quite otherwise than ourselves. He had, as it were, the means within himself of increasing physical forces when he required them for his own use. It is only possible to picture the Atlanteans correctly when one knows that they had conceptions of fatigue and the loss of strength absolutely different from our own.

An Atlantean settlement, as may be gathered from what has already been said, bore a character in no way resembling that of a modern town. But there was a much closer resemblance between it and Nature. We can only give a faint suggestion of the real picture when we say that in early Atlantean times — till about the middle of the third sub-race — a settlement resembled a garden in which the houses formed themselves out of trees whose branches were intertwined in an artistic manner. Whatever the hand of man fashioned at that time grew naturally in like manner. Man, too, felt himself entirely akin to Nature, and so it arose that his social instinct was quite different from our own. Nature is indeed the common property of all men; and whatever the Atlantean built up with Nature for its foundation, he regarded as common property, precisely as the man of to-day thinks it only natural to regard as his own private property that which his acuteness and his reason have produced.

Anyone who familiarises himself with the idea that the Atlanteans were endowed with such mental and physical powers as have been depicted, will likewise learn to understand that at still earlier periods mankind presents an aspect which but very faintly reminds us of what we are accustomed to see to-day. And not only man, but Nature which surrounds him, has also changed enormously in the course of time. [With regard to the time-periods at which the conditions shown held sway, something more will be said in the course of these communications. For the present the reader is warned not be surprised if the few figures given him in the previous chapter seem to contradict what he finds elsewhere.] The forms of plant and animal have altered; the whole of terrestrial Nature has undergone a transformation.

Regions of the earth which were formerly inhabited have been destroyed, and others have arisen.

The forefathers of the Atlanteans lived on a part of the earth which has disappeared, the principal portion of which lay to the south of what is Asia to-day. In Theosophical literature they are called Lemurians. After passing through various stages of evolution the greater number fell into decadence. They became a stunted race, whose descendants, the so-called savages, inhabit certain portions of the earth even now. Only a small number of the Lemurians were capable of advancing in their evolution, and it was from these that the Atlantean Race developed. Still later something similar occurred. The great mass of the inhabitants of Atlantis fell into decadence; and the so-called Âryans, to which race belongs the humanity of our present civilisation, sprang from a small division of these Atlanteans. According to the nomenclature of the "Secret Doctrine," *Lemurians*, *Atlanteans*, and *Âryans* are *Root-Races* of humanity. If we think of two such Root-Races preceding the Lemurian, and two following the Âryan in the future, we have altogether *seven*. The one always arises out of the other in the manner pointed out in the case of the Lemurian, Atlantean, and Âryan Races. And each Root-Race has physical and mental qualities entirely different from those of that which precedes it. While, for example, the Atlantean brought his memory and everything in connection with it to a high degree of development, the duty of the Âryan of the present is to develop thought-power and all that appertains thereto.

But each Root-Race itself must pass through different stages, and these again are always sevenfold. At the beginning of a time-period belonging to a Root-Race, its leading characteristics appear in an immature state; they gradually reach maturity, and then at last decadence. Thus, the members of a Root-Race are divided into seven sub-races. However, it must not be imagined that one sub-race immediately disappeared on the development of a new one. On the contrary, every one of them continued to exist for a long time, while others flourished beside it. Thus there are always dwellers on the earth, living side by side, but showing the most varied stages of evolution.

The first sub-race of the Atlanteans arose from a portion of the Lemurian Race which was greatly advanced and capable of further evolution. For instance, in this latter race the gift of memory showed itself only in its very earliest beginnings, and even so much did not appear until the latest stages of its evolution. It must be realised that a Lemurian could indeed make images of his experiences, but could not preserve them as recollections; he immediately forgot what he had pictured to himself. That, in spite of this, he lived to a certain extent a civilised life; for instance, that he possessed tools, erected buildings, and so on, was not due to his own imagination, but to an inner mental force which was instinctive. Yet we must not imagine an instinct similar to that which animals possess at the present time, but an instinct of another order.

The first sub-race of the Atlanteans is called in Theosophical literature the Rmoahal. The memory of this race was especially derived from vivid sense-impressions. Colours which the eye had seen, tones which the ear had heard, continued to operate long within the soul. This was manifested in the fact that the Rmoahals developed *feelings* quite unknown to their Lemurian ancestors. For instance, adherence to that which had been experienced in the past constituted part of such feelings.

Now the development of speech depended on that of memory. As long as man did not remember the past, there could be no narration of experiences by means of speech. And because the first rudiments of a memory appeared in the latest Lemurian period, it was only then possible that the ability to give names to things heard and seen could begin to appear. It is only those who have the faculty of recollection who can make any use of a *name* which has been given to an object; and consequently it was in the Atlantean period that speech found its development. And with speech a tie was formed between the human soul and things exterior to man, since he then produced the spoken word from within himself, and this spoken word appertained to the objects of the outer world. Through communication by means of speech a new bond also arose between man and man. All this, indeed, was still in an elementary form at the time of the Rmoahals; but nevertheless it distinguished them profoundly from their Lemurian ancestors.

Now the forces in the souls of these first Atlanteans still retained something of the force of Nature. Man was then in a certain manner more nearly related to the Nature-spirits surrounding him than were his descendants. Their soul forces were more Nature forces than are those of the men of the present, and so, too, the spoken word which they uttered had something of the might of Nature. Not only did they name objects, but their words contained a power over things and over their fellow-creatures. The word of the Rmoahal possessed more than mere meaning; it had also power. When we speak of the magic force of words we indicate something which was a far greater reality at that time, and for those men, than it is for men of the present. When a Rmoahal pronounced a word, this word developed a force akin to that of the object designated by it. Hence it is that words had the power of healing at that time, and that they could hasten the growth of plants, tame the rage of animals, and produce other such effects. All this force gradually faded away among the later Atlantean sub-races. It might be said that that fullness of strength which was a product of Nature wasted away little by little. The men of the Rmoahal race regarded such fullness of strength altogether as a gift from mighty Nature herself; and this relation of theirs with Nature bore for them a religious character. Speech was, to them, something especially sacred, and the misuse of certain tones in which dwelt a significant power was to them an impossibility. Every individual felt that such misuse must bring him terrible injury. The magic of such words, they thought, would change into its opposite; that which rightly used would cause a blessing would bring the author to ruin if wrongly employed. In a certain innocence of feeling the Rmoahals ascribed their power less to themselves than to Divine Nature working in them.

It was otherwise in the second sub-race (the so-called Tlavatli peoples). The men of this race began to feel their own personal value. Ambition, an unknown quality among the Rmoahals, showed itself in them. We might say that the faculty of memory grew into the comprehension of life in communities. He who could look back on certain deeds demanded from his fellow-men some recognition of his ability. He claimed that his work should be held in remembrance, and it was this memory of deeds that was the basis on which rested the election, by a group of men allied to each other, of a certain one as leader. A kind of kingship arose. Indeed, this recognition extended beyond death. The remembrance, the commemoration of forefathers, or of those who, during life, had one merit, arose in this way, and thus in single family groups there grew up a kind of religious reverence for the dead — in other words, ancestor-worship. This has continued to spread into much later times and has taken the most varied forms. Among the Rmoahals a man was still esteemed only according to the degree in which for the moment he was able to make himself valuable by the greatness of his power. Did anyone want recognition for what he had done in former days, then he must show by new deeds that he still possessed the old power. He must call to remembrance his old achievements by the performance of new ones. That which had once been done was valueless in itself. Not until the second sub-race was the personal character of a man of so much account that his past life was taken into consideration in the estimation of it.

A further result of the power of thought in drawing men to live together appeared in the fact that groups of men were formed who were united by the remembrance of deeds done in company. The forming of such groups originally depended wholly upon the forces of Nature, on their common

13

parentage. By his own intelligence man had as yet added nothing to that which Nature had made of him. One mighty personality now enlisted a great company to share in a common undertaking; and the remembrance of this work, being retained by all, built up a social group.

This manner of living together in social groups only impressed itself forcibly when the third sub-race (the Toltec) was reached. It was therefore the men of this race who first founded what may be called a commonwealth, the earliest kind of statecraft. The leadership, the government, of this commonwealth passed from ancestors to descendants. That which had formerly continued only in the memory of their fellow-men, the father now transferred to the son. The deeds of their forefathers would be kept in remembrance by the whole race. The achievements of an ancestor continued to be cherished by his descendants. However, we must clearly understand that in those times men really had the power to transfer their gifts to their offspring. Education was based upon the representation of life in comprehensive pictures, and the efficacy of this education depended on the personal force which proceeded from the teacher. It was not an intellectual power which he sought to excite, but rather those gifts which were more instinctive in character. By such a system of education the father's ability was really, in most cases, transferred to the son.

Under conditions like these, *personal experience* won for itself more and more importance in the third sub-race. When one group of human beings severed itself from another group, it brought with it for the foundation of its new community the vivid recollection of what it had experienced in its former surroundings. But all the same, these memories contained something with which they were not in sympathy, something in which they did not feel at ease. In this connection, therefore, they sought something new, and thus conditions improved with every new settlement of the kind. And it was only natural that the improved conditions should find imitators. These were the facts on which rested the foundation of those flourishing commonwealths that arose in the time of the third sub-race, and are described in Theosophical literature. The personal experiences undergone found support from those who were *initiated* into the eternal laws of mental development. Mighty rulers received initiation in order that personal ability might have its full provision. A man gradually prepares himself for initiation by his personal ability. He must first develop his forces from below upwards, so that enlightenment may then be imparted to him from above. Thus arose the King-Initiates and Leaders of the people among the Atlanteans. In their hands lay a tremendous amount of power, and great, too, was the reverence paid to them.

But in this fact lay also the cause of their fall. The development of memory led to enormous personal power. The individual began to wish for influence by means of this power of his; and the greater the power grew, the more did he desire to use it for himself. The ambition which he had developed became selfishness, and this gave rise to a misuse of forces. When we consider what the Atlanteans were able to do by their command of the life-force, we can understand that such misuse must have had tremendous consequences. An enormous power over Nature could be placed at the service of personal self-love.

And this was what happened in full measure during the period of the fourth sub-race (the original Turanians). The members belonging to this race, who were instructed in the mastery of the forces mentioned, made manifold use of these to satisfy their wayward wishes and desires. But these forces put to such a use naturally destroy one another in their action. It is as if the feet of a man wilfully moved forwards while at the same time the upper part of his body desired to go backwards.

Such destructive action could only be arrested by the cultivation of a higher force in man. This was thought-power. The effect of logical thinking is to restrain selfish personal wishes. We must seek the origin of this logical thought in the fifth sub-race (the original Semites). Men began to go beyond the simple remembrance of the past, they began to *compare* their various experiences. The faculty of judgment developed, and wishes and desires were regulated according to this discernment. Man began to calculate, to combine. He learnt to work in thoughts. Whereas formerly he had abandoned himself to every wish, he now asked himself whether, on reflection, he approved of the wish. While the men of the fourth sub-race wildly rushed after the satisfaction of their desires, those of the fifth began to hearken to the inner voice. And this inner voice had the effect of checking the desires, even if it could not crush the demands of the selfish personality.

Thus did the fifth sub-race implant within the human soul the interior impulses of action. In his own soul man must decide what to do and what to leave undone. But, while man thus gained thought-power inwardly, his command over the external forces of Nature was being lost. The forces of the mineral kingdom can be controlled only by means of this combining thought, not by the life-power. It was therefore at the cost of the mastery of the life-force that the fifth sub-race developed thought-power. But it was just by so doing that they created the germs of a further evolution of humanity. Now it is no longer possible for thought alone, working entirely within the man, and no longer able to command Nature directly, to bring about such devastating results as did the misused forces of earlier times, even if the personality, self-love, and selfishness were ever so great. Out of this fifth sub-race was chosen its most gifted portion, which outlived the destruction of the Fourth Race and formed the nucleus of the Fifth, — the Âryan race, whose task it is to bring to perfection the power of thought and all that belongs thereto.

The men of the sixth sub-race — the Akkadian — trained their thought-power still more highly than did the fifth. They distinguished themselves from the so-called original Semites by bringing into use in a wider sense the faculty mentioned. It has been said that the development of thought-power did not indeed allow the demands of the selfish personality to attain such destructive results as were possible in earlier races; but that, nevertheless, these demands were not killed out by it. The original Semites at first regulated their personal affairs as their reason suggested. In place of crude desires and lust, prudence appeared. Other conditions of life presented themselves. Whereas the races of former times inclined to recognize as their leader him whose deeds were deeply engraved in the memory, or who could look back on a life rich in recollections, such a *rôle* was now rather adjudged to the wise man; and if formerly that was considered decisive which was still fresh in the memory, so now that was regarded as best which appealed most strongly to the reason. Under the influence of thought men once clung to a thing till it was considered insufficient, and then in the latter case it came about naturally that he who had a novelty capable of supplying a want should find a hearing. A love of novelty and a longing for change were, however, developed by this thought-power. Everyone wanted to carry out what his own sagacity suggested; and thus it is that restlessness begins to appear in the fifth sub-race, leading in the sixth to the necessity of placing under general laws the capricious ideas of the single individual. The glory of the states of the third sub-race lay in the order and harmony caused by a common memory. In the sixth this order had to be obtained by deliberately constructed laws. Thus in the sixth sub-race must be sought the origin of law and legislation. And during the third sub-race the segregation of a group of human beings took place only when in a manner they were compelled to leave, because they no longer felt comfortable within the prevailing conditions, brought about by recollection. It was essentially different in the sixth. The calculating power of thought sought novelty as such; it urged men to enterprise and new undertakings. Thus the Akkadians were an enterprising people inclined towards colonization. It was commerce especially that fed the young and germinating power of thought and judgment.

In the seventh sub-race — the Mongolian — thought-power also developed; but in them existed qualities of the earlier sub-races, especially of the fourth, in a much greater degree than in the fifth and sixth. They remained true to their sense of memory. And so they came to the conclusion that the most ancient must also be the wisest, must be that which could best defend itself against the attack of thought. They had indeed lost the command of the life-force, but that which developed in them as thought-power had in itself something of the power of this life-force. It is true they had lost the power over life, but never the direct, instinctive belief in the existence of such a power. This force, indeed, became to them their God in Whose service they performed everything which they considered right. Thus they appeared to their neighbours to be possessed of a mystic power, and the latter yielded to it in blind faith. Their descendants in Asia and in some European regions showed, and still show, much of this peculiarity.

The power of thought implanted in man could only attain its full value in evolution when, in the Fifth Race, it acquired a new impulse. After all, the Fourth could only place this power at the service of that which had been fostered by the gift of memory. It was not until the Fifth was reached that such forms of life were attained as could find their instrument in the faculty of thought.

III. TRANSITION OF THE ATLANTEAN INTO THE ÂRYAN ROOT-RACE

THE following communications refer to the transition of the fourth (Atlantean) Root-Race into the fifth (Âryan), to which belongs civilised mankind of the present day. He only will estimate them correctly who is able to grasp the idea of evolution in its fullest meaning. Everything that comes to the notice of man in his surroundings is in a condition of development. And it must also be remembered that the peculiar characteristic of men of our fifth Root-Race, consisting in the use of *thought*, has but just been developed. Indeed, it is this Root-Race that slowly and gradually brings the power of thought to maturity. The man of the present makes up his mind and carries out his decision on the strength of his own thought. With the Atlanteans this capacity was only in preparation. Not their *own* thoughts, but those which flowed in upon them from Beings of a higher kind, influenced their will, which was thus guided, in a sense, from without. He who makes himself familiar with this conception of evolution in regard to man, and who learns to admit that he was, in prehistoric times and as an inhabitant of the earth, of an altogether different constitution, will also be able to advance to the conception of those wholly different Beings to whom reference is made in these communications. The development which is under consideration occupied enormous periods of time. Details of this will be shown more circumstantially in the following communications.

What has previously been said about the fourth Root-Race, the Atlantean, refers to the great general mass of mankind. But the latter found themselves under leaders who towered high above them in ability. The wisdom possessed by these leaders, and the powers of which they were masters, could not be obtained through any earthly education, but were imparted to them by entities of a high rank, and not pertaining directly to the earth. It was, therefore, quite natural that the great mass of mankind regarded these, their leaders, as Beings of a higher kind, as "messengers" of the gods. For that which these leaders knew and were able to achieve could not have been accomplished by means of human sense-organs or human understanding. They were worshipped as "Divine Messengers," and their precepts, commands, and instructions were accepted. By such Beings mankind was instructed in sciences, arts, and the construction of tools. And such "Divine Messengers" either directed the communities themselves, or instructed such men as were sufficiently developed in the arts of governing. These leaders were said "to hold intercourse with gods," and to be initiated by these themselves in the laws according to which mankind was to develop. And this was in accordance with fact. This initiation, this intercourse with the gods, occurred at places quite unknown to the populace. "Temples of Mysteries" was the name given to these places of initiation, and it was from their midst that mankind was governed.

That which took place in the Temples of Mysteries was, accordingly, incomprehensible to the populace, and only very slightly did the latter understand the purposes of their great leaders. The people could, indeed, understand with their senses only what happened immediately on the earth, not what was revealed from higher worlds. Consequently the teachings of the leaders had also to be clad in a form which was unlike the form used in the communication of earthly matters. The language used in the mysteries between the gods and their messengers was, indeed, no earthly tongue, nor were the forms assumed by the gods in their manifestations of an earthly kind. "In fiery clouds" did they, the higher spirits, appear to their messengers, in order to instruct them how men were to be guided. Only a man can appear in human form; entities whose faculties surpass the human level must manifest under forms which are not to be found among those of earth.

The fact that the "Messengers of the Gods" could receive the revelations was owing to their attainment of the highest degree of development among their human brothers. They had already, in earlier stages of evolution, gone through what the majority of men have yet to experience. Only in a special way did they belong to this contemporaneous mankind. They could assume the human form, but their psycho-spiritual faculties were superhuman in character. They were, therefore, divine-human, double entities. Hence they might also be described as higher spirits who had assumed human bodies, in order to help mankind further along its earthly path. Their true home was not on the earth. These entities guided man without being able to communicate to him the principles according to which they were leading him. For up to the fifth sub-race of the Atlanteans, the Original Semites, men had absolutely no capacity whatever wherewith to grasp these principles. Not till the power of thought began to develop in this sub-race did such capacity exist. But this faculty developed slowly and gradually. Even the last sub-races of the Atlanteans could as yet understand very little of the principles of their divine leaders. They began by having a very vague presentiment of such principles. Consequently, their conceptions and also the laws mentioned in connection with their civic institutions were intuitive rather than definitely thought out.

The chief leader of the fifth Atlantean sub-race had for his object to bring it gradually to such a point that it could, later on, and after the disappearance of the Atlantean mode of living, initiate a new one, such as would be completely regulated by the power of thought.

Now we must realise that the end of the Atlantean era is characterized by these groups of human entities. There are, firstly, the so-called "Messengers of the Gods," who were advanced far beyond the great mass of people, teaching Divine Wisdom and performing divine deeds. Secondly, there was the great mass itself, in which the power of thought was in a state of torpor, although it possessed other natural faculties which have since been lost. Thirdly, there was a smaller number of such as developed the thinking capacity. These, it is true, gradually lost the primeval faculties of the Atlanteans; but they developed instead the capacity to grasp in thought the principles of the "Messengers of the Gods." The second group of human entities was destined to die out gradually. The third, however, admitted of such an education by the entities of the first group that it could henceforward take over its own guidance.

From the midst of this third group selection was made by the aforesaid chief leader (who is known in Theosophical literature by the name of the Manu) of those most capable of forming the nucleus of a new mankind.

These fittest people were to be found in the fifth sub-race. The thought-power of the sixth and seventh sub-races was in a certain way already on the downward path, and no longer fit for further development. The best qualities of the best men were to be developed. This was achieved by the leader sequestering the elect in a particular spot of the earth — in Central Asia — and freeing them from every influence of those left behind or gone astray. The task undertaken by the leader was to conduct his disciples so far on that they could grasp in their own souls and through their own thought the principles according to which they were previously directed and which they faintly understood. Men were now meant to understand the divine powers which they had formerly followed blindly. So far, the gods had led men through their messengers; henceforth men should *know* of these divine Beings. They were to consider themselves as the executive organs of divine Providence.

This isolated group had to face an important change. The divine leader was in their midst in human form. From such divine messengers mankind had previously received directions or commands as to what was to be done or left undone. It had been taught in sciences which referred to what could be observed by the senses. Men suspected the fact of a divine government of the world, they felt as much in their own actions, but they had no clear knowledge of this fact. Their leader now spoke to them quite differently. He taught them that invisible powers governed what was visibly before them; and that they themselves were servants of these invisible powers; that, with their thoughts, they had to execute the laws of these powers; and that the invisible spiritual element was the Creator and Preserver of the visible material world. Hitherto they had looked up to their visible messengers of the gods, to those superhuman Initiates of whom he who talked to them thus was himself one, and by whom they were directed as to what to do or to avoid. Now however they were found worthy of being instructed by the divine messenger of the gods. Powerful was the injunction impressed again and again on his followers: "Hitherto ye have seen those who were your leaders, but there are higher Leaders whom ye see not, and ye are subject to these Leaders. Fulfil the commands of the God whom ye see not, and obey Him of whom ye can make to yourselves no image." Thus sounded, from the lips of the great Leader, the new and highest commandment, prescribing the worship of a God whom no image, visible to the senses, could resemble, of whom, therefore, none such should be made. An echo of this great primary commandment of the fifth race is heard in the well-known phrase: "Thou shalt have no other gods before me. Thou shalt not make unto thee any graven image, or any likeness of any thing that is in

20

heaven above, or that is in the earth beneath, or that is in the water under the earth." (**Exodus, chapter xx, 3 and 4.**)

Assisting the chief leader (Manu), there were other messengers of the gods who executed his designs with regard to particular branches of life, and helped in the development of the new race. For the object was to arrange the whole of life conformably with the new conception of a divine government of the world. The thoughts of men were to be turned in every respect from the visible to the invisible. Life is determined by natural forces. The course of this human life depends on day and night, winter and summer, sunshine and rain. How these momentous visible facts are connected with the invisible (divine) forces, and how man should act so as to live in accordance with these invisible powers — all this was shown to him. All knowledge and all work were to be pursued in this sense. In the course of the stars and in atmospheric conditions, man was to see the decrees of Providence, the expression of divine Wisdom. Astronomy and meteorology were taught in this sense. And man was to bring his work, his moral life, into harmony with the laws of the divine, that are so rich in wisdom. Life was ordered according to divine commandments, since in the course of the stars, in meteorological conditions, etc., divine thoughts were fathomed. Man was to bring his works into harmony with dispositions of the gods through sacrificial deeds.

It was the intention of the Manu to direct everything in human life towards the higher worlds. All human action, all arrangements were to bear a religious character. In this way the Manu wished to lead the way to that which constitutes the special task of the fifth Root-Race. This Race was to learn to guide itself onward through its own thoughts. Such self-determination, however, can lead to salvation only when man gives his own self also to the service of the higher powers. Man should make use of his thinking capacity; but this power of thought should be uplifted by mindfulness of the Divine.

To grasp completely what happened at that time, it is also necessary to know that the development of the thinking capacity, beginning with the fifth sub-race of the Atlanteans, brought about a still further consequence. In a certain direction men acquired branches of knowledge and performed acts which were in no immediate connection with what the Manu had to consider as his proper task. These acquirements and arts lacked, first of all, the religious character. They dawned on man at a time when his only thought was to exploit them for his own advantage, for his personal wants. — To such acquirements belongs, for instance, that of Fire in its application to human industry. At the beginning of the Atlantean era man had no need of fire, as the vital force was still at his disposal. With this decrease of his ability to avail himself of this force, he was obliged to learn how to fashion his tools and implements from so-called lifeless things. Here the use of fire became most advantageous, and it was the same with regard to other natural forces. Man had also learned to make use of these forces without being conscious of their divine origin. This, indeed, was inevitable. Man was not to be *forced* to link these things, which assisted his own mentality, with the divine order of things. This he was rather meant to do voluntarily in his thoughts. The intention of the Manu was, then, to evoke in men a spontaneous need to establish a connection between such things and the higher order of the world. Men could, as it were, choose whether they would exploit the acquired knowledge for purely personal benefit, or use it in the religious service of a higher world. Just as man had previously been forced to consider himself as a part of the divine ruling of the world, from which there flowed in on him, for instance, the mastery of the vital force without any need of mental effort, so now he could also make use of natural forces without giving thought to the divine. Of those whom the Manu had gathered round himself, all were not ripe for the change. Indeed, very few of them were so. And only from these could the nucleus of the new race be actually formed by the Manu. It was, then, only with this small number that the Manu retired, in order to further their development, while the rest became merged in the general mass of mankind. It was then from this small number of men, thus finally grouped round the Manu, that all the true germs of progress in the fifth Root-Race up to the present time were derived. Thus, however, it becomes plain that the whole development of this fifth Root-Race displays two characteristic features. One of these distinguishes those who are animated by higher ideals, and who consider themselves as children of a divine universal power; the other appears in those who make everything subservient only to personal interests, to selfish ends.

This little band remained with the Manu until it had become strong enough to act in the new spirit, and until its members could set forth to impart this new spirit to that portion of mankind which remained over from the preceding races. This new spirit naturally assumed a different character with various nations, according to the different phases of their development. The old surviving characteristics became mixed with what the messengers of the Manu brought into the various parts of the world, and in this way manifold new cultures and civilizations arose.

The fittest personalities of those surrounding the Manu were chosen to become initiated little by little into his divine wisdom, so that they might become teachers to the rest. Thus it was that along with the old messengers of the gods there now arose a new kind of Initiates. These were they who developed their mentality in exactly the same manner as the rest of their fellow-men. The divine messengers of old — and the Manu — had not done so. Their development belongs to higher worlds. They brought their higher wisdom into earthly relations. What they gave to mankind was "a gift from on high." Before the middle of the Atlantean era men were not advanced far enough to grasp with their own faculties the import of divine decrees. Now, in the period indicated, they were to reach this stage. Their earthly thought was to rise to the conception of the divine. Human Initiates united themselves with those who were superhuman. This signifies an important change in the development of humanity. The first Atlanteans had not yet the choice of viewing their leaders as divine messengers, or of not doing so. For what these accomplished appeared, perforce, as a deed of the higher worlds. A divine origin was stamped on it. On account of their power, the divine messengers of the Atlantean era were therefore sanctified Beings, surrounded by the lustre conferred on them by this power. The human Initiates of the subsequent era, if considered externally, are men among men. To be sure, they remained in touch with the higher worlds, receptive of the revelations and appearances of the messengers of the gods. Only on exceptional occasions, in the case of a higher necessity, they made use of certain powers, conferred on them from that source. Then did they perform feats which men failed to interpret in terms of the known laws and therefore rightly viewed as miracles. Nevertheless it is the higher purpose of all this to place men on their own feet, to develop perfectly their mentality. The human Initiates are now the mediators between the people and the higher powers; and Initiation alone qualifies one for intercourse with the messengers of the gods.

The human Initiates, the holy teachers, became, then, in the beginning of the fifth Root-Race, the leaders of the rest of mankind. The great priest-kings of prehistoric times — attested to, if not historically, at least mythologically — belong to this class of Initiates. The higher messengers of the gods gradually withdrew from this earth, handing over the leadership to these human Initiates, but still assisting them by deed and word. Were this not so, man would not attain to a free use of his mentality. The world stands under divine guidance; but man should not be forced to acknowledge this fact, but should do so in consequence of the free exercise of his mental capacity. Only when he has attained to this do the Initiates gradually unveil to him their secrets. But this cannot be attained suddenly. Rather is the whole development of the fifth Root-Race a slow path to this goal. At first the Manu himself still led his flock like children, but afterwards the leadership was gradually transferred to human Initiates. And, to-day, the progress still continues to consist in a mingling of conscious and unconscious acting and thinking on the part of men. Only at the end of the fifth Root-Race, when, after the progress made in the course of the sixth and seventh sub-races, a sufficiently large number of men will be ready to receive knowledge, the greatest Initiate will be able to reveal himself to them publicly. And this human Initiate will then be able to take over the further general leadership, just as the Manu had done at the end of the fourth Root-Race. The education of the fifth Root-Race has therefore as its aim the production of a larger portion of mankind who shall attain so far as to follow freely a human Manu, just as was done by the nucleus of this fifth race with regard to the divine Manu.

IV. THE LEMURIAN ERA

THE following contains a fragment from the Âkâshic Records which refers to a very remote prehistoric epoch in the development of mankind. This epoch precedes that which has been delineated in the previous chapters. The subject is the third human Root-Race, which in Theosophical books is said to have dwelt on the Lemurian continent. This continent lay — according to these books — in the south of Asia, but extended roughly from Ceylon to Madagascar. Also the modern southern Asia and parts of Africa belonged to it. Although in the reading of the Âkâshic Records all possible precaution has been observed, it must nevertheless be emphasized that in no case must a dogmatic character be claimed for these communications. Merely to read of things and happenings so far removed from the present is by no means easy, but a translation of what has been seen and deciphered into the language of our time entails almost insuperable obstacles. Dates will be given later. They will be better grasped when we have given an account of the whole Lemurian era, and also of that which embraces the fifth Root-Race up to the present time. The things which are here communicated are surprising even to the occultist when he reads them for the first time — although the word "surprise" does not quite suit the case. This, however, is why he is allowed to communicate them only after a most careful examination.

* * *

The fourth (Atlantean) Root-Race was preceded by the so-called *Lemurian*. In the course of its development the earth and mankind underwent transformations of the greatest significance. Nevertheless, something will first be said about the character of this Root-Race subsequently to these transformations, a delineation of which will follow.

24

This Root-Race as a whole had not yet developed memory. Men were able, it is true, to form conceptions of things and events; but these conceptions did not remain in the memory, and in consequence men did not possess language in its true sense. What they could produce in this connection were rather natural sounds which expressed their sensations of pleasure, joy, pain, and so on, but which did not designate external things. Their mental conceptions, however, had quite a different power from those of later men. They influenced their surroundings by means of this power. Other men, animals, plants, and even inanimate objects could feel this action and were worked upon by mere mind-images. Thus the Lemurian could communicate with his fellow-men without the need of speech. This intercourse consisted in a kind of "thought-reading." The power of his conceptions was derived by the Lemurian immediately from the things that surrounded him. It flowed on him from the power of growth in plants, from the vital energy in animals. Thus did he understand plants and animals in their inner working and life. Indeed, he thus understood even the physical and chemical forces of inanimate things. In building anything, he did not need first to calculate the bearing-capacity of a trunk or the weight of a block of stone: he could see how much the trunk could bear, how the block would settle through its weight. The Lemurian built in this way without any art of engineering, but with the certainty of a kind of instinct working out as imagination. And withal he had his body under great control. If necessary he could steel his arm through a mere effort of will. Consequently he could, for instance, raise enormous burdens. Just as the Atlantean disposed of the vital energy, so the Lemurian was master of his will. He was — let not the expression be misunderstood — a born magician in all spheres of the lower human activities.

The main object, too, of the Lemurians was to develop the will and the power of conception. This was the ruling motive in the education of children. Boys were hardened in the most energetic manner. They had to learn to face dangers, to overcome pain, to perform daring deeds. Those who could not bear tortures or face dangers were not considered useful members of society, but were allowed to perish in the course of their hardships. What the Âkâshic Records show in regard to this method of rearing children surpasses all that present-day man can picture to himself in his wildest fancy. The endurance of heat up to scorching point, and the piercing of the body with sharp points, were quite common occurrences. — The training of girls was different. It is true that hardening was also their lot, but the chief aim lay here in the development of a powerful imagination. For instance, girls were exposed to a storm that they might feel its terrible beauty with calmness; they had to witness fights between men fearlessly, feeling only admiration for the display of strength and prowess. A disposition to dreaming, to revelling in fancy, was in this way fostered in girls; but this disposition was exceptionally prized, and in the absence of memory there was no chance of its degeneration. These dreamy or imaginative conceptions lasted only while there was an external occasion for them. So far, then, they were well equipped for external things. They did not lose themselves in the fathomless. It was the imaginative and visionary in Nature herself that sank deep into the soul of woman.

Until the end of their era the Lemurians had no dwellings in our sense of the word. They lived in natural shelters; for instance, in caves which they modified according to their needs. At a later period they built such caves in the earth; and then they developed great skill in such building. But it must not be thought that they did not also erect artificial buildings, although these did not serve as dwellings. They originated in the earlier period from the need of giving to the things of nature a form moulded by man. Hills were remoulded so that man might find pleasure and gratification in their form. For the same reason stones were joined together, and this was done also with the aim of making them serve some useful purpose. The places where children were hardened were surrounded by walls of this kind. But ever grander and more ingenious, toward the end of this epoch, became the structures devoted to the worship of "divine Wisdom and divine Art." These edifices were in every respect different from what served, at a later stage, as temples, for they were also places of instruction and scientific study. Whoever was found fit was permitted to become initiated into the science of universal laws and the application of these laws. Whereas the Lemurian was a born magician, this talent for art and insight was here cultivated. Only those could be admitted who, through every process of hardening, had become invincible in the highest degree. That which transpired in these institutions remained the most profound secret to all but the few. Here the knowledge and mastery of natural forces was learnt by immediate perception, but this cognisance was a kind of transformation of the natural forces into the power of will in man. Thereby he could himself achieve what Nature achieves. What mankind accomplished later by means of reflection or combination was then a kind of instinctive activity. Of course, in this connection, the word "instinct" must not be used in the sense in which it is usually applied to the animal world, for the achievements of the Lemurians rank immeasurably higher than all that the animal world can produce instinctively. They far surpassed all that mankind, through memory, intellect, and imagination, has since acquired in arts and sciences. To make this more clearly understood one might call these teaching-places "High-schools of the powers of will and of the clairvoyant power of forming conceptions." From them proceeded such men as became in every respect rulers of the others. It is difficult to-day to give in words a correct conception of all these conditions, for everything on earth has since undergone a change. Nature herself and all human life were different then; and consequently human labour and the relation of man to man were quite otherwise than what is customary now.

The atmosphere was as yet much denser than later during the Atlantean era; and water was much more fluid. Also that which now forms our firm earth-crust was not yet hardened to the same extent as later. The vegetable and animal worlds were advanced only to the stage of amphibious animals, of birds and the lower mammals, and of growths analogous to our palms and similar trees. But all forms were different from those of the present. What is now found small in size was then developed to gigantic proportions. Our small ferns were then trees which formed mighty forests. The higher mammals of to-day were not in existence at that time. On the other hand, a great portion of mankind was at so low a stage of development that it must be described as altogether animal. In fact, the foregoing description of men applies only to a small number. The remainder lived on the animal level. Indeed, these animal-men were, in their external form, and in their mode of living, altogether different from that small number. They hardly differed from the lower mammals, whom in a way they also resembled in form.

A few words must also be added as to the significance of the places of worship previously mentioned. It was not exactly religion that was fostered there. It was "divine Wisdom and Art." Man felt what was given him there to be a direct gift from the spiritual world-powers, and when he shared in this gift he looked upon himself as a "servant" of these universal powers. He felt himself "consecrated" in opposition to all that was unholy. If one would speak of religion at this stage of mankind, one might call it "religion of the will." Religious feeling and consecration lay in this, that a man guarded the powers conferred on him as a "secret" deep and divine, and that he led such a life as sanctified his power. Very great were the awe and reverence with which persons possessed of such powers were regarded by others; nor was this enjoined by laws or in any other way, but was the result of the direct power exercised by such men. One who was not initiated found himself quite naturally under the magical influence of the Initiates, and as a matter of course the latter considered themselves consecrated persons. For in their temples they were in a true sense partakers in the working of natural forces. They gazed into the creative laboratory of Nature. What they experienced was intercourse with the Beings who work at the building of the world itself. This may be called an intercourse with the gods, and what developed later as "Initiation" or "Mysteries" sprang from this original mode of intercourse between men and the gods. In later times this intercourse was bound to undergo a transformation, because the human conception, the human spirit, assumed other forms.

Special importance attaches to one point connected with the progress of the Lemurian development, in consequence of the mode of life which was pursued by the women. They developed, by this way of living, special human powers. The unity of their imaginative power with Nature became the basis of a higher development of the imaginative life. Through their senses they drew into themselves the forces of Nature, and allowed these to react on their souls. Thus were the germs of memory formed. And with memory there entered into the world the capacity to form the first and very simplest of moral conceptions. The culture of the will in the masculine element brought, at the outset, no development of the mind. Man followed instinctively either natural impulses or influences emanating from the Initiates. Womankind gave birth to the first conceptions of "good and evil." Here they began on the one hand to love that which made a special impression on their imaginative life, and on the other hand to hate its opposite. While the rule exercised by the masculine element was directed more to the external effect of the powers of will, to the management of natural powers, in the feminine element there arose at the same time an impulse through the feelings, through the inner personal human powers. He only can comprehend the development of mankind correctly who realizes that the first steps forward in the sphere of imagination were made by women. The development of habits dependent on the meditative, imaginative life, on the cultivation of memory which formed the nucleus of a life of order, of a sort of moral life, came from this side. Whereas man perceived and employed natural forces, woman became the first *interpreter* of these. It was a new and special mode of life that here arose — that of Thought. This mode had something far more personal than that of men. Now we must understand that this feminine mode was itself really a kind of clairvoyance, even though it differed from the magic of the will on the part of man. Woman was, in her soul, responsive to another kind of spiritual power, — to such as appealed more to the element of feeling, and less to the spiritual element to which man was subjected. There emanated thus from men an influence which was more naturally divine, from women one that was more psychically divine.

V. WOMAN IN THE THIRD ROOT-RACE

THE development undergone by woman during the Lemurian era qualified her for an important *rôle* on the earth in connection with the beginning of the next Atlantean Root-Race. This was ushered in under the influence of highly developed entities who were acquainted with the laws of the moulding of races, and who were capable of turning the existing forces of human nature into such courses as led to the formation of a new race. Later on, a special reference will be made to these entities. For the present suffice it to say that superhuman wisdom and power were immanent in them. They separated a small number of the Lemurian men and appointed them to become the progenitors of the subsequent Atlantean Race. The place chosen lay in the torrid zone. The men of this little clan attained, under their guidance, the mastery of Nature's forces. They were full of energy, and knew how to wrest from Nature treasures of many kinds. They knew how to cultivate fields and how to utilize their fruits. Through the training to which they had been subjected (compare previous chapter), they had become men of strong will. It was in woman, however, that the mind and the soul were developed, for it was in her that memory and imagination, and all connected therewith, were found to have been already fostered.

The leaders to whom reference has been made brought about an arrangement of the little flock into small groups, and to woman they entrusted the ordering and arranging of these groups. Women had acquired, by means of their memory, the faculty of utilizing for the future all the experiences that they had once known. That which had proved valuable yesterday was turned by them to present advantage; and they were clearly aware that it would likewise be useful to-morrow. The arrangements of the communal life came thus from women. Under their influence the notions of "good and evil" were developed. Through their reflective life they had acquired an understanding of Nature. Out of their observations of Nature grew the ideas according to which they guided the actions of men. The leaders arranged things in such wise that the will-power and superabundant energy of men were ennobled and purified by the "soul" in woman. Of course, all this is to be considered as at an elementary stage. The words of our languages are too apt to suggest ideas derived from contemporary life.

Indirectly, through the awakened psychical life of women, did the leaders develop that of the men. In the above-mentioned colony, the influence of women was therefore very great. They were consulted whenever it was desired to interpret the signs of Nature. The whole mode of their psychic life was, however, still such that it was ruled by the "secret" psychic powers of men. To give an approximate, if not quite adequate, conception of this state, one might speak of a somnambulistic perception on the part of these women. The secrets of Nature were revealed to them, and the impulses of their actions were imparted in a kind of higher dream-state. Everything to them was the expression of spiritual powers, and appeared in the form of psychic faculties and visions. They abandoned themselves to the mystic working of their psychic powers. They were prompted to their actions by "inner voices" or by that which was told them by plants, animals, and stones, the wind and the clouds, or the rustling of the trees.

From soul-conditions of such a kind arose that which may be called human religion. The psychic element in Nature and in human life came gradually to be reverenced and worshipped. Some women attained to special predominance, because they were able to interpret from certain mysterious depths the phenomena of the world. So it came to pass that with these women that which was within them transposed itself into a kind of Nature-speech. For the beginning of speech lies in something akin to song. The power of thought converted itself into that of audible sound. The inner rhythm of Nature resounded through the life of "wise" women. People gathered round such women, and their song-like utterances were felt as the expression of higher powers. Thus did divine worship take its inception among men. It would be an error to consider that there was any "sense" in the spoken word at that time. Only the sound, tone, and rhythm were felt. No one had any aim other than that of drawing strength into the soul from what was heard. The whole procedure was under the guidance of the higher leaders. They had inspired the "wise" priestesses with tones and rhythms in a manner which cannot be described here, and it was thus that women were able to affect the souls of men in such a way as to ennoble them. It may be said that it was altogether in this manner that the true soul-life was awakened.

The Âkâshic Records reveal what are in this respect scenes of much beauty. One of these shall be described. We are in a wood close to a gigantic tree. The sun has just risen in the east. Mighty are the shadows thrown by the palm-like tree across the cleared space round it. With her face to the east, and in a state of exaltation, we discern a priestess on a seat prepared of curious natural objects and plants. Slowly and in a rhythmic cadence flow from her lips certain wondrous sounds which are repeated again and again. Ranged in large circles, a number of men and women sit round her with dreamy faces, absorbing inner life from the sounds. Still other scenes may be witnessed. At another place, arranged in like manner, a priestess chants in a similar way, but her tones have in them something more mighty, more powerful, and the men around her move in rhythmic dances. For this was the other method by means of which the "soul" entered mankind. The mysterious rhythms which man had caught from Nature were imitated in the movements of his own limbs. Thus was it that man felt himself at one with Nature and with the Powers that ruled her.

The part of the earth on which was reared the germ of the coming human race was particularly adapted for this purpose. It was situated where the still agitated and stormy earth had more or less settled down. For Lemuria was greatly troubled by storms. The earth had not then reached its later density. The thin soil was everywhere undermined by volcanic forces bursting forth in smaller or greater streams. Mighty volcanoes were found nearly everywhere, and continually exercised a devastating activity. In all their arrangements men were accustomed to take this fiery agency into consideration. They even turned the fire to advantage in respect of their works and enterprises. The state of things was such that this natural fire could be turned to account in human labour just as is the case to-day with artificial fire. It was the activity of volcanic fire that also brought about the ruin of the Lemurian continent. The portion of Lemuria in which the Root-Race of the Atlanteans was to appear had, it is true, a hot climate, but nevertheless it was exempt, on the whole, from subjection to volcanic agency. Human nature could develop itself here more calmly and peacefully. The more nomadic life of former times was abandoned, and fixed settlements increased in number.

One has to remember that the human body was at this time still very plastic and flexible. It was still in a state of formation, in keeping with man's inner changes. At a recent era, for instance, men were still quite different as to their external appearance. The external influence of the country and of the climate continued to affect their form. But in the specified colony the body became increasingly an expression of the inner psychic life. This colony contained at the same time a species of men who were advanced, and of a finer external form. It should be said that the true human form was created by what had been clone by the leaders. The work was certainly very slow and gradual, but the progress began with the unfolding of the psychic life in man; and the still soft and plastic body adapted itself accordingly. It is a law of human development that the transforming influence of man on his physical body decreases with progress. Indeed, that physical body only acquired a fairly firm form through the development of intellectual power, and contemporaneously with the solidification of the stony, mineral and metallic formations of the earth, which were connected with this development. For in the Lemurian, and even in the Atlantean era also, stones and metals were far softer than they afterwards became. This is not in contradiction with the fact that there still exist descendants of the last Lemurians and Atlanteans who even now display forms no less solid than those of the later human races. These remainders had to adapt themselves to the altered conditions surrounding them, and consequently became more rigid. This is precisely the cause of their gradual extinction. They did not mould themselves from within, but their less developed inner nature was forced from without into rigidity and thereby brought to a standstill. And this standstill is truly a retrogression, for even the inner life deteriorated because it could not live itself out in the solidified external body.

Animal life displayed a still greater capacity for change. (Reference will be made later on to the kinds of animals present at the time of the earliest races, both as to their origin and also as to the appearance of new forms of animals during the subsequent history of men. Suffice it here to say that the existing animal species were in a state of constant transformation, and that new species continued to arise.) This transformation was naturally gradual. The reasons of the transformation lay, partly, in the change of domicile and mode of life. Animals had an extraordinarily quick capacity for adaptation to new conditions. The plastic body altered its organs with comparative quickness, so that, after a longer or shorter time, the descendants of a particular species well-nigh ceased to resemble their progenitors. It was also thus with plants, but in a more pronounced degree. The greatest influence on the transformation of man and animals was due to man himself, by his either instinctively bringing living beings into such surroundings that they assumed definite forms, or by attempting to produce changes by breeding. The transforming influence of man on nature was, at that time, incalculably greater than is the case at present, and this was especially the case in the colony described. For here this transformation was guided by the leaders in a manner which was not realized by men. So it came about that, when men went forth to found the various Atlantean races, they took with them highly advanced knowledge as to the breeding of animals and plants. The growth of civilization was, then, essentially a consequence of the knowledge which they had brought with them. Nevertheless it must be emphasized that these instructions were only instinctive in character, and in essence they still remained so among the first Atlantean races.

·

The predominance of the woman-soul, already indicated, is particularly strong in the last Lemurian epoch, and continues into the Atlantean era, when the fourth sub-race was in preparation. It must not, however, be thought that this was the case with the whole of mankind; but it holds true as regards that portion of the earthly population from which came forth, at a later period, the truly advanced races. This influence was most potent on all that is "unconscious" in, or about man. The acquisition of certain habitual gestures, the subtleties of sense perception, the feeling for beauty, a good deal of the sensitive and emotional life common to men in general, emanated originally from the soul of woman. It is not saying too much if we interpret the communications of the Âkâshic Records to this effect: "Civilized nations have a bodily structure and a bodily expression, as well as certain bases of the physically psychic life, which have been stamped on them by woman."

VI. HUMANITY BEFORE THE DIVISION OF SEX

ALTHOUGH the form of man, in those ancient times which have been already described, was very different from his present form, yet, if we go still further back in the history of humanity, we find conditions differing even much more widely. For it was only in the course of time that the forms of man and woman arose from an earlier, original form in which the human being was neither the one nor the other, but both at the same time. He who would gain for himself a conception of those primeval ages must free himself entirely from those customary ideas which are drawn from present conditions. The times to which we are looking back lie somewhat before the middle of that epoch called in the preceding extracts the Lemurian. The human body then consisted of soft plastic matter; and the rest of the earthly forms also were both soft and plastic. Compared with its later firmness, the earth was still in a bubbling and more fluid state. The human soul, being embodied in that matter, could then adapt itself in a much greater degree than later. For the clothing of the soul in a male or female body is due to the fact that the one or the other is forced upon it by the development of external nature. So long as matter had not become firm, the soul could enforce its own laws upon it. It moulded the body in its own likeness; but when matter had grown dense the soul had to suit itself to the laws stamped on that matter by external nature. So long as the soul was master of matter, it formed its body neither male nor female, but gave to it qualities common to both. For the soul is at once both male and female. In itself it bears these two natures. Its male element is related to that which we call Will, its female element to what is designated Imagination. The external formation of the earth has led the body to adopt a one-sided evolution. The male body has assumed a form determined by the element of Will; the female, on the contrary, bears rather the impress of Imagination. Thus it is that the bisexual male-female soul inhabits a unisexual male or female body. And so the body had in the course of evolution assumed so decided a form through the influence of external earth-forces that thereafter it was no longer possible for the soul to pour its entire force into this body. It had to retain within itself something of the force that belonged to it, and could allow only a part to flow into the body.

When we study the Âkâshic Records we see that, at a period in the far past, human forms appear soft, plastic, and quite unlike those of later times. They still retain in equal measure the nature of man and woman. As time passes and matter densifies, the human body appears in two forms, one of which resembles the man's later form, the other the woman's. Before the appearance of these differentiated forms, every human being could of itself bring forth another. The fructification was no outer process, but one which took place within the human body itself. When the body took on a male or a female form, it lost the possibility of self-fructification. Co-operation with another body was necessary in order to produce a new human being.

The separation of the sexes appears when the earth attains a certain condition of density. The density of matter partly checks the power of reproduction, and that portion of the reproductive force which is still effective requires completion from outside by the opposite force in another human being. But the soul must retain within itself a part of its earlier force, in man as well as in woman. It cannot expend this part in the outer corporeal world. Now this portion of his force is directed inwards in man. It cannot appear outwardly; therefore it is set free for the use of inner organs — and here comes an important point in the evolution of mankind. Before it, that which we call mind — the ability to think — could have found no place in man, for this capacity would have had no organ through which to act. The soul turned its whole force outwards to the building up of the body. But now the soul-force, which cannot find an object for its activity without, can unite itself with the mind-force; and, by such union, those organs of the body are evolved which, at a later period, make man a thinking being. Thus could man direct a part of the force that in earlier times he had turned to the bringing forth of his kind, to the perfecting of his own being. The force by means of which mankind formed for itself a thinking brain is the same force by which, in ancient times, man fructified himself. Thought is attained by unisexuality. Since man no longer fructifies himself, but the opposite sexes fructify one another, they can turn a part of their productive force inwards and become thinking beings. Thus the male and female bodies respectively present externally an imperfect picture of the soul, but because of this they become inwardly more perfect beings.

Very slowly and gradually this change is accomplished in man. Little by little the later single-sexed human forms appear side by side with those of the double sex.

It is again a kind of fructification which takes place in man on his becoming a thinking being. The inner organs which can be built up by the superfluous soul-force are fructified by the mind. The soul is in itself two-fold — male-female, and so in ancient times it also formed its body. At a later period it can only give to its body a form that can co-operate with another externally; for itself it retains the ability to co-operate with the mind. From this time forward man is fructified from without for the exterior part, — from within and for the interior part of his nature by the mind. It may be said, then, that the male body has a female soul, the female body a male soul. This inner one-sidedness in man is now balanced by the fructification of the mind. The one-sidedness is removed. The male soul in the female body and the female soul in the male body both become bisexual again through fructification by the mind. Thus do man and woman differ in their outer form, and, within, the one-sidedness of the soul unites itself in both sexes to a harmonious whole. Within, mind and soul melt into unity. The mind affects as female the male soul in woman, and thus makes it male-female; it works upon the female soul in man, as male, and so forms it female-male. The bisexuality in man has withdrawn from the outer world, where it existed in pre-Lemurian times, to his inner self.

We see that the higher inner man has nothing to do with male and female. Nevertheless the inner uniformity comes from a male soul in a woman and in like manner from a female soul in a man. The union with the mind brings uniformity at last; but the fact that before the appearance of this uniformity there exists difference, this fact contains a mystery of human nature. The knowledge of this mystery is of great importance to all occult science, for it is the key to weighty problems of life. For the present it is forbidden to raise further the veil that covers this mystery.

Thus did physical man develop from the bisexual body to the unisexual, — to the separation into man and woman. And because of this, man has become a being endowed with mentality, such as he now is. But it must not be imagined that there were not intelligent beings in connection with the earth even before this period. If we search the Âkâshic Records, we certainly see that in the first Lemurian period the physical man of the future was a very different being from that which we call man to-day. He was unable to connect any sense-perceptions with thoughts: he did not think. His life was one of instinct. His soul expressed itself simply in instincts, desires, animal wishes, and so on. His consciousness was dreamy; he lived in a kind of stupor. But there were other beings in the midst of this humanity. These were, of course, also bisexual; for with the prevailing conditions in the evolution of the earth at that time, no male or female human body could be brought forth. The external conditions were still wanting. But there were other beings who, in spite of their double sex, were able to acquire knowledge and wisdom. This was possible, because these beings had undergone an entirely different evolution at a still more remote period of the past. It had become possible for their souls to fertilize themselves with mind, without waiting for the development of the inner organs of the human physical body. It is only by the help of the brain that contemporary man is able to ponder upon those impressions which he receives from outside and through the senses. It is the evolution of the soul of man that caused this. The human soul had to wait till there was a brain to co-operate with the mind. The soul would have remained mindless had it not taken this indirect path. It would have remained at the stage of dream-consciousness.

It was different with the superhuman beings already mentioned. The soul of such beings had at earlier stages developed soul-organs which required nothing physical to enable them to unite themselves with the mind. Their knowledge and wisdom were supersensually acquired. Such knowledge is called intuitive. It is not until a later stage of his evolution that the man of the present attains to this intuition, which enables him to come into touch with mind, apart from the assistance of the senses. He must reach it indirectly through the material senses. This indirect course is called the descent of the human soul into matter, or popularly "The Fall" (into sin). Owing to an earlier evolution of a different kind, these superhuman beings did not need to undergo this descent into matter. As the soul of such beings had already attained a higher stage, their consciousness was not dreamy but inwardly luminous, and the comprehension of knowledge and wisdom by them was clairvoyance which needed no senses and no organs of thought. The Wisdom by which the world was built streamed directly into their soul.

Thus were they able to be the leaders of young humanity, still sunk in apathy. They were the bearers of an Ancient Wisdom, to comprehend which man must struggle upwards by the roundabout path described. They differed from what is called "man" by the fact that Wisdom poured out its rays on them "from above" as a free gift, just as the sunlight streams down on us. It was not so with "man." He had to acquire wisdom for himself by the labour of the senses and of the organ of thought. It did not at first come to him as a free gift. He must desire it. Only when the longing for wisdom is alive in man does he strive to attain it for himself through his senses and thought-organ. So a new impulse must awaken in the soul, — desire, the longing for knowledge. The human soul could not possess this longing in its earlier stages. Its impulses were only towards embodiment in that which took on an outer form, in that in which it lived as a dreamy life, but not towards the knowledge of an outer world, not towards understanding. With the separation of the sexes first appeared the desire for knowledge.

It was just because the superhuman beings did not desire it, that wisdom became known to them by the path of clairvoyance. They waited till wisdom streamed into them, as we wait for the sunshine that we cannot create by night, but which must come to us of itself in the morning.

The longing for knowledge is evoked in this way, in order that the soul may build up inner organs (the brain, etc.) by which it comes into possession of knowledge. This result follows, because part of the soul-force works no longer from without but from within. But the superhuman beings who have not accomplished this separation of their soul-forces direct their entire soul-energy outwards.

They have thus also at their service, for the outer fructification by the mind, that force which man turns inward for the building up of his organs of knowledge. Now that force by means of which man turns outwards to unite himself with another is Love. The superhuman beings directed their whole love outwards to let the wisdom of the worlds stream into their souls. But man can turn outward only a part. Man became sensual, and thus his love grew sensual too. He withdrew from the outer world a part of his being which he then directed towards his inner building. And this produced what is called "selfishness." When man became man or woman in his physical body he could only surrender a part of his being; with the other part he separated himself from the surrounding world. He became selfish. And his outer activity, as well as his striving for inward development, became selfish. He loved, because he desired, and he thought, because again he desired, — in this case, knowledge. In contrast to a childish and selfish humanity stood the leaders in their all-loving, unselfish natures. The soul which in them inhabits neither a male nor a female body is itself male-female. It loves without desire. The innocent soul of man loved thus before the separation of the sexes; nevertheless, it could not at that time know, for the very reason that it was still at a lower stage — in dream-consciousness. Thus too does the soul of the higher beings love; nevertheless, these beings can know in spite of this and on account of their advanced development. "Man" must pass through selfishness in order once more to reach unselfishness at a higher stage, but this time with an absolutely clear consciousness.

This, then, was the task of the superhuman beings, of the great leaders, — to stamp upon the young humanity their own character, that of love. They could do so only with that part of the soul-force which was directed outwards. Thus arose sensual love. And hence the latter accompanies the soul's activity in a male or female body. Sensual love became the force for human physical development. This love brings man and woman together in so far as they are physical beings. On this love rests the progress of physical humanity. It was over this love only that the so-called superhuman beings had power. That part of the human soul-force which turns inwards and must gain knowledge by the indirect path of sensuality withdraws itself from the power of those superhuman beings. They themselves had never descended to the development of corresponding inner organs. They could clothe the outward impulse in love, because they possessed as their very essence the love that was outwardly active. Thus there was a gulf between them and the young humanity. They could implant love in man, at first in a sensual form; knowledge they could not give, because their own knowledge had never taken the by-path through those inner organs which man was now developing in himself. They could speak no language which a being with brains could understand.

Now the said inner organs of man were, it is true, not ripe for contact with mind till that stage of earthly existence was reached which lies in the middle of the Lemurian period; but once before, at a much earlier period of development, they had been cultivated into an imperfect first beginning. For the soul had already passed through physical embodiments in times long gone by. It had lived, not indeed on the earth, but on other celestial bodies in densified matter. More exact information on this subject cannot be given till later. Only so much as this may now be said, — the beings of earth had formerly inhabited another planet, and, according to the conditions existing on it, they had developed to the stage at which they stood when they reached the earth. They laid aside the matter of the preceding planet like a garment, and became pure soul-germs at the stage of development reached then, — capable of sensation, of feeling, and so on; in short, able to lead that dreamlike life which still belonged to them in the first stages of their earth existence. But the superhuman beings spoken of, the leaders in the domain of love, had also lived on the preceding planets, and were even there so perfect that they no longer needed to descend in order to develop the first beginnings of those inner organs.

But there were other beings, not so far advanced as these Leaders of Love, but who might rather be counted as men on the preceding planet, who nevertheless outstripped mankind at that time. They were thus indeed, at the beginning of the earth formation, further advanced than man, but nevertheless still at the stage at which knowledge must be acquired through inner organs. These beings were in a peculiar position. They were too far advanced to pass through the physical human body, either male or female, and yet not far enough to be able to act by means of perfect clairvoyance, as were the Leaders of Love. They could not be, as yet, *Beings of Love*; and at the same time they could no longer be "men." So it was only possible for them as semi-superhuman beings to continue their own evolution, but with the help of man. They could converse with the beings with brains in a language these understood. By this means the human soul-force directed inwards was aroused, and they were enabled to unite themselves to knowledge and wisdom. It was indeed only thus that wisdom of a human sort came to the earth. The "semi-superhuman" beings spoken of were able to absorb this human wisdom, and thus reach that perfection which they themselves still lacked. They thus became the creators of human wisdom. For this reason they were called "light bringers" (Lucifer). Thus had infant humanity leaders of two kinds — Beings of Love and Beings of Wisdom, — human nature was yoked between Love and Wisdom, when it assumed its present form on the earth. By the Beings of Love it was stimulated to physical development, by the Beings of Wisdom to the perfection of its inner self. In consequence of its physical development, mankind advanced from generation to generation, forming new tribes and races; through its inner development the individuals increased in inward perfection; they became scholars, sages, artists, technical scientists, etc. From race to race physical humanity advances; each race throughout its physical evolution transfers, to the following one, such of its qualities as are perceptible to the senses. Here the law of heredity reigns. The children bear the physical characteristics of their fathers. Beyond this lies an evolution towards perfection of mind and soul which can only be accomplished by the development of the soul itself. And here we are confronted with the law of the evolution of the soul within the bounds of earthly existence.

VII. THE BEGINNINGS OF SEX DUALITY

A DESCRIPTION of the constitution of man before the division into male and female sexes must now be given. The body consisted then of a soft, plastic mass. Over it the will-power was far more potent than was the case with mankind subsequently. On his separation from the parent being, man appeared, it is true, as an organism with members, but incomplete. His organs continued their further development apart from the parent body. Much of that which at a later period ripened within the maternal organism was then brought to perfection by an external force akin to our will-power. The parent's fostering care was necessary to promote such a ripening from without. Man brought with him into the world certain organs which he afterwards discarded. Others, still quite imperfect at his first appearance, completed their development. The whole process permits of a comparison with liberation from an egg-form and the casting off of an outer covering; but we must here not think of a hard and egg-like shell.

Man's body was warm-blooded. This must be distinctly stated, for in former times it was otherwise, as will afterwards be shown. The process of maturing apart from the mother-entity was accomplished under the influence of increased warmth, conveyed in like manner from without. But by no means must we imagine a hatching-out of the egg-shaped man — so named for the sake of brevity. The conditions of warmth and fire on the earth were different then from those of later times. By means of his own force a man could constrain and confine within a certain space fire or warmth. In short, he could concentrate heat. He was thus in a position to supply warmth to the young creature that required it for his development.

The organs of motion were at that time man's most highly developed organs. The sense-organs of to-day were then quite unevolved. The most advanced were the organ of hearing and the organs for the perception of cold and heat (the sense of feeling); still far behind was the perception of light. Man was born with the senses of hearing and of touch, and then, somewhat later, the light-perception was evolved.

All that is stated here refers to the latest period before the separation of the sexes. The latter proceeded slowly and gradually. For a long time before its actual appearance, mankind began to develop in such a way that one individual was born with more of the masculine, the other with more of the feminine character. Nevertheless, the characteristics of the opposite sex were present in every individual, so that spontaneous generation was possible, though not at all times, for it was dependent upon the influences of external conditions at certain seasons of the year. In diverse matters mankind as a whole depended to a large extent on such external circumstances. For that reason he had to regulate all his undertakings in accordance with such outer conditions; in accordance, for example, with the course of sun and moon. This regulation did not, however, take place consciously, in the present sense of the term, but was carried out in a manner which must rather be called instinctive, a term indicating the mental life of the man of that time.

This mental life cannot be described as an actual inner life. Bodily and mental activities and qualities were not as yet rigidly separated from one another. The outer life of Nature was still experienced by the soul. It was above all on the sense of hearing that every single vibration from without made a powerful impression. Every quiver in the air, every movement in his surroundings was "heard." The wind and the water expressed in their motions what to man was an "eloquent language." It was a perception of the mysterious weaving and working in Nature which thus penetrated man. And this weaving and working resounded again in his soul. His activity was an echo of these influences. He transformed the perception of sound into his own activity. He lived amid those surgings of sound, and brought them into expression by means of his own will. In like manner was he impelled to accomplish all his daily work. To a somewhat less degree, indeed, he was affected by the energy playing upon his feelings. Nevertheless these too acted an important part. The surroundings were sensed by him within his own body and he acted accordingly. By the activities of his feelings he knew when and how he ought to work. By these he knew where to settle, or recognised the dangers threatening his life, and so avoided them. He regulated the taking of sustenance accordingly.

Altogether different from that of later times was the course taken by the rest of his mental life. Pictures lived in his soul, but not as representations of external things. When, for example, the man moved from a colder into a warmer place, there arose in his soul a definite colour-picture, but this colour-picture had nothing to do with any external object. It sprang from an inner force akin to the will. Pictures like these continually filled the soul. The whole can only be compared with the rising and falling dream-visions of man. Only at that time the pictures were not unregulated, but in conformity with laws; and for that reason we must not speak, at this stage of humanity, of a dream-consciousness, but rather of a picture-consciousness. In the main it was colour-pictures with which this consciousness was filled, but these were not the only kind. Thus man wandered through the world, experiencing its events by means of his senses of hearing and feeling, but in his inner life this world was reflected in pictures, very unlike those existing in the outer world. Pleasure and pain were bound up with these soul-pictures in a much smaller degree than is the case with man's ideas to-day, which reflect his perceptions in the world outside. Doubtless one picture caused him pleasure, another disgust; the one hatred, and the other love; but these sensations bore a much fainter character. On the other hand strong feelings were produced by something else. Man was then much more agile, much more active than later. Everything in his surroundings, as well as the pictures in his soul, stirred him to activity, to movement. Now when his activity, unhindered, had free play, he experienced a sensation of well-being; when, however, this activity was checked in any direction, he was overcome by unhappiness and discomfort. The absence or presence of opposition to his will determined the content of his life of feeling, his pleasure and his pain. And this pleasure or this pain discharged itself again in his own soul as a living world of pictures. Clear, bright, beautiful pictures lived within him when he was able to expand unhindered; gloomy and misshapen were those which appeared in his soul when his movements were hampered.

So far the average man has been described. In the case of those who had developed into a kind of superhuman state, the inner life was different. With them the soul-life was not of this instinctive character. What they perceived through their senses of hearing and of feeling were Nature's deeper secrets, and these they could consciously interpret. In the roaring of the wind, in the rustling of the trees, the laws and the wisdom of Nature were disclosed; and in their soul-pictures these were not mere reflections of an outer world, but images of the spiritual powers in the world. It was not the things of sense which they perceived, but spiritual intelligences. If the average man, for example, experienced a sensation of fear, a hideous sinister picture would arise in his soul. The superhuman being received by means of such pictures information, revelation from the spiritual beings of the world. The processes of Nature did not appear to him as they do to the naturalist of to-day, dependent on lifeless natural laws, but rather as the deeds of spiritual beings. The outer reality did not as yet exist, for there were no outer senses, but to the higher beings the inner reality revealed itself. The spirit poured its rays into them as the sunlight streams into the physical eye of the man of to-day. In these beings was knowledge in its fullest sense, that which is called intuitive knowledge. There was no such thing as combining and speculating among them, but a direct contemplation of the working of spiritual beings. These superhuman individualities could thus absorb directly, into their wills, communications coming from the spiritual world. Consciously they led the others. They received their mission from the spiritual world and acted in accordance with it.

Now when the time arrived at which the sexes separated, these beings naturally considered it their task to influence the new life in conformity with their mission. The regulation of sexual life originated with them. All arrangements which had to do with the generation of mankind had their source in them. In this they acted with perfect consciousness, but the other human beings were sensible of the impulse only as an instinct implanted in them. Sexual love was implanted in man by direct thought-transference; and all its expressions were at first of the noblest kind. Everything in this domain which has taken on an ugly character dates from a later period, when man had become more independent, and when he had sullied a desire originally pure. In these early times there was no such thing as a satisfaction of sexual desire for its own sake. Everything then was a service of sacrifice for the continuance of human existence. Generation was regarded as a sacred thing, as a service which man owed to the world, and sacrificial priests were the leaders and rulers in this domain.

Of another kind were the influences of the semi-superhuman beings. The latter were not developed to the stage at which they could receive the revelations of the spiritual world in all their purity. In their soul-pictures there arose besides the impressions of the spiritual world the activities also of the world of sense. Those who were in the fullest sense superhuman beings had no sensation of either pleasure or pain from the external world. They abandoned themselves entirely to the revelations of the spiritual powers. Wisdom flowed into them as light flows into the creatures of sense. Their will was directed towards nothing else but to action in accordance with this wisdom, and in action of this kind lay their highest pleasure. Wisdom, Will, and Activity composed their very being. It was otherwise with the semi-superhuman beings. They felt the desire to receive impressions from without, and connected pleasure with the satisfaction of this desire, disappointment with its lack. They were thus distinguishable from the superhuman beings. For the latter, impressions from without were nothing more than confirmation of spiritual revelations. They might behold the outer world and receive nothing more than a reflection of that which they had already received through the spirit. The semi-superhuman beings experienced something new to them, and on that account they were able to be the leaders of mankind, when the latter began to change the mere pictures in the soul into images, into representations of outer objects. This happened when a part of the earlier human generative force turned inwards and when beings possessing a brain were evolved. For with the brain man also developed the capacity to change external sense-impressions into mind-conceptions. It must be said, therefore, that man was impelled by semi-superhuman beings to turn his soul towards the external world of sense. It was, indeed, denied him to expose his own soul-pictures directly to pure spiritual influences. The ability to generate his kind was implanted in him as an instinctive impulse by the superhuman beings. Mentally he would have had to lead a sort of dream-existence at first, had not the semi-superhuman beings interfered. Swayed by them, his soul-pictures were directed to the world outside. He became a being self-conscious in the world of sense. And thus man achieved the ability to guide his actions consciously and according to his perceptions in the world of sense. Once he had acted from a kind of instinct, under the sway of his external surroundings and the energizing forces playing upon him from higher individualities. Now he began to follow the urgings, the allurements, of his own conceptions. And with this the free will of mankind appeared in the world. That was the beginning of "Good and Evil."

Before advancing further in this direction something must be said about man's environment on the earth. Side by side with man there existed animals as well, which according to their kind were at the same stage of development as he was. In accordance with our present conceptions they would be counted as reptiles. Besides these there were lower forms of the animal world. Now there was an essential difference between man and the animals. On account of his still plastic body, man could only live in those regions of the earth which had not as yet reached the densest material form, and in these regions animals possessing a like plastic body lived with him. In other regions, however, animals lived which had already dense bodies and which had also already developed unisexuality and their sense organs. Whence they came will be shown later. They could develop no farther because their bodies had taken on the denser matter too soon. Some species among them have disappeared, some have developed further after their kind into the present forms. Man was able to reach higher forms because he remained in those regions which at that time suited his structure. On that account his body remained so flexible and soft that he was able to single out of himself those organs which were capable of fructification by the mind. His external body had then advanced so far that it could densify and become a protecting sheath for the finer mental organs. But all human bodies were not so far developed. Those that were so advanced were few. These were first of all vivified by the mind. Others were not vivified. Had the mind entered the latter as well, it would only have been able partially to evolve, because of the imperfect inner organs. And so these human personalities had for the time being to continue their development as a kind of mindless creature. A third kind had proceeded so far that feeble mental impulses could make themselves felt. These stood between the other two kinds. Their mental activity remained dull. They had to be led by higher mental powers. Between these three kinds were all possible grades of

44

transition. Further development was now only possible if one part of mankind should educate itself more highly at the cost of another part. First of all, the absolutely mindless had to be sacrificed. An intermingling with them for the purpose of propagation would only have dragged the more advanced down to their level. And so all who had received the mind principle were singled out from among them. Therefore they fell more and more to the level of animality. Thus, side by side with mankind, animals resembling man evolved themselves further.

Man left, as it were, a portion of his brothers behind him on the path, so that he might himself mount higher. This process was, however, by no means at an end here. Those men also of dull mentality, who stood rather higher, could only advance further by being drawn into association with higher beings and by separating themselves from the less mentally gifted. Only by these means could they develop bodies afterwards suited for the reception of the entire human intelligence. Not until after the lapse of a certain time had physical evolution advanced so far that, in this direction, a sort of pause set in, during which all lying beyond a fixed limit belonged to the human domain. The conditions of life on the earth had meantime so changed that a further rejection would have resulted in the production, not of animal-like beings, but of such as were not even fit to live. But what was thrust down into a state of animality has either died out or lives on in the various higher animals. In such therefore we must recognize creatures which had to remain behind, at an earlier stage of human development. Only they have not retained the same form which they had at the time of their separation, but have degenerated from a higher to a lower type. Thus monkeys are retrograde human beings of a bygone age. Just as man was at one time less perfect than he is to-day, so were these at one time more perfect than at present. And that which remained within the domain of man has undergone a like process, within its own limits. In many a savage tribe we may see the degraded descendants of human forms which were at one time more exalted. These have not sunk to the level of the brute, but only to that of the savage.

That which in man is eternal is the mind. It has been shown at what period the mind entered the body. Before that time the mind belonged to other regions. It could not unite itself with the body till the latter had attained a certain stage of development. Only when there is a perfect comprehension of the way in which this union took place can the meaning of birth and death be understood, or the character of the everlasting mind become known.

VIII. MAN'S FIRST ANCESTORS

THE observations of the Âkâshic Record, which will be described in the following pages, date from a period immediately preceding the incidents related in the previous chapter. In view of the materialistic tendency of thought at the present day, the risk attending the publication of the following facts is even greater than that incurred by the descriptions given in the preceding chapters. One is so liable in these days, when dealing with matters of this kind, to be dubbed fantastic, or accused of groundless speculation, that nothing but the conviction that the information we offer with regard to spiritual experience is true and accurate could induce us to publish these statements, knowing, as we do only too well, that any one who is versed in the teachings of Physical Science, as accepted by the present generation, will be unable even to approach the matter in a serious attitude of mind. Nothing is herein stated, but what has been carefully tested according to the methods employed by Spiritual Science; and all we ask of the ordinary scientist is that he shall accord to the student of the Higher Science the same tolerance as the latter shows to the mode of thought of Physical Science. (See my *Welt- und Lebensanschauungen im Neunzehnten Jahrhundert*, where I think I have shown my appreciation of the views held by materialistic Science.)

Nevertheless, for the benefit of any who may be sympathetically inclined towards the teachings of the Higher Science, I would add a further special remark with reference to the present expositions: we shall here touch upon matters of very great significance, pertaining to an age now long past, matters which, portrayed by the Records of Âkâsha, it is by no means an easy task to decipher. The writer, indeed, makes no claim on blind faith; he merely sets forth the results of investigations on which the utmost care has been bestowed, and any correction, if based on a practical knowledge of such matters, would be welcomed. The signs of the times are such as to impress him with a sense of duty, nay, urgency, in making known these events in the evolution of mankind. Moreover, we shall first have to sketch briefly an extensive period of existence, in order to gain at the outset a good general idea. Many things, therefore, which are now merely indicated, will receive a more detailed exposition in later chapters.

It is, however, difficult to translate the inscriptions of the Âkâshic Records into everyday language. It were easier to decipher the occult language of symbolical signs used in occult schools, but this is not yet permitted in our time. The reader is therefore begged to give a hearing to much that may seem obscure and hard to understand, to make a valiant endeavour to grasp their meaning, as the author, on his part, has striven to devise a mode of interpretation capable of being understood by all. The trouble expended in mastering many a difficult passage will be rewarded by the insight gained into the profound mysteries, the momentous problems of humanity herein revealed. These Âkâshic Records — which, for the occult investigator, are as much an undeniable reality as mountains and rivers are for the physical eye — constitute for man the basis of a true knowledge of self. An error of perception is, of course, as possible for the one as for the other.

It must be remembered that the present chapter relates only to the evolution of man. As a matter of course, the other kingdoms of Nature, the mineral, the plant, and the animal, are evolving side by side with humanity, and these other evolutions will be dealt with in future chapters. In these we shall discuss certain other subjects destined to illumine and to render more comprehensible the details given concerning man's evolution. On the other hand, we shall not be able to study the evolution of the other terrestrial kingdoms from the occult standpoint until the gradual development of man has been shown.

When we retrace still further the earth's evolutionary history — further back even than we have done in the foregoing pages — we find our celestial globe composed of ever finer conditions of matter. The matter which later became solid was, at a previous stage, liquid; before that, gaseous and of the nature of vapour; while at a still remoter period we find it in its finest form, that is to say, as ether. The decrease of temperature, however, caused the gradual solidification of matter.

In our present studies we shall go back to the time when our earthly dwelling-place was composed of matter in its finest etheric state. In that epoch of the earth's evolution man began his earthly career. In earlier times he had lived in other worlds, which will be the subject of study elsewhere. [See *An Outline Of Occult Science*, by Rudolf Steiner, Ph.D.] We will here only say a word or two about the existence which immediately preceded his earth-life. It was what we should call an astral or spiritual world, peopled with beings who had no outer, that is to say, no physical, corporeal existence. Neither had man. He had by that time perfected the picture-consciousness, or dream-consciousness, which was described in a foregoing chapter. He possessed feelings and desires, but all confined in a soul-body: a human being at that stage would only have been visible to clairvoyant sight.

47

It is true that the more highly evolved human beings of that period possessed such sight, though it was of a rather vague and dreamy description; it was *not* self-conscious clairvoyance. These astral beings are, in a certain sense, man's ancestors; for what to-day we call "Man" contains an indwelling, self-conscious Spirit. This Spirit became united to the being which descended from that ancestor about the middle of the Lemurian phase of civilisation. (This union of the Soul-Ancestor with the Physical-Ancestor has already been mentioned in earlier chapters. The subject will be taken up again, and treated more explicitly, after we have followed the evolution of man's ancestors up to that point.)

The astral or Soul-Ancestors of man were transplanted to the subtle matter of the etheric world. They absorbed this subtle matter into themselves — roughly putting it — something after the manner of a sponge. Thus, by permeating themselves with etheric matter their etheric bodies were formed. They were elongated, and elliptic in form; yet subtle differentiations of matter, tendencies to form limbs and other organs to be developed at a later period, were even then perceptible. The whole process perceptible in the mass of etheric matter was, however, purely physico-chemical, though regulated and controlled by the soul.

When one of these ovoids of matter had reached a certain size, it split into two, forming two new masses each resembling the one which gave it birth, and reproducing the same activities which were at work in the parent form. Every one of these new forms possessed a soul similar to that of the mother-being. The reason of this was that not only a definite number of human souls incarnated on the physical plane, but there was what we might call a Soul-Tree (or Group Soul), which was able, as it were, to give off innumerable individual souls, sprung from its common root. Just as a plant springs up again and again from numberless seeds, so did the soul-life reincarnate in the countless offshoots which were created as the result of these continual cleavings. (Of course, there existed from the beginning a very limited number of soul species, but within these species, evolution proceeded in the manner described, every soul species putting forth innumerable scions.)

With incarnation in physical matter a most important change came over the souls themselves. As long as the souls remained unconnected with the material world, no outward material occurrence could affect them. All influences affecting them were purely psychic, or clairvoyant. Thus in their life they shared the astral influences of their surroundings, and it was in this way that they took part in, or experienced, everything that existed at that time. The impressions made by stones, plants, and animals, then also existing in a purely astral (Soul) form, were felt as inner experiences of the soul. On entering the plane of our earth, something quite new was added. Outer material events brought influences to bear upon the soul, which had thus robed itself in a garment of etheric matter. At first these influences consisted of motions in the outer material world which caused corresponding activity in the etheric body. In the same way as the vibrations of the air now affect us in the form of sound, so were those etheric beings affected by the vibrations of the etheric matter surrounding them. Such a being was, in fact, a single organ of hearing. This sense was the first to be developed; but from this we see that the separated organ of hearing was formed at a later period.

With the increasing solidification of physical matter, the soul-nature gradually lost control over its formation. The bodies already formed could only reproduce bodies after their own image. A change now occurs in the manner of generation, that is to say, the offspring of the mother-being appears considerably smaller, only growing gradually to the size of the parent. Organs of generation now begin to appear, whereas hitherto they had not existed. Henceforward it is no mere physico-chemical process which takes place within the form. Such a process is now no longer sufficient for the purpose of generation: for the outer matter, growing denser and denser, is no longer capable of being directly influenced by the soul. A special portion within the form is therefore set apart for this function, being withdrawn from the immediate influence of the outside material world. Only the body, exclusive of the specialised part, is still exposed to these influences; and it remains in the condition which was formerly that of the whole body. In the specialised part the psychic nature continues to work, and the soul becomes at this point the vehicle of the life-principle (called in Theosophical literature "Prâna").

We now find the physical human ancestor in possession of two principles: one being the physical body, which is subject to the chemical and physical laws of the world surrounding it; and the second, the sum total of the organs directly controlled by the individual life-principle. In this manner a part of the activity of the soul has been liberated. No longer retaining power over the physical sheath, the soul turns this part of its activity inwards, transforming part of the body into special organs; and so begins an inner life of the body. It no longer merely participates in the vibrations from without, but begins to feel them inwardly as individual experiences. Here sensation begins. At first, the sensation somewhat resembles the sense of touch: the subject *feels* the movements of the outer world, the pressure caused by substances, and so on; also a sensation of heat and cold began now to be developed.

At this point man has reached an important stage in his evolution. The direct influence of the soul has been withdrawn from the physical body, the latter being entirely surrendered to the physical and chemical activities of the material world. The moment the soul, at work in the other principles, relaxes its hold over the body, the latter dissolves. This is the beginning of what we call "death." We cannot speak of death in reference to previous states. In the simple case of separation, the life of the mother-form is continued in the offspring, for in the latter are at work all the transformed soul-forces which hitherto had sought expression in the one parent-form: after the separation, nothing remains that is soulless.

A change now takes place: as soon as the soul ceases to retain its power over the physical body, the latter is subject to the chemical and physical laws of the outer world, that is to say, it decays. The field of activity for the soul-powers is limited to generation and the developed inner life; for through this generative power, descendants are brought forth, which are in their turn endowed with a surplus of organ-forming power. In this surplus the soul always returns to life again. As the whole body was formerly filled with psychic activity at the separation, so were now the organs of reproduction and of sensation. We must recognise in this nothing less than a *Rebirth* of the soul-life in the new growing organism.

Theosophical literature describes these two evolutionary stages of man as the first two Root-Races of our earth. The first is called the Polar Race, the second the Hyperborean Race.

We must bear in mind that the field of sensation possessed by these human forefathers was of a general character and as yet quite vague and indefinite. So far, only two of the kinds of sensation we now possess were differentiated: the sense of hearing and that of touch. By reason of the changes, however, which the body was undergoing, as well as its physical environment, the whole human form was no longer capable of acting, so to speak, as "all ear." Henceforward a specialised part of the body retained the power of responding to the delicate vibrations, and supplied the material from which was gradually developed the organ of hearing we now possess, whilst the rest of the body remained almost entirely an organ of touch.

Obviously, the whole process of the evolution of man has hitherto been connected with the alteration in the degree of warmth of our earth; it was, in fact, due to the heat in his surroundings that man evolved to the stage we have just described. The heat from without, however, had now reached a point at which further progress in the formation of the human body was no longer possible. Thus, with the cooling off of the earth, a corresponding reaction set in within the form itself, and man became the generator of his own supply of heat, whereas hitherto his temperature had been that of his surroundings. Organs now appear in him, enabling him to generate for himself the degree of heat necessary for his life. Up till now, currents of substances had circulated within him, dependent on the environment for the necessary heat; but now he could generate his own heat, for these substances and the fluids of the body turned into warm blood. Thus he had attained a far greater degree of self-dependence as a physical being than ever before, and his whole inner life was intensified. Sensation still depended entirely upon the effects of the outer world. The filling of the body with its own warmth gave it an independent physical inner life. The soul had now a field of activity within the body, where it could unfold an existence which would no longer be a mere sharing in the life of the outer world.

By this proceeding, the astral, or soul life, was drawn into the sphere of physical matter. Hitherto desires, longings and passions, joy and sorrow of soul, could only arise through psychic influences; and attraction and aversion were awakened, passions excited, and so on, by that which proceeded from one soul to another. No other external physical object could have produced such effects. Now, for the first time, the possibility arose that such outer objects had a significance for the soul. For the quickening of the inner life which followed the power of generating its own heat caused it to experience the sensation of pleasure, while the disturbance of this inner life caused it discomfort; an outer object qualified to maintain bodily comfort could become an object of desire, or longing. The astral, or desire body — known as "Kâma" in Theosophical literature, — was united with terrestrial man, and the objects of the senses became objects capable of being desired; man was thus bound through his desire body to earthly existence.

The foregoing fact coincides with a great cosmic event, with which it is causally connected. Till now there had been no material separation between sun, earth, and moon: these three affected man as a single body. At this point separation occurs: the finer matter, including all that which had hitherto conferred on the soul the power of directly giving life, was separated off as sun; the grossest matter went forth as moon; while the earth, with its materiality, occupied a position between the two. Of course, the separation did not occur suddenly; for the whole process was gradually taking place while man was advancing from the stage of generation by cleavage to that just described. The advance in man's evolution was, indeed, accomplished just through the cosmic happenings mentioned. First, the sun withdrew its substance from the common globe. The soul was thereby deprived of the possibility of directly vivifying the earth substance left behind. Then the moon began to take form, in this way bringing about a condition of the earth favourable to the growth of the capacity for sensation just as we have already described.

In conjunction with this occurrence, a new sense was developed. The conditions of warmth of the earth became such that the bodies gradually took on a definite outline, dividing the transparent matter from the opaque. The sun, which had withdrawn from the earth-body, now assumed its task as light-giver, and awoke in the human body the sense of sight. It was not at first what we know as sight to-day. Light and darkness were perceptible to man as vague sensations. For instance, he was aware that under certain conditions light gave him a sense of comfort and well-being, quickening the life in his body; therefore he sought it and strove towards it.

Meanwhile the actual soul-life continued to run its course in the form of dreamlike pictures. Colour-pictures came and went in this life, without having any particular connection with the things of the outer world, and these colour-pictures were still attributed by man to soul activities. Light colour-pictures appeared to him when his astral experiences were pleasant; sombre pictures when he was affected by disagreeable astral influences. That which was effected as the result of self-generated heat we have called in the foregoing the "inner life." Nevertheless, we see that it was not an inner life in the sense of later human development. All things advance step by step, and so does the evolution of the inner life. In the sense in which it has been spoken of in a former chapter, this true inner life only begins when the fructification by the mind takes place, when man begins to think about these outer influences. All that has been described here does but show how man climbed upward to the state depicted in the preceding chapter. And we really live over again the times there described when we picture to ourselves the following. More and more the soul learns to relate to the outer bodily existence that which it formerly lived through in itself and which it only attributed to soul influences.

The same thing now happened with regard to the colour-pictures. Just as before the impression of a sympathetic psychic influence was connected in the individual soul with a bright colour-picture, so did it now become a brilliant light-impression from outside. The soul began to perceive in colours the objects surrounding it. This was in conjunction with the development of new organs of sight. At its previous stages the body had one eye, which does not exist to-day, by means of which it vaguely sensed the light and the darkness. (The legend of the Cyclops with one eye is a reminiscence of this state.)

The two eyes developed when the soul began to associate the external light-impressions more intimately with its own life, and thus was lost the capacity of perception of the surrounding astral world. The soul became more and more a mirror of the outer world, the latter being reproduced within it as an image; and simultaneously with this the separation of the sexes appeared. On the one hand, the human body became capable of fecundation only by another human being, while on the other hand there developed in the body "soul-organs" (the nervous system), by which the sense-impressions of the outer world were reflected in the soul, thereby preparing the way for the mind, or thinking principle, in the human body.

IX. THE FIRST, OR POLAR, RACE

WE will now trace the Âkâshic Records back to the primeval past, when our earth, as it is now, began to exist. By earth we mean that condition of our planet by reason of which it is the bearer of minerals, plants, animals, and men, in their present form; for this state was preceded by others in which the above-named kingdoms of Nature existed under essentially different forms.

The earth, as we know it, had undergone many transformations before it could become the bearer of our present world of minerals, plants, animals, and human beings. Minerals also existed in those earlier conditions, but they had quite a different appearance from the minerals of our day. These past conditions will be dealt with later, but for the time being we shall merely refer to the way in which the condition immediately preceding the present was transformed into the latter.

We may form a faint idea of such a transformation by comparison with the passage of the plant nature through the germinal state. Imagine a plant with its roots, stem, leaves, blossoms, and fruit: it draws matter from its surroundings and expels it again. But everything belonging to it of the nature of substance, form, and growth disappears — all but the tiny germ; through it the life quickens, to spring up again next year in a similar form. In the same way all that existed on our earth in its previous state disappeared, but only to arise again in its present form. That which might be called mineral, plant, animal, in the former condition, has passed away, as the roots, stem, and different parts of the plant have passed away; and in one case as in the other, the germ-state has remained out of which the old form is built up anew, for within the germ lie concealed the forces which cause the new form to proceed from it.

In the period which we are just about to describe, we have to deal, therefore, with a kind of earth-germ, containing within it the forces which gave rise to the earth of to-day, forces which were acquired by virtue of its former conditions. We must not imagine, however, that this earth-seed consisted of dense matter like the plant-seed: it was rather of a psychic nature, and composed of that fine, vibrating, plastic matter which is called "astral" in Theosophical literature.

This astral germ of the earth at first contained the embryonic human being, the beginnings of the future human souls. Everything which existed in previous states as minerals, plants, and animals, had been absorbed by these human germs — merged in them. So, before man trod the physical earth, he was a soul — an astral being, — and as such he finds himself on the physical earth, which then consisted of the finest matter — called in Theosophical literature the finest etheric matter.

The origin of this etheric earth will be explained in another chapter. The astral human beings drew this ether round them, imprinting on it, as it were, their own nature, so that it became a copy of the astral human being. Thus, at the first stage, we have to deal with an etheric earth, which is really only composed of this etheric humanity, and is nothing but a conglomerate of it. The astral body, or soul of man, is actually, for the most part, outside the etheric body and organizes it from without. To the occult investigator the earth appears somewhat as follows: it is a sphere composed in its turn of countless tiny etheric spheres — etheric humanity — and surrounded by an astral covering, as the present earth is surrounded by a covering of air. In this astral envelope (atmosphere) astral humanity lives, and from there it works on its etheric images. The astral human souls create organs in their etheric images, in whom they effect a human etheric existence. Within the whole earth there is only one condition of matter, and that is the subtle vital ether. This primeval humanity is called in Theosophical books the Polar, or First, Root-Race.

The further evolution of the earth now consists in the development of the one condition of matter into two; a denser matter separates off, leaving a finer substance behind. The denser substance is similar to our air, while the finer substance resembles that which effects the formation of chemical elements from their previously undifferentiated substance. In addition to these, a remnant of the earlier matter — the vitalised ether — continued to exist. Only a part of the latter was incorporated with the two conditions of matter just described.

We find, then, at this time three kinds of matter in the physical earth. While formerly the activities of the astral human beings were confined to one substance in the earth-shell, they now had to work upon three, their work being carried on in the following manner. That part which had become gaseous at first offered resistance to the work of the astral beings; it would not assimilate all the latent possibilities contained in the perfect astral beings; consequently, the astral humanity is forced to divide into two groups. One group is that which elaborates the gaseous matter, and creates in it its own image; the other group is able to do more: it can work upon the two other kinds of matter; it can create an image of itself composed both of the vitalised ether and the other kind of ether, thus giving rise to the chemical elements. In the present work we shall call this kind of ether "chemical ether."

But this second group of astral beings has only acquired this higher faculty by throwing off a part — the first group — of the astral essence, and condemning it to perform lower work. Had it retained in itself those forces which accomplished the meaner task, it could not have risen higher itself. Here we have an event arising from the fact that something higher procures its own advancement at the cost of another, which it severs from itself.

This is the picture which now presents itself within the physical earth: two kinds of beings exist. Firstly, those having a gaseous body, on which astral beings belonging to it work from outside. These beings are of the nature of animals, and form a first animal kingdom on the earth. Were we to describe the forms of these animals, the man of to-day would think them rather strange. Their form — we must bear in mind that it consisted only of gaseous substance — resembles none of the animal forms existing now; they have, perhaps, a distant resemblance to the shells of certain snails or shell-fish of the present day.

Side by side with these animal forms, man's physical development progresses. Astral humanity, now risen a step higher, creates a physical image of itself consisting of two kinds of matter, of vital ether and of chemical ether. Thus we have before us a human being consisting of an astral body, who is working upon an etheric body, which is again composed of two kinds of ether, vital and chemical ether.

By means of the life-ether this physical image of man has the power of reproduction, of bringing forth beings like itself. By means of the chemical ether it develops certain forces, similar to the chemical forces known to us at the present day as attraction and repulsion. Thereby this human image has the power of attracting certain substances in its surroundings and of uniting them with itself — afterwards to throw them out again by the power of repulsion. Such matter can, of course, only be drawn from the animal kingdom described above, and from the human kingdom. Here we discover the origin of nutrition. These first human images were thus animal and man-eaters. There still existed simultaneously with these the descendants of the former, merely life-ether beings, but they became stunted, having to adapt themselves to the new terrestrial conditions. From these are formed at a later period, after many transformations undergone by them, the unicellular creatures, as also the cells which afterwards went to the formation of the more complicated beings.

The next step forward is this: the gaseous matter divides in two, the denser part becoming watery and the other remaining gaseous. But the chemical ether also divides into two conditions of matter; the one becomes denser, and forms what we shall here call light-ether; it confers on the beings in whom it is contained the gift of becoming luminous. But a part of the chemical ether retains its original form. We have henceforth to deal with a physical earth composed of the following kinds of matter: water, air, light-ether, chemical ether, and life-ether. Now, to enable the astral beings to influence these kinds of matter again, another occurrence takes place, involving the progress of something higher at the expense of something lower thrown off from it. This process gives rise to physical beings of the character we shall now describe.

Firstly, there were those whose physical body was made up of water and air, who are now worked upon by coarse astral beings belonging to those who had been thrown out. So there arises a new group of animals composed of denser matter than the former ones. Secondly, another new group of physical beings came into existence, possessing a body which may consist of air and light-ether mixed with water. These are plant-like beings, but differing greatly in form from the plants of the present time. Only in the third new group do we find the man of that time represented. His physical body is composed of three kinds of ether, light-ether, chemical ether, and life-ether. When we consider that descendants of the old groups still continue to exist, we can gauge the multiplicity of living beings which already existed when our earth was at that stage of development.

A momentous cosmic event here occurs. The sun withdraws, and simultaneously certain forces leave the earth altogether. These forces are composed of a part of that which was present on the earth hitherto in the form of life-, chemical-, and light-ether. Thus these forces were withdrawn, as it were, from the earth as it had existed up to the present. Thereby a radical change took place in all the groups of terrestrial beings who had hitherto contained these forces within themselves. They underwent transformation. The first to be so transformed were what we called above the plant beings, who were deprived of the forces they had possessed by means of the light-ether, so that they could now only develop as living beings when acted upon from without by the light forces taken from them, and in this way plants came under the influence of sunlight.

Something of a similar nature happened to the human bodies as well. Their light-ether had to co-operate henceforth with the light-ether of the sun, in order to be capable of life. But not only those beings from whom the light-ether had been directly withdrawn were affected; others were also influenced; for everything in the world works together. The animal forms, too, which did not themselves contain light-ether had once been irradiated by their fellow-beings on the earth, and developed under the influence of the light received from them; and they now came also indirectly under the influence of the sun from without.

The human body, however, in particular, developed organs which are susceptible to the sunlight — the first rudiments of the human eye.

The result of the sun's separation was a further condensation of the matter of the earth. Solid matter began to develop from the liquid; in like manner the light-ether differentiates into a second kind of light-ether and an ether which enables bodies to develop warmth. The earth thus becomes a being which generates heat within itself. All its inhabitants were brought under the influence of heat. Again, in the astral world a similar process to the former one must occur: certain beings progressed at the expense of others. A certain number of beings, suited to work upon the gross solid matter, were separated off, and this was the origin of the firm skeleton of the earth, the mineral kingdom.

At first the higher kingdoms of Nature did not all exercise their influence on this solid, mineral, bony mass, so that we find on the earth a mineral kingdom which is hard and a vegetable kingdom in which the densest matter is water and air. For in this kingdom the gaseous body itself had been densified to a water-body by the events described; and, besides these, there were animals of the most multifarious forms, some with water- and some with air-bodies. The human body itself had undergone a process of densification. Its firmest corporeality had solidified to the density of water. The heat-ether having arisen, this water-body of man's was pervaded by it, imparting to it a kind of matter which might, perhaps, be described as

57

of the nature of gas. This condition of matter of the human body is described in works on Occult Science as that of "firemist." In this body of firemist man was incorporated.

X. THE SECOND, OR HYPERBOREAN, RACE

IN the last chapter the Âkâshic studies are carried to that point of time at which man's soul is incarnated in the subtle matter of the firemist. We must understand very clearly that man only assumed dense matter, which he now regards as his own, at a later date, and then only very gradually. If we wish to form an idea of his bodily appearance at the stage of his development just depicted, we can best do so by thinking of it as water-vapour, or as a cloud floating in the air; but this representation is, of course, on which merely approaches the reality superficially; for the fiery-cloud "man" is inwardly vitalized and organized. But in comparison to that which he becomes later, we must picture him at this stage as psychically slumbering, as yet but dimly conscious. All that we can call intelligence, understanding, and reason are yet lacking in him. He moves about with a floating, rather than pacing, motion, by means of four limb-like organs, forwards, backwards, sideways, and in all directions. But as regards the soul of this being something has already been said.

We must not think, however, that the movements, or other expressions of life evinced by these beings, were irrational or unregulated. On the contrary, they were perfectly regulated, and nothing happened without purpose and meaning, the only difference being that the guiding power, or understanding, was not within the beings themselves; rather were they controlled by an intelligence outside themselves. Higher beings, more fully developed than they, hovered round them, as it were, and guided them; for that is the all-important and fundamental quality of the firemist, that human beings at this stage of evolution could incarnate in it, while at the same time higher beings could also incorporate therein, and could thus be in full intercommunication with man. Man had developed his inclinations, instincts, and passions, up to a point at which they could clothe themselves in the firemist; but the other order of beings here mentioned could, by the power of their reason, create within this firemist, by means of their intelligent activity. For these latter possessed still higher faculties by means of which they could reach up to higher regions. From these regions their determinations and impulses emanated, but the actual effects of these determinations were apparent in the firemist. All that was done on the earth by man originated in the regulated intercourse of the human firemist body with that of those higher beings.

58

We can therefore say that man strove to climb upwards; in the firemist he was to evolve higher qualities — in a human sense — than he had possessed before. The other beings, however, strove downwards towards the material. Their course of evolution was to seek expression for their creative forces in ever denser and denser material forms; but in a wider sense this in no wise meant a degradation for them. We must come to a very clear understanding on this point: it requires higher power and capacity to control denser than rarer forms of matter. These higher beings, too, had in former periods of their evolution a power as limited in extent as that of man at the present time. And they, like man to-day, once had dominion only over that which took place within them; they had no control over the outer coarse matter. They now strove to reach a condition in which they should magically direct external things, and were, therefore, at this period ahead of man in evolution. Man reached upwards, striving first to embody the mind in finer substances, so that it could afterwards direct its activity outwards. He had already assimilated reason, and now became possessed of magic power in order to permeate with reason the surrounding world. Thus man advanced upwards through the stage of the firemist, while his companions pressed downwards through the same stage in order to increase their power.

The forces which above all others were most effective in the firemist were those known to men as lower passions and impulses. Man, as well as the higher beings, makes use of these forces at the firemist period described; and these forces, working at that stage within the human form, have the effect of developing organs which enabled man to think, and thus to develop his personality. In the higher beings, however, these forces worked, at the stage with which we are now dealing, in such a manner that the beings mentioned could make use of them in order impersonally to bring about terrestrial conditions through their medium. By this means there arose on the earth, through these beings, forms which were themselves an image of the laws of reason. Thus, through the activity of the passional forces, there appeared in man the personal reasoning organs, and round about him, by means of the same forces, organisations replete with intelligence were formed.

Let us now think of this process as a little further advanced, or rather, let us bring before us what we find registered in the Âkâshic Records, when we glance at a somewhat later period: The moon has separated from the earth; a great revolution has thereby been accomplished. A great part of the heat has escaped from the objects surrounding man, whereby these objects have passed into a coarser and denser order of matter. Man must live in this colder environment, and he can only do so by altering his own matter; and a change of form goes hand in hand with this densification of substance. For the condition of firemist on earth has itself given place to one which is entirely different. The result of this is that the higher beings spoken of no longer have the firemist as a medium for their activity. Nor can they consequently any longer exercise an influence over the expression of man's soul-life, formerly their chief sphere of activity. But they have obtained power over the human form which they themselves had before created from the firemist.

This change of activities goes hand in hand with a transformation of the human form. One half of the latter, with two motory organs, has been transformed into the lower half of the body, which has thus become mainly the vehicle of nutrition and generation. The other half is, as it were, directed upwards. Out of the two other organs of motion grow rudimentary hands. And such organs as had once also served for nutrition and generation are remodelled into organs of speech and thought. Man stands upright. That is the immediate consequence of the moon's exit. And together with the moon the terrestrial globe is deprived of all those forces which, in the period of the firemist, had enabled man to practise self-fructification and to bring forth beings like himself without external influence. The whole lower half of his body — that which we often call his lower nature — is now subject to the formative influence, governed by reason, of those higher beings. That which these beings had themselves been able to regulate before in man, while the volume of forces, henceforth withdrawn into the moon, were still united with the earth, must now be organized by them with the co-operation of the two sexes. This explains why the moon has been regarded by Initiates as the symbol of generative forces, these forces clinging to it, as it were.

The higher beings, described above, being akin to the moon, are in a certain sense, moon-gods. Before the separation of the moon, they worked by its force in man; afterwards their forces worked from outside to effect the propagation of man. We may also truly say that those exalted spiritual forces which were formerly acting upon man's still higher instincts through the medium of the firemist have now descended to unfold their powers in the realm of reproduction. Lofty, divine forces are actually at work in regulating and organising this function.

In this we have the expression of an important teaching of Occult Science, which says that the high and sublime god-like forces are akin to the — apparently — lower forces of human nature. The word "apparently" must here be understood in its full significance; for it would be a complete misconception of occult truths to regard the force of generation in itself as something ignoble. It is only when man misuses this force and compels it

60

to serve his passions and desires that evil lurks in it; but not when he ennobles it by the thought that it contains divine, spiritual strength. Then will he place these forces at the service of the evolution of the earth, and will carry out the plans of those higher beings by means of his own generative forces. To raise this entire domain and place it under divine laws — not to destroy it — is what Occult Science teaches us. The latter can be the only result of superficially understood occult principles, distorted into mistaken asceticism.

We see that man had developed in the upper half of his body something over which the higher beings we spoke of had no influence; over this part other beings now obtain authority. They are those who had, indeed, at earlier stages of development advanced beyond humanity, but had not yet risen so high as the moon-gods. They could, so far, develop no power in the firemist; but now that a later condition has appeared in which, through the firemist, something in man's reasoning organs had attained development, something to which they themselves had approached earlier — now their time has come.

In the case of the moon-gods the stage at which reason worked and organized outwardly had arrived earlier. In them this reason was present at the beginning of the firemist epoch. They could act outwardly on terrestrial objects, but the beings just described had not at an earlier period attained the development of an outwardly active reason, and therefore the firemist period found them unprepared. Now, however, reason is there. It is present in man, and they seize this human reason in order that they may work upon the things of earth through it. Just as formerly the moon-gods had worked upon the whole man, these work now on his lower half only, whereas the influence of the lower beings spoken of is at work upon his upper half.

Thus man is subject to a twofold guidance. In his lower nature he is subject to the power of the moon-gods, but in his evolved personality he has come under the leadership of those beings called collectively by the name of their regent "Lucifer." For the Lucifer-beings complete their own evolution by making use of the awakened forces of man's reason. They could not attain this stage earlier. But they confer on man at the same time the disposition towards freedom, the tendency to distinguish "good" from "evil." Under the sole guidance of the moon-gods the human reasoning organ is indeed formed, but these gods would have allowed the organ to slumber; they would have had no interest in using it for themselves. They had their own powers of reason. The Lucifer-beings had an interest in developing human reason, in guiding it to the objects of earth for their own sake, and therefore they became for humanity the teachers of all that can be accomplished through man's reason. They could, however, be no more than instigators. For they could not develop reason in themselves, but, as we have seen, they could only do so in man. There arose thus a twofold stream of activity on earth. The one, arising from the direct influence of the moon-deities, was regulated from the beginning by law and reason; for the moon-gods, having already finished their time of apprenticeship, were now beyond the possibility of error. On the other hand, the Lucifer-gods, who had intercourse with man, had first of all to work their way to the light of such knowledge. Under their guidance man had to learn the laws of his nature; under the guidance of Lucifer he must himself become as "a god among gods."

The question arises: if the Lucifer-beings had not progressed in their evolution to the point of intelligent creation in the firemist, where did they fall behind? Up to what stage in the earth's evolution were they able to co-operate with the moon-gods? The Âkâshic Records show us that they were able to take part in earthly creation up to the period at which the sun separated from the earth. We are shown that up to this time they performed what, it is true, was work of a somewhat inferior nature to that of the moon-gods, but nevertheless they belonged to the band of divine creators. After the separation of earth and sun, an activity — the work in the firemist — began on the former for which the moon-deities, but not the Lucifer-Spirits, were prepared. For these a period of inactivity and waiting then began.

Now, when the universal firemist had rolled away and the human beings began to work on the formation of their intellectual organs, the Lucifer-Spirits could again emerge from their period of rest. For the creation of reason is correlated with solar activity, and the dawn of intelligence in human nature is the rise of an inner sun. This is affirmed not merely figuratively, but in an absolutely real sense. These beings found thus an opportunity of resuming their activity within the human being, in conjunction with the sun, when the firemist epoch had passed away from earth. From this it is easy to see the origin of the name "Lucifer" — that is, "Light-bearer" — and to understand why these beings are characterised in Occult Science as "sun-gods."

The readings from the Âkâshic Records describing the first beginnings of our earth and its inhabitants are to be found in *An Outline Of Occult Science* — the most important of Dr Steiner's works which has so far appeared — in the fifth chapter entitled "The Evolution of the World and Man." The reader will there find the present studies of the Âkâshic Records carried back to the origins of what we find in the worlds to-day. THE END

BOOK TWO.
THE STORY OF ATLANTIS
& THE LOST LEMURIA

(W. SCOTT-ELLIOT & CHARLES LEADBEATER)
PREFACE.

For readers unacquainted with the progress that has been made in recent years by earnest students of occultism attached to the Theosophical Society, the significance of the statement embodied in the following pages would be misapprehended without some preliminary explanation. Historical research has depended for western civilisation hitherto, on written records of one kind or another. When literary memoranda have fallen short, stone monuments have sometimes been available, and fossil remains have given us a few unequivocal, though inarticulate assurances concerning the antiquity of the human race; but modern culture has lost sight of or has overlooked possibilities connected with the investigation of past events, which are independent of fallible evidence transmitted to us by ancient writers. The world at large is thus at present so imperfectly alive to the resources of human faculty, that by most people as yet, the very existence, even as a potentiality, of psychic powers, which some of us all the while are consciously exercising every day, is scornfully denied and derided. The situation is sadly ludicrous from the point of view of those who appreciate the prospects of evolution, because mankind is thus wilfully holding at arm's length, the knowledge that is essential to its own ulterior progress. The maximum cultivation of which the human intellect is susceptible while it denies itself all the resources of its higher spiritual consciousness, can never be more than a preparatory process as compared with that which may set in when the faculties are sufficiently enlarged to enter into conscious relationship with the super-physical planes or aspects of Nature.

For anyone who will have the patience to study the published results of psychic investigation during the last fifty years, the reality of clairvoyance as an occasional phenomenon of human intelligence must establish itself on an immovable foundation. For those who, without being occultists—students that is to say of Nature's loftier aspects, in a position to obtain better teaching than that which any written books can give—for those who merely avail themselves of recorded evidence, a declaration on the part of others of a disbelief in the possibility of clairvoyance, is on a level with the proverbial African's disbelief in ice. But the experiences of clairvoyance that have accumulated on the hands of those who have studied it in connection with mesmerism, do no more than prove the existence in human nature of a capacity for cognizing physical phenomena distant either in space or time, in some way which has nothing to do with the physical senses. Those who have studied the mysteries of clairvoyance in connection with theosophic teaching have been enabled to realize that the ultimate resources of that faculty range as far beyond its humbler manifestations, dealt with by unassisted enquirers, as the resources of the higher mathematics exceed those of the abacus. Clairvoyance, indeed, is of many kinds, all of which fall easily into their places when we appreciate the manner in which human consciousness functions on different planes of Nature. The faculty of reading the pages of a closed book, or of discerning objects blindfold, or at a distance from the observer, is quite a different faculty from that employed on the cognition of past events. That last is the kind of which it is necessary to say something here, in order that the true character of the present treatise on Atlantis may be understood, but I allude to the others merely that the explanation I have to give may not be mistaken for a complete theory of clairvoyance in all its varieties.

We may best be helped to a comprehension of clairvoyance as related to past events, by considering in the first instance the phenomena of memory. The theory of memory which relates it to an imaginary rearrangement of physical molecules of brain matter, going on at every instant of our lives, is one that presents itself as plausible to no one who can ascend one degree above the thinking level of the uncompromising atheistical materialist. To every one who accepts, as even a reasonable hypothesis, the idea that a man is something more than a carcase in a state of animation, it must be a reasonable hypothesis that memory has to do with that principle in man which is super-physical. His memory in short, is a function of some other than the physical plane. The pictures of memory are imprinted, it is clear, on some non-physical medium, and are accessible to the embodied thinker in ordinary cases by virtue of some effort he makes in as much unconsciousness as to its precise character, as he is unconscious of the brain impulse which actuates the muscles of his heart. The events with which he has had to do in the past are photographed by Nature on some imperishable page of super-physical matter, and by making an appropriate interior effort, he is capable of bringing them again, when he requires them, within the area of some interior sense which reflects its perception on the physical brain. We are not all of us able to make this effort equally well, so that memory is sometimes dim, but even in the experience of mesmeric research, the occasional super-excitation of memory under mesmerism is a familiar fact. The circumstances plainly show that the record of Nature is accessible if we know how to recover it, or even if our own capacity to make an effort for its recovery is somehow improved without our having an improved knowledge of the method employed. And from this thought we may arrive by an easy transition at the idea, that in truth the records of Nature are not separate collections of individual property, but constitute the all-embracing memory of Nature herself, on which different people are in a position to make drafts according to their several capacities.

I do not say that the one thought necessarily ensues as a logical consequence of the other. Occultists know that what I have stated is the fact, but my present purpose is to show the reader who is not an Occultist, how the accomplished Occultist arrives at his results, without hoping to epitomize all the stages of his mental progress in this brief explanation. Theosophical literature at large must be consulted by those who would seek a fuller elucidation of the magnificent prospects and practical demonstrations of its teaching in many directions, which, in the course of the Theosophical development, have been laid before the world for the benefit of all who are competent to profit by them.

The memory of Nature is in reality a stupendous unity, just as in another way all mankind is found to constitute a spiritual unity if we ascend to a sufficiently elevated plane of Nature in search of the wonderful convergence where unity is reached without the loss of individuality. For ordinary humanity, however, at the early stage of its evolution represented at present by the majority, the interior spiritual capacities ranging beyond those which the brain is an instrument for expressing, are as yet too imperfectly developed to enable them to get touch with any other records in the vast archives of Nature's memory, except those with which they have individually been in contact at their creation. The blindfold interior effort they are competent to make, will not, as a rule, call up any others. But in a flickering fashion we have experience in ordinary life of efforts that are a little more effectual. "Thought Transference" is a humble example. In that case "impressions on the mind" of one person—Nature's memory pictures, with which he is in normal relationship, are caught up by someone else who is just able, however unconscious of the method he uses—to range Nature's memory under favourable conditions, a little beyond the area with which he himself is in normal relationship. Such a person has begun, however slightly, to exercise the faculty of astral clairvoyance. That term may be conveniently used to denote the kind of clairvoyance I am now endeavouring to elucidate, the kind which, in some of its more magnificent developments, has been employed to carry out the investigations on the basis of which the present account of Atlantis has been compiled.

There is no limit really to the resources of astral clairvoyance in investigations concerning the past history of the earth, whether we are concerned with the events that have befallen the human race in prehistoric epochs, or with the growth of the planet itself through geological periods which antedated the advent of man, or with more recent events, current narrations of which have been distorted by careless or perverse historians. The memory of Nature is infallibly accurate and inexhaustibly minute. A time will come as certainly as the precession of the equinoxes, when the literary method of historical research will be laid aside as out of date, in the case of all original work. People among us who are capable of exercising astral clairvoyance in full perfection—but have not yet been called away to higher functions in connexion with the promotion of human progress, of which ordinary humanity at present knows even less than an Indian ryot knows of cabinet councils—are still very few. Those who know what the few can do, and through what processes of training and self-discipline they have passed in pursuit of interior ideals, of which when attained astral clairvoyance is but an individual circumstance, are many, but still a small minority as compared with the modern cultivated world. But as time goes on, and within a measurable future, some of us have reason to feel sure that the numbers of those who are competent to exercise astral clairvoyance will increase sufficiently to extend the circle of those who are aware of their capacities, till it comes to embrace all the intelligence and culture of civilised mankind only a few generations hence. Meanwhile the present volume is the first that has been put forward as the pioneer essay of the new method of historical research. It is amusing to all who are concerned with it, to think how inevitably it will be mistaken—for some little while as yet, by materialistic readers, unable to accept the frank explanation here given of the principle on which it has been prepared—for a work of imagination.

For the benefit of others who may be more intuitive it may be well to say a word or two that may guard them from supposing that because historical research by means of astral clairvoyance is not impeded by having to deal with periods removed from our own by hundreds of thousands of years, it is on that account a process which involves no trouble. Every fact stated in the present volume has been picked up bit by bit with watchful and attentive care, in the course of an investigation on which more than one qualified person has been engaged, in the intervals of other activity, for some years past. And to promote the success of their work they have been allowed access to some maps and other records physically preserved from the remote periods concerned—though in safer keeping than in that of the turbulent races occupied in Europe with the development of civilisation in brief intervals of leisure from warfare, and hard pressed by the fanaticism that so long treated science as sacrilegious during the middle ages of Europe.

Laborious as the task has been however, it will be recognized as amply repaying the trouble taken, by everyone who is able to perceive how absolutely necessary to a proper comprehension of the world as we find it, is a proper comprehension of its preceding Atlantean phase. Without this knowledge all speculations concerning ethnology are futile and misleading. The course of race development is chaos and confusion without the key furnished by the character of Atlantean civilization and the configuration of the earth at Atlantean periods. Geologists know that land and ocean surfaces must have repeatedly changed places during the period at which they also know—from the situation of human remains in the various strata—that the lands were inhabited. And yet for want of accurate knowledge as to the dates at which the changes took place, they discard the whole theory from their practical thinking, and except for certain hypotheses started by naturalists dealing with the southern hemisphere, have generally endeavoured to harmonize race migrations with the configuration of the earth in existence at the present time.

In this way nonsense is made of the whole retrospect; and the ethnological scheme remains so vague and shadowy that it fails to displace crude conceptions of mankind's beginning which still dominate religious thinking, and keep back the spiritual progress of the age. The decadence and ultimate disappearance of Atlantean civilisation is in turn as instructive as its rise and glory; but I have now accomplished the main purpose with which I sought leave to introduce the work now before the world, with a brief prefatory explanation, and if its contents fail to convey a sense of its importance to any listeners I am now addressing, that result could hardly be accomplished by further recommendations of mine.

A. P. SINNETT.

I. THE STORY OF ATLANTIS

A Geographical, Historical and Ethnological Sketch.

The general scope of the subject before us will best be realized by considering the amount of information that is obtainable about the various nations who compose our great Fifth or Aryan Race.

From the time of the Greeks and the Romans onwards volumes have been written about every people who in their turn have filled the stage of history. The political institutions, the religious beliefs, the social and domestic manners and customs have all been analyzed and catalogued, and countless works in many tongues record for our benefit the march of progress.

Further, it must be remembered that of the history of this Fifth Race we possess but a fragment—the record merely of the last family races of the Keltic sub-race, and the first family races of our own Teutonic stock.

But the hundreds of thousands of years which elapsed from the time when the earliest Aryans left their home on the shores of the central Asian Sea to the time of the Greeks and Romans, bore witness to the rise and fall of innumerable civilizations. Of the 1st sub-race of our Aryan Race who inhabited India and colonial Egypt in prehistoric times we know practically nothing, and the same may be said of the Chaldean, Babylonian, and Assyrian nations who composed the 2nd sub-race—for the fragments of knowledge obtained from the recently deciphered hieroglyphs or cuneiform inscriptions on Egyptian tombs or Babylonian tablets can scarcely be said to constitute history. The Persians who belonged to the 3rd or Iranian sub-race have it is true, left a few more traces, but of the earlier civilizations of the Keltic or 4th sub-race we have no records at all. It is only with the rise of the last family shoots of this Keltic stock, *viz.*, the Greek and Roman peoples, that we come upon historic times.

In addition also to the blank period in the past, there is the blank period in the future. For of the seven sub-races required to complete the history of a great Root Race, five only have so far come into existence. Our own Teutonic or 5th sub-race has already developed many nations, but has not yet run its course, while the 6th and 7th sub-races, who will be developed on the continents of North and South America, will have thousands of years of history to give to the world.

In attempting, therefore, to summarize in a few pages information about the world's progress during a period which must have occupied at least as great a stretch of years as that above referred to, it must be realized how slight a sketch this must inevitably be.

A record of the world's progress during the period of the Fourth or Atlantean Race must embrace the history of many nations, and register the rise and fall of many civilizations.

Catastrophes, too, on a scale such as have not yet been experienced during the life of our present Fifth Race, took place on more than one occasion during the progress of the Fourth. The destruction of Atlantis was accomplished by a series of catastrophes varying in character from great cataclysms in which whole territories and populations perished, to comparatively unimportant landslips such as occur on our own coasts to-day. When the destruction was once inaugurated by the first great catastrophe there was no intermission of the minor landslips which continued slowly but steadily to eat away the continent. Four of the great catastrophes stand out above the rest in magnitude. The first took place in the Miocene age, about 800,000 years ago. The second, which was of minor importance, occurred about 200,000 years ago. The third—about 80,000 years ago—was a very great one. It destroyed all that remained of the Atlantean continent, with the exception of the island to which Plato gave the name of Poseidonis, which in its turn was submerged in the fourth and final great catastrophe of 9,564 B.C.

Now the testimony of the oldest writers and of modern scientific research alike bear witness to the existence of an ancient continent occupying the site of the lost Atlantis.

Before proceeding to the consideration of the subject itself, it is proposed cursorily to glance at the generally known sources which supply corroborative evidence. These may be grouped into the five following classes:

First, the testimony of the deep-sea soundings.

Second, the distribution of fauna and flora.

Third, the similarity of language and of ethnological type.

Fourth, the similarity of religious belief, ritual, and architecture.

Fifth, the testimony of ancient writers, of early race traditions, and of archaic flood-legends.

In the first place, then, the testimony of the deep-sea soundings may be summarized in a few words. Thanks chiefly to the expeditions of the British and American gunboats, "Challenger" and "Dolphin" (though Germany also was associated in this scientific exploration) the bed of the whole Atlantic Ocean is now mapped out, with the result that an immense bank or ridge of great elevation is shewn to exist in mid-Atlantic. This ridge stretches in a south-westerly direction from about fifty degrees north towards the coast of South America, then in a south-easterly direction towards the coast of Africa, changing its direction again about Ascension Island, and running due south to Tristan d'Acunha. The ridge rises almost sheer about 9,000 feet from the ocean depths around it, while the Azores, St. Paul, Ascension, and Tristan d'Acunha are the peaks of this land which still remain above water. A line of 3,500 fathoms, or say, 21,000 feet, is required to sound the deepest parts of the Atlantic, but the higher parts of the ridge are only a hundred to a few hundred fathoms beneath the sea.

The soundings too showed that the ridge is covered with volcanic *débris* of which traces are to be found right across the ocean to the American coasts. Indeed the fact that the ocean bed, particularly about the Azores, has been the scene of volcanic disturbance on a gigantic scale, and that within a quite measurable period of geologic time, is conclusively proved by the investigations made during the above named expeditions.

Mr. Starkie Gardner is of opinion that in the Eocene times the British Islands formed part of a larger island or continent stretching into the Atlantic, and "that a great tract of land formerly existed where the sea now is, and that Cornwall, the Scilly and Channel Islands, Ireland and Brittany are the remains of its highest summits" (*Pop. Sc. Review*, July, 1878).

Second.—The proved existence on continents separated by great oceans of similar or identical species of fauna and flora is the standing puzzle to biologists and botanists alike. But if a link between these continents once existed allowing for the natural migration of such animals and plants, the puzzle is solved. Now the fossil remains of the camel are found in India, Africa, South America and Kansas: but it is one of the generally accepted hypotheses of naturalists that every species of animal and plant originated in but one part of the globe, from which centre it gradually overran the other portions. How then can the facts of such fossil remains be accounted for without the existence of land communication in some remote age? Recent discoveries in the fossil beds of Nebraska seem also to prove that the horse originated in the Western Hemisphere, for that is the only part of the world where fossil remains have been discovered, showing the various intermediate forms which have been identified as the precursors of the true horse. It would therefore be difficult to account for the presence of the horse in Europe except on the hypothesis of continuous land communication between the two continents, seeing that it is certain that the horse existed in a wild state in Europe and Asia before his domestication by man, which may be traced back almost to the stone age. Cattle and sheep as we now

70

know them have an equally remote ancestry. Darwin finds domesticated cattle in Europe in the earliest part of the stone age, having long before developed out of wild forms akin to the buffalo of America. Remains of the cave-lion of Europe are also found in North America.

Turning now from the animal to the vegetable kingdom it appears that the greater part of the flora of the Miocene age in Europe—found chiefly in the fossil beds of Switzerland—exist at the present day in America, some of them in Africa. But the noteworthy fact about America is that while the greater proportion are to be found in the Eastern States, very many are wanting on the Pacific coast. This seems to show that it was from the Atlantic side that they entered the continent. Professor Asa Gray says that out of 66 genera and 155 species found in the forest east of the Rocky Mountains, only 31 genera and 78 species are found west of these heights.

But the greatest problem of all is the plantain or banana. Professor Kuntze, an eminent German botanist, asks, "In what way was this plant" (a native of tropical Asia and Africa) "which cannot stand a voyage through the temperate zone, carried to America?" As he points out, the plant is seedless, it cannot be propagated by cuttings, neither has it a tuber which could be easily transported. Its root is tree-like. To transport it special care would be required, nor could it stand a long transit. The only way in which he can account for its appearance in America is to suppose that it must have been transported by civilized man at a time when the polar regions had a tropical climate! He adds, "a cultivated plant which does not possess seeds must have been under culture for a *very long period* ... it is perhaps fair to infer that these plants were cultivated as early as the beginning of the Diluvial period." Why, it may be asked, should not this inference take us back to still earlier times, and where did the civilization necessary for the plant's cultivation exist, or the climate and circumstances requisite for its transportation, unless there were at some time a link between the old world and the new?

Professor Wallace in his delightful *Island Life* as well as other writers in many important works, have put forward ingenious hypotheses to account for the identity of flora and fauna on widely separated lands, and for their transit across the ocean, but all are unconvincing, and all break down at different points.

It is well known that wheat as we know it has never existed in a truly wild state, nor is there any evidence tracing its descent from fossil species. Five varieties of wheat were *already cultivated* in Europe in the stone age— one variety found in the "Lake dwellings" being known as Egyptian wheat, from which Darwin argues that the Lake dwellers "either still kept up commercial intercourse with some southern people, or had originally proceeded as colonists from the south." He concludes that wheat, barley, oats, etc., are descended from various *species now extinct*, or so widely different as to escape identification in which case he says: "Man must have cultivated cereals from an enormously remote period." The regions where these extinct species flourished, and the civilization under which they were cultivated by intelligent selection, are both supplied by the lost continent whose colonists carried them east and west.

Third.—From the fauna and flora we now turn to man.

Language.—The Basque language stands alone amongst European tongues, having affinity with none of them. According to Farrar, "there never has been any doubt that this isolated language, preserving its identity in a western corner of Europe, between two mighty kingdoms, resembles in its structure the aboriginal languages of the vast opposite continent (America) and those alone" (*Families of Speech*, p. 132).

The Phoenicians apparently were the first nation in the Eastern Hemisphere to use a phonetic alphabet, the characters being regarded as mere signs for sounds. It is a curious fact that at an equally early date we find a phonetic alphabet in Central America amongst the Mayas of Yucatan, whose traditions ascribe the origin of their civilization to a land across the sea to the east. Le Plongeon, the great authority on this subject, writes: "One-third of this tongue (the Maya) is pure Greek. Who brought the dialect of Homer to America? or who took to Greece that of the Mayas? Greek is the off-spring of the Sanskrit. Is Maya? or are they coeval?" Still more surprising is it to find thirteen letters out of the Maya alphabet bearing most distinct relation to the Egyptian hieroglyphic signs for the same letters. It is probable that the earliest form of alphabet was hieroglyphic, "the writing of the Gods," as the Egyptians called it, and that it developed later in Atlantis into the phonetic. It would be natural to assume that the Egyptians were an early colony from Atlantis (as they actually were) and that they carried away with them the primitive type of writing which has thus left its traces on both hemispheres, while the Phoenicians, who were a sea-going people, obtained and assimilated the later form of alphabet during their trading voyages with the people of the west.

One more point may be noticed, *viz.*, the extraordinary resemblance between many words in the Hebrew language and words bearing precisely the same meaning in the tongue of the Chiapenecs—a branch of the Maya race, and amongst the most ancient in Central America. A list of these words is given in *North Americans of Antiquity*, p. 475.

The similarity of language among the various savages races of the Pacific islands has been used as an argument by writers on this subject. The existence of similar languages among races separated by leagues of ocean, across which in historic time they are known to have had no means of transport, is certainly an argument in favour of their descent from a single race occupying a single continent, but the argument cannot be used here, for the continent in question was not Atlantis, but the still earlier Lemuria.

Ethnological Types.—Atlantis as we shall see is said to have been inhabited by red, yellow, white and black races. It is now proved by the researches of Le Plongeon, De Quatrefages, Bancroft and others that black populations of negroid type existed even up to recent times in America. Many of the monuments of Central America are decorated with negro faces, and some of the idols found there are clearly intended to represent negros, with small skulls, short woolly hair and thick lips. The Popul Vuh, speaking of the first home of the Guatemalan race, says that "black and white men together" lived in this happy land "in great peace," speaking "one language." (See Bancroft's *Native Races*, p. 547.) The Popul Vuh goes on to relate how the people migrated from their ancestral home, how their language *became altered*, and how some went to the east, while other travelled west (to Central America).

Professor Retzius, in his *Smithsonian Report*, considers that the primitive dolichocephalæ of America are nearly related to the Guanches of the Canary Islands, and to the population on the Atlantic seaboard of Africa, which Latham comprises under the name of Egyptian-Atlantidæ. The same form of skull is found in the Canary Islands off the African coast and the Caribe Islands off the American coast, while the colour of the skin in both is that of a reddish-brown.

The ancient Egyptians depicted themselves as red men of much the same complexion as exists to-day among some tribes of American Indians.

"The ancient Peruvians," says Short, "appear from numerous examples of hair found in their tombs to have been an auburn-haired race."

A remarkable fact about the American Indians, and one which is a standing puzzle to ethnologists, is the wide range of colour and complexion to be found among them. From the white tint of the Menominee, Dakota, Mandan and Zuni tribes, many of whom have auburn hair and blue eyes, to the almost negro blackness of the Karos of Kansas and the now extinct tribes of California, the Indian races run through every shade of red-brown, copper, olive, cinnamon, and bronze. (See Short's *North Americans of Antiquity*, Winchell's *Pre-Adamites*, and Catlin's *Indians of North America*; see also *Atlantis*, by Ignatius Donnelly who has collected a great mass of evidence under this and other heads.) We shall see by and by how the diversity of complexion on the American continent is accounted for by the original race-tints on the parent continent of Atlantis.

Fourth.—Nothing seems to have surprised the first Spanish adventurers in Mexico and Peru more than the extraordinary similarity to those of the old world, of the religious beliefs, rites, and emblems which they found established in the new. The Spanish priests regarded this similarity as the work of the devil. The worship of the cross by the natives, and its constant presence in all religious buildings and ceremonies, was the principal subject of their amazement; and indeed nowhere—not even in India and Egypt— was this symbol held in more profound veneration than amongst the primitive tribes of the American continents, while the meaning underlying its worship was identical. In the west, as in the east, the cross was the symbol of life—sometimes of life physical, more often of life eternal.

In like manner in both hemispheres the worship of the sun-disk or circle, and of the serpent, was universal, and more surprising still is the similarity of the word signifying "God" in the principal languages of east and west. Compare the Sanscrit "Dyaus" or "Dyaus-pitar," the Greek "Theos" and Zeus, the Latin "Deus" and "Jupiter," the Keltic "Dia" and "Ta," pronounced "Thyah" (seeming to bear affinity to the Egyptian Tau), the Jewish "Jah" or "Yah" and lastly the Mexican "Teo" or "Zeo."

Baptismal rites were practised by all nations. In Babylon and Egypt the candidates for initiation into the Mysteries were first baptized. Tertullian in his *De Baptismo* says that they were promised in consequence "regeneration and the pardon of all their perjuries." The Scandinavian nations practised baptism of new-born children; and when we turn to Mexico and Peru we find infant baptism there as a solemn ceremonial, consisting of water sprinkling, the sign of the cross, and prayers for the washing away of sin (see Humboldt's *Mexican Researches* and Prescott's *Mexico*).

In addition to baptism, the tribes of Mexico, Central America and Peru resembled the nations of the old world in their rites of confession, absolution, fasting, and marriage before priests by joining hands. They had even a ceremony resembling the Eucharist, in which cakes marked with the Tau (an Egyptian form of cross) were eaten, the people calling them the flesh of their God. These exactly resemble the sacred cakes of Egypt and other eastern nations. Like these nations too, the people of the new world had monastic orders, male and female, in which broken vows were punished with death. Like the Egyptians they embalmed their dead, they worshipped sun, moon, and planets, but over and above these adored a Deity "omnipresent, who knoweth all things ... invisible, incorporeal, one God of perfect perfection" (see Sahagun's *Historia de Nueva Espâna*, lib. vi.).

They too had their virgin-mother goddess, "Our Lady" whose son, the "Lord of Light," was called the "Saviour," bearing an accurate correspondence to Isis, Beltis and the many other virgin-goddesses of the east with their divine sons.

Their rites of sun and fire worship closely resembled those of the early Kelts of Britain and Ireland, and like the latter they claimed to be the "children of the sun." An ark or argha was one of the universal sacred symbols which we find alike in India, Chaldea, Assyria, Egypt, Greece and amongst the Keltic peoples. Lord Kingsborough in his *Mexican Antiquities* (vol. viii. p. 250) says: "As among the Jews the ark was a sort of portable temple in which the deity was supposed to be continually present, so among the Mexicans, the Cherokees and the Indians of Michoacan and Honduras, an ark was held in the highest veneration and was considered an object too sacred to be touched by any but the priests."

As to religious architecture, we find on both sides of the Atlantic that one of the earliest sacred buildings is the pyramid. Doubtful as are the uses for which these structures were originally intended, one thing is clear, that they were closely connected with some religious idea or group of ideas. The identity of design in the pyramids of Egypt and those of Mexico and Central America is too striking to be a mere coincidence. True some—the greater number—of the American pyramids are of the truncated or flattened form, yet according to Bancroft and others, many of those found in Yucatan, and notably those near Palenque, are pointed at the top in true Egyptian fashion, while on the other hand we have some of the Egyptian pyramids of the stepped and flattened type. Cholula has been compared to the groups of Dachour, Sakkara and the step pyramid of Médourn. Alike in orientation, in structure, and even in their internal galleries and chambers, these mysterious monuments of the east and of the west stand as witnesses to some common source whence their builders drew their plan.

The vast remains of cities and temples in Mexico and Yucatan also strangely resemble those of Egypt, the ruins of Teotihuacan having frequently been compared to those of Karnak. The "false arch"—horizontal courses of stone, each slightly overlapping the other—is found to be identical in Central America, in the oldest buildings of Greece, and in Etruscan remains. The mound builders of both eastern and western continents formed similar tumuli over their dead, and laid the bodies in similar stone coffins. Both continents have their great serpent-mounds; compare that of Adams Co., Ohio, with the fine serpent-mound discovered in Argyleshire, or the less perfect specimen at Avebury in Wilts. The very carving and decoration of the temples of America, Egypt and India have much in common, while some of the mural decorations are absolutely identical.

Fifth.—It only remains now to summarize some of the evidence obtainable from ancient writers, from early race traditions, and from archaic flood-legends.

Aelian in his *Varia Historia* (lib. iii. ch. xviii.), states that Theopompus (400 B.C.) recorded an interview between the King of Phrygia and Silenus, in which the latter referred to the existence of a great continent beyond the Atlantic, larger than Asia, Europe and Libya together.

Proclus quotes an extract from an ancient writer who refers to the islands in the sea beyond the Pillars of Hercules (Straits of Gibraltar), and says that the inhabitants of one of these islands had a tradition from their ancestors of an extremely large island called Atlantis, which for a long time ruled over all the islands of the Atlantic Ocean.

Marcellus speaks of seven islands in the Atlantic, and states that their inhabitants preserve the memory of a much greater island, Atlantis, "which had for a long time exercised dominion over the smaller ones."

Diodorus Siculus relates that the Phœnicians discovered "a large island in the Atlantic Ocean beyond the Pillars of Hercules several days' sail from the coast of Africa."

But the greatest authority on this subject is Plato. In the *Timæus* he refers to the island continent, while the *Critias* or *Atlanticus* is nothing less than a detailed account of the history, arts, manners and customs of the people. In the *Timæus* he refers to "a mighty warlike power, rushing from the Atlantic sea and spreading itself with hostile fury over all Europe and Asia. For at that time the Atlantic sea was navigable and had an island before that mouth which is called by you the Pillars of Hercules. But this island was greater than both Libya and all Asia together, and afforded an easy passage to other neighbouring islands, as it was likewise easy to pass from those islands to all the continents which border on this Atlantic sea."

There is so much of value in the *Critias* that it is not easy to choose, but the following extract is given, as it bears on the material resources of the country: "They had likewise everything provided for them which both in a city and every other place is sought after as useful for the purposes of life. And they were supplied indeed with many things from foreign countries, on account of their extensive empire; but the island afforded them the greater part of everything of which they stood in need. In the first place the island supplied them with such things as are dug out of mines in a solid state, and with such as are melted: and orichalcum, which is now but seldom mentioned, but then was much celebrated, was dug out of the earth in many parts of the island, and was considered as the most honourable of all metals except gold. Whatever, too, the woods afforded for builders the island produced in abundance. There were likewise sufficient pastures there for tame and savage animals; together with a prodigious number of elephants. For there were pastures for all such animals as are fed in lakes and rivers, on mountains and in plains. And in like manner there was sufficient aliment for the largest and most voracious kind of animals. Besides this, whatever of odoriferous the earth nourishes at present, whether roots, or grass, or wood, or juices, or gums, flowers or fruits—these the island produced and produced them well."

The Gauls possessed traditions of Atlantis which were collected by the Roman historian, Timagenes, who lived in the first century, B.C. Three distinct peoples apparently dwelt in Gaul. First, the indigenous population (probably the remains of a Lemurian race), second, the invaders from the distant island of Atlantis, and third, the Aryan Gauls (see *Pre-Adamites*, p. 380).

The Toltecs of Mexico traced themselves back to a starting-point called Atlan or Aztlan; the Aztecs also claimed to come from Aztlan (see Bancroft's *Native Races*, vol. v. pp. 221 and 321).

The Popul Vuh (p. 294) speaks of a visit paid by three sons of the King of the Quiches to a land "in the east on the shores of the sea whence their fathers had come," from which they brought back amongst other things "a system of writing" (see also Bancroft, vol. v. p. 553).

Amongst the Indians of North America there is a very general legend that their forefathers came from a land "toward the sun-rising." The Iowa and Dakota Indians, according to Major J. Lind, believed that "all the tribes of Indians were formerly one and dwelt together *on an island* ... towards the sunrise." They crossed the sea from thence "in huge skiffs in which the Dakotas of old floated for weeks, finally gaining dry land."

The Central American books state that a part of the American continent extended far into the Atlantic Ocean, and that this region was destroyed by a series of frightful cataclysms at long intervals apart. *Three* of these are frequently referred to (see Baldwin's *Ancient America*, p. 176). It is a curious confirmation that the Kelts of Britain had a legend that part of *their* country once extended far into the Atlantic and was destroyed. Three catastrophes are mentioned in the Welsh traditions.

Quetzalcoatl, the Mexican Deity, is said to have come from "the distant east." He is described as a white man with a flowing beard. (N.B.—The Indians of North and South America are beardless.) He originated letters and regulated the Mexican calendar. After having taught them many peaceful arts and lessons he sailed away *to the east* in a canoe of serpent skins (see Short's *North Americans of Antiquity*, pp. 268-271). The same story is told of Zamna, the author of civilization in Yucatan.

The marvellous uniformity of the flood legends on all parts of the globe, alone remains to be dealt with. Whether these are some archaic versions of the story of the lost Atlantis and its submergence, or whether they are echoes of a great cosmic parable once taught and held in reverence in some common centre whence they have reverberated throughout the world, does not immediately concern us. Sufficient for our purpose is it to show the universal acceptance of these legends. It would be needless waste of time and space to go over these flood stories one by one. Suffice it to say, that in India, Chaldea, Babylon, Media, Greece, Scandinavia, China, amongst the Jews and amongst the Keltic tribes of Britain, the legend is absolutely identical in all essentials. Now turn to the west and what do we find? The same story in its every detail preserved amongst the Mexicans (each tribe having its own version), the people of Guatemala, Honduras, Peru, and almost every tribe of North American Indians. It is puerile to suggest that mere coincidence can account for this fundamental identity.

The following quotation from Le Plongeon's translation of the famous Troano MS., which may be seen in the British Museum, will appropriately bring this part of the subject to a close. The Troano MS. appears to have been written about 3,500 years ago, among the Mayas of Yucatan, and the following is its description of the catastrophe that submerged the island of Poseidonis:—"In the year 6 Kan, on the 11th Muluc in the month Zac, there occurred terrible earthquakes, which continued without interruption until the 13th Chuen. The country of the hills of mud, the land of Mu was sacrificed: being twice upheaved it suddenly disappeared during the night, the basin being continually shaken by volcanic forces. Being confined, these caused the land to sink and to rise several times and in various places. At last the surface gave way and ten countries were torn asunder and scattered. Unable to stand the force of the convulsions, they sank with their 64,000,000 of inhabitants 8060 years before the writing of this book."

But enough space has now been devoted to the fragments of evidence— all more or less convincing—which the world so far has been in possession of. Those interested in pursuing any special line of investigation are referred to the various works above named or quoted.

The subject in hand must now be dealt with. Drawn as they have been from contemporary records which were compiled in and handed down through the ages we have to deal with, the facts here collected are based upon no assumption or conjecture. The writer may have failed fully to comprehend the facts, and so may have partially misstated them. But the original records are open for investigation to the duly qualified, and those who are disposed to undertake the necessary training may obtain the powers to check and verify.

But even were *all* the occult records open to our inspection, it should be realized how fragmentary must be the sketch that attempts to summarize in a few pages the history of races and of nations extending over at least many hundreds of thousands of years. However, any details on such a subject—disconnected though they are—must be new, and should therefore be interesting to the world at large.

Among the records above referred to there are maps of the world at various periods of its history, and it has been the great privilege of the writer to be allowed to obtain copies—more or less complete—of four of these. All four represent Atlantis and the surrounding lands at different epochs of their history. These epochs correspond approximately with the periods that lay between the catastrophes referred to above, and into the periods thus represented by the four maps the records of the Atlantean Race will naturally group themselves.

Before beginning the history of the race, however, a few remarks may be made about the geography of the four different epochs.

The first map represents the land surface of the earth as it existed about a million years ago, when the Atlantean Race was at its height, and before the first great submergence took place about 800,000 years ago. The continent of Atlantis itself, it will be observed, extended from a point a few degrees east of Iceland to about the site now occupied by Rio de Janeiro, in South America. Embracing Texas and the Gulf of Mexico, the Southern and Eastern States of America, up to and including Labrador, it stretched across the ocean to our own islands—Scotland and Ireland, and a small portion of the north of England forming one of its promontories—while its equatorial lands embraced Brazil and the whole stretch of ocean to the African Gold Coast. Scattered fragments of what eventually became the continents of Europe, Africa and America, as well as remains of the still older, and once wide-spread continent of Lemuria, are also shown on this map. The remains of the still older Hyperborean continent which was inhabited by the Second Root Race, are also given, and like Lemuria, coloured blue.

As will be seen from the second map the catastrophe of 800,000 years ago caused very great changes in the land distribution of the globe. The great continent is now shorn of its northern regions, and its remaining portion has been still further rent. The now growing American continent is separated by a chasm from its parent continent of Atlantis, and this no longer comprises any of the lands now existing, but occupies the bulk of the Atlantic basin from about 50° north to a few degrees south of the equator. The subsidences and upheavals in other parts of the world have also been considerable—the British Islands for example, now being part of a huge island which also embraces the Scandinavian peninsula, the north of France, and all the intervening and some of the surrounding seas. The dimensions of the remains of Lemuria it will be observed, have been further curtailed, while Europe, Africa and America have received accretions of territory.

The third map shows the results of the catastrophe which took place about 200,000 years ago. With the exception of the rents in the continents both of Atlantis and America, and the submergence of Egypt, it will be seen how relatively unimportant were the subsidences and upheavals at this epoch, indeed the fact that this catastrophe has not always been considered as one of the great ones, is apparent from the quotation already given from the sacred book of the Guatemalans—three great ones only being there mentioned. The Scandinavian island however, appears now as joined to the mainland. The two islands into which Atlantis was now split were known by the names of Ruta and Daitya.

The stupendous character of the natural convulsion that took place about 80,000 years ago, will be apparent from the fourth map. Daitya, the smaller and more southerly of the islands, has almost entirely disappeared, while of Ruta there only remains the relatively small island of Poseidonis. This map was compiled about 75,000 years ago, and it no doubt fairly represents the land surface of the earth from that period onwards till the final submergence of Poseidonis in 9564 B.C., though during that period minor changes must have taken place. It will be noted that the land outlines had then begun to assume roughly the same appearance they do to-day, though the British Islands were still joined to the European continent, while the Baltic Sea was non-existent, and the Sahara desert then formed part of the ocean floor.

Some reference to the very mystical subject of the Manus is a necessary preliminary to the consideration of the origin of a Root Race. In Transaction No. 26, of the London Lodge, reference was made to the work done by these very exalted Beings, which embraces not only the planning of the types of the whole Manvantara, but the superintending the formation and education of each Root Race in turn. The following quotation refers to these arrangements: "There are also Manus whose duty it is to act in a similar way for each Root Race on each Planet of the Round, the Seed Manu planning the improvement in type which each successive Root Race inaugurates and the Root Manu actually incarnating amongst the new Race as a leader and teacher to direct the development and ensure the improvement."

The way in which the necessary segregation of the picked specimens is effected by the Manu in charge, and his subsequent care of the growing community, may be dealt with in a future Transaction. The merest reference to the mode of procedure is all that is necessary here.

It was of course from one of the sub-races of the Third Root Race on the continent which is spoken of as Lemuria, that the segregation was effected which was destined to produce the Fourth Root Race.

Following where necessary the history of the Race through the four periods represented by the four maps, it is proposed to divide the subject under the following headings:

1.Origin and territorial location of the different sub-races.

2. The political institutions they respectively evolved.

3. Their emigrations to other parts of the world.

4. The arts and sciences they developed.

5. The manners and customs they adopted.

6. The rise and decline amongst them of religious ideas.

The names of the different sub-races must first be given—

1. Rmoahal.

2. Tlavatli.

3. Toltec.

4. First Turanian.

5. Original Semite.

6. Akkadian.

7. Mongolian.

Some explanation is necessary as to the principle on which these names are chosen. Wherever modern ethnologists have discovered traces of one of these sub-races, or even identified a small part of one, the name they have given to it is used for the sake of simplicity, but in the case of the first two sub-races there are hardly any traces left for science to seize upon, so the names by which they called themselves have been adopted.

Now the period represented by the first map shows the land surface of the earth as it existed about one million years ago, but the Rmoahal race came into existence between four and five million years ago, at which period large portions of the great southern continent of Lemuria still existed, while the continent of Atlantis had not assumed the proportions it ultimately attained. It was upon a spur of this Lemurian land that the Rmoahal race was born. Roughly it may be located at latitude 7° north and longitude 5° west, which a reference to any modern atlas will show to lie on the Ashanti coast of to-day. It was a hot, moist country, where huge antediluvian animals lived in reedy swamps and dank forests. The fossil remains of such plants are to-day found in the coal measures. The Rmoahals were a dark race—their complexion being a sort of mahogany black. Their height in these early days was about ten or twelve feet—truly a race of giants—but through the centuries their stature gradually dwindled, as did that of all the races in turn, and later on we shall find they had shrunk to the stature of the "Furfooz man." They ultimately migrated to the southern shores of Atlantis, where they were engaged in constant warfare with the sixth and seventh sub-races of the Lemurians then inhabiting that country. A large part of the tribe eventually moved north, while the remainder settled down and intermarried with these black Lemurian aborigines. The result was that at the period we are dealing with—the first map period—there was no pure blood left in the south, and as we shall see it was from these dark races who inhabited the equatorial provinces, and the extreme south of the continent, that the Toltec conquerors subsequently drew their supplies of slaves. The remainder of the race, however, reached the extreme north-eastern promontories contiguous with Iceland, and dwelling there for untold generations, they gradually became lighter in colour, until at the date of the first map period we find them a tolerably fair people. Their descendants eventually became subject, at least nominally, to the Semite kings.

That they dwelt there for untold generations is not meant to imply that their occupation was unbroken, for stress of circumstances at intervals of time drove them south. The cold of the glacial epochs of course operated alike with the other races, but the few words to be said on this subject may as well come in here.

Without going into the question of the different rotations which this earth performs, or the varying degrees of eccentricity of its orbit, a combination of which is sometimes held to be the cause of the glacial epochs, it is a fact—and one already recognized by some astronomers—that a minor glacial epoch occurs about every 30,000 years. But in addition to these there were two occasions in the history of Atlantis when the ice-belt desolated not merely the northern regions, but, invading the bulk of the continent, forced all life to migrate to equatorial lands. The first of these was in process during the Rmoahal days, about 3,000,000 years ago, while the second took place in the Toltec ascendency about 850,000 years ago.

With reference to all glacial epochs it should be stated that though the inhabitants of northern lands were forced to settle during the winter far south of the ice-belt, there yet were great districts to which in summer they could return, and where for the sake of the hunting they encamped until driven south again by the winter cold.

The place of origin of the Tlavatli or 2nd sub-race was an island off the west coast of Atlantis. The spot is marked on the first map with the figure 2. Thence they spread into Atlantis proper, chiefly across the middle of the continent, gradually however tending northwards towards the stretch of coast facing the promontory of Greenland. Physically they were a powerful and hardy race of a red-brown colour, but they were not quite so tall as the Rmoahals whom they drove still further north. They were always a mountain-loving people, and their chief settlements were in the mountainous districts of the interior, which a comparison of the first map and the fourth map will show to be approximately conterminous with what ultimately became the island of Poseidonis. At this first map period they also—as just stated—peopled the northern coasts, whilst a mixture of Tlavatli and Toltec race inhabited the western islands, which subsequently formed part of the American continent.

We now come to the Toltec or 3rd sub-race. This was a magnificent development. It ruled the whole continent of Atlantis for thousands of years in great material power and glory. Indeed so dominant and so endowed with vitality was this race that intermarriages with the following sub-races failed to modify the type, which still remained essentially Toltec; and hundreds of thousands of years later we find one of their remote family races ruling magnificently in Mexico and Peru, long ages before their degenerate descendants were conquered by the fiercer Aztec tribes from the north. The complexion of this race was also a red-brown, but they were redder or more copper-coloured than the Tlavatli. They also were a tall race, averaging about eight feet during the period of their ascendency, but of course dwindling, as all races did, to the dimensions that are common to-day. The type was an improvement on the two previous sub-races, the features being straight and well marked, not unlike the ancient Greek. The approximate birthplace of this race may be seen, marked with the figure 3, on the first map. It lay near the west coast of Atlantis about latitude 30° North, and the whole of the surrounding country, embracing the bulk of the west coast of the continent, was peopled with a pure Toltec race. But as we shall see when dealing with the political organization, their territory eventually extended right across the continent, and it was from their great capital on the eastern coast that the Toltec emperors held their almost world-wide sway.

These first three sub-races are spoken of as the "red races," between whom and the four following there was not at first much mixture of blood. These four, though differing considerably from each other, have been called "yellow," and this colour may appropriately define the complexion of the Turanian and Mongolian, but the Semite and Akkadian were comparatively white.

The Turanian or 4th sub-race had their origin on the eastern side of the continent, south of the mountainous district inhabited by the Tlavatli people. This spot is marked 4 on the first map. The Turanians were colonists from the earliest days, and great numbers migrated to the lands lying to the east of Atlantis. They were never a thoroughly dominant race on the mother-continent, though some of their tribes and family races became fairly powerful. The great central regions of the continent lying west and south of the Tlavatli mountainous district was their special though not their exclusive home, for they shared these lands with the Toltecs. The curious political and social experiments made by this sub-race will be dealt with later on.

As regards the original Semite or 5th sub-race ethnologists have been somewhat confused, as indeed it is extremely natural they should be considering the very insufficient data they have to go upon. This sub-race had its origin in the mountainous country which formed the more southerly of the two north-eastern peninsulas which, as we have seen, is now represented by Scotland, Ireland, and some of the surrounding seas. The site is marked 5 in the first map. In this least desirable portion of the great continent the race grew and flourished, for centuries maintaining its independence against aggressive southern kings, till the time came for it in turn to spread abroad and colonize. It must be remembered that by the time the Semites rose to power hundreds of thousands of years had passed and the 2nd map period had been reached. They were a turbulent, discontented race, always at war with their neighbours, especially with the then growing power of the Akkadians.

The birthplace of the Akkadian or 6th sub-race will be found on map #2 (marked there with the figure 6), for it was after the great catastrophe of 800,000 years ago that this race first came into existence. It took its rise in the land east of Atlantis, about the middle of the great peninsula whose south-eastern extremity stretched out towards the old continent. The spot may be located approximately at latitude 42° North and longitude 10° East. They did not for long, however, confine themselves to the land of their birth, but overran the now diminished continent of Atlantis. They fought with the Semites in many battles both on land and sea, and very considerable fleets were used on both sides. Finally about 100,000 years ago they completely vanquished the Semites, and from that time onwards an Akkadian dynasty was set up in the old Semite capital, and ruled the country wisely for several hundred years. They were a great trading, sea-going, and colonizing people, and they established many centres of communication with distant lands.

The Mongolian or 7th sub-race seems to be the only one that had absolutely no touch with the mother-continent. Having its origin on the plains of Tartary (marked No. 7 on the second map) at about latitude 63° North and longitude 140° East, it was directly developed from descendants of the Turanian race, which it gradually supplanted over the greater part of Asia. This sub-race multiplied exceedingly, and even at the present day a majority of the earth's inhabitants technically belong to it, though many of its divisions are so deeply coloured with the blood of earlier races as to be scarcely distinguishable from them.

Political Institutions.—In such a summary as this it would be impossible to describe how each sub-race was further sub-divided into nations, each having its distinct type and characteristics. All that can be here attempted is to sketch in broad outline the varying political institutions throughout the great epochs of the race.

While recognizing that each sub-race as well as each Root Race is destined to stand in some respects at a higher level than the one before it, the cyclic nature of the development must be recognized as leading the race like the man through the various phases of infancy, youth, and manhood back to the infancy of old age again. Evolution necessarily means ultimate progress, even though the turning back of its ascending spiral may seem to make the history of politics or of religion a record not merely of development and progress but also of degradation and decay.

In making the statement therefore that the 1st sub-race started under the most perfect government conceivable, it must be understood that this was owing to the necessities of their childhood, not to the merits of their matured manhood. For the Rmoahals were incapable of developing any plan of settled government, nor did they ever reach even as high a point of civilization as the 6th and 7th Lemurian sub-races. But the Manu who effected the segregation actually incarnated in the race and ruled it as king. Even when he no longer took visible part in the government of the race, Adept or Divine rulers were, when the times required it, still provided for the infant community. As students of Theosophy know, our humanity had not then reached the stage of development necessary to produce fully initiated Adepts. The rulers above referred to, including the Manu himself, were therefore necessarily the product of evolution on other systems of worlds.

The Tlavatli people showed some signs of advance in the art of government. Their various tribes or nations were ruled by chiefs or kings who generally received their authority by acclamation of the people. Naturally the most powerful individuals and greatest warriors were so chosen. A considerable empire was eventually established among them, in which one king became the nominal head, but his suzerainty consisted rather in titular honour than in actual authority.

It was the Toltec race who developed the highest civilization and organized the most powerful empire of any of the Atlantean peoples, and it was then that the principle of hereditary succession was for the first time established. The race was at first divided into a number of petty independent kingdoms, constantly at war with each other, and all at war with the Lemurio-Rmoahals of the south. These were gradually conquered and made subject peoples—many of their tribes being reduced to slavery. About one million years ago, however, these separate kingdoms united in a great federation with a recognized emperor at its head. This was of course inaugurated by great wars, but the outcome was peace and prosperity for the race.

It must be remembered that humanity was still for the most part possessed of psychic attributes, and by this time the most advanced had undergone the necessary training in the occult schools, and had attained various stages of initiation—some even reaching to Adeptship. Now the second of these emperors was an Adept, and for thousands of years the

Divine dynasty ruled not only all the kingdoms into which Atlantis was divided but the islands on the west and the southern portion of the adjacent land lying to the east. When necessary, this dynasty was recruited from the Lodge of Initiates, but as a rule the power was handed down from father to son, all being more or less qualified, and the son in some cases receiving a further degree at the hands of his father. During all this period these Initiate rulers retained connection with the Occult Hierarchy which governs the world, submitting to its laws, and acting in harmony with its plans. This was the golden age of the Toltec race. The government was just and beneficent; the arts and sciences were cultivated—indeed the workers in these fields, guided as they were by occult knowledge, achieved tremendous results; religious belief and ritual was still comparatively pure—in fact the civilization of Atlantis had by this time reached its height.

After about 100,000 years of this golden age the degeneracy and decay of the race set in. Many of the tributary kings, and large numbers of the priests and people ceased to use their faculties and powers in accordance with the laws made by their Divine rulers, whose precepts and advice were now disregarded. Their connection with the Occult Hierarchy was broken. Personal aggrandisement, the attainment of wealth and authority, the humiliation and ruin of their enemies became more and more the objects towards which their occult powers were directed: and thus turned from their lawful use, and practised for all sorts of selfish and malevolent purposes, they inevitably led to what we must call by the name of sorcery.

Surrounded as this word is with the odium which credulity on the one hand and imposture on the other have during many centuries of superstition and ignorance gradually caused it to be associated, let us consider for a moment its real meaning, and the terrible effects which its practice is ever destined to bring on the world.

Partly through their psychic faculties, which were not yet quenched in the depths of materiality to which the race afterwards descended, and partly through their scientific attainments during this culmination of Atlantean civilization, the most intellectual and energetic members of the race gradually obtained more and more insight into the working of Nature's laws, and more and more control over some of her hidden forces. Now the desecration of this knowledge and its use for selfish ends is what constitutes sorcery. The awful effects, too, of such desecration are well enough exemplified in the terrible catastrophes that overtook the race. For when once the black practice was inaugurated it was destined to spread in ever widening circles. The higher spiritual guidance being thus withdrawn, the Kamic principle, which being the fourth, naturally reached its zenith during

87

the Fourth Root Race, asserted itself more and more in humanity. Lust, brutality and ferocity were all on the increase, and the animal nature in man was approaching its most degraded expression. It was a moral question which from the very earliest times divided the Atlantean Race into two hostile camps, and what was begun in the Rmoahal times was terribly accentuated in the Toltec era. The battle of Armageddon is fought over and over again in every age of the world's history.

No longer submitting to the wise rule of the Initiate emperors, the followers of the "black arts" rose in rebellion and set up a rival emperor, who after much struggle and fighting drove the white emperor from his capital, the "City of the Golden Gates," and established himself on his throne.

The white emperor driven northward re-established himself in a city originally founded by the Tlavatli on the southern edge of the mountainous district, but which was now the seat of one of the tributary Toltec kings. He gladly welcomed the white emperor and placed the city at his disposal. A few more of the tributary kings also remained loyal to him, but most transferred their allegiance to the new emperor reigning at the old capital. These, however, did not long remain faithful. Constant assertions of independence were made by the tributary kings, and continual battles were fought in different parts of the empire, the practice of sorcery being largely resorted to, to supplement the powers of destruction possessed by the armies.

These events took place about 50,000 years before the first great catastrophe.

From this time onwards things went from bad to worse. The sorcerers used their powers more and more recklessly, and greater and greater numbers of people acquired and practised these terrible "black arts."

Then came the awful retribution when millions upon millions perished. The great "City of the Golden Gates" had by this time become a perfect den of iniquity. The waves swept over it and destroyed its inhabitants, and the "black" emperor and his dynasty fell to rise no more. The emperor of the north as well as the initiated priests throughout the whole continent had long been fully aware of the evil days at hand, and subsequent pages will tell of the many priest-led emigrations which preceded this catastrophe, as well as those of later date.

The continent was now terribly rent. But the actual amount of territory submerged by no means represented the damage done, for tidal waves swept over great tracts of land and left them desolate swamps. Whole provinces were rendered barren, and remained for generations in an uncultivated and desert condition.

The remaining population too had received a terrible warning. It was taken to heart, and sorcery was for a time less prevalent among them. A long period elapsed before any new powerful rule was established. We shall eventually find a Semite dynasty of sorcerers enthroned in the "City of the Golden Gates," but no Toltec power rose to eminence during the second map period. There were considerable Toltec populations still, but little of the pure blood remained on the mother continent.

On the island of Ruta however, in the third map period, a Toltec dynasty again rose to power and ruled through its tributary kings a large portion of the island. This dynasty was addicted to the black craft, which it must be understood became more and more prevalent during all the four periods, until it culminated in the inevitable catastrophe, which to a great extent purified the earth of the monstrous evil. It must also be borne in mind that down to the very end when Poseidonis disappeared, an Intitiate emperor or king—or at least one acknowledging the "good law"—held sway in some part of the island continent, acting under the guidance of the Occult Hierarchy in controlling where possible the evil sorcerers, and in guiding and instructing the small minority who were still willing to lead pure and wholesome lives. In later days this "white" king was as a rule elected by the priests—the handful, that is, who still followed the "good law."

Little more remains to be said about the Toltecs. In Poseidonis the population of the whole island was more or less mixed. Two kingdoms and one small republic in the west divided the island between them. The northern portion was ruled by an Initiate king. In the south too the hereditary principle had given way to election by the people. Exclusive race-dynasties were at an end, but kings of Toltec blood occasionally rose to power both in the north and south, the northern kingdom being constantly encroached upon by its southern rival, and more and more of its territory annexed.

Having dealt at some length with the state of things under the Toltecs, the leading political characteristics of the four following sub-races need not long detain us, for none of them reached the heights of civilization that the Toltecs did—in fact the degeneration of the race had set in.

It seems to have been some sort of feudal system that the natural bent of the Turanian race tended to develop. Each chief was supreme on his own territory, and the king was only *primus inter pares*. The chiefs who formed his council occasionally murdered their king and set up one of their own number in his place. They were a turbulent and lawless race—brutal and cruel also. The fact that at some periods of their history regiments of women took part in their wars is significant of the last named characteristics.

But the strange experiment they made in social life which, but for its political origin, would more naturally have been dealt with under "manners and customs," is the most interesting fact in their record. Being continually worsted in war with their Toltec neighbours, knowing themselves to be greatly outnumbered, and desiring above all things increase of population, laws were passed, by which every man was relieved from the direct burden of maintaining his family. The State took charge of and provided for the children, and they were looked upon as its property. This naturally tended to increase the birth-rate amongst the Turanians, and the ceremony of marriage came to be disregarded. The ties of family life, and the feeling of parental love were of course destroyed, and the scheme having been found to be a failure, was ultimately given up. Other attempts at finding socialistic solutions of economical problems which still vex us to-day, were tried and abandoned by this race.

The original Semites, who were a quarrelsome marauding and energetic race, always leant towards a patriarchal form of government. Their colonists, who generally took to the nomadic life, almost exclusively adopted this form, but as we have seen they developed a considerable empire in the days of the second map period, and possessed the great "City of the Golden Gates." They ultimately, however, had to give way before the growing power of the Akkadians.

It was in the third map period, about 100,000 years ago, that the Akkadians finally overthrew the Semite power. This 6th sub-race were a much more law-abiding people than their predecessors. Traders and sailors, they lived in settled communities, and naturally produced an oligarchical form of government. A peculiarity of theirs, of which Sparta is the only modern example, was the dual system of two kings reigning in one city. As a result probably of their sea-going taste, the study of the stars became a characteristic pursuit, and this race made great advances both in astronomy and astrology.

The Mongolian people were an improvement on their immediate ancestors of the brutal Turanian stock. Born as they were on the wide steppes of Eastern Siberia, they never had any touch with the mother-continent, and owing, doubtless, to their environment, they became a nomadic people. More psychic and more religious than the Turanians from whom they sprang, the form of government towards which they gravitated required a suzerain in the background who should be supreme both as a territorial ruler and as a chief high priest.

Emigrations.—Three causes contributed to produce emigrations. The Turanian race, as we have seen, was from its very start imbued with the spirit of colonizing, which it carried out on a considerable scale. The Semites and Akkadians were also to a certain extent colonizing races.

Then, as time went on and population tended more and more to outrun the limits of subsistence, necessity operated with the least well-to-do in every race alike, and drove them to seek for a livelihood in less thickly populated countries. For it should be realized that when the Atlanteans reached their zenith in the Toltec era, the proportion of population to the square mile on the continent of Atlantis probably equalled, even if it did not exceed, our modern experience in England and Belgium. It is at all events certain that the vacant spaces available for colonization were very much larger in that age than in ours, while the total population of the world, which at the present moment is probably not more than twelve hundred to fifteen hundred millions, amounted in those days to the big figure of about two thousand millions.

Lastly, there were the priest-led emigrations which took place prior to each catastrophe—and there were many more of these than the four great ones referred to above. The initiated kings and priests who followed the "good law" were aware beforehand of the impending calamities. Each one, therefore, naturally became a centre of prophetic warning, and ultimately a leader of a band of colonists. It may be noted here that in later days the rulers of the country deeply resented these priest-led emigrations, as tending to impoverish and depopulate their kingdoms, and it became necessary for the emigrants to get on board ship secretly during the night.

In roughly tracing the lines of emigration followed by each sub-race in turn, we shall of necessity ultimately reach the lands which their respective descendants to-day occupy.

For the earliest emigrations we must go back to the Rmoahal days. It will be remembered that that portion of the race which inhabited the north-eastern coasts alone retained its purity of blood. Harried on their southern borders and driven further north by the Tlavatli warriors, they began to overflow to the neighbouring land to the east, and to the still nearer promontory of Greenland. In the second map period no pure Rmoahals were left on the then reduced mother-continent, but the northern promontory of the continent then rising on the west was occupied by them, as well as the Greenland cape already mentioned, and the western shores of the great Scandinavian island. There was also a colony on the land lying north of the central Asian sea.

Brittany and Picardy then formed part of the Scandinavian island, while the island itself became in the third map period part of the growing continent of Europe. Now it is in France that remains of this race have been found in the quaternary strata, and the brachycephalous, or round-headed specimen known as the "Furfooz man," may be taken as a fair average of the type of the race in its decay.

Many times forced to move south by the rigours of a glacial epoch, many times driven north by the greed of their more powerful neighbours, the scattered and degraded remnants of this race may be found to-day in the modern Lapps, though even here there was some infusion of other blood. And so it comes to pass that these faded and stunted specimens of humanity are the lineal descendants of the black race of giants who arose on the equatorial lands of Lemuria well-nigh five million years ago.

The Tlavatli colonists seem to have spread out towards every point of the compass. By the second map period their descendants were settled on the western shores of the then growing American continent (California) as well as on its extreme southern coasts (Rio de Janeiro). We also find them occupying the eastern shores of the Scandinavian island, while numbers of them sailed across the ocean, rounded the coast of Africa, and reached India. There, mixing with the indigenous Lemurian population, they formed the Dravidian race. In later days this in its turn received an infusion of Aryan or Fifth Race blood, from which results the complexity of type found in India to-day. In fact we have here a very fair example of the extreme difficulty of deciding any question of race upon merely physical evidence, for it would be quite possible to have Fifth Race egos incarnate among the Brahmans, Fourth Race egos among the lower castes, and some lingering Third Race among the hill tribes.

By the fourth map period we find a Tlavatli people occupying the southern parts of South America, from which it may be inferred that the Patagonians probably had remote Tlavatli ancestry.

Remains of this race, as of the Rmoahals, have been found in the quaternary strata of Central Europe, and the dolichocephalous "Cro-Magnon man" (*) may be taken as an average specimen of the race in its decadence, while the "Lake-Dwellers" of Switzerland formed an even earlier and not quite pure offshoot. The only people who can be cited as fairly pure-blooded specimens of the race at the present day are some of the brown tribes of Indians of South America. The Burmese and Siamese have also

Tlavatli blood in their veins, but in their case it was mixed with, and therefore dominated by, the nobler stock of one of the Aryan sub-races. *(*) Students of geology and palæontology will know that these sciences regard the "Cro-Magnon man" as prior to the "Furfooz," and seeing that the two races ran alongside each other for vast periods of time, it may quite well be that the individual "Cro-Magnon" skeleton, though representative of the second race, was deposited in the quaternary strata thousands of years before the individual Furfooz man lived on the earth.*

We now come to the Toltecs. It was chiefly to the west that their emigrations tended, and the neighbouring coasts of the American continent were in the second map period peopled by a pure Toltec race, the greater part of those left on the mother-continent being then of very mixed blood. It was on the continents of North and South America that this race spread abroad and flourished, and on which thousands of years later were established the empires of Mexico and Peru. The greatness of these empires is a matter of history, or at least of tradition supplemented by such evidence as is afforded by magnificent architectural remains. It may here be noted that while the Mexican empire was for centuries great and powerful in all that is usually regarded as power and greatness in our civilization of to-day, it never reached the height attained by the Peruvians about 14,000 years ago under their Inca sovereigns, for as regards the general well-being of the people, the justice and beneficence of the government, the equitable nature of the land tenure, and the pure and religious life of the inhabitants, the Peruvian empire of those days might be considered a traditional though faint echo of the golden age of the Toltecs on the mother-continent of Atlantis.

The average Red Indian of North or South America is the best representative to-day of the Toltec people, but of course bears no comparison with the highly civilized individual of the race at its zenith.

Egypt must now be referred to, and the consideration of this subject should let in a flood of light upon its early history. Although the first settlement in that country was not in the strict sense of the term a colony, it was from the Toltec race that was subsequently drawn the first great body of emigrants intended to mix with and dominate the aboriginal people.

In the first instance it was the transfer of a great Lodge of initiates. This took place about 400,000 years ago. The golden age of the Toltecs was long past. The first great catastrophe had taken place. The moral degradation of the people and the consequent practice of the "black arts" were becoming more accentuated and widely spread. Purer surroundings for the White Lodge were needed. Egypt was isolated and was thinly peopled, and therefore Egypt was chosen. The settlement so made answered its purpose, and undisturbed by adverse conditions the Lodge of Initiates for nearly 200,000 years did its work.

About 210,000 years ago, when the time was ripe, the Occult Lodge founded an empire—the first "Divine Dynasty" of Egypt—and began to teach the people. Then it was that the first great body of colonists was brought from Atlantis, and some time during the ten thousand years that led up to the second catastrophe, the two great Pyramids of Gizeh were built, partly to provide permanent Halls of Initiation, but also to act as treasure-house and shrine for some great talisman of power during the submergence which the Initiates knew to be impending. Map No. 3 shows Egypt at that date as under water. It remained so for a considerable period, but on its re-emergence it was again peopled by the descendants of many of its old inhabitants who had retired to the Abyssinian mountains (shown in Map No. 3 as an island) as well as by fresh bands of Atlantean colonists from various parts of the world. A considerable immigration of Akkadians then helped to modify the Egyptian type. This is the era of the second "Divine Dynasty" of Egypt—the rulers of the country being again Initiated Adepts.

The catastrophe of 80,000 years ago again laid the country under water, but this time it was only a temporary wave. When it receded the third "Divine Dynasty"—that mentioned by Manetho—began its rule, and it was under the early kings of this dynasty that the great Temple of Karnak and many of the more ancient buildings still standing in Egypt were constructed. In fact with the exception of the two pyramids no building in Egypt predates the catastrophe of 80,000 years ago.

The final submergence of Poseidonis sent another tidal wave over Egypt. This too, was only a temporary calamity, but it brought the Divine Dynasties to an end, for the Lodge of Initiates had transferred its quarters to other lands.

Various points here left untouched have already been dealt with in the *Transaction of the London Lodge*, "The Pyramids and Stonehenge."

The Turanians who in the first map period had colonized the northern parts of the land lying immediately to the east of Atlantis, occupied in the second map period its southern shores (which included the present Morocco and Algeria). We also find them wandering eastwards, and both the east and west coasts of the central Asian sea were peopled by them.

Bands of them ultimately moved still further east, and the nearest approximation to the type of this race is to-day to be found in the inland Chinese. A curious freak of destiny must be recorded about one of their western offshoots. Dominated all through the centuries by their more powerful Toltec neighbours, it was yet reserved for a small branch of the Turanian stock to conquer and replace the last great empire that the Toltecs raised, for the brutal and barely civilized Aztecs were of pure Turanian blood.

The Semite emigrations were of two kinds, first, those which were controlled by the natural impulse of the race: second, that special emigration which was effected under the direct guidance of the Manu; for, strange as it may seem, it was not from the Toltecs but from this lawless and turbulent though vigorous and energetic sub-race that was chosen the nucleus destined to be developed into our great Fifth or Aryan Race. The reason, no doubt, lay in the Mânasic characteristic with which the number five is always associated. The sub-race of that number was inevitably developing its physical brain power and intellect; although at the expense of the psychic perceptions, while that same development of intellect to infinitely higher levels is at once the glory and the destined goal of our Fifth Root Race.

Dealing first with the natural emigrations we find that in the second map period while still leaving powerful nations on the mother-continent, the Semites had spread both west and east—west to the lands now forming the United States, and thus accounting for the Semitic type to be found in some of the Indian races, and east to the northern shores of the neighbouring continent, which combined all there then was of Europe, Africa and Asia. The type of the ancient Egyptians, as well as of other neighbouring nations, was to some extent modified by this original Semite blood; but with the exception of the Jews, the only representatives of comparatively unmixed race at the present day are the lighter coloured Kabyles of the Algerian mountains.

The tribes resulting from the segregation effected by the Manu for the formation of the new Root Race eventually found their way to the southern shores of the central Asian sea, and there the first great Aryan kingdom was established. When the Transaction dealing with the origin of a Root Race comes to be written, it will be seen that many of the peoples we are accustomed to call Semitic are really Aryan in blood. The world will also be enlightened as to what constitutes the claim of the Hebrews to be considered a "chosen people." Shortly it may be stated that they constitute an abnormal and unnatural link between the Fourth and Fifth Root Races.

95

The Akkadians, though eventually becoming supreme rulers on the mother-continent of Atlantis, owed their birthplace as we have seen in the second map period, to the neighbouring continent—that part occupied by the basin of the Mediterranean about the present island of Sardinia being their special home. From this centre they spread eastwards, occupying what eventually became the shores of the Levant, and reaching as far as Persia and Arabia. As we have seen, they also helped to people Egypt. The early Etruscans, the Phœnicians, including the Carthaginians and the Shumero-Akkads, were branches of this race, while the Basques of to-day have probably more of the Akkadian than of any other blood which flows in their veins.

A reference to the early inhabitants of our own islands may appropriately be made here, for it was in the early Akkadian days, about 100,000 years ago, that the colony of Initiates who founded Stonehenge landed on these shores—"these shores" being, of course, the shores of the Scandinavian part of the continent of Europe, as shown in Map No. 3. The initiated priests and their followers appear to have belonged to a very early strain of the Akkadian race—they were taller, fairer, and longer headed than the aborigines of the country, who were a very mixed race, but mostly degenerate remnants of the Rmoahals. As readers of the *Transaction of the London Lodge* on the "Pyramids and Stonehenge," will know, the rude simplicity of Stonehenge was intended as a protest against the extravagant ornament and over-decoration of the existing temples in Atlantis, where the debased worship of their own images was being carried on by the inhabitants.

The Mongolians, as we have seen, never had any touch with the mother-continent. Born on the wide plains of Tartary, their emigrations for long found ample scope within those regions; but more than once tribes of Mongol descent have overflowed from northern Asia to America, across Behring's Straits, and the last of such emigrations—that of the Kitans, some 1,300 years ago—has left traces which some western savants have been able to follow. The presence of Mongolian blood in some tribes of North American Indians has also been recognized by various writers on ethnology. The Hungarians and Malays are both known to be offshoots of this race, ennobled in the one case by a strain of Aryan blood, degraded in the other by mixture with the effete Lemurians. But the interesting fact about the Mongolians is that its last family race is still in full force—it has not in fact yet reached its zenith—and the Japanese nation has still got history to give to the world.

Arts and Sciences.—It must primarily be recognized that our own Aryan race has naturally achieved far greater results in almost every direction than did the Atlanteans, but even where they failed to reach our level, the records of what they accomplished are of interest as representing the high water mark which their tide of civilization reached. On the other hand, the character of the scientific achievements in which they did outstrip us are of so dazzling a nature, that bewilderment at such unequal development is apt to be the feeling left.

The arts and sciences, as practised by the first two races, were, of course, crude in the extreme, but we do not propose to follow the progress achieved by each sub-race separately. The history of the Atlantean, as of the Aryan race, was interspersed with periods of progress and of decay. Eras of culture were followed by times of lawlessness, during which all artistic and scientific development was lost, these again being succeeded by civilizations reaching to still higher levels. It must naturally be with the periods of culture that the following remarks will deal, chief among which stands out the great Toltec era.

Architecture and sculpture, painting and music were all practised in Atlantis. The music even at the best of times was crude, and the instruments of the most primitive type. All the Atlantean races were fond of colour, and brilliant hues decorated both the insides and the outsides of their houses, but painting as a fine art was never well established, though in the later days some kind of drawing and painting was taught in the schools. Sculpture on the other hand, which was also taught in the schools, was widely practised, and reached great excellence. As we shall see later on under the head of "Religion" it became customary for every man who could afford it to place in one of the temples an image of himself. These were sometimes carved in wood or in hard black stone like basalt, but among the wealthy it became the fashion to have their statues cast in one of the precious metals, aurichalcum, gold or silver. A very fair resemblance of the individual usually resulted, while in some cases a striking likeness was achieved.

Architecture, however, was naturally the most widely practised of these arts. Their buildings were massive structures of gigantic proportions. The dwelling houses in the cities were not, as ours are, closely crowded together in streets. Like their country houses some stood in their own garden grounds, others were separated by plots of common land, but all were isolated structures. In the case of houses of any importance four blocks of building surrounded a central courtyard, in the centre of which generally stood one of the fountains whose number in the "City of the Golden Gates" gained for it the second appellation of the "City of Waters." There was no exhibition of goods for sale as in modern streets. All transactions of buying and selling took place privately, except at stated times, when large public fairs were held in the open spaces of the cities. But the characteristic feature of the Toltec house was the tower that rose from one of its corners or from the centre of one of the blocks. A spiral staircase built outside led to the upper stories, and a pointed dome terminated the tower—this upper portion being very commonly used as an observatory. As already stated the houses were decorated with bright colours. Some were ornamented with carvings, others with frescoes or painted patterns. The window-spaces were-filled with some manufactured article similar to, but less transparent than, glass. The interiors were not furnished with the elaborate detail of our modern dwellings, but the life was highly civilized of its kind.

The temples were huge halls resembling more than anything else the gigantic piles of Egypt, but built on a still more stupendous scale. The pillars supporting the roof were generally square, seldom circular. In the days of the decadence the aisles were surrounded with innumerable chapels in which were enshrined the statues of the more important inhabitants. These side shrines indeed were occasionally of such considerable size as to admit a whole retinue of priests whom some specially great man might have in his service for the ceremonial worship of his image. Like the private houses the temples too were never complete without the dome-capped towers, which of course were of corresponding size and magnificence. These were used for astronomical observations and for sun-worship.

The precious metals were largely used in the adornment of the temples, the interiors being often not merely inlaid but plated with gold. Gold and silver were highly valued, but as we shall see later on when the subject of the currency is dealt with, the uses to which they were put were entirely artistic and had nothing to do with coinage, while the great quantities that were then produced by the chemists—or as we should now-a-days call them alchemists—may be said to have taken them out of the category of the precious metals. This power of transmutation of metals was not universal, but it was so widely possessed that enormous quantities were made. In fact the production of the wished-for metals may be regarded as one of the industrial enterprises of those days by which these alchemists gained their living. Gold was admired even more than silver, and was consequently produced in much greater quantity.

Education.—A few words on the subject of language will fitly prelude a consideration of the training in the schools and colleges of Atlantis. During the first map period Toltec was the universal language, not only throughout the continent but in the western islands and that part of the eastern

98

continent which recognized the emperor's rule. Remains of the Rmoahal and Tlavatli speech survived it is true in out-of-the-way parts, just as the Keltic and Cymric speech survives to-day among us in Ireland and Wales. The Tlavatli tongue was the basis used by the Turanians, who introduced such modifications that an entirely different language was in time produced; while the Semites and Akkadians, adopting a Toltec ground-work, modified it in their respective ways, and so produced two divergent varieties. Thus in the later days of Poseidonis there were several entirely different languages—all however belonging to the agglutinative type—for it was not till Fifth Race days that the descendants of the Semites and Akkadians developed inflectional speech. All through the ages, however, the Toltec language fairly maintained its purity, and the same tongue that was spoken in Atlantis in the days of its splendour was used, with but slight alterations, thousands of years later in Mexico and Peru.

The schools and colleges of Atlantis in the great Toltec days, as well as in subsequent eras of culture, were all endowed by the State. Though every child was required to pass through the primary schools, the subsequent training differed very widely. The primary schools formed a sort of winnowing ground. Those who showed real aptitude for study were, along with the children of the dominant classes who naturally had greater abilities, drafted into the higher schools at about the age of twelve. Reading and writing, which were regarded as mere preliminaries, had already been taught them in the primary schools.

But reading and writing were not considered necessary for the great masses of the inhabitants who had to spend their lives in tilling the land, or in handicrafts, the practice of which was required by the community. The great majority of the children therefore were at once passed on to the technical schools best suited to their various abilities. Chief among these were the agricultural schools. Some branches of mechanics also formed part of the training, while in outlying districts and by the sea-side hunting and fishing were naturally included. And so the children all received the education or training which was most appropriate for them.

The children of superior abilities, who as we have seen had been taught to read and write, had a much more elaborate education. The properties of plants and their healing qualities formed an important branch of study. There were no recognized physicians in those days—every educated man knew more or less of medicine as well as of magnetic healing. Chemistry, mathematics and astronomy were also taught. The training in such studies finds its analogy among ourselves, but the object towards which the teachers' efforts were mainly directed, was the development of the pupil's

99

psychic faculties and his instruction in the more hidden forces of nature. The occult properties of plants, metals, and precious stones, as well as the alchemical processes of transmutation, were included in this category. But as time went on it became more and more the personal power, which Bulwer Lytton calls vril, and the operation of which he has fairly accurately described in his *Coming Race*, that the colleges for the higher training of the youth of Atlantis were specially occupied in developing. The marked change which took place when the decadence of the race set in was, that instead of merit and aptitude being regarded as warrants for advancement to the higher grades of instruction, the dominant classes becoming more and more exclusive allowed none but their own children to graduate in the higher knowledge which gave so much power.

In such an empire as the Toltec, agriculture naturally received much attention. Not only were the labourers taught their duties in technical schools, but colleges were established in which the knowledge necessary for carrying out experiments in the crossing both of animals and plants, were taught to fitting students.

As readers of Theosophic literature may know, *wheat* was not evolved on this planet at all. It was the gift of the Manu who brought it from another globe outside our chain of worlds. But oats and some of our other cereals are the results of crosses between wheat and the indigenous grasses of the earth. Now the experiments which gave these results were carried out in the agricultural schools of Atlantis. Of course such experiments were guided by high knowledge. But the most notable achievement to be recorded of the Atlantean agriculturists was the evolution of the plantain or banana. In the original wild state it was like an elongated melon with scarcely any pulp, but full of seeds as a melon is. It was of course only by centuries (if not thousands of years) of continuous selection and elimination that the present seedless plant was evolved.

Among the domesticated animals of the Toltec days were creatures that looked like very small tapirs. They naturally fed upon roots or herbage, but like the pigs of to-day, which they resembled in more than one particular, they were not over cleanly, and ate whatever came in their way. Large cat-like animals and the wolf-like ancestors of the dog might also be met about human habitations. The Toltec carts appear to have been drawn by creatures somewhat resembling small camels. The Peruvian llamas of to-day are probably their descendants. The ancestors of the Irish elk, too, roamed in herds about the hill sides in much the same way as our Highland cattle do now—too wild to allow of easy approach, but still under the control of man.

Constant experiments were made in breeding and cross-breeding different kinds of animals, and, curious though it may seem to us, artificial heat was largely used to force their development, so that the results of crossing and interbreeding might be more quickly apparent. The use, too, of different coloured lights in the chambers where such experiments were carried on were adopted in order to obtain varying results.

This control and moulding at will by man of the animal forms brings us to a rather startling and very mysterious subject. Reference has been made above to the work done by the Manus. Now it is in the mind of the Manu that originates all improvements in type and the potentialities latent in every form of being. In order to work out in detail the improvements in the animal forms, the help and co-operation of man were required. The amphibian and reptile forms which then abounded had about run their course, and were ready to assume the more advanced type of bird or mammal. These forms constituted the inchoate material placed at man's disposal, and the clay was ready to assume whatever shape the potter's hands might mould it into. It was specially with animals in the intermediate stage that so many of the experiments above referred to were tried, and doubtless the domesticated animals like the horse, which are now of such service to man, are the result of these experiments in which the men of those days acted in co-operation with the Manu and his ministers. But the co-operation was too soon withdrawn. Selfishness obtained the upper hand, and war and discord brought the Golden Age of the Toltecs to a close. When instead of working loyally for a common end, under the guidance of their Initiate kings, men began to prey upon each other, the beasts which might gradually have assumed, under the care of man, more and more useful and domesticated forms, being left to the guidance of their own instincts naturally followed the example of their monarch, and began to prey upon each other. Some indeed had actually already been trained and used by men in their hunting expeditions, and thus the semi-domesticated cat-like animals above referred to naturally became the ancestors of the leopards and jaguars.

One illustration of what some may be tempted to call a fantastic theory, though it may not elucidate the problem, will at least point the moral contained in this supplement to our knowledge regarding the mysterious manner in which our evolution has proceeded. The lion it would appear might have had a gentler nature and a less fierce aspect had the men of those days completed the task that was given them to perform. Whether or not he is fated eventually "to lie down with the lamb and eat straw like the ox," the destiny in store for him as pictured in the mind of the Manu has not yet been realized, for the picture was that of a powerful but domesticated animal—a strong level-backed creature, with large intelligent eyes, intended to act as man's most powerful servant for purposes of traction.

The "City of the Golden Gates" and its surroundings must be described before we come to consider the marvellous system by which its inhabitants were supplied with water. It lay, as we have seen, on the east coast of the continent close to the sea, and about 15° north of the equator. A beautifully-wooded park-like country surrounded the city. Scattered over a large area of this were the villa residences of the wealthier classes. To the west lay a range of mountains, from which the water supply of the city was drawn. The city itself was built on the slopes of a hill, which rose from the plain about 500 feet. On the summit of this hill lay the emperor's palace and gardens, in the centre of which welled up from the earth a never-ending stream of water, supplying first the palace and the fountains in the gardens, thence flowing in the four directions and falling in cascades into a canal or moat which encompassed the palace grounds, and thus separated them from the city which lay below on every side. From this canal four channels led the water through four quarters of the city to cascades which in their turn supplied another encircling canal at a lower level. There were three such canals forming concentric circles, the outermost and lowest of which was still above the level of the plain. A fourth canal at this lowest level, but on a rectangular plan, received the constantly flowing waters, and in its turn discharged them into the sea. The city extended over part of the plain, up to the edge of this great outermost moat, which surrounded and defended it with a line of waterways extending about twelve miles by ten miles square.

It will thus be seen that the city was divided into three great belts, each hemmed in by its canals. The characteristic feature of the upper belt that lay just below the palace grounds, was a circular race-course and large public gardens. Most of the houses of the court officials also lay on this belt, and here also was an institution of which we have no parallel in modern times. The term "Strangers' Home" amongst us suggests a mean appearance and sordid surroundings, but this was a palace where all strangers who might come to the city were entertained as long as they might choose to stay—being treated all the time as guests of the Government. The detached houses of the inhabitants and the various temples scattered throughout the city occupied the other two belts. In the days of the Toltec greatness there seems to have been no real poverty—even the retinue of slaves attached to most houses being well fed and clothed—but there were a number of comparatively poor houses in the lowest belt to the north, as well as outside the outermost canal towards the sea. The inhabitants of this part were mostly connected with the shipping, and their houses though detached were built closer together than in other districts.

It will be seen from the above that the inhabitants had thus a never-failing supply of pure clear water constantly coursing through the city, while the upper belts and the emperor's palace were protected by lines of moats, each one at a higher level as the centre was approached.

Now it does not require much mechanical knowledge in order to realize how stupendous must have been the works needed to provide this supply, for in the days of its greatness the "City of the Golden Gates" embraced within its four circles of moats over two million inhabitants. No such system of water supply has ever been attempted in Greek, Roman or modern times—indeed it is very doubtful whether our ablest engineers, even at the expenditure of untold wealth, could produce such a result.

A description of some of its leading features will be of interest. It was from a lake which lay among the mountains to the west of the city, at an elevation of about 2,600 feet, that the supply was drawn. The main aqueduct which was of oval section, measuring fifty feet by thirty feet, led underground to an enormous heart-shaped reservoir. This lay deep below the palace, in fact at the very base of the hill on which the palace and the city stood. From this reservoir a perpendicular shaft of about 500 feet up through the solid rock gave passage to the water which welled up in the palace grounds, and thence was distributed throughout the city. Various pipes from the central reservoir also led to different parts of the city to supply drinking water and the public fountains. Systems of sluices of course also existed to control or cut off the supply of the different districts.

From the above it will be apparent to any one possessed of some little knowledge of mechanics that the pressure in the subterranean aqueduct and the central reservoir from which the water naturally rose to the basin in the palace gardens, must have been enormous, and the resisting power of the material used in their construction consequently prodigious.

If the system of water supply in the "City of the Golden Gates" was wonderful, the Atlantean methods of locomotion must be recognised as still more marvellous, for the air-ship or flying-machine which Keely in America, and Maxim in this country are now attempting to produce, was then a realized fact. It was not at any time a common means of transport. The slaves, the servants, and the masses who laboured with their hands, had to trudge along the country tracks, or travel in rude carts with solid wheels drawn by uncouth animals. The air-boats may be considered as the private carriages of those days, or rather the private yachts, if we regard the relative number of those who possessed them, for they must have been at all times difficult and costly to produce. They were not as a rule built to accommodate many persons. Numbers were constructed for only two, some allowed for six or eight passengers. In the later days when war and strife had brought the Golden Age to an end, battle ships that could navigate the air had to a great extent replaced the battle ships at sea—having naturally proved far more powerful engines of destruction. These were constructed to carry as many as fifty, and in some cases even up to a hundred fighting men.

The material of which the air boats were constructed was either wood or metal. The earlier ones were built of wood—the boards used being exceedingly thin, but the injection of some substance which did not add materially to the weight while it gave leather-like toughness, provided the necessary combination of lightness and strength. When metal was used it was generally an alloy—two white-coloured metals and one red one entering into its composition. The resultant was white-coloured, like aluminium, and even lighter in weight. Over the rough framework of the air-boat was extended a large sheet of this metal which was then beaten into shape and electrically welded where necessary. But whether built of metal or wood their outside surface was apparently seamless and perfectly smooth, and they shone in the dark as if coated with luminous paint.

In shape they were boat-like, but they were invariably decked over, for when at full speed it could not have been convenient, even if safe, for any on board to remain on the upper deck. Their propelling and steering gear could be brought into use at either end.

But the all-interesting question is that relating to the power by which they were propelled. In the earlier times it seems to have been personal vril that supplied the motive power—whether used in conjunction with any mechanical contrivance matters not much—but in the later days this was replaced by a force which, though generated in what is to us an unknown manner, operated nevertheless through definite mechanical arrangements. This force, though not yet discovered by science, more nearly approached that which Keely in America is learning to handle than the electric power used by Maxim. It was in fact of an etheric nature, but though we are no nearer to the solution of the problem, its method of operation can be described. The mechanical arrangements no doubt differed somewhat in different vessels. The following description is taken from an air-boat in which on one occasion three ambassadors from the king who ruled over the northern part of Poseidonis made the journey to the court of the southern kingdom. A strong heavy metal chest which lay in the centre of the boat was the generator. Thence the force flowed through two large flexible tubes to either end of the vessel, as well as through eight subsidiary tubes fixed fore and aft to the bulwarks. These had double openings pointing vertically both up and down. When the journey was about to begin the valves of the eight bulwark tubes which pointed downwards were opened—all the other valves being closed. The current rushing through these impinged on the earth with such force as to drive the boat upwards, while the air itself continued to supply the necessary fulcrum. When a sufficient elevation was reached the flexible tube at that end of the vessel which pointed away from the desired destination, was brought into action, while by the partial closing of the valves the current rushing through the eight vertical tubes was reduced to the small amount required to maintain the elevation reached. The great volume of the current, being now directed through the large tube pointing downwards from the stern at an angle of about forty-five degrees, while helping to maintain the elevation, provided also the great motive power to propel the vessel through the air. The steering was accomplished by the discharge of the current through this tube, for the slightest change in its direction at once caused an alteration in the vessel's course. But constant supervision was not required. When a long journey had to be taken the tube could be fixed so as to need no handling till the destination was almost reached. The maximum speed attained was about one hundred miles an hour, the course of flight never being a straight line, but always in the form of long waves, now approaching and now receding from the earth. The elevation at which the vessels travelled was only a few hundred feet— indeed, when high mountains lay in the line of their track it was necessary to change their course and go round them—the more rarefied air no longer supplying the necessary fulcrum. Hills of about one thousand feet were the highest they could cross. The means by which the vessel was brought to a stop on reaching its destination—and this could be done equally well in mid-air—was to give escape to some of the current force through the tube at that end of the boat which pointed towards its destination, and the current impinging on the land or air in front, acted as a drag, while the propelling force behind was gradually reduced by the closing of the valve. The reason has still to be given for the existence of the eight tubes pointing upwards from the bulwarks. This had more specially to do with the aerial warfare. Having so powerful a force at their disposal, the warships naturally directed the current against each other. Now this was apt to destroy the equilibrium of the ship so struck and to turn it upside down—a situation sure to be taken advantage of by the enemy's vessel to make an attack with her ram. There was also the further danger of being precipitated to the ground, unless the shutting and opening of the necessary valves were quickly attended to. In whatever position the vessel might be, the tubes pointing towards the earth were naturally those through which the current should be rushing, while the tubes pointing upwards should be closed. The means by which a vessel turned upside down might be righted and placed again on a level keel, was accomplished by using the four tubes pointing downwards at one side of the vessel only, while the four at the other side were kept closed.

The Atlanteans had also sea-going vessels which were propelled by some power analogous to that above mentioned, but the current force which was eventually found to be most effective in this case had a denser appearance than that used in the air-boats.

Manners and Customs.—There was doubtless as much variety in the manners and customs of the Atlanteans at different epochs of their history, as there has been among the various nations which compose our Aryan race. With the fluctuating fashion of the centuries we are not concerned. The following remarks will attempt to deal merely with the leading characteristics which differentiate their habits from our own, and these will be chosen as much as possible from the great Toltec era.

With regard to marriage and the relations of the sexes the experiments made by the Turanians have already been referred to. Polygamous customs were prevalent at different times among all the sub-races, but in the Toltec days while two wives were allowed by the law, great numbers of men had only one wife. Nor were the women—as in countries now-a-days where polygamy prevails—regarded as inferiors, or in the least oppressed. Their position was quite equal to that of the men, while the aptitude many of them displayed in acquiring the vril-power made them fully the equals if not the superiors of the other sex. This equality indeed was recognised from infancy, and there was no separation of the sexes in schools or colleges. Boys and girls were taught together. It was the rule, too, and not the exception, for complete harmony to prevail in the dual households, and the mothers taught their children to look equally to their father's wives for love and protection. Nor were women debarred from taking part in the government. Sometimes they were members of the councils, and occasionally even were chosen by the Adept emperor to represent him in the various provinces as the local sovereigns.

The writing material of the Atlanteans consisted of thin sheets of metal, on the white porcelain-like surface of which the words were written. They also had the means of reproducing the written text by placing on the inscribed sheet another thin metal plate which had previously been dipped in some liquid. The text thus graven on the second plate could be reproduced at will on other sheets, a great number of which fastened together constituted a book.

A custom which differs considerably from our own must be instanced next, in their choice of food. It is an unpleasant subject, but can scarcely be passed over. The flesh of the animals they usually discarded, while the parts which among us are avoided as food, were by them devoured. The blood also they drank—often hot from the animal—and various cooked dishes were also made of it.

It must not, however, be thought that they were without the lighter, and to us, more palatable, kinds of food. The seas and rivers provided them with fish, the flesh of which they ate, though often in such an advanced stage of decomposition as would be to us revolting. The different grains were largely cultivated, of which were made bread and cakes. They also had milk, fruit and vegetables.

A small minority of the inhabitants, it is true, never adopted the revolting customs above referred to. This was the case with the Adept kings and emperors and the initiated priesthood throughout the whole empire. They were entirely vegetarian in their habits, but though many of the emperor's counsellors and the officials about the court affected to prefer the purer diet, they often indulged in secret their grosser tastes.

Nor were strong drinks unknown in those days. Fermented liquor of a very potent sort was at one time much in vogue. But it was so apt to make these who drank it dangerously excited that a law was passed absolutely forbidding its consumption.

The weapons of warfare and the chase differed considerably at different epochs. Swords and spears, bows and arrows sufficed as a rule for the Rmoahals and the Tlavatli. The beasts which they hunted at that very early period were mammoths with long woolly hair, elephants and hippopotami. Marsupials also abounded as well as survivals of intermediate types—some being half reptile and half mammal, others half reptile and half bird.

The use of explosives was adopted at an early period, and carried to great perfection in later times. Some appear to have been made to explode on concussion, others after a certain interval of time, but in either case the destruction to life seems to have resulted from the release of some poisonous vapour, not from the impact of bullets. So powerful indeed must have become these explosives in later Atlantean times, that we hear of whole companies of men being destroyed in battle by the noxious gas generated by the explosion of one of these bombs above their heads, thrown there by some sort of lever.

The monetary system must now be considered. During the first three sub-races at all events, such a thing as a State coinage was unknown. Small pieces of metal or leather stamped with some given value were, it is true, used as tokens. Having a perforation in the centre they were strung together, and were usually carried at the girdle. But each man was as it were his own coiner, and the leather or metal token fabricated by him, and exchanged with another for value received, was but a personal acknowledgment of indebtedness, such as a promissory note is among us. No man was entitled to fabricate more of these tokens than he was able to redeem by the transfer of goods in his possession. The tokens did not circulate as coinage does, while the holder of the token had the means to estimate with perfect accuracy the resources of his debtor by the clairvoyant faculty which all then possessed to a greater or less degree, and which in any case of doubt was instantly directed to ascertain the actual state of the facts.

It must be stated, however, that in the later days of Poseidonis, a system approximating to our own currency was adopted, and the triple mountain visible from the great southern capital was the favourite representation on the State coinage.

But the system of land tenure is the most important subject under this heading. Among the Rmoahal and Tlavatli, who lived chiefly by hunting and fishing, the question naturally did not arise, though some system of village cultivation was recognized in the Tlavatli days.

It was with the increase of population and civilization in the early Toltec times that land first became worth fighting for. It is not proposed to trace the system or want of system prevalent in the troublous times anterior to the advent of the Golden Age. But the records of that epoch present to the consideration, not only of political economists, but of all who regard the welfare of the race, a subject of the utmost interest and importance.

The population it must be remembered had been steadily increasing, and under the government of the Adept emperors it had reached the very large figure already quoted; nevertheless poverty and want were things undreamt of in those days, and this social well-being was no doubt partly due to the system of land tenure.

Not only was all the land and its produce regarded as belonging to the emperor, but all the flocks and herds upon it were his as well. The country was divided into different provinces or districts, each province having at its head one of the subsidiary kings or viceroys appointed by the emperor. Each of these viceroys was held responsible for the government and well-being of all the inhabitants under his rule. The tillage of the land, the harvesting of the crops, and the pasturage of the herds lay within his sphere of superintendence, as well as the conducting of such agricultural experiments as have been already referred to.

Each viceroy had round him a council of agricultural advisers and coadjutors, who had amongst their other duties to be well versed in astronomy, for it was not a barren science in those days. The occult influences on plant and animal life were then studied and taken advantage of. The power, too, of producing rain at will was not uncommon then, while the effects of a glacial epoch were on more than one occasion partly neutralized in the northern parts of the continent by occult science. The right day for beginning every agricultural operation was of course duly calculated, and the work carried into effect by the officials whose duty it was to supervise every detail.

The produce raised in each district or kingdom was as a rule consumed in it, but an exchange of agricultural commodities was sometimes arranged between the rulers.

After a small share had been put aside for the emperor and the central government at the "City of the Golden Gates," the produce of the whole district or kingdom was divided among the inhabitants—the local viceroy and his retinue of officials naturally receiving the larger portions, but the meanest agricultural labourer getting enough to secure him competence and comfort. Any increase in the productive capacity of the land, or in the mineral wealth which it yielded, was divided proportionately amongst all concerned—all, therefore, were interested in making the result of their combined labour as lucrative as possible.

This system worked admirably for a very long period. But as time went on negligence and self-seeking crept in. Those whose duty it was to superintend, threw more and more responsibility on their inferiors in office, and in time it became rare for the rulers to interfere or to interest themselves in any of the operations. This was the beginning of the evil days. The members of the dominant class who had previously given all their time to the state duties began to think about making their own lives more pleasant. The elaboration of luxury was setting in.

There was one cause in particular which produced great discontent amongst the lower classes. The system under which the youth of the nation was drafted into the technical schools has already been referred to. Now it was always one of the superior class whose psychic faculties had been duly cultivated, to whom the duty was assigned of selecting the children so that each one should receive the training, and ultimately be devoted to the occupation, for which he was naturally most fitted. But when those possessed of the clairvoyant vision, by which alone such choice could be made, delegated their duties to inferiors who were wanting in such psychic attributes, the results ensuing were that the children were often thrust into wrong grooves, and those whose capacity and taste lay in one direction often found themselves tied for life to an occupation which they disliked, and in which, therefore, they were rarely successful.

The systems of land tenure which ensued in different parts of the empire on the breaking up of the great Toltec dynasty were many and various. But it is not necessary to follow them. In the later days of Poseidonis they had, as a rule, given place to the system of individual ownership which we know so well.

Reference has already been made, under the head of "Emigrations," to the system of land tenure which prevailed during that glorious period of Peruvian history when the Incas held sway about 14,000 years ago. A short summary of this may be of interest as demonstrating the source from which its ground-work was doubtless derived, as well as instancing the variations which had been adopted in this somewhat more complicated system.

All title to land was derived in the first instance from the Inca, but half of it was assigned to the cultivators, who of course constituted the great bulk of the population. The other half was divided between the Inca and the priesthood who celebrated the worship of the sun.

Out of the proceeds of his specially allotted lands the Inca had to keep up the army, the roads throughout the whole empire, and all the machinery of government. This was conducted by a special governing class all more or less closely related to the Inca himself, and representing a civilization and a culture much in advance of the great masses of the population.

The remaining fourth—"the lands of the sun"—provided not only for the priests who conducted the public worship throughout the empire, but for the entire education of the people in schools and colleges, for all sick and infirm persons, and finally, for every inhabitant (exclusive, of course, of the governing class for whom there was no cessation of work) on reaching the age of forty-five, that being the age arranged for the hard work of life to cease, and for leisure and enjoyment to begin.

Religion.—The only subject that now remains to be dealt with is the evolution of religious ideas. Between the spiritual aspiration of a rude but simple race and the degraded ritual of an intellectually cultured but spiritually dead people, lies a gulf which only the term religion, used in its widest acceptation, can span. Nevertheless it is this consecutive process of generation and degeneration which has to be traced in the history of the Atlantean people.

It will be remembered that the government under which the Rmoahals came into existence, was described as the most perfect conceivable, for it was the Manu himself who acted as their king. The memory of this divine ruler was naturally preserved in the annals of the race, and in due time he came to be regarded as a god, among a people who were naturally psychic, and had consequently glimpses of those states of consciousness which transcend our ordinary waking condition. Retaining these higher attributes, it was only natural that this primitive people should adopt a religion, which, though in no way representative of any exalted philosophy, was of a type far from ignoble. In later days this phase of religious belief passed into a kind of ancestor-worship.

The Tlavatli while inheriting the traditional reverence and worship for the Manu, were taught by Adept instructors of the existence of a Supreme Being whose symbol was recognized as the sun. They thus developed a sort of sun worship, for the practice of which they repaired to the hill tops. There they built great circles of upright monoliths. These were intended to be symbolical of the sun's yearly course, but they were also used for astronomical purposes—being placed so that, to one standing at the high altar, the sun would rise at the winter solstice behind one of these monoliths, at the vernal equinox behind another, and so on throughout the year. Astronomical observations of a still more complex character connected with the more distant constellations were also helped by these stone circles.

We have already seen under the head of emigrations how a later sub-race—the Akkadians—in the erection of Stonehenge, reverted to this primitive building of monoliths.

Endowed though the Tlavatli were with somewhat greater capacity for intellectual development than the previous sub-race, their cult was still of a very primitive type.

With the wider diffusion of knowledge in the days of the Toltecs, and more especially with the establishment later on of an initiated priesthood and an Adept emperor, increased opportunities were offered to the people for the attainment of a truer conception of the divine. The few who were ready to take full advantage of the teaching offered, after having been tried and tested, were doubtless admitted into the ranks of the priesthood which then constituted an immense occult fraternity. With these, however, who had so outstripped the mass of humanity, as to be ready to begin the progress of the occult path, we are not here concerned, the religions practised by the inhabitants of Atlantis generally being the subject of our investigation.

The power to rise to philosophic heights of thought was of course wanting to the masses of those days, as it is similarly wanting to the great majority of the inhabitants of the world to-day. The nearest approach which the most gifted teacher could make in attempting to convey any idea of the nameless and all-pervading essence of the Kosmos was necessarily imparted in the form of symbols, and the sun naturally enough was the first symbol adopted. As in our own days too the more cultivated and spiritually minded would see through the symbol, and might sometimes rise on the wings of devotion to the Father of our spirits, that

"Motive and centre of our soul's desire, Object and refuge of our journey's end"

while the grosser multitude would see nothing but the symbol, and would worship it, as the carved Madonna or the wooden image of the crucified one is to-day worshipped throughout Catholic Europe.

Sun and fire worship then became the cult for the celebration of which magnificent temples were reared throughout the length and breadth of the continent of Atlantis, but more especially in the great "City of the Golden Gates"—the temple service being performed by retinues of priests endowed by the State for that purpose.

In those early days no image of the Deity was permitted. The sun-disk was considered the only appropriate emblem of the godhead, and as such was used in every temple, a golden disk being generally placed so as to catch the first rays of the rising sun at the vernal equinox or at the summer solstice.

An interesting example of the almost unalloyed survival of this worship of the sun-disk may be instanced in the Shinto ceremonies of Japan. All other representation of Deity is in this faith regarded as impious, and even the circular mirror of polished metal is hidden from the vulgar gaze save on ceremonial occasions. Unlike the gorgeous temple decorations of Atlantis however, the Shinto temples are characterized by an entire absence of decoration—the exquisite finish of the plain wood-work being unrelieved by any carving, paint or varnish.

But the sun-disk did not always remain the only permissible emblem of Deity. The image of a man—an archetypal man—was in after days placed in the temples and adored as the highest representation of the divine. In some ways this might be considered a reversion to the Rmoahal worship of the Manu. Even then the religion was comparatively pure, and the occult fraternity of the "Good Law" of course did their utmost to keep alive in the hearts of the people the spiritual life.

The evil days, however, were drawing near when no altruistic idea should remain to redeem the race from the abyss of selfishness in which it was destined to be overwhelmed. The decay of the ethical idea was the necessary prelude to the perversion of the spiritual. The hand of every man fought for himself alone, and his knowledge was used for purely selfish ends, till it became an established belief that there was nothing in the universe greater or higher than themselves. Each man was his own "Law, and Lord and God," and the very worship of the temples ceased to be the worship of any ideal, but became the mere adoration of man as he was known and seen to be. As is written in the *Book of Dzyan*, "Then the Fourth became tall with pride. We are the kings it was said; we are the Gods.... They built huge cities. Of rare earths and metals they built, and out of the fires vomited, out of the white stone of the mountains and of the black stone, they cut their own images in their size and likeness, and worshipped them." Shrines were placed in temples in which the statue of each man, wrought in gold or silver, or carved in stone or wood, was adored by himself. The richer men kept whole trains of priests in their employ for the cult and care of their shrines, and offerings were made to these statues as to gods. The apotheosis of self could go no further.

It must be remembered that every true religious idea that has ever entered into the mind of man, has been consciously suggested to him by the divine Instructors or the Initiates of the Occult Lodges, who throughout all the ages have been the guardians of the divine mysteries, and of the facts of the supersensual states of consciousness.

Mankind generally has but slowly become capable of assimilating a few of these divine ideas, while the monstrous growths and hideous distortions to which every religion on earth stands as witness, must be traced to man's own lower nature. It would seem indeed that he has not always even been fit to be entrusted with knowledge as to the mere symbols under which were veiled the light of Deity, for in the days of the Turanian supremacy some of this knowledge was wrongfully divulged.

We have seen how the life and light giving attributes of the sun were in early times used as the symbol to bring before the minds of the people all that they were capable of conceiving of the great First Cause. But other symbols of far deeper and more real significance were known and guarded within the ranks of the priesthood. One of these was the conception of a Trinity in Unity. The Trinities of most sacred significance were never divulged to the people, but the Trinity personifying the cosmic powers of the universe as Creator, Preserver, and Destroyer, became publicly known in some irregular manner in the Turanian days. This idea was still further materialized and degraded by the Semites into a strictly anthropomorphic Trinity consisting of father, mother and child.

A further and rather terrible development of the Turanian times must still be referred to. With the practice of sorcery many of the inhabitants had, of course, become aware of the existence of powerful elementals—creatures who had been called into being, or at least animated by their own powerful wills, which being directed towards maleficent ends, naturally produced the elementals of power and malignity. So degraded had then become man's feelings of reverence and worship, that they actually began to adore these semi-conscious creations of their own malignant thought. The ritual with which these beings were worshipped was blood-stained from the very start, and of course every sacrifice offered at their shrine gave vitality and persistence to these vampire-like creations—so much so, that even to the present day in various parts of the world, the elementals formed by the powerful will of these old Atlantean sorcerers still continue to exact their tribute from unoffending village communities.

Though inaugurated and widely practised by the brutal Turanians, this blood-stained ritual seems never to have spread to any extent among the other sub-races, though human sacrifices appear to have been not uncommon among some branches of the Semites.

In the great Toltec empire of Mexico the sun-worship of their forefathers was still the national religion, while the bloodless offerings to their beneficent Deity, Quetzalcoatl, consisted merely of flowers and fruit. It was only with the coming of the savage Aztecs that the harmless Mexican ritual was supplemented with the blood of human sacrifices, which drenched the altars of their war-god, Huitzilopochtli, and the tearing out of the hearts of the victims on the summit of the Teocali may be regarded as a direct survival of the elemental-worship of their Turanian ancestors in Atlantis.

It will be seen then that as in our own days, the religious life of the people embraced the most varied forms of belief and worship. From the small minority who aspired to initiation, and had touch with the higher spiritual life—who knew that good will towards all men, control of thought, and purity of life and action were the necessary preliminaries to the attainment of the highest states of consciousness and the widest realms of vision—innumerable phases led down through the more or less blind worship of cosmic powers, or of anthropomorphic gods, to the degraded but most widely extended ritual in which each man adored his own image, and to the blood-stained rites of the elemental worship.

It must be remembered throughout that we are dealing with the Atlantean race only, so that any reference would be out of place that bore on the still more degraded fetish-worship that even then existed—as it still does—amongst the debased representatives of the Lemurian peoples.

All through the centuries then the various rituals composed to celebrate these various forms of worship were carried on, till the final submergence of Poseidonis, by which time the countless hosts of Atlantean emigrants had already established on foreign lands the various cults of the mother-continent.

To trace the rise and follow the progress in detail of the archaic religions, which in historic times have blossomed into such diverse and antagonistic forms, would be an undertaking of great difficulty, but the illumination it would throw on matters of transcendent importance may some day induce the attempt.

In conclusion, it would be vain to attempt to summarize what is already too much of a summary. Rather let us hope that the foregoing may lend itself as the text from which may be developed histories of the many offshoots of the various sub-races—histories which may analytically examine political and social developments which have been here touched on in the most fragmentary manner.

One word, however, may still be said about that evolution of the race—that progress which all creation, with mankind at its head, is ever destined to achieve century by century, millennium by millennium, manvantara by manvantara, and kalpa by kalpa.

The descent of spirit into matter—these two poles of the one eternal substance—is the process which occupies the first half of every cycle. Now the period we have been contemplating in the foregoing pages—the period during which the Atlantean race was running its course—was the very middle or turning point of this present manvantara.

The process of evolution which in our present Fifth Race has now set in—the return, that is, of matter into spirit—had in those days revealed itself in but a few isolated individual cases—forerunners of the resurrection of the spirit.

But the problem, which all who have given the subject any amount of consideration must have felt to be still awaiting a solution, is the surprising contrast in the attributes of the Atlantean race. Side by side with their brutal passions, their degraded animal propensities, were their psychic faculties, their godlike intuition.

Now the solution of this apparently insoluble enigma lies in the fact that the building of the bridge had only then been begun—the bridge of Manas, or mind, destined to unite in the perfected individual the upward surging forces of the animal and the downward cycling spirit of the God. The animal kingdom of to-day exhibits a field of nature where the building of that bridge has not yet been begun, and even among mankind in the days of Atlantis the connection was so slight that the spiritual attributes had but little controlling power over the lower animal nature. The touch of mind they had was sufficient to add zest to the gratification of the senses, but was not enough to vitalize the still dormant spiritual faculties, which in the perfected individual will have to become the absolute monarch. Our metaphor of the bridge may carry us a little further if we consider it as now in process of construction, but as destined to remain incomplete for mankind in general for untold millenniums—in fact, until Humanity has completed another circle of the seven planets and the great Fifth Round is half way through its course.

Though it was during the latter half of the Third Root Race and the beginning of the Fourth that the Manasaputra descended to endow with mind the bulk of Humanity who were still without the spark, yet so feebly burned the light all through the Atlantean days that few could be said to have attained to the powers of abstract thought. On the other hand the functioning of the mind on concrete things came well within their grasp, and as we have seen it was in the practical concerns of their every-day life, especially when their psychic faculties were directed towards the same objects, that they achieved such remarkable and stupendous results.

It must also be remembered that Kama, the fourth principle, naturally obtained its culminating development in the Fourth Race. This would account for the depths of animal grossness to which they sank, whilst the approach of the cycle to its nadir inevitably accentuated this downward movement, so that there is little to be surprised at in the gradual loss by the race of the psychic faculties, and in its descent to selfishness and materialism.

Rather should all this be regarded as part of the great cyclic process in obedience to the eternal law.

We have all gone through those evil days, and the experiences we then accumulated go to make up the characters we now possess.

But a brighter sun now shines on the Aryan race than that which lit the path of their Atlantean forefathers. Less dominated by the passions of the senses, more open to the influence of mind, the men of our race have obtained, and are obtaining, a firmer grasp of knowledge, a wider range of intellect. This upward arc of the great Manvantaric cycle will naturally lead increasing numbers towards the entrance of the Occult Path, and will lend more and more attraction to the transcendent opportunities it offers for the continued strengthening and purification of the character—strengthening and purification no longer directed by mere spasmodic effort, and continually interrupted by misleading attractions, but guided and guarded at every step by the Masters of Wisdom, so that the upward climb when once begun should no longer be halting and uncertain, but lead direct to the glorious goal.

The psychic faculties too, and the godlike intuition, lost for a time but still the rightful heritage of the race, only await the individual effort of re-attainment, to give to the character still deeper insight and more transcendent powers. So shall the ranks of the Adept instructors—the Masters of Wisdom—be ever strengthened and recruited, and even amongst us to-day there must certainly be some, indistinguishable save by the deathless enthusiasm with which they are animated, who will, before the next Root Race is established on this planet, stand themselves as Masters of Wisdom to help the race in its upward progress.

II. THE LOST LEMURIA

FOREWORD.

The object of this paper is not so much to bring forward new and startling information about the lost continent of Lemuria and its inhabitants, as to establish by the evidence obtainable from geology and from the study of the relative distribution of living and extinct animals and plants, as well as from the observed processes of physical evolution in the lower kingdoms, the facts stated in the "Secret Doctrine" and in other works with reference to these now submerged lands.

The Lost Lemuria.

It is generally recognised by science that what is now dry land, on the surface of our globe, was once the ocean floor, and that what is now the ocean floor was once dry land. Geologists have in some cases been able to specify the exact portions of the earth's surface where these subsidences and upheavals have taken place, and although the lost continent of Atlantis has so far received scant recognition from the world of science, the general concensus of opinion has for long pointed to the existence, at some prehistoric time, of a vast southern continent to which the name of Lemuria has been assigned.

Evidence supplied by Geology and by the relative distribution of living and extinct Animals and Plants.

"The history of the earth's development shows us that the distribution of land and water on its surface is ever and continually changing. In consequence of geological changes of the earth's crust, *elevations* and *depressions* of the ground take place everywhere, sometimes more strongly marked in one place, sometimes in another. Even if they happen so slowly that in the course of centuries the seashore rises or sinks only a few inches, or even only a few lines, still they nevertheless effect great results in the course of long periods of time. And long—immeasurably long—periods of time have not been wanting in the earth's history. During the course of many millions of years, ever since organic life existed on the earth, land and water have perpetually struggled for supremacy. Continents and islands have sunk into the sea, and new ones have arisen out of its bosom. Lakes and seas have been slowly raised and dried up, and new water basins have arisen by the sinking of the ground. Peninsulas have become islands by the narrow neck of land which connected them with the mainland sinking into the water. The islands of an archipelago have become the peaks of a continuous chain of mountains by the whole floor of their sea being considerably raised.

"Thus the Mediterranean at one time was an inland sea, when in the place of the Straits of Gibraltar, an isthmus connected Africa with Spain. England even during the more recent history of the earth, when man already existed, has repeatedly been connected with the European continent and been repeatedly separated from it. Nay, even Europe and North America have been directly connected. The South Sea at one time formed a large Pacific Continent, and the numerous little islands which now lie scattered in it were simply the highest peaks of the mountains covering that continent. The Indian Ocean formed a continent which extended from the Sunda Islands along the southern coast of Asia to the east coast of Africa. This large continent of former times Sclater, an Englishman, has called *Lemuria*, from the monkey-like animals which inhabited it, and it is at the same time of great importance from being the probable cradle of the human race, which in all likelihood here first developed out of anthropoid apes.* *Haeckel is correct enough in his surmise that Lemuria was the cradle of the human race as it now exists, but it was not out of Anthropoid apes that mankind developed. A reference will be made later on to the position in nature which the Anthropoid apes really occupy.*

The important proof which Alfred Wallace has furnished, by the help of chorological facts, that the present Malayan Archipelago consists in reality of two completely different divisions, is particularly interesting. The western division, the Indo-Malayan Archipelago, comprising the large islands of Borneo, Java and Sumatra, was formerly connected by Malacca with the Asiatic continent, and probably also with the Lemurian continent just mentioned. The eastern division on the other hand, the Austro-Malayan Archipelago, comprising Celebes, the Moluccas, New Guinea, Solomon's Islands, etc., was formerly directly connected with Australia. Both divisions were formerly two continents separated by a strait, but they have now for the most part sunk below the level of the sea. Wallace, solely on the ground of his accurate chorological observations, has been able in the most accurate manner to determine the position of this former strait, the south end of which passes between Balij and Lombok.

"Thus, ever since liquid water existed on the earth, the boundaries of water and land have eternally changed, and we may assert that the outlines of continents and islands have never remained for an hour, nay, even for a minute, exactly the same. For the waves eternally and perpetually break on the edge of the coast, and whatever the land in these places loses in extent, it gains in other places by the accumulation of mud, which condenses into

119

solid stone and again rises above the level of the sea as new land. Nothing can be more erroneous than the idea of a firm and unchangeable outline of our continents, such as is impressed upon us in early youth by defective lessons on geography, which are devoid of a geological basis."* *Ernst Haeckel's "Hist. of Creation," 2nd ed., 1876, Vol. 1., pp. 360-62.

The name Lemuria, as above stated, was originally adopted by Mr. Sclater in recognition of the fact that it was probably on this continent that animals of the Lemuroid type were developed.

"This," writes A. R. Wallace, "is undoubtedly a legitimate and highly probable supposition, and it is an example of the way in which a study of the geographical distribution of animals may enable us to reconstruct the geography of a bygone age....

"It [this continent] represents what was probably a primary zoological region in some past geological epoch; but what that epoch was and what were the limits of the region in question, we are quite unable to say. If we are to suppose that it comprised the whole area now inhabited by Lemuroid animals, we must make it extend from West Africa to Burmah, South China and Celebes, an area which it possibly did once occupy." (*) Alfred Russell Wallace's "The Geographical Distribution of Animals—with a study of the relations of living and extinct Faunas as elucidating the past changes of the Earth's Surface." London: Macmillan & Co., 1876. Vol. 1., pp. 76-7.

"We have already had occasion," he elsewhere writes, "to refer to an ancient connection between this sub-region (the Ethiopian) and Madagascar, in order to explain the distribution of the Lemurine type, and some other curious affinities between the two countries. This view is supported by the geology of India, which shows us Ceylon and South India consisting mainly of granite and old-metamorphic rocks, while the greater part of the peninsula is of tertiary formation, with a few isolated patches of secondary rocks. It is evident, therefore, that during much of the tertiary period. (*) Ceylon and South India, it is true, have been bounded on the north by a considerable extent of sea, but that was at a much earlier date than the Tertiary period.

Ceylon and South India were bounded on the north by a considerable extent of sea, and probably formed part of an extensive Southern Continent or great island. The very numerous and remarkable cases of affinity with Malaya, require, however, some closer approximation with these islands, which probably occurred at a later period. When, still later, the great plains and tablelands of Hindostan were formed, and a permanent land communication effected with the rich and highly developed Himalo-

Chinese fauna, a rapid immigration of new types took place, and many of the less specialised forms of mammalia and birds became extinct. Among reptiles and insects the competition was less severe, or the older forms were too well adapted to local conditions to be expelled; so that it is among these groups alone that we find any considerable number of what are probably the remains of the ancient fauna of a now submerged Southern Continent." (*) *Wallace's "Geographical Distribution, etc." Vol. 1., pp. 328-9.*

After stating that during the whole of the tertiary and perhaps during much of the secondary periods, the great land masses of the earth were probably situated in the Northern Hemisphere, Wallace proceeds, "In the Southern Hemisphere there appear to have been three considerable and very ancient land masses, varying in extent from time to time, but always keeping distinct from each other, and represented more or less completely by Australia, South Africa and South America of our time. Into these flowed successive waves of life as they each in turn became temporarily united with some part of the Northern land." (*) *Wallace's "Geographical Distribution, etc.," Vol. ii., p. 155.*

Although, apparently in vindication of some conclusions of his which had been criticised by Dr. Hartlaub, Wallace subsequently denied the necessity of postulating the existence of such a continent, his general recognition of the facts of subsidences and upheavals of great portions of the earth's surface, as well as the inferences which he draws from the acknowledged relations of living and extinct faunas as above stated, remain of course unaltered.

The following extracts from Mr. H. F. Blandford's[1] most interesting paper read before a meeting of the Geological Society deals with the subject in still greater detail:— "The affinities between the fossils of both animals and plants of the Beaufort group of Africa and those of the Indian Panchets and Kathmis are such as to suggest the former existence of a land connexion between the two areas. But the resemblance of the African and Indian fossil faunas does not cease with Permian and Triassic times. The plant beds of the Uitenhage group have furnished eleven forms of plants, two of which Mr. Tate has identified with Indian Rájmahál plants. The Indian Jurassic fossils have yet to be described (with a few exceptions), but it has been stated that Dr. Stoliezka was much struck with the affinities of certain of the Cutch fossils to African forms; and Dr. Stoliezka and Mr. Griesbach have

---

[1] *"On the age and correlations of the Plant-bearing series of India and the former existence of an Indo-Oceanic Continent," see Quarterly Journal of the Geological Society, Vol. xxxi., 1875, pp. 534-540.*

shown that of the Cretaceous fossils of the Umtafuni river in Natal, the majority (22 out of 35 described forms) are identical with species from Southern India. Now the plant-bearing series of India and the Karoo and part of the Uitenhage formation of Africa are in all probability of freshwater origin, both indicating the existence of a large land area around, from the waste of which these deposits are derived. Was this land continuous between the two regions? And is there anything in the present physical geography of the Indian Ocean which would suggest its probable position? Further, what was the connexion between this land and Australia which we must equally assume to have existed in Permian times? And, lastly, are there any peculiarities in the existing fauna and flora of India, Africa and the intervening islands which would lend support to the idea of a former connexion more direct than that which now exists between Africa and South India and the Malay peninsula? The speculation here put forward is no new one. It has long been a subject of thought in the minds of some Indian and European naturalists, among the former of whom I may mention my brother [Mr. Blandford] and Dr. Stoliezka, their speculations being grounded on the relationship and partialidentity of the faunas and floras of past times, not less than on that existing community of forms which has led Mr. Andrew Murray, Mr. Searles, V. Wood, jun., and Professor Huxley to infer the existence of a Miocene continent occupying a part of the Indian Ocean. Indeed, all that I can pretend to aim at in this paper is to endeavour to give some additional definition and extension to the conception of its geological aspect.

"With regard to the geographical evidence, a glance at the map will show that from the neighbourhood of the West Coast of India to that of the Seychelles, Madagascar, and the Mauritius, extends a line of coral atolls and banks, including Adas bank, the Laccadives, Maldives, the Chagos group and the Saya de Mulha, all indicating the existence of a submerged mountain range or ranges. The Seychelles, too, are mentioned by Mr. Darwin as rising from an extensive and tolerably level bank having a depth of between 30 and 40 fathoms; so that, although now partly encircled by fringing reefs, they may be regarded as a virtual extension of the same submerged axis. Further west the Cosmoledo and Comoro Islands consist of atolls and islands surrounded by barrier reefs; and these bring us pretty close to the present shores of Africa and Madagascar. It seems at least probable that in this chain of atolls, banks, and barrier reefs we have indicated the position of an ancient mountain chain, which possibly formed the back-bone of a tract of later Palæozoic, Mesozoic, and early Tertiary land, being related to it much as the Alpine and Himálayan system is to the

Europæo-Asiatic continent, and the Rocky Mountains and Andes to the two Americas. As it is desirable to designate this Mesozoic land by a name, I would propose that of Indo-Oceana. [The name given to it by Mr. Sclater, viz., Lemuria, is, however, the one which has been most generally adopted.] Professor Huxley has suggested on palæontological grounds that a land connexion existed in this region (or rather between Abyssinia and India) during the Miocene epoch. From what has been said above it will be seen that I infer its existence from a far earlier date. *(*) A reference to the maps will show that Mr. Blandford's estimate of date is the more correct of the two.*

With regard to its depression, the only present evidence relates to its northern extremity, and shows that it was in this region, later than the great trap-flows of the Dakhan. These enormous sheets of volcanic rock are remarkably horizontal to the east of the Gháts and the Sakyádri range, but to the west of this they begin to dip seawards, so that the island of Bombay is composed of the higher parts of the formation. This indicates only that the depression to the westward has taken place in Tertiary times; and to that extent Professor Huxley's inference, that it was after the Miocene period, is quite consistent with the geological evidence."

After proceeding at some length to instance the close relationship of many of the fauna in the lands under consideration (Lion, Hyæna, Jackal, Leopard, Antelope, Gazelle, Sand-grouse, Indian Bustard, many Land Molusca, and notably the Lemur and the Scaly Anteater) the writer proceeds as follows:—

"Palæontology, physical geography and geology, equally with the ascertained distribution of living animals and plants, offer thus their concurrent testimony to the former close connexion of Africa and India, including the tropical islands of the Indian Ocean. This Indo-Oceanic land appears to have existed from at least early Permian times, probably (as Professor Huxley has pointed out) up to the close of the Miocene epoch[2] and South Africa and Peninsular India are the existing remnants of that ancient land. It may not have been absolutely continuous during the whole of this long period. Indeed, the Cretaceous rocks of Southern India and Southern Africa, and the marine Jurassic beds of the same regions, prove that some portions of it were, for longer or shorter periods, invaded by the sea; but any break of continuity was probably not prolonged; for Mr. Wallace's investigations in the Eastern Archipelago have shown how

---

[2] *Parts of the continent of course endured, but the dismemberment of Lemuria is said to have taken place before the beginning of the Eocene Age.)*

narrow a sea may offer an insuperable barrier to the migration of land animals. In Palæozoic times this land must have been connected with Australia, and in Tertiary times with Malayana, since the Malayan forms with African alliances are in several cases distinct from those of India. We know as yet too little of the geology of the eastern peninsula to say from what epoch dates its connexion with Indo-Oceanic land. Mr. Theobald has ascertained the existence of Triassic, Cretaceous, and Nummulitic rocks in the Arabian coast range; and Carboniferous limestone is known to occur from Moulmein southward, while the range east of the Irrawadi is formed of younger Tertiary rocks. From this it would appear that a considerable part of the Malay peninsula must have been occupied by the sea during the greater part of the Mesozoic and Eocene periods. Plant-bearing rocks of Rániganj age have been identified as forming the outer spurs of the Sikkim Himálaya; the ancient land must therefore have extended some distance to the north of the present Gangetic delta. Coal both of Cretaceous and Tertiary age occurs in the Khasi hills, and also in Upper Assam, but in both cases associated with marine beds; so that it would appear that in this region the boundaries of land and sea oscillated somewhat during Cretaceous and Eocene times. To the north-west of India the existence of great formations of Cretaceous and Nummulitic age, stretching far through Baluchistán and Persia, and entering into the structure of the north-west Himálaya, prove that in the later Mesozoic and Eocene ages India had no direct communication with western Asia; while the Jurassic rocks of Cutch, the Salt range, and the northern Himálaya, show that in the preceding period the sea covered a large part of the present Indus basin; and the Triassic, Carboniferous, and still more recent marine formations of the Himálaya, indicate that from very early times till the upheaval of that great chain, much of its present site was for ages covered by the sea.

"To sum up the views advanced in this paper.

"1st. The plant-bearing series of India ranges from early Permian to the latest Jurassic times, indicating (except in a few cases and locally) the uninterrupted continuity of land and fresh water conditions. These may have prevailed from much earlier times.

"2nd. In the early Permian, as in the Postpliocene age, a cold climate prevailed down to low latitudes, and I am inclined to believe in both hemispheres simultaneously. With the decrease of cold the flora and reptilian fauna of Permian times were diffused to Africa, India, and possibly Australia; or the flora may have existed in Australia somewhat earlier, and have been diffused thence.

"3rd. India, South Africa and Australia were connected by an Indo-Oceanic Continent in the Permian epoch; and the two former countries remained connected (with at the utmost only short interruptions) up to the end of the Miocene period. During the latter part of the time this land was also connected with Malayana.

"4th. In common with some previous writers, I consider that the position of this land was defined by the range of coral reefs and banks that now exist between the Arabian sea and East Africa.

"5th. Up to the end of the Nummulitic epoch no direct connexion (except possibly for short periods) existed between India and Western Asia."

In the discussion which followed the reading of the paper, Professor Ramsay "agreed with the author in the belief in the junction of Africa with India and Australia in geological times."

Mr. Woodward "was pleased to find that the author had added further evidence, derived from the fossil flora of the mesozoic series of India, in corroboration of the views of Huxley, Sclater and others as to the former existence of an old submerged continent ('Lemuria') which Darwin's researches on coral reefs had long since foreshadowed."

"Of the five now existing continents," writes Ernst Haeckel, in his great work "The History of Creation, *Vol ii., pp. 325-6,* neither Australia, nor America, nor Europe can have been this primæval home [of man], or the so-called 'Paradise,' the 'cradle of the human race.' Most circumstances indicate Southern Asia as the locality in question. Besides Southern Asia, the only other of the now existing continents which might be viewed in this light is Africa. But there are a number of circumstances (especially chorological facts) which suggest that the primeval home of man was a continent now sunk below the surface of the Indian Ocean, which extended along the south of Asia, as it is at present (and probably in direct connection with it), towards the east, as far as Further India and the Sunda Islands; towards the west, as far as Madagascar and the south-eastern shores of Africa. We have already mentioned that many facts in animal and vegetable geography render the former existence of such a South Indian continent very probable. Sclater has given this continent the name of Lemuria, from the semi-apes which were characteristic of it. By assuming this Lemuria to have been man's primæval home, we greatly facilitate the explanation of the geographical distribution of the human species by migration." In a subsequent work, "The Pedigree of Man," Haeckel asserts the existence of Lemuria at some early epoch of the earth's history as an acknowledged fact.

The following quotation from Dr. Hartlaub's [3]writings may bring to a close this portion of the evidence in favour of the existence of the lost Lemuria:—"Five and thirty years ago, Isidore Geoffrey St. Hilaire remarked that, if one had to classify the Island of Madagascar exclusively on zoological considerations, and without reference to its geographical situation, it could be shown to be neither Asiatic nor African, but quite different from either, and almost a fourth continent. And this fourth continent could be further proved to be, as regards its fauna, much more different from Africa, which lies so near to it, than from India which is so far away. With these words the correctness and pregnancy of which later investigations tend to bring into their full light, the French naturalist first stated the interesting problem for the solution of which an hypothesis based on scientific knowledge has recently been propounded, for this fourth continent of Isidore Geoffrey is Sclater's 'Lemuria'—that sunken land which, containing parts of Africa, must have extended far eastwards over Southern India and Ceylon, and the highest points of which we recognise in the volcanic peaks of Bourbon and Mauritius, and in the central range of Madagascar itself—the last resorts of the almost extinct Lemurine race which formerly peopled it."

Evidence obtained from Archaic Records.

The further evidence we have with regard to Lemuria and its inhabitants has been obtained from the same source and in the same manner as that which resulted in the writing of the *Story of Atlantis*. In this case also the author has been privileged to obtain copies of two maps, one representing Lemuria (and the adjoining lands) during the period of that continent's greatest expansion, the other exhibiting its outlines after its dismemberment by great catastrophes, but long before its final destruction.

It was never professed that the maps of Atlantis were correct *to a single degree* of latitude, or longitude, but, with the far greater difficulty of obtaining the information in the present case, it must be stated that still less must these maps of Lemuria be taken as absolutely accurate. In the former case there was a globe, a good bas-relief in terra-cotta, and a well-preserved map on parchment, or skin of some sort, to copy from. In the present case there was only a broken terra-cotta model and a very badly preserved and crumpled map, so that the difficulty of carrying back the remembrance of all the details, and consequently of reproducing exact copies, has been far greater.

---

[3] Dr. G. Hartlaub "On the Avifauna of Madagascar and the Mascarene Islands," see "The Ibis," a Quarterly Journal of Ornithology. Fourth Series, Vol. i., 1877, p. 334.

We were told that it was by mighty Adepts in the days of Atlantis that the Atlantean maps were produced, but we are not aware whether the Lemurian maps were fashioned by some of the divine instructors in the days when Lemuria still existed, or in still later days of the Atlantean epoch.

But while guarding against over-confidence in the absolute accuracy of the maps in question, the transcriber of the archaic originals believes that they may in all important particulars, be taken as approximately correct.

Probable Duration of the Continent of Lemuria.

A period—speaking roughly—of between four and five million years probably represents the life of the continent of Atlantis, for it is about that time since the Rmoahals, the first sub-race of the Fourth Root Race who inhabited Atlantis, arose on a portion of the Lemurian Continent which at that time still existed. Remembering that in the evolutionary process the figure four invariably represents not only the nadir of the cycle, but the period of shortest duration, whether in the case of a Manvantaraor of a race, it may be assumed that the number of millions of years assignable as the life-limit of the continent of Lemuria must be very much greater than that representing the life of Atlantis, the continent of the Fourth Root Race. But in the case of Lemuria no dates can be stated with even approximate accuracy. Geological epochs, so far as they are known to modern science, will be a better medium for contemporary reference, and they alone will be dealt with.

The Maps.

But not even geological epochs, it will be observed, are assigned to the maps. If, however, an inference may be drawn from all the evidence before us, it would seem probable that the older of the two Lemurian maps represented the earth's configuration from the Permian, through the Triassic and into the Jurassic epoch, while the second map probably represents the earth's configuration through the Cretaceous and into the Eocene period.

From the older of the two maps it may be seen that the equatorial continent of Lemuria at the time of its greatest expansion nearly girdled the globe, extending as it then did from the site of the present Cape Verd Islands a few miles from the coast of Sierra Leone, in a south-easterly direction through Africa, Australia, the Society Islands and all the intervening seas, to a point but a few miles distant from a great island continent (about the size of the present South America) which spread over the remainder of the Pacific Ocean, and included Cape Horn and parts of Patagonia.

A remarkable feature in the second map of Lemuria is the great length, and at parts the extreme narrowness, of the straits which separated the two great blocks of land into which the continent had by this time been split, and it will be observed that the straits at present existing between the islands of Bali and Lomboc coincide with a portion of the straits which then divided these two continents. It will also be seen that these straits continued in a northerly direction by the west, not by the east coast of Borneo, as conjectured by Ernst Haeckel.

With reference to the distribution of fauna and flora, and the existence of so many types common to India and Africa alike, pointed out by Mr. Blandford, it will be observed that between parts of India and great tracts of Africa there was direct land communication during the first map period, and that similar communication was partially maintained in the second map period also; while a comparison of the maps of Atlantis with those of Lemuria will demonstrate that continuous land communication existed, now at one epoch, and now at another, between so many different parts of the earth's surface, at present separated by sea, that the existing distribution of fauna and flora in the two Americas, in Europe and in Eastern lands, which has been such a puzzle to naturalists, may with perfect ease be accounted for.

The island indicated in the earlier Lemurian map as existing to the north-west of the extreme promontory of that continent, and due west of the present coast of Spain, was probably a centre from which proceeded, during long ages, the distribution of fauna and flora above referred to. For— and this is a most interesting fact—it will be seen that this island must have been the nucleus, from first to last, of the subsequent great continent of Atlantis. It existed, as we see, in these earliest Lemurian times. It was joined in the second map period to land which had previously formed part of the great Lemurian continent; and indeed, so many accretions of territory had it by this time received that it might more appropriately be called a continent than an island. It was the great mountainous region of Atlantis at its prime, when Atlantis embraced great tracts of land which have now become North and South America. It remained the mountainous region of Atlantis in its decadence, and of Ruta in the Ruta and Daitya epoch, and it practically constituted the island of Poseidonis—the last remnant of the continent of Atlantis—the final submergence of which took place in the year 9564 B.C.

A comparison of the two maps here given, along with the four maps of Atlantis, will also show that Australia and New Zealand, Madagascar, parts of Somaliland, the south of Africa, and the extreme southern portion of

Patagonia are lands which have *probably* existed through all the intervening catastrophes since the early days of the Lemurian period. The same may be said of the southern parts of India and Ceylon, with the exception in the case of Ceylon, of a temporary submergence in the Ruta and Daitya epoch.

It is true there are also remains still existing of the even earlier Hyperborean continent, and they of course are the oldest known lands on the face of the earth. These are Greenland, Iceland, Spitzbergen, the most northerly parts of Norway and Sweden, and the extreme north cape of Siberia.

Japan is shown by the maps to have been above water, whether as an island, or as part of a continent, since the date of the second Lemurian map. Spain, too, has doubtless existed since that time. Spain is, therefore, with the exception of the most northerly parts of Norway and Sweden, *probably* the oldest land in Europe.

The indeterminate character of the statements just made is rendered necessary by our knowledge that there *did* occur subsidences and upheavals of different portions of the earth's surface during the ages which lay between the periods represented by the maps.

For example, soon after the date of the second Lemurian map we are informed that the whole Malay Peninsula was submerged and remained so for a long time, but a subsequent upheaval of that region must have taken place before the date of the first Atlantean map, for, what is now the Malay Peninsula is there exhibited as part of a great continent. Similarly there have been repeated minor subsidences and upheavals nearer home in more recent times, and Haeckel is perfectly correct in saying that England—he might with greater accuracy have said the islands of Great Britain and Ireland, which were then joined together—"has repeatedly been connected with the European continent, and been repeatedly separated from it."

In order to bring the subject more dearly before the mind, a tabular statement is here annexed which supplies a condensed history of the animal and plant life on our globe, bracketed—according to Haeckel—with the contemporary rock strata. Two other columns give the contemporary races of man, and such of the great cataclysms as are known to occult students.

Reptiles and Pine Forests.

From this statement it will be seen that Lemurian man lived in the age of Reptiles and Pine Forests. The amphibious monsters and the gigantic tree-ferns of the Permian age still flourished in the warm damp climates. Plesiosauri and Icthyosauri swarmed in the tepid marshes of the Mesolithic

129

epoch, but, with the drying up of many of the inland seas, the Dinosauria—the monstrous land reptiles—gradually became the dominant type, while the Pterodactyls—the Saurians which developed bat-like wings—not only crawled on the earth, but flew through the air. The smallest of these latter were about the size of a sparrow; the largest, however, with a breadth of wing of more than sixteen feet, exceeding the largest of our living birds of to-day; while most of the Dinosauria—the Dragons—were terrible beasts of prey, colossal reptiles which attained a length of from forty to fifty feet.(*) *Ernst Haeckel's "History of Creation," Vol. ii., pp. 22-56.*

Subsequent excavations have laid bare skeletons of an even larger size. Professor Ray Lankester, at a meeting of the Royal Institution on 7th January, 1904, is reported to have referred to a brontosaurus skeleton of sixty-five feet long, which had been discovered in the Oolite deposit in the southern part of the United States of America.

As it is written in the stanzas of the archaic Book of Dzyan, "Animals with bones, dragons of the deep, and flying sarpas were added to the creeping things. They that creep on the ground got wings. They of the long necks in the water became the progenitors of the fowls of the air." Modern science records her endorsement. "The class of birds as already remarked is so closely allied to Reptiles in internal structure and by embryonal development that they undoubtedly originated out of a branch of this class.... The derivation of birds from reptiles first took place in the Mesolithic epoch, and this moreover probably during the Trias." (*) *Ernst Haeckel's "History of Creation," Vol. ii., pp. 226-7.*

In the vegetable kingdom this epoch also saw the pine and the palm-tree gradually displace the giant tree ferns. In the later days of the Mesolithic epoch, mammals for the first time came into existence, but the fossil remains of the mammoth and mastodon, which were their earliest representatives, are chiefly found in the subsequent strata of the Eocene and Miocene times.

The Human Kingdom.

Before making any reference to what must, even at this early date, be called the human kingdom, it must be stated that none of those who, at the present day, can lay claim to even a moderate amount of mental or spiritual culture *can* have lived in these ages. It was only with the advent of the last three sub-races of this Third Root Race that the least progressed of the first group of the Lunar Pitris began to return to incarnation, while the most advanced among them did not take birth till the early sub-races of the Atlantean period.

Indeed, Lemurian man, during at least the first half of the race, must be regarded rather as an animal destined to reach humanity than as human according to our understanding of the term; for though the second and third groups of Pitris, who constituted the inhabitants of Lemuria during its first four sub-races, had achieved sufficient self-consciousness in the Lunar Manvantara to differentiate them from the animal kingdom, they had not yet received the Divine Spark which should endow them with mind and individuality—in other words, make them truly human.

Size and Consistency of Man's Body.

The evolution of this Lemurian race, therefore, constitutes one of the most obscure, as well as one of the most interesting, chapters of man's development, for during this period not only did he reach true humanity, but his body underwent the greatest physical changes, while the processes of reproduction were twice altered.

In explanation of the surprising statements which will have to be made in regard to the size and consistency of man's body at this early period it must be remembered that while the animal, vegetable and mineral kingdoms pursued the normal course, on this the fourth globe, during the Fourth Round of this Manvantara, it was ordained that humanity should run over in rapid succession the various stages through which its evolution had passed during the previous rounds of the present Manvantara. Thus the bodies of the First Root Race in which these almost mindless beings were destined to gain experience, would have appeared to us as gigantic phantoms—if indeed we could have seen them at all, for their bodies were formed of astral matter. The astral forms of the First Root Race were then gradually enveloped in a more physical casing. But though the Second Root Race may be called physical—their bodies being composed of ether—they would have been equally invisible to eyesight as it at present exists.

It was, we are told, in order that the Manu, and the Beings who aided him, might take means for improving the physical type of humanity that this epitome of the process of evolution was ordained. The highest development which the type had so far reached was the huge ape-like creature which had existed on the three physical planets, Mars, the Earth and Mercury in the Third Round. On the arrival of the human life-wave on the Earth in this the Fourth Round, a certain number, naturally, of these ape-like creatures were found in occupation—the residuum left on the planet during its period of obscuration. These, of course, joined the in-coming human stream as soon as the race became fully physical. Their bodies may not then have been absolutely discarded; they may have been utilized for purposes of reincarnation for the most backward entities, but it was an improvement on this type which was required, and this was most easily achieved by the Manu, through working out on the astral plane in the first instance, the architype originally formed in the mind of the Logos.

From the Etheric Second Race, then, was evolved the Third—the Lemurian. Their bodies had become material, being composed of the gases, liquids and solids which constitute the three lowest sub-divisions of the physical plane, but the gases and liquids still predominated, for as yet their vertebrate structure had not solidified into bones such as ours, and they could not, therefore, stand erect. Their bones in fact were pliable as the bones of young infants now are. It was not until the middle of the Lemurian period that man developed a solid bony structure.

To explain the possibility of the process by which the etheric form evolved into a more physical form, and the soft-boned physical form ultimately developed into a structure such as man possesses to-day, it is only necessary to refer to the permanent physical atom. *(*) For a further account of the permanent atoms on all the planes, and the potentialities contained in them with reference to the processes of death and re-birth, see "Man's Place in Universe." pp. 76-80.*

Containing as it does the essence of all the forms through which man has passed on the physical plane, it contained consequently the potentiality of a hard-boned physical structure such as had been attained during the course of the Third Round, as well as the potentiality of an etheric form and all the phases which lie between, for it must be remembered that the physical plane consists of four grades of ether as well as the gases, liquids and solids which so many are apt to regard as alone constituting the physical. Thus, every stage of the development was a natural process, for it was a process which had been accomplished in ages long past, and all that was needed was for the Manu and the Beings who aided him, to gather round the permanent atom the appropriate kind of matter.

Organs of Vision.

The organs of vision of these creatures before they developed bones were of a rudimentary nature, at least such was the condition of the two eyes in front with which they sought for their food upon the ground. But there was a third eye at the back of the head, the atrophied remnant of which is now known as the *pineal gland*. This, as we know, is *now* a centre solely of astral vision, but at the epoch of which we are speaking it was the chief centre not only of astral but of physical sight. Referring to reptiles which had become extinct, Professor Ray Lankester, in a recent lecture at the Royal Institution, is reported to have drawn special attention "to the size of the parietal foramen in the skull which showed that in the ichthyosaurs the parietal or pineal eye on the top of the head must have been very large." In this respect he went on to say mankind were inferior to these big sea lizards, "for we had lost the third eye which might be studied in the common lizard, or better in the great blue lizard of the South of France." (*) *The "Standard," 8th Jan., 1904.*

Somewhat before the middle of the Lemurian period, probably during the evolution of the third sub-race, the gigantic gelatinous body began slowly to solidify and the soft-boned limbs developed into a bony structure. These primitive creatures were now able to stand upright, and the two eyes in the face gradually became the chief organs of physical sight, though the third eye still remained to some extent an organ of physical sight also, and this it did till the very end of the Lemurian epoch. It, of course, remained an actual organ, as it still is a potential focus, of psychic vision. This psychic vision continued to be an attribute of the race not only throughout the whole Lemurian period, but well into the days of Atlantis.

A curious fact to note is that when the race first attained the power of standing and moving in an upright position, they could walk backwards with almost as great ease as forwards. This may be accounted for not only by the capacity for vision possessed by the third eye, but doubtless also by the curious projection at the heels which will presently be referred to.

Description of Lemurian Man.

The following is a description of a man who belonged to one of the later sub-races—probably the fifth. "His stature was gigantic, somewhere between twelve and fifteen feet. His skin was very dark, being of a yellowish brown colour. He had a long lower jaw, a strangely flattened face, eyes small but piercing and set curiously far apart, so that he could see sideways as well as in front, while the eye at the back of the head—on which part of the head no hair, of course, grew—enabled him to see in that direction also. He had no forehead, but there seemed to be a roll of flesh where it should have been. The head sloped backwards and upwards in a rather curious way. The arms and legs (especially the former) were longer in proportion than ours, and could not be perfectly straightened either at elbows or knees; the hands and feet were enormous, and the heels projected backwards in an ungainly way. The figure was draped in a loose robe of skin, something like rhinoceros hide, but more scaly, probably the skin of some animal of which we now know only through its fossil remains. Round his head, on which the hair was quite short, was twisted another piece of skin to which were attached tassels of bright red, blue and other colours. In his left hand he held a sharpened staff, which was doubtless used for defence or attack. It was about the height of his own body, *viz.*, twelve to fifteen feet. In his right hand was twisted the end of a long rope made of some sort of creeping plant, by which he led a huge and hideous reptile, somewhat resembling the Plesiosaurus. The Lemurians actually domesticated these creatures, and trained them to employ their strength in hunting other animals. The appearance of the man gave an unpleasant sensation, but he was not entirely uncivilised, being an average common-place specimen of his day."

Many were even less human in appearance than the individual here described, but the seventh sub-race developed a superior type, though very unlike any living men of the present time. While retaining the projecting lower jaw, the thick heavy lips, the flattened face, and the uncanny looking eyes, they had by this time developed something which might be called a forehead, while the curious projection of the heel had been considerably reduced. In one branch of this seventh sub-race, the head might be described as almost egg-shaped—the small end of the egg being uppermost, with the eyes wide apart and very near the top. The stature had perceptibly decreased, and the appearance of the hands, feet and limbs generally had become more like those of the negroes of to-day. These people developed an important and long-lasting civilisation, and for thousands of years dominated most of the other tribes who dwelt on the vast Lemurian continent, and even at the end, when racial decay seemed to be overtaking them, they secured another long lease of life and power by inter-marriage with the Rmoahals—the first sub-race of the Atlanteans. The progeny, while retaining many Third Race characteristics, of course, really belonged to the Fourth Race, and thus naturally acquired fresh power of development. Their general appearance now became not unlike that of some American Indians, except that their skin had a curious bluish tinge not now to be seen.

But surprising as were the changes in the size, consistency, and appearance of man's body during this period, the alterations in the process of reproduction are still more astounding. A reference to the systems which now obtain among the lower kingdoms of nature may help us in the consideration of the subject.

Processes of Reproduction.

After instancing the simplest processes of propagation by self-division, and by the formation of buds (Gemmatio), Haeckel proceeds, "A third mode of non-sexual propagation, that of the formation of germ-buds (Polysporogonia) is intimately connected with the formation of buds. In the case of the lower, imperfect organisms, among animals, especially in the case of the plant-like animals and worms, we very frequently find that in the interior of an individual composed of many cells, a small group of cells separates itself from those surrounding it, and that this small isolated group gradually develops itself into an individual, which becomes like the parent and sooner or later comes out of it.... The formation of germ buds is evidently but little different from real budding. But, on the other hand, it is connected with a fourth kind of non-sexual propagation, which almost forms a transition to sexual reproduction, namely, the formation of germ cells (Monosporogonia). In this case it is no longer a group of cells but a single cell, which separates itself from the surrounding cells in the interior of the producing organism, and which becomes further developed after it has come out of its parent.... Sexual or amphigonic propagation (Amphigonia) is the usual method of propagation among all higher animals and plants. It is evident that it has only developed at a very late period of the earth's history, from non-sexual propagation, and apparently in the first instance from the method of propagation by germ-cells.... In all the chief forms of non-sexual propagation mentioned above—in fission, in the formation of buds, germ-buds, and germ-cells—the separated cell or group of cells was able by itself to develop into a new individual, but in the case of sexual propagation, the cell must first be fructified by another generative substance. The fructifying sperm must first mix with the germ-cell (the egg) before the latter can develop into a new individual. These two generative substances, the sperm and the egg, are either produced by one and the same individual hermaphrodite (Hermaphroditismus) or by two different individuals (sexual-separation).

"The simpler and more ancient form of sexual propagation is through double-sexed individuals. It occurs in the great majority of plants, but only in a minority of animals, for example, in the garden snails, leeches, earth-worms, and many other worms. Every single individual among hermaphrodites produces within itself materials of both sexes—eggs and sperm. In most of the higher plants every blossom contains both the male organ (stamens and anther) and the female organ (style and germ). Every garden snail produces in one part of its sexual gland eggs, and in another part sperm. Many hermaphrodites can fructify themselves; in others, however, reciprocal fructification of both hermaphrodites is necessary for causing the development of the eggs. This latter case is evidently a transition to sexual separation.

"Sexual separation, which characterises the more complicated of the two kinds of sexual reproduction, has evidently been developed from the

135

condition of hermaphroditism at a late period of the organic history of the world. It is at present the universal method of propagation of the higher animals.... The so-called virginal reproduction (Parthenogenesis) offers an interesting form of transition from sexual reproduction to the non-sexual formation of germ-cells which most resembles it.... In this case germ-cells which otherwise appear and are formed exactly like egg-cells, become capable of developing themselves into new individuals without requiring the fructifying seed. The most remarkable and the most instructive of the different parthenogenetic phenomena are furnished by those cases in which the same germ-cells, according as they are fructified or not, produce different kinds of individuals. Among our common honey bees, a male individual (a drone) arises out of the eggs of the queen, if the egg has not been fructified; a female (a queen, or working bee) if the egg has been fructified. It is evident from this, that in reality there exists no wide chasm between sexual and non-sexual reproduction, but that both modes of reproduction are directly connected." *(Ernst Haeckel's "The History of Creation," 2nd ed., Vol. i., pp. 193-8.)*

Now, the interesting fact in connection with the evolution of Third Race man on Lemuria, is that his mode of reproduction ran through phases which were closely analogous with some of the processes above described. Sweat-born, egg-born and Androgyne are the terms used in the Secret Doctrine. "Almost sexless, in its early beginnings, it became bisexual or androgynous; very gradually, of course. The passage from the former to the latter transformation required numberless generations, during which the simple cell that issued from the earliest parent (the two in one), first developed into a bisexual being; and then the cell, becoming a regular egg, gave forth a unisexual creature. The Third Race mankind is the most mysterious of all the hitherto developed five Races. The mystery of the 'How' of the generation of the distinct sexes must, of course, be very obscure here, as it is the business of an embryologist and a specialist, the present work giving only faint outlines of the process. But it is evident that the units of the Third Race humanity began to separate in their pre-natal shells, or eggs, and to issue out of them as distinct male and female babes, ages after the appearance of its early progenitors. And, as time rolled on its geological periods, the newly born sub-races began to lose their natal capacities. Toward the end of the fourth *sub-race*, the babe lost its faculty of walking as soon as liberated from its shell, and by the end of the fifth, mankind was born under the same conditions and by the same identical process as our historical generations. This required, of course, millions of years." *("The Secret Doctrine," Vol. ii., p. 197.)*

Lemurian Races still Inhabiting the Earth.

It may be as well again to repeat that the almost mindless creatures who inhabited such bodies as have been above described during the early sub-races of the Lemurian period can scarcely be regarded as completely human. It was only after the separation of the sexes, when their bodies had become densely physical, that they became human even in appearance. It must be remembered that the beings we are speaking of, though embracing the second and third groups of the Lunar Pitris, must also have been largely recruited from the animal kingdom of that (the Lunar) Manvantara. The degraded remnants of the Third Root Race who still inhabit the earth may be recognised in the aborigines of Australia, the Andaman Islanders, some hill tribes of India, the Tierra-del-Fuegans, the Bushmen of Africa, and some other savage tribes. The entities now inhabiting these bodies must have belonged to the animal kingdom in the early part of *this* Manvantara. It was probably during the evolution of the Lemurian race and before the "door was shut" on the entities thronging up from below, that these attained the human kingdom.

Sin of the Mindless.

The shameful acts of the mindless men at the first separation of the sexes had best be referred to in the words of the stanzas of the archaic Book of Dzyan. No commentary is needed. "During the Third Race the boneless animals grew and changed, they became animals with bones, their chayas became solid. The animals separated first. They began to breed. The two-fold man separated also. He said, 'Let us as they; let us unite and make creatures.' They did.

"And those that had no spark took huge she-animals unto them. They begat upon them dumb races. Dumb they were themselves. But their tongues untied. The tongues of their progeny remained still. Monsters they bred. A race of crooked red-hair-covered monsters going on all fours. A dumb race to keep the shame untold." (And an ancient commentary adds 'when the Third separated and fell into sin by breeding men-animals, these (the animals) became ferocious, and men and they mutually destructive. Till then, there was no sin, no life taken.').

"Seeing which the Lhas who had not built men, wept, saying. 'The Amanasa [mindless] have defiled our future abodes. This is Karma. Let us dwell in the others. Let us teach them better lest worse should happen.' They did.

"Then all men became endowed with Manas. They saw the sin of the mindless."

Origin of the Pithecoid and the Anthropoid Apes.

The anatomical resemblance between Man and the higher Ape, so frequently cited by Darwinists as pointing to some ancestors common to both, presents an interesting problem, the proper solution of which is to be sought for in the esoteric explanation of the genesis of the pithecoid stocks.

Now, we gather from the Secret Doctrine (*Vol. ii., pp. 683 and 689*) that the descendants of these semi-human monsters described above as originating in the sin of the "mindless," having through long centuries dwindled in size and become more densely physical, culminated in a race of Apes at the time of the Miocene period, from which in their turn are descended the pithecoids of to-day. With these Apes of the Miocene period, however, the Atlanteans of that age renewed the sin of the "mindless"—this time with full responsibility, and the resultants of their crime are the species of Apes now known as Anthropoid.

We are given to understand that in the coming Sixth Root Race, these anthropoids will obtain human incarnation, in the bodies doubtless of the lowest races then existing upon earth.

That part of the Lemurian continent where the separation of the sexes took place, and where both the fourth and the fifth sub-races flourished, is to be found in the earlier of the two maps. It lay to the east of the mountainous region of which the present Island of Madagascar formed a part, and thus occupied a central position around the smaller of the two great lakes.

Origin of Language.

As stated in the stanzas of Dzyan above quoted, the men of that epoch, even though they had become completely physical, still remained speechless. Naturally the astral and etherial ancestors of this Third Root Race had no need to produce a series of sounds in order to convey their thoughts, living as they did in astral and etherial conditions, but when man became physical he could not for long remain dumb. We are told that the sounds which these primitive men made to express their thoughts were at first composed entirely of vowels. In the slow course of evolution the consonant sounds gradually came into use, but the development of language from first to last on the continent of Lemuria never reached beyond the monosyllabic phase. The Chinese language of to-day is the sole great lineal descendant of ancient Lemurian speech ((*) *It must, however, be noted that the Chinese people are mainly descended from the fourth or Turanian sub-race of the Fourth Root Race)* for "the whole human race was at that time of one language and of one lip." (*) "Secret Doctrine," Vol. ii., p. 198.

In Humboldt's classification of language, the Chinese, as we know, is called the *isolating* as distinguished from the more highly evolved *agglutinative*, and the still more highly evolved *inflectional*. Readers of the *Story of Atlantis* may remember that many different languages were developed on that continent, but all belonged to the *agglutinative*, or, as Max Müller prefers to call it, the *combinatory* type, while the still higher development of *inflectional* speech, in the Aryan and Semitic tongues, was reserved for our own era of the Fifth Root Race.

The First Taking of Life.

The first instance of sin, the first taking of life—quoted above from an old commentary on the stanzas of Dzyan, may be taken as indicative of the attitude which was then inaugurated between the human and the animal kingdom, and which has since attained such awful proportions, not only between men and animals, but between the different races of men themselves. And this opens up a most interesting avenue of thought.

The fact that Kings and Emperors consider it necessary or appropriate, on all state occasions, to appear in the garb of one of the fighting branches of their service, is a significant indication of the apotheosis reached by the combative qualities in man! The custom doubtless comes down from a time when the King was the warrior-chief, and when his kingship was acknowledged solely in virtue of his being the chief warrior. But now that the Fifth Root Race is in ascendency, whose chief characteristic and function is the development of intellect, it might have been expected that the dominant attribute of the Fourth Root Race would have been a little less conspicuously paraded. But the era of one race overlaps another, and though, as we know, the leading races of the world all belong to the Fifth Root Race, the vast majority of its inhabitants still belong to the Fourth, and it would appear that the Fifth Root Race has not yet outstripped Fourth Race characteristics, for it is by infinitely slow degrees that man's evolution is accomplished.

It will be interesting here to summarise the history of this strife and bloodshed from its genesis during these far-off ages on Lemuria.

From the information placed before the writer it would seem that the antagonism between men and animals was developed first. With the evolution of man's physical body, suitable food for that body naturally became an urgent need, so that in addition to the antagonism brought about by the necessity of self-defence against the now ferocious animals, the

139

desire of food also urged men to their slaughter, and as we have seen above, one of the first uses they made of their budding mentality was to train animals to act as hunters in the chase.

The element of strife having once been kindled, men soon began to use weapons of offence against each other. The causes of aggression were naturally the same as those which exist to-day among savage communities. The possession of any desirable object by one of his fellows was sufficient inducement for a man to attempt to take it by force. Nor was strife limited to single acts of aggression. As among savages to-day, bands of marauders would attack and pillage the communities who dwelt at a distance from their own village. But to this extent only, we are told, was warfare organised on Lemuria, even down to the end of its seventh sub-race.

It was reserved for the Atlanteans to develop the principle of strife on organised lines—to collect and to drill armies and to build navies. This principle of strife was indeed the fundamental characteristic of the Fourth Root Race. All through the Atlantean period, as we know, warfare was the order of the day, and battles were constantly fought on land and sea. And so deeply rooted in man's nature during the Atlantean period did this principle of strife become, that even now the most intellectually developed of the Aryan races are ready to war upon each other.

The Arts.

To trace the development of the Arts among the Lemurians, we must start with the history of the fifth sub-race. The separation of the sexes was now fully accomplished, and man inhabited a completely physical body, though it was still of gigantic stature. The offensive and defensive war with the monstrous beasts of prey had already begun, and men had taken to living in huts. To build their huts they tore down trees, and piled them up in a rude fashion. At first each separate family lived in its own clearing in the jungle, but they soon found it safer, as a defence against the wild beasts, to draw together and live in small communities. Their huts, too, which had been formed of rude trunks of trees, they now learnt to build with boulders of stone, while the weapons with which they attacked, or defended themselves against the Dinosauria and other wild beasts, were spears of sharpened wood, similar to the staff held by the man whose appearance is described above. Up to this time agriculture was unknown, and the uses of fire had not been discovered. The food of their boneless ancestors who crawled on the earth were such things as they could find on the surface of the ground or just below it. Now that they walked erect many of the wild forest trees provided them with nuts and berries, but their chief article of food was the flesh of the beasts and reptiles which they slew, tore in pieces, and devoured.

Teachers of the Lemurian Race.

But now there occurred an event pregnant with consequences the most momentous in the history of the human race. An event too full of mystical import, for its narration brings into view Beings who belonged to entirely different systems of evolution, and who nevertheless came at this epoch to be associated with our humanity.

The lament of the Lhas "who had not built men" at seeing their future abodes defiled, is at first sight far from intelligible. Though the descent of these Beings into human bodies is not the chief event to which we have to refer, some explanation of its cause and its result must first be attempted. Now, we are given to understand that these Lhas were the highly evolved humanity of some system of evolution which had run its course at a period in the infinitely far-off past. They had reached a high stage of development on their chain of worlds, and since its dissolution had passed the intervening ages in the bliss of some Nirvanic condition. But their karma now necessitated a return to some field of action and of physical causes, and as they had not yet fully learnt the lesson of compassion, their temporary task now lay in becoming guides and teachers of the Lemurian race, who then required all the help and guidance they could get.

But other Beings also took up the task—in this case voluntarily. These came from the scheme of evolution which has Venus as its one physical planet. That scheme has already reached the Seventh Round of its planets in its Fifth Manvantara; its humanity therefore stands at a far higher level than ordinary mankind on this earth has yet attained. They are "divine" while we are only "human." The Lemurians, as we have seen, were then merely on the verge of attaining true manhood. It was to supply a temporary need—the education of our infant humanity—that these divine Beings came—as we possibly, long ages hence, may similarly be called to give a helping hand to the beings struggling up to manhood on the Jupiter or the Saturn chain. Under their guidance and influence the Lemurians rapidly advanced in mental growth. The stirring of their minds with feelings of love and reverence for those whom they felt to be infinitely wiser and greater than themselves naturally resulted in efforts of imitation, and so the necessary advance in mental growth was achieved which transformed the higher mental sheath into a vehicle capable of carrying over the human characteristics from life to life, thus warranting that outpouring of the Divine Life which endowed the recipient with individual immortality. As expressed in the archaic stanzas of Dzyan, "Then all men became endowed with Manas."

A great distinction, however, must be noted between the coming of the exalted Beings from the Venus scheme and that of those described as the highly evolved humanity of some previous system of evolution. The former, as we have seen, were under no karmic impulse. They came as men to live and work among them, but they were not required to assume their physical limitations, being in a position to provide appropriate vehicles for themselves.

The Lhas on the other hand had actually to be born in the bodies of the race as it then existed. Better would it have been both for them and for the race if there had been no hesitation or delay on their part in taking up their Karmic task, for the sin of the mindless and all its consequences would have been avoided. Their task, too, would have been an easier one, for it consisted not only in acting as guides and teachers, but in improving the racial type—in short, in evolving out of the half-human, half-animal form then existing, the physical body of the man to be.

It must be remembered that up to this time the Lemurian race consisted of the second and third groups of the Lunar Pitris. But now that they were approaching the level reached on the Lunar chain by the first group of Pitris, it became necessary for these again to return to incarnation, and this they did all through the fifth, sixth and seventh sub-races (indeed, some did not take birth till the Atlantean period), so that the impetus given to the progress of the race was a cumulative force.

The positions occupied by the divine beings from the Venus chain were naturally those of rulers, instructors in religion, and teachers of the arts, and it is in this latter capacity that a reference to the arts taught by them comes to our aid in the consideration of the history of this early race.

The Arts continued.

Under the guidance of their divine teachers the people began to learn the use of fire, and the means by which it could be obtained, at first by friction, and later on by the use of flints and iron. They were taught to explore for metals, to smelt and to mould them, and instead of spears of sharpened wood they now began to use spears tipped with sharpened metal.

They were also taught to dig and till the ground and to cultivate the seeds of wild grain till it improved in type. This cultivation carried on through the vast ages which have since elapsed has resulted in the evolution of the various cereals which we now possess—barley, oats, maize, millet, etc. But an exception must here be noted. Wheat was not evolved upon this

142

planet like the other cereals. It was a gift of the divine beings who brought it from Venus ready for the food of man. Nor was wheat their only gift. The one animal form whose type has not been evolved on our chain of worlds is that of the bee. It, too, was brought from Venus.

The Lemurians now also began to learn the art of spinning and weaving fabrics with which to clothe themselves. These were made of the coarse hair of a species of animal now extinct, but which bore some resemblance to the llamas of to-day, the ancestors of which they may possibly have been. We have seen above that the earliest articles of clothing of Lemurian man were robes of skin stripped from the beasts he had slain. These skins he still continued to wear on the colder parts of the continent, but he now learnt to cure and dress the skin in some rude fashion.

One of the first things the people were taught was the use of fire in the preparation of their food, and whether it was the flesh of animals they slew or the pounded grains of wheat, their modes of cooking were closely analogous to those we hear of as existing to-day among savage communities. With reference to the gift of wheat so marvellously brought from Venus, the divine rulers doubtless realised the advisability of at once procuring such food for the people, for they must have known that it would take many generations before the cultivation of the wild seeds could provide an adequate supply.

Rude and barbarous as were the people during the period of the fifth and sixth sub-races, such of them as had the privilege of coming in contact with their divine teachers were naturally inspired with such feelings of reverence and worship as helped to lift them out of their savage condition. The constant influx, too, of more intelligent beings from the first group of the Lunar Pitris, who were then beginning to return to incarnation, helped the attainment of a more civilised state.

Great Cities and Statues.

During the later part of the sixth, and the seventh sub-race they learnt to build great cities. These appear to have been of cyclopean architecture, corresponding with the gigantic bodies of the race. The first cities were built on that extended mountainous region of the continent which included, as will be seen in the first map, the present Island of Madagascar. Another great city is described in the "Secret Doctrine" *Vol. ii., p. 317.,* as having been entirely built of blocks of lava. It lay some 30 miles west of the present Easter Island, and it was subsequently destroyed by a series of volcanic eruptions. The gigantic statues of Easter Island—measuring as most of them do about 27 feet in height by 8 feet across the shoulders—were probably intended to be representative not only of the features, but of the height of those who carved them, or it may be of their ancestors, for it was probably in the later ages of the Lemuro-Atlanteans that the statues were erected. It will be observed that by the second map period, the continent of which Easter Island formed a part had been broken up and Easter Island itself had become a comparatively small island, though of considerably greater dimensions than it retains to-day.

Civilisations of comparative importance arose on different parts of the continent and the great islands where the inhabitants built cities and dwelt in settled communities, but large tribes who were also partially civilised continued to lead a nomadic and patriarchial life; while other parts of the land—in many cases the least accessible, as in our own times—were peopled by tribes of extremely low type.

Religion.

With so primitive a race of men, at the best, there was but little in the shape of religion that they could be taught. Simple rules of conduct and the most elementary precepts of morality were all that they were fitted to understand or to practise. During the evolution of the seventh sub-race, it is true that their divine instructors taught them some primitive form of worship and imparted the knowledge of a Supreme Being whose symbol was represented as the Sun.

Destruction of the Continent.

Unlike the subsequent fate of Atlantis, which was submerged by great tidal waves, the continent of Lemuria perished by volcanic action. It was raked by the burning ashes and the red-hot dust from numberless volcanoes. Earthquakes and volcanic eruptions, it is true, heralded each of the great catastrophes which overtook Atlantis, but when the land had been shaken and rent, the sea rushed in and completed the work, and most of the inhabitants perished by drowning. The Lemurians, on the other hand, met their doom chiefly by fire or suffocation. Another marked contrast between the fate of Lemuria and Atlantis was that while four great catastrophes completed the destruction of the latter, the former was slowly eaten away by internal fires, for, from the time when the disintegrating process began towards the end of the first map period, there was no cessation from the fiery activity, and whether in one part of the continent or another, the volcanic action was incessant, while the invariable sequence was the subsidence and total disappearance of the land, just as in the case of Krakatoa in 1883.

So closely analogous was the eruption of Mount Pelée, which caused the destruction of St. Pièrre, the capital of Martinique, about two years ago, to the whole series of volcanic catastrophes on the continent of Lemuria, that the description of the former given by some of the survivors may be of interest. "An immense black cloud had suddenly burst forth from the crater of Mont Pelée and rushed with terrific velocity upon the city, destroying everything—inhabitants, houses and vegetation alike—that it found in its path. In two or three minutes it passed over, and the city was a blazing pyre of ruins. In both islands [Martinique and St. Vincent] the eruptions were characterised by the sudden discharge of immense quantities of red-hot dust, mixed with steam, which flowed down the steep hillsides with an ever-increasing velocity. In St. Vincent this had filled many valleys to a depth of between 100 feet and 200 feet, and months after the eruptions was still very hot, and the heavy rains which then fell thereon caused enormous explosions, producing clouds of steam and dust that shot upwards to a height of from 1500 feet to 2000 feet, and filled the rivers with black boiling mud." Captain Freeman, of the "Roddam," then described "a thrilling experience which he and his party had at Martinique. One night, when they were lying at anchor in a little sloop about a mile from St. Pièrre, the mountain exploded in a way that was apparently an exact repetition of the original eruption. It was not entirely without warning; hence they were enabled to sail at once a mile or two further away, and thus probably saved their lives. In the darkness they saw the summit glow with a bright red light; then soon, with loud detonations, great red-hot stones were projected into the air and rolled down the slopes. A few minutes later a prolonged rumbling noise was heard, and in an instant was followed by a red-hot avalanche of dust, which rushed out of the crater and rolled down the side with a terrific speed, which they estimated at about 100 miles an hour, with a temperature of 1000° centigrade. As to the probable explanation of these phenomena, no lava, he said, had been seen to flow from either of the volcanoes, but only steam and fine hot dust. The volcanoes were, therefore, of the explosive type; and from all his observations he had concluded that the absence of lava-flows was due to the material within the crater being partly solid, or at least highly viscous, so that it could not flow like an ordinary lava-stream. Since his return this theory had received striking confirmation, for it was now known that within the crater of Mont Pelée there was no lake of molten lava, but that a solid pillar of red-hot rock was slowly rising upwards in a great conical, sharp-pointed hill, until it might finally overtop the old summit of the mountain. It was nearly 1000 feet high, and slowly grew as it was forced upwards by pressure from beneath, while every now and then explosions of steam took place, dislodging large pieces from its summit or its sides. Steam was set free within this mass as it cooled, and the rock then passed into a dangerous and highly explosive condition, such that an explosion must sooner or later take place, which shivered a great part of the mass into fine red-hot dust." *(The "Times," 14th Sept., 1903.)*

A reference to the first Lemurian map will show that in the lake lying to the south-east of the extensive mountainous region there was an island which consisted of little more than one great mountain. This mountain was a very active volcano. The four mountains which lay to the south-west of the lake were also active volcanoes, and in this region it was that the disruption of the continent began. The seismic cataclysms which followed the volcanic eruptions caused such wide-spread damage that by the second map period a large portion of the southern part of the continent had been submerged.

A marked characteristic of the land surface in early Lemurian times was the great number of lakes and marshes, as well as the innumerable volcanoes. Of course, all these are not shown on the map. Only some of the great mountains which were volcanoes, and only some of the largest lakes are there indicated.

Another volcano on the north-east coast of the continent began its destructive work at an early date. Earthquakes completed the disruption, and it seems probable that the sea shown in the second map as dotted with small islands to the south-east of the present Japan, indicates the area of seismic disturbance.

In the first map it will be seen that there were lakes in the centre of what is now the island-continent of Australia—lakes where the land is at present exceedingly dry and parched. By the second map period those lakes had disappeared, and it seems natural to conjecture that the districts where those lakes lay, must, during the eruptions of the great volcanoes which lay to the south-east (between the present Australia and New Zealand), have been so raked with red-hot volcanic dust that the very water-springs were dried up.

Founding of the Atlantean Race.

In concluding this sketch, a reference to the process by which the Fourth Root Race was brought into existence, will appropriately bring to an end what we know of the story of Lemuria and link it on to that of Atlantis.

It may be remembered from previous writings on the subject that it was from the *fifth* or Semitic sub-race of the Fourth Root Race that was chosen the nucleus destined to become our great Fifth or Aryan Root Race. It was

146

not, however, until the time of the *seventh* sub-race on Lemuria that humanity was sufficiently developed physiologically to warrant the choice of individuals fit to become the parents of a new Root Race. So it was from the seventh sub-race that the segregation was effected. The colony was first settled on land which occupied the site of the present Ashantee and Western Nigeria. A reference to the second map will show this as a promontory lying to the north-west of the island-continent which embraced the Cape of Good Hope and parts of western Africa. Having been guarded for generations from any admixture with a lower type, the colony gradually increased in numbers, and the time came when it was ready to receive and to hand on the new impulse to physical heredity which the Manu was destined to impart.

Students of Theosophy are aware that, up to the present day, no one belonging to our humanity has been in a position to undertake the exalted office of Manu, though it is stated that the founding of the coming Sixth Root Race will be entrusted to the guidance of one of our Masters of Wisdom—one who, while belonging to our humanity, has nevertheless reached a most exalted level in the Divine Hierarchy.

In the case we are considering—the founding of the Fourth Root Race— it was one of the Adepts from Venus who undertook the duties of the Manu. Naturally he belonged to a very high order, for it must be understood that the Beings who came from the Venus system as rulers and teachers of our infant humanity did *not* all stand at the same level. It is this circumstance which furnishes a reason for the remarkable fact that may, in conclusion, be stated—namely, that there existed in Lemuria a Lodge of Initiation.

A Lodge of Initiation.

Naturally it was not for the benefit of the Lemurian race that the Lodge was founded. Such of them as were sufficiently advanced were, it is true, taught by the Adept Gurus, but the instruction they required was limited to the explanation of a few physical phenomena, such as the fact that the earth moves round the sun, or to the explanation of the different appearance which physical objects assumed for them when subjected alternately to their physical sight and their astral vision.

It was, of course, for the sake of those who, while endowed with the stupendous powers of transferring their consciousness from the planet Venus to this our earth, and of providing for their use and their work while here appropriate vehicles in which to function, were yet pursuing the course of their own evolution.(*) *The heights reached by them will find their parallel when our humanity will, countless aeons hence, have reached the*

Sixth Round of our chain of worlds, and the same transcendent powers will be the possession of ordinary mankind in those far-off ages)

For their sake it was—for the sake of those who, having entered the Path, had only reached the lower grades, that this Lodge of Initiation was founded.

Though, as we know, the goal of normal evolution is greater and more glorious than can, from our present standpoint, be well imagined, it is by no means synonymous with that expansion of consciousness which, combined with and alone made possible by, the purification and ennoblement of character, constitute the heights to which the Pathway of Initiation leads.

The investigation into what constitutes this purification and ennoblement of character, and the endeavour to realise what that expansion of consciousness really means are subjects which have been written of elsewhere. Suffice it now to point out that the founding of a Lodge of Initiation for the sake of Beings who came from another scheme of evolution is an indication of the unity of object and of aim in the government and the guidance of *all* the schemes of evolution brought into existence by our Solar Logos.

Apart from the normal course in our own scheme, there is, we know, a Path by which He may be directly reached, which every son of man in his progress through the ages is privileged to hear of, and to tread, if he so chooses. We find that this was so in the Venus scheme also, and we may presume it is or will be so in all the schemes which form part of our Solar system. This Path is the Path of Initiation, and the end to which leads is the same for all, and that end is Union with God.

Rock Strata.		Depth of Strata Feet.	Races of Men.	Cataclysms.	Animals.	Plants.
Laurentian, Cambrian, Silurian	Archlithic or Primordial	70,000	First Root Race which being Astral could leave no fossil remains.		Skull-less Animals.	Forests of gigantic Tangles and other Thallus Plants.
Devonian, Coal, Permian	Palæolithic or Primary.	44,000	Second Root Race which was Etheric.		Fish.	Fern Forests.
Triassic, Jurassic, Cretaceous	Mesolithic or Secondary	15,000	Third Root Race or Lemurian.	Lemuria is said to have perished before the beginning of the Eocene age.	Reptiles.	Pine and Palm Forests.
Eocene, Miocene, Pliocene	Cenolithic or Tertiary.	5,000	Fourth Root Race or Atlantean.	The main Continent of Atlantis was destroyed in the Miocene period about 800,000 years ago. Second great catastrophe ? about 200,000 years ago.	Mammals.	Forests of Deciduous Trees.
Diluvial or Pleistocene, Alluvial	Quaternary or Anthropolithic	500	Fifth Root Race or Aryan.	Third great catastrophe about 80,000 years ago. Final submergence of Poseidonis 9564 B.C.	More differentiated Mammals.	Cultivated Forests.

MAPS

NO. 1 THE WORLD ABOUT 1,000,000 YEARS AGO, DURING MANY PREVIOUS AGES, AND UP TO THE CATASTROPHE OF ABOUT 800, 000 YEARS AGO ATLANTIS AT ITS PRIME

NO 2 THE WORLD AFTER THE CATASTROPHE OF 800,000 YEARS AGO AND UP TO THE CATASTROPHE OF ABOUT 200,000 YEARS AGO ATLANTIS IN ITS DECADENCE

NO 3 THE WORLD AFTER THE CATASTROPHE OF 200,000 YEARS AGO AND UP TO THE CATASTROPHE OF ABOUT 80,000 YEARS AGO
RUTA & DAITYA

NO 4 THE WORLD AFTER THE CATASTROPHE OF 80000 YEARS AGO AND UP TO THE FINAL SUBMERGENCE OF POSEIDONIS IN 9,564 B.C

No.1 LEMURIA at its greatest extent

No.2 LEMURIA at a later period

BOOK THREE.
ATLANTIS: THE ANTEDILUVIAN WORLD.

BY IGNATIUS DONNELLY.

The world has made such comet-like advance
Lately on science, we may almost hope,
Before we die of sheer decay, to learn
Something about our infancy; when lived
That great, original, broad-eyed, sunken race,
Whose knowledge, like the sea-sustaining rocks,
Hath formed the base of this world's fluctuous lore
FESTUS.

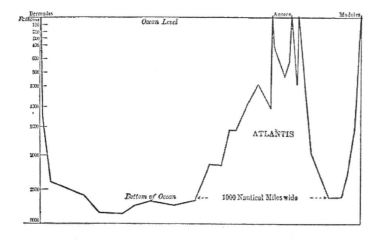

The Profile of Atlantis

PART I. THE HISTORY OF ATLANTIS.
CHAPTER I. THE PURPOSE OF THE BOOK.

This book is an attempt to demonstrate several distinct and novel propositions. These are:

1. That there once existed in the Atlantic Ocean, opposite the mouth of the Mediterranean Sea, a large island, which was the remnant of an Atlantic continent, and known to the ancient world as Atlantis.

2. That the description of this island given by Plato is not, as has been long supposed, fable, but veritable history.

3. That Atlantis was the region where man first rose from a state of barbarism to civilization.

4. That it became, in the course of ages, a populous and mighty nation, from whose overflowings the shores of the Gulf of Mexico, the Mississippi River, the Amazon, the Pacific coast of South America, the Mediterranean, the west coast of Europe and Africa, the Baltic, the Black Sea, and the Caspian were populated by civilized nations.

5. That it was the true Antediluvian world; the Garden of Eden; the Gardens of the Hesperides; the Elysian Fields; the Gardens of Alcinous; the Mesomphalos; the Olympos; the Asgard of the traditions of the ancient nations; representing a universal memory of a great land, where early mankind dwelt for ages in peace and happiness.

6. That the gods and goddesses of the ancient Greeks, the Phoenicians, the Hindoos, and the Scandinavians were simply the kings, queens, and heroes of Atlantis; and the acts attributed to them in mythology are a confused recollection of real historical events.

7. That the mythology of Egypt and Peru represented the original religion of Atlantis, which was sun-worship.

8. That the oldest colony formed by the Atlanteans was probably in Egypt, whose civilization was a reproduction of that of the Atlantic island.

9. That the implements of the "Bronze Age" of Europe were derived from Atlantis. The Atlanteans were also the first manufacturers of iron.

10. That the Phoenician alphabet, parent of all the European alphabets, was derived from an Atlantis alphabet, which was also conveyed from Atlantis to the Mayas of Central America.

11. That Atlantis was the original seat of the Aryan or Indo-European family of nations, as well as of the Semitic peoples, and possibly also of the Turanian races.

12. That Atlantis perished in a terrible convulsion of nature, in which the whole island sunk into the ocean, with nearly all its inhabitants.

13. That a few persons escaped in ships and on rafts, and, carried to the nations east and west the tidings of the appalling catastrophe, which has survived to our own time in the Flood and Deluge legends of the different nations of the old and new worlds.

If these propositions can be proved, they will solve many problems which now perplex mankind; they will confirm in many respects the statements in the opening chapters of Genesis; they will widen the area of human history; they will explain the remarkable resemblances which exist between the ancient civilizations found upon the opposite shores of the Atlantic Ocean, in the old and new worlds; and they will aid us to rehabilitate the fathers of our civilization, our blood, and our fundamental ideas-the men who lived, loved, and labored ages before the Aryans descended upon India, or the Phoenician had settled in Syria, or the Goth had reached the shores of the Baltic.

The fact that the story of Atlantis was for thousands of years regarded as a fable proves nothing. There is an unbelief which grows out of ignorance, as well as a scepticism which is born of intelligence. The people nearest to the past are not always those who are best informed concerning the past.

For a thousand years it was believed that the legends of the buried cities of Pompeii and Herculaneum were myths: they were spoken of as "the fabulous cities." For a thousand years the educated world did not credit the accounts given by Herodotus of the wonders of the ancient civilizations of the Nile and of Chaldea. He was called "the father of liars." Even Plutarch sneered at him. Now, in the language of Frederick Schlegel, "the deeper and more comprehensive the researches of the moderns have been, the more their regard and esteem for Herodotus has increased." Buckle says, "His minute information about Egypt and Asia Minor is admitted by all geographers."

There was a time when the expedition sent out by Pharaoh Necho to circumnavigate Africa was doubted, because the explorers stated that after they had progressed a certain distance the sun was north of them; this circumstance, which then aroused suspicion, now proves to us that the Egyptian navigators had really passed the equator, and anticipated by 2100 years Vasquez de Gama in his discovery of the Cape of Good Hope.

If I succeed in demonstrating the truth of the somewhat startling propositions with which I commenced this chapter, it will only be by bringing to bear upon the question of Atlantis a thousand converging lines of light from a multitude of researches made by scholars in different fields of modern thought. Further investigations and discoveries will, I trust, confirm the correctness of the conclusions at which I have arrived.

CHAPTER II. PLATO'S HISTORY OF ATLANTIS.

Plato has preserved for us the history of Atlantis. If our views are correct, it is one of the most valuable records which have come down to us from antiquity.

Plato lived 400 years before the birth of Christ. His ancestor, Solon, was the great law-giver of Athens 600 years before the Christian era. Solon visited Egypt. Plutarch says, "Solon attempted in verse a large description, or rather fabulous account of the Atlantic Island, which he had learned from the wise men of Sais, and which particularly concerned the Athenians; but by reason of his age, not want of leisure (as Plato would have it), he was apprehensive the work would be too much for him, and therefore did not go through with it. These verses are a proof that business was not the hinderance:

"'I grow in learning as I grow in age.'

And again:

"'Wine, wit, and beauty still their charms bestow,

Light all the shades of life, and cheer us as we go.'

"Plato, ambitious to cultivate and adorn the subject of the Atlantic Island, as a delightful spot in some fair field unoccupied, to which also he had some claim by reason of his being related to Solon, laid out magnificent courts and enclosures, and erected a grand entrance to it, such as no other story, fable, or Poem ever had. But, as he began it late, he ended his life before the work, so that the more the reader is delighted with the part that is written, the more regret he has to find it unfinished."

There can be no question that Solon visited Egypt. The causes of his departure from Athens, for a period of ten years, are fully explained by Plutarch. He dwelt, he tells us,

"On the Canopian shore, by Nile's deep mouth."

There he conversed upon points of philosophy and history with the most learned of the Egyptian priests. He was a man of extraordinary force and penetration of mind, as his laws and his sayings, which have been preserved to us, testify. There is no improbability in the statement that he commenced in verse a history and description of Atlantis, which he left unfinished at his death; and it requires no great stretch of the imagination to believe that this manuscript reached the hands of his successor and

155

descendant, Plato; a scholar, thinker, and historian like himself, and, like himself, one of the profoundest minds of the ancient world. The Egyptian priest had said to Solon, "You have no antiquity of history, and no history of antiquity;" and Solon doubtless realized fully the vast importance of a record which carried human history back, not only thousands of years before the era of Greek civilization, but many thousands of years before even the establishment of the kingdom of Egypt; and he was anxious to preserve for his half-civilized countrymen this inestimable record of the past.

We know of no better way to commence a book about Atlantis than by giving in full the record preserved by Plato. It is as follows:

Critias. Then listen, Socrates, to a strange tale, which is, however, certainly true, as Solon, who was the wisest of the seven sages, declared. He was a relative and great friend of my great-grandfather, Dropidas, as he himself says in several of his poems; and Dropidas told Critias, my grandfather, who remembered, and told us, that there were of old great and marvellous actions of the Athenians, which have passed into oblivion through time and the destruction of the human race and one in particular, which was the greatest of them all, the recital of which will be a suitable testimony of our gratitude to you....

Socrates. Very good; and what is this ancient famous action of which Critias spoke, not as a mere legend, but as a veritable action of the Athenian State, which Solon recounted!

Critias. I will tell an old-world story which I heard from an aged man; for Critias was, as he said, at that time nearly ninety years of age, and I was about ten years of age. Now the day was that day of the Apaturia which is called the registration of youth; at which, according to custom, our parents gave prizes for recitations, and the poems of several poets were recited by us boys, and many of us sung the poems of Solon, which were new at the time. One of our tribe, either because this was his real opinion, or because he thought that he would please Critias, said that, in his judgment, Solon was not only the wisest of men but the noblest of poets. The old man, I well remember, brightened up at this, and said, smiling: "Yes, Amynander, if Solon had only, like other poets, made poetry the business of his life, and had completed the tale which he brought with him from Egypt, and had not been compelled, by reason of the factions and troubles which he found stirring in this country when he came home, to attend to other matters, in my opinion he would have been as famous as Homer, or Hesiod, or any poet."

"And what was that poem about, Critias?" said the person who addressed him.

"About the greatest action which the Athenians ever did, and which ought to have been most famous, but which, through the lapse of time and the destruction of the actors, has not come down to us."

"Tell us," said the other, "the whole story, and how and from whom Solon heard this veritable tradition."

He replied: "At the head of the Egyptian Delta, where the river Nile divides, there is a certain district which is called the district of Sais, and the great city of the district is also called Sais, and is the city from which Amasis the king was sprung. And the citizens have a deity who is their foundress: she is called in the Egyptian tongue Neith, which is asserted by them to be the same whom the Hellenes called Athene. Now, the citizens of this city are great lovers of the Athenians, and say that they are in some way related to them. Thither came Solon, who was received by them with great honor; and he asked the priests, who were most skilful in such matters, about antiquity, and made the discovery that neither he nor any other Hellene knew anything worth mentioning about the times of old. On one occasion, when he was drawing them on to speak of antiquity, he began to tell about the most ancient things in our part of the world—about Phoroneus, who is called 'the first,' and about Niobe; and, after the Deluge, to tell of the lives of Deucalion and Pyrrha; and he traced the genealogy of their descendants, and attempted to reckon how many years old were the events of which he was speaking, and to give the dates. Thereupon, one of the priests, who was of very great age; said, 'O Solon, Solon, you Hellenes are but children, and there is never an old man who is an Hellene.' Solon, bearing this, said, 'What do you mean?' 'I mean to say,' he replied, 'that in mind you are all young; there is no old opinion handed down among you by ancient tradition, nor any science which is hoary with age. And I will tell you the reason of this: there have been, and there will be again, many destructions of mankind arising out of many causes. There is a story which even you have preserved, that once upon a time Phaëthon, the son of Helios, having yoked the steeds in his father's chariot, because he was not able to drive them in the path of his father, burnt up all that was upon the earth, and was himself destroyed by a thunderbolt. Now, this has the form of a myth, but really signifies a declination of the bodies moving around the earth and in the heavens, and a great conflagration of things upon the earth recurring at long intervals of time: when this happens, those who live upon the mountains and in dry and lofty places are more liable to destruction than those who dwell by rivers or on the sea-shore; and from this calamity the Nile, who is our never-failing savior, saves and delivers us. When, on the other hand, the gods purge the earth with a deluge of water, among you herdsmen and shepherds on the mountains are the survivors, whereas those of you who live in cities are carried by the rivers into the sea; but in this country neither at that time nor at any other does the water come from above on the fields, having always a tendency to come up from below, for which reason the things preserved here are said to be the oldest. The fact is, that wherever the extremity of winter frost or of summer sun does not prevent, the human race is always increasing at times, and at other times diminishing in numbers. And whatever happened either in your country or in ours, or in any other region of which we are informed—if any action which is noble or great, or in any other way remarkable has taken place, all that has been written down of old, and is preserved in our temples; whereas you and other nations are just being provided with letters and the other things which States require; and then, at the usual period, the stream from heaven descends like a pestilence, and leaves only those of you who are destitute of letters and education; and thus you have to begin all over again as children, and know nothing of what happened in ancient times, either among us or among yourselves. As for those genealogies of yours which you have recounted to us, Solon, they are no better than the tales of children; for, in the first place, you remember one deluge only, whereas there were many of them; and, in the next place, you do not know that there dwelt in your land the fairest and noblest race of men which ever lived, of whom you and your whole city are but a seed or remnant. And this was unknown to you, because for many generations the survivors of that destruction died and made no sign. For there was a time, Solon, before that great deluge of all, when the city which now is Athens was first in war, and was preeminent for the excellence of her laws, and is said to have performed the noblest deeds, and to have had the fairest constitution of any of which tradition tells, under the face of heaven.' Solon marvelled at this, and earnestly requested the priest to inform him exactly and in order about these former citizens. 'You are welcome to hear about them, Solon,' said the priest, 'both for your own sake and for that of the city; and, above all, for the sake of the goddess who is the common patron and protector and educator of both our cities. She founded your city a thousand years before ours, receiving from the Earth and Hephæstus the seed of your race, and then she founded ours, the constitution of which is set down in our sacred registers as 8000 years old. As touching the citizens of 9000 years ago, I will briefly inform you of their laws and of the noblest of their actions; and the exact particulars of the whole we will hereafter go through at our leisure, in the sacred registers themselves. If you compare these very laws with your own, you will find that many of ours are the counterpart of yours, as they were in the olden time. In the first place, there is the caste of priests, which is separated from all the others; next there are the artificers, who exercise their several crafts by themselves, and without admixture of any other; and also there is the class of shepherds and that of hunters, as well as that of husbandmen; and you will observe, too, that the warriors in Egypt are separated from all the other classes, and are commanded by the law only to engage in war; moreover, the weapons with which they are equipped are shields and spears, and this the goddess taught first among you, and then in Asiatic countries, and we among the Asiatics first adopted.

"'Then, as to wisdom, do you observe what care the law took from the very first, searching out and comprehending the whole order of things down to prophecy and medicine (the latter with a view to health); and out of these divine elements drawing what was needful for human life, and adding every sort of knowledge which was connected with them. All this order and arrangement the goddess first imparted to you when establishing your city; and she chose the spot of earth in which you were born, because she saw that the happy temperament of the seasons in that land would produce the wisest of men. Wherefore the goddess, who was a lover both of war and of wisdom, selected, and first of all settled that spot which was the most likely to produce men likest herself. And there you dwelt, having such laws as these and still better ones, and excelled all mankind in all virtue, as became the children and disciples of the gods. Many great and wonderful deeds are recorded of your State in our histories; but one of them exceeds all the rest in greatness and valor; for these histories tell of a mighty power which was aggressing wantonly against the whole of Europe and Asia, and to which your city put an end. This power came forth out of the Atlantic Ocean, for in those days the Atlantic was navigable; and there was an island situated in front of the straits which you call the Columns of Heracles: the island was larger than Libya and Asia put together, and was the way to other islands, and from the islands you might pass through the whole of the opposite continent which surrounded the true ocean; for this sea which is within the Straits of Heracles is only a harbor, having a narrow entrance, but that other is a real sea, and the surrounding land may be most truly called a continent. Now, in the island of Atlantis there was a great and wonderful empire, which had rule over the whole island and several others, as well as over parts of the continent; and, besides these, they subjected the parts of Libya within the Columns of Heracles as far as Egypt, and of Europe as far as Tyrrhenia. The vast power thus gathered into one, endeavored to subdue at one blow our country and yours, and the whole of the land which was within the straits; and then, Solon, your country shone forth, in the excellence of her virtue and strength, among all mankind; for she was the first in courage and military skill, and was the leader of the Hellenes. And when the rest fell off from her, being compelled to stand alone, after having undergone the very extremity of danger, she defeated and triumphed over the invaders, and preserved from slavery those who were not yet subjected, and freely liberated all the others who dwelt within the limits of Heracles. But afterward there occurred violent earthquakes and floods, and in a single day and night of rain all your warlike men in a body sunk into the earth, and the island of Atlantis in like manner disappeared, and was sunk beneath the sea. And that is the reason why the sea in those parts is impassable and impenetrable, because there is such a quantity of shallow mud in the way; and this was caused by the subsidence of the island.' ("Plato's Dialogues," ii., 617, Timæus.)...

"But in addition to the gods whom you have mentioned, I would specially invoke Mnemosyne; for all the important part of what I have to tell is dependent on her favor, and if I can recollect and recite enough of what was said by the priests, and brought hither by Solon, I doubt not that I shall satisfy the requirements of this theatre. To that task, then, I will at once address myself.

"Let me begin by observing, first of all, that nine thousand was the sum of years which had elapsed since the war which was said to have taken place between all those who dwelt outside the Pillars of Heracles and those who dwelt within them: this war I am now to describe. Of the combatants on the one side the city of Athens was reported to have been the ruler, and to have directed the contest; the combatants on the other side were led by the kings of the islands of Atlantis, which, as I was saying, once had an extent greater than that of Libya and Asia; and, when afterward sunk by an earthquake, became an impassable barrier of mud to voyagers sailing from hence to the ocean. The progress of the history will unfold the various tribes of barbarians and Hellenes which then existed, as they successively appear on the scene; but I must begin by describing, first of all, the Athenians as they were in that day, and their enemies who fought with them; and I shall have to tell of the power and form of government of both of them. Let us give the precedence to Athens....

"Many great deluges have taken place during the nine thousand years, for that is the number of years which have elapsed since the time of which I am speaking; and in all the ages and changes of things there has never been any settlement of the earth flowing down from the mountains, as in other places, which is worth speaking of; it has always been carried round in a circle, and disappeared in the depths below. The consequence is that, in comparison of what then was, there are remaining in small islets only the bones of the wasted body, as they may be called, all the richer and softer parts of the soil having fallen away, and the mere skeleton of the country being left....

"And next, if I have not forgotten what I heard when I was a child, I will impart to you the character and origin of their adversaries; for friends should not keep their stories to themselves, but have them in common. Yet, before proceeding farther in the narrative, I ought to warn you that you must not be surprised if you should bear Hellenic names given to foreigners. I will tell you the reason of this: Solon, who was intending to use the tale for his poem, made an investigation into the meaning of the names, and found that the early Egyptians, in writing them down, had translated them into their own language, and he recovered the meaning of the several names and retranslated them, and copied them out again in our language. My great-grandfather, Dropidas, had the original writing, which is still in my possession, and was carefully studied by me when I was a child. Therefore, if you bear names such as are used in this country, you must not be surprised, for I have told you the reason of them.

"The tale, which was of great length, began as follows: I have before remarked, in speaking of the allotments of the gods, that they distributed the whole earth into portions differing in extent, and made themselves temples and sacrifices. And Poseidon, receiving for his lot the island of Atlantis, begat children by a mortal woman, and settled them in a part of the island which I will proceed to describe. On the side toward the sea, and in the centre of the whole island, there was a plain which is said to have been the fairest of all plains, and very fertile. Near the plain again, and also in the centre of the island, at a distance of about fifty stadia, there was a mountain, not very high on any side. In this mountain there dwelt one of the earth-born primeval men of that country, whose name was Evenor, and he had a wife named Leucippe, and they had an only daughter, who was named Cleito. The maiden was growing up to womanhood when her father and mother died; Poseidon fell in love with her, and had intercourse with her; and, breaking the ground, enclosed the hill in which she dwelt all round, making alternate zones of sea and land, larger and smaller, encircling one another; there were two of land and three of water, which he turned as with a lathe out of the centre of the island, equidistant every way, so that no man could get to the island, for ships and voyages were not yet heard of. He himself, as he was a god, found no difficulty in making special arrangements for the centre island, bringing two streams of water under

161

the earth, which he caused to ascend as springs, one of warm water and the other of cold, and making every variety of food to spring up abundantly in the earth. He also begat and brought up five pairs of male children, dividing the island of Atlantis into ten portions: he gave to the first-born of the eldest pair his mother's dwelling and the surrounding allotment, which was the largest and best, and made him king over the rest; the others he made princes, and gave them rule over many men and a large territory. And he named them all: the eldest, who was king, he named Atlas, and from him the whole island and the ocean received the name of Atlantic. To his twin-brother, who was born after him, and obtained as his lot the extremity of the island toward the Pillars of Heracles, as far as the country which is still called the region of Gades in that part of the world, he gave the name which in the Hellenic language is Eumelus, in the language of the country which is named after him, Gadeirus. Of the second pair of twins, he called one Ampheres and the other Evæmon. To the third pair of twins he gave the name Mneseus to the elder, and Autochthon to the one who followed him. Of the fourth pair of twins he called the elder Elasippus and the younger Mestor. And of the fifth pair he gave to the elder the name of Azaes, and to the younger Diaprepes. All these and their descendants were the inhabitants and rulers of divers islands in the open sea; and also, as has been already said, they held sway in the other direction over the country within the Pillars as far as Egypt and Tyrrhenia. Now Atlas had a numerous and honorable family, and his eldest branch always retained the kingdom, which the eldest son handed on to his eldest for many generations; and they had such an amount of wealth as was never before possessed by kings and potentates, and is not likely ever to be again, and they were furnished with everything which they could have, both in city and country. For, because of the greatness of their empire, many things were brought to them from foreign countries, and the island itself provided much of what was required by them for the uses of life. In the first place, they dug out of the earth whatever was to be found there, mineral as well as metal, and that which is now only a name, and was then something more than a name—orichalcum—was dug out of the earth in many parts of the island, and, with the exception of gold, was esteemed the most precious of metals among the men of those days. There was an abundance of wood for carpenters' work, and sufficient maintenance for tame and wild animals. Moreover, there were a great number of elephants in the island, and there was provision for animals of every kind, both for those which live in lakes and marshes and rivers, and also for those which live in mountains and on plains, and therefore for the animal which is the largest and most voracious of them.

Also, whatever fragrant things there are in the earth, whether roots, or herbage, or woods, or distilling drops of flowers or fruits, grew and thrived in that land; and again, the cultivated fruit of the earth, both the dry edible fruit and other species of food, which we call by the general name of legumes, and the fruits having a hard rind, affording drinks, and meats, and ointments, and good store of chestnuts and the like, which may be used to play with, and are fruits which spoil with keeping—and the pleasant kinds of dessert which console us after dinner, when we are full and tired of eating—all these that sacred island lying beneath the sun brought forth fair and wondrous in infinite abundance. All these things they received from the earth, and they employed themselves in constructing their temples, and palaces, and harbors, and docks; and they arranged the whole country in the following manner: First of all they bridged over the zones of sea which surrounded the ancient metropolis, and made a passage into and out of they began to build the palace in the royal palace; and then the habitation of the god and of their ancestors. This they continued to ornament in successive generations, every king surpassing the one who came before him to the utmost of his power, until they made the building a marvel to behold for size and for beauty. And, beginning from the sea, they dug a canal three hundred feet in width and one hundred feet in depth, and fifty stadia in length, which they carried through to the outermost zone, making a passage from the sea up to this, which became a harbor, and leaving an opening sufficient to enable the largest vessels to find ingress. Moreover, they divided the zones of land which parted the zones of sea, constructing bridges of such a width as would leave a passage for a single trireme to pass out of one into another, and roofed them over; and there was a way underneath for the ships, for the banks of the zones were raised considerably above the water. Now the largest of the zones into which a passage was cut from the sea was three stadia in breadth, and the zone of land which came next of equal breadth; but the next two, as well the zone of water as of land, were two stadia, and the one which surrounded the central island was a stadium only in width. The island in which the palace was situated had a diameter of five stadia. This, and the zones and the bridge, which was the sixth part of a stadium in width, they surrounded by a stone wall, on either side placing towers, and gates on the bridges where the sea passed in. The stone which was used in the work they quarried from underneath the centre island and from underneath the zones, on the outer as well as the inner side. One kind of stone was white, another black, and a third red; and, as they quarried, they at the same time hollowed out docks double within, having roofs formed out of the native rock. Some of their buildings were simple, but in others they put together different stones, which they intermingled for the sake of ornament, to be a natural source of delight. The entire circuit of the wall which went round the outermost one they covered with a coating of brass, and the circuit of the next wall they coated with tin, and the third, which encompassed the citadel flashed with the red light of orichalcum. The palaces in the interior of the citadel were constructed in this wise: In the centre was a holy temple dedicated to Cleito and Poseidon, which remained inaccessible, and was surrounded by an enclosure of gold; this was the spot in which they originally begat the race of the ten princes, and thither they annually brought the fruits of the earth in their season from all the ten portions, and performed sacrifices to each of them. Here, too, was Poiseidon's own temple, of a stadium in length and half a stadium in width, and of a proportionate height, having a sort of barbaric splendor. All the outside of the temple, with the exception of the pinnacles, they covered with silver, and the pinnacles with gold. In the interior of the temple the roof was of ivory, adorned everywhere with gold and silver and orichalcum; all the other parts of the walls and pillars and floor they lined with orichalcum. In the temple they placed statues of gold: there was the god himself standing in a chariot—the charioteer of six winged horses—and of such a size that he touched the roof of the building with his head; around him there were a hundred Nereids riding on dolphins, for such was thought to be the number of them in that day. There were also in the interior of the temple other images which had been dedicated by private individuals. And around the temple on the outside were placed statues of gold of all the ten kings and of their wives; and there were many other great offerings, both of kings and of private individuals, coming both from the city itself and the foreign cities over which they held sway. There was an altar, too, which in size and workmanship corresponded to the rest of the work, and there were palaces in like manner which answered to the greatness of the kingdom and the glory of the temple.

"In the next place, they used fountains both of cold and hot springs; these were very abundant, and both kinds wonderfully adapted to use by reason of the sweetness and excellence of their waters. They constructed buildings about them, and planted suitable trees; also cisterns, some open to the heaven, other which they roofed over, to be used in winter as warm baths, there were the king's baths, and the baths of private persons, which were kept apart; also separate baths for women, and others again for horses and cattle, and to them they gave as much adornment as was suitable for them. The water which ran off they carried, some to the grove of Poseidon, where were growing all manner of trees of wonderful height and beauty, owing to the excellence of the soil; the remainder was conveyed by aqueducts which passed over the bridges to the outer circles: and there were many temples built and dedicated to many gods; also gardens and places of exercise, some for men, and some set apart for horses, in both of the two islands formed by the zones; and in the centre of the larger of the two there was a race-course of a stadium in width, and in length allowed to extend all round the island, for horses to race in. Also there were guard-houses at intervals for the body-guard, the more trusted of whom had their duties appointed to them in the lesser zone, which was nearer the Acropolis; while the most trusted of all had houses given them within the citadel, and about the persons of the kings. The docks were full of triremes and naval stores, and all things were quite ready for use. Enough of the plan of the royal palace. Crossing the outer harbors, which were three in number, you would come to a wall which began at the sea and went all round: this was everywhere distant fifty stadia from the largest zone and harbor, and enclosed the whole, meeting at the mouth of the channel toward the sea. The entire area was densely crowded with habitations; and the canal and the largest of the harbors were full of vessels and merchants coming from all parts, who, from their numbers, kept up a multitudinous sound of human voices and din of all sorts night and day. I have repeated his descriptions of the city and the parts about the ancient palace nearly as he gave them, and now I must endeavor to describe the nature and arrangement of the rest of the country. The whole country was described as being very lofty and precipitous on the side of the sea, but the country immediately about and surrounding the city was a level plain, itself surrounded by mountains which descended toward the sea; it was smooth and even, but of an oblong shape, extending in one direction three thousand stadia, and going up the country from the sea through the centre of the island two thousand stadia; the whole region of the island lies toward the south, and is sheltered from the north. The surrounding mountains he celebrated for their number and size and beauty, in which they exceeded all that are now to be seen anywhere; having in them also many wealthy inhabited villages, and rivers and lakes, and meadows supplying food enough for every animal, wild or tame, and wood of various sorts, abundant for every kind of work. I will now describe the plain, which had been cultivated during many ages by many generations of kings. It was rectangular, and for the most part straight and oblong; and what it wanted of the straight line followed the line of the circular ditch. The depth and width and length of this ditch were incredible and gave the impression that such a work, in addition to so many other works, could hardly have been wrought by the hand of man. But I must say what I have heard. It was excavated to the depth of a hundred feet, and its breadth was a stadium everywhere; it was carried round the whole of the plain, and was ten thousand stadia in length. It received the streams which came down from the mountains, and winding round the plain, and touching the city at various points, was there let off into the sea. From above, likewise, straight canals of a hundred feet in width were cut in the plain, and again let off into the ditch, toward the sea; these canals were at intervals of a hundred stadia, and by them they brought, down the wood from the mountains to the city, and conveyed the fruits of the earth in ships, cutting transverse passages from one canal into another, and to the city. Twice in the year they gathered the fruits of the earth—in winter having the benefit of the rains, and in summer introducing the water of the canals. As to the population, each of the lots in the plain had an appointed chief of men who were fit for military service, and the size of the lot was to be a square of ten stadia each way, and the total number of all the lots was sixty thousand.

"And of the inhabitants of the mountains and of the rest of the country there was also a vast multitude having leaders, to whom they were assigned according to their dwellings and villages. The leader was required to furnish for the war the sixth portion of a war-chariot, so as to make up a total of ten thousand chariots; also two horses and riders upon them, and a light chariot without a seat, accompanied by a fighting man on foot carrying a small shield, and having a charioteer mounted to guide the horses; also, he was bound to furnish two heavy-armed men, two archers, two slingers, three stone-shooters, and three javelin men, who were skirmishers, and four sailors to make up a complement of twelve hundred ships. Such was the order of war in the royal city—that of the other nine governments was different in each of them, and would be wearisome to narrate. As to offices and honors, the following was the arrangement from the first: Each of the ten kings, in his own division and in his own city, had the absolute control of the citizens, and in many cases of the laws, punishing and slaying whomsoever he would.

"Now the relations of their governments to one another were regulated by the injunctions of Poseidon as the law had handed them down. These were inscribed by the first men on a column of orichalcum, which was situated in the middle of the island, at the temple of Poseidon, whither the people were gathered together every fifth and sixth years alternately, thus giving equal honor to the odd and to the even number. And when they were gathered together they consulted about public affairs, and inquired if any one had transgressed in anything, and passed judgment on him accordingly—and before they passed judgment they gave their pledges to one another in this wise: There were bulls who had the range of the temple of Poseidon; and the ten who were left alone in the temple, after they had offered prayers to the gods that they might take the sacrifices which were acceptable to them, hunted the bulls without weapons, but with staves and nooses; and the bull which they caught they led up to the column; the victim was then struck on the head by them, and slain over the sacred inscription. Now on the column, besides the law, there was inscribed an oath invoking mighty curses on the disobedient. When, therefore, after offering sacrifice according to their customs, they had burnt the limbs of the bull, they mingled a cup and cast in a clot of blood for each of them; the rest of the victim they took to the fire, after having made a purification of the column all round. Then they drew from the cup in golden vessels, and, pouring a libation on the fire, they swore that they would judge according to the laws on the column, and would punish any one who had previously transgressed, and that for the future they would not, if they could help, transgress any of the inscriptions, and would not command or obey any ruler who commanded them to act otherwise than according to the laws of their father Poseidon. This was the prayer which each of them offered up for himself and for his family, at the same time drinking, and dedicating the vessel in the temple of the god; and, after spending some necessary time at supper, when darkness came on and the fire about the sacrifice was cool, all of them put on most beautiful azure robes, and, sitting on the ground at night near the embers of the sacrifices on which they had sworn, and extinguishing all the fire about the temple, they received and gave judgement, if any of them had any accusation to bring against any one; and, when they had given judgment, at daybreak they wrote down their sentences on a golden tablet, and deposited them as memorials with their robes. There were many special laws which the several kings had inscribed about the temples, but the most important was the following: That they were not to take up arms against one another, and they were all to come to the rescue if any one in any city attempted to over-throw the royal house. Like their ancestors, they were to deliberate in common about war and other matters, giving the supremacy to the family of Atlas; and the king was not to have the power of life and death over any of his kinsmen, unless he had the assent of the majority of the ten kings.

"Such was the vast power which the god settled in the lost island of Atlantis; and this he afterward directed against our land on the following pretext, as traditions tell: For many generations, as long as the divine nature lasted in them, they were obedient to the laws, and well-affectioned toward the gods, who were their kinsmen; for they possessed true and in every way great spirits, practising gentleness and wisdom in the various chances of life, and in their intercourse with one another. They despised everything but virtue, not caring for their present state of life, and thinking lightly on the possession of gold and other property, which seemed only a burden to them; neither were they intoxicated by luxury; nor did wealth deprive them of their self-control; but they were sober, and saw clearly that all these goods are increased by virtuous friendship with one another, and that by excessive zeal for them, and honor of them, the good of them is lost, and friendship perishes with them.

"By such reflections, and by the continuance in them of a divine nature, all that which we have described waxed and increased in them; but when this divine portion began to fade away in them, and became diluted too often, and with too much of the mortal admixture, and the human nature got the upper-hand, then, they being unable to bear their fortune, became unseemly, and to him who had an eye to see, they began to appear base, and had lost the fairest of their precious gifts; but to those who had no eye to see the true happiness, they still appeared glorious and blessed at the very time when they were filled with unrighteous avarice and power. Zeus, the god of gods, who rules with law, and is able to see into such things, perceiving that an honorable race was in a most wretched state, and wanting to inflict punishment on them, that they might be chastened and improved, collected all the gods into his most holy habitation, which, being placed in the centre of the world, sees all things that partake of generation. And when he had called them together he spake as follows:" [Here Plato's story abruptly ends.]

CHAPTER III. THE PROBABILITIES OF PLATO'S STORY.

There is nothing improbable in this narrative, so far as it describes a great, rich, cultured, and educated people. Almost every part of Plato's story can be paralleled by descriptions of the people of Egypt or Peru; in fact, in some respects Plato's account of Atlantis falls short of Herodotus's description of the grandeur of Egypt, or Prescott's picture of the wealth and civilization of Peru. For instance, Prescott, in his "Conquest of Peru" (vol. i., p. 95), says:

"The most renowned of the Peruvian temples, the pride of the capital and the wonder of the empire, was at Cuzco, where, under the munificence of successive sovereigns, it had become so enriched that it received the name of Coricancha, or 'the Place of Gold.'... The interior of the temple was literally a mine of gold. On the western wall was emblazoned a representation of the Deity, consisting of a human countenance looking forth from amid innumerable rays of light, which emanated from it in every direction, in the same manner as the sun is often personified with us. The figure was engraved on a massive plate of gold, of enormous dimensions, thickly powdered with emeralds and precious stones.... The walls and ceilings were everywhere incrusted with golden ornaments; every part of the interior of the temple glowed with burnished plates and studs of the precious metal; the cornices were of the same material."

There are in Plato's narrative no marvels; no myths; no tales of gods, gorgons, hobgoblins, or giants. It is a plain and reasonable history of a people who built temples, ships, and canals; who lived by agriculture and commerce: who in pursuit of trade, reached out to all the countries around them. The early history of most nations begins with gods and demons, while here we have nothing of the kind; we see an immigrant enter the country, marry one of the native women, and settle down; in time a great nation grows up around him. It reminds one of the information given by the Egyptian priests to Herodotus. "During the space of eleven thousand three hundred and forty years they assert," says Herodotus, "that no divinity has appeared in human shape, ... they absolutely denied the possibility of a human being's descent from a god." If Plato had sought to draw from his imagination a wonderful and pleasing story, we should not have had so plain and reasonable a narrative. He would have given us a history like the legends of Greek mythology, full of the adventures of gods and goddesses, nymphs, fauns, and satyrs.

Neither is there any evidence on the face of this history that Plato sought to convey in it a moral or political lesson, in the guise of a fable, as did Bacon in the "New Atlantis," and More in the "Kingdom of Nowhere." There is no ideal republic delineated here. It is a straightforward, reasonable history of a people ruled over by their kings, living and progressing as other nations have lived and progressed since their day.

Plato says that in Atlantis there was "a great and wonderful empire," which "aggressed wantonly against the whole of Europe and Asia," thus testifying to the extent of its dominion. It not only subjugated Africa as far as Egypt, and Europe as far as Italy, but it ruled "as well over parts of the continent," to wit, "the opposite continent" of America, "which surrounded the true ocean." Those parts of America over which it ruled were, as we will show hereafter, Central America, Peru, and the Valley of the Mississippi, occupied by the "Mound Builders."

169

Moreover, he tells us that "this vast power was gathered into one;" that is to say, from Egypt to Peru it was one consolidated empire. We will see hereafter that the legends of the Hindoos as to Deva Nahusha distinctly refer to this vast empire, which covered the whole of the known world.

Another corroboration of the truth of Plato's narrative is found in the fact that upon the Azores black lava rocks, and rocks red and white in color, are now found. He says they built with white, red, and black stone. Sir C. Wyville Thomson describes a narrow neck of land between Fayal and Monte da Guia, called "Monte Queimada" (the burnt mountain), as follows: "It is formed partly of stratified tufa of a dark chocolate color, and partly of lumps of black lava, porous, and each with a large cavity in the centre, which must have been ejected as volcanic bombs in a glorious display of fireworks at some period beyond the records of Acorean history, but late in the geological annals of the island." ("Voyage of the Challenger," vol. ii., p. 24). He also describes immense walls of black volcanic rock in the island.

The plain of Atlantis, Plato tells us, "had been cultivated during many ages by many generations of kings." If, as we believe, agriculture, the domestication of the horse, ox, sheep, goat, and hog, and the discovery or development of wheat, oats, rye, and barley originated in this region, then this language of Plato in reference to "the many ages, and the successive generations of kings," accords with the great periods of time which were necessary to bring man from a savage to a civilized condition.

In the great ditch surrounding the whole land like a circle, and into which streams flowed down from the mountains, we probably see the original of the four rivers of Paradise, and the emblem of the cross surrounded by a circle, which, as we will show hereafter, was, from the earliest pre-Christian ages, accepted as the emblem of the Garden of Eden.

We know that Plato did not invent the name of Poseidon, for the worship of Poseidon was universal in the earliest ages of Europe; "Poseidon-worship seems to have been a peculiarity of all the colonies previous to the time of Sidon." ("Prehistoric Nations," p. 148.) This worship "was carried to Spain, and to Northern Africa, but most abundantly to Italy, to many of the islands, and to the regions around the Ægean Sea; also to Thrace." (Ibid., p. 155.)

Poseidon, or Neptune, is represented in Greek mythology as a sea-god; but he is figured as standing in a war-chariot drawn by horses. The association of the horse (a land animal) with a sea-god is inexplicable, except with the light given by Plato. Poseidon was a sea-god because he ruled over a great land in the sea, and was the national god of a maritime people; he is associated with horses, because in Atlantis the horse was first domesticated; and, as Plato shows, the Atlanteans had great race-courses for the development of speed in horses; and Poseidon is represented as standing in a war-chariot, because doubtless wheeled vehicles were first invented by the same people who tamed the horse; and they transmitted these war-chariots to their descendants from Egypt to Britain. We know that horses were the favorite objects chosen for sacrifice to Poseidon by the nations of antiquity within the Historical Period; they were killed, and cast into the sea from high precipices. The religious horse-feasts of the pagan Scandinavians were a survival of this Poseidon-worship, which once prevailed along all the coasts of Europe; they continued until the conversion of the people to Christianity, and were then suppressed by the Church with great difficulty.

We find in Plato's narrative the names of some of the Phoenician deities among the kings of Atlantis. Where did the Greek, Plato, get these names if the story is a fable?

Does Plato, in speaking of "the fruits having a hard rind, affording drinks and meats and ointments," refer to the cocoa nut?

Again: Plato tells us that Atlantis abounded in both cold and hot springs. How did he come to hit upon the hot springs if he was drawing a picture from his imagination? It is a singular confirmation of his story that hot springs abound in the Azores, which are the surviving fragments of Atlantis; and an experience wider than that possessed by Plato has taught scientific men that hot springs are a common feature of regions subject to volcanic convulsions.

Plato tells us, "The whole country was very lofty and precipitous on the side of the sea, but the country immediately about and surrounding the city was a level plain, itself surrounded by mountains which descended toward the sea." One has but to look at the profile of the "Dolphin's Ridge," as revealed by the deep-sea soundings of the Challenger, given as the frontispiece to this volume, to see that this is a faithful description of that precipitous elevation. "The surrounding mountains," which sheltered the plain from the north, are represented in the present towering peaks of the Azores.

Plato tells us that the destruction of Atlantis filled the sea with mud, and interfered with navigation. For thousands of years the ancients believed the Atlantic Ocean to be "a muddy, shallow, dark, and misty sea, Mare tenebrosum." ("Cosmos," vol. ii., p. 151.)

The three-pronged sceptre or trident of Poseidon reappears constantly in ancient history. We find it in the hands of Hindoo gods, and at the base of all the religious beliefs of antiquity.

"Among the numerals the sacred three has ever been considered the mark of perfection, and was therefore exclusively ascribed to the Supreme Deity, or to its earthly representative—a king, emperor, or any sovereign. For this reason triple emblems of various shapes are found on the belts, neckties, or any encircling fixture, as can be seen on the works of ancient art in Yucatan, Guatemala, Chiapas, Mexico, etc., whenever the object has reference to divine supremacy." (Dr. Arthur Schott, "Smith. Rep.," 1869, p. 391.)

We are reminded of the "tiara," and the "triple round of sovereignty."

In the same manner the ten kingdoms of Atlantis are perpetuated in all the ancient traditions.

"In the number given by the Bible for the Antediluvian patriarchs we have the first instance of a striking agreement with the traditions of various nations. Ten are mentioned in the Book of Genesis. Other nations, to whatever epoch they carry back their ancestors, whether before or after the Deluge, whether the mythical or historical character prevail, they are constant to this sacred number ten, which some have vainly attempted to connect with the speculations of later religious philosophers on the mystical value of numbers. In Chaldea, Berosus enumerates ten Antediluvian kings whose fabulous reign extended to thousands of years. The legends of the Iranian race commence with the reign of ten Peisdadien (Poseidon?) kings, 'men of the ancient law, who lived on pure Homa (water of life)' (nectar?), 'and who preserved their sanctity.' In India we meet with the nine Brahmadikas, who, with Brahma, their founder, make ten, and who are called the Ten Petris, or Fathers. The Chinese count ten emperors, partakers of the divine nature, before the dawn of historical times. The Germans believed in the ten ancestors of Odin, and the Arabs in the ten mythical kings of the Adites." (Lenormant and Chevallier, "Anc. Hist. of the East," vol. i., p. 13.)

The story of Plato finds confirmation from other sources. An extract preserved in Proclus, taken from a work now lost, which is quoted by Boeckh in his commentary on Plato, mentions islands in the exterior sea, beyond the Pillars of Hercules, and says it was known that in one of these islands "the inhabitants preserved from their ancestors a remembrance of Atlantis, an extremely large island, which for a long time held dominion over all the islands of the Atlantic Ocean." Ælian, in his "Varia Historia" (book iii., chap. xviii.), tells us that Theopompus (400 B.C.) related the particulars of an interview between Midas, King of Phrygia, and Silenus, in which Silenus reported the existence of a great continent beyond the Atlantic, "larger than Asia, Europe, and Libya together." He stated that a race of men called Meropes dwelt there, and had extensive cities. They were persuaded that their country alone was a continent. Out of curiosity some of them crossed the ocean and visited the Hyperboreans.

"The Gauls possessed traditions upon the subject of Atlantis which were collected by the Roman historian Timagenes, who lived in the first century before Christ. He represents that three distinct people dwelt in Gaul: 1. The indigenous population, which I suppose to be Mongoloids, who had long dwelt in Europe; 2. The invaders from a distant island, which I understand to be Atlantis; 3. The Aryan Gauls." ("Preadamites," p. 380.)

Marcellus, in a work on the Ethiopians, speaks of seven islands lying in the Atlantic Ocean—probably the Canaries—and the inhabitants of these islands, he says, preserve the memory of a much greater island, Atlantis, "which had for a long time exercised dominion over the smaller ones." (Didot Müller, "Fragmenta Historicorum Græcorum," vol. iv., p. 443.)

Diodorus Siculus relates that the Phoenicians discovered "a large island in the Atlantic Ocean, beyond the Pillars of Hercules, several days' sail from the coast of Africa. This island abounded in all manner of riches. The soil was exceedingly fertile; the scenery was diversified by rivers, mountains, and forests. It was the custom of the inhabitants to retire during the summer to magnificent country-houses, which stood in the midst of beautiful gardens. Fish and game were found in great abundance; the climate was delicious, and the trees bore fruit at all seasons of the year." Homer, Plutarch, and other ancient writers mention islands situated in the Atlantic, "several thousand stadia from the Pillars of Hercules." Silenus tells Midas that there was another continent besides Europe, Asia, and Africa— "a country where gold and silver are so plentiful that they are esteemed no more than we esteem iron." St. Clement, in his Epistle to the Corinthians, says that there were other worlds beyond the ocean.

Attention may here be called to the extraordinary number of instances in which allusion is made in the Old Testament to the "islands of the sea," especially in Isaiah and Ezekiel. What had an inland people, like the Jews, to do with seas and islands? Did these references grow out of vague traditions linking their race with "islands in the sea?"

The Orphic Argonaut sings of the division of the ancient Lyktonia into separate islands. He says, "When the dark-haired Poseidon, in anger with Father Kronion, struck Lyktonia with the golden trident."

Plato states that the Egyptians told Solon that the destruction of Atlantis occurred 9000 years before that date, to wit, about 9600 years before the Christian era. This looks like an extraordinarily long period of time, but it must be remembered that geologists claim that the remains of man found in the caves of Europe date back 500,000 years; and the fossil Calaveras skull was found deep under the base of Table Mountain, California, the whole mountain having been formed since the man to whom it belonged lived and died.

"M. Oppert read an essay at the Brussels Congress to show, from the astronomical observations of the Egyptians and Assyrians, that 11,542 years before our era man existed on the earth at such a stage of civilization as to be able to take note of astronomical phenomena, and to calculate with considerable accuracy the length of the year. The Egyptians, says he, calculated by cycles of 1460 years—zodiacal cycles, as they were called. Their year consisted of 365 days, which caused them to lose one day in every four solar years, and, consequently, they would attain their original starting-point again only after 1460 years (365 x 4). Therefore, the zodiacal cycle ending in the year 139 of our era commenced in the year 1322 B.C. On the other hand, the Assyrian cycle was 1805 years, or 22,325 lunations. An Assyrian cycle began 712 B.C. The Chaldeans state that between the Deluge and their first historic dynasty there was a period of 39,180 years. Now, what means, this number? It stands for 12 Egyptian zodiacal cycles plus 12 Assyrian lunar cycles. 12 X 1460 = 17,520

$$12 \text{ X } 1805 = 21,660 \qquad = 39,180$$

"These two modes of calculating time are in agreement with each other, and were known simultaneously to one people, the Chaldeans. Let us now build up the series of both cycles, starting from our era, and the result will be as follows:

Zodiacal Cycle.	Lunar Cycle.
1,460	1,805
1,822	712
---	---
2,782	2,517
4,242	4,322
5,702	6,127
7,162	7,932
8,622	9,737
110,082	11,542
11,542	

"At the year 11,542 B.C. the two cycles came together, and consequently they had on that year their common origin in one and the same astronomical observation."

That observation was probably made in Atlantis.

The wide divergence of languages which is found to exist among the Atlanteans at the beginning of the Historical Period implies a vast lapse of time. The fact that the nations of the Old World remembered so little of Atlantis, except the colossal fact of its sudden and overwhelming destruction, would also seem to remove that event into a remote past.

Herodotus tells us that he learned from the Egyptians that Hercules was one of their most ancient deities, and that he was one of the twelve produced from the eight gods, 17,000 years before the reign of Amasis.

In short, I fail to see why this story of Plato, told as history, derived from the Egyptians, a people who, it is known, preserved most ancient records, and who were able to trace their existence back to a vast antiquity, should have been contemptuously set aside as a fable by Greeks, Romans, and the modern world. It can only be because our predecessors, with their limited knowledge of the geological history of the world, did not believe it possible that any large part of the earth's surface could have been thus suddenly swallowed up by the sea.

Let us then first address ourselves to that question.

CHAPTER IV. WAS SUCH A CATASTROPHE POSSIBLE?

All that is needed to answer this question is to briefly refer to some of the facts revealed by the study of geology.

In the first place, the earth's surface is a record of successive risings and fallings of the land. The accompanying picture represents a section of the anthracite coal-measures of Pennsylvania. Each of the coal deposits here shown, indicated by the black lines, was created when the land had risen sufficiently above the sea to maintain vegetation; each of the strata of rock, many of them hundreds of feet in thickness, was deposited under water. Here we have twenty-three different changes of the level of the land during the formation of 2000 feet of rock and coal; and these changes took place over vast areas, embracing thousands of square miles.

All the continents which now exist were, it is well understood, once, under water, and the rocks of which they are composed were deposited beneath the water; more than this, most of the rocks so deposited were the detritus or washings of other continents, which then stood where the oceans now roll, and whose mountains and plains were ground down by the action of volcanoes and earthquakes, and frost, ice, wind, and rain, and washed into the sea, to form the rocks upon which the nations now dwell; so that we have changed the conditions of land and water: that which is now continent was once sea, and that which is now sea was formerly continent. There can be no question that the Australian Archipelago is simply the mountain-tops of a drowned continent, which once reached from India to South America. Science has gone so far as to even give it a name; it is called "Lemuria," and here, it is claimed, the human race originated. An examination of the geological formation of our Atlantic States proves beyond a doubt, from the manner in which the sedimentary rocks, the sand, gravel, and mud—aggregating a thickness of 45,000 feet—are deposited, that they came from the north and east. "They represent the detritus of pre-existing lands, the washings of rain, rivers, coast-currents, and other agencies of erosion; and since the areas supplying the waste could scarcely have been of less extent than the new strata it formed, it is reasonably inferred that land masses of continental magnitude must have occupied the region now covered by the North Atlantic before America began to be, and onward at least through the palæozoic ages of American history. The proof of this fact is that the great strata of rocks are thicker the nearer we approach their source in the east: the maximum thickness of the palæozoic rocks of the Appalachian formation is 25,000 to 35,000 feet in Pennsylvania and Virginia, while their minimum thickness in Illinois and Missouri is from 3000 to 4000 feet; the rougher and grosser-textured rocks predominate in the east, while the farther west we go the finer the deposits were of which the rocks are composed; the finer materials were carried farther west by the water." ("New Amer. Cyclop.," art. Coal.)

The history of the growth of the European Continent, as recounted by Professor Geikie, gives an instructive illustration of the relations of geology to geography. The earliest European land, he says, appears to have existed in the north and north-west, comprising Scandinavia, Finland, and the northwest of the British area, and to have extended thence through boreal and arctic latitudes into North America. Of the height and mass of this primeval land some idea may be formed by considering the enormous bulk of the material derived from its disintegration. In the Silurian formations of the British Islands alone there is a mass of rock, worn from the land, which would form a mountain-chain extending from Marseilles to the North Cape (1800 miles), with a mean breadth of over thirty-three miles, and an average height of 16,000 feet.

As the great continent which stood where the Atlantic Ocean now is wore away, the continents of America and Europe were formed; and there seems to have been from remote times a continuous rising, still going on, of the new lands, and a sinking of the old ones. Within five thousand years, or since the age of the "polished stone," the shores of Sweden, Denmark, and Norway have risen from 200 to 600 feet.

Professor Winchell says ("The Preadamites," p. 437):

"We are in the midst of great changes, and are scarcely conscious of it. We have seen worlds in flames, and have felt a comet strike the earth. We have seen the whole coast of South America lifted up bodily ten or fifteen feet and let down again in an hour. We have seen the Andes sink 220 feet in seventy years.... Vast transpositions have taken place in the coast-line of China. The ancient capital, located, in all probability, in an accessible position near the centre of the empire, has now become nearly surrounded by water, and its site is on the peninsula of Corea.... There was a time when the rocky barriers of the Thracian Bosphorus gave way and the Black Sea subsided. It had covered a vast area in the north and east. Now this area became drained, and was known as the ancient Lectonia: it is now the prairie region of Russia, and the granary of Europe."

There is ample geological evidence that at one time the entire area of Great Britain was submerged to the depth of at least seventeen hundred feet. Over the face of the submerged land was strewn thick beds of sand, gravel, and clay, termed by geologists "the Northern Drift." The British Islands rose again from the sea, bearing these water-deposits on their bosom. What is now Sicily once lay deep beneath the sea: It subsequently rose 3000 feet above the sea-level. The Desert of Sahara was once under water, and its now burning sands are a deposit of the sea.

Geologically speaking, the submergence of Atlantis, within the historical period, was simply the last of a number of vast changes, by which the continent which once occupied the greater part of the Atlantic had gradually sunk under the ocean, while the new lands were rising on both sides of it.

We come now to the second question, Is it possible that Atlantis could have been suddenly destroyed by such a convulsion of nature as is described by Plato? The ancients regarded this part of his story as a fable. With the wider knowledge which scientific research has afforded the modern world, we can affirm that such an event is not only possible, but that the history of even the last two centuries has furnished us with striking parallels for it. We now possess the record of numerous islands lifted above the waters, and others sunk beneath the waves, accompanied by storms and earthquakes similar to those which marked the destruction of Atlantis.

In 1783 Iceland was visited by convulsions more tremendous than any recorded in the modern annals of that country. About a month previous to the eruption on the main-land a submarine volcano burst forth in the sea, at a distance of thirty miles from the shore. It ejected so much pumice that the sea was covered with it for a distance of 150 miles, and ships were considerably impeded in their course. A new island was thrown up, consisting of high cliffs, which was claimed by his Danish Majesty, and named "Nyöe," or the New Island; but before a year had elapsed it sunk beneath the sea, leaving a reef of rocks thirty fathoms under water.

The earthquake of 1783 in Iceland destroyed 9000 people out of a population of 50,000; twenty villages were consumed by fire or inundated by water, and a mass of lava thrown out "greater than the entire bulk of Mont Blanc."

On the 8th of October, 1822, a great earthquake occurred on the island of Java, near the mountain of Galung Gung. "A loud explosion was heard, the earth shook, and immense columns of hot water and boiling mud, mixed with burning brimstone, ashes, and lapilli, of the size of nuts, were projected from the mountain like a water-spout, with such prodigious violence that large quantities fell beyond the river Tandoi, which is forty miles distant.... The first eruption lasted nearly five hours; and on the following days the rain fell in torrents, and the rivers, densely charged with mud, deluged the country far and wide. At the end of four days (October 12th), a second eruption occurred, more violent than the first, in which hot water and mud were again vomited, and great blocks of basalt were thrown to the distance of seven miles from the volcano. There was at the same time a violent earthquake, the face of the mountain was utterly changed, its summits broken down, and one side, which had been covered with trees, became an enormous gulf in the form of a semicircle. Over 4000 persons were killed and 114 villages destroyed." (Lyell's "Principles of Geology," p. 430.)

In 1831 a new island was born in the Mediterranean, near the coast of Sicily. It was called Graham's Island. It came up with an earthquake, and "a water-spout sixty feet high and eight hundred yards in circumference rising from the sea." In about a month the island was two hundred feet high and three miles in circumference; it soon, however, sank beneath the sea.

The Canary Islands were probably a part of the original empire of Atlantis. On the 1st of September, 1730, the earth split open near Yaiza, in the island of Lancerota. In one night a considerable hill of ejected matter was thrown up; in a few days another vent opened and gave out a lava stream which overran several villages. It flowed at first rapidly, like water, but became afterward heavy and slow, like honey. On the 11th of September more lava flowed out, covering up a village, and precipitating itself with a horrible roar into the sea. Dead fish floated on the waters in indescribable multitudes, or were thrown dying on the shore; the cattle throughout the country dropped lifeless to the ground, suffocated by putrid vapors, which condensed and fell down in drops. These manifestations were accompanied by a storm such as the people of the country had never known before. These dreadful commotions lasted for five years. The lavas thrown out covered one-third of the whole island of Lancerota.

The Gulf of Santorin, in the Grecian Archipelago, has been for two thousand years a scene of active volcanic operations. Pliny informs us that in the year 186 B.C. the island of "Old Kaimeni," or the Sacred Isle, was lifted up from the sea; and in A.D. 19 the island of "Thia" (the Divine) made its appearance. In A.D. 1573 another island was created, called "the small sunburnt island." In 1848 a volcanic convulsion of three months' duration created a great shoal; an earthquake destroyed many houses in Thera, and the sulphur and hydrogen issuing from the sea killed 50 persons and 1000 domestic animals. A recent examination of these islands shows that the whole mass of Santorin has sunk, since its projection from the sea, over 1200 feet.

The fort and village of Sindree, on the eastern arm of the Indus, above Luckput, was submerged in 1819 by an earthquake, together with a tract of country 2000 square miles in extent.

"In 1828 Sir A. Burnes went in a boat to the ruins of Sindree, where a single remaining tower was seen in the midst of a wide expanse of sea. The tops of the ruined walls still rose two or three feet above the level of the water; and, standing on one of these, he could behold nothing in the horizon but water, except in one direction, where a blue streak of land to the north indicated the Ullah Bund. This scene," says Lyell ("Principles of Geology," p. 462), "presents to the imagination a lively picture of the revolutions now in progress on the earth—a waste of waters where a few years before all was land, and the only land visible consisting of ground uplifted by a recent earthquake."

We give from Lyell's great work the following curious pictures of the appearance of the Fort of Sindree before and after the inundation.

In April, 1815, one of the most frightful eruptions recorded in history occurred in the province of Tomboro, in the island of Sumbawa, about two hundred miles from the eastern extremity of Java. It lasted from April 5th to July of that year; but was most violent on the 11th and 12th of July. The sound of the explosions was heard for nearly one thousand miles. Out of a population of 12,000, in the province of Tombora, only twenty-six individuals escaped. "Violent whirlwinds carried up men, horses, and cattle into the air, tore up the largest trees by the roots, and covered the whole sea with floating timber." (Raffles's "History of Java," vol. i., p. 28.) The ashes darkened the air; "the floating cinders to the westward of Sumatra formed, on the 12th of April, a mass two feet thick and several miles in extent, through which ships with difficulty forced their way." The darkness in daytime was more profound than the blackest night. "The town called Tomboro, on the west side of Sumbawa, was overflowed by the sea, which encroached upon the shore, so that the water remained permanently eighteen feet deep in places where there was land before." The area covered by the convulsion was 1000 English miles in circumference. "In the island of Amboyna, in the same month and year, the ground opened, threw out water and then closed again." (Raffles's "History of Java," vol. i., p. 25.)

But it is at that point of the European coast nearest to the site of Atlantis at Lisbon that the most tremendous earthquake of modern times has occurred. On the 1st of November, 1775, a sound of thunder was heard underground, and immediately afterward a violent shock threw down the greater part of the city. In six minutes 60,000 persons perished. A great concourse of people had collected for safety upon a new quay, built entirely of marble; but suddenly it sunk down with all the people on it, and not one of the dead bodies ever floated to the surface. A great number of small boats and vessels anchored near it, and, full of people, were swallowed up as in a whirlpool. No fragments of these wrecks ever rose again to the surface; the water where the quay went down is now 600 feet deep. The area covered by this earthquake was very great. Humboldt says that a portion of the earth's surface, four times as great as the size of Europe, was simultaneously shaken. It extended from the Baltic to the West Indies, and from Canada to Algiers. At eight leagues from Morocco the ground opened and swallowed a village of 10,000 inhabitants, and closed again over them.

It is very probable that the centre of the convulsion was in the bed of the Atlantic, at or near the buried island of Atlantis, and that it was a successor of the great earth throe which, thousands of years before, had brought destruction upon that land.

Ireland also lies near the axis of this great volcanic area, reaching from the Canaries to Iceland, and it has been many times in the past the seat of disturbance. The ancient annals contain numerous accounts of eruptions, preceded by volcanic action. In 1490, at the Ox Mountains, Sligo, one occurred by which one hundred persons and numbers of cattle were destroyed; and a volcanic eruption in May, 1788, on the hill of Knocklade, Antrim, poured a stream of lava sixty yards wide for thirty-nine hours, and destroyed the village of Ballyowen and all the inhabitants, save a man and his wife and two children. ("Amer. Cyclop.," art. Ireland.)

While we find Lisbon and Ireland, east of Atlantis, subjected to these great earthquake shocks, the West India Islands, west of the same centre, have been repeatedly visited in a similar manner. In 1692 Jamaica suffered from a violent earthquake. The earth opened, and great quantities of water were cast out; many people were swallowed up in these rents; the earth caught some of them by the middle and squeezed them to death; the heads of others only appeared above-ground. A tract of land near the town of Port Royal, about a thousand acres in extent, sunk down in less than one minute, and the sea immediately rolled in.

The Azore Islands are undoubtedly the peaks of the mountains of Atlantis. They are even yet the centre of great volcanic activity. They have suffered severely from eruptions and earthquakes. In 1808 a volcano rose suddenly in San Jorge to the height of 3500 feet, and burnt for six days, desolating the entire island. In 1811 a volcano rose from the sea, near San Miguel, creating an island 300 feet high, which was named Sambrina, but which soon sunk beneath the sea. Similar volcanic eruptions occurred in the Azores in 1691 and 1720.

Along a great line, a mighty fracture in the surface of the globe, stretching north and south through the Atlantic, we find a continuous series of active or extinct volcanoes. In Iceland we have Oerafa, Hecla, and Rauda Kamba; another in Pico, in the Azores; the peak of Teneriffe; Fogo, in one of the Cape de Verde Islands: while of extinct volcanoes we have several in Iceland, and two in Madeira; while Fernando de Noronha, the island of Ascension, St. Helena, and Tristan d'Acunha are all of volcanic origin. ("Cosmos," vol. v., p. 331.)

The following singular passage we quote entire from Lyell's "Principles of Geology," p. 436: "In the Nautical Magazine for 1835, p. 642, and for 1838, p. 361, and in the Comptes Rendus, April, 1838, accounts are given of a series of volcanic phenomena, earthquakes, troubled water, floating scoria, and columns of smoke, which have been observed at intervals since the middle of the last century, in a space of open sea between longitudes 20° and 22' W., about half a degree south of the equator. These facts, says Mr. Darwin, seem to show that an island or archipelago is in process of formation in the middle of the Atlantic. A line joining St. Helena and Ascension would, if prolonged, intersect this slowly nascent focus of volcanic action. Should land be eventually formed here, it will not be the first that has been produced by igneous action in this ocean since it was inhabited by the existing species of testacea. At Porto Praya, in St. Jago, one of the Azores, a horizontal, calcareous stratum occurs, containing shells of recent marine species, covered by a great sheet of basalt eighty feet thick. It would be difficult to estimate too highly the commercial and political importance which a group of islands might acquire if, in the next two or three thousand years, they should rise in mid-ocean between St. Helena and Ascension."

These facts would seem to show that the great fires which destroyed Atlantis are still smouldering in the depths of the ocean; that the vast oscillations which carried Plato's continent beneath the sea may again bring it, with all its buried treasures, to the light; and that even the wild imagination of Jules Verne, when he described Captain Nemo, in his diving armor, looking down upon the temples and towers of the lost island, lit by the fires of submarine volcanoes, had some groundwork of possibility to build upon.

But who will say, in the presence of all the facts here enumerated, that the submergence of Atlantis, in some great world-shaking cataclysm, is either impossible or improbable? As will be shown hereafter, when we come to discuss the Flood legends, every particular which has come down to us of the destruction of Atlantis has been duplicated in some of the accounts just given.

We conclude, therefore: 1. That it is proven beyond question, by geological evidence, that vast masses of land once existed in the region where Atlantis is located by Plato, and that therefore such an island must have existed; 2. That there is nothing improbable or impossible in the statement that it was destroyed suddenly by an earthquake "in one dreadful night and day."

CHAPTER. V. THE TESTIMONY OF THE SEA.

Suppose we were to find in mid-Atlantic, in front of the Mediterranean, in the neighborhood of the Azores, the remains of an immense island, sunk beneath the sea—one thousand miles in width, and two or three thousand miles long—would it not go far to confirm the statement of Plato that, "beyond the strait where you place the Pillars of Hercules, there was an island larger than Asia (Minor) and Libya combined," called Atlantis? And suppose we found that the Azores were the mountain peaks of this drowned island, and were torn and rent by tremendous volcanic convulsions; while around them, descending into the sea, were found great strata of lava; and the whole face of the sunken land was covered for thousands of miles with volcanic débris, would we not be obliged to confess that these facts furnished strong corroborative proofs of the truth of Plato's statement, that "in one day and one fatal night there came mighty earthquakes and inundations which ingulfed that mighty people? Atlantis disappeared beneath the sea; and then that sea became inaccessible on account of the quantity of mud which the ingulfed island left in its place."

MAP OF ATLANTIS, WITH ITS ISLANDS AND CONNECTING RIDGES, FROM DEEP-SEA SOUNDINGS

And all these things recent investigation has proved conclusively. Deep-sea soundings have been made by ships of different nations; the United States ship Dolphin, the German frigate Gazelle, and the British ships Hydra, Porcupine, and Challenger have mapped out the bottom of the Atlantic, and the result is the revelation of a great elevation, reaching from a point on the coast of the British Islands southwardly to the coast of South America, at Cape Orange, thence south-eastwardly to the coast of Africa, and thence southwardly to Tristan d'Acunha. I give one map showing the profile of this elevation in the frontispiece, and another map, showing the outlines of the submerged land, on page 47. It rises about 9000 feet above the great Atlantic depths around it, and in the

Azores, St. Paul's Rocks, Ascension, and Tristan d'Acunha it reaches the surface of the ocean.

Evidence that this elevation was once dry land is found in the fact that "the inequalities, the mountains and valleys of its surface, could never have been produced in accordance with any laws for the deposition of sediment, nor by submarine elevation; but, on the contrary, must have been carved by agencies acting above the water level." (Scientific American, July 28th, 1877.)

Mr. J. Starke Gardner, the eminent English geologist, is of the opinion that in the Eocene Period a great extension of land existed to the west of Cornwall. Referring to the location of the "Dolphin" and "Challenger" ridges, he asserts that "a great tract of land formerly existed where the sea now is, and that Cornwall, the Scilly and Channel Islands, Ireland and Brittany, are the remains of its highest summits." (Popular Science Review, July, 1878.)

Here, then, we have the backbone of the ancient continent which once occupied the whole of the Atlantic Ocean, and from whose washings Europe and America were constructed; the deepest parts of the ocean, 3500 fathoms deep, represent those portions which sunk first, to wit, the plains to the east and west of the central mountain range; some of the loftiest peaks of this range—the Azores, St. Paul's, Ascension, Tristan d'Acunba— are still above the ocean level; while the great body of Atlantis lies a few hundred fathoms beneath the sea. In these "connecting ridges" we see the pathway which once extended between the New World and the Old, and by means of which the plants and animals of one continent travelled to the other; and by the same avenues black men found their way, as we will show hereafter, from Africa to America, and red men from America to Africa.

And, as I have shown, the same great law which gradually depressed the Atlantic continent, and raised the lands east and west of it, is still at work: the coast of Greenland, which may be regarded as the northern extremity of the Atlantic continent, is still sinking "so rapidly that ancient buildings on low rock-islands are now submerged, and the Greenlander has learned by experience never to build near the water's edge," ("North Amer. of Antiq.," p. 504.) The same subsidence is going on along the shore of South Carolina and Georgia, while the north of Europe and the Atlantic coast of South America are rising rapidly. Along the latter raised beaches, 1180 miles long and from 100 to 1300 feet high, have been traced.

When these connecting ridges extended from America to Europe and Africa, they shut off the flow of the tropical waters of the ocean to the north:

there was then no "Gulf Stream;" the land-locked ocean that laved the shores of Northern Europe was then intensely cold; and the result was the Glacial Period. When the barriers of Atlantis sunk sufficiently to permit the natural expansion of the heated water of the tropics to the north, the ice and snow which covered Europe gradually disappeared; the Gulf Stream flowed around Atlantis, and it still retains the circular motion first imparted to it by the presence of that island.

The officers of the Challenger found the entire ridge of Atlantis covered with volcanic deposits; these are the subsided mud which, as Plato tells us,

rendered the sea impassable after the destruction of the island.

It does not follow that, at the time Atlantis was finally ingulfed, the ridges connecting it with America and Africa rose above the water-level; these may have gradually subsided into the sea, or have gone down in cataclysms such as are described in the Central American books. The Atlantis of Plato may have been confined to the "Dolphin Ridge" of our map.

ANCIENT ISLANDS BETWEEN ATLANTIS AND THE MEDITERRANEAN, FROM DEEP-SEA SOUNDINGS

The United States sloop Gettysburg has also made some remarkable discoveries in a neighboring field. I quote from John James Wild (in Nature, March 1st, 1877, p. 377):

"The recently announced discovery by Commander Gorringe, of the United States sloop Gettysburg, of a bank of soundings bearing N. 85° W., and distant 130 miles from Cape St. Vincent, during the last voyage of the vessel across the Atlantic, taken in connection with previous soundings obtained in the same region of the North Atlantic, suggests the probable existence of a submarine ridge or plateau connecting the island of Madeira with the coast of Portugal, and the probable subaerial connection in prehistoric times of that island with the south-western extremity of Europe."... "These soundings reveal the existence of a channel of an average depth of from 2000 to 3000 fathoms, extending in a northeasterly direction from its entrance between Madeira and the Canary Islands toward Cape St. Vincent.... Commander Gorringe, when about 150 miles from the Strait of Gibraltar, found that the soundings decreased from 2700 fathoms to 1600 fathoms in the distance of a few miles. The subsequent soundings (five miles apart) gave 900, 500, 400, and 100 fathoms; and eventually a depth of 32 fathoms was obtained, in which the vessel anchored. The bottom was found to consist of live pink coral, and the position of the bank in lat. 36° 29' N., long. 11° 33' W."

The map on page 51 shows the position of these elevations. They must have been originally islands;—stepping-stones, as it were, between Atlantis and the coast of Europe.

Sir C. Wyville Thomson found that the specimens of the fauna of the coast of Brazil, brought up in his dredging-machine, are similar to those of the western coast of Southern Europe. This is accounted for by the connecting ridges reaching from Europe to South America.

A member of the Challenger staff, in a lecture delivered in London, soon after the termination of the expedition, gave it as his opinion that the great submarine plateau is the remains of "the lost Atlantis."

CHAPTER VI. THE TESTIMONY OF THE FLORA AND FAUNA.

Proofs are abundant that there must have been at one time uninterrupted land communication between Europe and America. In the words of a writer upon this subject: "When the animals and plants of the Old and New World are compared, one cannot but be struck with their identity; all or nearly all belong to the same genera, while many, even of the species, are common to both continents. This is most important in its bearing on our theory, as indicating that they radiated from a common centre after the Glacial Period.... The hairy mammoth, woolly-haired rhinoceros, the Irish elk, the musk-ox, the reindeer, the glutton, the lemming, etc., more or less accompanied this flora, and their remains are always found in the post-glacial deposits of Europe as low down as the South of France. In the New World beds of the same age contain similar remains, indicating that they came from a common centre, and were spread out over both continents alike." (Westminster Review, January, 1872, p.19.)

Recent discoveries in the fossil beds of the Bad Lands of Nebraska prove that the horse originated in America. Professor Marsh, of Yale College, has identified the several preceding forms from which it was developed, rising, in the course of ages, from a creature not larger than a fox until, by successive steps, it developed into the true horse. How did the wild horse pass from America to Europe and Asia if there was not continuous land communication between the two continents? He seems to have existed in Europe in a wild state prior to his domestication by man.

The fossil remains of the camel are found in India, Africa, South America, and in Kansas. The existing alpacas and llamas of South America are but varieties of the camel family.

The cave bear, whose remains are found associated with the bones of the mammoth and the bones and works of man in the caves of Europe, was identical with the grizzly bear of our Rocky Mountains. The musk-ox, whose relics are found in the same deposits, now roams the wilds of Arctic America. The glutton of Northern Europe, in the Stone Age, is identical with the wolverine of the United States. According to Rutimeyer, the ancient bison (Bos priscus) of Europe was identical with the existing American buffalo. "Every stage between the ancient cave bison and the European aurochs can be traced." The Norway elk, now nearly extinct, is identical with the American moose. The Cervus Americanus found in Kentucky was as large as the Irish elk, which it greatly resembled. The lagomys, or tailless hare, of the European caves, is now found in the colder regions of North America. The reindeer, which once occupied Europe as far down as France, was the same as the reindeer of America. Remains of the cave lion of Europe (Felix speloæ), a larger beast than the largest of the existing species, have been found at Natchez, Mississippi. The European cave wolf was identical with the American wolf.

Cattle were domesticated among the people of Switzerland during the earliest part of the Stone Period (Darwin's "Animals Under Domestication," vol. i., p. 103), that is to say, before the Bronze Age and the Age of Iron. Even at that remote period they had already, by long-continued selection, been developed out of wild forms akin to the American buffalo. M. Gervais ("Hist. Nat. des Mammifores," vol. xi., p. 191) concludes that the wild race from which our domestic sheep was derived is now extinct. The remains of domestic sheep are found in the debris of the Swiss lake-dwellings during the Stone Age. The domestic horse, ass, lion, and goat also date back to a like great antiquity. We have historical records 7000 years old, and during that time no similar domestication of a wild animal has been made. This fact speaks volumes as to the vast period, of time during which man must

187

have lived in a civilized state to effect the domestication of so many and such useful animals.

And when we turn from the fauna to the flora, we find the same state of things. An examination of the fossil beds of Switzerland of the Miocene Age reveals the remains of more than eight hundred different species of flower-bearing plants, besides mosses, ferns, etc. The total number of fossil plants catalogued from those beds, cryptogamous as well as phænogamous, is upward of three thousand. The majority of these species have migrated to America. There were others that passed into Asia, Africa, and even to Australia. The American types are, however, in the largest proportion. The analogues of the flora of the Miocene Age of Europe now grow in the forests of Virginia, North and South Carolina, and Florida; they include such familiar examples as magnolias, tulip-trees, evergreen oaks, maples, plane-trees, robinas, sequoias, etc. It would seem to be impossible that these trees could have migrated from Switzerland to America unless there was unbroken land communication between the two continents.

It is a still more remarkable fact that a comparison of the flora of the Old World and New goes to show that not only was there communication by land, over which the plants of one continent could extend to another, but that man must have existed, and have helped this transmigration, in the case of certain plants that were incapable of making the journey unaided.

Otto Kuntze, a distinguished German botanist, who has spent many years in the tropics, announces his conclusion that "In America and in Asia the principal domesticated tropical plants are represented by the same species." He instances the Manihot utilissima, whose roots yield a fine flour; the tarro (Colocasia esculenta), the Spanish or red pepper, the tomato, the bamboo, the guava, the mango-fruit, and especially the banana. He denies that the American origin of tobacco, maize, and the cocoa-nut is proved. He refers to the Paritium tiliaceum, a malvaceous plant, hardly noticed by Europeans, but very highly prized by the natives of the tropics, and cultivated everywhere in the East and West Indies; it supplies to the natives of these regions so far apart their ropes and cordage. It is always seedless in a cultivated state. It existed in America before the arrival of Columbus.

But Professor Kuntze pays especial attention to the banana, or plantain. The banana is seedless. It is found throughout tropical Asia and Africa. Professor Kuntze asks, "In what way was this plant, which cannot stand a voyage through the temperate zone, carried to America?" And yet it was generally cultivated in America before 1492. Says Professor Kuntze, "It must be remembered that the plantain is a tree-like, herbaceous plant,

188

possessing no easily transportable bulbs, like the potato or the dahlia, nor propagable by cuttings, like the willow or the poplar. It has only a perennial root, which, once planted, needs hardly any care, and yet produces the most abundant crop of any known tropical plant." He then proceeds to discuss how it could have passed from Asia to America. He admits that the roots must have been transported from one country to the other by civilized man. He argues that it could not have crossed the Pacific from Asia to America, because the Pacific is nearly thrice or four times as wide as the Atlantic. The only way he can account for the plantain reaching America is to suppose that it was carried there when the North Pole had a tropical climate! Is there any proof that civilized man existed at the North Pole when it possessed the climate of Africa?

Is it not more reasonable to suppose that the plantain, or banana, was cultivated by the people of Atlantis, and carried by their civilized agricultural colonies to the east and the west? Do we not find a confirmation of this view in the fact alluded to by Professor Kuntze in these words: "A cultivated plant which does not possess seeds must have been under culture for a very long period—we have not in Europe a single exclusively seedless, berry-bearing, cultivated plant—and hence it is perhaps fair to infer that these plants were cultivated as early as the beginning of the middle of the Diluvial Period."

Is it possible that a plant of this kind could have been cultivated for this immense period of time in both Asia and America? Where are the two nations, agricultural and highly civilized, on those continents by whom it was so cultivated? What has become of them? Where are the traces of their civilization? All the civilizations of Europe, Asia, and Africa radiated from the Mediterranean; the Hindoo-Aryans advanced from the north-west; they were kindred to the Persians, who were next-door neighbors to the Arabians (cousins of the Phoenicians), and who lived along-side of the Egyptians, who had in turn derived their civilization from the Phoenicians.

It would be a marvel of marvels if one nation, on one continent, had cultivated the banana for such a vast period of time until it became seedless; the nation retaining a peaceful, continuous, agricultural civilization during all that time. But to suppose that two nations could have cultivated the same plant, under the same circumstances, on two different continents, for the same unparalleled lapse of time, is supposing an impossibility.

We find just such a civilization as was necessary, according to Plato, and under just such a climate, in Atlantis and nowhere else. We have found it reaching, by its contiguous islands, within one hundred and fifty miles of the coast of Europe on the one side, and almost touching the West India Islands on the other, while, by its connecting ridges, it bound together Brazil and Africa.

But it may be said these animals and plants may have passed from Asia to America across the Pacific by the continent of Lemuria; or there may have been continuous land communication at one time at Behring's Strait. True; but an examination of the flora of the Pacific States shows that very many of the trees and plants common to Europe and the Atlantic States are not to be seen west of the Rocky Mountains. The magnificent magnolias, the tulip-trees, the plane-trees, etc., which were found existing in the Miocene Age in Switzerland, and are found at the present day in the United States, are altogether lacking on the Pacific coast. The sources of supply of that region seem to have been far inferior to the sources of supply of the Atlantic States. Professor Asa Gray tells us that, out of sixty-six genera and one hundred and fifty-five species found in the forests cast of the Rocky Mountains, only thirty-one genera and seventy-eight species are found west of the mountains. The Pacific coast possesses no papaw, no linden or basswood, no locust-trees, no cherry-tree large enough for a timber tree, no gum-trees, no sorrel-tree, nor kalmia; no persimmon-trees, not a holly, only one ash that may be called a timber tree, no catalpa or sassafras, not a single elm or hackberry, not a mulberry, not a hickory, or a beech, or a true chestnut. These facts would seem to indicate that the forest flora of North America entered it from the east, and that the Pacific States possess only those fragments of it that were able to struggle over or around the great dividing mountain-chain.

We thus see that the flora and fauna of America and Europe testify not only to the existence of Atlantis, but to the fact that in an earlier age it must have extended from the shores of one continent to those of the other; and by this bridge of land the plants and animals of one region passed to the other.

The cultivation of the cotton-plant and the manufacture of its product was known to both the Old and New World. Herodotus describes it (450 B.C.) as the tree of India that bears a fleece more beautiful than that of the sheep. Columbus found the natives of the West Indies using cotton cloth. It was also found in Mexico and Peru. It is a significant fact that the cotton-plant has been found growing wild in many parts of America, but never in the Old World. This would seem to indicate that the plant was a native of America; and this is confirmed by the superiority of American cotton, and the further fact that the plants taken from America to India constantly degenerate, while those taken from India to America as constantly improve.

There is a question whether the potato, maize, and tobacco were not cultivated in China ages before Columbus discovered America. A recent traveller says, "The interior of China, along the course of the Yang-tse-Kiang, is a land full of wonders. In one place piscicultural nurseries line the banks for nearly fifty miles. All sorts of inventions, the cotton-gin included, claimed by Europeans and Americans, are to be found there forty centuries old. Plants, yielding drugs of great value, without number, the familiar tobacco and potato, maize, white and yellow corn, and other plants believed to be indigenous to America, have been cultivated there from time immemorial."

Bonafous ("Histoire Naturelle du Mais," Paris, 1826) attributes a European or Asiatic origin to maize. The word maize, (Indian corn) is derived from mahiz or mahis, the name of the plant in the language of the Island of Hayti. And yet, strange to say, in the Lettish and Livonian languages, in the north of Europe, mayse signifies bread; in Irish, maise is food, and in the Old High German, maz is meat. May not likewise the Spanish maiz have antedated the time of Columbus, and borne testimony to early intercommunication between the people of the Old and New Worlds?

It is to Atlantis we must look for the origin of nearly all our valuable plants. Darwin says ("Animals and Plants under Domestication," vol. i., p. 374), "It has often been remarked that we do not owe a single useful plant to Australia, or the Cape of Good Hope—countries abounding to an unparalleled degree with endemic species—or to New Zealand, or to America south of the Plata; and, according to some authors, not to America north of Mexico." In other words, the domesticated plants are only found within the limits of what I shall show hereafter was the Empire of Atlantis and its colonies; for only here was to be found an ancient, long-continuing civilization, capable of developing from a wild state those plants which were valuable to man, including all the cereals on which to-day civilized man depends for subsistence. M. Alphonse de Candolle tells us that we owe 33 useful plants to Mexico, Peru, and Chili. According to the same high authority, of 157 valuable cultivated plants 85 can be traced back to their wild state; as to 40, there is doubt as to their origin; while 32 are utterly unknown in their aboriginal condition. ("Geograph. Botan. Raisonnée," 1855, pp. 810-991.) Certain roses—the imperial lily, the tuberose and the lilac—are said to have been cultivated from such a vast antiquity that they are not known in their wild state. (Darwin, "Animals and Plants," vol. i., p. 370.) And these facts are the more remarkable because, as De Candolle has shown, all the plants historically known to have been first cultivated in

Europe still exist there in the wild state. (Ibid.) The inference is strong that the great cereals—wheat, oats, barley, rye, and maize—must have been first domesticated in a vast antiquity, or in some continent which has since disappeared, carrying the original wild plants with it.

Darwin quotes approvingly the opinion of Mr. Bentham ("Hist. Notes Cult. Plants"), "as the result of all the most reliable evidence that none of the Ceralia—wheat, rye, barley, and oats—exist or have existed truly wild in their present state." In the Stone Age of Europe five varieties of wheat and three of barley were cultivated. (Darwin, "Animals and Plants," vol. i., p. 382.) He says that it may be inferred, from the presence in the lake habitations of Switzerland of a variety of wheat known as the Egyptian wheat, and from the nature of the weeds that grew among their crops, "that the lake inhabitants either still kept up commercial intercourse with some southern people, or had originally proceeded as colonists from the south." I should argue that they were colonists from the land where wheat and barley were first domesticated, to wit, Atlantis. And when the Bronze Age came, we find oats and rye making their appearance with the weapons of bronze, together with a peculiar kind of pea. Darwin concludes (Ibid., vol. i., p. 385) that wheat, barley, rye, and oats were either descended from ten or fifteen distinct species, "most of which are now unknown or extinct," or from four or eight species closely resembling our present forms, or so "widely different as to escape identification;" in which latter case, he says, "man must have cultivated the cereals at an enormously remote period," and at that time practised "some degree of selection."

Rawlinson ("Ancient Monarchies," vol. i., p. 578) expresses the opinion that the ancient Assyrians possessed the pineapple. "The representation on the monuments is so exact that I can scarcely doubt the pineapple being intended." (See Layard's "Nineveh and Babylon," p. 338.) The pineapple (Bromelia ananassa) is supposed to be of American origin, and unknown to Europe before the time of Columbus; and yet, apart from the revelations of the Assyrian monuments, there has been some dispute upon this point. ("Amer. Cyclop.," vol. xiii., p. 528.)

ANCIENT IRISH PIPES

It is not even certain that the use of tobacco was not known to the colonists from Atlantis settled in Ireland in an age long prior to Sir Walter Raleigh. Great numbers of pipes have been found in the raths and tumuli of Ireland, which, there is every reason to believe, were placed there by men of the Prehistoric Period. The illustration on p. 63 represents some of the so-called "Danes' pipes" now in the collection of the Royal Irish Academy. The Danes entered Ireland many centuries before the time of Columbus, and if the pipes are theirs, they must have used tobacco, or some substitute for it, at that early period. It is probable, however, that the tumuli of Ireland antedate the Danes thousands of years.

ANCIENT INDIAN PIPE, NEW JERSEY

Compare these pipes from the ancient mounds of Ireland with the accompanying picture of an Indian pipe of the Stone Age of New Jersey. ("Smithsonian Rep.," 1875, p. 342.)

Recent Portuguese travellers have found the most remote tribes of savage negroes in Africa, holding no commercial intercourse with Europeans, using strangely shaped pipes, in which they smoked a plant of the country. Investigations in America lead to the conclusion that tobacco was first burnt as an incense to the gods, the priest alone using the pipe; and from this beginning the extraordinary practice spread to the people, and thence over all the world. It may have crossed the Atlantic in a remote age, and have subsequently disappeared with the failure of retrograding colonists to raise the tobacco-plant.

PART II. THE DELUGE.

CHAPTER I. THE DESTRUCTION OF ATLANTIS DESCRIBED IN THE DELUGE LEGENDS.

Having demonstrated, as we think successfully, that there is no improbability in the statement of Plato that a large island, almost a continent, existed in the past in the Atlantic Ocean, nay, more, that it is a geological certainty that it did exist; and having further shown that it is not improbable but very possible that it may have sunk beneath the sea in the manner described by Plato, we come now to the next question, Is the memory of this gigantic catastrophe preserved among the traditions of mankind? We think there can be no doubt that an affirmative answer must be given to this question.

An event, which in a few hours destroyed, amid horrible convulsions, an entire country, with all its vast population—that Population the ancestors of the great races of both continents, and they themselves the custodians of the civilization of their age—could not fail to impress with terrible force the minds of men, and to project its gloomy shadow over all human history. And hence, whether we turn to the Hebrews, the Aryans, the Phoenicians, the Greeks, the Cushites, or the inhabitants of America, we find everywhere traditions of the Deluge; and we shall see that all these traditions point unmistakably to the destruction of Atlantis.

François Lenormant says (Contemp. Rev., Nov., 1879): "The result authorizes us to affirm the story of the Deluge to be a universal tradition among all branches of the human race, with the one exception, however, of the black. Now, a recollection thus precise and concordant cannot be a myth voluntarily invented. No religious or cosmogonic myth presents this character of universality. It must arise from the reminiscence of a real and terrible event, so powerfully impressing the imagination of the first ancestors of our race as never to have been forgotten by their descendants. This cataclysm must have occurred near the first cradle of mankind, and before the dispersion of the families from which the principal races were to spring; for it would be at once improbable and uncritical to admit that, at as many different points of the globe as we should have to assume in order to explain the wide spread of these traditions, local phenomena so exactly alike should have occurred, their memory having assumed an identical form, and presenting circumstances that need not necessarily have occurred to the mind in such cases.

"Let us observe, however, that probably the diluvian tradition is not primitive, but imported in America; that it undoubtedly wears the aspect of an importation among the rare populations of the yellow race where it is found; and lastly, that it is doubtful among the Polynesians of Oceania. There will still remain three great races to which it is undoubtedly peculiar, who have not borrowed it from each other, but among whom the tradition is primitive, and goes back to the most ancient times, and these three races are precisely the only ones of which the Bible speaks as being descended from Noah—those of which it gives the ethnic filiation in the tenth chapter of Genesis. This observation, which I hold to be undeniable, attaches a singularly historic and exact value to the tradition as recorded by the Sacred

Book, even if, on the other hand, it may lead to giving it a more limited geographical and ethnological significance....

"But, as the case now stands, we do not hesitate to declare that, far from being a myth, the Biblical Deluge is a real and historical fact, having, to say the least, left its impress on the ancestors of three races—Aryan, or Indo-European, Semitic, or Syro-Arabian, Chamitic, or Cushite—that is to say, on the three great civilized races of the ancient world, those which constitute the higher humanity—before the ancestors of those races had as yet separated, and in the part of Asia they together inhabited."

Such profound scholars and sincere Christians as M. Schoebel (Paris, 1858), and M. Omalius d'Halloy (Bruxelles, 1866), deny the universality of the Deluge, and claim that "it extended only to the principal centre of humanity, to those who remained near its primitive cradle, without reaching the scattered tribes who had already spread themselves far away in almost desert regions. It is certain that the Bible narrative commences by relating facts common to the whole human species, confining itself subsequently to the annals of the race peculiarly chosen by the designs of Providence." (Lenormant and Chevallier, "Anc. Hist. of the East," p. 44.) This theory is supported by that eminent authority on anthropology, M. de Quatrefages, as well as by Cuvier; the Rev. R. p. Bellynck, S.J., admits that it has nothing expressly opposed to orthodoxy.

Plato identifies "the great deluge of all" with the destruction of Atlantis. The priest of Sais told Solon that before "the great deluge of all" Athens possessed a noble race, who performed many noble deeds, the last and greatest of which was resisting the attempts of Atlantis to subjugate them; and after this came the destruction of Atlantis, and the same great convulsion which overwhelmed that island destroyed a number of the Greeks. So that the Egyptians, who possessed the memory of many partial deluges, regarded this as "the great deluge of all."

CHAPTER II. THE DELUGE OF THE BIBLE

We give first the Bible history of the Deluge, as found in Genesis (chap. vi. to chap. viii.):

"And it came to pass, when men began to multiply on the face of the earth, and daughters were born unto them, that the sons of God saw the daughters of men that they were fair; and they took them wives of all which they chose.

"And the Lord said, My Spirit shall not always strive with man, for that he also is flesh: yet his days shall be a hundred and twenty years.

195

"There were giants in the earth in those days; and also after that, when the sons of God came in unto the daughters of men, and they bare children to them, the same became mighty men which were of old, men of renown.

"And God saw that the wickedness of man was great in the earth, and that every imagination of the thoughts of his heart was only evil continually. And it repented the Lord that he had made man on the earth, and it grieved him at his heart. And the Lord said, I will destroy man whom I have created from the face of the earth; both man, and beast, and the creeping thing, and the fowls of the air; for it repenteth me that I have made them. But Noah found grace in the eyes of the Lord.

["These are the generations of Noah: Noah was a just man and perfect in his generations, and Noah walked with God. And Noah begat three sons, Shem, Ham, and Japheth.]

"The earth also was corrupt before God; and the earth was filled with violence. And God looked upon the earth, and, behold, it was corrupt; for all flesh had corrupted his way upon the earth. And God said unto Noah, The end of all flesh is come before me; for the earth is filled with violence through them; and, behold, I will destroy them with the earth. Make thee an ark of gopher wood; rooms shalt thou make in the ark, and shalt pitch it within and without with pitch. And this is the fashion which thou shalt make it of: The length of the ark shall be three hundred cubits, the breadth of it fifty cubits, and the height of it thirty cubits. A window shalt thou make to the ark, and in a cubit shalt thou finish it above; and the door of the ark shalt thou set in the side thereof; with lower, second, and third stories shalt thou make it. And, behold, I, even I, do bring a flood of waters upon the earth, to destroy all flesh, wherein is the breath of life, from under heaven; and everything that is in the earth shall die. But with thee will I establish my covenant; and thou shalt come into the ark, thou, and thy sons, and thy wife, and thy sons' wives with thee. And of every living thing of all flesh, two of every sort shalt thou bring into the ark, to keep them alive with thee; they shall be male and female. Of fowls after their kind, and of cattle after their kind, of every creeping thing of the earth after his kind; two of every sort shall come unto thee, to keep them alive. And take thou unto thee of all food that is eaten, and thou shalt gather it to thee; and it shall be for food for thee, and for them.

"Thus did Noah; according to all that God commanded him, so did he.

"And the Lord said unto Noah, Come thou and all thy house into the ark; for thee have I seen righteous before me in this generation. Of every clean beast thou shalt take to thee by sevens, the male and his female: and of beasts that are not clean by two, the male and his female. Of fowls also of the air by sevens, the male and the female; to keep seed alive upon the face of all the earth. For yet seven days, and I will cause it to rain upon the earth forty days and forty nights; and every living substance that I have made will I destroy from off the face of the earth.

"And Noah did according unto all that the Lord commanded him. And Noah was six hundred years old when the flood of waters was upon the earth.

"And Noah went in, and his sons, and his wife, and his sons' wives with him, into the ark, because of the waters of the flood. Of clean beasts, and of beasts that are not clean, and of fowls, and of everything that creepeth upon the earth, there went in two and two unto Noah into the ark, the male and the female, as God had commanded Noah.

"And it came to pass after seven days, that the waters of the flood were upon the earth. In the six hundredth year of Noah's life, in the second month, the seventeenth day of the month, the same day were all the fountains of the great deep broken up, and the windows of heaven were opened. And the rain was upon the earth forty days and forty nights. In the selfsame day entered Noah, and Shem, and Ham, and Japheth, the sons of Noah, and Noah's wife, and the three wives of his sons with them, into the ark; they, and every beast after his kind, and all the cattle after their kind, and every creeping thing that creepeth upon the earth after his kind, and every fowl after his kind, every bird of every sort. And they went in unto Noah into the ark, two and two of all flesh, wherein is the breath of life. And they that went in, went in male and female of all flesh, as God had commanded him: and the Lord shut him in.

"And the flood was forty days upon the earth; and the waters increased, and bare up the ark, and it was lifted up above the earth. And the waters prevailed, and were increased greatly upon the earth; and the ark went upon the face of the waters. And the waters prevailed exceedingly upon the earth; and all the high hills, that were under the whole heaven, were covered. Fifteen cubits upward did the waters prevail; and the mountains were covered. And all flesh died that moved upon the earth, both of fowl, and of cattle, and of beast, and of every creeping thing that creepeth upon the earth, and every man: all in whose nostrils was the breath of life, of all that was in the dry land, died. And every living substance was destroyed which was upon the face of the ground, both man, and cattle, and the creeping things, and the fowl of the heaven; and they were destroyed from the earth: and Noah only remained alive, and they that were with him in the ark. And the waters prevailed upon the earth a hundred and fifty days.

"And God remembered Noah, and every living thing, and all the cattle that was with him in the ark: and God made a wind to pass over the earth, and the waters assuaged. The fountains also of the deep and the windows of heaven were stopped, and the rain from heaven was restrained. And the waters returned from off the earth continually: and after the end of the hundred and fifty days the waters were abated. And the ark rested in the seventh mouth, on the seventeenth day of the month, upon the mountains of Ararat. And the waters decreased continually until the tenth month: in the tenth month, on the first day of the mouth, were the tops of the mountains seen.

"And it came to pass at the end of forty days, that Noah opened the window of the ark which he had made: and he sent forth a raven, which went forth to and fro, until the waters were dried up from off the earth. Also he sent forth a dove from him, to see if the waters were abated from off the face of the ground. But the dove found no rest for the sole of her foot, and she returned unto him into the ark; for the waters were on the face of the whole earth. Then he put forth his hand, and took her, and pulled her in unto him into the ark. And he stayed yet other seven days; and again he sent forth the dove out of the ark. And the dove came in to him in the evening, and, lo, in her mouth was an olive leaf plucked off: so Noah knew that the waters were abated from off the earth. And he stayed yet other seven days, and sent forth the dove, which returned not again unto him any more.

"And it came to pass in the six hundredth and first year, in the first month, the first day of the month, the waters were dried up from off the earth: and Noah removed the covering of the ark, and looked, and, behold, the face of the ground was dry. And in the second month, on the seven and twentieth day of the month, was the earth dried.

"And God spake unto Noah, saying, Go forth of the ark, thou, and thy wife, and thy sons, and thy sons' wives with thee. Bring forth with thee every living thing that is with thee, of all flesh, both of fowl and of cattle, and of every creeping thing that creepeth upon the earth; that they may breed abundantly in the earth, and be fruitful, and multiply upon the earth.

"And Noah went forth, and his sons, and his wife, and his sons' wives with him: every beast, every creeping thing, and every fowl, and whatsoever creepeth upon the earth, after their kinds, went forth out of the ark.

"And Noah builded an altar unto the Lord; and took of every clean beast, and of every clean fowl, and offered burnt offerings on the altar. And the

Lord smelled a sweet savour; and the Lord said in his heart, I will not again curse the ground any more for man's sake; for the imagination of man's heart is evil from his youth: neither will I again smite any more every thing living, as I have done. While the earth remaineth, seedtime and harvest, and cold and heat, and summer and winter, and day and night shall not cease."

Let us briefly consider this record.

It shows, taken in connection with the opening chapters of Genesis:

1. That the land destroyed by water was the country in which the civilization of the human race originated. Adam was at first naked (Gen., chap. iii., 7); then he clothed himself in leaves; then in the skins of animals (chap. iii., 21): he was the first that tilled the earth, having emerged from a more primitive condition in which he lived upon the fruits of the forest (chap. ii., 16); his son Abel was the first of those that kept flocks of sheep (chap. iv., 2); his son Cain was the builder of the first city (chap. iv., 17); his descendant, Tubal-cain, was the first metallurgist (chap. iv., 22); Jabal was the first that erected tents and kept cattle (chap. iv., 20); Jubal was the first that made musical instruments. We have here the successive steps by which a savage race advances to civilization. We will see hereafter that the Atlanteans passed through precisely similar stages of development.

2. The Bible agrees with Plato in the statement that these Antediluvians had reached great populousness and wickedness, and that it was on account of their wickedness God resolved to destroy them.

3. In both cases the inhabitants of the doomed land were destroyed in a great catastrophe by the agency of water; they were drowned.

4. The Bible tells us that in an earlier age, before their destruction, mankind had dwelt in a happy, peaceful, sinless condition in a Garden of Eden. Plato tells us the same thing of the earlier ages of the Atlanteans.

6. In both the Bible history and Plato's story the destruction of the people was largely caused by the intermarriage of the superior or divine race, "the sons of God," with an inferior stock, "the children of men," whereby they were degraded and rendered wicked.

We will see hereafter that the Hebrews and their Flood legend are closely connected with the Phoenicians, whose connection with Atlantis is established in many ways.

It is now conceded by scholars that the genealogical table given in the Bible (Gen., chap. x.) is not intended to include the true negro races, or the Chinese, the Japanese, the Finns or Lapps, the Australians, or the American red men. It refers altogether to the Mediterranean races, the Aryans, the Cushites, the Phoenicians, the Hebrews, and the Egyptians. "The sons of

Ham" were not true negroes, but the dark-brown races. (See Winchell's "Preadamites," chap. vii.)

If these races (the Chinese, Australians, Americans, etc.) are not descended from Noah they could not have been included in the Deluge. If neither China, Japan, America, Northern Europe, nor Australia were depopulated by the Deluge, the Deluge could not have been universal. But as it is alleged that it did destroy a country, and drowned all the people thereof except Noah and his family, the country so destroyed could not have been Europe, Asia, Africa, America, or Australia, for there has been no universal destruction of the people of those regions; or, if there had been, how can we account for the existence to-day of people on all of those continents whose descent Genesis does not trace back to Noah, and, in fact, about whom the writer of Genesis seems to have known nothing?

We are thus driven to one of two alternative conclusions: either the Deluge record of the Bible is altogether fabulous, or it relates to some land other than Europe, Asia, Africa, or Australia, some land that was destroyed by water. It is not fabulous; and the land it refers to is not Europe, Asia, Africa, or Australia—but Atlantis. No other land is known to history or tradition that was overthrown in a great catastrophe by the agency of water; that was civilized, populous, powerful, and given over to wickedness.

That high and orthodox authority, François Lenormant, says ("Ancient Hist. of the East," vol. i., p. 64), "The descendants of Shem, Ham, and Japhet, so admirably catalogued by Moses, include one only of the races of humanity, the white race, whose three chief divisions he gives us as now recognized by anthropologists. The other three races—yellow, black, and red—have no place in the Bible list of nations sprung from Noah." As, therefore, the Deluge of the Bible destroyed only the land and people of Noah, it could not have been universal. The religious world does not pretend to fix the location of the Garden of Eden. The Rev. George Leo Haydock says, "The precise situation cannot be ascertained; how great might be its extent we do not know;" and we will see hereafter that the unwritten traditions of the Church pointed to a region in the west, beyond the ocean which bounds Europe in that direction, as the locality in which "mankind dwelt before the Deluge."

It will be more and more evident, as we proceed in the consideration of the Flood legends of other nations, that the Antediluvian World was none other than Atlantis.

CHAPTER III. THE DELUGE OF THE CHALDEANS.

We have two versions of the Chaldean story—unequally developed, indeed, but exhibiting a remarkable agreement. The one most anciently known, and also the shorter, is that which Berosus took from the sacred books of Babylon, and introduced into the history that he wrote for the use of the Greeks. After speaking of the last nine antediluvian kings, the Chaldean priest continues thus.

"Obartès Elbaratutu being dead, his son Xisuthros (Khasisatra) reigned eighteen sares (64,800 years). It was under him that the Great Deluge took place, the history of which is told in the sacred documents as follows: Cronos (Ea) appeared to him in his sleep, and announced that on the fifteenth of the month of Daisios (the Assyrian month Sivan—a little before the summer solstice) all men should perish by a flood. He therefore commanded him to take the beginning, the middle, and the end of whatever was consigned to writing, and to bury it in the City of the Sun, at Sippara; then to build a vessel, and to enter it with his family and dearest friends; to place in this vessel provisions to eat and drink, and to cause animals, birds, and quadrupeds to enter it; lastly, to prepare everything for navigation. And when Xisuthros inquired in what direction he should steer his bark, he was answered, 'toward the gods,' and enjoined to pray that good might come of it for men.

"Xisuthros obeyed, and constructed a vessel five stadia long and five broad; he collected all that had been prescribed to him, and embarked his wife, his children, and his intimate friends.

"The Deluge having come, and soon going down, Xisuthros loosed some of the birds. These, finding no food nor place to alight on, returned to the ship. A few days later Xisuthros again let them free, but they returned again to the vessel, their feet full of mud. Finally, loosed the third time, the birds came no more back. Then Xisuthros understood that the earth was bare. He made an opening in the roof of the ship, and saw that it had grounded on the top of a mountain. He then descended with his wife, his daughter, and his pilot, who worshipped the earth, raised an altar, and there sacrificed to the gods; at the same moment he vanished with those who accompanied him.

"Meanwhile those who had remained in the vessel, not seeing Xisutbros return, descended too, and began to seek him, calling him by his name. They saw Xisuthros no more; but a voice from heaven was heard commanding them piety toward the gods; that he, indeed, was receiving the reward of his piety in being carried away to dwell thenceforth in the midst of the gods, and that his wife, his daughter, and the pilot of the ship shared the same honor. The voice further said that they were to return to Babylon, and, conformably to the decrees of fate, disinter the writings buried at Sippara in order to transmit them to men. It added that the country in which they found themselves was Armenia. These, then, having heard the voice, sacrificed to the gods and returned on foot to Babylon. Of the vessel of Xisuthros, which had finally landed in Armenia, a portion is still to be found in the Gordyan Mountains in Armenia, and pilgrims bring thence asphalte that they have scraped from its fragments. It is used to keep off the influence of witchcraft. As to the companions of Xisuthros, they came to Babylon, disinterred the writings left at Sippara, founded numerous cities, built temples, and restored Babylon."

"By the side of this version," says Lenormant, "which, interesting though it be, is, after all, second-hand, we are now able to place an original Chaldeo-Babylonian edition, which the lamented George Smith was the first to decipher on the cuneiform tablets exhumed at Nineveh, and now in the British Museum. Here the narrative of the Deluge appears as an episode in the eleventh tablet, or eleventh chant of the great epic of the town of Uruk. The hero of this poem, a kind of Hercules, whose name has not as yet been made out with certainty, being attacked by disease (a kind of leprosy), goes, with a view to its cure, to consult the patriarch saved from the Deluge, Khasisatra, in the distant land to which the gods have transported him, there to enjoy eternal felicity. He asks Khasisatra to reveal the secret of the events which led to his obtaining the privilege of immortality, and thus the patriarch is induced to relate the cataclysm.

"By a comparison of the three copies of the poem that the library of the palace of Nineveh contained, it has been possible to restore the narrative with hardly any breaks. These three copies were, by order of the King of Assyria, Asshurbanabal, made in the eighth century B.C., from a very ancient specimen in the sacerdotal library of the town of Uruk, founded by the monarchs of the first Chaldean empire. It is difficult precisely to fix the date of the original, copied by Assyrian scribes, but it certainly goes back to the ancient empire, seventeen centuries at least before our era, and even probably beyond; it was therefore much anterior to Moses, and nearly contemporaneous with Abraham. The variations presented by the three existing copies prove that the original was in the primitive mode of writing called the hieratic, a character which must have already become difficult to decipher in the eighth century B.C., as the copyists have differed as to the interpretation to be given to certain signs, and in other cases have simply reproduced exactly the forms of such as they did not understand. Finally, it results from a comparison of these variations, that the original, transcribed by order of Asshurbanabal, must itself have been a copy of some still more ancient manuscript, it, which the original text had already received interlinear comments. Some of the copyists have introduced these into their text, others have omitted them. With these preliminary observations, I proceed to give integrally the narrative ascribed in the poem to Khasisatra:

"'I will reveal to thee, O Izdhubar, the history of my preservation—and tell to thee the decision of the gods.

"'The town of Shurippak, a town which thou knowest, is situated on the Euphrates—it was ancient, and in it [men did not honor] the gods. [I alone, I was] their servant, to the great gods—[The gods took counsel on the appeal of] Ann—[a deluge was proposed by] Bel—[and approved by Nabon, Nergal and] Adar.

"'And the god [Ea], the immutable lord, repeated this command in a dream.—I listened to the decree of fate that he announced, and he said to me:—" Man of Shurippak, son of Ubaratutu—thou, build a vessel and finish it [quickly].—[By a deluge] I will destroy substance and life.—Cause thou to go up into the vessel the substance of all that has life.—The vessel thou shall build—600 cubits shall be the measure of its length—and 60 cubits the amount of its breadth and of its height. [Launch it] thus on the ocean, and cover it with a roof."—I understood, and I said to Ea, my lord:—"[The vessel] that thou commandest me to build thus—[when] I shall do it,—young and old [shall laugh at me.]"—[Ea opened his mouth and] spoke.—He said to me, his servant:—"[If they laugh at thee] thou shalt say to them:—[shall be punished] he who has insulted me, [for the protection of the gods] is over me.— ... like to caverns ... — ... I will exercise my judgment on that which is on high and that which is below ... — ... Close the vessel ... — ... At a given moment that I shall cause thee to know,—enter into it, and draw the door of the ship toward thee.—Within it, thy grains, thy furniture, thy provisions, thy riches, thy men-servants, and thy maid-servants, and thy young people—the cattle of the field, and the wild beasts of the plain that I will assemble—and that I will send thee, shall be kept behind thy door."—Khasisatra opened his mouth and spoke;—he said to Ea, his lord:—"No one has made [such a] ship.—On the prow I will fix ... —I shall see ... and the vessel ... —the vessel thou commandest me to build [thus] which in...."

"'On the fifth day [the two sides of the bark] were raised.—In its covering fourteen in all were its rafters—fourteen in all did it count above.—I placed

203

its roof, and I covered it.—I embarked in it on the sixth day; I divided its floors on the seventh;—I divided the interior compartments on the eighth. I stopped up the chinks through which the water entered in;—I visited the chinks, and added what was wanting.—I poured on the exterior three times 3600 measures of asphalte,—and three times 3600 measures of asphalte within.—Three times 3600 men, porters, brought on their heads the chests of provisions.—I kept 3600 chests for the nourishment of my family,—and the mariners divided among themselves twice 3600 chests.—For [provisioning] I had oxen slain;—I instituted [rations] for each day.—In [anticipation of the need of] drinks, of barrels, and of wine—[I collected in quantity] like to the waters of a river, [of provisions] in quantity like to the dust of the earth.—[To arrange them in] the chests I set my hand to.— ... of the sun ... the vessel was completed.— ... strong and—I had carried above and below the furniture of the ship.—[This lading filled the two-thirds.]

"'All that I possessed I gathered together; all I possessed of silver I gathered together; all that I possessed of gold I gathered—all that I possessed of the substance of life of every kind I gathered together.—I made all ascend into the vessel; my servants, male and female,—the cattle of the fields, the wild beasts of the plains, and the sons of the people, I made them all ascend.

"'Shamash (the sun) made the moment determined, and he announced it in these terms:—"In the evening I will cause it to rain abundantly from heaven; enter into the vessel and close the door."—The fixed moment had arrived, which he announced in these terms:—"In the evening I will cause it to rain abundantly from heaven."—When the evening of that day arrived, I was afraid,—I entered into the vessel and shut my door.—In shutting the vessel, to Buzur-shadi-rabi, the pilot,—I confided this dwelling, with all that it contained.

"'Mu-sheri-ina-namari—rose from the foundations of heaven in a black cloud;—Ramman thundered in the midst of the cloud,—and Nabon and Sharru marched before;—they marched, devastating the mountain and the plain;—Nergal the powerful dragged chastisements after him;—Adar advanced, overthrowing;—before him;—the archangels of the abyss brought destruction,—in their terrors they agitated the earth.—The inundation of Ramman swelled up to the sky,—and [the earth] became without lustre, was changed into a desert.

"'They broke ... of the surface of the earth like...;—[they destroyed] the living beings of the surface of the earth.—The terrible [Deluge] on men swelled up to [heaven]. The brother no longer saw his brother; men no longer knew each other. In heaven—the gods became afraid of the water-spout, and—sought a refuge; they mounted up to the heaven of Anu.—The gods were stretched out motionless, pressing one against another like dogs.—Ishtar wailed like a child, the great goddess pronounced her discourse:—"Here is humanity returned into mud, and—this is the misfortune that I have announced in the presence of the gods.—So I announced the misfortune in the presence of the gods,—for the evil I announced the terrible [chastisement] of men who are mine.—I am the mother who gave birth to men, and—like to the race of fishes, there they are filling the sea;—and the gods, by reason of that—which the archangels of the abyss are doing, weep with me."—The gods on their seats were seated in tears,—and they held their lips closed, [revolving] future things.

"'Six days and as many nights passed; the wind, the water-spout, and the diluvian rain were in all their strength. At the approach of the seventh day the diluvian rain grew weaker, the terrible water-spout—which had assailed after the fashion of an earthquake—grew calm, the sea inclined to dry up, and the wind and the water-spout came to an end. I looked at the sea, attentively observing—and the whole of humanity had returned to mud; like unto sea-weeds the corpses floated. I opened the window, and the light smote on my face. I was seized with sadness; I sat down and I wept;-and my tears came over my face.

"'I looked at the regions bounding the sea: toward the twelve points of the horizon; not any continent.—The vessel was borne above the land of Nizir,—the mountain of Nizir arrested the vessel, and did not permit it to pass over.—A day and a second day the mountain of Nizir arrested the vessel, and did not permit it to pass over;—the third and fourth day the mountain of Nizir arrested the vessel, and did not permit it to pass over;—the fifth and sixth day the mountain of Nizir arrested the vessel, and did not permit it to pass over. At the approach of the seventh day, I sent out and loosed a dove. The dove went, turned, and—found no place to light on, and it came back. I sent out and loosed a swallow; the swallow went, turned, and—found no place to light on, and it came back. I sent out and loosed a raven; the raven went and saw the corpses on the waters; it ate, rested, turned, and came not back.

"'I then sent out (what was in the vessel) toward the four winds, and I offered a sacrifice. I raised the pile of my burnt-offering on the peak of the mountain; seven by seven I disposed the measured vases,—and beneath I spread rushes, cedar, and juniper-wood. The gods were seized with the desire of it—the gods were seized with a benevolent desire of it;—and the gods assembled like flies above the master of the sacrifice. From afar, in approaching, the great goddess raised the great zones that Anu has made for their glory (the gods). These gods, luminous crystal before me, I will never leave them; in that day I prayed that I might never leave them. "Let the gods come to my sacrificial pile!—but never may Bel come to my sacrificial pile! for he did not master himself, and he has made the water-spout for the Deluge, and he has numbered my men for the pit."

"'From far, in drawing near, Bel—saw the vessel, and Bel stopped;—he was filled with anger against the gods and the celestial archangels:—

"'"No one shall come out alive! No man shall be preserved from the abyss!"—Adar opened his mouth and said; he said to the warrior Bel:— "What other than Ea should have formed this resolution?—for Ea possesses knowledge, and [he foresees] all."—Ea opened his mouth and spake; he said to the warrior Bel:—"O thou, herald of the gods, warrior,—as thou didst not master thyself, thou hast made the water-spout of the Deluge.—Let the sinner carry the weight of his sins, the blasphemer the weight of his blasphemy.—Please thyself with this good pleasure, and it shall never be infringed; faith in it never [shall be violated].—Instead of thy making a new deluge, let lions appear and reduce the number of men;—instead of thy making a new deluge, let hyenas appear and reduce the number of men;— instead of thy making a new deluge, let there be famine, and let the earth be [devastated];—instead of thy making a new deluge, let Dibbara appear, and let men be [mown down]. I have not revealed the decision of the great gods;—it is Khasisatra who interpreted a dream and comprehended what the gods had decided."

"'Then, when his resolve was arrested, Bel entered into the vessel.—He took my hand and made me rise.—He made my wife rise, and made her place herself at my side—He turned around us and stopped short; he approached our group.—"Until now Khasisatra has made part of perishable humanity;—but lo, now Khasisatra and his wife are going to be carried away to live like the gods,—and Khasisatra will reside afar at the mouth of the rivers."—They carried me away, and established me in a remote place at the mouth of the streams.'"

"This narrative," says Lenormant, "follows with great exactness the same course as that, or, rather, as those of Genesis; and the analogies are, on both sides, striking."

When we consider these two forms of the same legend, we see many points wherein the story points directly to Atlantis.

1. In the first place, Berosus tells us that the god who gave warning of the coming of the Deluge was Chronos. Chronos, it is well known, was the

same as Saturn. Saturn was an ancient king of Italy, who, far anterior to the founding of Rome, introduced civilization from some other country to the Italians. He established industry and social order, filled the land with plenty, and created the golden age of Italy. He was suddenly removed to the abodes of the gods. His name is connected, in the mythological legends, with "a great Saturnian continent" in the Atlantic Ocean, and a great kingdom which, in the remote ages, embraced Northern Africa and the European coast of the Mediterranean as far as the peninsula of Italy, and "certain islands in the sea;" agreeing, in this respect, with the story of Plato as to the dominions of Atlantis. The Romans called the Atlantic Ocean "Chronium Mare," the Sea of Chronos, thus identifying Chronos with that ocean. The pillars of Hercules were also called by the ancients "the pillars of Chronos."

Here, then, we have convincing testimony that the country referred to in the Chaldean legends was the land of Chronos, or Saturn—the ocean world, the dominion of Atlantis.

2. Hea or Ea, the god of the Nineveh tablets, was a fish-god: he was represented in the Chaldean monuments as half man and half fish; he was described as the god, not of the rivers and seas, but of "the abyss"—to wit, the ocean. He it was who was said to have brought civilization and letters to the ancestors of the Assyrians. He clearly represented an ancient, maritime, civilized nation; he came from the ocean, and was associated with some land and people that had been destroyed by rain and inundations. The fact that the scene of the Deluge is located on the Euphrates proves nothing, for we will see hereafter that almost every nation had its especial mountain on which, according to its traditions, the ark rested; just as every Greek tribe had its own particular mountain of Olympos. The god Bel of the legend was the Baal of the Phoenicians, who, as we shall show, were of Atlantean origin. Bel, or Baal, was worshipped on the western and northern coasts of Europe, and gave his name to the Baltic, the Great and Little Belt, Balesbaugen, Balestranden, etc.; and to many localities, in the British Islands, as, for instance, Belan and the Baal hills in Yorkshire.

3. In those respects wherein the Chaldean legend, evidently the older form of the tradition, differs from the Biblical record, we see that in each instance we approach nearer to Atlantis. The account given in Genesis is the form of the tradition that would be natural to an inland people. Although there is an allusion to "the breaking up of the fountains of the great deep" (about which I shall speak more fully hereafter), the principal destruction seems to have been accomplished by rain; hence the greater period allowed for the Deluge, to give time enough for the rain to fall, and subsequently

207

drain off from the land. A people dwelling in the midst of a continent could not conceive the possibility of a whole world sinking beneath the sea; they therefore supposed the destruction to have been caused by a continuous down-pour of rain for forty days and forty nights.

In the Chaldean legend, on the contrary, the rain lasted but seven days; and we see that the writer had a glimpse of the fact that the destruction occurred in the midst of or near the sea. The ark of Genesis (têbâh) was simply a chest, a coffer, a big box, such as might be imagined by an inland people. The ark of the Chaldeans was a veritable ship; it had a prow, a helm, and a pilot, and men to manage it; and it navigated "the sea."

4. The Chaldean legend represents not a mere rain-storm, but a tremendous cataclysm. There was rain, it is true, but there was also thunder, lightning, earthquakes, wind, a water-spout, and a devastation of mountain and land by the war of the elements. All the dreadful forces of nature were fighting together over the doomed land: "the archangel of the abyss brought destruction," "the water rose to the sky," "the brother no longer saw his brother; men no longer knew each other;" the men "filled the sea like fishes;" the sea was filled with mud, and "the corpses floated like sea-weed." When the storm abated the land had totally disappeared-there was no longer "any continent." Does not all this accord with "that dreadful day and night" described by Plato?

5. In the original it appears that Izdhubar, when he started to find the deified Khasisatra, travelled first, for nine days' journey, to the sea; then secured the services of a boatman, and, entering a ship, sailed for fifteen days before finding the Chaldean Noah. This would show that Khasisatra dwelt in a far country, one only attainable by crossing the water; and this, too, seems like a reminiscence of the real site of Atlantis. The sea which a sailing-vessel required fifteen days to cross must have been a very large body of water; in fact, an ocean.

CHAPTER IV. THE DELUGE LEGENDS OF OTHER NATIONS.

A collection of the Deluge legends of other nations will throw light upon the Biblical and Chaldean records of that great event.

The author of the treatise "On the Syrian Goddess" acquaints us with the diluvian tradition of the Arameans, directly derived from that of Chaldea, as it was narrated in the celebrated Sanctuary of Hierapolis, or Bambyce.

"The generality of people," he says, "tells us that the founder of the temple was Deucalion Sisythes—that Deucalion in whose time the great inundation occurred. I have also heard the account given by the Greeks themselves of Deucalion; the myth runs thus: The actual race of men is not the first, for there was a previous one, all the members of which perished. We belong to a second race, descended from Deucalion, and multiplied in the course of time. As to the former men, they are said to have been full of insolence and pride, committing many crimes, disregarding their oath, neglecting the rights of hospitality, unsparing to suppliants; accordingly, they were punished by an immense disaster. All on a sudden enormous volumes of water issued from the earth, and rains of extraordinary abundance began to fall; the rivers left their beds, and the sea overflowed its shores; the whole earth was covered with water, and all men perished. Deucalion alone, because of his virtue and piety, was preserved alive to give birth to a new race. This is how he was saved: He placed himself, his children, and his wives in a great coffer that he had, in which pigs, horses, lions, serpents, and all other terrestrial animals came to seek refuge with him. He received them all; and while they were in the coffer Zeus inspired them with reciprocal amity, which prevented their devouring one another. In this manner, shut up within one single coffer, they floated as long as the waters remained in force. Such is the account given by the Greeks of Deucalion.

"But to this, which they equally tell, the people of Hierapolis add a marvellous narrative: That in their country a great chasm opened, into which all the waters of the Deluge poured. Then Deucalion raised an altar, and dedicated a temple to Hera (Atargatis) close to this very chasm. I have seen it; it is very narrow, and situated under the temple. Whether it was once large, and has now shrunk, I do not know; but I have seen it, and it is quite small. In memory of the event the following is the rite accomplished: Twice a year sea-water is brought to the temple. This is not only done by the priests, but numerous pilgrims come from the whole of Syria and Arabia, and even from beyond the Euphrates, bringing water. It is poured out in the temple and goes into the cleft, which, narrow as it is, swallows up a considerable quantity. This is said to be in virtue of a religious law instituted by Deucalion to preserve the memory of the catastrophe, and of the benefits that he received from the gods. Such is the ancient tradition of the temple."

"It appears to me difficult," says Lenormant, "not to recognize an echo of fables popular in all Semitic countries about this chasm of Hierapolis, and the part it played in the Deluge, in the enigmatic expressions of the Koran respecting the oven (tannur) which began to bubble and disgorge water all around at the commencement of the Deluge. We know that this tannur has been the occasion of most grotesque imaginings of Mussulman commentators, who had lost the tradition of the story to which Mohammed made allusion. And, moreover, the Koran formally states that the waters of the Deluge were absorbed in the bosom of the earth."

Here the Xisuthros of Berosus becomes Deucalion-Sisythes. The animals are not collected together by Deucalion, as in the case of Noah and Khasisatra, but they crowded into the vessel of their own accord, driven by the terror with which the storm had inspired them; as in great calamities the creatures of the forest have been known to seek refuge in the houses of men.

India affords us an account of the Deluge which, by its poverty, strikingly contrasts with that of the Bible and the Chaldeans. Its most simple and ancient form is found in the Çatapatha Brâhmana of the Rig-Veda. It has been translated for the first time by Max Müller.

"One morning water for washing was brought to Mann, and when he had washed himself a fish remained in his hands, and it addressed these words to him: 'Protect me, and I will save thee.' 'From what wilt thou save me?' 'A deluge will sweep all creatures away;ʻit is from that I will save thee.' 'How shall I protect thee?' The fish replied, 'While we are small we run great dangers, for fish swallow fish. Keep me at first in a vase; when I become too large for it, dig a basin to put me into. When I shall have grown still more, throw me into the ocean; then I shall be preserved from destruction.' Soon it grew a large fish. It said to Mann, 'The very year I shall have reached my full growth the Deluge will happen. Then build a vessel and worship me. When the waters rise, enter the vessel, and I will save thee.'

"After keeping him thus, Mann carried the fish to the sea. In the year indicated Mann built a vessel and worshipped the fish. And when the Deluge came he entered the vessel. Then the fish came swimming up to him, and Mann fastened the cable of the ship to the horn of the fish, by which means the latter made it pass over the Mountain of the North. The fish said, 'I have saved thee; fasten the vessel to a tree, that the water may not sweep it away while thou art on the mountain; and in proportion as the waters decrease thou shalt descend.' Mann descended with the waters, and this is what is called the descent of Mann on the Mountain of the North. The Deluge had carried away all creatures, and Mann remained alone."

There is another form of the Hindoo legend in the Purânas. Lenormant says:

"We must also remark that in the Purânas it is no longer Mann Vaivasata that the divine fish saves from the Deluge, but a different personage, the King of the Dâstas—i. e., fisher—Satyravata, 'the man who loves justice and truth,' strikingly corresponding to the Chaldean Khasisatra. Nor is the Puranic version of the Legend of the Deluge to be despised, though it be of recent date, and full of fantastic and often puerile details. In certain aspects it is less Aryanized than that of Brâhmana or than the Mahâbhârata; and, above all, it gives some circumstances omitted in these earlier versions, which must yet have belonged to the original foundation, since they appear in the Babylonian legend; a circumstance preserved, no doubt, by the oral tradition—popular, and not Brahmanic— with which the Purânas are so deeply imbued. This has already been observed by Pictet, who lays due stress on the following passage of the Bhâgavata-Purâna: 'In seven days,' said Vishnu to Satyravata, 'the three worlds shall be submerged.' There is nothing like this in the Brâhmana nor the Mahâbhârata, but in Genesis the Lord says to Noah, 'Yet seven days and I will cause it to rain upon the earth;' and a little farther we read, 'After seven days the waters of the flood were upon the earth.'... Nor must we pay less attention to the directions given by the fish-god to Satyravata for the placing of the sacred Scriptures in a safe place, in order to preserve them from Hayagriva, a marine horse dwelling in the abyss.... We recognize in it, under an Indian garb, the very tradition of the interment of the sacred writings at Sippara by Khasisatra, such as we have seen it in the fragment of Berosus."

The references to "the three worlds" and the "fish-god" in these legends point to Atlantis. The "three worlds" probably refers to the great empire of Atlantis, described by Plato, to wit, the western continent, America, the eastern continent, Europe and Africa, considered as one, and the island of Atlantis. As we have seen, Poseidon, the founder of the civilization of Atlantis, is identical with Neptune, who is always represented riding a dolphin, bearing a trident, or three-pronged symbol, in his hand, emblematical probably of the triple kingdom. He is thus a sea-god, or fish-god, and he comes to save the representative of his country.

And we have also a new and singular form of the legend in the following. Lenormant says:

"Among the Iranians, in the sacred books containing the fundamental Zoroastrian doctrines, and dating very far back, we meet with a tradition which must assuredly be looked upon as a variety of that of the Deluge, though possessing a special character, and diverging in some essential particulars from those we have been examining. It relates how Yima, who, in the original and primitive conception, was the father of the human race, was warned by Ahuramazda, the good deity, of the earth being about to be devastated by a flood. The god ordered Yima to construct a refuge, a square garden, vara, protected by an enclosure, and to cause the germs of men, beasts, and plants to enter it, in order to escape annihilation. Accordingly, when the inundation occurred, the garden of Yima, with all that it contained, was alone spared, and the message of safety was brought thither by the bird Karshipta, the envoy of Ahuramazda." ("Vendûdid," vol. ii., p. 46.)

This clearly signifies that, prior to the destruction of Atlantis, a colony had been sent out to some neighboring country. These emigrants built a walled town, and brought to it the grains and domestic animals of the mother country; and when the island of Atlantis sunk in the ocean, a messenger brought the terrible tidings to them in a ship.

"The Greeks had two principal legends as to the cataclysm by which primitive humanity was destroyed. The first was connected with the name of Ogyges, the most ancient of the kings of Boeotia or Attica—a quite mythical personage, lost in the night of ages, his very name seemingly derived from one signifying deluge in Aryan idioms, in Sanscrit Angha. It is said that in his time the whole land was covered by a flood, whose waters reached the sky, and from which he, together with some companions, escaped in a vessel.

"The second tradition is the Thessalian legend of Deucalion. Zeus having worked to destroy the men of the age of bronze, with whose crimes he was wroth, Deucalion, by the advice of Prometheus, his father, constructed a coffer, in which he took refuge with his wife, Pyrrha. The Deluge came; the chest, or coffer, floated at the mercy of the waves for nine days and nine nights, and was finally stranded on Mount Parnassus. Deucalion and Pyrrha leave it, offer sacrifice, and, according to the command of Zeus, repeople the world by throwing behind them 'the bones of the earth'—namely, stones, which change into men. This Deluge of Deucalion is, in Grecian tradition, what most resembles a universal deluge. Many authors affirm that it extended to the whole earth, and that the whole human race perished. At Athens, in memory of the event, and to appease the manes of its victims, a ceremony called Hydrophoria was observed, having so close a resemblance to that in use at Hierapolis, in Syria, that we can hardly fail to look upon it as a Syro-Phoenician importation, and the result of an assimilation established in remote antiquity between the Deluge of Deucalion and that of Khasisatra, as described by the author of the treatise 'On the Syrian Goddess.' Close to the temple of the Olympian

Zeus a fissure in the soil was shown, in length but one cubit, through which it was said the waters of the Deluge had been swallowed up. Thus, every year, on the third day of the festival of the Anthestéria, a day of mourning consecrated to the dead—that is, on the thirteenth of the month of Anthestérion, toward the beginning of March—it was customary, as at Bambyce, to pour water into the fissure, together with flour mixed with honey, poured also into the trench dug to the west of the tomb, in the funeral sacrifices of the Athenians."

In this legend, also, there are passages which point to Atlantis. We will see hereafter that the Greek god Zeus was one of the kings of Atlantis. "The men of the age of bronze" indicates the civilization of the doomed people; they were the great metallurgists of their day, who, as we will see, were probably the source of the great number of implements and weapons of bronze found all over Europe. Here, also, while no length of time is assigned to the duration of the storm, we find that the ark floated but nine days and nights. Noah was one year and ten days in the ark, Khasisatra was not half that time, while Deucalion was afloat only nine days.

At Megara, in Greece, it was the eponym of the city, Megaros, son of Zeus and one of the nymphs, Sithnides, who, warned by the cry of cranes of the imminence of the danger of the coming flood, took refuge on Mount Geranien. Again, there was the Thessalian Cerambos, who was said to have escaped the flood by rising into the air on wings given him by the nymphs; and it was Perirrhoos, son of Eolus, that Zeus Naios had preserved at Dodona. For the inhabitants of the Isle of Cos the hero of the Deluge was Merops, son of Hyas, who there assembled under his rule the remnant of humanity preserved with him. The traditions of Rhodes only supposed the Telchines, those of Crete Sasion, to have escaped the cataclysm. In Samothracia the same character was attributed to Saon, said to be the son of Zeus or of Hermes.

It will be observed that in all these legends the name of Zeus, King of Atlantis, reappears. It would appear probable that many parties had escaped from the catastrophe, and had landed at the different points named in the traditions; or else that colonies had already been established by the Atlanteans at those places. It would appear impossible that a maritime people could be totally destroyed; doubtless many were on shipboard in the harbors, and others going and coming on distant voyages.

"The invasion of the East," says Baldwin ('Prehistoric Nations,' p. 396), "to which the story of Atlantis refers, seems to have given rise to the Panathenæ, the oldest, greatest, and most splendid festivals in honor of

Athena celebrated in Attica. These festivals are said to have been established by Erichthonis in the most ancient times remembered by the historical traditions of Athens. Boeckh says of them, in his 'Commentary on Plato:'

"'In the greater Panathenæ there was carried in procession a peplum of Minerva, representing the war with the giants and the victory of the gods of Olympus. In the lesser Panathenæ they carried another peplum (covered with symbolic devices), which showed how the Athenians, supported by Minerva, had the advantage in the war with the Atlantes.' A scholia quoted from Proclus by Humboldt and Boeckh says: 'The historians who speak of the islands of the exterior sea tell us that in their time there were seven islands consecrated to Proserpine, and three others of immense extent, of which the first was consecrated to Pluto, the second to Ammon, and the third to Neptune. The inhabitants of the latter had preserved a recollection (transmitted to them by their ancestors) of the island of Atlantis, which was extremely large, and for a long time held sway over all the islands of the Atlantic Ocean. Atlantis was also consecrated to Neptune.'" (See Humboldt's "Histoire de la Géographie du Nouveau Continent," vol. i.)

No one can read these legends and doubt that the Flood was an historical reality. It is impossible that in two different places in the Old World, remote from each other, religious ceremonies should have been established and perpetuated from age to age in memory of an event which never occurred. We have seen that at Athens and at Hierapolis, in Syria, pilgrims came from a distance to appease the god of the earthquake, by pouring offerings into fissures of the earth said to have been made at the time Atlantis was destroyed.

More than this, we know from Plato's history that the Athenians long preserved in their books the memory of a victory won over the Atlanteans in the early ages, and celebrated it by national festivals, with processions and religious ceremonies.

It is too much to ask us to believe that Biblical history, Chaldean, Iranian, and Greek legends signify nothing, and that even religious pilgrimages and national festivities were based upon a myth.

I would call attention to the farther fact that in the Deluge legend of the Isle of Cos the hero of the affair was Merops. Now we have seen that, according to Theopompus, one of the names of the people of Atlantis was "Meropes."

But we have not reached the end of our Flood legends. The Persian Magi possessed a tradition in which the waters issued from the oven of an old woman. Mohammed borrowed this story, and in the Koran he refers to the Deluge as coming from an oven. "All men were drowned save Noah and his family; and then God said, 'O earth, swallow up thy waters; and thou, O heaven, withhold thy rain;' and immediately the waters abated."

In the bardic poems of Wales we have a tradition of the Deluge which, although recent, under the concise forms of the triads, is still deserving of attention. As usual, the legend is localized in the country, and the Deluge counts among three terrible catastrophes of the island of Prydian, or Britain, the other two consisting of devastation by fire and by drought.

"The first of these events," it is said, "was the eruption of Llyn-llion, or 'the lake of waves,' and the inundation (bawdd) of the whole country, by which all mankind was drowned with the exception of Dwyfam and Dwyfach, who saved themselves in a vessel without rigging, and it was by them that the island of Prydian was repeopled."

Pictet here observes:

"Although the triads in their actual form hardly date farther than the thirteenth or fourteenth century, some of them are undoubtedly connected with very ancient traditions, and nothing here points to a borrowing from Genesis.

"But it is not so, perhaps, with another triad, speaking of the vessel Nefyddnaf-Neifion, which at the time of the overflow of Llyon-llion, bore a pair of all living creatures, and rather too much resembles the ark of Noah. The very name of the patriarch may have suggested this triple epithet, obscure as to its meaning, but evidently formed on the principle of Cymric alliteration. In the same triad we have the enigmatic story of the horned oxen (ychain banog) of Hu the mighty, who drew out of Llyon-llion the avanc (beaver or crocodile?), in order that the lake should not overflow. The meaning of these enigmas could only be hoped from deciphering the chaos of barbaric monuments of the Welsh middle age; but meanwhile we cannot doubt that the Cymri possessed an indigenous tradition of the Deluge."

We also find a vestige of the same tradition in the Scandinavian Edda. Here the story is combined with a cosmogonic myth. The three sons of Borr—Othin, Wili, and We—grandsons of Buri, the first man, slay Ymir, the father of the Hrimthursar, or ice giants, and his body serves them for the construction of the world. Blood flows from his wounds in such abundance that all the race of giants is drowned in it except Bergelmir, who saves himself, with his wife, in a boat, and reproduces the race.

In the Edda of Soemund, "The Vala's Prophecy" (stz. 48-56, p. 9), we seem to catch traditional glimpses of a terrible catastrophe, which reminds us of the Chaldean legend:

"Then trembles Yggdrasil's ash yet standing, groans that ancient tree, and the Jötun Loki is loosed. The shadows groan on the ways of Hel (the goddess of death), until the fire of Surt has consumed the tree. Hyrm steers from the east, the waters rise, the mundane snake is coiled in jötun-rage. The worm beats the water and the eagle screams; the pale of beak tears carcasses; (the ship) Naglfar is loosed. Surt from the south comes with flickering flame; shines from his sword the Valgod's sun. The stony hills are dashed together, the giantesses totter; men tread the path of Hel, and heaven is cloven. The sun darkens, earth in ocean sinks, fall from heaven the bright stars, fire's breath assails the all-nourishing, towering fire plays against heaven itself."

Egypt does not contain a single allusion to the Flood. Lenormant says:

"While the tradition of the Deluge holds so considerable a place in the legendary memories of all branches of the Aryan race, the monuments and original texts of Egypt, with their many cosmogonic speculations, have not afforded one, even distant, allusion to this cataclysm. When the Greeks told the Egyptian priests of the Deluge of Deucalion, their reply was that they had been preserved from it as well as from the conflagration produced by Phaëthon; they even added that the Hellenes were childish in attaching so much importance to that event, as there had been several other local catastrophes resembling it. According to a passage in Manetho, much suspected, however, of being an interpolation, Thoth, or Hermes Trismegistus, had himself, before the cataclysm, inscribed on stelæ, in hieroglyphical and sacred language, the principles of all knowledge. After it the second Thoth translated into the vulgar tongue the contents of these stelæ. This would be the only Egyptian mention of the Deluge, the same Manetho not speaking of it in what remains to us of his 'Dynasties,' his only complete authentic work. The silence of all other myths of the Pharaonic religion on this head render it very likely that the above is merely a foreign tradition, recently introduced, and no doubt of Asiatic and Chaldean origin."

To my mind the explanation of this singular omission is very plain. The Egyptians had preserved in their annals the precise history of the destruction of Atlantis, out of which the Flood legends grew; and, as they told the Greeks, there had been no universal flood, but only local catastrophes. Possessing the real history of the local catastrophe which destroyed Atlantis, they did not indulge in any myths about a universal deluge covering the mountain-tops of all the world. They had no Ararat in their neighborhood.

The traditions of the early Christian ages touching the Deluge pointed to the quarter of the world in which Atlantis was situated.

There was a quaint old monk named Cosmos, who, about one thousand years ago, published a book, "Topographia Christiana," accompanied by a map, in which he gives his view of the world as it was then understood. It was a body surrounded by water, and resting on nothing. "The earth," says Cosmos, "presses downward, but the igneous parts tend upward," and between the conflicting forces the earth hangs suspended,, like Mohammed's coffin in the old story. The accompanying illustration

represents the earth surrounded by the ocean, and beyond this ocean was "the land where men dwelt before the Deluge."

THE WORLD ACCORDING TO COSMOS

He then gives us a more accurate map, in detail, of the known world of his day.

I copy this map, not to show how much more we know than poor Cosmos, but because be taught that all around this habitable world there was yet another world, adhering closely on all sides to the circumscribing walls of heaven. "Upon the eastern side of this transmarine land he judges man was created; and that there the paradise of gladness was located, such as here on the eastern edge is described, where it received our first parents, driven out of Paradise to that extreme point of land on the sea-shore.

MAP OF EUROPE, AFTER COSMOS.

Hence, upon the coming of the Deluge, Noah and his sons were borne by the ark to the earth we now inhabit.

The four rivers he supposes to be gushing up the spouts of Paradise." They are depicted on the above map: O is the Mediterranean Sea; P, the Arabian Gulf; L, the Caspian Sea; Q, the Tigris; M, the river Pison; "and J, the land where men dwelt before the Flood."

It will be observed that, while he locates Paradise in the east, he places the scene of the Deluge in the west; and he supposes that Noah came from the scene of the Deluge to Europe.

This shows that the traditions in the time of Cosmos looked to the west as the place of the Deluge, and that after the Deluge Noah came to the shores of the Mediterranean. The fact, too, that there was land in the west beyond the ocean is recognized by Cosmos, and is probably a dim echo from Atlantean times.

The following rude cut, from Cosmos, represents the high mountain in the north behind which the sun hid himself at night, thus producing the alternations of day and night. His solar majesty is just getting behind the mountain, while Luna looks calmly on at the operation. The mountain is as

crooked as Culhuacan, the crooked mountain of Atzlan described by the Aztecs.

THE MOUNTAIN THE SUN GOES BEHIND AT NIGHT.

CHAPTER V. THE DELUGE LEGENDS OF AMERICA.

"It is a very remarkable fact," says Alfred Maury, "that we find in America traditions of the Deluge coming infinitely nearer to that of the Bible and the Chaldean religion than among any people of the Old World. It is difficult to suppose that the emigration that certainly took place from Asia into North America by the Kourile and Aleutian Islands, and still does so in our day, should have brought in these memories, since no trace is found of them among those Mongol or Siberian populations which were fused with the natives of the New World.... The attempts that have been made to trace the origin of Mexican civilization to Asia have not as yet led to any sufficiently conclusive facts. Besides, had Buddhism, which we doubt, made its way into America, it could not have introduced a myth not found in its own scriptures. The cause of these similarities between the diluvian traditions of the nations of the New World and that of the Bible remains therefore unexplained."

The cause of these similarities can be easily explained: the legends of the Flood did not pass into America by way of the Aleutian Islands, or through the Buddhists of Asia, but were derived from an actual knowledge of Atlantis possessed by the people of America.

Atlantis and the western continent had from an immemorial age held intercourse with each other: the great nations of America were simply colonies from Atlantis, sharing in its civilization, language, religion, and blood. From Mexico to the peninsula of Yucatan, from the shores of Brazil to the heights of Bolivia and Peru, from the Gulf of Mexico to the head-waters of the Mississippi River, the colonies of Atlantis extended; and therefore it is not strange to find, as Alfred Maury says, American traditions of the Deluge coming nearer to that of the Bible and the Chaldean record than those of any people of the Old World.

"The most important among the American traditions are the Mexican, for they appear to have been definitively fixed by symbolic and mnemonic paintings before any contact with Europeans. According to these documents, the Noah of the Mexican cataclysm was Coxcox, called by certain peoples Teocipactli or Tezpi. He had saved himself, together with his wife Xochiquetzal, in a bark, or, according to other traditions, on a raft made of cypress-wood (Cupressus disticha). Paintings retracing the deluge of Coxcox have been discovered among the Aztecs, Miztecs, Zapotecs, Tlascaltecs, and Mechoacaneses. The tradition of the latter is still more strikingly in conformity with the story as we have it in Genesis, and in Chaldean sources. It tells how Tezpi embarked in a spacious vessel with his wife, his children, and several animals, and grain, whose preservation was essential to the subsistence of the human race. When the great god Tezcatlipoca decreed that the waters should retire, Tezpi sent a vulture from the bark. The bird, feeding on the carcasses with which the earth was laden, did not return. Tezpi sent out other birds, of which the humming-bird only came back with a leafy branch in its beak. Then Tezpi, seeing that the country began to vegetate, left his bark on the mountain of Colhuacan.

"The document, however, that gives the most valuable information," says Lenormant, "as to the cosmogony of the Mexicans is one known as 'Codex Vaticanus,' from the library where it is preserved. It consists of four symbolic pictures, representing the four ages of the world preceding the actual one. They were copied at Chobula from a manuscript anterior to the conquest, and accompanied by the explanatory commentary of Pedro de los

Rios, a Dominican monk, who, in 1566, less than fifty years after the arrival of Cortez, devoted himself to the research of indigenous traditions as being necessary to his missionary work."

There were, according to this document, four ages of the world. The first was an age of giants (the great mammalia?) who were destroyed by famine; the second age ended in a conflagration; the third age was an age of monkeys.

"Then comes the fourth age, Atonatiuh, 'Sun of Water,' whose number is 10 X 400 + 8, or 4008. It ends by a great inundation, a veritable deluge. All mankind are changed into fish, with the exception of one man and his wife, who save themselves in a bark made of the trunk of a cypress-tree. The picture represents Matlalcueye, goddess of waters, and consort of Tlaloc, god of rain, as darting down toward earth. Coxcox and Xochiquetzal, the two human beings preserved, are seen seated on a tree-trunk and floating in the midst of the waters. This flood is represented as the last cataclysm that devastates the earth."

The learned Abbé Brasseur de Bourbourg translates from the Aztec language of the "Codex Chimalpopoca" the following Flood legend:

"This is the sun called Nahui-atl, '4 water.' Now the water was tranquil for forty years, plus twelve, and men lived for the third and fourth times. When the sun Nahui-atl came there had passed away four hundred years, plus two ages, plus seventy-six years. Then all mankind was lost and drowned, and found themselves changed into fish. The sky came nearer the water. In a single day all was lost, and the day Nahui-xochitl, '4 flower,' destroyed all our flesh.

"And that year was that of cé-calli, '1 house,' and the day Nahui-atl all was lost. Even the mountains sunk into the water, and the water remained tranquil for fifty-two springs.

"Now at the end of the year the god Titlacahuan had warned Nata and his spouse Nena, saying, 'Make no more wine of Agave, but begin to hollow out a great cypress, and you will enter into it when in the month Tozontli the water approaches the sky.'

"Then they entered in, and when the god had closed the door, he said, 'Thou shalt eat but one ear of maize, and thy wife one also.'

"But as soon as they had finished they went out, and the water remained calm, for the wood no longer moved, and, on opening it, they began to see fish.

"Then they lit a fire, by rubbing together pieces of wood, and they roasted fish.

"The gods Citlallinicué and Citlalatonac, instantly looking down said: 'Divine Lord, what is that fire that is making there? Why do they thus smoke the sky?' At once Titlacahuan-Tezcatlipoca descended. He began to chide, saying, 'Who has made this fire here?' And, seizing hold of the fish, he shaped their loins and heads, and they were transformed into dogs (chichime)."

Here we note a remarkable approximation to Plato's account of the destruction of Atlantis. "In one day and one fatal night," says Plato, "there came mighty earthquakes and inundations that ingulfed that warlike people." "In a single day all was lost," says the Aztec legend. And, instead of a rainfall of forty days and forty nights, as represented in the Bible, here we see "in a single day ... even the mountains sunk into the water;" not only the land on which the people dwelt who were turned into fish, but the very mountains of that land sunk into the water. Does not this describe the fate of Atlantis? In the Chaldean legend "the great goddess Ishtar wailed like a child," saying, "I am the mother who gave birth to men, and, like to the race of fishes, they are filling the sea."

In the account in Genesis, Noah "built an altar unto the Lord, and took of every clean beast, and of every clean fowl, and offered burnt offerings on the altar. And the Lord smelled a sweet savor; and the Lord said in his heart, 'I will not again curse the ground any more for man's sake.'" In the Chaldean legend we are told that Khasisatra also offered a sacrifice, a burnt offering, "and the gods assembled like flies above the master of the sacrifice." But Bel came in a high state of indignation, just as the Aztec god did, and was about to finish the work of the Deluge, when the great god Ea took pity in his heart and interfered to save the remnant of mankind.

These resemblances cannot be accidental; neither can they be the interpolations of Christian missionaries, for it will be observed the Aztec legends differ from the Bible in points where they resemble on the one hand Plato's record, and on the other the Chaldean legend.

The name of the hero of the Aztec story, Nata, pronounced with the broad sound of the a, is not far from the name of Noah or Noe. The Deluge of Genesis is a Phoenician, Semitic, or Hebraic legend, and yet, strange to say, the name of Noah, which occurs in it, bears no appropriate meaning in those tongues, but is derived from Aryan sources; its fundamental root is Na, to which in all the Aryan language is attached the meaning of water— {Greek} na'ein, to flow; {Greek} na~ma, water; Nympha, Neptunus, water deities. (Lenormant and Chevallier, "Anc. Hist. of the East," vol. i., p. 15.)

We find the root Na repeated in the name of this Central American Noah, Na-ta, and probably in the word "Na-hui-atl"—the age of water.

But still more striking analogies exist between the Chaldean legend and the story of the Deluge as told in the "Popul Vuh" (the Sacred Book) of the Central Americans:

"Then the waters were agitated by the will of the Heart of Heaven (Hurakan), and a great inundation came upon the heads of these creatures.... They were ingulfed, and a resinous thickness descended from heaven; ... the face of the earth was obscured, and a heavy darkening rain commenced—rain by day and rain by night.... There was heard a great noise above their heads, as if produced by fire. Then were men seen running, pushing each other, filled with despair; they wished to climb upon their houses, and the houses, tumbling down, fell to the ground; they wished to climb upon the trees, and the trees shook them off; they wished to enter into the grottoes (caves), and the grottoes closed themselves before them.... Water and fire contributed to the universal ruin at the time of the last great cataclysm which preceded the fourth creation."

Observe the similarities here to the Chaldean legend. There is the same graphic description of a terrible event. The "black cloud" is referred to in both instances; also the dreadful noises, the rising water, the earthquake rocking the trees, overthrowing the houses, and crushing even the mountain caverns; "the men running and pushing each other, filled with despair," says the "Popul Vuh;" "the brother no longer saw his brother," says the Assyrian legend.

And here I may note that this word hurakan—the spirit of the abyss, the god of storm, the hurricane—is very suggestive, and testifies to an early intercourse between the opposite shores of the Atlantic. We find in Spanish the word huracan; in Portuguese, furacan; in French, ouragan; in German, Danish, and Swedish, orcan—all of them signifying a storm; while in Latin furo, or furio, means to rage. And are not the old Swedish hurra, to be driven along; our own word hurried; the Icelandic word hurra, to be rattled over frozen ground, all derived from the same root from which the god of the abyss, Hurakan, obtained his name? The last thing a people forgets is the name of their god; we retain to this day, in the names of the days of the week, the designations of four Scandinavian gods and one Roman deity.

It seems to me certain the above are simply two versions of the same event; that while ships from Atlantis carried terrified passengers to tell the story of the dreadful catastrophe to the people of the Mediterranean shores, other ships, flying from the tempest, bore similar awful tidings to the civilized races around the Gulf of Mexico.

The native Mexican historian, Ixtlilxochitl, gave this as the Toltec legend of the Flood:

It is found in the histories of the Toltecs that this age and first world, as they call it, lasted 1716 years; that men were destroyed by tremendous rains and lightning from the sky, and even all the land, without the exception of anything, and the highest mountains, were covered up and submerged in water fifteen cubits (caxtolmolatli); and here they added other fables of how men came to multiply from the few who escaped from this destruction in a "toptlipetlocali;" that this word nearly signifies a close chest; and how, after men had multiplied, they erected a very high "zacuali," which is to-day a tower of great height, in order to take refuge in it should the second world (age) be destroyed. Presently their languages were confused, and, not being able to understand each other, they went to different parts of the earth.

"The Toltecs, consisting of seven friends, with their wives, who understood the same language, came to these parts, having first passed great land and seas, having lived in caves, and having endured great hardships in order to reach this land; ... they wandered 104 years through different parts of the world before they reached Hue Hue Tlapalan, which was in Ce Tecpatl, 520 years after the Flood." ("Ixtlilxochitl Relaciones," in Kingsborough's "Mex. Ant.," vol. ix., pp. 321, 322.)

It will of course be said that this account, in those particulars where it agrees with the Bible, was derived from the teachings of the Spanish priests; but it must be remembered that Ixtlilxochitl was an Indian, a native of Tezeuco, a son of the queen, and that his "Relaciones" were drawn from the archives of his family and the ancient writings of his nation: he had no motive to falsify documents that were probably in the hands of hundreds at that time.

Here we see that the depth of the water over the earth, "fifteen cubits," given in the Toltec legend, is precisely the same as that named in the Bible: "fifteen cubits upward did the waters prevail." (Gen., chap. vii., 20.)

In the two curious picture-histories of the Aztecs preserved in the Boturini collection, and published by Gamelli Careri and others, there is a record of their migrations from their original location through various parts of the North American continent until their arrival in Mexico. In both cases their starting-point is an island, from which they pass in a boat; and the island contains in one case a mountain, and in the other a high temple in the midst thereof. These things seem to be reminiscences of their origin in Atlantis.

THE STARTING POINT OF THE AZTECS
GAMELLI CARERI PICTURED.

BOTURINI PICTURED WRITING

In each case we see the crooked mountain of the Aztec legends, the Calhuacan, looking not unlike the bent mountain of the monk, Cosmos.

In the legends of the Chibchas of Bogota we seem to have distinct reminiscences of Atlantis. Bochica was their leading divinity. During two thousand years he employed himself in elevating his subjects. He lived in the sun, while his wife Chia occupied the moon. This would appear to be an allusion to the worship of the sun and moon. Beneath Bochica in their mythology was Chibchacum. In an angry mood he brought a deluge on the people of the table-land. Bochica punished him for this act, and obliged him ever after, like Atlas, to bear the burden of the earth on his back. Occasionally be shifts the earth from one shoulder to another, and this causes earthquakes!

Here we have allusions to an ancient people who, during thousands of years, were elevated in the scale of civilization, and were destroyed by a deluge; and with this is associated an Atlantean god bearing the world on his back. We find even the rainbow appearing in connection with this legend. When Bochica appeared in answer to prayer to quell the deluge he is seated on a rainbow. He opened a breach in the earth at Tequendama, through which the waters of the flood escaped, precisely as we have seen them disappearing through the crevice in the earth near Bambyce, in Greece.

The Toltecs traced their migrations back to a starting-point called "Aztlan," or "Atlan." This could be no other than, Atlantis. (Bancroft's "Native Races," vol. v., p. 221.) "The original home of the Nahuatlacas was Aztlan, the location of which has been the subject of much discussion. The causes that led to their exodus from that country can only be conjectured; but they may be supposed to have been driven out by their enemies, for Aztlan is described as a land too fair and beautiful to be left willingly in the mere hope of finding a better." (Bancroft's "Native Races," vol. v., p. 306.) The Aztecs also claimed to have come originally from Aztlan. (Ibid., p. 321.) Their very name, Aztecs, was derived from Aztlan. (Ibid., vol. ii., p. 125). They were Atlanteans.

The "Popul Vuh" tells us that after the migration from Aztlan three sons of the King of the Quiches, upon the death of their father, "determined to go as their fathers had ordered to the East, on the shores of the sea whence their fathers had come, to receive the royalty, 'bidding adieu to their brothers and friends, and promising to return.' Doubtless they passed over the sea when they went to the East to receive the royalty. Now this is the name of the lord, of the monarch of the people of the East where they went. And when they arrived before the lord Nacxit, the name of the great lord, the only judge, whose power was without limit, behold he granted them the sign of royalty and all that represents it ... and the insignia of royalty ... all the things, in fact, which they brought on their return, and which they went to receive from the other side of the sea—the art of painting from Tulan, a system of writing, they said, for the things recorded in their histories." (Bancroft's "Native Races," vol. v., p. 553 "Popul Vuh," p. 294.)

This legend not only points to the East as the place of origin of these races, but also proves that this land of the East, this Aztlan, this Atlantis, exercised dominion over the colonies in Central America, and furnished them with the essentials of civilization. How completely does this agree with the statement of Plato that the kings of Atlantis held dominion over parts of "the great opposite continent!"

Professor Valentini ("Maya Archæol.," p. 23) describes an Aztec picture in the work of Gemelli ("Il giro del mondo," vol. vi.) of the migration of the Aztecs from Aztlan:

"Out of a sheet of water there projects the peak of a mountain; on it stands a tree, and on the tree a bird spreads its wings. At the foot of the mountain-peak there comes out of the water the heads of a man and a woman. The one wears on his head the symbol of his name, Coxcox, a pheasant. The other head bears that of a hand with a bouquet (xochitl, a flower, and quetzal, shining in green gold). In the foreground is a boat, out of which a naked man stretches out his hand imploringly to heaven. Now turn to the sculpture in the Flood tablet (on the great Calendar stone). There you will find represented the Flood, and with great emphasis, by the accumulation of all those symbols with which the ancient Mexicans conveyed the idea of water: a tub of standing water, drops springing out— not two, as heretofore in the symbol for Atl, water—but four drops; the picture for moisture, a snail; above, a crocodile, the king of the rivers. In the midst of these symbols you notice the profile of a man with a fillet, and a smaller one of a woman. There can be no doubt these are the Mexican Noah, Coxcox, and his wife, Xochiquetzal; and at the same time it is evident (the Calendar stone, we know, was made in A.D., 1478) that the story of them, and the pictures representing the story, have not been invented by the Catholic clergy, but really existed among these nations long before the Conquest."

The above figure represents the Flood tablet on the great Calendar stone.

When we turn to the uncivilized Indians of America, while we still find legends referring to the Deluge, they are, with one exception, in such garbled and uncouth forms that we can only see glimpses of the truth shining through a mass of fable.

The following tradition was current among the Indians of the Great Lakes:

"In former times the father of the Indian tribes dwelt toward the rising sun. Having been warned in a dream that a deluge was coming upon the earth, he built a raft, on which he saved himself, with his family and all the animals. He floated thus for several months. The animals, who at that time spoke, loudly complained and murmured against him. At last a new earth appeared, on which he landed with all the animals, who from that time lost the power of speech, as a punishment for their murmurs against their deliverer."

According to Father Charlevoix, the tribes of Canada and the valley of the Mississippi relate in their rude legends that all mankind was destroyed by a flood, and that the Good Spirit, to repeople the earth, had changed animals into men. It is to J. S. Kohl we owe our acquaintance with the version of the Chippeways—full of grotesque and perplexing touches—in which the man saved from the Deluge is called Menaboshu. To know if the earth be drying, he sends a bird, the diver, out of his bark; then becomes the restorer of the human race and the founder of existing society.

A clergyman who visited the Indians north-west of the Ohio in 1764 met, at a treaty, a party of Indians from the west of the Mississippi.

"They informed him that one of their most ancient traditions was that, a great while ago, they had a common father, who lived toward the rising of the sun, and governed the whole world; that all the white people's heads were under his feet; that he had twelve sons, by whom he administered the government; that the twelve sons behaved very bad, and tyrannized over the people, abusing their power; that the Great Spirit, being thus angry with them, suffered the white people to introduce spirituous liquors among them, made them drunk, stole the special gift of the Great Spirit from them, and by this means usurped power over them; and ever since the Indians' heads were under the white people's feet." (Boudinot's "Star in the West," p. 111.)

Here we note that they looked "toward the rising sun"—toward Atlantis—for the original home of their race; that this region governed "the whole world;" that it contained white people, who were at first a subject race, but who subsequently rebelled, and acquired dominion over the darker races. We will see reason hereafter to conclude that Atlantis had a composite population, and that the rebellion of the Titans in Greek mythology was the rising up of a subject population.

In 1836 C. S. Rafinesque published in Philadelphia, Pa., a work called "The American Nations," in which he gives the historical songs or chants of the Lenni-Lenapi, or Delaware Indians, the tribe that originally dwelt along the Delaware River. After describing a time "when there was nothing but sea-water on top of the land," and the creation of sun, moon, stars, earth, and man, the legend depicts the Golden Age and the Fall in these words: "All were willingly pleased, all were easy-thinking, and all were well-happified. But after a while a snake-priest, Powako, brings on earth secretly the snake-worship (Initako) of the god of the snakes, Wakon. And there came wickedness, crime, and unhappiness. And bad weather was coming, distemper was coming, with death was coming. All this happened very long ago, at the first land, Netamaki, beyond the great ocean Kitahikau." Then follows the Song of the Flood:

"There was, long ago, a powerful snake, Maskanako, when the men had become bad beings, Makowini. This strong snake had become the foe of the Jins, and they became troubled, hating each other. Both were fighting, both were spoiling, both were never peaceful. And they were fighting, least man Mattapewi with dead-keeper Nihaulowit. And the strong snake readily

227

resolved to destroy or fight the beings or the men. The dark snake he brought, the monster (Amanyam) he brought, snake-rushing water he brought (it). Much water is rushing, much go to hills, much penetrate, much destroying. Meanwhile at Tula (this is the same Tula referred to in the Central American legends), at THAT ISLAND, Nana-Bush (the great hare Nana) becomes the ancestor of beings and men. Being born creeping, he is ready to move and dwell at Tula. The beings and men all go forth from the flood creeping in shallow water or swimming afloat, asking which is the way to the turtle-back, Tula-pin. But there are many monsters in the way, and some men were devoured by them. But the daughter of a spirit helped them in a boat, saying, 'Come, come;' they were coming and were helped. The name of the boat or raft is Mokol.... Water running off, it is drying; in the plains and the mountains, at the path of the cave, elsewhere went the powerful action or motion." Then follows Song 3, describing the condition of mankind after the Flood. Like the Aryans, they moved into a cold country: "It freezes was there; it snows was there; it is cold was there." They move to a milder region to hunt cattle; they divided their forces into tillers and hunters. "The good and the holy were the hunters; they spread themselves north, south, east, and west." Meantime all the snakes were afraid in their huts, and the Snake-priest Nakopowa said to all, 'Let us go.' Eastwardly they go forth at Snakeland (Akhokink), and they went away earnestly grieving." Afterward the fathers of the Delawares, who "were always boating and navigating," find that the Snake-people have taken possession of a fine country; and they collect together the people from north, south, east, and west, and attempt "to pass over the waters of the frozen sea to possess that land." They seem to travel in the dark of an Arctic winter until they come to a gap of open sea. They can go no farther; but some tarry at Firland, while the rest return to where they started from, "the old turtle land."

Here we find that the land that was destroyed was the "first land;" that it was an island "beyond the great ocean." In an early age the people were happy and peaceful; they became wicked; "snake worship" was introduced, and was associated, as in Genesis, with the "fall of man;" Nana-Bush became the ancestor of the new race; his name reminds us of the Toltec Nata and the Hebrew Noah. After the flood came a dispersing of the people, and a separation into hunters and tillers of the soil.

Among the Mandan Indians we not only find flood legends, but, more remarkable still, we find an image of the ark preserved from generation to generation, and a religious ceremony performed which refers plainly to the destruction of Atlantis, and to the arrival of one of those who escaped from the Flood, bringing the dreadful tidings of the disaster. It must be remembered, as we will show hereafter, that many of these Mandan Indians were white men, with hazel, gray, and blue eyes, and all shades of color of the hair from black to pure white; that they dwelt in houses in fortified towns, and manufactured earthen-ware pots in which they could boil water—an art unknown to the ordinary Indians, who boiled water by putting heated stones into it.

I quote the very interesting account of George Catlin, who visited the Mandans nearly fifty years ago, lately republished in London in the "North American Indians," a very curious and valuable work. He says (vol. i., p. 88): "In the centre of the village is an open space, or public square, 150 feet in diameter and circular in form, which is used for all public games and festivals, shows and exhibitions. The lodges around this open space front in, with their doors toward the centre; and in the middle of this stands an object of great religious veneration, on account of the importance it has in connection with the annual religious ceremonies. This object is in the form of a large hogshead, some eight or ten feet high, made of planks and hoops, containing within it some of their choicest mysteries or medicines. They call it the 'Big Canoe.'"

This is a representation of the ark; the ancient Jews venerated a similar image, and some of the ancient Greek States followed in processions a model of the ark of Deucalion. But it is indeed surprising to find this practice perpetuated, even to our own times, by a race of Indians in the heart of America. On page 158 of the first volume of the same work Catlin describes the great annual mysteries and religious ceremonials of which this image of the ark was the centre. He says:

"On the day set apart for the commencement of the ceremonies a solitary figure is seen approaching the village.

"During the deafening din and confusion within the pickets of the village the figure discovered on the prairie continued to approach with a dignified step, and in a right line toward the village; all eyes were upon him, and he at length made his appearance within the pickets, and proceeded toward the centre of the village, where all the chiefs and braves stood ready to receive him, which they did in a cordial manner by shaking hands, recognizing him as an old acquaintance, and pronouncing his name, Nu-mohk-muck-a-nah (the first or only man). The body of this strange personage, which was chiefly naked, was painted with white clay, so as to resemble at a distance a white man. He enters the medicine lodge, and goes through certain mysterious ceremonies.

"During the whole of this day Nu-mohk-muck-a-nah (the first or only man) travelled through the village, stopping in front of each man's lodge, and crying until the owner of the lodge came out and asked who he was, and what was the matter? To which he replied by narrating the sad catastrophe which had happened on the earth's surface by the overflowing of the waters, saying that 'he was the only person saved from the universal calamity; that he landed his big canoe on a high mountain in the west, where he now resides; that he has come to open the medicine lodge, which must needs receive a present of an edged tool from the owner of every wigwam, that it may be sacrificed to the water; for,' he says, 'if this is not done there will be another flood, and no one will be saved, as it was with such tools that the big canoe was made.'

"Having visited every lodge in the village during the day, and having received such a present from each as a hatchet, a knife, etc. (which is undoubtedly always prepared ready for the occasion), be places them in the medicine lodge; and, on the last day of the ceremony, they are thrown into a deep place in the river—'sacrificed to the Spirit of the Waters.'"

Among the sacred articles kept in the great medicine lodge are four sacks of water, called Eeh-teeh-ka, sewed together, each of them in the form of a tortoise lying on its back, with a bunch of eagle feathers attached to its tail. "These four tortoises," they told me, "contained the waters from the four quarters of the world—that those waters had been contained therein ever since the settling down of the waters," "I did not," says Catlin, who knew nothing of an Atlantis theory, "think it best to advance anything against such a ridiculous belief." Catlin tried to purchase one of these water-sacks, but could not obtain it for any price; he was told they were "a society property."

He then describes a dance by twelve men around the ark: "They arrange themselves according to the four cardinal points; two are painted perfectly black, two are vermilion color, some were painted partially white. They dance a dance called Bel-lohck-na-pie,'" with horns on their heads, like those used in Europe as symbolical of Bel, or Baal.

Could anything be more evident than the connection of these ceremonies with the destruction of Atlantis? Here we have the image of the ark; here we have a white man coming with the news that "the waters had overflowed the land," and that all the people were destroyed except himself; here we have the sacrifice to appease the spirit that caused the Flood, just as we find the Flood terminating, in the Hebrew, Chaldean, and Central American legends, with a sacrifice. Here, too, we have the image of the tortoise, which we find in other flood legends of the Indians, and which is a very natural symbol for an island. As one of our own poets has expressed it,

"Very fair and full of promise
Lay the island of St. Thomas;
Like a great green turtle slumbered
On the sea which it encumbered."

Here we have, too, the four quarters of Atlantis, divided by its four rivers, as we shall see a little farther on, represented in a dance, where the dancers arrange themselves according to the four cardinal points of the compass; the dancers are painted to represent the black and red races, while "the first and only man" represents the white race; and the name of the dance is a reminiscence of Baal, the ancient god of the races derived from Atlantis.

But this is not all. The Mandans were evidently of the race of Atlantis. They have another singular legend, which we find in the account of Lewis and Clarke: "Their belief in a future state is connected with this theory of their origin: The whole nation resided in one large village, underground, near a subterranean lake. A grape-vine extended its roots down to their habitation, and gave them a view of the light. Some of the most adventurous climbed up the vine, and were delighted with the sight of the earth, which they found covered with buffalo, and rich with every kind of fruit. Returning with the grapes they had gathered, their countrymen were so pleased with the taste of them that the whole nation resolved to leave their dull residence for the charms of the upper region. Men, women, and children ascended by means of the vine, but, when about half the nation had reached the surface of the earth, a corpulent woman, who was clambering up the vine, broke it with her weight, and closed upon herself and the rest of the nation the light of the sun."

This curious tradition means that the present nation dwelt in a large settlement underground, that is, beyond the land, in the sea; the sea being represented by "the subterranean lake." At one time the people had free intercourse between this "large village" and the American continent, and they founded extensive colonies on this continent; whereupon some mishap cut them off from the mother country. This explanation is confirmed by the fact that in the legends of the Iowa Indians, who were a branch of the Dakotas, or Sioux Indians, and relatives of the Mandans (according to Major James W. Lynd), "all the tribes of Indians were formerly one, and all dwelt together on an island, or at least across a large water toward the east or sunrise. They crossed this water in skin canoes, or by swimming; but they know not how long they were in crossing, or whether the water was salt or fresh." While the Dakotas, according to Major Lynd, who lived among them for nine years, possessed legends of "huge skiffs, in which the Dakotas of old floated for weeks, finally gaining dry land"—a reminiscence of ships and long sea-voyages.

The Mandans celebrated their great religious festival above described in the season when the willow is first in leaf, and a dove is mixed up in the ceremonies; and they further relate a legend that "the world was once a great tortoise, borne on the waters, and covered with earth, and that when one day, in digging the soil, a tribe of white men, who had made holes in the earth to a great depth digging for badgers, at length pierced the shell of the tortoise, it sank, and the water covering it drowned all men with the exception of one, who saved himself in a boat; and when the earth re-emerged, sent out a dove, who returned with a branch of willow in its beak."

The holes dug to find badgers were a savage's recollection of mining operations; and when the great disaster came, and the island sunk in the sea amid volcanic convulsions, doubtless men said it was due to the deep mines, which had opened the way to the central fires. But the recurrence of "white men" as the miners, and of a white man as "the last and only man," and the presence of white blood in the veins of the people, all point to the same conclusion—that the Mandans were colonists from Atlantis.

And here I might add that Catlin found the following singular resemblances between the Mandan tongue and the Welsh:

English.	Mandan.	Welsh.	Pronounced.
I	Me.	Mi.	Me.
You.	Ne.	Chwi.	Chwe.
He.	E.	A.	A.
She.	Ea.	E.	A.
It.	Ount.	Hwynt.	Hooynt.
We.	Noo.	Ni.	Ne.
They.	Eonah.	Hona, *fem.*	Hona.
No; or there is not.	Megosh.	Nagoes.	Nagosh.
No.		Na.	
Head.	Pan.	Pen.	Pan.
The Great Spirit.	Maho Peneta.	Mawr Penæthir.	Mosoor Panæther.

Major Lynd found the following resemblances between the Dakota tongue and the languages of the Old World:

Latin.	English.	Saxon	Sanscrit.	German.	Danish.	Sioux.	Other Languages.	Primary Signification.
	See, seen	Seon		Sehen	Sigt	Sin		Appearing, visible.
Pinso	Pound	Punian				Pau	W., Pwynian	Beating
Vado	Went Wend	Wendan				Winta		Passage.
	Town	Tun		Zaun	Tun	Tonwe	Gaelic, Dun	
Qui	Who	Hwa	Kwas	Wir		Tuwe		
	Weapon	Wepn		Wapen	Vaapen	Wipe		Sioux dimin. Wipena
Ego	I	Ic	Agam	Ich	Jeg	Mish		
Cor	Core					Co	Gr., Kear	Centre, heart
	Eight	Achta	Aute	Acht	Otte	Shaktogan	Gr., Okto	
Canna	Cane					Can	Heb., Can W., Cawn	Reed, weed, wood.
Pock	Pock	Poc		Pocke	Pukkel	Poka	Dutch, Poca	Swelling.
	With	With		Wider		Wita	Goth., Gewithan.	
	Doughty	Dohtig		Taugen	Digtig	Dita Ditaya		Hot, brave, daring.
	Tight	Tian		Dicht	Digt	Titan		Strain.
Tango Tactus	Touch Take	Taecan		Ticken	Tekkan	Tan Htaka		Touch, take.
	Child	Cild		Kind	Kuld	Cin		Progeny.
	Work	Wercan				Woccas Hecon	Dutch, Werk Span.,Hecho	Labor, motion.
	Shackle	Seoacul				Shka	Ar., Schakala, Dutch, Schakel Teton, Shakalan	to bind (a link).
Query						Kuiva		
Shabby				Schabig	Schabbig	Shabya		

COMPARISON OF DAKOTA, OR SIOUX, WITH OTHER LANGUAGES.

According to Major Lynd, the Dakotas, or Sioux, belonged to the same race as the Mandans; hence the interest which attaches to these verbal similarities.

"Among the Iroquois there is a tradition that the sea and waters infringed upon the land, so that all human life was destroyed. The Chickasaws assert that the world was once destroyed by water, but that one family was saved, and two animals of every kind. The Sioux say there was a time when there was no dry land, and all men had disappeared from existence." (See Lynd's "MS. History of the Dakotas," Library of Historical Society of Minnesota.)

"The Okanagaus have a god, Skyappe, and also one called Chacha, who appear to be endowed with omniscience; but their principal divinity is their great mythical ruler and heroine, Scomalt. Long ago, when the sun was no bigger than a star, this strong medicine-woman ruled over what appears to have now become a lost island. At last the peace of the island was destroyed by war, and the noise of battle was heard, with which Scomalt was exceeding wroth, whereupon she rose up in her might and drove her rebellious subjects to one end of the island, and broke off the piece of land on which they were huddled and pushed it out to sea, to drift whither it would. This floating island was tossed to and fro and buffeted by the winds till all but two died. A man and woman escaped in a canoe, and arrived on the mainland; and from these the Okanagaus are descended." (Bancroft's "Native Races," vol. iii., p. 149.)

Here we have the Flood legend clearly connected with a lost island.

The Nicaraguans believed "that ages ago the world was destroyed by a flood, in which the most part of mankind perished. Afterward the teotes, or gods, restored the earth as at the beginning." (Ibid., p. 75.) The wild Apaches, "wild from their natal hour," have a legend that "the first days of the world were happy and peaceful days;" then came a great flood, from which Montezuma and the coyote alone escaped. Montezuma became then very wicked, and attempted to build a house that would reach to heaven, but the Great Spirit destroyed it with thunderbolts. (Bancroft's "Native Races," vol. iii., p. 76.)

The Pimas, an Indian tribe allied to the Papagos, have a peculiar flood legend. The son of the Creator was called Szeu-kha (Ze-us?). An eagle prophesied the deluge to the prophet of the people three times in succession, but his warning was despised; "then in the twinkling of an eye there came a peal of thunder and an awful crash, and a green mound of water reared itself over the plain. It seemed to stand upright for a second, then, cut incessantly by the lightning, goaded on like a great beast, it flung itself upon the prophet's hut. When the morning broke there was nothing to be seen alive but one man—if indeed he were a man; Szeu-kha, the son of the Creator, had saved himself by floating on a ball of gum or resin." This instantaneous catastrophe reminds one forcibly of the destruction of Atlantis. Szeu-kha killed the eagle, restored its victims to life, and repeopled the earth with them, as Deucalion repeopled the earth with the stones.

CHAPTER VI. SOME CONSIDERATION OF THE DELUGE LEGENDS.

The Fountains of the Great Deep.—As Atlantis perished in a volcanic convulsion, it must have possessed volcanoes. This is rendered the more probable when we remember that the ridge of land of which it was a part, stretching from north to south, from Iceland to St. Helena, contains even now great volcanoes—as in Iceland, the Azores, the Canaries, etc.—and that the very sea-bed along the line of its original axis is, to this day, as we have shown, the scene of great volcanic disturbances.

If, then, the mountains of Atlantis contained volcanoes, of which the peaks of the Azores are the surviving representatives, it is not improbable that the convulsion which drowned it in the sea was accompanied by great discharges of water. We have seen that such discharges occurred in the island of Java, when four thousand people perished. "Immense columns of hot water and boiling mud were thrown out" of the volcano of Galung Gung; the water was projected from the mountain "like a water-spout." When a volcanic island was created near Sicily in 1831, it was accompanied by "a waterspout sixty feet high."

In the island of Dominica, one of the islands constituting the Leeward group of the West Indies, and nearest to the site of Atlantis, on the 4th of January, 1880, occurred a series of convulsions which reminds us forcibly of the destruction of Plato's island; and the similarity extends to another particular: Dominica contains, like Atlantis, we are told, numerous hot and sulphur springs. I abridge the account given by the New York Herald of January 28th, 1880:

"A little after 11 o'clock A.M., soon after high-mass in the Roman Catholic cathedral, and while divine service was still going on in the Anglican and Wesleyan chapels, all the indications of an approaching thunder-storm suddenly showed themselves; the atmosphere, which just previously had been cool and pleasant—slight showers falling since early morning—became at once nearly stifling hot; the rumbling of distant thunder was heard, and the light-blue and fleecy white of the sky turned into a heavy and lowering black. Soon the thunder-peals came near and loud, the lightning flashes, of a blue and red color, more frequent and vivid; and the rain, first with a few heavy drops, commenced to pour as if the floodgates of heaven were open. In a moment it darkened, as if night had come; a strong, nearly overpowering smell of sulphur announced itself; and people who happened to be out in the streets felt the rain-drops falling on their heads, backs, and shoulders like showers of hailstones. The cause of this was to be noted by looking at the spouts, from which the water was rushing like so many cataracts of molten lead, while the gutters below ran swollen streams of thick gray mud, looking like nothing ever seen in them before. In the mean time the Roseau River had worked itself into a state of mad fury, overflowing its banks, carrying down rocks and large trees, and threatening destruction to the bridges over it and the houses in its neighborhood. When the storm ceased—it lasted till twelve, mid-day—the roofs and walls of the buildings in town, the street pavement, the door-steps and back-yards were found covered with a deposit of volcanic débris, holding together like clay, dark-gray in color, and in some places more than an inch thick, with small, shining metallic particles on the surface, which could be easily identified as iron pyrites. Scraping up some of the stuff, it required only a slight examination to determine its main constituents— sandstone and magnesia, the pyrites being slightly mixed, and silver showing itself in even smaller quantity. This is, in fact, the composition of the volcanic mud thrown up by the soufrières at Watton Waven and in the Boiling Lake country, and it is found in solution as well in the lake water. The Devil's Billiard-table, within half a mile of the Boiling Lake, is composed wholly of this substance, which there assumes the character of stone in formation. Inquiries instituted on Monday morning revealed the fact that, except on the south-east, the mud shower had not extended beyond the limits of the town. On the north-west, in the direction of Fond Colo and Morne Daniel, nothing but pure rain-water had fallen, and neither Loubière nor Pointe Michel had seen any signs of volcanic disturbance....

"But what happened at Pointe Mulâtre enables us to spot the locale of the eruption. Pointe Mulâtre lies at the foot of the range of mountains on the top of which the Boiling Lake frets and seethes. The only outlet of the lake is a cascade which falls into one of the branches of the Pointe Mulâtre River, the color and temperature of which, at one time and another, shows the existence or otherwise of volcanic activity in the lake-country. We may observe, en passant, that the fall of the water from the lake is similar in appearance to the falls on the sides of Roairama, in the interior of British Guiana; there, is no continuous stream, but the water overleaps its basin like a kettle boiling over, and comes down in detached cascades from the top. May there not be a boiling lake on the unapproachable summit of Roairama? The phenomena noted at Pointe Mulâtre on Sunday were similar to what we witnessed in Roseau, but with every feature more strongly marked. The fall of mud was heavier, covering all the fields; the atmospheric disturbance was greater, and the change in the appearance of the running water about the place more surprising. The Pointe Mulâtre River suddenly began to run volcanic mud and water; then the mud predominated, and almost buried the stream under its weight, and the odor of sulphur in the air became positively oppressive. Soon the fish in the water—brochet, camoo, meye, crocro, mullet, down to the eel, the crawfish, the loche, the tétar, and the dormer—died, and were thrown on the banks. The mud carried down by the river has formed a bank at the month which nearly dams up the stream, and threatens to throw it back over the low-lying lands of the Pointe Mulâtre estate. The reports from the Laudat section of the Boiling Lake district are curious. The Bachelor and Admiral rivers, and the numerous mineral springs which arise in that part of the island, are all running a thick white flood, like cream milk. The face of the entire country, from the Admiral River to the Solfatera Plain, has undergone some portentous change, which the frightened peasants who bring the news to Roseau seem unable clearly and connectedly to describe, and the volcanic activity still continues."

From this account it appears that the rain of water and mud came from a boiling lake on the mountains; it must have risen to a great height, "like a water-spout," and then fallen in showers over the face of the country. We are reminded, in this Boiling Lake of Dominica, of the Welsh legend of the eruption of the Llyn-llion, "the Lake of Waves," which "inundated the whole country." On the top of a mountain in the county of Kerry, Ireland, called Mangerton, there is a deep lake known as Poulle-i-feron, which signifies Hell-hole; it frequently overflows, and rolls down the mountain in frightful torrents. On Slieve-donart, in the territory of Mourne, in the county of Down, Ireland, a lake occupies the mountain-top, and its overflowings help to form rivers.

If we suppose the destruction of Atlantis to have been, in like manner, accompanied by a tremendous outpour of water from one or more of its volcanoes, thrown to a great height, and deluging the land, we can

237

understand the description in the Chaldean legend of "the terrible water-spout," which even "the gods grew afraid of," and which "rose to the sky," and which seems to have been one of the chief causes, together with the earthquake, of the destruction of the country. And in this view we are confirmed by the Aramæan legend of the Deluge, probably derived at an earlier age from the Chaldean tradition. In it we are told, "All on a sudden enormous volumes of water issued from the earth, and rains of extraordinary abundance began to fall; the rivers left their beds, and the ocean overflowed its banks." The disturbance in Dominica duplicates this description exactly: "In a moment" the water and mud burst from the mountains, "the floodgates of heaven were opened," and "the river overflowed its banks."

And here, again, we are reminded of the expression in Genesis, "the same day were all the fountains of the great deep broken up" (chap. vii., 11). That this does not refer to the rain is clear from the manner in which it is stated: "The same day were all the fountains of the great deep broken up, and the windows of heaven were opened. And the rain was upon the earth," etc. And when the work of destruction is finished, we are told "the fountains also of the deep and the windows of heaven were stopped." This is a reminiscence by an inland people, living where such tremendous volcanic disturbances were nearly unknown, of the terrible water-spout which "rose to the sky," of the Chaldean legend, and of "the enormous volumes of water issuing from the earth" of the Aramæan tradition. The Hindoo legend of the Flood speaks of "the marine god Hayagriva, who dwelt in the abyss," who produced the cataclysm. This is doubtless "the archangel of the abyss" spoken of in the Chaldean tradition.

The Mountains of the North.—We have in Plato the following reference to the mountains of Atlantis:

"The whole country was described as being very lofty and precipitous on the side of the sea.... The whole region of the island lies toward the south, and is sheltered from the north.... The surrounding mountains exceeded all that are to be seen now anywhere."

These mountains were the present Azores. One has but to contemplate their present elevation, and remember the depth to which they descend in the ocean, to realize their tremendous altitude and the correctness of the description given by Plato.

In the Hindoo legend we find the fish-god, who represents Poseidon, father of Atlantis, helping Mann over "the Mountain of the North." In the

Chaldean legend Khasisatra's vessel is stopped by "the Mountain of Nizir" until the sea goes down.

THE GOD OF THE FLOOD
(From "The Walls of Ninevah.")

The Mud which Stopped Navigation.—We are told by Plato, "Atlantis disappeared beneath the sea, and then that sea became inaccessible, so that navigation on it ceased, on account of the quantity of mud which the ingulfed island left in its place." This is one of the points of Plato's story which provoked the incredulity and ridicule of the ancient, and even of the modern, world. We find in the Chaldean legend something of the same kind: Khasisatra says, "I looked at the sea attentively, observing, and the whole of humanity had returned to mud." In the "Popol Vuh" we are told that a "resinous thickness descended from heaven," even as in Dominica the rain was full of "thick gray mud," accompanied by an "overpowering smell of sulphur."

The explorations of the ship Challenger show that the whole of the submerged ridge of which Atlantis is a part is to this day thickly covered with volcanic débris.

We have but to remember the cities of Pompeii and Herculaneum, which were covered with such a mass of volcanic ashes from the eruption of A.D. 79 that for seventeen centuries they remained buried at a depth of from fifteen to thirty feet; a new population lived and labored above them; an aqueduct was constructed over their heads; and it was only when a farmer, in digging for a well, penetrated the roof of a house, that they were once more brought to the light of day and the knowledge of mankind.

We have seen that, in 1783, the volcanic eruption in Iceland covered the sea with pumice for a distance of one hundred and fifty miles, "and ships were considerably impeded in their course."

The eruption in the island of Sumbawa, in April, 1815, threw out such masses of ashes as to darken the air. "The floating cinders to the west of Sumatra formed, on the 12th of April, a mass two feet thick and several miles in extent, through which ships with difficulty forced their way."

It thus appears that the very statement of Plato which has provoked the ridicule of scholars is in itself one of the corroborating features of his story. It is probable that the ships of the Atlanteans, when they returned after the tempest to look for their country, found the sea impassable from the masses of volcanic ashes and pumice. They returned terrified to the shores of Europe; and the shock inflicted by the destruction of Atlantis upon the civilization of the world probably led to one of those retrograde periods in the history of our race in which they lost all intercourse with the Western continent.

The Preservation of a Record.—There is a singular coincidence in the stories of the Deluge in another particular.

The legends of the Phoenicians, preserved by Sanchoniathon, tell us that Taautos, or Taut, was the inventor of the alphabet and of the art of writing.

Now, we find in the Egyptian legends a passage of Manetho, in which Thoth (or Hermes Trismegistus), before the Deluge, inscribed on stelæ, or tablets, in hieroglyphics, or sacred characters, the principles of all knowledge. After the Deluge the second Thoth translated the contents of these stelæ into the vulgar tongue.

Josephus tells us that "The patriarch Seth, in order that wisdom and astronomical knowledge should not perish, erected, in prevision of the double destruction by fire and water predicted by Adam, two columns, one of brick, the other of stone, on which this knowledge was engraved, and which existed in the Siriadic country."

In the Chaldean legends the god Ea ordered Khasisatra to inscribe the divine learning, and the principles of all sciences, on tables of terra-cotta, and bury them, before the Deluge, "in the City of the Sun at Sippara."

Berosus, in his version of the Chaldean flood, says:

"The deity, Chronos, appeared to him (Xisuthros) in a vision, and warned him that, upon the 15th day of the month Doesius, there would be a flood by which mankind would be destroyed. He therefore enjoined him to write a history of the beginning, procedure, and conclusion of all things, and to bury it in the City of the Sun at Sippara, and to build a vessel," etc.

The Hindoo Bhâgavata-Purâna tells us that the fish-god, who warned Satyravata of the coming of the Flood, directed him to place the sacred Scriptures in a safe place, "in order to preserve them from Hayagriva, a marine horse dwelling in the abyss."

Are we to find the original of these legends in the following passage from Plato's history of Atlantis?

"Now, the relations of their governments to one another were regulated by the injunctions of Poseidon, as the law had handed them down. These were inscribed by the first then on a column of orichalcum, which was situated in the middle of the island, at the Temple of Poseidon, whither the people were gathered together.... They received and gave judgments, and at daybreak they wrote down their sentences on a golden tablet, and deposited them as memorials with their robes. There were many special laws which the several kings had inscribed about the temples." (Critias, p. 120.)

A Succession of Disasters.—The Central American books, translated by De Bourbourg, state that originally a part of the American continent extended far into the Atlantic Ocean. This tradition is strikingly confirmed by the explorations of the ship Challenger, which show that the "Dolphin's Ridge" was connected with the shore of South America north of the mouth of the Amazon. The Central American books tell us that this region of the continent was destroyed by a succession of frightful convulsions, probably at long intervals apart; three of these catastrophes are constantly mentioned, and sometimes there is reference to one or two more.

"The land," in these convulsions, "was shaken by frightful earthquakes, and the waves of the sea combined with volcanic fires to overwhelm and ingulf it.... Each convulsion swept away portions of the land until the whole disappeared, leaving the line of coast as it now is. Most of the inhabitants, overtaken amid their regular employments, were destroyed; but some escaped in ships, and some fled for safety to the summits of high mountains, or to portions of the land which for a time escaped immediate destruction." (Baldwin's "Ancient America," p. 176.)

This accords precisely with the teachings of geology. We know that the land from which America and Europe were formed once covered nearly or quite the whole space now occupied by the Atlantic between the continents; and it is reasonable to believe that it went down piecemeal, and that Atlantis was but the stump of the ancient continent, which at last perished from the same causes and in the same way.

The fact that this tradition existed among the inhabitants of America is proven by the existence of festivals, "especially one in the month Izcalli, which were instituted to commemorate this frightful destruction of land and people, and in which, say the sacred books, 'princes and people humbled themselves before the divinity, and besought him to withhold a return of such terrible calamities.'"

Can we doubt the reality of events which we thus find confirmed by religious ceremonies at Athens, in Syria, and on the shores of Central America?

And we find this succession of great destructions of the Atlantic continent in the triads of Wales, where traditions are preserved of "three terrible catastrophes." We are told by the explorations of the ship Challenger that the higher lands reach in the direction of the British

Islands; and the Celts had traditions that a part of their country once extended far out into the Atlantic, and was subsequently destroyed.

And the same succession of destructions is referred to in the Greek legends, where a deluge of Ogyges—"the most ancient of the kings of Boeotia or Attica, a quite mythical person, lost in the night of ages"—preceded that of Deucalion.

We will find hereafter the most ancient hymns of the Aryans praying God to hold the land firm. The people of Atlantis, having seen their country thus destroyed, section by section, and judging that their own time must inevitably come, must have lived under a great and perpetual terror, which will go far to explain the origin of primeval religion, and the hold which it took upon the minds of men; and this condition of things may furnish us a solution of the legends which have come down to us of their efforts to perpetuate their learning on pillars, and also an explanation of that other legend of the Tower of Babel, which, as I will show hereafter, was common to both continents, and in which they sought to build a tower high enough to escape the Deluge.

All the legends of the preservation of a record prove that the united voice of antiquity taught that the antediluvians had advanced so far in civilization as to possess an alphabet and a system of writing; a conclusion which, as we will see hereafter, finds confirmation in the original identity of the alphabetical signs used in the old world and the new.

PART III. THE CIVILIZATION OF THE OLD WORLD AND NEW COMPARED.

CHAPTER I. CIVILIZATION AN INHERITANCE.

Material civilization might be defined to be the result of a series of inventions and discoveries, whereby man improves his condition, and controls the forces of nature for his own advantage.

The savage man is a pitiable creature; as Menabosbu says, in the Chippeway legends, he is pursued by a "perpetual hunger;" he is exposed unprotected to the blasts of winter and the heats of summer. A great terror sits upon his soul; for every manifestation of nature—the storm, the wind, the thunder, the lightning, the cold, the heat—all are threatening and dangerous demons. The seasons bring him neither seed-time nor harvest; pinched with hunger, appeasing in part the everlasting craving of his stomach with seeds, berries, and creeping things, he sees the animals of the forest dash by him, and he has no means to arrest their flight. He is powerless and miserable in the midst of plenty. Every step toward civilization is a step of conquest over nature. The invention of the bow and arrow was, in its time, a far greater stride forward for the human race than the steam-engine or the telegraph. The savage could now reach his game—his insatiable hunger could be satisfied; the very eagle, "towering in its pride of place," was not beyond the reach of this new and wonderful weapon. The discovery of fire and the art of cooking was another immense step forward. The savage, having nothing but wooden vessels in which to cook, covered the wood with clay; the day hardened in the fire. The savage gradually learned that he could dispense with the wood, and thus pottery was invented. Then some one (if we are to believe the Chippeway legends, on the shores of Lake Superior) found fragments of the pure copper of that region, beat them into shape, and the art of metallurgy was begun; iron was first worked in the same way by shaping meteoric iron into spear-heads.

But it must not be supposed that these inventions followed one another in rapid succession. Thousands, and perhaps tens of thousands, of years intervened between each step; many savage races have not to this day achieved some of these steps. Prof. Richard Owen says, "Unprepossessed and sober experience teaches that arts, language, literature are of slow growth, the results of gradual development."

I shall undertake to show hereafter that nearly all the arts essential to civilization which we possess date back to the time of Atlantis—certainly to that ancient Egyptian civilization which was coeval with, and an outgrowth from, Atlantis.

In six thousand years the world made no advance on the civilization which it received from Atlantis.

Phoenicia, Egypt, Chaldea, India, Greece, and Rome passed the torch of civilization from one to the other; but in all that lapse of time they added nothing to the arts which existed at the earliest period of Egyptian history. In architecture, sculpture, painting, engraving, mining, metallurgy, navigation, pottery, glass-ware, the construction of canals, roads, and aqueducts, the arts of Phoenicia and Egypt extended, without material change or improvement, to a period but two or three hundred years ago. The present age has entered upon a new era; it has added a series of wonderful inventions to the Atlantean list; it has subjugated steam and electricity to the uses of man. And its work has but commenced: it will continue until it lifts man to a plane as much higher than the present as the present is above the barbaric condition; and in the future it will be said that between the birth of civilization in Atlantis and the new civilization there stretches a period of many thousands of years, during which mankind did not invent, but simply perpetuated.

Herodotus tells us ("Euterpe," cxlii.) that, according to the information he received from the Egyptian priests, their written history dated back 11,340 years before his era, or nearly 14,000 years prior to this time. They introduced him into a spacious temple, and showed him the statues of 341 high-priests who had in turn succeeded each other; and yet the age of Columbus possessed no arts, except that of printing (which was ancient in China), which was not known to the Egyptians; and the civilization of Egypt at its first appearance was of a higher order than at any subsequent period of its history, thus testifying that it drew its greatness from a fountain higher than itself. It was in its early days that Egypt worshipped one only God; in the later ages this simple and sublime belief was buried under the corruptions of polytheism. The greatest pyramids were built by the Fourth Dynasty, and so universal was education at that time among the people that the stones with which they were built retain to this day the writing of the workmen. The first king was Menes.

"At the epoch of Menes," says Winchell, "the Egyptians were already a civilized and numerous people. Manetho tells us that Athotis, the son of this first king, Menes, built the palace at Memphis; that he was a physician, and left anatomical books. All these statements imply that even at this early period the Egyptians were in a high state of civilization." (Winchell's "Preadamites," p. 120.) "In the time of Menes the Egyptians had long been architects, sculptors, painters, mythologists, and theologians." Professor Richard Owen says, "Egypt is recorded to have been a civilized and governed community before the time of Menes. The pastoral community of a group of nomad families, as portrayed in the Pentateuch, may be admitted as an early step in civilization. But how far in advance of this stage is a nation administered by a kingly government, consisting of grades of society, with divisions of labor, of which one kind, assigned to the priesthood, was to record or chronicle the names and dynasties of the kings, the duration and chief events of their reigns!" Ernest Renan points out that "Egypt at the beginning appears mature, old, and entirely without mythical and heroic ages, as if the country had never known youth. Its civilization has no infancy, and its art no archaic period. The civilization of the Old Monarchy did not begin with infancy. It was already mature."

We shall attempt to show that it matured in Atlantis, and that the Egyptian people were unable to maintain it at the high standard at which they had received it, as depicted in the pages of Plato. What king of Assyria, or Greece, or Rome, or even of these modern nations, has ever devoted himself to the study of medicine and the writing of medical books for the benefit of mankind? Their mission has been to kill, not to heal the people; yet here, at the very dawn of Mediterranean history, we find the son of the first king of Egypt recorded "as a physician, and as having left anatomical books."

I hold it to be incontestable that, in some region of the earth, primitive mankind must have existed during vast spaces of time, and under most favorable circumstances, to create, invent, and discover those arts and things which constitute civilization. When we have it before our eyes that for six thousand years mankind in Europe, Asia, and Africa, even when led by great nations, and illuminated by marvellous minds, did not advance one inch beyond the arts of Egypt, we may conceive what lapses, what aeons, of time it must have required to bring savage man to that condition of refinement and civilization possessed by Egypt when it first comes within the purview of history.

That illustrious Frenchman, H. A. Taine ("History of English Literature," p. 23), sees the unity of the Indo-European races manifest in their languages, literature, and philosophies, and argues that these pre-eminent traits are "the great marks of an original model," and that when we meet with them "fifteen, twenty, thirty centuries before our era, in an Aryan, an Egyptian, a Chinese, they represent the work of a great many ages, perhaps of several myriads of centuries.... Such is the first and richest source of these master faculties from which historical events take their rise; and one sees that if it be powerful it is because this is no simple spring, but a kind of lake, a deep reservoir, wherein other springs have, for a multitude of centuries, discharged their several streams." In other words, the capacity of the Egyptian, Aryan, Chaldean, Chinese, Saxon, and Celt to maintain civilization is simply the result of civilized training during "myriads of centuries" in some original home of the race.

I cannot believe that the great inventions were duplicated spontaneously, as some would have us believe, in different countries; there is no truth in the theory that men pressed by necessity will always hit upon the same invention to relieve their wants. If this were so, all savages would

245

have invented the boomerang; all savages would possess pottery, bows and arrows, slings, tents, and canoes; in short, all races would have risen to civilization, for certainly the comforts of life are as agreeable to one people as another.

Civilization is not communicable to all; many savage tribes are incapable of it. There are two great divisions of mankind, the civilized and the savage; and, as we shall show, every civilized race in the world has had something of civilization from the earliest ages; and as "all roads lead to Rome," so all the converging lines of civilization lead to Atlantis. The abyss between the civilized man and the savage is simply incalculable; it represents not alone a difference in arts and methods of life, but in the mental constitution, the instincts, and the predispositions of the soul. The child of the civilized races in his sports manufactures water-wheels, wagons, and houses of cobs; the savage boy amuses himself with bows and arrows: the one belongs to a building and creating race; the other to a wild, hunting stock. This abyss between savagery and civilization has never been passed by any nation through its own original force, and without external influences, during the Historic Period; those who were savages at the dawn of history are savages still; barbarian slaves may have been taught something of the arts of their masters, and conquered races have shared some of the advantages possessed by their conquerors; but we will seek in vain for any example of a savage people developing civilization of and among themselves. I may be reminded of the Gauls, Goths, and Britons; but these were not savages, they possessed written languages, poetry, oratory, and history; they were controlled by religious ideas; they believed in God and the immortality of the soul, and in a state of rewards and punishments after death. Wherever the Romans came in contact with Gauls, or Britons, or German tribes, they found them armed with weapons of iron. The Scots, according to Tacitus, used chariots and iron swords in the battle of the Grampians—"enormes gladii sine mucrone." The Celts of Gaul are stated by Diodorus Siculus to have used iron-headed spears and coats-of-mail, and the Gauls who encountered the Roman arms in B.C. 222 were armed with soft iron swords, as well as at the time when Cæsar conquered their country. Among the Gauls men would lend money to be repaid in the next world, and, we need not add, that no Christian people has yet reached that sublime height of faith; they cultivated the ground, built houses and walled towns, wove cloth, and employed wheeled vehicles; they possessed nearly all the cereals and domestic animals we have, and they wrought in iron, bronze, and steel. The Gauls had even invented a machine on wheels to cut their grain, thus anticipating our reapers and mowers by two thousand years. The difference between the civilization of the Romans under Julius Cæsar and the Gauls under Vercingetorix was a difference in degree and not in kind. The Roman civilization was simply a development and perfection of the civilization possessed by all the European populations; it was drawn from the common fountain of Atlantis.

If we find on both sides of the Atlantic precisely the same arts, sciences, religious beliefs, habits, customs, and traditions, it is absurd to say that the peoples of the two continents arrived separately, by precisely the same steps, at precisely the same ends. When we consider the resemblance of the civilizations of the Mediterranean nations to one another, no man is silly enough to pretend that Rome, Greece, Egypt, Assyria, Phoenicia, each spontaneously and separately invented the arts, sciences, habits, and opinions in which they agreed; but we proceed to trace out the thread of descent or connection from one to another. Why should a rule of interpretation prevail, as between the two sides of the Atlantic, different from that which holds good as to the two sides of the Mediterranean Sea? If, in the one case, similarity of origin has unquestionably produced similarity of arts, customs, and condition, why, in the other, should not similarity of arts, customs, and condition prove similarity of origin? Is there any instance in the world of two peoples, without knowledge of or intercourse with each other, happening upon the same invention, whether that invention be an arrow-head or a steam-engine? If it required of mankind a lapse of at least six thousand years before it began anew the work of invention, and took up the thread of original thought where Atlantis dropped it, what probability is there of three or four separate nations all advancing at the same speed to precisely the same arts and opinions? The proposition is untenable.

If, then, we prove that, on both sides of the Atlantic, civilizations were found substantially identical, we have demonstrated that they must have descended one from the other, or have radiated from some common source.

CHAPTER II. THE IDENTITY OF THE CIVILIZATIONS OF THE OLD WORLD AND THE NEW

Architecture.—Plato tells us that the Atlanteans possessed architecture; that they built walls, temples, and palaces.

We need not add that this art was found in Egypt and all the civilized countries of Europe, as well as in Peru, Mexico, and Central America.

Among both the Peruvians and Egyptians the walls receded inward, and the doors were narrower at the top than at the threshold.

The obelisks of Egypt, covered with hieroglyphics, are paralleled by the round columns of Central America, and both are supposed to have originated in Phallus-worship. "The usual symbol of the Phallus was an erect stone, often in its rough state, sometimes sculptured." (Squier, "Serpent Symbol," p. 49; Bancroft's "Native Races," vol. iii., p. 504.) The worship of Priapus was found in Asia, Egypt, along the European shore of the Mediterranean, and in the forests of Central America.

The mounds of Europe and Asia were made in the same way and for the same purposes as those of America. Herodotus describes the burial of a Scythian king; he says, "After this they set to work to raise a vast mound above the grave, all of them vying with each other, and seeking to make it as tall as possible." "It must be confessed," says Foster ("Prehistoric Races," p. 193), "that these Scythic burial rites have a strong resemblance to those of the Mound Builders." Homer describes the erection of a great symmetrical mound over Achilles, also one over Hector. Alexander the Great raised a great mound over his friend Hephæstion, at a cost of more than a million dollars; and Semiramis raised a similar mound over her husband. The pyramids of Egypt, Assyria, and Phoenicia had their duplicates in Mexico and Central America.

The grave-cists made of stone of the American mounds are exactly like the stone chests, or kistvaen for the dead, found in the British mounds. (Fosters "Prehistoric Races," p. 109.) Tumuli have been found in Yorkshire enclosing wooden coffins, precisely as in the mounds of the Mississippi Valley. (Ibid., p. 185.) The articles associated with the dead are the same in both continents: arms, trinkets, food, clothes, and funeral urns. In both the Mississippi Valley and among the Chaldeans vases were constructed around the bones, the neck of the vase being too small to permit the extraction of the skull. (Foster's "Prehistoric Races," p. 200.)

The use of cement was known alike to the European and American nations.

The use of the arch was known on both sides of the Atlantic.

The manufacture of bricks was known in both the Old and New Worlds.

The style of ornamentation in architecture was much the same on both hemispheres, as shown in the preceding designs, pages 137, 139.

Metallurgy.—The Atlanteans mined ores, and worked in metals; they used copper, tin, bronze, gold, and silver, and probably iron.

The American nations possessed all these metals. The age of bronze, or of copper combined with tin, was preceded in America, and nowhere else, by a simpler age of copper; and, therefore, the working of metals probably originated in America, or in some region to which it was tributary. The Mexicans manufactured bronze, and the Incas mined iron near Lake Titicaca; and the civilization of this latter region, as we will show, probably dated back to Atlantean times. The Peruvians called gold the tears of the sun: it was sacred to the sun, as silver was to the moon.

Sculpture.—The Atlanteans possessed this art; so did the American and Mediterranean nations.

Dr. Arthur Schott ("Smith. Rep.," 1869, p. 391), in describing the "Cara Gigantesca," or gigantic face, a monument of Yzamal, in Yucatan, says, "Behind and on both sides, from under the mitre, a short veil falls upon the shoulders, so as to protect the back of the head and the neck. This particular appendage vividly calls to mind the same feature in the symbolic adornments of Egyptian and Hindoo priests, and even those of the Hebrew hierarchy." Dr. Schott sees in the orbicular wheel-like plates of this statue the wheel symbol of Kronos and Saturn; and, in turn, it may be supposed that the wheel of Kronos was simply the cross of Atlantis, surrounded by its encircling ring.

Painting.—This art was known on both sides of the Atlantic. The paintings upon the walls of some of the temples of Central America reveal a state of the art as high as that of Egypt.

Engraving.—Plato tells us that the Atlanteans engraved upon pillars. The American nations also had this art in common with Egypt, Phoenicia, and Assyria.

Agriculture.—The people of Atlantis were pre-eminently an agricultural people; so were the civilized nations of America and the Egyptians. In Egypt the king put his hand to the plough at an annual festival, thus dignifying and consecrating the occupation of husbandry. In Peru precisely the same custom prevailed. In both the plough was known; in Egypt it was drawn by oxen, and in Peru by men. It was drawn by men in the North of Europe down to a comparatively recent period.

Public Works.—The American nations built public works as great as or greater than any known in Europe. The Peruvians had public roads, one thousand five hundred to two thousand miles long, made so thoroughly as to elicit the astonishment of the Spaniards. At every few miles taverns or hotels were established for the accommodation of travellers. Humboldt pronounced these Peruvian roads "among the most useful and stupendous works ever executed by man." They built aqueducts for purposes of irrigation some of which were five hundred miles long. They constructed magnificent bridges of stone, and had even invented suspension bridges thousands of years before they were introduced into Europe. They had, both in Peru and Mexico, a system of posts, by means of which news was transmitted hundreds of miles in a day, precisely like those known among the Persians in the time of Herodotus, and subsequently among the Romans. Stones similar to mile-stones were placed along the roads in Peru. (See Prescott's "Peru,")

Navigation.—Sailing vessels were known to the Peruvians and the Central Americans. Columbus met, in 1502, at an island near Honduras, a party of the Mayas in a large vessel, equipped with sails, and loaded with a variety of textile fabrics of divers colors.

ANCIENT IRISH VASE OF THE BRONZE AGE

Mannfactures.—The American nations manufactured woollen and cotton goods; they made pottery as beautiful as the wares of Egypt; they manufactured glass; they engraved gems and precious stones. The Peruvians had such immense numbers of vessels and ornaments of gold that the Inca paid with them a ransom for himself to Pizarro of the value of fifteen million dollars.

Music.—It has been pointed out that there is great resemblance between the five-toned music of the Highland Scotch and that of the Chinese and other Eastern nations. ("Anthropology," p. 292.)

Weapons.—The weapons of the New World were identically the same as those of the Old World; they consisted of bows and arrows, spears, darts, short swords, battle-axes, and slings; and both peoples used shields or bucklers, and casques of wood or hide covered with metal. If these weapons had been derived from separate sources of invention, one country or the other would have possessed implements not known to the other, like the blow-pipe, the boomerang, etc. Absolute identity in so many weapons strongly argues identity of origin.

Religion.—The religion of the Atlanteans, as Plato tells us, was pure and simple; they made no regular sacrifices but fruits and flowers; they worshipped the sun.

In Peru a single deity was worshipped, and the sun, his most glorious work, was honored as his representative. Quetzalcoatl, the founder of the Aztecs, condemned all sacrifice but that of fruits and flowers. The first religion of Egypt was pure and simple; its sacrifices were fruits and flowers; temples were erected to the sun, Ra, throughout Egypt. In Peru the great festival of the sun was called Ra-mi. The Phoenicians worshipped Baal and Moloch; the one represented the beneficent, and the other the injurious powers of the sun.

Religious Beliefs.—The Guanches of the Canary Islands, who were probably a fragment of the old Atlantean population, believed in the immortality of the soul and the resurrection of the body, and preserved their dead as mummies. The Egyptians believed in the immortality of the soul and the resurrection of the body, and preserved the bodies of the dead by embalming them. The Peruvians believed in the immortality of the soul and the resurrection of the body, and they too preserved the bodies of their dead by embalming them. "A few mummies in remarkable preservation have been found among the Chinooks and Flatheads." (Schoolcraft, vol. v., p. 693.) The embalmment of the body was also practised in Central America and among the Aztecs. The Aztecs, like the Egyptians, mummified their dead by taking out the bowels and replacing them with aromatic substances. (Dorman, "Origin Prim. Superst.," p. 173.) The bodies of the kings of the Virginia Indians were preserved by embalming. (Beverly, p. 47.)

Here are different races, separated by immense distances of land and ocean, uniting in the same beliefs, and in the same practical and logical application of those beliefs.

The use of confession and penance was known in the religious ceremonies of some of the American nations. Baptism was a religious ceremony with them, and the bodies of the dead were sprinkled with water.

Vestal virgins were found in organized communities on both sides of the Atlantic; they were in each case pledged to celibacy, and devoted to death if they violated their vows. In both hemispheres the recreant were destroyed by being buried alive. The Peruvians, Mexicans, Central Americans, Egyptians, Phoenicians, and Hebrews each had a powerful hereditary priesthood.

The Phoenicians believed in an evil spirit called Zebub; the Peruvians had a devil called Cupay. The Peruvians burnt incense in their temples. The Peruvians, when they sacrificed animals, examined their entrails, and from these prognosticated the future.

I need not add that all these nations preserved traditions of the

Deluge; and all of them possessed systems of writing.

The Egyptian priest of Sais told Solon that the myth of Phaëthon, the son of Helios, having attempted to drive the chariot of the sun, and thereby burning up the earth, referred to "a declination of the bodies moving round the earth and in the heavens" (comets), which caused a "great conflagration upon the earth," from which those only escaped who lived near rivers and seas. The "Codex Chimalpopoca"—a Nahua, Central American record—tells us that the third era of the world, or "third sun," is called, Quia Tonatiuh, or sun of rain, "because in this age there fell a rain of fire, all which existed burned, and there fell a rain of gravel;" the rocks "boiled with tumult, and there also arose the rocks of vermilion color." In other words, the traditions of these people go back to a great cataclysm of fire, when the earth possibly encountered, as in the Egyptian story, one of "the bodies moving round the earth and in the heavens;" they had also memories of "the Drift Period," and of the outburst of Plutonic rocks. If man has existed on the earth as long as science asserts, he must have passed through many of the great catastrophes which are written upon the face of the planet; and it is very natural that in myths and legends he should preserve some recollection of events so appalling and destructive.

Among the early Greeks Pan was the ancient god; his wife was Maia. The Abbé Brasseur de Bourbourg calls attention to the fact that Pan was adored in all parts of Mexico and Central America; and at Panuco, or Panca, literally Panopolis, the Spaniards found, upon their entrance into Mexico, superb temples and images of Pan. (Brasseur's Introduction in Landa's "Relacion.") The names of both Pan and Maya enter extensively into the Maya vocabulary, Maia being the same as Maya, the principal name of the peninsula; and pan, added to Maya, makes the name of the ancient capital Mayapan. In the Nahua language pan, or pani, signifies "equality to that which is above," and Pentecatl was the progenitor of all beings. ("North Americans of Antiquity," p. 467.)

The ancient Mexicans believed that the sun-god would destroy the world in the last night of the fifty-second year, and that he would never come back. They offered sacrifices to him at that time to propitiate him; they extinguished all the fires in the kingdom; they broke all their household furniture; they bung black masks before their faces; they prayed and fasted; and on the evening of the last night they formed a great procession to a neighboring mountain. A human being was sacrificed exactly at midnight; a block of wood was laid at once on the body, and fire was then produced by rapidly revolving another piece of wood upon it; a spark was carried to a funeral pile, whose rising flame proclaimed to the anxious people the promise of the god not to destroy the world for another fifty-two years. Precisely the same custom obtained among the nations of Asia Minor and other parts of the continent of Asia, wherever sun-worship prevailed, at the periodical reproduction of the sacred fire, but not with the same bloody rites as in Mexico. (Valentini, "Maya Archaeology," p. 21.)

To this day the Brahman of India "churns" his sacred fire out of a board by boring into it with a stick; the Romans renewed their sacred fire in the same way; and in Sweden even now a "need-fire is kindled in this manner when cholera or other pestilence is about." (Tylor's "Anthropology," p. 262.)

A belief in ghosts is found on both continents. The American Indians think that the spirits of the dead retain the form and features which they wore while living; that there is a hell and a heaven; that hell is below the earth, and heaven above the clouds; that the souls of the wicked sometimes wander the face of the earth, appearing occasionally to mortals. The story of Tantalus is found among the Chippewayans, who believed that bad souls stand up to their chins in water in sight of the spirit-land, which they can never enter. The dead passed to heaven across a stream of water by means of a narrow and slippery bridge, from which many were lost. The Zuñis set apart a day in each year which they spent among the graves of their dead, communing with their spirits, and bringing them presents—a kind of All-souls-day. (Dorman, "Prim. Superst.," p. 35.) The Stygian flood, and Scylla and Charybdis, are found among the legends of the Caribs. (Ibid., p. 37.) Even the boat of Charon reappears in the traditions of the Chippewayans.

The Oriental belief in the transmigration of souls is found in every American tribe. The souls of men passed into animals or other men.

(Schoolcraft, vol. i., p. 33.) The souls of the wicked passed into toads and wild beasts. (Dorman, "Prim. Superst.," p. 50.)

Among both the Germans and the American Indians lycanthropy, or the metamorphosis of men into wolves, was believed in. In British Columbia the men-wolves have often been seen seated around a fire, with their wolf-hides hung upon sticks to dry! The Irish legend of hunters pursuing an animal which suddenly disappears, whereupon a human being appears in its place is found among all the American tribes.

That timid and harmless animal, the hare, was, singularly enough, an object of superstitious reverence and fear in Europe, Asia, and America. The ancient Irish killed all the hares they found on May-day among their cattle, believing them to be witches. Cæsar gives an account of the horror in which this animal was held by the Britons. The Calmucks regarded the rabbit with fear and reverence. Divine honors were paid to the hare in Mexico. Wabasso was changed into a white rabbit, and canonized in that form.

The white bull, Apis, of the Egyptians, reappears in the Sacred white buffalo of the Dakotas, which was supposed to possess supernatural power, and after death became a god. The white doe of European legend had its representative in the white deer of the Housatonic Valley, whose death brought misery to the tribe. The transmission of spirits by the laying on of hands, and the exorcism of demons, were part of the religion of the American tribes.

The witches of Scandinavia, who produced tempests by their incantations, are duplicated in America. A Cree sorcerer sold three days of fair weather for one pound of tobacco! The Indian sorcerers around Freshwater Bay kept the winds in leather bags, and disposed of them as they pleased.

Among the American Indians it is believed that those who are insane or epileptic are "possessed of devils." (Tylor, "Prim. Cult.," vol. ii., pp. 123-126.) Sickness is caused by evil spirits entering into the sick person. (Eastman's "Sioux.") The spirits of animals are much feared, and their departure out of the body of the invalid is a cause of thanksgiving. Thus an Omaha, after an eructation, says, "Thank you, animal." (Dorman, "Prim. Superst.," p. 55.) The confession of their sins was with a view to satisfy the evil spirit and induce him to leave them. (Ibid., p. 57.)

In both continents burnt-offerings were sacrificed to the gods. In both continents the priests divined the future from the condition of the internal organs of the man or animal sacrificed. (Ibid., pp. 214, 226.) In both continents the future was revealed by the flight of birds and by dreams. In Peru and Mexico there were colleges of augurs, as in Rome, who practised divination by watching the movements and songs of birds. (Ibid., p. 261.)

Animals were worshipped in Central America and on the banks of the Nile. (Ibid., p. 259.)

The Ojibbeways believed that the barking of a fox was ominous of ill. (Ibid., p. 225). The peasantry of Western Europe have the same belief as to the howling of a dog.

The belief in satyrs, and other creatures half man and half animal, survived in America. The Kickapoos are Darwinians. "They think their ancestors had tails, and when they lost them the impudent fox sent every morning to ask how their tails were, and the bear shook his fat sides at the joke." (Ibid., p. 232.) Among the natives of Brazil the father cut a stick at the wedding of his daughter; "this was done to cut off the tails of any future grandchildren." (Tylor, vol. i., p. 384.)

Jove, with the thunder-bolts in his hand, is duplicated in the Mexican god of thunder, Mixcoatl, who is represented holding a bundle of arrows.

"He rode upon a tornado, and scattered the lightnings." (Dorman, "Prim. Superst.," p. 98.)

Dionysus, or Bacchus, is represented by the Mexican god Texcatzoncatl, the god of wine. (Bancroft, vol. iii., p. 418.)

Atlas reappears in Chibchacum, the deity of the Chibchas; he bears the world on his shoulders, and when be shifts the burden from one shoulder to another severe earthquakes are produced. (Bollært, pp.12-13.)

Deucalion repeopling the world is repeated in Xololt, who, after the destruction of the world, descended to Mictlan, the realm of the dead, and brought thence a bone of the perished race. This, sprinkled with blood, grew into a youth, the father of the present race. The Quiche hero-gods, Hunaphu and Xblanque, died; their bodies were burnt, their bones ground to powder and thrown into the waters, whereupon they changed into handsome youths, with the same features as before. (Dorman, "Prim. Superst.," p. 193.)

Witches and warlocks, mermaids and mermen, are part of the mythology of the American tribes, as they were of the European races. (Ibid., p. 79.) The mermaid of the Ottawas was "woman to the waist and fair;" thence fish-like. (Ibid., p. 278.)

The snake-locks of Medusa are represented in the snake-locks of

At-otarho, an ancient culture-hero of the Iroquois.

A belief in the incarnation of gods in men, and the physical translation of heroes to heaven, is part of the mythology of the Hindoos and the American races. Hiawatha, we are told, rose to heaven in the presence of the multitude, and vanished from sight in the midst of sweet music.

The vocal statues and oracles of Egypt and Greece were duplicated in America. In Peru, in the valley of Rimac, there was an idol which answered questions and became famous as an oracle. (Dorman, "Prim. Superst.," p. 124.)

The Peruvians believed that men were sometimes metamorphosed into stones. The Oneidas claimed descent from a stone, as the Greeks from the stones of Deucalion. (Ibid., p. 132.)

Witchcraft is an article of faith among all the American races. Among the Illinois Indians "they made small images to represent those whose days they have a mind to shorten, and which they stab to the heart," whereupon the person represented is expected to die. (Charlevoix, vol. ii., p. 166.) The witches of Europe made figures of wax of their enemies, and gradually melted them at the fire, and as they diminished the victim was supposed to sicken and die.

A writer in the Popular Science Monthly (April, 1881, p. 828) points out the fact that there is an absolute identity between the folk-lore of the negroes on the plantations of the South and the myths and stories of certain tribes of Indians in South America, as revealed by Mr. Herbert Smith's "Brazil, the Amazons, and the Coast." (New York: Scribner, 1879.) Mr. Harris, the author of a work on the folk-lore of the negroes, asks this question, "When did the negro or the North American Indian come in contact with the tribes of South America?"

Customs.—Both peoples manufactured a fermented, intoxicating drink, the one deriving it from barley, the other from maize. Both drank toasts. Both had the institution of marriage, an important part of the ceremony consisting in the joining of hands; both recognized divorce, and the Peruvians and Mexicans established special courts to decide cases of this kind. Both the Americans and Europeans erected arches, and had triumphal processions for their victorious kings, and both strewed the ground before them with leaves and flowers. Both celebrated important events with bonfires and illuminations; both used banners, both invoked blessings. The Phoenicians, Hebrews, and Egyptians practised circumcision. Palacio relates that at Azori, in Honduras, the natives circumcised boys before an idol called Icelca. ("Carta," p. 84.) Lord Kingsborough tells us the Central Americans used the same rite, and McKenzie (quoted by Retzius) says he saw the ceremony performed by the Chippeways. Both had bards and minstrels, who on great festivals sung the deeds of kings and heroes. Both the Egyptians and the Peruvians held agricultural fairs; both took a census of the people. Among both the land was divided per capita among the people; in Judea a new division was made every fifty years. The Peruvians renewed every year all the fires of the kingdom from the Temple of the Sun, the new fire being kindled from concave mirrors by the sun's rays. The Romans under Numa had precisely the same custom. The Peruvians had theatrical plays. They chewed the leaves of the coca mixed with lime, as the Hindoo to-day chews the leaves of the betel mixed with lime. Both the American and European nations were divided into castes; both practised planet-worship; both used scales and weights and mirrors. The Peruvians, Egyptians, and Chaldeans divided the year into twelve months, and the months into lesser divisions of weeks.

Both inserted additional days, so as to give the year three hundred and sixty-five days. The Mexicans added five intercalary days; and the Egyptians, in the time of Amunoph I., had already the same practice.

Humboldt, whose high authority cannot be questioned, by an elaborate discussion ("Vues des Cordilleras," p. 148 et. seq., ed. 1870), has shown the relative likeness of the Nahua calendar to that of Asia. He cites the fact that the Chinese, Japanese, Calmucks, Mongols, Mantchou, and other hordes of Tartars have cycles of sixty years' duration, divided into five brief periods of twelve years each. The method of citing a date by means of signs and numbers is quite similar with Asiatics and Mexicans. He further shows satisfactorily that the majority of the names of the twenty days employed by the Aztecs are those of a zodiac used since the most remote antiquity among the peoples of Eastern Asia.

Cabera thinks he finds analogies between the Mexican and Egyptian calendars. Adopting the view of several writers that the Mexican year began on the 26th of February, he finds the date to correspond with the beginning of the Egyptian year.

The American nations believed in four great primeval ages, as the Hindoo does to this day.

"In the Greeks of Homer," says Volney, "I find the customs, discourse, and manners of the Iroquois, Delawares, and Miamis. The tragedies of Sophocles and Euripides paint to me almost literally the sentiments of the red men respecting necessity, fatality, the miseries of human life, and the rigor of blind destiny." (Volney's "View of the United States.")

The Mexicans represent an eclipse of the moon as the moon being devoured by a dragon; and the Hindoos have precisely the same figure; and both nations continued to use this expression long after they had discovered the real meaning of an eclipse.

The Tartars believe that if they cut with an axe near a fire, or stick a knife into a burning stick, or touch the fire with a knife, they will "cut the top off the fire." The Sioux Indians will not stick an awl or a needle into a stick of wood on the fire, or chop on it with an axe or a knife.

Cremation was extensively practised in the New World. The dead were burnt, and their ashes collected and placed in vases and urns, as in Europe. Wooden statues of the dead were made.

There is a very curious and apparently inexplicable custom, called the "Couvade," which extends from China to the Mississippi Valley; it demands "that, when a child is born, the father must take to his bed, while the mother attends to all the duties of the household." Marco Polo found the custom among the Chinese in the thirteenth century.

The widow tells Hudibras—

"Chineses thus are said

To lie-in in their ladies' stead."

The practice remarked by Marco Polo continues to this day among the hill-tribes of China. "The father of a new-born child, as soon as the mother has become strong enough to leave her couch, gets into bed himself, and there receives the congratulations of his acquaintances." (Max Müller's "Chips from a German Workshop," vol. ii., p. 272.) Strabo (vol. iii., pp. 4, 17) mentions that, among the Iberians of the North of Spain, the women, after the birth of a child, tend their husbands, putting them to bed instead of going themselves. The same custom existed among the Basques only a few years ago. "In Biscay," says M. F. Michel, "the women rise immediately after childbirth and attend to the duties of the household, while the husband goes to bed, taking the baby with him, and thus receives the neighbors' compliments." The same custom was found in France, and is said to exist to this day in some cantons of Béarn. Diodorus Siculus tells us that among the Corsicans the wife was neglected, and the husband put to bed and treated as the patient. Apollonius Rhodius says that among the Tibereni, at the south of the Black Sea, "when a child was born the father lay groaning, with his head tied up, while the mother tended him with food and prepared his baths." The same absurd custom extends throughout the tribes of North and South America. Among the Caribs in the West Indies (and the Caribs, Brasseur de Bourbourg says, were the same as the ancient Carians of the Mediterranean Sea) the man takes to his bed as soon as a child is born, and kills no animals. And herein we find an explanation of a custom otherwise inexplicable. Among the American Indians it is believed that, if the father kills an animal during the infancy of the child, the spirit of the animal will revenge itself by inflicting some disease upon the helpless little one. "For six months the Carib father must not eat birds or fish, for what ever animals he eats will impress their likeness on the child, or produce disease by entering its body." (Dorman, "Prim. Superst.," p. 58.) Among the Abipones the husband goes to bed, fasts a number of days, "and you would think," says Dobrizboffer, "that it was he that had had the child." The Brazilian father takes to his hammock during and after the birth of the child, and for fifteen days eats no meat and hunts no game. Among the Esquimaux the husbands forbear hunting during the lying-in of their wives and for some time thereafter.

Here, then, we have a very extraordinary and unnatural custom, existing to this day on both sides of the Atlantic, reaching back to a vast antiquity, and finding its explanation only in the superstition of the American races. A practice so absurd could scarcely have originated separately in the two continents; its existence is a very strong proof of unity of origin of the races on the opposite sides of the Atlantic; and the fact that the custom and the reason for it are both found in America, while the custom remains in Europe without the reason, would imply that the American population was the older of the two.

The Indian practice of depositing weapons and food with the dead was universal in ancient Europe, and in German villages nowadays a needle and thread is placed in the coffin for the dead to mend their torn clothes with; "while all over Europe the dead man had a piece of money put in his hand to pay his way with." ("Anthropology," p. 347.)

The American Indian leaves food with the dead; the Russian peasant puts crumbs of bread behind the saints' pictures on the little iron shelf, and believes that the souls of his forefathers creep in and out and eat them. At the cemetery of Père-la-Chaise, Paris, on All-souls-day, they "still put cakes and sweetmeats on the graves; and in Brittany the peasants that night do not forget to make up the fire and leave the fragments of the supper on the table for the souls of the dead." (Ibid., p. 351.)

The Indian prays to the spirits of his forefathers; the Chinese religion is largely "ancestor-worship;" and the rites paid to the dead ancestors, or lares, held the Roman family together." ("Anthropology," p. 351.)

We find the Indian practice of burying the dead in a sitting posture in use among the Nasamonians, tribe of Libyans. Herodotus, speaking of the wandering tribes of Northern Africa, says, "They bury their dead according to the fashion of the Greeks.... They bury them sitting, and are right careful, when the sick man is at the point of giving up the ghost, to make him sit, and not let him die lying down."

The dead bodies of the caciques of Bogota were protected from desecration by diverting the course of a river and making the grave in its bed, and then letting the stream return to its natural course. Alaric, the leader of the Goths, was secretly buried in the same way. (Dorman, "Prim. Superst.," p. 195.)

Among the American tribes no man is permitted to marry a wife of the same clan-name or totem as himself. In India a Brahman is not allowed to marry a wife whose clan-name (her "cow-stall," as they say) is the same as his own; nor may a Chinaman take a wife of his own surname.

("Anthropology," p. 403.) "Throughout India the hill-tribes are divided into septs or clans, and a man may not marry a woman belonging to his own clan. The Calmucks of Tartary are divided into hordes, and a man may not marry a girl of his own horde. The same custom prevails among the Circassians and the Samoyeds of Siberia. The Ostyaks and Yakuts regard it as a crime to marry a woman of the same family, or even of the same name." (Sir John Lubbock, "Smith. Rep.," p. 347, 1869.)

Sutteeism—the burning of the widow upon the funeral-pile of the husband—was extensively practised in America (West's "Journal," p. 141); as was also the practice of sacrificing warriors, servants, and animals at the funeral of a great chief (Dorman, pp. 210-211.) Beautiful girls were sacrificed to appease the anger of the gods, as among the Mediterranean races. (Bancroft, vol. iii., p. 471.) Fathers offered up their children for a like purpose, as among the Carthaginians.

The poisoned arrows of America had their representatives in Europe. Odysseus went to Ephyra for the man-slaying drug with which to smear his bronze-tipped arrows. (Tylor's "Anthropology," p. 237.)

"The bark canoe of America was not unknown in Asia and Africa" (Ibid., p. 254), while the skin canoes of our Indians and the Esquimaux were found on the shores of the Thames and the Euphrates. In Peru and on the Euphrates commerce was carried on upon rafts supported by inflated skins. They are still used on the Tigris.

The Indian boils his meat by dropping red-hot stones into a water-vessel made of hide; and Linnæus found the Both land people brewing beer in this way—"and to this day the rude Carinthian boor drinks such stone-beer, as it is called." (Ibid., p. 266.)

In the buffalo dance of the Mandan Indians the dancers covered their heads with a mask made of the head and horns of the buffalo. To-day in the temples of India, or among the lamas of Thibet, the priests dance the demons out, or the new year in, arrayed in animal masks (Ibid., p. 297); and the "mummers" at Yule-tide, in England, are a survival of the same custom. (Ibid., p. 298.) The North American dog and bear dances, wherein the dancers acted the part of those animals, had their prototype in the Greek dances at the festivals of Dionysia. (Ibid., p. 298.)

Tattooing was practised in both continents. Among the Indians it was fetichistic in its origin; "every Indian had the image of an animal tattooed on his breast or arm, to charm away evil spirits." (Dorman, "Prim. Superst.," p. 156.) The sailors of Europe and America preserve to this day a custom which was once universal among the ancient races. Banners, flags, and armorial bearings are supposed to be survivals of the old totemic tattooing. The Arab woman still tattoos her face, arms, and ankles. The war-paint of the American savage reappeared in the woad with which the ancient Briton stained his body; and Tylor suggests that the painted stripes on the circus clown are a survival of a custom once universal. (Tylor's "Anthropology," p. 327.)

In America, as in the Old World, the temples of worship were built over the dead., (Dorman, "Prim. Superst.," p. 178.) Says Prudentius, the Roman bard, "there were as many temples of gods as sepulchres."

The Etruscan belief that evil spirits strove for the possession of the dead was found among the Mosquito Indians. (Bancroft, "Native Races," vol. i., p. 744)

The belief in fairies, which forms so large a part of the folklore of Western Europe, is found among the American races. The Ojibbeways see thousands of fairies dancing in a sunbeam; during a rain myriads of them bide in the flowers. When disturbed they disappear underground. They have their dances, like the Irish fairies; and, like them, they kill the domestic animals of those who offend them. The Dakotas also believe in fairies. The Otoes located the "little people" in a mound at the mouth of Whitestone River; they were eighteen inches high, with very large heads; they were armed with bows and arrows, and killed those who approached their residence. (See Dorman's "Origin of Primitive Superstitions," p. 23.) "The Shoshone legends people the mountains of Montana with little imps, called Nirumbees, two feet long, naked, and with a tail." They stole the children of the Indians, and left in their stead the young of their own baneful race, who resembled the stolen children so much that the mothers were deceived and suckled them, whereupon they died. This greatly resembles the European belief in "changelings." (Ibid., p. 24.)

In both continents we find tree-worship. In Mexico and Central America cypresses and palms were planted near the temples, generally in groups of threes; they were tended with great care, and received offerings of incense and gifts. The same custom prevailed among the Romans—the cypress was dedicated to Pluto, and the palm to Victory.

Not only infant baptism by water was found both in the old Babylonian religion and among the Mexicans, but an offering of cakes, which is recorded by the prophet Jeremiah as part of the worship of the Babylonian goddess-mother, "the Queen of Heaven," was also found in the ritual of the Aztecs. ("Builders of Babel," p. 78.)

In Babylonia, China, and Mexico the caste at the bottom of the social scale lived upon floating islands of reeds or rafts, covered with earth, on the lakes and rivers.

In Peru and Babylonia marriages were made but once a year, at a public festival.

Among the Romans, the Chinese, the Abyssinians, and the Indians of Canada the singular custom prevails of lifting the bride over the door-step of her husband's home. The bride-cake which so invariably accompanies a wedding among ourselves, and which must always be cut by the bride, may be traced back to the old Roman form of marriage by 'conferreatio,' or eating together. So, also, among the Iroquois the bride and bridegroom used to partake together of a cake of sagamite, which the bride always offered to her husband." (Sir John Lubbock, "Smith. Rep.," 1869, p. 352.)

Among many American tribes, notably in Brazil, the husband captured the wife by main force, as the men of Benjamin carried off the daughters of Shiloh at the feast, and as the Romans captured the Sabine women. "Within a few generations the same old habit was kept up in Wales, where the bridegroom and his friends, mounted and armed as for war, carried off the bride; and in Ireland they used even to hurl spears at the bride's people, though at such a distance that no one was hurt, except now and then by accident—as happened when one Lord Hoath lost an eye, which mischance put an end to this curious relic of antiquity." (Tylor's "Anthropology," p. 409.)

Marriage in Mexico was performed by the priest. He exhorted them to maintain peace and harmony, and tied the end of the man's mantle to the dress of the woman; he perfumed them, and placed on each a shawl on which was painted a skeleton, "as a symbol that only death could now separate them from one another." (Dorman, "Prim. Superst.," p. 379.)

The priesthood was thoroughly organized in Mexico and Peru. They were prophets as well as priests. "They brought the newly-born infant into the religious society; they directed their training and education; they determined the entrance of the young men into the service of the state; they consecrated marriage by their blessing; they comforted the sick and assisted the dying." (Ibid., p. 374.) There were five thousand priests in the temples of Mexico. They confessed and absolved the sinners, arranged the festivals, and managed the choirs in the churches. They lived in conventual discipline, but were allowed to marry; they practised flagellation and fasting, and prayed at regular hours. There were great preachers and exhorters among them. There were also convents into which females were admitted. The novice had her hair cut off and took vows of celibacy; they lived holy and pious lives. (Ibid., pp. 375, 376.) The king was the high-priest of the religious orders. A new king ascended the temple naked, except his girdle; he was sprinkled four times with water which had been blessed; he was then clothed in a mantle, and on his knees took an oath to maintain the ancient religion. The priests then instructed him in his royal duties. (Ibid., p. 378.) Besides the regular priesthood there were monks who were confined in cloisters. (Ibid., p. 390.) Cortes says the Mexican priests were very strict in the practice of honesty and chastity, and any deviation was punished with death. They wore long white robes and burned incense. (Dorman, "Prim. Superst.," p. 379.) The first fruits of the earth were devoted to the support of the priesthood. (Ibid., p. 383.) The priests of the Isthmus were sworn to perpetual chastity.

The American doctors practised phlebotomy. They bled the sick man because they believed the evil spirit which afflicted him would come away with the blood. In Europe phlebotomy only continued to a late period, but the original superstition out of which it arose, in this case as in many others, was forgotten.

There is opportunity here for the philosopher to meditate upon the perversity of human nature and the persistence of hereditary error. The superstition of one age becomes the science of another; men were first bled to withdraw the evil spirit, then to cure the disease; and a practice whose origin is lost in the night of ages is continued into the midst of civilization, and only overthrown after it has sent millions of human beings to untimely graves. Dr. Sangrado could have found the explanation of his profession only among the red men of America.

Folk-lore.—Says Max Müller: "Not only do we find the same words and the same terminations in Sanscrit and Gothic; not only do we find the same name for Zeus in Sanscrit, Latin, and German; not only is the abstract name for God the same in India, Greece, and Italy; but these very stories, these 'Mährchen' which nurses still tell, with almost the same words, in the Thuringian forest and in the Norwegian villages, and to which crowds of children listen under the Pippal-trees of India—these stories, too, belonged to the common heirloom of the Indo-European race, and their origin carries us back to the same distant past, when no Greek had set foot in Europe, no Hindoo had bathed in the sacred waters of the Ganges."

And we find that an identity of origin can be established between the folk-lore or fairy tales of America and those of the Old World, precisely such as exists between the, legends of Norway and India.

Mr. Tylor tells us the story of the two brothers in Central America who, starting on their dangerous journey to the land of Xibalba, where their father had perished, plant each a cane in the middle of their grandmother's house, that she may know by its flourishing or withering whether they are alive or dead. Exactly the same conception occurs in Grimm's "Mährchen," when the two gold-children wish to see the world and to leave their father; and when their father is sad, and asks them how he shall bear news of them, they tell him, "We leave you the two golden lilies; from these you can see how we fare. If they are fresh, we are well; if they fade, we are ill; if they fall, we are dead." Grimm traces the same idea in Hindoo stories. "Now this," says Max Müller, "is strange enough, and its occurrence in India, Germany, and Central America is stranger still."

Compare the following stories, which we print in parallel columns, one from the Ojibbeway Indians, the other from Ireland:

THE OJIBBEWAY STORY.

The birds met together one day to try which could fly the highest. Some flew up very swift, but soon got tired, and were passed by others of stronger wing. But the eagle went up beyond them all, and was ready to claim the victory, when the gray linnet, a very small bird, flew from the eagle's back, where it had perched unperceived, and, being fresh and unexhausted, succeeded in going the highest. When the birds came down and met in council to award the prize it was given to the eagle, because that bird had not only gone up nearer to the sun than any of the larger birds, but it had carried the linnet on its back.

For this reason the eagle's feathers became the most honorable marks of distinction a warrior could bear.

THE IRISH STORY.

The birds all met together one day, and settled among themselves that whichever of them could fly highest was to be the king of all. Well, just as they were on the hinges of being off, what does the little rogue of a wren do but hop up and perch himself unbeknown on the eagle's tail. So they flew and flew ever so high, till the eagle was miles above all the rest, and could not fly another stroke, he was so tired. "Then," says he, "I'm king of the birds." "You lie!" says the wren, darting up a perch and a half above the big fellow. Well, the eagle was so mad to think how he was done, that when the wren was coming down he gave him a stroke of his wing, and from that day to this the wren was never able to fly farther than a hawthorn-bush.

Compare the following stories:

THE ASIATIC STORY.

In Hindoo mythology Urvasi came down from heaven and became the wife of the son of Buddha only on condition that two pet rams should never be taken from her bedside, and that she should never behold her lord undressed. The immortals, however, wishing Urvasi back in heaven, contrived to steal the rams; and, as the king pursued the robbers with his sword in the dark, the lightning revealed his person, the compact was broken, and Urvasi disappeared. This same story is found in different forms among many people of Aryan and Turanian descent, the central idea being that of a man marrying some one of an aerial or aquatic origin, and living happily with her till he breaks the condition on which her residence with him depends, stories exactly parallel to that of Raymond of Toulouse, who chances in the hunt upon the beautiful Melusina at a fountain, and lives with her happily until he discovers her fish-nature and she vanishes.

THE AMERICAN STORY.

Wampee, a great hunter, once came to a strange prairie, where be heard faint sounds of music, and looking up saw a speck in the sky, which proved itself to be a basket containing twelve most beautiful maidens, who, on reaching the earth, forthwith set themselves to dance. He tried to catch the youngest, but in vain; ultimately he succeeded by assuming the disguise of a mouse. He was very attentive to his new wife, who was really a daughter of one of the stars, but she wished to return home, so she made a wicker basket secretly, and, by help of a charm she remembered, ascended to her father.

If the legend of Cadmus recovering Europa, after she has been carried away by the white bull, the spotless cloud, means that "the sun must journey westward until he sees again the beautiful tints which greeted his eyes in the morning," it is curious to find a story current in North America to the effect that a man once had a beautiful daughter, 'whom he forbade to leave the lodge lest she should be carried off by the king of the buffaloes; and that as she sat, notwithstanding, outside the house combing her hair, "all of a sudden the king of the buffaloes came dashing on, with his herd of followers, and, taking her between his horns, away be cantered over plains, plunged into a river which bounded his land, and carried her safely to his lodge on the other side," whence she was finally recovered by her father.

Games.—The same games and sports extended from India to the shores of Lake Superior. The game of the Hindoos, called pachisi, is played upon a cross-shaped board or cloth; it is a combination of checkers and draughts, with the throwing of dice, the dice determining the number of moves; when the Spaniards entered Mexico they found the Aztecs playing a game called patolli, identical with the Hindoo pachisi, on a similar cross-shaped board. The game of ball, which the Indians of America were in the habit of playing at the time of the discovery of the country, from California to the Atlantic, was identical with the European chueca, crosse, or hockey.

One may well pause, after reading this catalogue, and ask himself, wherein do these peoples differ? It is absurd to pretend that all these similarities could have been the result of accidental coincidences.

These two peoples, separated by the great ocean, were baptized alike in infancy with blessed water; they prayed alike to the gods; they worshipped together the sun, moon, and stars; they confessed their sins alike; they were instructed alike by an established priesthood; they were married in the same way and by the joining of hands; they armed themselves with the same weapons; when children came, the man, on both continents, went to bed and left his wife to do the honors of the household; they tattooed and painted themselves in the same fashion; they became intoxicated on kindred drinks; their dresses were alike; they cooked in the same manner; they used the same metals; they employed the same exorcisms and bleedings for disease; they believed alike in ghosts, demons, and fairies; they listened to the same stories; they played the same games; they used the same musical instruments; they danced the same dances, and when they died they were embalmed in the same way and buried sitting; while over them were erected, on both continents, the same mounds, pyramids, obelisks, and temples. And yet we are asked to believe that there was no relationship between them, and that they had never had any ante-Columbian intercourse with each other.

If our knowledge of Atlantis was more thorough, it would no doubt appear that, in every instance wherein the people of Europe accord with the people of America, they were both in accord with the people of Atlantis; and that Atlantis was the common centre from which both peoples derived their arts, sciences, customs, and opinions. It will be seen that in every case where Plato gives us any information in this respect as to Atlantis, we find this agreement to exist. It existed in architecture, sculpture, navigation, engraving, writing, an established priesthood, the mode of worship, agriculture, the construction of roads and canals; and it is reasonable to suppose that the same correspondence extended down to all the minor details treated of in this chapter.

CHAPTER III. AMERICAN EVIDENCES OF INTERCOURSE WITH EUROPE OR ATLANTIS.

1. ON the monuments of Central America there are representations of bearded men. How could the beardless American Indians have imagined a bearded race?

2. All the traditions of the civilized races of Central America point to an Eastern origin.

The leader and civilizer of the Nahua family was Quetzalcoatl. This is the legend respecting him:

"From the distant East, from the fabulous Hue Hue Tlapalan, this mysterious person came to Tula, and became the patron god and high-priest of the ancestors of the Toltecs. He is described as having been a white man, with strong formation of body, broad forehead, large eyes, and flowing beard. He wore a mitre on his head, and was dressed in a long white robe reaching to his feet, and covered with red crosses. In his hand he held a sickle. His habits were ascetic, he never married, was most chaste and pure in life, and is said to have endured penance in a neighboring mountain, not for its effects upon himself, but as a warning to others. He condemned sacrifices, except of fruits and flowers, and was known as the god of peace; for, when addressed on the subject of war, he is reported to have stopped his ears with his fingers." ("North Amer. of Antiq.," p. 268.)

"He was skilled in many arts: he invented" (that is, imported) "gem-cutting and metal-casting; he originated letters, and invented the Mexican calendar. He finally returned to the land in the East from which he came: leaving the American coast at Vera Cruz, he embarked in a canoe made of serpent-skins, and 'sailed away into the east.'" (Ibid., p. 271.)

Dr. Le Plongeon says of the columns at Chichen:

"The base is formed by the head of Cukulcan, the shaft of the body of

ANCIENT MEXICAN VASE.

the serpent, with its feathers beautifully carved to the very chapiter. On the chapiters of the columns that support the portico, at the entrance of the castle in Chichen Itza, may be seen the carved figures of long-bearded men, with upraised hands, in the act of worshipping sacred trees. They forcibly recall to mind the same worship in Assyria."

In the accompanying cut of an ancient vase from Tula, we see a bearded figure grasping a beardless man.

In the cut given below we see a face that might be duplicated among the old men of any part of Europe.

The Cakchiquel MS. says: "Four persons came from Tulan, from the *direction of the rising sun*--that is one Tulan. There is another Tulan in Xibalbay, and another where the sun sets, *and it is there that we came*; and in the direction of the setting sun there is another, where is the god; so that there are four Tulans; and it is where the sun sets that we came to Tulan, *from the other side of the sea*, where this Tulan is; and it is there that we were conceived and begotten by our mothers and fathers."

That is to say, the birthplace of the race was in the East, across the sea, at a place called Tulan and when they emigrated they called their first stopping-place on the American continent Tulan also; and besides this there were two other Tulans.

BEARDED HEAD TEOTEHUACAN

"Of the Nahua predecessors of the Toltecs in Mexico the Olmecs and Xicalaucans were the most important. They were the forerunners of the great races that followed. According to Ixtlilxochitl, these people—which are conceded to be the ones who occupied the world in the third age; they came from the East in ships or barks to the land of Potonchan, which they commenced to populate."

3. The Abbé Brasseur de Bourbourg, in one of the notes of the Introduction of the "Popol Vuh," presents a very remarkable analogy between the kingdom of Xibalba, described in that work, and Atlantis. He says: "Both countries are magnificent, exceedingly fertile, and abound in the precious metals. The empire of Atlantis was divided into ten kingdoms, governed by five couples of twin sons of Poseidon, the eldest being supreme over the others; and the ten constituted a tribunal that managed the affairs of the empire. Their descendants governed after them. The ten kings of Xibalba, who reigned (in couples) under Hun-Came and Vukub-Came (and who together constituted a grand council of the kingdom), certainly furnish curious points of comparison. And there is wanting neither a catastrophe—for Xibalba had a terrific inundation—nor the name of Atlas, of which the etymology is found only in the Nahuatl tongue: it comes from atl, water; and we know that a city of Atlan (near the water) still existed on the Atlantic side of the Isthmus of Panama at the time of the Conquest."

"In Yucatan the traditions all point to an Eastern and foreign origin for the race. The early writers report that the natives believe their ancestors to have crossed the sea by a passage which was opened for them." (Landa's "Relacion," p. 28.)

"It was also believed that part of the population came into the country from the West. Lizana says that the smaller portion, 'the little descent,' came from the East, while the greater portion, 'the great descent,' came from the West. Cogolluda considers the Eastern colony to have been the larger.... The culture-hero Zamna, the author of all civilization in Yucatan, is described as the teacher of letters, and the leader of the people from their ancient home.... He was the leader of a colony from the East." ("North Amer. of Antiq.," p. 229.)

The ancient Mexican legends say that, after the Flood, Coxcox and his wife, after wandering one hundred and four years, landed at Antlan, and passed thence to Capultepec, and thence to Culhuacan, and lastly to Mexico.

Coming from Atlantis, they named their first landing-place Antlan.

All the races that settled Mexico, we are told, traced their origin back to an Aztlan (Atlan-tis). Duran describes Aztlan as "a most attractive land." ("North Amer. of Antiq.," p. 257.)

Samé, the great name of Brazilian legend, came across the ocean from the rising sun. He had power over the elements and tempests; the trees of the forests would recede to make room for him (cutting down the trees); the animals used to crouch before him (domesticated animals); lakes and rivers became solid for him (boats and bridges); and he taught the use of agriculture and magic. Like him, Bochica, the great law-giver of the Muyscas, and son of the sun—he who invented for them the calendar and regulated their festivals—had a white beard, a detail in which all the American culture-heroes agree. The "Samé" of Brazil was probably the "Zamna" of Yucatan.

4. We find in America numerous representations of the elephant. We are forced to one of two conclusions: either the monuments date back to the time of the mammoth in North America, or these people held intercourse at some time in the past with races who possessed the elephant, and from whom they obtained pictures of that singular animal. Plato tells us that the Atlanteans possessed great numbers of elephants.

There are in Wisconsin a number of mounds of earth representing different animals-men, birds, and quadrupeds. Among the latter is a mound representing an elephant, "so perfect in its proportions, and complete in its representation of an elephant, that its builders must have been well acquainted with all the physical characteristics of the animal which they delineated."

ELEPHANT MOUND, WISCONSIN.

On a farm in Louisa County, Iowa, a pipe was ploughed up which also represents an elephant. We are indebted to the valuable work of John T. Short ("The North Americans of Antiquity," p. 530) for a picture of this singular object. It was found in a section where the ancient mounds were very abundant and rich in relies. The pipe is of sandstone, of the ordinary Mound-Builder's type, and has every appearance of age and usage.

ELEPHANT PIPE, LOISA COUNTY, IOWA.

There can be no doubt of its genuineness. The finder had no conception of its archæological value.

In the ruined city of Palenque we find, in one of the palaces, a stucco bass-relief of a priest. His elaborate head-dress or helmet represents very faithfully the head of an elephant. The cut on page 169 is from a drawing made by Waldeck.

ELEPHANT-TRUNK HEAD-DRESS, PALENQUE

The decoration known as "elephant-trunks" is found in many parts of the ancient ruins of Central America, projecting from above the door-ways of the buildings. In Tylor's "Researches into the Early History of Mankind," p. 313, I find a remarkable

representation of an elephant, taken from an ancient Mexican manuscript.

CHAPTER IV. CORROBORATING CIRCUMSTANCES.

1. Lenormant insists that the human race issued from Ups Merou, and adds that some Greek traditions point to "this locality—particularly the expression me'ropes a?'nðwpoi, which can only mean 'the men sprung from Merou.'" ("Mannal," p. 21.)

Theopompus tells us that the people who inhabited Atlantis were the Meropes, the people of Merou.

2. Whence comes the word Atlantic? The dictionaries tell us that the ocean is named after the mountains of Atlas; but whence did the Atlas mountains get their name?

"The words Atlas and Atlantic have no satisfactory etymology in any language known to Europe. They are not Greek, and cannot be referred to any known language of the Old World. But in the Nahuatl language we find immediately the radical a, atl, which signifies water, war, and the top of the head. (Molina, "Vocab. en lengua Mexicana y Castellana.") From this comes a series of words, such as atlan—on the border of or amid the water—from which we have the adjective Atlantic. We have also atlaça, to combat, or be in agony; it means likewise to hurl or dart from the water, and in the preterit makes Atlaz. A city named Atlan existed when the continent was discovered by Columbus, at the entrance of the Gulf of Uraba, in Darien. With a good harbor, it is now reduced to an unimportant pueblo named Acla." (Baldwin's "Ancient America," p. 179.)

Plato tells us that Atlantis and the Atlantic Ocean were named after Atlas, the eldest son of Poseidon, the founder of the kingdom.

3. Upon that part of the African continent nearest to the site of Atlantis we find a chain of mountains, known from the most ancient times as the Atlas Mountains. Whence this name Atlas, if it be not from the name of the great king of Atlantis? And if this be not its origin, how comes it that we find it in the most north-western corner of Africa? And how does it happen that in the time of Herodotus there dwelt near this mountain-chain a people called the Atlantes, probably a remnant of a colony from Solon's island? How comes it that the people of the Barbary States were known to the Greeks, Romans, and Carthaginians as the "Atlantes," this name being especially applied to the inhabitants of Fezzan and Bilma? Where did they get the name from? There is no etymology for it east of the Atlantic Ocean. (Lenormants "Anc. Hist. of the East," p. 253.)

Look at it! An "Atlas" mountain on the shore of Africa; an "Atlan" town on the shore of America; the "Atlantes" living along the north and west coast of Africa; an Aztec people from Aztlan, in Central America; an ocean rolling between the two worlds called the "Atlantic;" a mythological deity called "Atlas" holding the world on his shoulders; and an immemorial tradition of an island of Atlantis. Can all these things be the result of accident?

4. Plato says that there was a "passage west from Atlantis to the rest of the islands, as well as from these islands to the whole opposite continent that surrounds that real sea." He calls it a real sea, as contradistinguished from the Mediterranean, which, as he says, is not a real sea (or ocean) but a landlocked body of water, like a harbor.

Now, Plato might have created Atlantis out of his imagination; but how could he have invented the islands beyond (the West India Islands), and the whole continent (America) enclosing that real sea? If we look at the map, we see that the continent of America does "surround" the ocean in a great half-circle. Could Plato have guessed all this? If there had been no Atlantis, and no series of voyages from it that revealed the half-circle of the continent from Newfoundland to Cape St. Roche, how could Plato have guessed it? And how could he have known that the Mediterranean was only a harbor compared with the magnitude of the great ocean surrounding Atlantis? Long sea-voyages were necessary to establish that fact, and the Greeks, who kept close to the shores in their short journeys, did not make such voyages.

5. How can we, without Atlantis, explain the presence of the Basques in Europe, who have no lingual affinities with any other race on the continent of Europe, but whose language is similar to the languages of America?

Plato tells us that the dominion of Gadeirus, one of the kings of Atlantis, extended "toward the pillars of Heracles (Hercules) as far as the country which is still called the region of Gades in that part of the world." Gades is the Cadiz of today, and the dominion of Gadeirus embraced the land of the Iberians or Basques, their chief city taking its name from a king of Atlantis, and they themselves being Atlanteans.

Dr. Farrar, referring to the Basque language, says:

"What is certain about it is, that its structure is polysynthetic, like the languages of America. Like them, it forms its compounds by the elimination of certain radicals in the simple words; so that ilhun, the twilight, is contracted from hill, dead, and egun, day; and belhaur, the knee, from belhar, front, and oin, leg.... The fact is indisputable, and is eminently noteworthy, that while the affinities of the Basque roots have never been conclusively elucidated, there has never been any doubt that this isolated language, preserving its identity in a western corner of Europe, between two mighty kingdoms, resembles, in its grammatical structure, the aboriginal languages of the vast opposite continent (America), and those alone." ("Families of Speech," p. 132.)

If there was an Atlantis, forming, with its connecting ridges, a continuous bridge of land from America to Africa, we can understand how the Basques could have passed from one continent to another; but if the wide Atlantic rolled at all times unbroken between the two continents, it is difficult to conceive of such an emigration by an uncivilized people.

6. Without Atlantis, how can we explain the fact that the early Egyptians were depicted by themselves as red men on their own monuments? And, on the other hand, how can we account for the representations of negroes on the monuments of Central America?

Dêsirè Charnay, now engaged in exploring those monuments, has published in the *North American Review* for December, 1880, photographs of a number of idols exhumed at San Juan de Teotihuacan, from which I select the following strikingly negroid faces:

NEGRO IDOLS FOUND IN MEXICO.

Dr. Le Plongeon says: "Besides the sculptures of long-bearded men seen by the explorer at Chichen Itza, there were tall figures of people with small heads, thick lips, and curly short hair or wool, regarded as negroes. 'We always see them as standard or parasol bearers, but never engaged in actual warfare.'" ("Maya Archæology," p. 62.)

273

The following cut is from the court of the Palace of Palenque, figured by Stephens. The face is strongly Ethiopian.

NEGROID FIGURE, PALENQUE.

The figure below represents a gigantic granite head, found near the volcano of Tuxtla, in the Mexican State of Vera Cruz, at Caxapa. The features are unmistakably negroid.

As the negroes have never been a sea-going race, the presence of these faces among the antiquities of Central America proves one of two things, either the existence of a land connection between America and Africa via Atlantis, as revealed by the deep-sea soundings of the *Challenger*, or commercial relations between America and Africa through the ships of the Atlanteans

NEGRO HEAD, VERA CRUZ

or some other civilized race, whereby the negroes were brought to America as slaves at a very remote epoch.

And we find some corroboration of the latter theory in that singular book of the Quiches, the "Popol Vuh," in which, after describing the creation of the first men "*in the region of the rising sun*" (Bancroft's "Native Races," vol. v., p. 548),

and enumerating their first generations, we are told, "All seem to have spoken one language, and to have lived in great peace, *black men and white together*. Here they awaited the rising of the sun, and prayed to the Heart of Heaven." (Bancroft's "Native Races," p. 547.) How did the red men of Central America know anything about "black men and white men?" The conclusion seems inevitable that these legends of a primitive, peaceful, and happy land, an Aztlan in the East, inhabited by black and white men, to which all the civilized nations of America traced their origin, could only refer to Atlantis--that bridge of land where the white, dark, and red races met. The "Popol Vuh" proceeds to tell how this first home of the race

274

became over-populous, and how the people under Balam-Quitze migrated; how their language became "confounded," in other words, broken up into dialects, in consequence of separation; and how some of the people "*went to the East*, and many came hither to Guatemala." (*Ibid.*, p. 547.)

M. A. de Quatrefages ("Human Species," p. 200) says, "Black populations have been found in America in very small numbers only, as isolated tribes in the midst of very different populations. Such are the Charruas, of Brazil, the Black Carribees of Saint Vincent, in the Gulf of Mexico; the Jamassi of Florida, and the dark-complexioned Californians.... Such, again, is the tribe that Balboa saw some representatives of in his passage of the Isthmus of Darien in 1513; ... they were true negroes."

7. How comes it that all the civilizations of the Old World radiate from the shores of the Mediterranean? The Mediterranean is a cul de sac, with Atlantis opposite its mouth. Every civilization on its shores possesses traditions that point to Atlantis. We hear of no civilization coming to the Mediterranean from Asia, Africa, or Europe—from north, south, or west; but north, south, east, and west we find civilization radiating from the Mediterranean to other lands. We see the Aryans descending upon Hindostan from the direction of the Mediterranean; and we find the Chinese borrowing inventions from Hindostan, and claiming descent from a region not far from the Mediterranean.

The Mediterranean has been the centre of the modern world, because it lay in the path of the extension of an older civilization, whose ships colonized its shores, as they did also the shores of America. Plato says, "the nations are gathered around the shores of the Mediterranean like frogs around a marsh."

Dr. McCausland says: "The obvious conclusion from these facts is, that at some time previous to these migrations a people speaking a language of a superior and complicated structure broke up their society, and, under some strong impulse, poured out in different directions, and gradually established themselves in all the lands now inhabited by the Caucasian race. Their territories extend from the Atlantic to the Ganges, and from Iceland to Ceylon, and are bordered on the north and east by the Asiatic Mongols, and on the south by the negro tribes of Central Africa. They present all the appearances of a later race, expanding itself between and into the territories of two pre-existing neighboring races, and forcibly appropriating the room required for its increasing population." (McCausland's "Adam and the Adamites," p. 280.)

Modern civilization is Atlantean. Without the thousands of years of development which were had in Atlantis modern civilization could not have existed. The inventive faculty of the present age is taking up the great delegated work of creation where Atlantis left it thousands of years ago.

8. How are we to explain the existence of the Semitic race in Europe without Atlantis? It is an intrusive race; a race colonized on sea-coasts. Where are its Old World affinities?

9. Why is it that the origin of wheat, barley, oats, maize, and rye—the essential plants of civilization—is totally lost in the mists of a vast antiquity? We have in the Greek mythology legends of the introduction of most of these by Atlantean kings or gods into Europe; but no European nation claims to have discovered or developed them, and it has been impossible to trace them to their wild originals. Out of the whole flora of the world mankind in the last seven thousand years has not developed a single food-plant to compare in importance to the human family with these. If a wise and scientific nation should propose nowadays to add to this list, it would have to form great botanical gardens, and, by systematic and long-continued experiments, develop useful plants from the humble productions of the field and forest. Was this done in the past on the island of Atlantis?

10. Why is it that we find in Ptolemy's "Geography of Asia Minor," in a list of cities in Armenia Major in A.D. 140, the names of five cities which have their counterparts in the names of localities in Central America?

Armenian Cities.	Central American Localities.
Chol.	Chol-ula
Colua.	Colua-can.
Zuivana.	Zuivan.
Cholima.	Colima.
Zalissa.	Xalisco.

(Short's "North Americans of Antiquity," p. 497.)

11. How comes it that the sandals upon the feet of the statue of Chacmol, discovered at Chichen Itza, are "exact representations of those found on the feet of the Guanches, the early inhabitants of the Canary Islands, whose mummies are occasionally discovered in the caves of Teneriffe?" Dr. Merritt deems the axe or chisel heads dug up at Chiriqui, Central America, "almost identical in form as well as material with specimens found in Suffolk County, England." (Bancroft's Native Races," vol. iv., p. 20.) The rock-carvings of Chiriqui are pronounced by Mr. Seemann to have a striking

resemblance to the ancient incised characters found on the rocks of Northumberland, England. (Ibid.)

"Some stones have recently been discovered in Hierro and Las Palmas (Canary Islands), bearing sculptured symbols similar to those found on the shores of Lake Superior; and this has led M. Bertholet, the historiographer of the Canary Islands, to conclude that the first inhabitants of the Canaries and those of the great West were one in race." (Benjamin, "The Atlantic Islands," p. 130.)

12. How comes it that that very high authority, Professor Retzius ("Smithsonian Report," 1859, p. 266), declares, "With regard to the primitive dolichocephalæ of America I entertain a hypothesis still more bold, namely, that they are nearly related to the Guanches in the Canary Islands, and to the Atlantic populations of Africa, the Moors, Tuaricks, Copts, etc., which Latham comprises under the name of Egyptian-Atlantidæ. We find one and the same form of skull in the Canary Islands, in front of the African coast, and in the Carib Islands, on the opposite coast, which faces Africa. The color of the skin on both sides of the Atlantic is represented in these populations as being of a reddish-brown."

13. The Barbarians who are alluded to by Homer and Thucydides were a race of ancient navigators and pirates called Cares, or Carians, who occupied the isles of Greece before the Pelasgi, and antedated the Phoenicians in the control of the sea. The Abbé Brasseur de Bourbourg claims that these Carians were identical with the Caribs of the West Indies, the Caras of Honduras, and the Gurani of South America. (Landa's "Relacion," pp. 52-65.)

14. When we consider it closely, one of the most extraordinary customs ever known to mankind is that to which I have already alluded in a preceding chapter, to wit, the embalming of the body of the dead man, with a purpose that the body itself may live again in a future state. To arrive at this practice several things must coexist:

a. The people must be highly religious, and possessed of an organized and influential priesthood, to perpetuate so troublesome a custom from age to age.

b. They must believe implicitly in the immortality of the soul; and this implies a belief in rewards and punishments after death; in a heaven and a hell.

c. They must believe in the immortality of the body, and its resurrection from the grave on some day of judgment in the distant future.

d. But a belief in the immortality of the soul and the resurrection of the body is not enough, for all Christian nations hold to these beliefs; they must supplement these with a determination that the body shall not perish; that the very flesh and blood in which the man died shall rise with him on the last day, and not a merely spiritual body.

Now all these four things must coexist before a people proceed to embalm their dead for religious purposes. The probability that all these four things should coexist by accident in several widely separated races is slight indeed. The doctrine of chances is all against it. There is here no common necessity driving men to the same expedient, with which so many resemblances have been explained; the practice is a religious ceremony, growing out of religious beliefs by no means common or universal, to wit, that the man who is dead shall live again, and live again in the very body in which he died. Not even all the Jews believed in these things.

If, then, it should appear that among the races which we claim were descended from Atlantis this practice of embalming the dead is found, and nowhere else, we have certainly furnished evidence which can only be explained by admitting the existence of Atlantis, and of some great religious race dwelling on Atlantis, who believed in the immortality of soul and body, and who embalmed their dead. We find, as I have shown:

First. That the Guanches of the Canary Islands, supposed to be a remnant of the Atlantean population, preserved their dead as mummies.

Second. That the Egyptians, the oldest colony of Atlantis, embalmed their dead in such vast multitudes that they are now exported by the ton to England, and ground up into manures to grow English turnips.

Third. That the Assyrians, the Ethiopians, the Persians, the Greeks, and even the Romans embalmed their dead.

Fourth. On the American continents we find that the Peruvians, the Central Americans, the Mexicans, and some of the Indian tribes, followed the same practice.

Is it possible to account for this singular custom, reaching through a belt of nations, and completely around the habitable world, without Atlantis?

15. All the traditions of the Mediterranean races look to the ocean as the source of men and gods. Homer sings of "Ocean, the origin of gods and Mother Tethys."

Orpheus says, "The fair river of Ocean was the first to marry, and he espoused his sister Tethys, who was his mothers daughter." (Plato's "Dialogues," Cratylus, p. 402.) The ancients always alluded to the ocean as a river encircling the earth, as in the map of Cosmos (see page 95 ante);

probably a reminiscence of the great canal described by Plato which surrounded the plain of Atlantis. Homer (Iliad, book xviii.) describes Tethys, "the mother goddess," coming to Achilles "from the deep abysses of the main:"

"The circling Nereids with their mistress weep,

And all the sea-green sisters of the deep."

Plato surrounds the great statue of Poseidon in Atlantis with the images of one hundred Nereids.

16. In the Deluge legends of the Hindoos (as given on page 87 ante), we have seen Mann saving a small fish, which subsequently grew to a great size, and warned him of the coming of the Flood. In this legend all the indications point to an ocean as the scene of the catastrophe. It says: "At the close of the last calpa there was a general destruction, caused by the sleep of Brahma, whence his creatures, in different worlds, were drowned in a vast ocean.... A holy king, named Satyavrata, then reigned, a servant of the spirit which moved on the waves" (Poseidon?), "and so devout that water was his only sustenance.... In seven days the three worlds" (remember Poseidon's trident) "shall be plunged in an ocean of death."... "'Thou shalt enter the spacious ark, and continue in it secure from the Flood on one immense ocean.'... The sea overwhelmed its shores, deluged the whole earth, augmented by showers from immense clouds." ("Asiatic Researches," vol. i., p. 230.)

All this reminds us of "the fountains of the great deep and the flood-gates of heaven," and seems to repeat precisely the story of Plato as to the sinking of Atlantis in the ocean.

17. While I do not attach much weight to verbal similarities in the languages of the two continents, nevertheless there are some that are very remarkable. We have seen the Pan and Maia of the Greeks reappearing in the Pan and Maya of the Mayas of Central America. The god of the Welsh triads, "Hu the mighty," is found in the Hu-nap-bu, the hero-god of the Quiches; in Hu-napu, a hero-god; and in Hu-hu-nap-hu, in Hu-ncam, in Hu-nbatz, semi-divine heroes of the Quiches. The Phoenician deity El "was subdivided into a number of hypostases called the Baalim, secondary divinities, emanating from the substance of the deity" ("Anc. Hist. East," vol. ii., p. 219); and this word Baalim we find appearing in the mythology of the Central Americans, applied to the semi-divine progenitors of the human race, Balam-Quitze, Balam-Agab, and Iqui-Balam.

CHAPTER V. THE QUESTION OF COMPLEXION.

The tendency of scientific thought in ethnology is in the direction of giving more and more importance to the race characteristics, such as height, color of the hair, eyes and skin, and the formation of the skull and body generally, than to language. The language possessed by a people may be merely the result of conquest or migration. For instance, in the United States to-day, white, black, and red men, the descendants of French, Spanish, Italians, Mexicans, Irish, Germans, Scandinavians, Africans, all speak the English language, and by the test of language they are all Englishmen; and yet none of them are connected by birth or descent with the country where that language was developed.

There is a general misconception as to the color of the European and American races. Europe is supposed to be peopled exclusively by white men; but in reality every shade of color is represented on that continent, from the fair complexion of the fairest of the Swedes to the dark-skinned inhabitants of the Mediterranean coast, only a shade lighter than the Berbers, or Moors, on the opposite side of that sea. Tacitus spoke of the "Black Celts," and the term, so far as complexion goes, might not inappropriately be applied to some of the Italians, Spaniards, and Portuguese, while the Basques are represented as of a still darker hue. Tylor says ("Anthropology," p. 67), "On the whole, it seems that the distinction of color, from the fairest Englishman to the darkest African, has no hard and fast lines, but varies gradually from one tint to another."

And when we turn to America we find that the popular opinion that all Indians are "red men," and of the same hue from Patagonia to Hudson's Bay, is a gross error.

Prichard says ("Researches into the Physical History of Mankind," vol. i., p. 269, 4th ed., 1841):

"It will be easy to show that the American races show nearly as great a variety in this respect as the nations of the old continent; there are among them white races with a florid complexion, and tribes black or of a very dark hue; that their stature, figure, and countenance are almost equally diversified."

John T. Short says ("North Americans of Antiquity," p. 189):

"The Menominees, sometimes called the 'White Indians,' formerly occupied the region bordering on Lake Michigan, around Green Bay. The whiteness of these Indians, which is compared to that of white mulattoes, early attracted the attention of the Jesuit missionaries, and has often been commented on by travellers. While it is true that hybridy has done much to lighten the color of many of the tribes, still the peculiarity of the complexion of this people has been marked since the first time a European encountered them. Almost every shade, from the ash-color of the Menominees through the cinnamon-red, copper, and bronze tints, may be found among the tribes formerly occupying the territory east of the Mississippi, until we reach the dark-skinned Kaws of Kansas, who are nearly as black as the negro. The variety of complexion is as great in South America as among the tribes of the northern part of the continent."

In foot-note of p. 107 of vol. iii. of "U. S. Explorations for a Railroad Route to the Pacific Ocean," we are told,

"Many of the Indians of Zuni (New Mexico) are white. They have a fair skin, blue eyes, chestnut or auburn hair, and are quite good-looking. They claim to be full-blooded Zunians, and have no tradition of intermarriage with any foreign race. The circumstance creates no surprise among this people, for from time immemorial a similar class of people has existed among the tribe."

Winchell says: "The ancient Indians of California, in the latitude of forty-two degrees, were as black as the negroes of Guinea, while in Mexico were tribes of an olive or reddish complexion, relatively light. Among the black races of tropical regions we find, generally, some light-colored tribes interspersed. These sometimes have light hair and blue eyes. This is the case with the Tuareg of the Sahara, the Afghans of India, and the aborigines of the banks of the Oronoco and the Amazon." (Winchell's "Preadamites," p. 185.)

William Penn said of the Indians of Pennsylvania, in his letter of August, 1683: "The natives ... are generally tall, straight, well-built, and of singular proportion; they tread strong and clever, and mostly walk with a lofty chin.... Their eye is little and black, not unlike a straight-looked Jew.... I have seen among them as comely European-like faces of both sexes as on your side of the sea; and truly an Italian complexion hath not much more of the white, and the noses of several of them have as much of the Roman.... For their original, I am ready to believe them to be of the Jewish race—I mean of the stock of the ten tribes—and that for the following reasons: first, in the next place, I find them to be of the like countenance, and their children of so lively a resemblance that a man would think himself in Duke's Place or Berry Street in London when he seeth them. But this is not all: they agree in rites, they reckon by moons, they offer their first-fruits, they have a kind of feast of tabernacles, they are said to lay their altars upon twelve stones, their mourning a year, customs of women, with many other things that do not now occur."

Upon this question of complexion Catlin, in his "Indians of North America," vol. i., p. 95, etc., gives us some curious information. We have already seen that the Mandans preserved an image of the ark, and possessed legends of a clearly Atlantean character. Catlin says:

"A stranger in the Mandan village is first struck with the different shades of complexion and various colors of hair which he sees in a crowd about him, and is at once disposed to exclaim, 'These are not Indians.' There are a great many of these people whose complexions appear as light as half-breeds; and among the women particularly there are many whose skins are almost white, with the most pleasing symmetry and proportion of feature; with hazel, with gray, and with blue eyes; with mildness and sweetness of expression and excessive modesty of demeanor, which render them exceedingly pleasing and beautiful. Why this diversity of complexion I cannot tell, nor can they themselves account for it. Their traditions, so far as I can learn them, afford us no information of their having had any knowledge of white men before the visit of Lewis and Clarke, made to their village thirty-three years ago. Since that time until now (1835) there have been very few visits of white men to this place, and surely not enough to have changed the complexions and customs of a nation. And I recollect perfectly well that Governor Clarke told me, before I started for this place, that I would find the Mandans a strange people and half white.

"Among the females may be seen every shade and color of hair that can be seen in our own country except red or auburn, which is not to be found.... There are very many of both sexes, and of every age, from infancy to manhood and old age, with hair of a bright silvery-gray, and in some instances almost perfectly white. This unaccountable phenomenon is not the result of disease or habit, but it is unquestionably an hereditary characteristic which runs in families, and indicates no inequality in disposition or intellect. And by passing this hair through my hands I have found it uniformly to be as coarse and harsh as a horse's mane, differing materially from the hair of other colors, which, among the Mandans, is generally as fine and soft as silk.

"The stature of the Mandans is rather below the ordinary size of man, with beautiful symmetry of form and proportion, and wonderful suppleness and elasticity."

Catlin gives a group (54) showing this great diversity in complexion: one of the figures is painted almost pure white, and with light hair. The faces are European.

Major James W. Lynd, who lived among the Dakota Indians for nine years, and was killed by them in the great outbreak of 1862, says (MS. "Hist. of Dakotas," Library, Historical Society, Minnesota, p. 47), after calling attention to the fact that the different tribes of the Sioux nation represent several different degrees of darkness of color:

"The Dakota child is of lighter complexion than the young brave; this one lighter than the middle-aged man, and the middle-aged man lighter than the superannuated homo, who, by smoke, paint, dirt, and a drying up of the vital juices, appears to be the true copper-colored Dakota. The color of the Dakotas varies with the nation, and also with the age and condition of the individual. It may be set down, however, as a shade lighter than olive; yet it becomes still lighter by change of condition or mode of life, and nearly vanishes, even in the child, under constant ablutions and avoiding of exposure. Those children in the Mission at Hazlewood, who are taken very young, and not allowed to expose themselves, lose almost entirely the olive shade, and become quite as white as the American child. The Mandans are as light as the peasants of Spain, while their brothers, the Crows, are as dark as the Arabs. Dr. Goodrich, in the 'Universal Traveller,' p. 154, says that the modern Peruvians, in the warmer regions of Peru, are as fair as the people of the south of Europe."

The Aymaras, the ancient inhabitants of the mountains of Peru and Bolivia, are described as having an olive-brown complexion, with regular features, large heads, and a thoughtful and melancholy cast of countenance. They practised in early times the deformation of the skull.

Professor Wilson describes the hair of the ancient Peruvians, as found upon their mummies, as "a lightish brown, and of a fineness of texture which equals that of the Anglo-Saxon race." "The ancient Peruvians," says Short ("North Americans of Antiquity," p. 187), "appear, from numerous examples of hair found in their tombs, to have been an auburn-haired race." Garcilasso, who had an opportunity of seeing the body of the king, Viracocha, describes the hair of that monarch as snow-white. Haywood tells us of the discovery, at the beginning of this century, of three mummies in a cave on the south side of the Cumberland River (Tennessee), who were buried in baskets, as the Peruvians were occasionally buried, and whose skin was fair and white, and their hair auburn, and of a fine texture. ("Natural and Aboriginal History of Tennessee," p. 191.)

CHOCTAW.   SHAWNEES. SAVONAROLA.

Neither is the common opinion correct which asserts all the American Indians to be of the same type of features. The portraits on this page and on pages 187 and 191, taken from the "Report of the U. S. Survey for a Route for a Pacific Railroad," present features very much like those of Europeans; in fact, every face here could be precisely matched among the inhabitants of the southern part of the old continent.

On the other hand, look at the portrait of the great Italian orator and reformer, Savonarola, on page 193. It looks more like the hunting Indians of North-western America than any of the preceding faces. In fact, if it was dressed with a scalp-lock it would pass muster anywhere as a portrait of the "Man-afraid-of-his-horses," or "Sitting Bull."

Adam was, it appears, a red man. Winchell tells us that Adam is derived from the red earth. The radical letters ÂDâM are found in ADaMaH, "something out of which vegetation was made to germinate," to wit, the earth. ÂDôM and ÂDOM signifies red, ruddy, bay-colored, as of a horse, the color of a red heifer. "ÂDâM, a man, a human being, male or female, red, ruddy." ("Preadamites," p. 161.)

"The Arabs distinguished mankind into two races, one red, ruddy, the other black." (Ibid.) They classed themselves among the red men.

Not only was Adam a red man, but there is evidence that, from the highest antiquity, red was a sacred color; the gods of the ancients were always painted red. The Wisdom of Solomon refers to this custom: "The carpenter carved it elegantly, and formed it by the skill of his understanding, and fashioned it to the shape of a man, or made it like some vile beast, laying it over with vermilion, and with paint, coloring it red, and covering every spot therein."

The idols of the Indians were also painted red, and red was the religious color. (Lynd's MS. "Hist. of Dakotas," Library, Hist. Society, Minn.)

The Cushites and Ethiopians, early branches of the Atlantean stock, took their name from their "sunburnt" complexion; they were red men.

The name of the Phoenicians signified red. Himyar, the prefix of the Himyaritic Arabians, also means red, and the Arabs were painted red on the Egyptian monuments.

The ancient Egyptians were red men. They recognized four races of men—the red, yellow, black, and white men. They themselves belonged to the "Rot," or red men; the yellow men they called "Namu"—it included the Asiatic races; the black men were called "Nahsu," and the white men "Tamhu." The following figures are copied from Nott and Gliddon's "Types of Mankind," p. 85, and were taken by them from the great works of Belzoni, Champollion, and Lepsius.

In later ages so desirous were the Egyptians of preserving the aristocratic distinction of the color of their skin, that they represented themselves on the monuments as of a crimson hue—an exaggeration of their original race complexion.

In the same way we find that the ancient Aryan writings divided mankind into four races—the white, red, yellow, and black: the four castes of India were founded upon these distinctions in color; in fact, the word for color in Sanscrit (varna) means caste. The red men, according to the Mahâbhârata, were the Kshatriyas—the warrior caste-who were afterward engaged in a fierce contest with the whites—the Brahmans—and were nearly exterminated, although some of them survived, and from their stock Buddha was born. So that not only the Mohammedan and Christian but the Buddhistic religion seem to be derived from branches of the Hamitic or red stock. The great Mann was also of the red race.

Red. Yellow. Black. White.

THE RACES OF MEN ACCORDING TO THE EGYPTIANS.

The Egyptians, while they painted themselves red-brown, represented the nations of Palestine as yellow-brown, and the Libyans yellow-white. The present inhabitants of Egypt range from a yellow color in the north parts to a deep bronze. Tylor is of opinion ("Anthropology," p. 95) that the ancient Egyptians belonged to a brown race, which embraced the Nubian tribes and, to some extent, the Berbers of Algiers and Tunis. He groups the Assyrians, Phoenicians, Persians, Greeks, Romans, Andalusians, Bretons, dark Welshmen, and people of the Caucasus into one body, and designates them as "dark whites." The Himyarite Arabs, as I have shown, derived their name originally from their red color, and they were constantly depicted on the Egyptian monuments as red or light brown. Herodotus tells us that there was a nation of Libyans, called the Maxyans, who claimed descent from the people of Troy (the walls of Troy, we shall see, were built by Poseidon; that is to say, Troy was an Atlantean colony). These Maxyans painted their whole bodies red. The Zavecians, the ancestors of the Zuavas of Algiers (the tribe that gave their name to the French Zouaves), also painted themselves red. Some of the Ethiopians were "copper-colored." ("'Amer. Cyclop.," art. Egypt, p. 464.) Tylor says ("Anthropology," p. 160): "The language of the ancient Egyptians, though it cannot be classed in the Semitic family with Hebrew, has important points of correspondence, whether due to the long intercourse between the two races in Egypt or to some deeper ancestral connection; and such analogies also appear in the Berber languages of North Africa."

These last were called by the ancients the Atlanteans.

"If a congregation of twelve representatives from Malacca, China, Japan, Mongolia, Sandwich Islands, Chili, Peru, Brazil, Chickasaws, Comanches, etc., were dressed alike, or undressed and unshaven, the most skilful anatomist could not, from their appearance, separate them." (Fontaine's "How the World was Peopled," pp. 147, 244.)

Ferdinand Columbus, in his relation of his father's voyages, compares the inhabitants of Guanaani to the Canary Islanders (an Atlantean race), and describes the inhabitants of San Domingo as still more beautiful and fair. In Peru the Charanzanis, studied by M. Angraud, also resemble the Canary Islanders. L'Abbé Brasseur de Bourbourg imagined himself surrounded by Arabs when all his Indians of Rabinal were around him; for they had, he said, their complexion, features, and beard. Pierre Martyr speaks of the Indians of the Parian Gulf as having fair hair. ("The Human Species," p. 201.) The same author believes that tribes belonging to the Semitic type are also found in America. He refers to "certain traditions of

Guiana, and the use in the country of a weapon entirely characteristic of the ancient Canary Islanders."

When science is able to disabuse itself of the Mortonian theory that the aborigines of America are all red men, and all belong to one race, we may hope that the confluence upon the continent of widely different races from different countries may come to be recognized and intelligently studied. There can be no doubt that red, white, black, and yellow men have united to form the original population of America. And there can be as little doubt that the entire population of Europe and the south shore of the Mediterranean is a mongrel race—a combination, in varying proportions, of a dark-brown or red race with a white race; the characteristics of the different nations depending upon the proportions in which the dark and light races are mingled, for peculiar mental and moral characteristics go with these complexions. The red-haired people are a distinct variety of the white stock; there were once whole tribes and nations with this color of hair; their blood is now intermingled with all the races of men, from Palestine to Iceland. Everything in Europe speaks of vast periods of time and long, continued and constant interfusion of bloods, until there is not a fair-skinned man on the Continent that has not the blood of the dark-haired race in his veins; nor scarcely a dark-skinned man that is not lighter in hue from intermixture with the white stock.

CHAPTER VI. GENESIS CONTAINS A HISTORY OF ATLANTIS

The Hebrews are a branch of the great family of which that powerful commercial race, the Phoenicians, who were the merchants of the world fifteen hundred years before the time of Christ, were a part. The Hebrews carried out from the common storehouse of their race a mass of traditions, many of which have come down to us in that oldest and most venerable of human compositions, the Book of Genesis. I have shown that the story of the Deluge plainly refers to the destruction of Atlantis, and that it agrees in many important particulars with the account given by Plato. The people destroyed were, in both instances, the ancient race that had created civilization; they had formerly been in a happy and sinless condition; they had become great and wicked; they were destroyed for their sins—they were destroyed by water.

But we can go farther, and it can be asserted that there is scarcely a prominent fact in the opening chapters of the Book of Genesis that cannot be duplicated from the legends of the American nations, and scarcely a custom known to the Jews that does not find its counterpart among the people of the New World.

Even in the history of the Creation we find these similarities:

The Bible tells us (Gen. i., 2) that in the beginning the earth was without form and void, and covered with water. In the Quiche legends we are told, "at first all was sea—no man, animal, bird, or green herb—there was nothing to be seen but the sea and the heavens."

The Bible says (Gen. i., 2), "And the Spirit of God moved upon the face of the waters." The Quiche legend says, "The Creator—the Former, the Dominator—the feathered serpent—those that give life, moved upon the waters like a glowing light."

The Bible says (Gen. i., 9), "And God said, Let the waters under the heaven be gathered together unto one place, and let the dry land appear: and it was so." The Quiche legend says, "The creative spirits cried out 'Earth!' and in an instant it was formed, and rose like a vapor-cloud; immediately the plains and the mountains arose, and the cypress and pine appeared."

The Bible tells us, "And God saw that it was good." The Quiche legend says, "Then Gucumatz was filled with joy, and cried out, 'Blessed be thy coming, O Heart of Heaven, Hurakan, thunder-bolt.'"

The order in which the vegetables, animals, and man were formed is the same in both records.

In Genesis (chap. ii., 7) we are told, "And the Lord God formed man of the dust of the ground." The Quiche legend says. "The first man was made of clay; but he had no intelligence, and was consumed in the water."

In Genesis the first man is represented as naked. The Aztec legend says, "The sun was much nearer the earth then than now, and his grateful warmth rendered clothing unnecessary."

Even the temptation of Eve reappears in the American legends. Lord Kingsborough says: "The Toltecs had paintings of a garden, with a single tree standing in the midst; round the root of the tree is entwined a serpent, whose head appearing above the foliage displays the face of a woman. Torquemada admits the existence of this tradition among them, and agrees with the Indian historians, who affirm that this was the first woman in the world, who bore children, and from whom all mankind are descended." ("Mexican Antiquities," vol. viii., p. 19.) There is also a legend of Suchiquecal, who disobediently gathered roses from a tree, and thereby disgraced and injured herself and all her posterity. ("Mexican Antiquities," vol. vi., p. 401.)

The legends of the Old World which underlie Genesis, and were used by Milton in the "Paradise Lost," appear in the Mexican legends of a war of angels in heaven, and the fall of Zou-tem-que (Soutem, Satan—Arabic, Shatana?) and the other rebellious spirits.

We have seen that the Central Americans possessed striking parallels to the account of the Deluge in Genesis.

There is also a clearly established legend which singularly resembles the Bible record of the Tower of Babel.

Father Duran, in his MS. "Historia Antiqua de la Nueva Espana," A.D. 1585, quotes from the lips of a native of Cholula, over one hundred years old, a version of the legend as to the building of the great pyramid of Cholula. It is as follows:

"In the beginning, before the light of the sun had been created, this land (Cholula) was in obscurity and darkness, and void of any created thing; all was a plain, without hill or elevation, encircled in every part by water, without tree or created thing; and immediately after the light and the sun arose in the east there appeared gigantic men of deformed stature and possessed the land, and desiring to see the nativity of the sun, as well as his occident, proposed to go and seek them. Dividing themselves into two parties, some journeyed to the west and others toward the east; these travelled; until the sea cut off their road, whereupon they determined to return to the place from which they started, and arriving at this place (Cholula), not finding the means of reaching the sun, enamored of his light and beauty, they determined to build a tower so high that its summit should reach the sky. Having collected materials for the purpose, they found a very adhesive clay and bitumen, with which they speedily commenced to build the tower; and having reared it to the greatest possible altitude, so that they say it reached to the sky, the Lord of the Heavens, enraged, said to the inhabitants of the sky, 'Have you observed how they of the earth have built a high and haughty tower to mount hither, being enamored of the light of the sun and his beauty? Come and confound them, because it is not right that they of the earth, living in the flesh, should mingle with us.' Immediately the inhabitants of the sky sallied forth like flashes of lightning; they destroyed the edifice, and divided and scattered its builders to all parts of the earth."

One can recognize in this legend the recollection, by a ruder race, of a highly civilized people; for only a highly civilized people would have attempted such a vast work. Their mental superiority and command of the arts gave them the character of giants who arrived from the East; who had

289

divided into two great emigrations, one moving eastward (toward Europe), the other westward (toward America). They were sun-worshippers; for we are told "they were enamored of the light and beauty of the sun," and they built a high place for his worship.

The pyramid of Cholula is one of the greatest constructions ever erected by human hands. It is even now, in its ruined condition, 160 feet high, 1400 feet square at the base, and covers forty-five acres; we have only to remember that the greatest pyramid of Egypt, Cheops, covers but twelve or thirteen acres, to form some conception of the magnitude of this American structure.

It must not be forgotten that this legend was taken down by a Catholic priest, shortly after the conquest of Mexico, from the lips of an old Indian who was born before Columbus sailed from Spain.

Observe the resemblances between this legend and the Bible account of the building of the Tower of Babel:

"All was a plain without hill or elevation," says the Indian legend. "They found a plain in the land of Shinar, and they dwelt there," says the Bible. They built of brick in both cases. "Let us build us a tower whose top may reach unto heaven," says the Bible. "They determined to build a tower so high that its summit should reach the sky," says the Indian legend. "And the Lord came down to see the city and the tower which the children of men had builded. And the Lord said, Behold ... nothing will be restrained from them which they have imagined to do. Go to, let us go down and confound them," says the Bible record. "The Lord of the Heavens, enraged, said to the inhabitants of the sky, 'Have you observed,' etc. Come and confound them," says the Indian record. "And the Lord scattered them abroad from thence on all the face of the earth," says the Bible. "They scattered its builders to all parts of the earth," says the Mexican legend.

Can any one doubt that these two legends must have sprung in some way from one another, or from some common source? There are enough points of difference to show that the American is not a servile copy of the Hebrew legend. In the former the story comes from a native of Cholula: it is told under the shadow of the mighty pyramid it commemorates; it is a local legend which he repeats. The men who built it, according to his account, were foreigners. They built it to reach the sun—that is to say, as a sun-temple; while in the Bible record Babel was built to perpetuate the glory of its architects. In the Indian legend the gods stop the work by a great storm, in the Bible account by confounding the speech of the people.

Both legends were probably derived from Atlantis, and referred to some gigantic structure of great height built by that people; and when the story emigrated to the east and west, it was in the one case affixed to the tower of the Chaldeans, and in the other to the pyramid of Cholula, precisely as we find the ark of the Deluge resting upon separate mountain-chains all the way from Greece to Armenia. In one form of the Tower of Babel legend, that of the Toltecs, we are told that the pyramid of Cholula was erected "as a means of escape from a second flood, should another occur."

But the resemblances between Genesis and the American legends do not stop here.

We are told (Gen. ii., 21) that "the Lord God caused a deep sleep to fall upon Adam," and while he slept God made Eve out of one of his ribs. According to the Quiche tradition, there were four men from whom the races of the world descended (probably a recollection of the red, black, yellow, and white races); and these men were without wives, and the Creator made wives for them "while they slept."

Some wicked misanthrope referred to these traditions when he said, "And man's first sleep became his last repose."

In Genesis (chap. iii., 22), "And the Lord God said, Behold, the man is become as one of us, to know good and evil: and now, lest he put forth his hand, and take also of the tree of life, and eat, and live forever:" therefore God drove him out of the garden. In the Quiche legends we are told, "The gods feared that they had made men too perfect, and they breathed a cloud of mist over their vision."

When the ancestors of the Quiches migrated to America the Divinity parted the sea for their passage, as the Red Sea was parted for the Israelites.

The story of Samson is paralleled in the history of a hero named Zipanca, told of in the "Popol Vuh," who, being captured by his enemies and placed in a pit, pulled down the building in which his captors had assembled, and killed four hundred of them.

"There were giants in those days," says the Bible. A great deal of the Central American history is taken up with the doings of an ancient race of giants called Quinames.

This parallelism runs through a hundred particulars:

Both the Jews and Mexicans worshipped toward the east.

Both called the south "the right hand of the world."

Both burnt incense toward the four corners of the earth.

Confession of sin and sacrifice of atonement were common to both peoples.

Both were punctilious about washings and ablutions.

Both believed in devils, and both were afflicted with leprosy.

Both considered women who died in childbirth as worthy of honor as soldiers who fell in battle.

Both punished adultery with stoning to death.

As David leaped and danced before the ark of the Lord, so did the

Mexican monarchs before their idols.

Both had an ark, the abiding-place of an invisible god.

Both had a species of serpent-worship.

Compare our representation of the great serpent-mound in Adams County, Ohio, with the following description of a great serpent-mound in Scotland:

"Serpent-worship in the West.—Some additional light appears to have been thrown upon ancient serpent-worship in the West by the recent archæological explorations of Mr. John S. Phené, F.G.S., F.R.G.S., in Scotland. Mr. Phené has just investigated a curious earthen mound in Glen Feechan, Argyleshire, referred to by him, at the late meeting of the British Association in Edinburgh, as being in the form of a serpent or saurian. The mound, says the Scotsman, is a most perfect one. The head is a large cairn, and the body of the earthen reptile 300 feet long; and in the centre of the head there were evidences, when Mr. Phené first visited it, of an altar having been placed there. The position with regard to Ben Cruachan is most remarkable. The three peaks are seen over the length of the reptile when a person is standing on the head, or cairn. The shape can only be seen so as to be understood when looked down upon from an elevation, as the outline cannot be understood unless the whole of it can be seen. This is most perfect when the spectator is on the head of the animal form, or on the lofty rock to the west of it. This mound corresponds almost entirely with one 700 feet long in America, an account of which was lately published, after careful survey, by Mr. Squier. The altar toward the head in each case agrees. In the American mound three rivers (also objects of worship with the ancients) were evidently identified. The number three was a sacred number in all ancient mythologies. The sinuous winding and articulations of the vertebral spinal arrangement are anatomically perfect in the Argyleshire mound. The gentlemen present with Mr. Phené during his investigation state that beneath the cairn forming the head of the animal was found a megalithic chamber, in which was a quantity of charcoal and burnt earth and charred

292

nutshells, a flint instrument, beautifully and minutely serrated at the edge, and burnt bones. The back or spine of the serpent, which, as already stated, is 300 feet long, was found, beneath the peat moss, to be formed by a careful adjustment of stones, the formation of which probably prevented the structure from being obliterated by time and weather." (Pall Mall Gazette.)

We find a striking likeness between the works of the Stone Age in America and Europe.

The same singular custom which is found among the Jews and the Hindoos, for "a man to raise up seed for his deceased brother by marrying his widow," was found among the Central American nations. (Las Casas, MS. "Hist. Apoloq.," cap. ccxiii., ccxv. Torquemada, "Monarq. Ind.," tom. ii., 377-8.)

No one but the Jewish high-priest might enter the Holy of Holies. A similar custom obtained in Peru. Both ate the flesh of the sacrifices of atonement; both poured the blood of the sacrifice on the earth; they sprinkled it, they marked persons with it, they smeared it upon walls and stones. The Mexican temple, like the Jewish, faced the east. "As among the Jews the ark was a sort of portable temple, in which the Deity was supposed to be continually present, so among the Mexicans, the Cherokees, and the Indians of Michoacan and Honduras, an ark was held in the highest veneration, and was considered an object too sacred to be touched by any but the priests." (Kingsborough, "Mex. Antiq., "vol. viii., p. 258.)

The Peruvians believed that the rainbow was a sign that the earth would not be again destroyed by a deluge. (Ibid., p. 25.)

The Jewish custom of laying the sins of the people upon the head of an animal, and turning him out into the wilderness, had its counterpart among the Mexicans, who, to cure a fever, formed a dog of maize paste and left it by the roadside, saying the first passer-by would carry away the illness. (Dorman, "Prim. Super.," p. 59.) Jacob's ladder had its duplicate in the vine or tree of the Ojibbeways, which led from the earth to heaven, up and down which the spirits passed. (Ibid., p. 67.)

Both Jews and Mexicans offered water to a stranger that he might wash his feet; both ate dust in token of humility; both anointed with oil; both sacrificed prisoners; both periodically separated the women, and both agreed in the strong and universal idea of uncleanness connected with that period.

Both believed in the occult power of water, and both practised baptism.

"Then the Mexican midwife gave the child to taste of the water, putting her moistened fingers in its mouth, and said, 'Take this; by this thou hast to live on the earth, to grow and to flourish; through this we get all things that support existence on the earth; receive it.' Then with moistened fingers she touched the breast of the child, and said, 'Behold the pure water that washes and cleanses thy heart, that removes all filthiness; receive it: may the goddess see good to purify and cleanse thine heart.' Then the midwife poured water upon the head of the child, saying, 'O my grandson—my son—take this water of the Lord of the world, which is thy life, invigorating and refreshing, washing and cleansing. I pray that this celestial water, blue and light blue, may enter into thy body, and there live; I pray that it may destroy in thee and put away from thee all the things evil and adverse that were given thee before the beginning of the world.... Wheresoever thou art in this child, O thou hurtful thing, begone! leave it, put thyself apart; for now does it live anew, and anew is it born; now again is it purified and cleansed; now again is it shaped and engendered by our mother, the goddess of water." (Bancroft's "Native Races," vol. iii., p. 372.)

Here we find many resemblances to the Christian ordinance of baptism: the pouring of the water on the head, the putting of the fingers in the mouth, the touching of the breast, the new birth, and the washing away of the original sin. The Christian rite, we know, was not a Christian invention, but was borrowed from ancient times, from the great storehouse of Asiatic traditions and beliefs.

The Mexicans hung up the heads of their sacrificed enemies; this was also a Jewish custom:

"And the Lord said unto Moses, Take all the heads of the people, and hang them up before the Lord against the sun, that the fierce anger of the Lord may be turned away from Israel. And Moses said unto the judges of Israel, Slay ye every one his men that were joined unto Baal-peor." (Numb., xxv., 4, 5.)

The Scythians, Herodotus tells us, scalped their enemies, and carried the scalp at the pommel of their saddles; the Jews probably scalped their enemies:

"But God shall wound the head of his enemies, and the hairy scalp of such a one as goeth on still in his trespasses." (Psa., lxviii., 21.)

The ancient Scandinavians practised scalping. When Harold Harefoot seized his rival, Alfred, with six hundred followers, he "had them maimed, blinded, hamstrung, scalped, or embowelled." (Taine's "Hist. Eng. Lit.," p. 35.)

Herodotus describes the Scythian mode of taking the scalp: "He makes a cut round the head near the ears, and shakes the skull out." This is

294

precisely the Indian custom. "The more scalps a man has," says Herodotus, "the more highly he is esteemed among them."

The Indian scalp-lock is found on the Egyptian monuments as one of the characteristics of the Japhetic Libyans, who shaved all the head except one lock in the middle.

The Mantchoos of Tartary wear a scalp-lock, as do the modern Chinese.

Byron describes the heads of the dead Tartars under the walls of Corinth, devoured by the wild dogs:

"Crimson and green were the shawls of their wear,

And each scalp had a single long tuft of hair,

All the rest was shaven and bare."

These resemblances are so striking and so numerous that repeated attempts have been made to prove that the inhabitants of America are the descendants of the Jews; some have claimed that they represented "the lost tribes" of that people. But the Jews were never a maritime or emigrating people; they formed no colonies; and it is impossible to believe (as has been asserted) that they left their flocks and herds, marched across the whole face of Asia, took ships and sailed across the greatest of the oceans to a continent of the existence of which they had no knowledge.

If we seek the origin of these extraordinary coincidences in opinions and habits, we must go far back to the time of the lost tribes. We must seek it in the relationship of the Jews to the family of Noah, and in the identity of the Noachic race destroyed in the Deluge with the people of the drowned Atlantis.

Nor need it surprise us to find traditions perpetuated for thousands upon thousands of years, especially among a people having a religious priesthood.

The essence of religion is conservatism; little is invented; nothing perishes; change comes from without; and even when one religion is supplanted by another its gods live on as the demons of the new faith, or they pass into the folk-lore and fairy stories of the people. We see Votan, a hero in America, become the god Odin or Woden in Scandinavia; and when his worship as a god dies out Odin survives (as Dr. Dasent has proved) in the Wild Huntsman of the Hartz, and in the Robin Hood (Oodin) of popular legend. The Hellequin of France becomes the Harlequin of our pantomimes. William Tell never existed; he is a myth; a survival of the sun-god Apollo, Indra, who was worshipped on the altars of Atlantis.

"Nothing here but it doth change into something rich and strange."

The rite of circumcision dates back to the first days of Phoenicia, Egypt, and the Cushites. It, too, was probably an Atlantean custom, invented in the Stone Age. Tens of thousands of years have passed since the Stone Age; the ages of copper, bronze, and iron have intervened; and yet to this day the Hebrew rabbi performs the ceremony of circumcision with a stone knife. Frothingham says, speaking of St. Peter's Cathedral, in Rome: "Into what depths of antiquity the ceremonies carried me back! To the mysteries of Eleusis; to the sacrificial rites of Phoenicia. The boys swung the censors as censors had been swung in the adoration of Bacchus. The girdle and cassock of the priests came from Persia; the veil and tonsure were from Egypt; the alb and chasuble were prescribed by Numa Pompilius; the stole was borrowed from the official who used to throw it on the back of the victim that was to be sacrificed; the white surplice was the same as described by Juvenal and Ovid."

Although it is evident that many thousands of years must have passed since the men who wrote in Sanscrit, in Northwestern India, could have dwelt in Europe, yet to this day they preserve among their ancient books maps and descriptions of the western coast of Europe, and even of England and Ireland; and we find among them a fuller knowledge of the vexed question of the sources of the Nile than was possessed by any nation in the world twenty-five years ago.

This perpetuation of forms and beliefs is illustrated in the fact that the formulas used in the Middle Ages in Europe to exorcise evil spirits were Assyrian words, imported probably thousands of years before from the magicians of Chaldea. When the European conjurer cried out to the demon, "Hilka, hilka, besha, besha," he had no idea that he was repeating the very words of a people who had perished ages before, and that they signified Go away, go away, evil one, evil one. (Lenormant, "Anc. Hist. East," vol. i., p. 448.)

Our circle of 360 degrees; the division of a chord of the circle equal to the radius into 60 equal parts, called degrees: the division of these into 60 minutes, of the minute into 60 seconds, and the second into 60 thirds; the division of the day into 24 hours, each hour into 60 minutes, each minute into 60 seconds; the division of the week into seven days, and the very order of the days—all have come down to us from the Chaldeo-Assyrians; and these things will probably be perpetuated among our posterity "to the last syllable of recorded time."

We need not be surprised, therefore, to find the same legends and beliefs cropping out among the nations of Central America and the people of Israel. Nay, it should teach us to regard the Book of Genesis with increased veneration, as a relic dating from the most ancient days of man's history on earth; its roots cross the great ocean; every line is valuable; a word, a letter, an accent may throw light upon the gravest problems of the birth of civilization.

The vital conviction which, during thousands of years, at all times pressed home upon the Israelites, was that they were a "chosen people," selected out of all the multitude of the earth, to perpetuate the great truth that there was but one God—an illimitable, omnipotent, paternal spirit, who rewarded the good and punished the wicked—in contradistinction from the multifarious, subordinate, animal and bestial demi-gods of the other nations of the earth. This sublime monotheism could only have been the outgrowth of a high civilization, for man's first religion is necessarily a worship of "stocks and stones," and history teaches us that the gods decrease in number as man increases in intelligence. It was probably in Atlantis that monotheism was first preached. The proverbs of "Ptah-hotep," the oldest book of the Egyptians, show that this most ancient colony from Atlantis received the pure faith from the mother-land at the very dawn of history: this book preached the doctrine of one God, "the rewarder of the good and the punisher of the wicked." (Reginald S. Poole, Contemporary Rev., Aug., 1881, p. 38.) "In the early days the Egyptians worshipped one only God, the maker of all things, without beginning and without end. To the last the priests preserved this doctrine and taught it privately to a select few." ("Amer. Encycl.," vol. vi., p. 463.) The Jews took up this great truth where the Egyptians dropped it, and over the heads and over the ruins of Egypt, Chaldea, Phoenicia, Greece, Rome, and India this handful of poor shepherds—ignorant, debased, and despised—have carried down to our own times a conception which could only have originated in the highest possible state of human society.

And even skepticism must pause before the miracle of the continued existence of this strange people, wading through the ages, bearing on their shoulders the burden of their great trust, and pressing forward under the force of a perpetual and irresistible impulse. The speech that may be heard to-day in the synagogues of Chicago and Melbourne resounded two thousand years ago in the streets of Rome; and, at a still earlier period, it could be heard in the palaces of Babylon and the shops of Thebes—in Tyre, in Sidon, in Gades, in Palmyra, in Nineveh. How many nations have perished, how many languages have ceased to exist, how many splendid civilizations have crumbled into ruin, how many temples and towers and towns have gone down to dust since the sublime frenzy of monotheism first seized this extraordinary people! All their kindred nomadic tribes are gone; their land of promise is in the hands of strangers; but Judaism, with its offspring, Christianity, is taking possession of the habitable world; and the continuous life of one people—one poor, obscure, and wretched people—spans the tremendous gulf between "Ptah-hotep" and this nineteenth century.

If the Spirit of which the universe is but an expression—of whose frame the stars are the infinite molecules—can be supposed ever to interfere with the laws of matter and reach down into the doings of men, would it not be to save from the wreck and waste of time the most sublime fruit of the civilization of the drowned Atlantis—a belief in the one, only, just God, the father of all life, the imposer of all moral obligations?

CHAPTER VII. THE ORIGIN OF OUR ALPHABET

One of the most marvellous inventions for the advancement of mankind is the phonetic alphabet, or a system of signs representing the sounds of human speech. Without it our present civilization could scarcely have been possible.

No solution of the origin of our European alphabet has yet been obtained: we can trace it back from nation to nation, and form to form, until we reach the Egyptians, and the archaic forms of the Phoenicians, Hebrews, and Cushites, but beyond this the light fails us.

The Egyptians spoke of their hieroglyphic system of writing not as their own invention, but as "the language of the gods." (Lenormant and Cheval, "Anc. Hist. of the East," vol. ii., p. 208.) "The gods" were, doubtless, their highly civilized ancestors—the people of Atlantis—who, as we shall hereafter see, became the gods of many of the Mediterranean races.

"According to the Phoenicians, the art of writing was invented by Taautus, or Taut, 'whom the Egyptians call Thouth,' and the Egyptians said it was invented by Thouth, or Thoth, otherwise called 'the first Hermes,' in which we clearly see that both the Phoenicians and Egyptians referred the invention to a period older than their own separate political existence, and to an older nation, from which both peoples received it." (Baldwin's "Prehistoric Nations," p. 91.)

The "first Hermes," here referred to (afterward called Mercury by the Romans), was a son of Zeus and Maia, a daughter of Atlas. This is the same Maia whom the Abbé Brasseur de Bourbourg identifies with the Maya of Central America.

Sir William Drummond, in his "Origines," said:

"There seems to be no way of accounting either for the early use of letters among so many different nations, or for the resemblance which existed between some of the graphic systems employed by those nations, than by supposing hieroglyphical writing, if I may be allowed the term, to have been in use among the Tsabaists in the first ages after the Flood, when Tsabaisin (planet-worship) was the religion of almost every country that was yet inhabited."

Sir Henry Rawlinson says:

"So great is the analogy between the first principles of the Science of writing, as it appears to have been pursued in Chaldea, and as we can actually trace its progress in Egypt, that we can hardly hesitate to assign the original invention to a period before the Hamitic race had broken up and divided."

It is not to be believed that such an extraordinary system of sound-signs could have been the invention of any one man or even of any one age. Like all our other acquisitions, it must have been the slow growth and accretion of ages; it must have risen step by step from picture-writing through an intermediate condition like that of the Chinese, where each word or thing was represented by a separate sign. The fact that so old and enlightened a people as the Chinese have never reached a phonetic alphabet, gives us some indication of the greatness of the people among whom it was invented, and the lapse of time before they attained to it.

Humboldt says: "According to the views which, since Champollion's great discovery, have been gradually adopted regarding the earlier condition of the development of alphabetical writing, the Phoenician as well as the Semitic characters are to be regarded as a phonetic alphabet that has originated from pictorial writing; as one in which the ideal signification of the symbols is wholly disregarded, and the characters are regarded as mere signs for sounds." ("Cosmos," vol. ii., p. 129.)

Baldwin says ("Prehistoric Nations," p. 93): "The nation that became mistress of the seas, established communication with every shore, and monopolized the commerce of the known world, must have substituted a phonetic alphabet for the hieroglyphics as it gradually grew to this eminence; while isolated Egypt, less affected by the practical wants and tendencies of commercial enterprise, retained the hieroglyphic system, and carried it to a marvellous height of perfection."

It must be remembered that some of the letters of our alphabet are inventions of the later nations. In the oldest alphabets there was no c, the g taking its place. The Romans converted the g into c; and then, finding the necessity for a g Sign, made one by adding a tail-piece to the c (C, G). The Greeks added to the ancient alphabet the upsilon, shaped like our V or Y, the two forms being used at first indifferently: they added the X sign; they converted the t of the Phoenicians into th, or theta; z and s into signs for double consonants; they turned the Phoenician y (yod) into i (iota). The Greeks converted the Phoenician alphabet, which was partly consonantal, into one purely phonetic—"a perfect instrument for the expression of spoken language." The w was also added to the Phoenician alphabet. The Romans added the y. At first i and j were both indicated by the same sound; a sign for j was afterward added. We have also, in common with other European languages, added a double U, that is, VV, or W, to represent the w sound.

The letters, then, which we owe to the Phoenicians, are A, B, C, D, E, H, I, K, L, M, N, O, P, Q, R, S, T, Z. If we are to trace out resemblances with the alphabet of any other country, it must be with these signs.

Is there any other country to which we can turn which possessed a phonetic alphabet in any respect kindred to this Phoenician alphabet? It cannot be the Chinese alphabet, which has more signs than words; it cannot be the cuneiform alphabet of Assyria, with its seven hundred arrow-shaped characters, none of which bear the slightest affinity to the Phoenician letters.

It is a surprising fact that we find in Central America a phonetic alphabet. This is in the alphabet of the Mayas, the ancient people of the peninsula of Yucatan, who claim that their civilization came to them across the sea in ships from the east, that is, from the direction of Atlantis. The Mayas succeeded to the Colhuas, whose era terminated one thousand years before the time of Christ; from them they received their alphabet. It has come to us through Bishop Landa, one of the early missionary bishops, who confesses to having burnt a great number of Maya books because they contained nothing but the works of the devil. He fortunately, however, preserved for posterity the alphabet of this people. We present it herewith.

Diego de Landa was the first bishop of Yucatan. He wrote a history of the Mayas and their country, which was preserved in manuscript at Madrid in the library of the Royal Academy of History.... It contains a description and explanation of the phonetic alphabet of the Mayas. Landa's manuscript seems to have lain neglected in the library, for little or nothing was heard of it until it was discovered by the French priest Brasseur de Bourbourg, who, by means of it, has deciphered some of the old American writings. He says, 'the alphabet and signs explained by Landa have been to me a Rosetta stone.' (Baldwin's "Ancient America," p. 191.)

LANDA'S ALPHABET (From "North Amer. of Antiquity," p. 434.)

When we observe, in the table of alphabets of different European nations which I give herewith, how greatly the forms of the Phoenician letters have been modified, it would surprise us to find any resemblance between the Maya alphabet of two or three centuries since and the ancient European forms. It must, however, be remembered that the Mayas are one of the most conservative peoples in the world. They still adhere with striking pertinacity to the language they spoke when Columbus landed on San Salvador; and it is believed that that language is the same as the one inscribed on the most ancient monuments of their country. Señor Pimental says of them, "The Indians have preserved this idiom with such tenacity that they will speak no other; it is necessary for the whites to address them in their own language to communicate with them." It is therefore probable, as their alphabet did not pass from nation to nation, as did the Phoenician, that it has not departed so widely from the original forms received from the Colhuas.

301

	Maya	Maya		Archaic Phoenician						Hieroglyph	Arch. Greek	Later Greek	
A													
B													
C													
D													
AE													
V													
Z													
CH													
T													
I													
K													
L													
M													
N													
NX													
O													
P													
Q													
R													
S													

The Alphabet

But when we consider the vast extent of time which has elapsed, and the fact that we are probably without the intermediate stages of the alphabet which preceded the archaic Phoenician, it will be astonishing if we find resemblances between any of the Maya letters and the European forms, even though we concede that they are related. If we find decided affinities between two or three letters, we may reasonably presume that similar coincidences existed as to many others which have disappeared under the attrition of centuries.

The first thought that occurs to us on examining the Landa alphabet is the complex and ornate character of the letters. Instead of the two or three strokes with which we indicate a sign for a sound, we have here rude pictures of objects. And we find that these are themselves simplifications of older forms of a still more complex character. Take, for instance, the letter

pp in Landa's alphabet, : here are evidently the traces of a face. The same appear, but not so plainly, in the sign for *x*, which is ![face glyph]. Now, if we turn to the ancient hieroglyphics upon the monuments of Central America, we will find the human face appearing in a great many of them, as in the following, which we copy from the Tablet of the Cross at Palenque. We take the hieroglyphs from the left-hand side

 of the inscription. Here it will be seen that, out of seven hieroglyphical figures, six contain human faces. And we find that in the whole inscription of the Tablet of the Cross there are 33 figures out of 108 that are made up in part of the human countenance.

We can see, therefore, in the Landa alphabet a tendency to simplification. And this is what we would naturally expect. When the emblems--which were probably first intended for religious inscriptions, where they could be slowly and carefully elaborated--were placed in the hands of a busy, active, commercial people, such as were the Atlanteans, and afterward the Phœnicians, men with whom time was valuable, the natural tendency would be to simplify and condense them; and when the original meaning of the picture was lost, they would naturally slur it, as we find in the letters *pp* and *x* of the Maya alphabet, where the figure of the human face remains only in rude lines.

The same tendency is plainly shown in the two forms of the letter *h*, as given in Landa's alphabet; the original form is more elaborate than the variation of it. The original form is ![glyph]. The variation is given as ![glyph]. Now let us suppose this simplification to be carried a step farther: we have seen the upper and lower parts of the first form shrink into a smaller and less elaborate shape; let us imagine that the same tendency does away with them altogether; we would then have the letter H of the Maya alphabet represented by this figure, ![glyph]; now, as it takes less time to make a single stroke than a double one, this would become in time ![glyph]. We turn now to the archaic Greek and the old Hebrew, and we find the letter *h* indicated by this sign, ![glyph], precisely the Maya letter *h* simplified. We turn to the archaic Hebrew, and we find ![glyph]. Now it is known that the Phœnicians wrote from right to left, and just as we in writing from left to right slope our letters to the right, so did the Phœnicians slope their letters to the left. Hence the

303

Maya sign becomes in the archaic Phœnician this, . In some of the Phœnician alphabets we even find the letter h made with the double strokes above and below, as in the Maya *h.* The Egyptian hieroglyph for *h* is while *ch* is . In time the Greeks carried the work of simplification still farther, and eliminated the top lines, as we have supposed the Atlanteans to have eliminated the double strokes, and they left the letter as it has come down to us, H.

Now it may be said that all this is coincidence. If it is, it is certainly remarkable. But let us go a step farther:

We have seen in Landa's alphabet that there are two forms of the letter *m.* The first is . But we find also an *m* combined with the letter *o, a,* or *e,* says Landa, in this form, . The *m* here is certainly indicated by the central part of this combination, the figure ; where does that come from? It is clearly taken from the heart of the original figure wherein it appears. What does this prove? That the Atlanteans, or Mayas, when they sought to simplify their letters and combine them with others, took from the centre of the ornate hieroglyphical figure some characteristic mark with which they represented the whole figure. Now let us apply this rule:

We have seen in the table of alphabets that in every language, from our own day to the time of the Phœnicians, *o* has been represented by a circle or a circle within a circle. Now where did the Phœnicians get it? Clearly from the Mayas. There are two figures for *o* in the Maya alphabet; they are and ; now, if we apply the rule which we have seen to exist in the case of the Maya *m* to these figures, the essential characteristic found in each is the circle, in the first case pendant from the hieroglyph; in the other, in the centre of the lower part of it. And that this circle was withdrawn from the hieroglyph, and used alone, as in the case of the *m,* is proved by the very sign used at the foot of Landa's alphabet, which is, . Landa calls this *ma, me,* or *mo;* it is probably the latter, and in it we have the circle detached from the hieroglyph.

We find the precise Maya *o* a circle in a circle, or a dot within a circle, repeated in the Phœnician forms for *o,* thus, and , and by exactly the same forms in the Egyptian hieroglyphics; in the Runic we have the circle in the circle; in one form of the Greek o the dot was placed along-side of the circle instead of below it, as in the Maya.

Are these another set of coincidences?

Take another letter:

The letter *n* of the Maya alphabet is represented by this sign, itself probably a simplification of some more ornate form, $\mathcal{S}$. This is something like our letter S, but quite unlike our N. But let us examine into the pedigree of our *n*. We find in the archaic Ethiopian, a language as old as the Egyptian, and which represents the Cushite branch of the Atlantean stock, the sign for *n* (*na*) is $\mathcal{Z}$; in archaic Phœnician it comes still closer to the S shape, thus, $\mathcal{S}$, or in this form, $\mathcal{S}$; we have but to curve these angles to approximate it very closely to the Maya *n*; in Troy this form was found, $\mathcal{S}$. The Samaritan makes it $\mathcal{P}$; the old Hebrew $\mathcal{S}$; the Moab stone inscription gives it $\mathcal{Y}$; the later Phœnicians simplified the archaic form still further, until it became $\mathcal{S}$; then it passed into $\mathcal{S}$: the archaic Greek form is $\mathcal{M}$; the later Greeks made $\mathcal{N}$, from which it passed into the present form, N. All these forms seem to be representations of a serpent; we turn to the valley of the Nile, and we find that the Egyptian hieroglyphic for *n* was the serpent, $\sim\!\!\sim$; the Pelasgian *n* was $\mathcal{Z}$; the Arcadian, $\mathcal{S}$; the Etruscan, $\mathcal{Z}$.

Can anything be more significant than to find the serpent the sign for *n* in Central America, and in all these Old World languages?

Now turn to the letter *k*. The Maya sign for *k* is ⊙. This does not look much like our letter K; but let us examine it. Following the precedent established for us by the Mayas in the case of the letter m, let us see what is the distinguishing feature here; it is clearly the figure of a serpent standing erect, with its tail doubled around its middle, forming a circle. It has already been remarked by Savolini that this erect serpent is very much like the

Egyptian *Uræus*, an erect serpent with an enlarged body--a sacred emblem found in the hair of their deities. We turn again to the valley of the Nile, and we find that the Egyptian hieroglyphic for *k* was a serpent with a convolution or protuberance in the middle, precisely as in the Maya, thus,

; this was transformed into the Egyptian letter ; the serpent and the protuberance reappear in one of the Phœnician forms of *k*, to wit,

; while in the Punic we have these forms, and . Now suppose a busy people trying to give this sign: instead of drawing the serpent in all

its details they would abbreviate it into something like this, ; now we

turn to the ancient Ethiopian sign for *k* (*ka*), and we have , or the

Himyaritic Arabian ; while in the Phœnician it becomes ; in the

archaic Greek, ; and in the later Greek, when they changed the writing

from left to right, K. So that the two lines projecting from the upright stroke of our English K are a reminiscence of the convolution of the serpent in the Maya original and the Egyptian copy.

Turn now to the Maya sign for *t*: it is . What is the distinctive mark

about this figure? It is the cross composed of two curved lines, thus, . It is probable that in the Maya sign the cross is united at the bottom, like a figure *8*. Here again we turn to the valley of the Nile, and we find that the

Egyptian hieroglyph for *t* is and ; and in the Syriac *t* it is . We even find the curved lines of the Maya *t* which give it something of the appearance of the numeral *8*, repeated accurately in the Mediterranean

alphabets; thus the Punic *t* repeats the Maya form almost exactly as

and . Now suppose a busy people compelled to make this mark every day for a thousand years, and generally in a hurry, and the cross would soon be made without curving the lines; it would become **X**. But before it reached even that simplified form it had crossed the Atlantic, and appeared in the archaic Ethiopian sign for *tsa*, thus, ⋈. In the archaic Phœnician the sign

for *t* is ⊕ and ✕; the oldest Greek form is ⊗ or ✕ and the later

Greeks gave it to the Romans ⊤, and modified this into ⊖; the old

Hebrew gave it as ✕ and ✝; the Moab stone as ✕; this became in

time ✝ and ⊤.

Take the letter *a*. In the Maya there are three forms given for this letter.

The first is ⌇; the third is ⌇. The first looks very much like the foot of
a lion or tiger; the third is plainly a foot or boot. If one were required to give
hurriedly a rude outline of either of these, would he not represent it thus,

ᶑ; and can we not conceive that this could have been in time modified

into the Phœnician *a*, which was ⋋? The hieratic Egyptian *a* was ᘔ; the

ancient Hebrew, which was ⵗ or ⵡ; the ancient Greek was the

foot reversed, ᐱ; the later Greek became our A.

Turn next to the Maya sign for *q* (*ku*): it is ◉. Now what is the
peculiarity of this hieroglyph? The circle below is not significant, for there
are many circular figures in the Maya alphabet. Clearly, if one was called
upon to simplify this, he would retain the two small circles joined side by
side at the top, and would indicate the lower circle with a line or dash. And

when we turn to the Egyptian *q* we find it in this shape, ⵗ; we turn

to the Ethiopian *q* (*khua*), and we find it ⵗ, as *qua*, ⵗ; while the

Phœnician comes still nearer the supposed Maya form in φ; the Moab

stone was φ; the Himyaritic Arabian form became φ; the Greek form

was φ, which graduated into the Roman Q. But a still more striking proof
of the descent of the Phœnician alphabet from the Maya is found in the

other form of the *q*, the Maya *cu*, which is . Now, if we apply the Maya

rule to this, and discard the outside circle, we have this left, . In time the curved line would be made straight, and the figure would assume this

form, ; the next step would be to make the cross on the straight line,

thus, . One of the ancient Phœnician forms is . Can all this be accident?

The letter *c* or *g* (for the two probably gave the same sound as in the

Phœnician) is given in the Maya alphabet as follows, . This would in time be simplified into a figure representing the two sides of a triangle with

the apex upward, thus, . This is precisely the form found by Dr.

Schliemann in the ruins of Troy, . What is the Phœnician form for *g* as

found on the Moab stone? It is . The Carthaginian Phœnicians gave it

more of a rounded form, thus, . The hieratic Egyptian figure for *g* was

; in the earlier Greek form the left limb of the figure was shortened,

thus, ; the later Greeks reversed it, and wrote it ; the Romans,

changed this into and it finally became C.

In the Maya we have one sign for *p*, and another for *pp*. The first

contains a curious figure, precisely like our *r* laid on its back , There is, apparently, no *r* in the Maya alphabet; and the Roman *r* grew out of the

later Phœnician *r* formed thus, ; it would appear that the earliest Phœnician alphabet did not contain the letter *r*. But if we now turn to the Phœnician alphabet, we will find one of the curious forms of the *p* given

thus, , a very fair representation of an *r* lying upon its face. Is it not another remarkable coincidence that the *p*, in both Maya and Phœnician, should contain this singular sign?

308

The form of *pp* in the Maya alphabet is this, . If we are asked, on the principle already indicated, to reduce this to its elements, we would use

a figure like this, ; in time the tendency would be to shorten one of these perpendicular lines, thus, and this we find is very much like the Phœnician

p, . The Greek *ph* is Φ.

The letter *l* in the Maya is in two forms; one of these is , the other

is . Now, if we again apply the rule which we observed to hold good with the letter *m*--that is, draw from the inside of the hieroglyph some symbol that will briefly indicate the whole letter--we will have one of two

forms, either a right-angled figure formed thus, , or an acute angle

formed by joining the two lines which are unconnected, thus, ; and either of these forms brings us quite close to the letter *l* of the Old World.

We find *l* on the Moab stone thus formed, . The archaic Phœnician form

of *l* was , or ; the archaic Hebrew was and ; the hieratic

Egyptian was ; the Greek form was --the Roman L.

The Maya letter *b* is shaped thus, . Now, if we turn to the Phœnician, we find that *b* is represented by the same crescent-like figure which we find in the middle of this hieroglyph, but reversed in the direction

of the writing, thus, ; while in the archaic Hebrew we have the same crescent figure as in the Maya, turned in the same direction, but

accompanied by a line drawn downward, and to the left, thus, ; a

similar form is also found in the Phœnician , and this in the earliest

Greek changed into , and in the later Greek into B. One of the Etruscan

signs for *b* was , while the Pelasgian *b* was represented thus, ;

the Chaldaic *b* was ⟨symbol⟩ ; the Syriac sign for *b* was ⟨symbol⟩ ?B; the Illyrian *b* was ⟨symbol⟩ .

The Maya *e* is ⟨symbol⟩ ; this became in time ⟨symbol⟩ ; then ⟨symbol⟩ (we see this form on the Maya monuments); the dots in time were indicated by strokes, and we reach the hieratic Egyptian form, ⟨symbol⟩ : we even find in some of the ancient Phœnician inscriptions the original Maya circles preserved in making the letter *e*, thus, ⟨symbol⟩ ; then we find the old Greek form, ⟨symbol⟩ ; the old Hebrew, ⟨symbol⟩ ; and the later Phœnician, ⟨symbol⟩ : when the direction of the writing was changed this became ⟨symbol⟩ . Dr. Schliemann found a form like this on inscriptions deep in the ruins of Troy, ⟨symbol⟩ . This is exactly the form found on the American monuments.

The Maya *i* is ⟨symbol⟩ ; this became in time ⟨symbol⟩ ; this developed into a still simpler form, ⟨symbol⟩ ; and this passed into the Phœnician form, ⟨symbol⟩ . The Samaritan *i* was formed thus, ⟨symbol⟩ ; the Egyptian letter *i* is ⟨symbol⟩ : gradually in all these the left-hand line was dropped, and we come to the figure used on the stone of Moab, ⟨symbol⟩ and ⟨symbol⟩ ; this in time became the old Hebrew ⟨symbol⟩ , or ⟨symbol⟩ ; and this developed into the Greek ⟨symbol⟩ .

We have seen the complicated symbol for *m* reduced by the Mayas themselves into this figure, ⟨symbol⟩ : if we attempt to write this rapidly, we find it very difficult to always keep the base lines horizontal; naturally we form something like this, ⟨symbol⟩ : the distinctive figure within the sign for *m* in the Maya is ٦ ?X or ⊏ . We see this repeated in the Egyptian hieroglyphics for *m*, ⊏ , and ⊔⊔⊔⊔ , and ⊐ ; and in the Chaldaic *m*, ٦ מ; and in the Ethiopic ⊓⊓ . We find one form of the Phœnician where the *m* is made thus, ⌐⊐ ; and in the Punic it appears thus, ⌐┘ ; and this is not unlike the *m* on the stone of Moab, ᴡ· , or the ancient Phœnician forms ᵐᶜ , ᶜᵧ , and the old Greek ᴍ , or the ancient Hebrew ᵐᶜ , ᵗᶜ .

The X, *x*, of the Maya alphabet is a hand pointing downward 🐦 , this, reduced to its elements, would be expressed some thing like this, ///∖ or ᴡᴧ∖ ; and this is very much like the *x* of the archaic Phœnician, ≢ ; or the Moab stone, ╤ ; or the later Phœnician ╤ or the Hebrew ᶾᵢ , ⧫ , or the old Greek, ⅂ : the later Greek form was Ξ.

The Maya alphabet contains no sign for the letter *s*; there is, however, a symbol called *ca* immediately above the letter *k*; it is probable that the sign *ca* stands for the soft sound of *c*, as, in our words *citron*, *circle*, *civil*, *circus*, etc. As it is written in the Maya alphabet *ca*, and not *k*, it evidently represents a different sound. The sign *ca* is this, ℰ . A somewhat similar sign is found in the body of the symbol for *k*, thus, ⊓⊓⊓ , this would appear to be a simplification of *ca*, but turned downward. If now we turn to the Egyptian letters we find the sign *k* represented by this figure ⟨⟨ , simplified again into ⊂ ; while the sign for *k* in the Phœnician inscription on the stone of Moab is ⅄ . If now we turn to the *s* sound, indicated by the Maya sign *ca*, ℰ , we find the resemblance still more

311

striking to kindred European letters. The Phœnician *s* is

; in the Greek this becomes ; the Hebrew is ; the Samaritan, . The Egyptian hieroglyph for *s* is ; the Egyptian letter *sis* ; the Ethiopic, ; the Chaldaic, ; and the Illyrian *s c* is .

We have thus traced back the forms of eighteen of the ancient letters to the Maya alphabet. In some cases the pedigree, is so plain as to be indisputable.

For instance, take the *h*:

Maya, ; old Greek, ; old Hebrew, ; Phœnician, .

Or take the letter *o*:

Maya, o; old Greek, o; old Hebrew, o; Phœnician, o.

Or take the letter *t*:

Maya, ; old Greek, ; old Phœnician, and .

Or take the letter *q*:

Maya, ; old Phœnician, and ; Greek, .

Or take the letter *k*:

Maya, ; Egyptian, ; Ethiopian, ; Phœnician, .

Or take the letter *n*:

Maya, ; Egyptian, ; Pelasgian , Arcadian, ;

Phœnician, .

Surely all this cannot be accident!

But we find another singular proof of the truth of this theory: It will be seen that the Maya alphabet lacks the letter *d* and the letter *r*. The Mexican alphabet possessed a *d*. The sounds *d* and *t* were probably indicated in the Maya tongue by the same sign, called *t* in the Landa alphabet. The Finns and Lapps do not distinguish between these two sounds. In the oldest known form of the Phœnician alphabet, that found on the Moab stone, we find in the same way but one sign to express the *d* and *t*. *D* does not occur on the Etruscan monuments, *t* being used in its place. It would, therefore, appear that after the Maya alphabet passed to the Phœnicians they added two new signs for the letters *d* and *r*; and it is a singular fact that their poverty of invention seems to have been such that they used to express both *d* and *r*, the same sign, with very little modification, which they had already obtained from the Maya alphabet as the symbol for *b*. To illustrate this we place the signs side by side:

It thus appears that the very signs *d* and *r*, in the Phœnician, early Greek, and ancient Hebrew, which are lacking in the Maya, were supplied by imitating the Maya sign for *b*; and it is a curious fact that while the Phœnician legends claim that Taaut invented the art of writing, yet they tell us that Taaut made records, and "delivered them to his successors and to foreigners, of whom one was Isiris (Osiris, the Egyptian god), *the inventor of the three letters.*" Did these three letters include the *d* and *r*, which they did not receive from the Atlantean alphabet, as represented to us by the Maya alphabet?

In the alphabetical table which we herewith append we have represented the sign V, or vau, or *f*, by the Maya sign for U. "In the present so-called Hebrew, as in the Syriac, Sabæic, Palmyrenic, and some other kindred writings, the *vau* takes the place of F, and indicates the sounds of *v* and *u*. F occurs in the same place also on the Idalian tablet of Cyprus, in Lycian, also in Tuarik (Berber), and some other writings." ("American Cyclopædia," art. F.)

Since writing the above, I find in the "Proceedings of the American Philosophical Society" for December, 1880, p. 154, an interesting article pointing out other resemblances between the Maya alphabet and the Egyptian. I quote:

It is astonishing to notice that while Landa's first B is, according to Valentini, represented by a footprint, and that path and footprint are pronounced *Be* in the Maya dictionary, the Egyptian sign for B was the human leg.

"Still more surprising is it that the H of Landa's alphabet is a tie of cord, while the Egyptian H is a twisted cord. . . . But the most striking coincidence of all occurs in the coiled or curled line representing Landa's U; *for it is absolutely identical with the Egyptian curled U.* The Mayan word for to wind or bend is Uuc; but why should Egyptians, confined as they were to the valley of the Nile, and abhorring as they did the sea and sailors, write their U precisely like Landa's alphabet U in Central America? There is one other remarkable coincidence between Landa's and the Egyptian alphabets; and, by-the-way, the English and other Teutonic dialects have a curious share in it. Landa's D (T) is a disk with lines inside the four quarters, the allowed Mexican symbol for a day or sun. So far as sound is concerned, the English *day* represents it; so far as the form is concerned, the Egyptian 'cake,' ideograph for (1) country and (2) the sun's orbit is essentially the same."

It would appear as if both the Phœnicians and Egyptians drew their alphabet from a common source, of which the Maya is a survival, but did not borrow from one another. They followed out different characteristics in the same original hieroglyph, as, for instance, in the letter *b.* And yet I have shown that the closest resemblances exist between the Maya alphabet and the Egyptian signs--in the *c, h,t, i, k, m, n, o, q,* and *s*--eleven letters in all; in some cases, as in the *n* and *k,* the signs are identical; the *k,* in both alphabets, is not only a serpent, but a serpent with a protuberance or convolution in the middle! If we add to the above the *b* and *u,* referred to in the "Proceedings of the American Philosophical Society," we have thirteen letters out of sixteen in the Maya and Egyptian related to each other. Can any theory of accidental coincidences account for all this? And it must be remembered that these resemblances are found between the only two phonetic systems of alphabet in the world.

Let us suppose that two men agree that each shall construct apart from the other a phonetic alphabet of sixteen letters; that they shall employ only simple forms--combinations of straight or curved lines--and that their signs shall not in anywise resemble the letters now in use. They go to work apart; they have a multitudinous array of forms to draw from the thousand possible combinations of lines, angles, circles, and curves; when they have finished, they bring their alphabets together for comparison. Under such circumstances it is possible that out of the sixteen signs one sign might appear in both alphabets; there is one chance in one hundred that such might be the case; but there is not one chance in five hundred that this sign should in both cases represent the same sound. It is barely possible that two men working thus apart should bit upon two or three identical forms, but altogether imposible that these forms should have the same significance; and by no stretch of the imagination can it be supposed that in these alphabets so created, without correspondence, thirteen out of sixteen signs should be the same in form and the same in meaning.

It is probable that a full study of the Central American monuments may throw stronger light upon the connection between the Maya and the European alphabets, and that further discoveries of inscriptions in Europe may approximate the alphabets of the New and Old World still more closely by supplying intermediate forms.

We find in the American hieroglyphs peculiar signs which take the place of pictures, and which probably, like the hieratic symbols mingled with the hieroglyphics of Egypt, represent alphabetical sounds. For instance, we find this sign on the walls of the palace of Palenque, ; this is not unlike the form of the Phœnician t used in writing, and ; we find also upon these monuments the letter o represented by a small circle, and entering into many of the hieroglyphs; we also find the tau sign (thus) often repeated; also the sign which we have supposed to represent b, ; also this sign, , which we think is the simplification of the letter k; also this sign, which we suppose to represent e, ; also this figure, ; and this . There is an evident tendency to reduce the complex figures to simple signs whenever the writers proceed to form words.

Although it has so far been found difficult, if not impossible, to translate the compound words formed from the Maya alphabet, yet we can go far enough to see that they used the system of simpler sounds for the whole hieroglyph to which we have referred.

Bishop Landa gives us, in addition to the alphabet, the signs which represent the days and months, and which are evidently compounds of the Maya letters. For instance, we have this figure as the representative of the month Mol . Here we see very plainly the letter ꜩ ?X for m, the sign

315

for *o*; and we will possibly find the sign for *l* in the right angle to the right of the*m* sign, and which is derived from the figure in the second sign for *l* in the Maya alphabet.

One of the most ancient races of Central America is the Chiapenec, a branch of the Mayas. They claim to be the first settlers of the country. They came, their legends tell us, from the East, from beyond the sea.

And even after the lapse of so many thousand years most remarkable resemblances have been found to exist between the Chiapenec language and the Hebrew, the living representative of the Phœnician tongue.

The Mexican scholar, Señor Melgar ("North Americans of Antiquity," p. 475) gives the following list of words taken from the Chiapenec and the Hebrew:

English.	Chiapenec.	Hebrew.
Son	Been	Ben.
Daughter	Batz	Bath.
Father	Abagh	Abba.
Star in Zodiac	Chimax	Chimah.
King	Molo	Maloc.
Name applied to Adam	Abagh	Abah.
Afflicted	Chanam	Chanan.
God	Elab	Elab.
September	Tsiquin	Tischiri.
More	Chic	Chi.
Rich	Chabin	Chabic.
Son of Seth	Enot	Enos.
To give	Votan	Votan.

Thus, while we find such extraordinary resemblances between the Maya alphabet and the Phœnician alphabet, we find equally surprising coincidences between the Chiapenec tongue, a branch of the Mayas, and the Hebrew, a branch of the Phœnician.

Attempts have been repeatedly made by European scholars to trace the letters of the Phœnician alphabet back to the elaborate hieroglyphics from which all authorities agree they must have been developed, but all such attempts have been failures. But here, in the Maya alphabet, we are not only able to extract from the heart of the hieroglyphic the typical sign for the sound, but we are able to go a step farther, and, by means of the inscriptions upon the monuments of Copan and Palenque, deduce the alphabetical hieroglyph itself from an older and more ornate figure; we thus not Only discover the relationship of the European alphabet to the American, but we trace its descent in the very mode in which reason tells us it must have been developed. All this proves that the similarities in question did not come from Phœnicians having accidentally visited the shores of America, but that we have before us the origin, the source, the very matrix in which the Phœnician alphabet was formed. In the light of such a discovery the inscriptions upon the monuments of Central America assume incalculable importance; they take us back to a civilization far anterior to the oldest known in Europe; they represent the language of antediluvian times.

It may be said that it is improbable that the use of an alphabet could have ascended to antediluvian times, or to that prehistoric age when intercourse existed between ancient Europe and America; but it must be remembered that if the Flood legends of Europe and Asia are worth anything they prove that the art of writing existed at the date of the Deluge, and that records of antediluvian learning were preserved by those who escaped the Flood; while Plato tells us that the people of Atlantis engraved their laws upon columns of bronze and plates of gold.

There was a general belief among the ancient nations that the art of writing was known to the antediluvians. The Druids believed in books more ancient than the Flood. They styled them "the books of Pheryllt," and "the writings of Pridian or Hu." "Ceridwen consults them before she prepares the mysterious caldron which shadows out the awful catastrophe of the Deluge." (Faber's "Pagan Idolatry," vol. ii., pp. 150, 151.)

In the first *Avatar* of Vishnu we are told that "the divine ordinances were stolen by the demon Haya-Griva. Vishnu became a fish; and after the Deluge, when the waters had subsided, he recovered the holy books *from the bottom of the ocean*." Berosus, speaking of the time before the Deluge, says: "Oannes wrote concerning the generations of mankind and their civil polity." The Hebrew commentators on Genesis say, "Our rabbins assert that Adam, our father of blessed memory, composed a book of precepts, which were delivered to him by God in Paradise." (Smith's "Sacred Annals," p. 49.) That is to say, the Hebrews preserved a tradition that the Ad-ami, the people of Ad, or Adlantis, possessed, while yet dwelling in Paradise, the art of writing. It has been suggested that without the use of letters it would have been impossible to preserve the many details as to dates, ages, and

317

measurements, as of the ark, handed down to us in Genesis. Josephus, quoting Jewish traditions, says, "The births and deaths of illustrious men, between Adam and Noah, were noted down at the time with great accuracy." (Ant., lib. 1, cap. iii., see. 3.) Suidas, a Greek lexicographer of the eleventh century, expresses tradition when he says, "Adam was the author of arts and letters." The Egyptians said that their god Anubis was an antediluvian, and it wrote annals *before* the Flood." The Chinese have traditions that the earliest race of their nation, prior to history, "taught all the arts of life and wrote books." "The Goths always had the use of letters;" and Le Grand affirms that before or soon after the Flood "there were found the acts of great men engraved in letters on large stones." (Fosbroke's "Encyclopædia of Antiquity," vol. i., p. 355.) Pliny says, "Letters were always in use." Strabo says, "The inhabitants of Spain possessed records *written before the Deluge*." (Jackson's "Chronicles of Antiquity," vol. iii., p. 85.) Mitford ("History of Greece," vol. i, p. 121) says, "Nothing appears to us so probable as that it (the alphabet) was derived from the antediluvian world."

CHAPTER VIII. THE BRONZE AGE IN EUROPE.

There exist in Europe the evidences of three different ages of human development:

1. The Stone Age, which dates back to a vast antiquity. It is subdivided into two periods: an age of rough stone implements; and a later age, when these implements were ground smooth and made in improved forms.

2. The Bronze Age, when the great mass of implements were manufactured of a compound metal, consisting of about nine parts of copper and one part of tin.

3. An age when iron superseded bronze for weapons and cutting tools, although bronze still remained in use for ornaments. This age continued down to what we call the Historical Period, and embraces our present civilization; its more ancient remains are mixed with coins of the Gauls, Greeks, and Romans.

The Bronze Period has been one of the perplexing problems of European scientists. Articles of bronze are found over nearly all that continent, but in especial abundance in Ireland and Scandinavia. They indicate very considerable refinement and civilization upon the part of the people who made them; and a wide diversity of opinion has prevailed as to who that people were and where they dwelt.

In the first place, it was observed that the age of bronze (a compound of copper and tin) must, in the natural order of things, have been preceded by an age when copper and tin were used separately, before the ancient metallurgists had discovered the art of combining them, and yet in Europe the remains of no such age have been found. Sir John Lubbock says ("Prehistoric Times," p. 59), "The absence of implements made either of copper or tin seems to me to indicate that the art of making bronze was introduced into, not invented in, Europe." The absence of articles of copper is especially marked, nearly all the European specimens of copper implements have been found in Ireland; and yet out of twelve hundred and eighty-three articles of the Bronze Age, in the great museum at Dublin, only thirty celts and one sword-blade are said to be made of pure copper; and even as to some of these there seems to be a question.

Where on the face of the earth are we to find a Copper Age? Is it in the barbaric depths of that Asia out of whose uncivilized tribes all civilization is said to have issued? By no means. Again we are compelled to turn to the West. In America, from Bolivia to Lake Superior, we find everywhere the traces of a long-enduring Copper Age; bronze existed, it is true, in Mexico, but it held the same relation to the copper as the copper held to the bronze in Europe—it was the exception as against the rule. And among the Chippeways of the shores of Lake Superior, and among them alone, we find any traditions of the origin of the manufacture of copper implements; and on the shores of that lake we find pure copper, out of which the first metal tools were probably hammered before man had learned to reduce the ore or run the metal into moulds. And on the shores of this same American lake we find the ancient mines from which some people, thousands of years ago, derived their supplies of copper.

Sir W. R. Wilde says, "It is remarkable that so few antique copper implements have been found (in Europe), although a knowledge of that metal must have been the preliminary stage in the manufacture of bronze." He thinks that this may be accounted for by supposing that "but a short time elapsed between the knowledge of smelting and casting copper ore and the introduction of tin, and the subsequent manufacture and use of bronze."

But here we have in America the evidence that thousands of years must have elapsed during which copper was used alone, before it was discovered that by adding one-tenth part of tin it gave a harder edge, and produced a superior metal.

The Bronze Age cannot be attributed to the Roman civilization. Sir John Lubbock shows ("Prehistoric Times," p. 21) that bronze weapons have never been found associated with Roman coins or pottery, or other remains of the Roman Period; that bronze articles have been found in the greatest abundance in countries like Ireland and Denmark, which were never invaded by Roman armies; and that the character of the ornamentation of the works of bronze is not Roman in character, and that the Roman bronze contained a large proportion of lead, which is never the case in that of the Bronze Age.

It has been customary to assume that the Bronze Age was due to the Phoenicians, but of late the highest authorities have taken issue with this opinion. Sir John Lubbock (Ibid., p. 73) gives the following reasons why the Phoenicians could not have been the authors of the Bronze Age: First, the ornamentation is different. In the Bronze Age "this always consists of geometrical figures, and we rarely, if ever, find upon them representations of animals and plants, while on the ornamented shields, etc., described by Homer, as well as in the decoration of Solomon's Temple, animals and plants were abundantly represented." In the next place, the form of burial is different in the Bronze Age from that of the Phoenicians. "In the third place, the Phoenicians, so far as we know them, were well acquainted with the use of iron; in Homer we find the warriors already armed with iron weapons, and the tools used in preparing the materials for Solomon's Temple were of this metal."

This view is also held by M. de Fallenberg, in the "Bulletin de la Société des Sciences" of Berne. (See "Smithsonian Rep.," 1865-66, p. 383.) He says, "It seems surprising that the nearest neighbors of the Phoenicians—the Greeks, the Egyptians, the Etruscans, and the Romans—should have manufactured plumbiferous bronzes, while the Phoenicians carried to the people of the North only pure bronzes without the alloy of lead. If the civilized people of the Mediterranean added lead to their bronzes, it can scarcely be doubted that the calculating Phoenicians would have done as much, and, at least, with distant and half-civilized tribes, have replaced the more costly tin by the cheaper metal.... On the whole, then, I consider that the first knowledge of bronze may have been conveyed to the populations of the period under review not only by the Phoenicians, but by other civilized people dwelling more to the south-east."

Professor E. Desor, in his work on the "Lacustrian Constructions of the Lake of Neuchatel," says,

"The Phoenicians certainly knew the use of iron, and it can scarcely be conceived why they should have excluded it from their commerce on the Scandinavian coasts.... The Etruscans, moreover, were acquainted with the use of iron as well as the Phoenicians, and it has already been seen that the composition of their bronzes is different, since it contains lead, which is entirely a stranger to our bronze epoch.... We must look, then, beyond both the Etruscans and Phoenicians in attempting to identify the commerce of the Bronze Age of our palafittes. It will be the province of the historian to inquire whether, exclusive of Phoenicians and Carthaginians, there may not have been some maritime and commercial people who carried on a traffic through the ports of Liguria with the populations of the age of bronze of the lakes of Italy before the discovery of iron. We may remark, in passing, that there is nothing to prove that the Phoenicians were the first navigators. History, on the contrary, positively mentions prisoners, under the name of Tokhari, who were vanquished in a naval battle fought by Rhamses III. in the thirteenth century before our era, and whose physiognomy, according to Morton, would indicate the Celtic type. Now there is room to suppose that if these Tokhari were energetic enough to measure their strength on the sea with one of the powerful kings of Egypt, they must, with stronger reason, have been in a condition to carry on a commerce along the coasts of the Mediterranean, and perhaps of the Atlantic. If such a commerce really existed before the time of the Phoenicians, it would not be limited to the southern slope of the Alps; it would have extended also to the people of the age of bronze in Switzerland. The introduction of bronze would thus ascend to a very high antiquity, doubtless beyond the limits of the most ancient European races."

For the merchants of the Bronze Age we must look beyond even the Tokhari, who were contemporaries of the Phoenicians.

The Tokhari, we have seen, are represented as taken prisoners, in a sea-fight with Rhamses III., of the twentieth dynasty, about the thirteenth century B.C. They are probably the Tochari of Strabo. The accompanying figure represents one of these people as they appear upon the Egyptian monuments. (See Nott and Gliddon's "Types of Mankind," p. 108.) Here we have, not an inhabitant of Atlantis, but probably a representative of one of the mixed races that sprung from its colonies.

Dr. Morton thinks these people, as painted on the Egyptian monuments, to have "strong Celtic features. Those familiar with the Scotch Highlanders may recognize a speaking likeness."

It is at least interesting to have a portrait of one of the daring race who more than three thousand years ago left the west of Europe in their ships to attack the mighty power of Egypt.

They were troublesome to the nations of the East for many centuries; for in 700 B.C. we find them depicted on the Assyrian monuments. This figure represents one of the Tokhari of the time of Sennacherib. It will be observed that the headdress (apparently of feathers) is the same in both portraits, al, though separated by a period of six hundred years.

It is more reasonable to suppose that the authors of the Bronze Age of Europe were the people described by Plato, who were workers in metal, who were highly civilized, who preceded in time all the nations which we call ancient. It was this people who passed through an age of copper before they reached the age of bronze, and whose colonies in America represented this older form of metallurgy as it existed for many generations.

Professor Desor says: "We are asked if the preparation of bronze was not an indigenous invention which had originated on the slopes of the Alps?... In this idea we acquiesced for a moment. But we are met by the objection that, if this were so, the natives, like the ancient tribes of America, would have commenced by manufacturing utensils of copper; yet thus far no utensils of this metal have been found except a few in the strand of Lake Garda. The great majority of metallic objects is of bronze, which necessitated the employment of tin, and this could not be obtained except by commerce, inasmuch as it is a stranger to the Alps. It would appear, therefore, more natural to admit that the art of combining tin with copper— in other words, that the manufacture of bronze—was of foreign importation." He then shows that, although copper ores are found in the Alps, the probability is that even "the copper also was of foreign importation. Now, in view of the prodigious quantity of bronze manufactured at that epoch, this single branch of commerce must itself have necessitated the most incessant commercial communications."

And as this commerce could not, as we have seen, have been carried on by the Romans, Greeks, Etruscans, or Phoenicians, because their civilizations flourished during the Iron Age, to which this age of bronze was anterior, where then are we to look for a great maritime and commercial people, who carried vast quantities of copper, tin, and bronze (unalloyed by the lead of the south of Europe) to Denmark, Norway, Sweden, Ireland, England, France, Spain, Switzerland, and Italy? Where can we find them save in that people of Atlantis, whose ships, docks, canals, and commerce provoked the astonishment of the ancient Egyptians, as recorded by Plato. The Toltec root for water is Atl; the Peruvian word for copper is Anti (from which, probably, the Andes derived their name, as there was a province of Anti on their slopes): may it not be that the name of Atlantis is derived from these originals, and signified the copper island, or the copper mountains in the sea? And from these came the thousands of tons of copper and tin that must, during the Bronze Age, have been introduced into Europe? There are no ancient works to indicate that the tin mines of Cornwall were worked for any length of time in the early days (see "Prehistoric Times," p. 74). Morlot has pointed out that the bronze implements of Hallstadt, in Austria, were of foreign origin, because they contain no lead or silver.

Or, if we are to seek for the source of the vast amount of copper brought into Europe somewhere else than in Atlantis, may it not be that these supplies were drawn in large part from the shores of Lake Superior in America? The mining operations of some ancient people were there carried on upon a gigantic scale, not only along the shores of the lake but even far out upon its islands. At Isle Royale vast works were found, reaching to a depth of sixty feet; great intelligence was shown in following up the richest veins even when interrupted; the excavations were drained by underground drains. On three sections of land on this island the amount of mining exceeded that mined in twenty years in one of our largest mines, with a numerous force constantly employed. In one place the excavations extended in a nearly continuous line for two miles. No remains of the dead and no mounds are found near these mines: it would seem, therefore, that the miners came from a distance, and carried their dead back with them. Henry Gillman ("Smithsonian Rep.," 1873, p. 387) supposes that the curious so-called "Garden Beds" of Michigan were the fields from which they drew their supplies of food. He adds,

"The discoveries in Isle Royale throw a new light on the character of the 'Mound Builders,' giving us a totally distinct conception of them, and dignifying them with something of the prowess and spirit of adventure which we associate with the higher races. The copper, the result of their mining, to be available, must, in all probability, have been conveyed in vessels, great or small, across a treacherous and stormy sea, whose dangers are formidable to us now, being dreaded even by our largest craft, and often proving their destruction. Leaving their homes, those men dared to face the unknown, to brave the hardships and perils of the deep and of the wilderness, actuated by an ambition which we to-day would not be ashamed to acknowledge."

Such vast works in so remote a land must have been inspired by the commercial necessities of some great civilization; and why not by that ancient and mighty people who covered Europe, Asia, and Africa with their manufactures of bronze—and who possessed, as Plato tells us, enormous fleets trading to all parts of the inhabited world—whose cities roared with the continual tumult of traffic, whose dominion extended to Italy and Egypt, and who held parts of "the great opposite continent" of America under their control? A continuous water-way led, from the island of Atlantis to the Gulf of Mexico, and thence up the Mississippi River and its tributaries almost to these very mines of Lake Superior.

Arthur Mitchell says ("The Past in the Present," p. 132),

"The discovery of bronze, and the knowledge of how to make it, may, as a mere intellectual effort, be regarded as rather above than below the effort which is involved in the discovery and use of iron. As regards bronze, there is first the discovery of copper, and the way of getting it from its ore; then the discovery of tin, and the way to get it from its ore; and then the further discovery that, by an admixture of tin with copper in proper proportions, an alloy with the qualities of a hard metal can be produced. It is surely no mistake to say that there goes quite as much thinking to this as to the getting of iron from its ore, and the conversion of that iron into steel. There is a considerable leap from stone to bronze, but the leap from bronze to iron is comparatively small.... It seems highly improbable, if not altogether absurd, that the human mind, at some particular stage of its development, should here, there, and everywhere—independently, and as the result of reaching that stage—discover that an alloy of copper and tin yields a hard metal useful in the manufacture of tools and weapons. There is nothing analogous to such an occurrence in the known history of human progress. It is infinitely more probable that bronze was discovered in one or more centres by one or more men, and that its first use was solely in such centre or centres. That the invention should then be perfected, and its various applications found out, and that it should thereafter spread more or less broadly over the face of the earth, is a thing easily understood."

We will find the knowledge of bronze wherever the colonies of Atlantis extended, and nowhere else; and Plato tells us that the people of Atlantis possessed and used that metal.

The indications are that the Bronze Age represents the coming in of a new people—a civilized people. With that era, it is believed, appears in Europe for the first time the domesticated animals—the horse, the ox, the sheep, the goat, and the hog. (Morlot, "Smithsonian Rep.," 1860, p. 311.) It was a small race, with very small hands; this is shown in the size of the sword-hilts: they are not large enough to be used by the present races of Europe. They were a race with long skulls, as contradistinguished from the round heads of the Stone Period. The drawings on the following page represent the types of the two races.

This people must have sent out colonies to the shores of France, Spain, Italy, Ireland, Denmark, and Norway, who bore with them the arts and implements of civilized life. They raised crops of grain, as is proved by the bronze sickles found in different parts of Europe.

It is not even certain that their explorations did not reach to Iceland. Says Humboldt, "When the Northmen first landed in Iceland (A.D. 875), although the country was uninhabited, they found there Irish books, mass-bells, and other objects which had been left behind by earlier visitors, called Papar; these papæ (fathers) were the clerici of Dicuil. If, then, as we may suppose from the testimony here referred to, these objects belonged to Irish monks (papar), who had come from the Faroe Islands, why should they have been termed in the native sagas 'West men' (Vestmen), 'who had come over the sea from the westward' (kommer til vestan um haf)?" (Humboldt's "Cosmos," vol. ii., 238.)

If they came "from the West" they could not have come from Ireland; and the Scandinavians may easily have mistaken Atlantean books and bells for Irish books and mass-bells. They do not say that there were any evidences that these relics belonged to a people who had recently visited the island; and, as they found the island uninhabited, it would be impossible for them to tell how many years or centuries had elapsed since the books and bells were left there.

`The fact that the implements of the Bronze Age came from some common centre, and did not originate independently in different countries, is proved by the striking similarity which exists between the bronze implements of regions as widely separated as Switzerland, Ireland, Denmark, and Africa. It is not to be supposed that any overland communication existed in that early age between these countries; and the coincidence of design which we find to exist can only be accounted for by the fact that the articles of bronze were obtained from some sea-going people, who carried on a commerce at the same time with all these regions. Compare, for instance, these two decorated bronze celts, the first from Ireland, the second from Denmark; and then compare both these with a

 stone celt found in a mound in Tennessee, given below. Here we have the same form precisely.

IRISH	CELT
DANISH	CELT
STONE	CELT,
MOUND IN TENNESSEE	

Compare the bronze swords in the four preceding illustrations—from Ireland, Sweden, Switzerland, and Denmark-and then observe the same very peculiar shape—the leaf-shape, as it is called—in the stone sword from Big Harpeth River, Tennessee.

We shall find, as we proceed, that the Phoenicians were unquestionably identified with Atlantis, and that it was probably from Atlantis they derived their god Baal, or Bel, or El, whose name crops out in the Bel of the Babylonians, the Elohim, and the Beelzebub of the Jews, and the Allah of the Arabians. And we find that this great deity, whose worship extended so widely among the Mediterranean races, was known and adored also upon the northern and western coasts of Europe. Professor Nilsson finds traces of Baal worship in Scandinavia; he tells us that the festival of Baal, or Balder, was celebrated on midsummer's night in Scania, and far up into Norway, almost to the Loffoden Islands, until within the last fifty years. The feast of Baal, or Beltinne, was celebrated in Ireland to a late period. I argue from these facts, not that the worship of Baal came to Ireland and Norway from Assyria or Arabia, but that the same great parent-race which carried the knowledge of Baal to the Mediterranean brought it also to the western coasts of Europe, and with the adoration of Baal they imported also the implements of bronze now found in such abundance in those regions.

The same similarity of form exists in the bronze knives from Denmark and Switzerland, as represented in the following illustrations. In the central figure we have a representation of an Egyptian-looking man holding a cup before him.

BRONZE KNIVES FROM DENMARK.

BRONZE KNIVES FROM SWITZERLAND.

We shall see, as we proceed, that the magnetic needle, or "mariner's compass," dates back to the days of Hercules, and that it consisted of a bar of magnetized iron floating upon a piece of wood *in a cup*. It is possible that in this ancient relic of the Bronze Age we have a representation of the magnetic cup. The magnetic needle must certainly have been an object of great interest to a people who, through its agency, were able to carry on commerce on all the shores of Europe, from the Mediterranean to the Baltic. The second knife represented above has upon its handle a wheel, or cross surrounded by a ring, which, we shall see here after, was pre-eminently the symbol of Atlantis.

HUT URN, ALBANO.

If we are satisfied that these implements of bronze were the work of the artisans of Atlantis--of the antediluvians--they must acquire additional and extraordinary interest in our eyes, and we turn to them to earn something of the habits and customs of "that great, original, broad-eyed, sunken race."

We find among the relics of the Bronze Age an urn, which probably gives us some idea of the houses of the Atlanteans: it is evidently made to represent a house, and shows us even the rude fashion in which they fastened their doors. The Mandan Indiana built round houses very much of this appearance.

327

BRONZE LAKE VILLAGE.

 The museum at Munich contains a very interesting piece of pottery, which is supposed to represent one of the lake villages or hamlets of the era when the people of Switzerland dwelt in houses erected on piles driven into the bottom of the lakes of that country. The accompanying illustration represents it. The double spiral ornament upon it shows that it belongs to the Bronze Age.

Among the curious relies of the Bronze Age are a number of razor-like knives; from which we may conclude that the habit of shaving the whole or some part of the face or head dates back to a great antiquity. The illustrations below represent them.

 These knives were found in Denmark. The figures upon them represent ships, and it is not impossible that their curious appendages may have been a primitive kind of sails.

An examination of the second of these bronze knives reveals a singular feature:

BRONZE RAZOR-KNIVES.

Upon the handle of the razor there are *ten* series of lines; the stars in the sky are *ten* in number; and there were probably *ten* rings at the left-hand side of the figure, two being obliterated. There were, we are told, ten sub-kingdoms in Atlantis; and precisely as the thirteen stripes on the American flag symbolize the thirteen original States of the Union, so the recurrence of the figure ten in the emblems upon this bronze implement may have reference to the ten subdivisions of Atlantis. The large object in the middle of this ship may be intended to represent a palm-tree--the symbol, as we shall see, in America, of Aztlan, or Atlantis.

We have but to compare the pictures of the ships upon these ancient razor-knives with the accompanying representations of a Roman galley and a ship of William the Conqueror's time, to see that there can be no question that they represented the galleys of that remote age. They are doubtless

 faithful portraits of the great vessels which Plato described as filling the harbors of Atlantis.

ANCIENT GALLEY, FROM A ROMAN COIN.

SHIP OF WILLIAM THE CONQUERER.

We give next a representation of a bronze dagger found in Ireland, a strongly-made weapon. The cut below it represents the only implement of the Bronze Age yet found containing an inscription. It has been impossible to decipher it, or even to tell to what group of languages its alphabet belongs.

IRISH BRONZE DAGGER.

It is proper to note, in connection with a discussion of the Bronze Age, that our word bronze is derived from the Basque, or Iberian*broncea*, from which the Spanish derive *bronce*, and the Italians *bronzo*. The copper mines of the Basques were extensively worked at a very early age of the world, either by the people of Atlantis or by the Basques themselves, a colony from Atlantis. The probabilities are that the name for bronze, as well as the metal itself, dates back to Plato's island.

INSCRIBED CELT.

I give some illustrations of ornaments and implements of the Bronze Age, which may serve to throw light upon the habits of the ancient people. It will be seen that they had reached a considerable degree of civilization; that they raised crops of grain, and cut them with sickles; that their women ornamented themselves with bracelets, armlets, earrings, finger-rings, hair-pins, and amulets; that their mechanics used hammers, adzes, and chisels; and that they possessed very fair specimens of pottery. Sir John Lubbock argues ("Prehistoric Times," pp. 14, 16, etc.): BRONZE HAIR PINS

"A new civilization is indicated not only by the mere presence of bronze but by the beauty and variety of the articles made from it. We find not only, as before, during the Stone Age, axes, arrows, and knives, but, in addition, swords, lances, sickles, fish-hooks, ear-rings, bracelets, pins, rings, and a variety of other articles."

If the bronze implements of Europe had been derived from the Phœnicians, Greeks, Etruscans, or Romans, the nearer we approached the site of those nations the greater should be the number of bronze weapons we would find; but the reverse is the case. Sir John Lubbock ("Prehistoric

Times," p. 20) shows that more than three hundred and fifty bronze swords have been found in Denmark, and that the Dublin Museum contains twelve hundred and eighty-three bronze weapons found in Ireland; "while," he says, "I have only been able to hear of six bronze swords in all Italy." This state of things is inexplicable unless we suppose that Ireland and Denmark received their bronze implements directly from some maritime nation whose site was practically as near their shores as it was to the shores of the Mediterranean. We have but to look at our map on page 43, *ante*, to see that Atlantis was considerably nearer to Ireland than it was to Italy.

The striking resemblance between the bronze implements found in the different portions of Europe is another proof that they were derived from one and the same source--from some great mercantile people who carried on their commerce at the same time with Denmark, Norway, Ireland, Spain, Greece, Italy, Egypt, Switzerland, and Hungary. Mr. Wright ("Essays on Archæology," p. 120) says, "Whenever we find the bronze swords or celts, whether in Ireland, in the far west, in Scotland, in distant Scandinavia, in Germany, or still farther east, in the Sclavonic countries, they are the same--*not similar in character, but identical.*" Says Sir John Lubbock ("Prehistoric Times," p. 59), "Not only are the several varieties of celts found throughout Europe alike, but some of the swords, knives, daggers, etc., are so similar that they seem as if they must have been cast by the same maker."

What race was there, other than the people of Atlantis, that existed before the Iron Age-before the Greek, Roman, Etruscan, and Phœnician-- that was civilized, that worked in metals, that carried on a commerce with all parts of Europe? Does history or tradition make mention of any such?

 We find a great resemblance between the pottery of the Bronze Age in Europe and the pottery of the ancient inhabitants of America. These two figures represent vases from one of the mounds of the Mississippi Valley. Compare them with the following from the lake dwellings of Switzerland:

VASES FROM SWITZERLAND.

It will be seen that these vases could scarcely stand upright unsupported; and we find that the ancient inhabitants of Switzerland had circles or rings of baked earth in which they placed them when in use, as in the annexed figure. The Mound Builders used the same contrivance.

ANCIENT SWISS VASE AND SUPPORTER.

The following illustrations of discoidal stones are from the "North Americans of Antiquity," p. 77.

  DISCOIDAL STONES, ILLINOIS.

The objects represented were taken from an ancient mound in Illinois. It would be indeed surprising if two distinct peoples, living in two different continents, thousands of miles apart, should, without any intercourse with each other, not only form their vases in the same inconvenient form, but should hit upon the same expedient as a remedy.

BRONZE CHISELS.

We observe, in the American spear-head and the Swiss hatchets, on the opposite page, the same overlapping), of the metal around the staff, or handle--a very peculiar mode of uniting them together, which has now passed out of use.

BRONZE HATCHETS, SWITZERLAND

A favorite design of the men of the Bronze Age in Europe is the spiral or double-spiral form. It appears on the face of the urn in the shape of a lake dwelling,; it also appears in the rock sculptures of Argyleshire, Scotland, here shown.

SPIRALS FROM SCOTLAND   SPIRAL, FROM NEW MEXICO.

We find the same figure in an ancient fragment of pottery from the Little Colorado, as given in the "United States Pacific Railroad Survey Report," vol. iii., p. 49, art. *Pottery*. It was part of a large vessel. The annexed illustration represents this.

The same design is also found in ancient rock etchings of the Zuñis of New Mexico, of which the following cut_is an illustration.

 SPIRAL, FROM NEW MEXICO.

We also find this figure repeated upon vase from a Mississippi Valley mound, which we give elsewhere.

It is found upon many of the monuments of Central America. In the Treasure House of Atreus, at Mycenæ, Greece, a fragment of a pillar was found which is literally covered with this double spiral design. (See "Rosengarten's Architectural Styles," p, 59.)

This Treasure House of Atreus is one of the oldest buildings in Greece.

 SHELL ORNAMENT, MOUND NEAR NASHVILLE, TENNESSEE.

We find the double-spiral figure upon a shell ornament found on the breast of a skeleton, in a carefully constructed stone coffin, in a mound near Nashville, Tennessee.

Lenormant remarks ("Anc. Civil.," vol. ii., p. 158) that the bronze implements found in Egypt, near Memphis, had been buried for six thousand years; and that at that time, as the Egyptians had a horror of the sea, some commercial nation must have brought the tin, of which the bronze was in part composed, from India, the Caucasus, or Spain, the nearest points to Egypt in which tin is found.

Heer has shown that the civilized plants of the lake dwellings are not of Asiatic, but of African, and, to a great extent, of Egyptian origin. Their stone axes are made largely of jade or nephrite, a mineral which, strange to say, geologists *have not found in place on the continent of Europe*." (Foster's "Prehistoric Races," p. 44.)

COPPER AXES

FROM A MOUND   WATEFORD IRELAND

NEAR LAPORTE,

INDIANA.

Compare this picture of a copper axe from a mound near Laporte, Indiana, with this representation of a copper axe of the Bronze Age, found near Waterford, Ireland. Professor Foster pronounces them almost identical.

Compare this specimen of pottery from the lake dwellings of Switzerland with the following specimen from San José, Mexico. Professor Foster calls attention to the striking resemblance in the designs of these two widely separated works of art, one belonging to the Bronze Age of Europe, the other to the Copper Age of America.

FRAGMENT OF POTTERY,

LAKE NEUFCHATEL, SWITZERLAND.

FRAGMENT OF POTTERY, SAN JOSÉ, MEXICO

These, then, in conclusion, are our reasons for believing that the Bronze Age of Europe has relation to Atlantis:

1. The admitted fact that it is anterior in time to the Iron Age relegates it to a great antiquity.

2. The fact that it is anterior in time to the Iron Age is conclusive that it is not due to any of the known European or Asiatic nations, all of which belong to the Iron Age.

3. The fact that there war. in Europe, Asia, or Africa no copper or tin age prior to the Bronze Age, is conclusive testimony that the manufacture of bronze was an importation into those continents from some foreign country.

4. The fact that in America alone of all the world is found the Copper Age, which must necessarily have preceded the Bronze Age, teaches us to look to the westward of Europe and beyond the sea for that foreign country.

5. We find many similarities in forms of implements between the Bronze Age of Europe and the Copper Age of America.

6. If Plato told the truth, the Atlanteans were a great commercial nation, trading to America and Europe, and, at the same time, they possessed bronze, and were great workers in the other metals.

7. We shall see hereafter that the mythological traditions of Greece referred to a Bronze Age which preceded an Iron Age, and placed this in the land of the gods, which was an island in the Atlantic Ocean, beyond the Pillars of Hercules; and this land was, as we shall see, clearly Atlantis.

8. As we find but a small development of the Bronze Age in America, it is reasonable to suppose that there must have been some intermediate station between America and Europe, where, during a long period of time, the Bronze Age was developed out of the Copper Age, and immense quantities of bronze implements were manufactured and carried to Europe.

CHAPTER IX. ARTIFICIAL DEFORMATION OF THE SKULL.

An examination of the American monuments shows (see figure on page 269) that the people represented were in the habit of flattening the skull by artificial means. The Greek and Roman writers had mentioned this practice, but it was long totally forgotten by the civilized world, until it was discovered, as an unheard-of wonder, to be the usage among the Carib Islanders, and several Indian tribes in North America. It was afterward found that the ancient Peruvians and Mexicans practised this art: several flattened Peruvian skulls are depicted in Morton's "Crania Americana." It is still in use among the Flat-head Indians of the north-western part of the United States.

In 1849 a remarkable memoir appeared from the pen of M. Rathke, showing that similar skulls had been found near Kertsch, in the Crimea, and calling attention to the book of Hippocrates, "De Aeris, Aquis et Locu," lib. iv., and a passage of Strabo, which speaks of the practice among the Scythians. In 1854 Dr. Fitzinger published a learned memoir on the skulls of the Avars, a branch of the Uralian race of Turks. He shows that the practice of flattening the head had existed from an early date throughout the East, and described an ancient skull, greatly distorted by artificial means, which had lately been found in Lower Austria. Skulls similarly flattened have been found in Switzerland and Savoy. The Huns under Attila had the same practice of flattening the heads. Professor Anders Retzius proved (see "Smithsonian Report," 1859) that the custom still exists in the south of France, and in parts of Turkey. "Not long since a French physician surprised the world by the fact that nurses in Normandy were still giving the children's heads a sugar-loaf shape by bandages and a tight cap, while in Brittany they preferred to press it round. No doubt they are doing so to this day." (Tylor's "Anthropology," p. 241.)

Professor Wilson remarks: "Trifling as it may appear, it is not without interest to have the fact brought under our notice, by the disclosures of ancient barrows and cysts, that the same practice of nursing the child and carrying it about, bound to a flat cradle-board, prevailed in Britain and the north of Europe long before the first notices of written history reveal the presence of man beyond the Baltic or the English Channel, and that in all probability the same custom prevailed continuously from the shores of the German Ocean to Behring's Strait." ("Smithsonian Report," 1862, p. 286.)

Dr. L. A. Gosse testifies to the prevalence of the same custom among the Caledonians and Scandinavians in the earliest times; and Dr. Thurman has treated of the same peculiarity among the Anglo-Saxons. ("Crania Britannica," chap. iv., p. 38.)

Here, then, is an extraordinary and unnatural practice which has existed from the highest antiquity, over vast regions of country, on both sides of the Atlantic, and which is perpetuated unto this day in races as widely separated as the Turks, the French, and the Flat-head Indians. Is it possible to explain this except by supposing that it originated from some common centre?

The annexed cut represents an ancient Swiss skull, from a cemetery near Lausanne, from a drawing of Frederick Troyon. Compare this with the illustration given on page 271, which represents a Peruvian flat-head, copied from Morton's "Ethnography and Archæology of the American Aborigines," 1846. This skull is shockingly distorted. The dotted lines indicate the course of the bandages by which the skull was deformed.

The following heads are from Del Rio's "Account of Palenque," copied into Nott and Gliddon's "Types of Mankind," p. 440. They show that the receding forehead was a natural characteristic of the ancient people of Central America. The same form of head has been found even in fossil skulls. We may therefore conclude that the skull-flattening, which we find to have been practised in both the Old and New Worlds, was an attempt of other races to imitate the form of skull of a people whose likenesses are found on the monuments of Egypt and of America. It has been shown that this peculiar form of the head was present even in the foetus of the Peruvian mummies.

Hippocrates tells us that the practice among the Scythians was for the purpose of giving a certain aristocratic distinction.

Amedée Thierry, in his "History of Attila," says the Huns used it for the same reason; and the same purpose influences the Indians of Oregon.

Dr. Lund, a Swedish naturalist, found in the bone caves of Minas-Geraes, Brazil, ancient human bones associated with the remains of extinct quadrupeds. "These skulls," says Lund, "show not only the peculiarity of the American race but in an excessive degree, even to the entire disappearance of the forehead." Sir Robert Schomburgh found on some of the affluents of the Orinoco a tribe known as Frog Indians, whose heads were flattened by Nature, as shown in newly-born children.

In the accompanying plate we show the difference in the conformation of the forehead in various races. The upper dotted line, A, represents the shape of the European forehead; the next line, B, that of the Australian; the next, C, that of the Mound Builder of the United States; the next, D, that of the Guanche of the Canary Islands; and the next, E, that of a skull from the Inca cemetery of Peru. We have but to compare these lines with the skulls of the Egyptians, Kurds, and the heroic type of heads in the statues of the gods of Greece, to see that there was formerly an ancient race marked by a receding forehead; and that the practice of flattening the skull was probably an attempt to approximate the shape of the head to this standard of an early civilized and dominant people.

Not only do we find the same receding forehead in the skulls of the ancient races of Europe and America, and the same attempt to imitate this natural and peculiar conformation by artificial flattening of the head, but it has been found (see Henry Gillman's "Ancient Man in Michigan," "Smithsonian Report," 1875, p. 242) that the Mound Builders and Peruvians of America, and the Neolithic people of France and the Canary Islands, had alike an extraordinary custom of boring a circular bole in the top of the skulls of their dead, so that the soul might readily pass in and out. More than this, it has been found that in all these ancient populations the skeletons exhibit a remarkable degree of platicnemism, or flattening of the tibiæ or leg bones. (Ibid., 1873, p. 367.) In this respect the Mound Builders of Michigan were identical with the man of Cro Magnon and the ancient inhabitants of Wales.

The annexed ancient Egyptian heads, copied from the monuments, indicate either that the people of the Nile deformed their heads by pressure upon the front of the skull, or that there was some race characteristic which gave this appearance to their heads. These heads are all the heads of priests, and therefore represented the aristocratic class.

The first illustration below is taken from a stucco relief found in a temple at Palenque, Central America. The second is from an Egyptian monument of the time of Rameses IV.

The outline drawing on the following page shows the form of the skull of the royal Inca line: the receding forehead here seems to be natural, and not the result of artificial compression.

Both illustrations at the bottom of the preceding page show the same receding form of the forehead, due to either artificial deformation of the skull or to a common race characteristic.

We must add the fact that the extraordinary practice of deforming the skull was found all over Europe and America to the catalogue of other proofs that the people of both continents were originally united in blood and race. With the couvade, the practice of circumcision, unity of religious beliefs and customs, folk-lore, and alphabetical signs, language and flood legends, we array together a mass of unanswerable proofs of prehistoric identity of race.

PART IV. THE MYTHOLOGIES OF THE OLD WORLD A RECOLLECTION OF ATLANTIS.

CHAPTER I. TRADITIONS OF ATLANTIS.

We find allusions to the Atlanteans in the most ancient traditions of many different races. The great antediluvian king of the Mussulman was Shedd-Ad-Ben-Ad, or Shed-Ad, the son of Ad, or Atlantis.

Among the Arabians the first inhabitants of that country are known as the Adites, from their progenitor, who is called Ad, the grandson of Ham. These Adites were probably the people of Atlantis or Ad-lantis. "They are personified by a monarch to whom everything is ascribed, and to whom is assigned several centuries of life." ("Ancient History of the East," Lenormant and Chevallier, vol. ii., p. 295.), Ad came from the northeast.

"He married a thousand wives, had four thousand sons, and lived twelve hundred years. His descendants multiplied considerably. After his death his sons Shadid and Shedad reigned in succession over the Adites. In the time of the latter the people of Ad were a thousand tribes, each composed of several thousands of men. Great conquests are attributed to Shedad; he subdued, it is said, all Arabia and Irak. The migration of the Canaanites, their establishment in Syria, and the Shepherd invasion of Egypt are, by many Arab writers, attributed to an expedition of Shedad." (Ibid., p. 296.)

Shedad built a palace ornamented with superb columns, and surrounded by a magnificent garden. It was called Irem. "It was a paradise that Shedad had built in imitation of the celestial Paradise, of whose delights he had heard." ("Ancient History of the East," p. 296.) In other words, an ancient, sun-worshipping, powerful, and conquering race overran Arabia at the very dawn of history; they were the sons of Adlantis: their king tried to create a palace and garden of Eden like that of Atlantis.

The Adites are remembered by the Arabians as a great and civilized race. "They are depicted as men of gigantic stature; their strength was equal to their size, and they easily moved enormous blocks of stone." (Ibid.) They were architects and builders. They raised many monuments of their power; and hence, among the Arabs, arose the custom of calling great ruins "buildings of the Adites." To this day the Arabs say "as old as Ad." In the Koran allusion is made to the edifices they built on "high places for vain uses;" expressions proving that their "idolatry was considered to have been tainted with Sabæism or star-worship." (Ibid.) "In these legends," says Lenormant, "we find traces of a wealthy nation, constructors of great buildings, with an advanced civilization, analogous to that of Chaldea, professing a religion similar to the Babylonian; a nation, in short, with whom material progress was allied to great moral depravity and obscene rites. These facts must be true and strictly historical, for they are everywhere met with among the Cushites, as among the Canaanites, their brothers by origin."

Nor is there wanting a great catastrophe which destroys the whole Adite nation, except a very few who escape because they had renounced idolatry. A black cloud assails their country, from which proceeds a terrible hurricane (the water-spout?) which sweeps away everything.

The first Adites were followed by a second Adite race; probably the colonists who had escaped the Deluge. The centre of its power was the country of Sheba proper. This empire endured for a thousand years. The Adites are represented upon the Egyptian monuments as very much like the

Egyptians themselves; in other words, they were a red or sunburnt race: their great temples were pyramidal, surmounted by buildings. ("Ancient History of the East," p. 321.) "The Sabæans," says Agatharchides ("De Mari Erythræo," p. 102), "have in their houses an incredible number of vases, and utensils of all sorts, of gold and silver, beds and tripods of silver, and all the furniture of astonishing richness. Their buildings have porticos with columns sheathed with gold, or surmounted by capitals of silver. On the friezes, ornaments, and the framework of the doors they place plates of gold incrusted with precious stones."

All this reminds one of the descriptions given by the Spaniards of the temples of the sun in Peru.

The Adites worshipped the gods of the Phoenicians under names but slightly changed; "their religion was especially solar... It was originally a religion without images, without idolatry, and without a priesthood." (Ibid., p. 325.) They "worshipped the sun from the tops of pyramids." (Ibid.) They believed in the immortality of the soul.

In all these things we see resemblances to the Atlanteans.

The great Ethiopian or Cushite Empire, which in the earliest ages prevailed, as Mr. Rawlinson says, "from the Caucasus to the Indian Ocean, from the shores of the Mediterranean to the mouth of the Ganges," was the empire of Dionysos, the empire of "Ad," the empire of Atlantis. El Eldrisi called the language spoken to this day by the Arabs of Mahrah, in Eastern Arabia, "the language of the people of Ad," and Dr. J. H. Carter, in the Bombay Journal of July, 1847, says, "It is the softest and sweetest language I have ever heard." It would be interesting to compare this primitive tongue with the languages of Central America.

The god Thoth of the Egyptians, who was the god of a foreign country, and who invented letters, was called At-hothes.

We turn now to another ancient race, the Indo-European family—the Aryan race.

In Sanscrit Adim, means first. Among the Hindoos the first man was Ad-ima, his wife was Heva. They dwelt upon an island, said to be Ceylon; they left the island and reached the main-land, when, by a great convulsion of nature, their communication with the parent land was forever cut off. (See "Bible in India.")

Here we seem to have a recollection of the destruction of Atlantis.

Mr. Bryant says, "Ad and Ada signify the first." The Persians called the first man "Ad-amah." "Adon" was one of the names of the Supreme God of the Phoenicians; from it was derived the name of the Greek god "Ad-onis."

The Arv-ad of Genesis was the Ar-Ad of the Cushites; it is now known as Ru-Ad. It is a series of connected cities twelve miles in length, along the coast, full of the most massive and gigantic ruins.

Sir William Jones gives the tradition of the Persians as to the earliest ages. He says: "Moshan assures us that in the opinion of the best informed Persians the first monarch of Iran, and of the whole earth, was Mashab-Ad; that he received from the Creator, and promulgated among men a sacred book, in a heavenly language, to which the Mussulman author gives the Arabic title of 'Desatir,' or 'Regulations.' Mashab-Ad was, in the opinion of the ancient Persians, the person left at the end of the last great cycle, and consequently the father of the present world. He and his wife having survived the former cycle, were blessed with a numerous progeny; he planted gardens, invented ornaments, forged weapons, taught men to take the fleece from sheep and make clothing; he built cities, constructed palaces, fortified towns, and introduced arts and commerce."

We have already seen that the primal gods of this people are identical with the gods of the Greek mythology, and were originally kings of Atlantis. But it seems that these ancient divinities are grouped together as "the Aditya;" and in this name "Ad-itya" we find a strong likeness to the Semitic "Adites," and another reminiscence of Atlantis, or Adlantis. In corroboration of this view we find,

1. The gods who are grouped together as the Aditya are the most ancient in the Hindoo mythology.

2. They are all gods of light, or solar gods. (Whitney's Oriental and Linguistic Studies," p. 39.)

3. There are twelve of them. (Ibid.)

4. These twelve gods presided over twelve months in the year.

5. They are a dim recollection of a very remote past. Says Whitney, "It seems as if here was an attempt on the part of the Indian religion to take a new development in a moral direction, which a change in the character and circumstances of the people has caused to fail in the midst, and fall back again into forgetfulness, while yet half finished and indistinct." (Ibid.)

6. These gods are called "the sons of Aditi," just as in the Bible we have allusions to "the sons of Adab," who were the first metallurgists and musicians. "Aditi is not a goddess. She is addressed as a queen's daughter, she of fair children."

7. The Aditya "are elevated above all imperfections; they do not sleep or wink." The Greeks represented their gods as equally wakeful and

omniscient. "Their character is all truth; they hate and punish guilt." We have seen the same traits ascribed by the Greeks to the Atlantean kings.

8. The sun is sometimes addressed as an Aditya.

9. Among the Aditya is Varuna, the equivalent of Uranos, whose identification with Atlantis I have shown. In the vedas Varuna is "the god of the ocean."

10. The Aditya represent an earlier and purer form of religion: "While in hymns to the other deities long life, wealth, power, are the objects commonly prayed for, of the Aditya is craved purity, forgiveness of sin, freedom from guilt, and repentance." ("Oriental and Linguistic Studies," p. 43.)

11. The Aditya, like the Adites, are identified with the doctrine of the immortality of the soul. Yama is the god of the abode beyond the grave. In the Persian story he appears as Yima, and "is made ruler of the golden age and founder of the Paradise." (Ibid., p. 45.) (See "Zamna," p. 167 ante.)

In view of all these facts, one cannot doubt that the legends of the "sons of Ad," "the Adites," and "the Aditya," all refer to Atlantis.

Mr. George Smith, in the Chaldean account of the Creation (p. 78), deciphered from the Babylonian tablets, shows that there was an original race of men at the beginning of Chaldean history, a dark race, the Zalmat-qaqadi, who were called Ad-mi, or Ad-ami; they were the race "who had fallen," and were contradistinguished from "the Sarku, or light race." The "fall" probably refers to their destruction by a deluge, in consequence of their moral degradation and the indignation of the gods. The name Adam is used in these legends, but as the name of a race, not of a man.

Genesis (chap. v., 2) distinctly says that God created man male and female, and "called their name Adam." That is to say, the people were the Ad-ami, the people of "Ad," or Atlantis. "The author of the Book of Genesis," says M. Schoebel, "in speaking of the men who were swallowed up by the Deluge, always describes them as 'Haadam,' 'Adamite humanity.'" The race of Cain lived and multiplied far away from the land of Seth; in other words, far from the land destroyed by the Deluge. Josephus, who gives us the primitive traditions of the Jews, tells us (chap. ii., p. 42) that "Cain travelled over many countries" before he came to the land of Nod. The Bible does not tell us that the race of Cain perished in the Deluge. "Cain went out from the presence of Jehovah;" he did not call on his name; the people that were destroyed were the "sons of Jehovah." All this indicates that large colonies had been sent out by the mother-land before it sunk in the sea.

Across the ocean we find the people of Guatemala claiming their descent from a goddess called At-tit, or grandmother, who lived for four hundred years, and first taught the worship of the true God, which they afterward forgot. (Bancroft's "Native Races," vol. iii., p. 75.) While the famous Mexican calendar stone shows that the sun was commonly called tonatiuh but when it was referred to as the god of the Deluge it was then called Atl-tona-ti-uh, or At-onatiuh. (Valentini's "Mexican Calendar Stone," art. Maya Archæology, p. 15.)

We thus find the sons of Ad at the base of all the most ancient races of men, to wit, the Hebrews, the Arabians, the Chaldeans, the Hindoos, the Persians, the Egyptians, the Ethiopians, the Mexicans, and the Central Americans; testimony that all these races traced their beginning back to a dimly remembered Ad-lantis.

CHAPTER II. THE KINGS OF ATLANTIS BECOME THE GODS OF THE GREEKS.

Lord Bacon said: "The mythology of the Greeks, which their oldest writers do not pretend to have invented, was no more than a light air, which had passed from a more ancient people into the flutes of the Greeks, which they modulated to such descants as best suited their fancies."

This profoundly wise and great man, who has illuminated every subject which he has touched, guessed very close to the truth in this utterance.

The Hon. W. E. Gladstone has had quite a debate of late with Mr. Cox as to whether the Greek mythology was underlaid by a nature worship, or a planetary or solar worship.

Peru, worshipping the sun and moon and planets, probably represents very closely the simple and primitive religion of Atlantis, with its sacrifices of fruits and flowers. This passed directly to their colony in Egypt. We find the Egyptians in their early ages sun and planet worshippers. Ptah was the object of their highest adoration. He is the father of the god of the sun, the ruler of the region of light. Ra was the sun-god. He was the supreme divinity at On, or Heliopolis, near Memphis. His symbol was the solar disk, supported by two rings. He created all that exists below the heavens.

The Babylonian trinity was composed of Idea, Anu, and Bel. Bel represented the sun, and was the favorite god. Sin was the goddess of the moon.

The Phoenicians were also sun-worshippers. The sun was represented by Baal-Samin, the great god, the god of light and the heavens, the creator and rejuvenator.

"The attributes of both Baal and Moloch (the good and bad powers of the sun) were united in the Phoenician god Melkart, "king of the city," whom the inhabitants of Tyre considered their special patron. The Greeks called him "Melicertes," and identified him with Hercules. By his great strength and power he turned evil into good, brought life out of destruction, pulled back the sun to the earth at the time of the solstices, lessened excessive heat and cold, and rectified the evil signs of the zodiac. In Phoenician legends he conquers the savage races of distant coasts, founds the ancient settlements on the Mediterranean, and plants the rocks in the Straits of Gibraltar." ("American Cyclopædia," art. Mythology.)

The Egyptians worshipped the sun under the name of Ra; the Hindoos worshipped the sun under the name of Rama; while the great festival of the sun, of the Peruvians, was called Ray-mi.

Sun-worship, as the ancient religion of Atlantis, underlies all the superstitions of the colonies of that country. The Samoyed woman says to the sun, "When thou, god, risest, I too rise from my bed." Every morning even now the Brahmans stand on one foot, with their hands held out before them and their faces turned to the east, adoring the sun. "In Germany or France one may still see the peasant take off his hat to the rising sun." ("Anthropology," p. 361.) The Romans, even, in later times, worshipped the sun at Emesa, under the name of Elagabalus, "typified in the form of a black conical stone, which it was believed had fallen from heaven." The conical stone was the emblem of Bel. Did it have relation to the mounds and pyramids?

Sun-worship was the primitive religion of the red men of America. It was found among all the tribes. (Dorman, "Origin of Primitive Superstitions," p. 338.) The Chichimecs called the sun their father. The Comanches have a similar belief.

But, compared with such ancient nations as the Egyptians and Babylonians, the Greeks were children. A priest of Sais said to Solon,

"You Greeks are novices in knowledge of antiquity. You are ignorant of what passed either here or among yourselves in days of old. The history of eight thousand years is deposited in our sacred books; but I can ascend to a much higher antiquity, and tell you what our fathers have done for nine thousand years; I mean their institutions, their laws, and their most brilliant achievements."

The Greeks, too young to have shared in the religion of Atlantis, but preserving some memory of that great country and its history, proceeded to convert its kings into gods, and to depict Atlantis itself as the heaven of the

343

human race. Thus we find a great solar or nature worship in the elder nations, while Greece has nothing but an incongruous jumble of gods and goddesses, who are born and eat and drink and make love and ravish and steal and die; and who are worshipped as immortal in presence of the very monuments that testify to their death.

"These deities, to whom the affairs of the world were intrusted, were, it is believed, immortal, though not eternal in their existence. In Crete there was even a story of the death of Zeus, his tomb being pointed out." (Murray's "Mythology," p. 2.)

The history of Atlantis is the key of the Greek mythology. There can be no question that these gods of Greece were human beings. The tendency to attach divine attributes to great earthly rulers is one deeply implanted in human nature. The savages who killed Captain Cook firmly believed that he was immortal, that he was yet alive, and would return to punish them. The highly civilized Romans made gods out of their dead emperors. Dr. Livingstone mentions that on one occasion, after talking to a Bushman for some time about the Deity, he found that the savage thought he was speaking of Sekomi, the principal chief of the district.

We find the barbarians of the coast of the Mediterranean regarding the civilized people of Atlantis with awe and wonder: "Their physical strength was extraordinary, the earth shaking sometimes under their tread. Whatever they did was done speedily. They moved through space almost without the loss of a moment of time." This probably alluded to the rapid motion of their sailing-vessels. "They were wise, and communicated their wisdom to men." That is to say, they civilized the people they came in contact with. They had a strict sense of justice, and punished crime rigorously, and rewarded noble actions, though it is true they were less conspicuous for the latter." (Murray's "Mythology," p. 4.) We should understand this to mean that where they colonized they established a government of law, as contradistinguished from the anarchy of barbarism.

"There were tales of personal visits and adventures of the gods among men, taking part in battles and appearing in dreams. They were conceived to possess the form of human beings, and to be, like men, subject to love and pain, but always characterized by the highest qualities and grandest forms that could be imagined." (Ibid.)

Another proof that the gods of the Greeks were but the deified kings of Atlantis is found in the fact that "the gods were not looked upon as having created the world." They succeeded to the management of a world already in existence.

The gods dwelt on Olympus. They lived together like human beings; they possessed palaces, storehouses, stables, horses, etc.; "they dwelt in a social state which was but a magnified reflection of the social system on earth. Quarrels, love passages, mutual assistance, and such instances as characterize human life, were ascribed to them." (Ibid., p. 10.)

Where was Olympus? It was in Atlantis. "The ocean encircled the earth with a great stream, and was a region of wonders of all kinds." (Ibid., p. 23.) It was a great island, the then civilized world. The encircling ocean "was spoken of in all the ancient legends. Okeanos lived there with his wife Tethys: these were the Islands of the Blessed, the garden of the gods, the sources of the nectar and ambrosia on which the gods lived." (Murray's "Mythology," p. 23.) Nectar was probably a fermented intoxicating liquor, and ambrosia bread made from wheat. Soma was a kind of whiskey, and the Hindoos deified it. "The gods lived on nectar and ambrosia" simply meant that the inhabitants of these blessed islands were civilized, and possessed a liquor of some kind and a species of food superior to anything in use among the barbarous tribes with whom they came in contact.

This blessed land answers to the description of Atlantis. It was an island full of wonders. It lay spread out in the ocean "like a disk, with the mountains rising from it." (Ibid.) On the highest point of this mountain dwelt Zeus (the king), "while the mansions of the other deities were arranged upon plateaus, or in ravines lower down the mountain. These deities, including Zeus, were twelve in number: Zeus (or Jupiter), Hera (or Juno), Poseidon (or Neptune), Demeter (or Ceres), Apollo, Artemis (or Diana), Hephæstos (or Vulcan), Pallas Athena (or Minerva), Ares (or Mars), Aphrodite (or Venus), Hermes (or Mercury), and Hestia (or Vesta)." These were doubtless the twelve gods from whom the Egyptians derived their kings. Where two names are given to a deity in the above list, the first name is that bestowed by the Greeks, the last that given by the Romans.

It is not impossible that our division of the year into twelve parts is a reminiscence of the twelve gods of Atlantis. Diodorus Siculus tells us that among the Babylonians there were twelve gods of the heavens, each personified by one of the signs of the zodiac, and worshipped in a certain month of the year. The Hindoos had twelve primal gods, "the Aditya." Moses erected twelve pillars at Sinai. The Mandan Indians celebrated the Flood with twelve typical characters, who danced around the ark. The Scandinavians believed in the twelve gods, the Aesir, who dwelt on Asgard, the Norse Olympus. Diligent investigation may yet reveal that the number of a modern jury, twelve, is a survival of the ancient council of Asgard.

345

"According to the traditions of the Phoenicians, the Gardens of the Hesperides were in the remote west." (Murray's "Mannal of Mythology," p. 258.) Atlas lived in these gardens. (Ibid., p. 259.) Atlas, we have seen, was king of Atlantis. "The Elysian Fields (the happy islands) were commonly placed in the remote west. They were ruled over by Chronos." (Ibid., p. 60.) Tartarus, the region of Hades, the gloomy home of the dead, was also located "under the mountains of an island in the midst of the ocean in the remote west." (Ibid., p. 58.) Atlas was described in Greek mythology as "an enormous giant, who stood upon the western confines of the earth, and supported the heavens on his shoulders, in a region of the west where the sun continued to shine after he had set upon Greece." (Ibid., p. 156.)

Greek tradition located the island in which Olympus was situated "in the far west," "in the ocean beyond Africa," "on the western boundary of the known world," "where the sun shone when it had ceased to shine on Greece," and where the mighty Atlas "held up the heavens." And Plato tells us that the land where Poseidon and Atlas ruled was Atlantis.

"The Garden of the Hesperides" (another name for the dwelling-place of the gods) "was situated at the extreme limit of Africa. Atlas was said to have surrounded it on every side with high mountains." (Smith's "Sacred Annals, Patriarchal Age," p. 131.) Here were found the golden apples.

This is very much like the description which Plato gives of the great plain of Atlantis, covered with fruit of every kind, and surrounded by precipitous mountains descending to the sea.

The Greek mythology, in speaking of the Garden of the Hesperides, tells us that "the outer edge of the garden was slightly raised, so that the water might not run in and overflow the land." Another reminiscence of the surrounding mountains of Atlantis as described by Plato, and as revealed by the deep-sea soundings of modern times.

Chronos, or Saturn, Dionysos, Hyperion, Atlas, Hercules, were all connected with "a great Saturnian continent;" they were kings that ruled over countries on the western shores of the Mediterranean, Africa and Spain. One account says:

"Hyperion, Atlas, and Saturn, or Chronos, were sons of Uranos, who reigned over a great kingdom composed of countries around the western part of the Mediterranean, with certain islands in the Atlantic. Hyperion succeeded his father, and was then killed by the Titans. The kingdom was then divided between Atlas and Saturn—Atlas taking Northern Africa, with the Atlantic islands, and Saturn the countries on the opposite shore of the Mediterranean to Italy and Sicily." (Baldwin's "Prehistoric Nations," p. 357.)

Plato says, speaking of the traditions of the Greeks ("Dialogues, Laws," c. iv., p. 713), "There is a tradition of the happy life of mankind in the days when all things were spontaneous and abundant.... In like manner God in his love of mankind placed over us the demons, who are a superior race, and they, with great care and pleasure to themselves and no less to us, taking care of us and giving us place and reverence and order and justice never failing, made the tribes of men happy and peaceful ... for Cronos knew that no human nature, invested with supreme power, is able to order human affairs and not overflow with insolence and wrong."

In other words, this tradition refers to an ancient time when the forefathers of the Greeks were governed by Chronos, of the Cronian Sea (the Atlantic), king of Atlantis, through civilized Atlantean governors, who by their wisdom preserved peace and created a golden age for all the populations under their control—they were the demons, that is, "the knowing ones," the civilized.

Plato puts into the mouth of Socrates these words ("Dialogues, Cratylus," p. 397): "My notion would be that the sun, moon, and stars, earth, and heaven, which are still the gods of many barbarians, were the only gods known to the aboriginal Hellenes.... What shall follow the gods? Must not demons and heroes and men come next?... Consider the real meaning of the word demons. You know Hesiod uses the word. He speaks of 'a golden race of men' who came first. He says of them,

> But now that fate has closed over this race,
> They are holy demons upon earth,
> Beneficent averters of ills, guardians of mortal men.'

He means by the golden men not men literally made of gold, but good and noble men; he says we are of the 'age of iron.' He called them demons because they were dah'mones (knowing or wise)."

This is made the more evident when we read that this region of the gods, of Chronos and Uranos and Zeus, passed through, first, a Golden Age, then a Silver Age—these constituting a great period of peace and happiness; then it reached a Bronze Age; then an Iron Age, and finally perished by a great flood, sent upon these people by Zeus as a punishment for their sins. We read:

"Men were rich then (in the Silver Age), as in the Golden Age of Chronos, and lived in plenty; but still they wanted the innocence and contentment which were the true sources of human happiness in the former age; and accordingly, while living in luxury and delicacy, they became overbearing in their manners to the highest degree, were never satisfied,

347

and forgot the gods, to whom, in their confidence of prosperity and comfort, they denied the reverence they owed.... Then followed the Bronze Age, a period of constant quarrelling and deeds of violence. Instead of cultivated lands, and a life of peaceful occupations and orderly habits, there came a day when every where might was right, and men, big and powerful as they were, became physically worn out.... Finally came the Iron Age, in which enfeebled mankind had to toil for bread with their hands, and, bent on gain, did their best to overreach each other. Dike, or Astræa, the goddess of justice and good faith, modesty and truth, turned her back on such scenes, and retired to Olympus, while Zeus determined to destroy the human race by a great flood. The whole of Greece lay under water, and none but Deucalion and his wife Pyrrha were saved." (Murray's "Mythology" p. 44.)

It is remarkable that we find here the same succession of the Iron Age after the Bronze Age that has been revealed to scientific men by the patient examination of the relics of antiquity in Europe. And this identification of the land that was destroyed by a flood—the land of Chronos and Poseidon and Zeus—with the Bronze Age, confirms the view expressed in Chapter VIII. (page 237, ante), that the bronze implements and weapons of Europe were mainly imported from Atlantis.

And here we find that the Flood that destroyed this land of the gods was the Flood of Deucalion, and the Flood of Deucalion was the Flood of the Bible, and this, as we have shown, was "the last great Deluge of all," according to the Egyptians, which destroyed Atlantis.

The foregoing description of the Golden Age of Chronos, when "men were rich and lived in plenty," reminds us of Plato's description of the happy age of Atlantis, when "men despised everything but virtue, not caring for their present state of life, and thinking lightly of the possession of gold and other property;" a time when, as the chants of the Delaware Indians stated it (page 109, ante), "all were willingly pleased, all were well-happified." While the description given by Murray in the above extract of the degeneracy of mankind in the land of the gods, "a period of constant quarrelling and deeds of violence, when might was right," agrees with Plato's account of the Atlanteans, when they became "aggressive," "unable to bear their fortune," "unseemly," "base," "filled with unrighteous avarice and power,"—and "in a most wretched state." And here again I might quote from the chant of the Delaware Indians—"they became troubled, hating each other; both were fighting, both were spoiling, both were never peaceful." And in all three instances the gods punished the depravity of mankind by a great deluge. Can all these precise coincidences be the result of accident?

May we not even suppose that the very word "Olympus" is a transformation from "Atlantis" in accordance with the laws that regulate the changes of letters of the same class into each other? Olympus was written by the Greeks "Olumpos." The letter a in Atlantis was sounded by the ancient world broad and full, like the a in our words all or altar; in these words it approximates very closely to the sound of o. It is not far to go to convert Otlontis into Oluntos, and this into Olumpos. We may, therefore, suppose that when the Greeks said that their gods dwelt in "Olympus," it was the same as if they said that they dwelt in "Atlantis."

Nearly all the gods of Greece are connected with Atlantis. We have seen the twelve principal gods all dwelling on the mountain of Olympus, in the midst of an island in the ocean in the far west, which was subsequently destroyed by a deluge on account of the wickedness of its people. And when we turn to Plato's description of Atlantis (p. 13, ante) we find that Poseidon and Atlas dwelt upon a mountain in the midst of the island; and on this mountain were their magnificent temples and palaces, where they lived, separated by great walls from their subjects.

It may be urged that Mount Olympus could not have referred to any mountain in Atlantis, because the Greeks gave that name to a group of mountains partly in Macedonia and partly in Thessaly. But in Mysia, Lycia, Cyprus, and elsewhere there were mountains called Olympus; and on the plain of Olympia, in Elis, there was an eminence bearing the same designation. There is a natural tendency among uncivilized peoples to give a "local habitation" to every general tradition.

"Many of the oldest myths," says Baldwin ("Prehistoric Nations," p. 376), "relate to Spain, North-western Africa, and other regions on the Atlantic, such as those concerning Hercules, the Cronidæ, the Hyperboreans, the Hesperides, and the Islands of the Blessed. Homer described the Atlantic region of Europe in his account of the wanderings of Ulysses…. In the ages previous to the decline of Phoenician influence in Greece and around the Ægean Sea, the people of those regions must have had a much better knowledge of Western Europe than prevailed there during the Ionian or Hellenic period."

The mythology of Greece is really a history of the kings of Atlantis. The Greek heaven was Atlantis. Hence the references to statues, swords, etc., that fell from heaven, and were preserved in the temples of the different states along the shores of the Mediterranean from a vast antiquity, and which were regarded as the most precious possessions of the people. They were relics of the lost race received in the early ages. Thus we read of the brazen or bronze anvil that was preserved in one city, which fell from heaven, and was nine days and nine nights in falling; in other words, it took nine days and nights of a sailing-voyage to bring it from Atlantis.

The modern theory that the gods of Greece never had any personal existence, but represented atmospheric and meteorological myths, the movements of clouds, planets, and the sun, is absurd. Rude nations repeat, they do not invent; to suppose a barbarous people creating their deities out of clouds and sunsets is to reverse nature. Men first worship stones, then other men, then spirits. Resemblances of names prove nothing; it is as if one would show that the name of the great Napoleon meant "the lion of the desert" (Napo-leon), and should thence argue that Napoleon never existed, that he was a myth, that he represented power in solitude, or some such stuff. When we read that Jove whipped his wife, and threw her son out of the window, the inference is that Jove was a man, and actually did something like the thing described; certainly gods, sublimated spirits, aerial sprites, do not act after this fashion; and it would puzzle the mythmakers to prove that the sun, moon, or stars whipped their wives or flung recalcitrant young men out of windows. The history of Atlantis could be in part reconstructed out of the mythology of Greece; it is a history of kings, queens, and princes; of love-making, adulteries, rebellions, wars, murders, sea-voyages, and colonizations; of palaces, temples, workshops, and forges; of sword-making, engraving and metallurgy; of wine, barley, wheat, cattle, sheep, horses, and agriculture generally. Who can doubt that it represents the history of a real people?

Uranos was the first god; that is to say, the first king of the great race. As he was at the commencement of all things, his symbol was the sky. He probably represented the race previous even to the settlement of Atlantis. He was a son of Gæa (the earth). He seems to have been the parent of three races—the Titans, the Hekatoncheires, and the Kyklopes or Cyclops.

I incline to the belief that these were civilized races, and that the peculiarities ascribed to the last two refer to the vessels in which they visited the shores of the barbarians.

THE EMPIRE OF ATLANTIS.

The empire of the Titans was clearly the empire of Atlantis. "The most judicious among our mythologists" (says Dr. Rees, "New British Cyclopædia," art. Titans)—"such as Gerard Vossius, Marsham, Bochart, and Father Thomassin—are of opinion that the partition of the world among the sons of Noah—Shem, Ham, and Japheth—was the original of the tradition of the same partition among Jupiter, Neptune, and Pluto," upon the breaking up of the great empire of the Titans. "The learned Pezron contends that the division which was made of this vast empire came, in after-times, to be taken for the partition of the whole world; that Asia remaining in the hands of Jupiter (Zeus), the most potent of the three brothers, made him looked upon as the god of Olympus; that the sea and islands which fell to Neptune occasioned their giving him the title of 'god of the sea;' and that Spain, the extremity of the then known world, thought to be a very low country in respect of Asia, and famous for its excellent mines of gold and silver, failing to Pluto, occasioned him to be taken for the 'god of the infernal regions.'" We should suppose that Pluto possibly ruled over the transatlantic possessions of Atlantis in America, over those "portions of the opposite continent" which Plato tells us were dominated by Atlas and his posterity, and which, being far beyond or below sunset, were the "under-world" of the ancients; while Atlantis, the Canaries, etc., constituted the island division with Western Africa and Spain. Murray tells us ("Mythology," p. 58) that Pluto's share of the kingdom was supposed to lie "in the remote west." The under-world of the dead was simply the world below the western horizon; "the home of the dead has to do with that far west region where the sun dies at night." ("Anthropology," p. 350.) "On the coast of Brittany, where Cape Raz stands out westward into the ocean, there is 'the Bay of Souls,' the launching-place where the departed spirits sail off across the sea." (Ibid.) In like manner, Odysseus found the land of the dead in the ocean beyond the Pillars of Hercules. There, indeed, was the land of the mighty dead, the grave of the drowned Atlanteans.

"However this be," continues F. Pezron, "the empire of the Titans, according to the ancients, was very extensive; they possessed Phrygia, Thrace, a part of Greece, the island of Crete, and several other provinces to the inmost recesses of Spain. To these Sanchoniathon seems to join Syria; and Diodorus adds a part of Africa, and the kingdoms of Mauritania." The kingdoms of Mauritania embraced all that north-western region of Africa nearest to Atlantis in which are the Atlas Mountains, and in which, in the days of Herodotus, dwelt the Atlantes.

Neptune, or Poseidon, says, in answer to a message from Jupiter,

No vassal god, nor of his train am I.

Three brothers, deities, from Saturn came,

And ancient Rhea, earth's immortal dame;

Assigned by lot our triple rule we know;

Infernal Pluto sways the shades below:

O'er the wide clouds, and o'er the starry plain

Ethereal Jove extends his high domain;

My court beneath the hoary waves I keep,

And hush the roaring of the sacred deep.

Iliad, book XVIII.

Homer alludes to Poseidon as

"The god whose liquid arms are hurled

Around the globe, whose earthquakes rock the world."

Mythology tells us that when the Titans were defeated by Saturn they retreated into the interior of Spain; Jupiter followed them up, and beat them for the last time near Tartessus, and thus terminated a ten-years' war. Here we have a real battle on an actual battle-field.

If we needed any further proof that the empire of the Titans was the empire of Atlantis, we would find it in the names of the Titans: among these were Oceanus, Saturn or Chronos, and Atlas; they were all the sons of Uranos. Oceanus was at the base of the Greek mythology. Plato says ("Dialogues," Timæus, vol. ii., p. 533): "Oceanus and Tethys were the children of Earth and Heaven, and from these sprung Phorcys, and Chronos, and Rhea, and many more with them; and from Chronos and Rhea sprung Zeus and Hera, and all those whom we know as their brethren, and others who were their children." In other words, all their gods came out of the ocean; they were rulers over some ocean realm; Chronos was the son of Oceanus, and Chronos was an Atlantean god, and from him the Atlantic Ocean was called by the ancients "the Chronian Sea." The elder Minos was called "the Son of the Ocean:" he first gave civilization to the Cretans; he engraved his laws on brass, precisely as Plato tells us the laws of Atlantis were engraved on pillars of brass.

The wanderings of Ulysses, as detailed in the "Odyssey" of Homer, are strangely connected with the Atlantic Ocean. The islands of the Phoenicians were apparently in mid-ocean:

We dwell apart, afar

Within the unmeasured deep, amid its waves

The most remote of men; no other race

Hath commerce with us.—Odyssey, book vi.

The description of the Phæacian walls, harbors, cities, palaces, ships, etc., seems like a recollection of Atlantis. The island of Calypso appears also to have been in the Atlantic Ocean, twenty days' sail from the Phæacian isles; and when Ulysses goes to the land of Pluto, "the under-world," the home of the dead, he

"Reached the far confines of Oceanus,"

beyond the Pillars of Hercules. It would be curious to inquire how far the poems of Homer are Atlantean in their relations and inspiration. Ulysses's wanderings were a prolonged struggle with Poseidon, the founder and god of Atlantis.

"The Hekatoncheires, or Cetimæni, beings each with a hundred hands, were three in number—Kottos, Gyges or Gyes, and Briareus—and represented the frightful crashing of waves, and its resemblance to the convulsions of earthquakes." (Murray's "Mythology," p. 26.) Are not these hundred arms the oars of the galleys, and the frightful crashing of the waves their movements in the water?

"The Kyklopes also were three in number—Brontes, with his thunder; Steropes, with his lightning; and Arges, with his stream of light. They were represented as having only one eye, which was placed at the juncture between the nose and brow. It was, however, a large, flashing eye, as became beings who were personifications of the storm-cloud, with its flashes of destructive lightning and peals of thunder."

We shall show hereafter that the invention of gunpowder dates back to the days of the Phoenicians, and may have been derived by them from Atlantis. It is not impossible that in this picture of the Kyklopes we see a tradition of sea-going ships, with a light burning at the prow, and armed with some explosive preparation, which, with a roar like thunder, and a flash like lightning, destroyed those against whom it was employed? It at least requires less strain upon our credulity to suppose these monsters were a barbarian's memory of great ships than to believe that human beings ever existed with a hundred arms, and with one eye in the middle of the forehead, and giving out thunder and lightning.

The natives of the West India Islands regarded the ships of Columbus as living creatures, and that their sails were wings.

Berosus tells us, speaking of the ancient days of Chaldea, "In the first year there appeared, from that part of the Erythræan Sea which borders upon Babylonia, an animal endowed with reason, by name Oannes, whose whole body (according to the account of Apollodorus) was that of a fish; that under the fish's head he had another head, with feet also below, similar to those of a man, subjoined to the fish's tail. His voice too and language was articulate and human, and a representation of him is preserved even unto this day. This being was accustomed to pass the day among men, but took no food at that season, and he gave them an insight into letters and arts of all kinds. He taught them to construct cities, to found temples, to compile laws, and explained to them the principles of geometrical knowledge. He made them distinguish the seeds of the earth, and showed them how to collect the fruits; in short, he instructed them in everything which could tend to soften manners and humanize their laws. From that time nothing material has been added by way of improvement to his instructions. And when the sun set, this being, Oannes, retired again into the sea, and passed the night in the deep, for he was amphibious. After this there appeared other animals like Oannes."

This is clearly the tradition preserved by a barbarous people of the great ships of a civilized nation, who colonized their coast and introduced the arts and sciences among them. And here we see the same tendency to represent the ship as a living thing, which converted the war-vessels of the Atlanteans (the Kyklopes) into men with one blazing eye in the middle of the forehead.

Uranos was deposed from the throne, and succeeded by his son Chronos. He was called "the ripener, the harvest-god," and was probably identified with the beginning of the Agricultural Period. He married his sister Rhea, who bore him Pluto, Poseidon, Zeus, Hestia, Demeter, and Hera. He anticipated that his sons would dethrone him, as he had dethroned his father, Uranos, and he swallowed his first five children, and would have swallowed the sixth child, Zeus, but that his wife Rhea deceived him with a stone image of the child; and Zeus was conveyed to the island of Crete, and there concealed in a cave and raised to manhood. Subsequently Chronos "yielded back to the light the children he had swallowed." This myth probably means that Chronos had his children raised in some secret place, where they could not be used by his enemies as the instruments of a rebellion against his throne; and the stone image of Zeus, palmed off upon him by Rhea, was probably some other child substituted for his own. His precautions seem to have been wise; for as soon as the children returned to the light they commenced a rebellion, and drove the old gentleman from his throne. A rebellion of the Titans followed. The struggle was a tremendous one, and seems to have been decided at last by the use of gunpowder, as I shall show farther on.

We have seen Chronos identified with the Atlantic, called by the Romans the "Chronian Sea." He was known to the Romans under the name of Saturn, and ruled over "a great Saturnian continent" in the Western Ocean. Saturn, or Chronos, came to Italy: he presented himself to the king, Janus, "and proceeded to instruct the subjects of the latter in agriculture, gardening, and many other arts then quite unknown to them; as, for example, how to tend and cultivate the vine. By such means he at length raised the people from a rude and comparatively barbarous condition to one of order and peaceful occupations, in consequence of which he was everywhere held in high esteem, and, in course of time, was selected by Janus to share with him the government of the country, which thereupon assumed the name of Saturnia—'a land of seed and fruit.' The period of Saturn's government was sung in later days by poets as a happy time, when sorrows were unknown, when innocence, freedom, and gladness reigned throughout the land in such a degree as to deserve the title of the Golden Age." (Murray's "Mythology," p. 32.)

All this accords with Plato's story. He tells us that the rule of the Atlanteans extended to Italy; that they were a civilized, agricultural, and commercial people. The civilization of Rome was therefore an outgrowth directly from the civilization of Atlantis.

The Roman Saturnalia was a remembrance of the Atlantean colonization. It was a period of joy and festivity; master and slave met as equals; the distinctions of poverty and wealth were forgotten; no punishments for crime were inflicted; servants and slaves went about dressed in the clothes of their masters; and children received presents from their parents or relatives. It was a time of jollity and mirth, a recollection of the Golden Age. We find a reminiscence of it in the Roman "Carnival."

The third and last on the throne of the highest god was Zeus. We shall see him, a little farther on, by the aid of some mysterious engine overthrowing the rebels, the Titans, who rose against his power, amid the flash of lightning and the roar of thunder. He was called "the thunderer," and "the mighty thunderer." He was represented with thunder-bolts in his hand and an eagle at his feet.

During the time of Zeus Atlantis seems to have reached its greatest height of power. He was recognized as the father of the whole world; he everywhere rewarded uprightness, truth, faithfulness, and kindness; he was merciful to the poor, and punished the cruel. To illustrate his rule on earth the following story is told:

"Philemon and Baukis, an aged couple of the poorer class, were living peacefully and full of piety toward the gods in their cottage in Phrygia, when Zeus, who often visited the earth, disguised, to inquire into the behavior of men, paid a visit, in passing through Phrygia on such a journey, to these poor old people, and was received by them very kindly as a weary traveller, which he pretended to be. Bidding him welcome to the house, they set about preparing for their guest, who was accompanied by Hermes, as excellent a meal as they could afford, and for this purpose were about to kill the only goose they had left, when Zeus interfered; for he was touched by their kindliness and genuine piety, and that all the more because he had observed among the other inhabitants of the district nothing but cruelty of disposition and a habit of reproaching and despising the gods. To punish this conduct he determined to visit the country with a flood, but to save from it Philemon and Baukis, the good aged couple, and to reward them in a striking manner. To this end he revealed himself to them before opening the gates of the great flood, transformed their poor cottage on the hill into a splendid temple, installed the aged pair as his priest and priestess, and granted their prayer that they might both die together. When, after many years, death overtook them, they were changed into two trees, that grew side by side in the neighborhood—an oak and a linden." (Murray's "Mythology," p. 38.)

Here we have another reference to the Flood, and another identification with Atlantis.

Zeus was a kind of Henry VIII., and took to himself a number of wives.

By Demeter (Ceres) he had Persephone (Proserpine); by Leto, Apollo and Artemis (Diana); by Dione, Aphrodite (Venus); by Semele, Dionysos (Bacchus); by Maia, Hermes (Mercury); by Alkmene, Hercules, etc., etc.

We have thus the whole family of gods and goddesses traced back to Atlantis.

Hera, or Juno, was the first and principal wife of Zeus. There were numerous conjugal rows between the royal pair, in which, say the poets, Juno was generally to blame. She was naturally jealous of the other wives of Zeus. Zeus on one occasion beat her, and threw her son Hephæstos out of Olympus; on another occasion he hung her out of Olympus with her arms tied and two great weights attached to her feet—a very brutal and ungentlemanly trick—but the Greeks transposed this into a beautiful symbol: the two weights, they say, represent the earth and sea, "an illustration of how all the phenomena of the visible sky were supposed to hang dependent on the highest god of heaven!" (Ibid., p. 47.) Juno probably regarded the transaction in an altogether different light; and she therefore united with Poseidon, the king's brother, and his daughter Athena, in a rebellion to put the old fellow in a strait-jacket, "and would have succeeded had not Thetis brought to his aid the sea-giant Ægæon," probably a war-ship. She seems in the main, however, to have been a good wife, and was the type of all the womanly virtues.

Poseidon, the first king of Atlantis, according to Plato, was, according to Greek mythology, a brother of Zeus, and a son of Chronos. In the division of the kingdom he fell heir to the ocean and its islands, and to the navigable rivers; in other words, he was king of a maritime and commercial people. His symbol was the horse. "He was the first to train and employ horses;" that is to say, his people first domesticated the horse. This agrees with what Plato tells us of the importance attached to the horse in Atlantis, and of the baths and race-courses provided for him. He was worshipped in the island of Tenos "in the character of a physician," showing that he represented an advanced civilization. He was also master of an agricultural people; "the ram with the golden fleece for which the Argonauts sailed was the offspring of Poseidon." He carried in his hand a three-pronged symbol, the trident, doubtless an emblem of the three continents that were embraced in the empire of Atlantis. He founded many colonies along the shores of the Mediterranean; "he helped to build the walls of Troy;" the tradition thus tracing the Trojan civilization to an Atlantean source. He settled Attica and founded Athens, named after his niece Athena, daughter of Zeus, who had no mother, but had sprung from the head of Zeus, which probably signified that her mother's name was not known—she was a foundling. Athena caused the first olive-tree to grow on the Acropolis of Athens, parent of all the olive-trees of Greece. Poseidon seems to have had settlements at Corinth, Ægina, Naxos, and Delphi. Temples were erected to his honor in nearly all the seaport towns of Greece. He sent a sea-monster, to wit, a slip, to ravage part of the Trojan territory.

In the "Iliad" Poseidon appears "as ruler of the sea, inhabiting a brilliant palace in its depths, traversing its surface in a chariot, or stirring the powerful billows until the earth shakes as they crash upon the shores.... He is also associated with well-watered plains and valleys." (Murray's "Mythology," p. 51.) The palace in the depths of the sea was the palace upon Olympus in Atlantis; the traversing of the sea referred to the movements of a mercantile race; the shaking of the earth was an association with earthquakes; the "well-watered plains and valleys" remind us of the great plain of Atlantis described by Plato.

POSEIDON, OR NEPTUNE.

All the traditions of the coming of civilization into Europe point to Atlantis.

For instance, Keleos, who lived at Eleusis, near Athens, hospitably received Demeter, the Greek Ceres, the daughter of Poseidon, when she landed; and in return she taught him the use of the plough, and presented his son with the seed of barley, and sent him out to teach mankind how to sow and utilize that grain. Dionysos, grandson of Poseidon, travelled "through all the known world, even into the remotest parts of India, instructing the people, as he proceeded, how to tend the vine, and how to practise many other arts of peace, besides teaching them the value of just and honorable dealings." (Murray's "Mythology," p. 119.) The Greeks celebrated great festivals in his honor down to the coming of Christianity.

"The Nymphs of Grecian mythology were a kind of middle beings between the gods and men, communicating with both, loved and respected by both; ... living like the gods on ambrosia. In extraordinary cases they were summoned, it was believed, to the councils of the Olympian gods; but they usually remained in their particular spheres, in secluded grottoes and peaceful valleys, occupied in spinning, weaving, bathing, singing sweet songs, dancing, sporting, or accompanying deities who passed through their territories—hunting with Artemis (Diana), rushing about with Dionysos (Bacchus), making merry with Apollo or Hermes (Mercury), but always in a hostile attitude toward the wanton and excited Satyrs."

The Nymphs were plainly the female inhabitants of Atlantis dwelling on the plains, while the aristocracy lived on the higher lands. And this is confirmed by the fact that part of them were called Atlantids, offspring of Atlantis. The Hesperides were also "daughters of Atlas;" their mother was Hesperis, a personification of "the region of the West." Their home was "an island in the ocean," Off the north or west coast of Africa.

And here we find a tradition which not only points to Atlantis, but also shows some kinship to the legend in Genesis of the tree and the serpent.

Titæa, "a goddess of the earth," gave Zeus a tree bearing golden apples on it. This tree was put in the care of the Hesperides, but they could not resist the temptation to pluck and eat its fruit; thereupon a serpent named Ladon was put to watch the tree. Hercules slew the serpent, and gave the apples to the Hesperides.

Heracles (Hercules), we have seen, was a son of Zeus, king of Atlantis. One of his twelve labors (the tenth) was the carrying off the cattle of Geryon. The meaning of Geryon is "the red glow of the sunset." He dwelt on the island of "Erythea, in the remote west, beyond the Pillars of Hercules." Hercules took a ship, and after encountering a storm, reached the island and placed himself on Mount Abas. Hercules killed Geryon, stole the cattle, put them on the ship, and landed them safely, driving them "through Iberia, Gaul, and over the Alps down into Italy." (Murray's "Mythology," p. 257.) This was simply the memory of a cattle raid made by an uncivilized race upon the civilized, cattle-raising people of Atlantis.

It is not necessary to pursue the study of the gods of Greece any farther. They were simply barbarian recollections of the rulers of a great civilized

358

people who in early days visited their shores, and brought with them the arts of peace.

Here then, in conclusion, are the proofs of our proposition that the gods of Greece had been the kings of Atlantis:

1. They were not the makers, but the rulers of the world.

2. They were human in their attributes; they loved, sinned, and fought battles, the very sites of which are given; they founded cities, and civilized the people of the shores of the Mediterranean.

3. They dwelt upon an island in the Atlantic," in the remote west.... where the sun shines after it has ceased to shine on Greece."

4. Their land was destroyed in a deluge.

5. They were ruled over by Poseidon and Atlas.

6. Their empire extended to Egypt and Italy and the shores of Africa, precisely as stated by Plato.

7. They existed during the Bronze Age and at the beginning of the Iron Age.

The entire Greek mythology is the recollection, by a degenerate race, of a vast, mighty, and highly civilized empire, which in a remote past covered large parts of Europe, Asia, Africa, and America.

CHAPTER III. THE GODS OF THE PHOENICIANS ALSO KINGS OF ATLANTIS.

Not alone were the gods of the Greeks the deified kings of Atlantis, but we find that the mythology of the Phoenicians was drawn from the same source.

For instance, we find in the Phoenician cosmogony that the Titans (Rephaim) derive their origin from the Phoenician gods Agrus and Agrotus. This connects the Phoenicians with that island in the remote west, in the midst of ocean, where, according to the Greeks, the Titans dwelt.

According to Sanchoniathon, Ouranos was the son of Autochthon, and, according to Plato, Autochthon was one of the ten kings of Atlantis. He married his sister Ge. He is the Uranos of the Greeks, who was the son of Gæa (the earth), whom he married. The Phoenicians tell us, "Ouranos had by Ge four sons: Ilus (El), who is called Chronos, and Betylus (Beth-El), and Dagon, which signifies bread-corn, and Atlas (Tammuz?)." Here, again, we have the names of two other kings of Atlantis. These four sons probably represented four races, the offspring of the earth. The Greek Uranos was the father of Chronos, and the ancestor of Atlas. The Phoenician god

Ouranos had a great many other wives: his wife Ge was jealous; they quarrelled, and he attempted to kill the children he had by her. This is the legend which the Greeks told of Zeus and Juno. In the Phoenician mythology Chronos raised a rebellion against Ouranos, and, after a great battle, dethroned him. In the Greek legends it is Zeus who attacks and overthrows his father, Chronos. Ouranos had a daughter called Astarte (Ashtoreth), another called Rhea. "And Dagon, after he had found out bread-corn and the plough, was called Zeus-Arotrius."

We find also, in the Phoenician legends, mention made of Poseidon, founder and king of Atlantis.

Chronos gave Attica to his daughter Athena, as in the Greek legends. In a time of plague he sacrificed his son to Ouranos, and "circumcised himself, and compelled his allies to do the same thing." It would thus appear that this singular rite, practised as we have seen by the Atlantidæ of the Old and New Worlds, the Egyptians, the Phoenicians, the Hebrews, the Ethiopians, the Mexicans, and the red men of America, dates back, as we might have expected, to Atlantis.

"Chronos visits the different regions of the habitable world."

He gave Egypt as a kingdom to the god Taaut, who had invented the alphabet. The Egyptians called him Thoth, and he was represented among them as "the god of letters, the clerk of the under-world," bearing a tablet, pen, and palm-branch.

This not only connects the Phoenicians with Atlantis, but shows the relations of Egyptian civilization to both Atlantis and the Phoenicians.

There can be no doubt that the royal personages who formed the gods of Greece were also the gods of the Phoenicians. We have seen the Autochthon of Plato reappearing in the Autochthon of the Phoenicians; the Atlas of Plato in the Atlas of the Phoenicians; the Poseidon of Plato in the Poseidon of the Phoenicians; while the kings Mestor and Mneseus of Plato are probably the gods Misor and Amynus of the Phoenicians.

Sanchoniathon tells us, after narrating all the discoveries by which the people advanced to civilization, that the Cabiri set down their records of the past by the command of the god Taaut, "and they delivered them to their successors and to foreigners, of whom one was Isiris (Osiris), the inventor of the three letters, the brother of Chua, who is called the first Phoenician." (Lenormant and Chevallier, "Ancient History of the East," vol. ii., p. 228.)

This would show that the first Phoenician came long after this line of the kings or gods, and that he was a foreigner, as compared with them; and, therefore, that it could not have been the Phoenicians proper who made the several inventions narrated by Sanchoniathon, but some other race, from whom the Phoenicians might have been descended.

And in the delivery of their records to the foreigner Osiris, the god of Egypt, we have another evidence that Egypt derived her civilization from Atlantis.

Max Müller says: "The Semitic languages also are all varieties of one form of speech. Though we do not know that primitive language from which the Semitic dialects diverged, yet we know that at one time such language must have existed.... We cannot derive Hebrew from Sanscrit, or Sanscrit from Hebrew; but we can well understand how both may have proceeded from one common source. They are both channels supplied from one river, and they carry, though not always on the surface, floating materials of language which challenge comparison, and have already yielded satisfactory results to careful analyzers." ("Outlines of Philosophy of History," vol. i., p. 475.)

There was an ancient tradition among the Persians that the Phoenicians migrated from the shores of the Erythræan Sea, and this has been supposed to mean the Persian Gulf; but there was a very old city of Erythia, in utter ruin in the time of Strabo, which was built in some ancient age, long before the founding of Gades, near the site of that town, on the Atlantic coast of Spain. May not this town of Erythia have given its name to the adjacent sea? And this may have been the starting-point of the Phoenicians in their European migrations. It would even appear that there was an island of Erythea. In the Greek mythology the tenth labor of Hercules consisted in driving away the cattle of Geryon, who lived in the island of Erythea, "an island somewhere in the remote west, beyond the Pillars of Hercules." (Murray's "Mythology," p. 257.) Hercules stole the cattle from this remote oceanic island, and, returning drove them "through Iberia, Gaul, over the Alps, and through Italy." (Ibid.) It is probable that a people emigrating from the Erythræan Sea, that is, from the Atlantic, first gave their name to a town on the coast of Spain, and at a later date to the Persian Gulf—as we have seen the name of York carried from England to the banks of the Hudson, and then to the Arctic Circle.

The builders of the Central American cities are reported to have been a bearded race. The Phoenicians, in common with the Indians, practised human sacrifices to a great extent; they worshipped fire and water, adopted the names of the animals whose skins they wore—that is to say, they had the totemic system—telegraphed by means of fires, poisoned their arrows, offered peace before beginning battle, and used drums. (Bancroft's "Native Races," vol. v., p. 77.)

The extent of country covered by the commerce of the Phoenicians represents to some degree the area of the old Atlantean Empire. Their colonies and trading-posts extended east and west from the shores of the Black Sea, through the Mediterranean to the west coast of Africa and of Spain, and around to Ireland and England; while from north to south they ranged from the Baltic to the Persian Gulf. They touched every point where civilization in later ages made its appearance. Strabo estimated that they had three hundred cities along the west coast of Africa. When Columbus sailed to discover a new world, or re-discover an old one, he took his departure from a Phoenician seaport, founded by that great race two thousand five hundred years previously. This Atlantean sailor, with his Phoenician features, sailing from an Atlantean port, simply re-opened the path of commerce and colonization which had been closed when Plato's island sunk in the sea. And it is a curious fact that Columbus had the antediluvian world in his mind's eye even then, for when he reached the mouth of the Orinoco he thought it was the river Gihon, that flowed out of Paradise, and he wrote home to Spain, "There are here great indications suggesting the proximity of the earthly Paradise, for not only does it correspond in mathematical position with the opinions of the holy and learned theologians, but all other signs concur to make it probable."

Sanchoniathon claims that the learning of Egypt, Greece, and Judæa was derived from the Phoenicians. It would appear probable that, while other races represent the conquests or colonizations of Atlantis, the Phoenicians succeeded to their arts, sciences, and especially their commercial supremacy; and hence the close resemblances which we have found to exist between the Hebrews, a branch of the Phoenician stock, and the people of America.

> Upon the Syrian sea the people live
> Who style themselves Phoenicians....
> These were the first great founders of the world—
> Founders of cities and of mighty states—
> Who showed a path through seas before unknown.
> In the first ages, when the sons of men
> Knew not which way to turn them, they assigned
> To each his first department; they bestowed
> Of land a portion and of sea a lot,

And sent each wandering tribe far off to share

A different soil and climate. Hence arose

The great diversity, so plainly seen,

'Mid nations widely severed.

Dyonysius of Susiana, A.D. 3.

CHAPTER IV. THE GOD ODIN, WODEN, OR WOTAN.

In the Scandinavian mythology the chief god was Odin, the Woden, Wotan, or Wuotan of the Germans. He is represented with many of the attributes of the Greek god Zeus, and is supposed by some to be identical with him. He dwelt with the twelve Æsir, or gods, upon Asgard, the Norse Olympus, which arose out of Midgard, a land half-way between the regions of frost and fire (to wit, in a temperate climate). The Scandinavian Olympus was probably Atlantis. Odin is represented as a grave-looking elderly man with a long beard, carrying in his hand a spear, and accompanied by two dogs and two ravens. He was the father of poetry, and the inventor of Runic writing.

The Chiapenese of Central America (the people whose language we have seen furnishing such remarkable resemblances to Hebrew) claim to have been the first people of the New World. Clavigero tells us ("Hist. Antiq. del Messico," Eng. trans., 1807, vol. i.) that according to the traditions of the Chiapenese there was a Votan who was the grandson of the man who built the ark to save himself and family from the Deluge; he was one of those who undertook to build the tower that should reach to heaven. The Lord ordered him to people America. "He came from the East." He brought seven families with him. He had been preceded in America by two others, Igh and Imox. He built a great city in America called "Nachan," City of the Serpents (the serpent that tempted Eve was Nahash), from his own race, which was named Chan, a serpent. This Nachan is supposed to have been Palenque. The date of his journey is placed in the legends in the year 3000 of the world, and in the tenth century B.C. He also founded three tributary monarchies, whose capitals were Tulan, Mayapan, and Chiquimala. He wrote a book containing a history of his deeds, and proofs that he belonged to the tribe of Chanes (serpents). He states that "he is the third of the Votans; that he conducted seven families from Valum-Votan to this continent, and assigned lands to them; that he determined to travel until he came to the root of heaven and found his relations, the Culebres, and made himself known to them; that he accordingly made four voyages to Chivim;

that he arrived in Spain; that he went to Rome; that he saw the house of God building; that he went by the road which his brethren, the Culebres, had bored; that he marked it, and that he passed by the houses of the thirteen Culebres. He relates that, in returning from one of his voyages, he found seven other families of the Tzequil nation who had joined the first inhabitants, and recognized in them the same origin as his own, that is, of the Culebres; he speaks of the place where they built the first town, which from its founders received the name of Tzequil; he affirms that, having taught them the refinement of manners in the use of the table, table-cloths, dishes, basins, cups, and napkins, they taught him the knowledge of God and his worship; his first ideas of a king, and obedience to him; that he was chosen captain of all these united families."

It is probable that Spain and Rome are interpolations. Cabrera claims that the Votanites were Carthaginians. He thinks the Chivim of Votan were the Hivim, or Givim, who were descended of Heth, son of Canaan, Phoenicians; they were the builders of Accaron, Azotus, Ascalon, and Gaza. The Scriptures refer to them as Hivites (Givim) in Deuteronomy (chap. ii., verse 32), and Joshua (chap. xiii., verse 4). He claims that Cadmus and his wife Hermione were of this stock; and according to Ovid they were metamorphosed into snakes (Culebres). The name Hivites in Phoenician signifies a snake.

Votan may not, possibly, have passed into Europe; he may have travelled altogether in Africa. His singular allusion to "a way which the Culebres had bored" seems at first inexplicable; but Dr. Livingstone's last letters, published 8th November, 1869, in the "Proceedings of the Royal Geographical Society," mention that "tribes live in underground houses in Rua. Some excavations are said to be thirty miles long, and have running rills in them; a whole district can stand a siege in them. The 'writings' therein, I have been told by some of the people, are drawings of animals, and not letters; otherwise I should have gone to see them. People very dark, well made, and outer angle of eyes slanting inward."

And Captain Grant, who accompanied Captain Speke in his famous exploration of the sources of the Nile, tells of a tunnel or subway under the river Kaoma, on the highway between Loowemba and Marunga, near Lake Tanganyika. His guide Manna describes it to him:

"I asked Manna if he had ever seen any country resembling it. His reply was, 'This country reminds me of what I saw in the country to the south of the Lake Tanganyika, when travelling with an Arab's caravan from Unjanyembeh. There is a river there called the Kaoma, running into the lake, the sides of which are similar in precipitousness to the rocks before us.' I then asked, 'Do the people cross this river in boats?' 'No; they have no boats; and even if they had, the people could not land, as the sides are too steep: they pass underneath the river by a natural tunnel, or subway.' He and all his party went through it on their way from Loowemba to Ooroongoo, and returned by it. He described its length as having taken them from sunrise till noon to pass through it, and so high that, if mounted upon camels, they could not touch the top. Tall reeds, the thickness of a walking-stick, grew inside, the road was strewed with white pebbles, and so wide—four hundred yards—that they could see their way tolerably well while passing through it. The rocks looked as if they had been planed by artificial means. Water never came through from the river overhead; it was procured by digging wells. Manna added that the people of Wambweh take shelter in this tunnel, and live there with their families and cattle, when molested by the Watuta, a warlike race, descended from the Zooloo Kafirs."

But it is interesting to find in this book of Votan, however little reliance we may place in its dates or details, evidence that there was actual intercourse between the Old World and the New in remote ages.

Humboldt remarks:

"We have fixed the special attention of our readers upon this Votan, or Wodan, an American who appears of the same family with the Wods or Odins of the Goths and of the people of Celtic origin. Since, according to the learned researches of Sir William Jones, Odin and Buddha are probably the same person, it is curious to see the names of Bondvar, Wodansday, and Votan designating in India, Scandinavia, and in Mexico the day of a brief period." ("Vues des Cordilleras," p. 148, ed. 1810.)

There are many things to connect the mythology of the Gothic nations with Atlantis; they had, as we have seen, flood legends; their gods Krodo and Satar were the Chronos and Saturn of Atlantis; their Baal was the Bel of the Phoenicians, who were closely connected with Poseidon and Atlas; and, as we shall see hereafter, their language has a distinct relationship with the tongues of the Arabians, Cushites, Chaldeans, and Phoenicians.

CHAPTER V. THE PYRAMID, THE CROSS, AND THE GARDEN OF EDEN.

No fact is better established than the reverence shown to the sign of the Cross in all the ages prior to Christianity. We cannot do better than quote from an able article in the Edinburgh Review of July, 1870, upon this question:

"From the dawn of organized Paganism in the Eastern world to the final establishment of Christianity in the Western, the Cross was undoubtedly one of the commonest and most sacred of symbolical monuments; and, to a remarkable extent, it is so still in almost every land where that of Calvary is unrecognized or unknown. Apart from any distinctions of social or intellectual superiority, of caste, color, nationality, or location in either hemisphere, it appears to have been the aboriginal possession of every people in antiquity—the elastic girdle, so to say, which embraced the most widely separated heathen communities—the most significant token of a universal brotherhood, to which all the families of mankind were severally and irresistibly drawn, and by which their common descent was emphatically expressed, or by means of which each and all preserved, amid every vicissitude of fortune, a knowledge of the primeval happiness and dignity of their species. Where authentic history is silent on the subject, the material relics of past and long since forgotten races are not wanting to confirm and strengthen this supposition. Diversified forms of the symbol are delineated more or less artistically, according to the progress achieved in civilization at the period, on the ruined walls of temples and palaces, on natural rocks and sepulchral galleries, on the hoariest monoliths and the rudest statuary; on coins, medals, and vases of every description; and, in not a few instances, are preserved in the architectural proportions of subterranean as well as superterranean structures, of tumuli as well as fanes. The extraordinary sanctity attaching to the symbol, in every age and under every variety of circumstance, justified any expenditure incurred in its fabrication or embellishment; hence the most persistent labor, the most consummate ingenuity, were lavished upon it. Populations of essentially different culture, tastes, and pursuits—the highly-civilized and the demi-civilized, the settled and nomadic—vied with each other in their efforts to extend the knowledge of its exceptional import and virtue among their latest posterities. The marvellous rock-hewn caves of Elephanta and Ellora, and the stately temples of Mathura and Terputty, in the East, may be cited as characteristic examples of one laborious method of exhibiting it; and the megalithic structures of Callernish and Newgrange, in the West, of another; while a third may be instanced in the great temple at Mitzla, 'the City of the Moon,' in Ojaaca, Central America, also excavated in the living rock, and manifesting the same stupendous labor and ingenuity as are observable in the cognate caverns of Salsette—of endeavors, we repeat, made by peoples as intellectually as geographically distinct, and followers withal of independent and unassociated deities, to magnify and perpetuate some grand primeval symbol....

"Of the several varieties of the Cross still in vogue, as national or ecclesiastical emblems, in this and other European states, and distinguished by the familiar appellations of St. George, St. Andrew, the Maltese, the Greek, the Latin, etc., etc., there is not one among them the existence of which may not be traced to the remotest antiquity. They were the common property of the Eastern nations. No revolution or other casualty has wrought any perceptible difference in their several forms or delineations; they have passed from one hemisphere to the other intact; have survived dynasties, empires, and races; have been borne on the crest of each successive wave of Aryan population in its course toward the West; and, having been reconsecrated in later times by their lineal descendants, are still recognized as military and national badges of distinction....

"Among the earliest known types is the crux ansata, vulgarly called 'the key of the Nile,' because of its being found sculptured or otherwise represented so frequently upon Egyptian and Coptic monuments. It has, however, a very much older and more sacred signification than this. It was the symbol of symbols, the mystical Tau, 'the hidden wisdom,' not only of the ancient Egyptians but also of the Chaldeans, Phoenicians, Mexicans, Peruvians, and of every other ancient people commemorated in history, in either hemisphere, and is formed very similarly to our letter T, with a roundlet, or oval, placed immediately above it. Thus it was figured on the gigantic emerald or glass statue of Serapis, which was transported (293 B.C.) by order of Ptolemy Soter from Sinope, on the southern shores of the Black Sea, re-erected within that famous labyrinth which encompassed the banks of Lake Moeris, and destroyed by the victorious army of Theodosius (A.D. 389), despite the earnest entreaties of the Egyptian priesthood to spare it, because it was the emblem of their god and of 'the life to come.' Sometimes, as may be seen on the breast of an Egyptian mummy in the museum of the London University, the simple T only is planted on the frustum of a cone; and sometimes it is represented as springing from a heart; in the first instance signifying goodness; in the second, hope or expectation of reward. As in the oldest temples and catacombs of Egypt, so this type likewise abounds in the ruined cities of Mexico and Central America, graven as well upon the most ancient cyclopean and polygonal walls as upon the more modern and perfect examples of masonry; and is displayed in an equally conspicuous manner upon the breasts of innumerable bronze statuettes which have been recently disinterred from the cemetery of Juigalpa (of unknown antiquity) in Nicaragua."

When the Spanish missionaries first set foot upon the soil of America, in the fifteenth century, they were amazed to find the Cross was as devoutly worshipped by the red Indians as by themselves, and were in doubt whether to ascribe the fact to the pious labors of St. Thomas or to the cunning device of the Evil One. The hallowed symbol challenged their attention on every hand and in almost every variety of form. It appeared on the bass-reliefs of ruined and deserted as well as on those of inhabited palaces, and was the most conspicuous ornament in the great temple of Gozumel, off the coast of Yucatan. According to the particular locality, and the purpose which it served, it was formed of various materials—of marble and gypsum in the open spaces of cities and by the way-side; of wood in the teocallis or chapels on pyramidal summits and in subterranean sanctuaries; and of emerald or jasper in the palaces of kings and nobles.

When we ask the question how it comes that the sign of the Cross has thus been reverenced from the highest antiquity by the races of the Old and New Worlds, we learn that it is a reminiscence of the Garden of Eden, in other words, of Atlantis.

Professor Hardwicke says:

"All these and similar traditions are but mocking satires of the old Hebrew story—jarred and broken notes of the same strain; but with all their exaggerations they intimate how in the background of man's vision lay a paradise of holy joy—a paradise secured from every kind of profanation, and made inaccessible to the guilty; a paradise full of objects that were calculated to delight the senses and to elevate the mind, a paradise that granted to its tenant rich and rare immunities, and that fed with its perennial streams the tree of life and immortality."

To quote again from the writer in the Edinburgh Review, already cited; "Its undoubted antiquity, no less than its extraordinary diffusion, evidences that it must have been, as it may be said to be still in unchristianized lands, emblematical of some fundamental doctrine or mystery. The reader will not have failed to observe that it is most usually associated with water; it was 'the key of the Nile,' that mystical instrument by means of which, in the popular judgment of his Egyptian devotees, Osiris produced the annual revivifying inundations of the sacred stream; it is discernible in that mysterious pitcher or vase portrayed on the brazen table of Bembus, before-mentioned, with its four lips discharging as many streams of water in opposite directions; it was the emblem of the water-deities of the Babylonians in the East and of the Gothic nations in the West, as well as that of the rain-deities respectively of the mixed population in America. We have seen with what peculiar rites the symbol was honored by those widely separated races in the western hemisphere; and the monumental slabs of

Nineveh, now in the museums of London and Paris, show us how it was similarly honored by the successors of the Chaldees in the eastern....

"In Egypt, Assyria, and Britain it was emblematical of creative power and eternity; in India, China, and Scandinavia, of heaven and immortality; in the two Americas, of rejuvenescence and freedom from physical suffering; while in both hemispheres it was the common symbol of the resurrection, or 'the sign of the life to come;' and, finally, in all heathen communities, without exception, it was the emphatic type, the sole enduring evidence, of the Divine Unity. This circumstance alone determines its extreme antiquity—an antiquity, in all likelihood, long antecedent to the foundation of either of the three great systems of religion in the East. And, lastly, we have seen how, as a rule, it is found in conjunction with a stream or streams of water, with exuberant vegetation, and with a hill or a mountainous region—in a word, with a land of beauty, fertility, and joy. Thus it was expressed upon those circular and sacred cakes of the Egyptians, composed of the richest materials—of flour, of honey, of milk—and with which the serpent and bull, as well as other reptiles and beasts consecrated to the service of Isis and their higher divinities, were daily fed; and upon certain festivals were eaten with extraordinary ceremony by the people and their priests. 'The cross-cake,' says Sir Gardner Wilkinson, 'was their hieroglyph for civilized land;' obviously a land superior to their own, as it was, indeed, to all other mundane territories; for it was that distant, traditional country of sempiternal contentment and repose, of exquisite delight and serenity, where Nature, unassisted by man, produces all that is necessary for his sustentation."

And this land was the Garden of Eden of our race. This was the Olympus of the Greeks, where

"This same mild season gives the blooms to blow,

The buds to harden and the fruits to grow."

In the midst of it was a sacred and glorious eminence—the umbilicus orbis terrarum—"toward which the heathen in all parts of the world, and in all ages, turned a wistful gaze in every act of devotion, and to which they hoped to be admitted, or, rather, to be restored, at the close of this transitory scene."

In this "glorious eminence" do we not see Plato's mountain in the middle of Atlantis, as he describes it:

"Near the plain and in the centre of the island there was a mountain, not very high on any side. In this mountain there dwelt one of the earth-born primeval men of that country, whose name was Evenor, and he had a

369

wife named Leucippe, and they had an only daughter, who was named Cleito. Poseidon married her. He enclosed the hill in which she dwelt all around, making alternate zones of sea and land, larger and smaller, encircling one another; there were two of land and three of water ... so that no man could get to the island.... He brought streams of water under the earth to this mountain-island, and made all manner of food to grow upon it. This island became the seat of Atlas, the over-king of the whole island; upon it they built the great temple of their nation; they continued to ornament it in successive generations, every king surpassing the one who came before him to the utmost of his power, until they made the building a marvel to behold for size and beauty.... And they had such an amount of wealth as was never before possessed by kings and potentates—as is not likely ever to be again."

The gardens of Alcinous and Laertes, of which we read in Homeric song, and those of Babylon, were probably transcripts of Atlantis. "The sacred eminence in the midst of a superabundant, happy region figures more or less distinctly in almost every mythology, ancient or modern. It was the Mesomphalos of the earlier Greeks, and the Omphalium of the Cretans, dominating the Elysian fields, upon whose tops, bathed in pure, brilliant, incomparable light, the gods passed their days in ceaseless joys."

"The Buddhists and Brahmans, who together constitute nearly half the population of the world, tell us that the decussated figure (the cross), whether in a simple or a complex form, symbolizes the traditional happy abode of their primeval ancestors—that 'Paradise of Eden toward the East,' as we find expressed in the Hebrew. And, let us ask, what better picture, or more significant characters, in the complicated alphabet of symbolism, could have been selected for the purpose than a circle and a cross: the one to denote a region of absolute purity and perpetual felicity; the other, those four perennial streams that divided and watered the several quarters of it?" (Edinburgh Review, January, 1870.)

And when we turn to the mythology of the Greeks, we find that the origin of the world was ascribed to Okeanos, the ocean. The world was at first an island surrounded by the ocean, as by a great stream:

"It was a region of wonders of all kinds; Okeanos lived there with his wife Tethys: these were the Islands of the Blessed, the gardens of the gods, the sources of nectar and ambrosia, on which the gods lived. Within this circle of water the earth lay spread out like a disk, with mountains rising from it, and the vault of heaven appearing to rest upon its outer edge all around." (Murray's "Mannal of Mythology," pp. 23, 24, et seq.)

On the mountains dwelt the gods; they had palaces on these mountains, with store-rooms, stabling, etc.

"The Gardens of the Hesperides, with their golden apples, were believed to exist in some island of the ocean, or, as it was sometimes thought, in the islands off the north or west coast of Africa. They were far famed in antiquity; for it was there that springs of nectar flowed by the couch of Zeus, and there that the earth displayed the rarest blessings of the gods; it was another Eden." (Ibid., p. 156.)

Homer described it in these words:

> "Stern winter smiles on that auspicious clime,
>
> The fields are florid with unfading prime,
>
> From the bleak pole no winds inclement blow.
>
> Mould the round hail, or flake the fleecy snow;
>
> But from the breezy deep the blessed inhale
>
> The fragrant murmurs of the western gale."

"It was the sacred Asgard of the Scandinavians, springing from the centre of a fruitful land, which was watered by four primeval rivers of milk, severally flowing in the direction of the cardinal points, 'the abode of happiness, and the height of bliss.' It is the Tien-Chan, 'the celestial mountain-land, ... the enchanted gardens' of the Chinese and Tartars, watered by the four perennial fountains of Tychin, or Immortality; it is the hill-encompassed Ilá of the Singhalese and Thibetians, 'the everlasting dwelling-place of the wise and just.' It is the Sineru of the Buddhist, on the summit of which is Tawrutisa, the habitation of Sekrá, the supreme god, from which proceed the four sacred streams, running in as many contrary directions.

It is the Slávratta, 'the celestial earth,' of the Hindoo, the summit of his golden mountain Meru, the city of Brahma, in the centre of Jambadwípa, and from the four sides of which gush forth the four primeval rivers, reflecting in their passage the colorific glories of their source, and severally flowing northward, southward, eastward, and westward."

It is the Garden of Eden of the Hebrews:

"And the Lord God planted a garden eastward in Eden; and there he put the man whom he had formed. And out of the ground made the Lord God to grow every tree that is pleasant to the sight, and good for food; the tree of life also in the midst of the garden, and the tree of knowledge of good and evil. And a river went out of Eden to water the garden; and from thence it was parted, and became into four heads. The name of the first is Pison; that

371

is it which compasseth the whole land of Havilah, where there is gold; and the gold of that land is good: there is bdellium and the onyx stone. And the name of the second river is Gihon: the same is it that compasseth the whole land of Ethiopia. And the name of the third river is Hiddekel: that is it which goeth toward the east of Assyria. And the fourth river is Euphrates. And the Lord God took the man and put him into the Garden of Eden to dress it and to keep it." (Gen. ii., 8-1-5.)

As the four rivers named in Genesis are not branches of any one stream, and head in very different regions, it is evident that there was an attempt, on the part of the writer of the Book, to adapt an ancient tradition concerning another country to the known features of the region in which he dwelt.

Josephus tells us (chap. i., p. 41), "Now the garden (of Eden) was watered by one river, which ran round about the whole earth, and was parted into four parts." Here in the four parts we see the origin of the Cross, while in the river running around the whole earth we have the wonderful canal of Atlantis, described by Plato, which was "carried around the whole of the plain," and received the streams which came down from the mountains. The streams named by Josephus would seem to represent the migrations of people from Atlantis to its colonies. "Phison," he tells us, "denotes a multitude; it ran into India; the Euphrates and Tigris go down into the Red Sea while the Geon runs through Egypt."

We are further told (chap. ii., p. 42) that when Cain, after the murder of Abel, left the land of Adam, "he travelled over many countries" before he reached the land of Nod; and the land of Nod was to the eastward of Adam's home. In other words, the original seat of mankind was in the West, that is to say, in the direction of Atlantis. Wilson tells us that the Aryans of India believed that they originally came "from the West." Thus the nations on the west of the Atlantic look to the east for their place of origin; while on the east of the Atlantic they look to the west: thus all the lines of tradition converge upon Atlantis.

But here is the same testimony that in the Garden of Eden there were four rivers radiating from one parent stream. And these four rivers, as we have seen, we find in the Scandinavian traditions, and in the legends of the Chinese, the Tartars, the Singhalese, the Thibetians, the Buddhists, the Hebrews, and the Brahmans.

And not only do we find this tradition of the Garden of Eden in the Old World, but it meets us also among the civilized races of America. The elder Montezuma said to Cortez, "Our fathers dwelt in that happy and prosperous place which they called Aztlan, which means whiteness.... In this place there is a great mountain in the middle of the water which is called Culhuacan, because it has the point somewhat turned over toward the bottom; and for this cause it is called Culhuacan, which means 'crooked mountain.'" He then proceeds to describe the charms of this favored land, abounding in birds, game, fish, trees, "fountains enclosed with elders and junipers, and alder-trees both large and beautiful." The people planted "maize, red peppers, tomatoes, beans, and all kinds of plants, in furrows."

Here we have the same mountain in the midst of the water which Plato describes—the same mountain to which all the legends of the most ancient races of Europe refer.

The inhabitants of Aztlan were boatmen. (Bancroft's "Native Races," vol. v., p. 325.) E. G. Squier, in his "Notes on Central America," p. 349, says, "It is a significant fact that in the map of their migrations, presented by Gemelli, the place of the origin of the Aztecs is designated by the sign of water, Atl standing for Atzlan, a pyramidal temple with grades, and near these a palm-tree." This circumstance did not escape the attention of Humboldt, who says, "I am astonished at finding a palm-tree near this teocalli. This tree certainly does not indicate a northern origin.... The possibility that an unskilful artist should unintentionally represent a tree of which he had no knowledge is so great, that any argument dependent on it hangs upon a slender thread." ("North Americans of Antiquity," p. 266.)

The Miztecs, a tribe dwelling on the outskirts of Mexico, had a tradition that the gods, "in the day of obscurity and darkness," built "a sumptuous palace, a masterpiece of skill, in which they made their abode upon a mountain. The rock was called 'The Place of Heaven;' there the gods first abode on earth, living many years in great rest and content, as in a happy and delicious land, though the world still lay in obscurity and darkness. The children of these gods made to themselves a garden, in which they put many trees, and fruit-trees, and flowers, and roses, and odorous herbs. Subsequently there came a great deluge, in which many of the sons and daughters of the gods perished." (Bancroft's "Native Races," vol. iii., p. 71.) Here we have a distinct reference to Olympus, the Garden of Plato, and the destruction of Atlantis.

And in Plato's account of Atlantis we have another description of the Garden of Eden and the Golden Age of the world:

"Also, whatever fragrant things there are in the earth, whether roots, or herbage, or woods, or distilling drops of flowers and fruits, grew and thrived in that land; and again the cultivated fruits of the earth, both the edible fruits and other species of food which we call by the name of legumes, and the fruits having a hard rind, affording drinks and meats and ointments ... all these that sacred island, lying beneath the sun, brought forth in abundance.... For many generations, as long as the divine nature lasted in them, they were obedient to the laws, and well affectioned toward the gods, who were their kinsmen; for they possessed true and in every way great spirits, practising gentleness and wisdom in the various chances of life, and in their intercourse with one another. They despised everything but virtue, not caring for their present state of life, and thinking lightly of the possession of gold and other property, which seemed only a burden to them; neither were they intoxicated by luxury; nor did wealth deprive them of their self-control; but they were sober, and saw clearly that all these goods were increased by virtuous friendship with one another, and that by excessive zeal for them, and honor of them, the good of them is lost, and friendship perishes with them."

All this cannot be a mere coincidence; it points to a common tradition of a veritable land, where four rivers flowed down in opposite directions from a central mountain-peak. And these four rivers, flowing to the north, south, east, and west, constitute the origin of that sign of the Cross which we have seen meeting us at every point among the races who were either descended from the people of Atlantis, or who, by commerce and colonization, received their opinions and civilization from them.

Let us look at the question of the identity of the Garden of Eden with Atlantis from another point of view:

If the alphabet of the Phoenicians is kindred with the Maya alphabet, as I think is clear, then the Phoenicians were of the same race, or of some race with which the Mayas were connected; in other words, they were from Atlantis.

Now we know that the Phoenicians and Hebrews were of the same stock, used the same alphabet, and spoke almost precisely the same language.

The Phoenicians preserved traditions, which have come down to us in the writings, of Sanchoniathon, of all the great essential inventions or discoveries which underlie civilization. The first two human beings, they tell us, were Protogonos and Aion (Adam and 'Havath), who produce Genos and Genea (Qên and Qênath), from whom again are descended three brothers, named Phos, Phur, and Phlox (Light, Fire, and Flame), because they "have discovered how to produce fire by the friction of two pieces of wood, and have taught the use of this element." In another fragment, at the origin of the human race we see in succession the fraternal couples of Autochthon and Technites (Adam and Quen—Cain?), inventors of the manufacture of bricks; Agros and Agrotes (Sade and Cêd), fathers of the agriculturists and hunters; then Amynos and Magos, "who taught to dwell in villages and rear flocks."

The connection between these Atlantean traditions and the Bible record is shown in many things. For instance, "the Greek text, in expressing the invention of Amynos, uses the words kw'mas kai` poi'mnas, which are precisely the same as the terms ôhel umiqneh, which the Bible uses in speaking of the dwellings of the descendants of Jabal (Gen., chap. iv., v. 20). In like manner Lamech, both in the signification of his name and also in the savage character attributed to him by the legend attached to his memory, is a true synonyme of Agrotes."

"And the title of A?lh~tai, given to Agros and Agrotes in the Greek of the Phoenician history, fits in wonderfully with the physiognomy of the race of the Cainites in the Bible narrative, whether we take a?lh~tai simply as a Hellenized transcription of the Semitic Elim, 'the strong, the mighty,' or whether we take it in its Greek acceptation, 'the wanderers;' for such is the destiny of Cain and his race according to the very terms of the condemnation which was inflicted upon him after his crime (Gen. iv., 14), and this is what is signified by the name of his grandson 'Yirad. Only, in Sanchoniathon the genealogy does not end with Amynos and Magos, as that of the Cainites in the Bible does with the three sons of Lamech. These two personages are succeeded by Misôr and Sydyk, 'the released and the just,' as Sanchoniathon translates them, but rather the 'upright and the just' (Mishôr and Çüdüq), 'who invent the use of salt.' To Misôr is born Taautos (Taût), to whom we owe letters; and to Sydyk the Cabiri or Corybantes, the institutors of navigation." (Lenormant, "Genealogies between Adam and the Deluge." Contemporary Review, April, 1880.)

We have, also, the fact that the Phoenician name for their goddess Astynome (Ashtar No'emâ), whom the Greeks called Nemaun, was the same as the name of the sister of the three sons of Lamech, as given in Genesis— Na'emah, or Na'amah.

If, then, the original seat of the Hebrews and Phoenicians was the Garden of Eden, to the west of Europe, and if the Phoenicians are shown to be connected, through their alphabets, with the Central Americans, who looked to an island in the sea, to the eastward, as their starting-point, the conclusion becomes irresistible that Atlantis and the Garden of Eden were one and the same.

The Pyramid.—Not only are the Cross and the Garden of Eden identified with Atlantis, but in Atlantis, the habitation of the gods, we find the original model of all those pyramids which extend from India to Peru.

This singular architectural construction dates back far beyond the birth of history. In the Purânas of the Hindoos we read of pyramids long anterior in time to any which have survived to our day. Cheops was preceded by a countless host of similar erections which have long since mouldered into ruins.

If the reader will turn to page 104 of this work he will see, in the midst of the picture of Aztlan, the starting-point of the Aztecs, according to the Botturini pictured writing, a pyramid with worshippers kneeling before it.

Fifty years ago Mr. Faber, in his "Origin of Pagan Idolatry," placed artificial tumuli, pyramids, and pagodas in the same category, conceiving that all were transcripts of the holy mountain which was generally supposed to have stood in the centre of Eden; or, rather, as intimated in more than one place by the Psalmist, the garden itself was situated on an eminence. (Psalms, chap. iii., v. 4, and chap. lxviii., vs. 15, 16, 18.)

The pyramid is one of the marvellous features of that problem which confronts us everywhere, and which is insoluble without Atlantis.

The Arabian traditions linked the pyramid with the Flood. In a manuscript preserved in the Bodleian Library, and translated by Dr. Sprenger, Abou Balkhi says: "The wise men, previous to the Flood, foreseeing an impending Judgment from heaven, either by submersion or fire, which would destroy every created thing, built upon the tops of the mountains in Upper Egypt many pyramids of stone, in order to have some refuge against the approaching calamity. Two of these buildings exceeded the rest in height, being four hundred cubits high and as many broad and as many long. They were built with large blocks of marble, and they were so well put together that the joints were scarcely perceptible. Upon the exterior of the building every charm and wonder of physic was inscribed."

This tradition locates these monster structures upon the mountains of Upper Egypt, but there are no buildings of such dimensions to be found anywhere in Egypt. Is it not probable that we have here another reference to the great record preserved in the land of the Deluge? Were not the pyramids of Egypt and America imitations of similar structures in Atlantis? Might not the building of such a gigantic edifice have given rise to the legends existing on both continents in regard to a Tower of Babel?

How did the human mind hit upon this singular edifice—the pyramid? By what process of development did it reach it? Why should these extraordinary structures crop out on the banks of the Nile, and amid the forests and plains of America? And why, in both countries, should they stand with their sides square to the four cardinal points of the compass? Are they in this, too, a reminiscence of the Cross, and of the four rivers of Atlantis that ran to the north, south, east, and west?

"There is yet a third combination that demands a specific notice. The decussated symbol is not unfrequently planted upon what Christian archæologists designate 'a calvary,' that is, upon a mount or a cone. Thus it is represented in both hemispheres. The megalithic structure of Callernish, in the island of Lewis before mentioned, is the most perfect example of the practice extant in Europe. The mount is preserved to this day. This, to be brief, was the recognized conventional mode of expressing a particular primitive truth or mystery from the days of the Chaldeans to those of the Gnostics, or from one extremity of the civilized world to the other. It is seen in the treatment of the ash Yggdrasill of the Scandinavians, as well as in that of the Bo-tree of the Buddhists. The prototype was not the Egyptian, but the Babylonian crux ansata, the lower member of which constitutes a conical support for the oval or sphere above it. With the Gnostics, who occupied the debatable ground between primitive Christianity and philosophic paganism, and who inscribed it upon their tombs, the cone symbolized death as well as life. In every heathen mythology it was the universal emblem of the goddess or mother of heaven, by whatsoever name she was addressed—whether as Mylitta, Astarte, Aphrodite, Isis, Mata, or Venus; and the several eminences consecrated to her worship were, like those upon which Jupiter was originally adored, of a conical or pyramidal shape. This, too, is the ordinary form of the altars dedicated to the Assyrian god of fertility. In exceptional instances the cone is introduced upon one or the other of the sides, or is distinguishable in the always accompanying mystical tree." (Edinburgh Review, July, 1870.)

If the reader will again turn to page 104 of this work he will see that the tree appears on the top of the pyramid or mountain in both the Aztec representations of Aztlan, the original island-home of the Central American races.

The writer just quoted believes that Mr. Faber is correct in his opinion that the pyramid is a transcript of the sacred mountain which stood in the midst of Eden, the Olympus of Atlantis. He adds: "Thomas Maurice, who is no mean authority, held the same view. He conceived the use to which pyramids in particular were anciently applied to have been threefold—namely, as tombs, temples, and observatories; and this view he labors to establish in the third volume of his 'Indian Antiquities.' Now, whatever may be their actual date, or with whatsoever people they may have originated, whether in Africa or Asia, in the lower valley of the Nile or in the plains of Chaldea, the pyramids of Egypt were unquestionably destined to very opposite purposes. According to Herodotus, they were introduced by the Hyksos; and Proclus, the Platonic philosopher, connects them with the science of astronomy—a science which, he adds, the Egyptians derived from the Chaldeans. Hence we may reasonably infer that they served as well for temples for planetary worship as for observatories. Subsequently to the descent of the shepherds, their hallowed precincts were invaded by royalty, from motives of pride and superstition; and the principal chamber in each was used as tombs."

The pyramidal imitations, dear to the hearts of colonists of the sacred mountain upon which their gods dwelt, was devoted, as perhaps the mountain itself was, to sun and fire worship. The same writer says:

"That Sabian worship once extensively prevailed in the New World is a well-authenticated fact; it is yet practised to some extent by the wandering tribes on the Northern continent, and was the national religion of the Peruvians at the time of the Conquest. That it was also the religion of their more highly civilized predecessors on the soil, south of the equator more especially, is evidenced by the remains of fire-altars, both round and square, scattered about the shores of lakes Umayu and Titicaca, and which are the counterparts of the Gueber dokh mehs overhanging the Caspian Sea. Accordingly, we find, among these and other vestiges of antiquity that indissolubly connected those long-since extinct populations in the New with the races of the Old World, the well-defined symbol of the Maltese Cross. On the Mexican feroher before alluded to, and which is most elaborately carved in bass-relief on a massive piece of polygonous granite, constituting a portion of a cyclopean wall, the cross is enclosed within the ring, and accompanying it are four tassel-like ornaments, graved equally well. Those accompaniments, however, are disposed without any particular regard to order, but the four arms of the cross, nevertheless, severally and accurately point to the cardinal quarters. The same regularity is observable on a much smaller but not less curious monument, which was discovered some time since in an ancient Peruvian huaca or catacomb—namely, a syrinx or pandean pipe, cut out of a solid mass of lapis ollaris, the sides of which are profusely ornamented, not only with Maltese crosses, but also with other symbols very similar in style to those inscribed on the obelisks of Egypt and on the monoliths of this country. The like figure occurs on the equally ancient Otrusco black pottery. But by far the most remarkable example of this form of the Cross in the New World is that which appears on a second type of the Mexican feroher, engraved on a tablet of gypsum, and which is described at length by its discoverer, Captain du Paix, and depicted by his friend, M. Baradère. Here the accompaniments—a shield, a hamlet, and a couple of bead-annulets or rosaries—are, with a single exception, identical in even the minutest particular with an Assyrian monument emblematical of the Deity....

"No country in the world can compare with India for the exposition of the pyramidal cross. There the stupendous labors of Egypt are rivalled, and sometimes surpassed. Indeed, but for the fact of such monuments of patient industry and unexampled skill being still in existence, the accounts of some others which have long since disappeared, having succumbed to the ravages of time and the fury of the bigoted Mussulman, would sound in our ears as incredible as the story of Porsenna's tomb, which 'o'ertopped old Pelion,' and made 'Ossa like a wart.' Yet something not very dissimilar in character to it was formerly the boast of the ancient city of Benares, on the banks of the Ganges. We allude to the great temple of Bindh Madhu, which was demolished in the seventeenth century by the Emperor Aurungzebe. Tavernier, the French baron, who travelled thither about the year 1680, has preserved a brief description of it. The body of the temple was constructed in the figure of a colossal cross (i. e., a St. Andrew's Cross), with a lofty dome at the centre, above which rose a massive structure of a pyramidal form. At the four extremities of the cross there were four other pyramids of proportionate dimensions, and which were ascended from the outside by steps, with balconies at stated distances for places of rest, reminding us of the temple of Belus, as described in the pages of Herodotus. The remains of a similar building are found at Mhuttra, on the banks of the Jumna. This and many others, including the subterranean temple at Elephanta and the caverns of Ellora and Salsette, are described at length in the well-known work by Maurice; who adds that, besides these, there was yet another device in which the Hindoo displayed the all-pervading sign; this was by pyramidal towers placed crosswise. At the famous temple of Chillambrum, on the Coromandel coast, there were seven lofty walls, one within the other, round the central quadrangle, and as many pyramidal gate-ways in the midst of each side which forms the limbs of a vast cross."

In Mexico pyramids were found everywhere. Cortez, in a letter to Charles V., states that he counted four hundred of them at Cholula. Their temples were on those "high-places." The most ancient pyramids in Mexico are at Teotihuacan, eight leagues from the city of Mexico; the two largest were dedicated to the sun and moon respectively, each built of cut stone, with a level area at the summit, and four stages leading up to it. The larger one is 680 feet square at the base, about 200 feet high, and covers an area of eleven acres. The Pyramid of Cholula, measured by Humboldt, is 160 feet high, 1400 feet square at the base, and covers forty five acres! The great pyramid of Egypt, Cheops, is 746 feet square, 450 feet high, and covers between twelve and thirteen acres. So that it appears that the base of the Teotihuacan structure is nearly as large as that of Cheops, while that of Cholula covers nearly four times as much space. The Cheops pyramid, however, exceeds very much in height both the American structures.

Señor Garcia y Cubas thinks the pyramids of Teotihuacan (Mexico) were built for the same purpose as those of Egypt. He considers the analogy established in eleven particulars, as follows: 1, the site chosen is the same; 2, the structures are orientated with slight variation; 3, the line through the centres of the structures is in the astronomical meridian; 4, the construction in grades and steps is the same; 5, in both cases the larger pyramids are dedicated to the sun; 6, the Nile has "a valley of the dead," as in Teotihuacan there is "a street of the dead;" 7, some monuments in each class have the nature of fortifications; 8, the smaller mounds are of the same nature and for the same purpose; 9, both pyramids have a small mound joined to one of their faces; 10, the openings discovered in the Pyramid of the Moon are also found in some Egyptian pyramids; 11, the interior arrangements of the pyramids are analogous. ("Ensayo de un Estudio.")

It is objected that the American edifices are different in form from the Egyptian, in that they are truncated, or flattened at the top; but this is not an universal rule.

"In many of the ruined cities of Yucatan one or more pyramids have been found upon the summit of which no traces of any building could be discovered, although upon surrounding pyramids such structures could be found. There is also some reason to believe that perfect pyramids have been found in America. Waldeck found near Palenque two pyramids in a state of perfect preservation, square at the base, pointed at the top, and thirty-one feet high, their sides forming equilateral triangles." (Bancroft's "Native Races," vol. v., p. 58.)

Bradford thinks that "some of the Egyptian pyramids, and those which with some reason it has been supposed are the most ancient, are precisely similar to the Mexican teocalli." ("North Americans of Antiquity" p. 423.)

And there is in Egypt another form of pyramid called the mastaba, which, like the Mexican, was flattened on the top; while in Assyria structures flattened like the Mexican are found. "In fact," says one writer, "this form of temple (the flat-topped) has been found from Mesopotamia to the Pacific Ocean." The Phoenicians also built pyramids. In the thirteenth century the Dominican Brocard visited the ruins of the Phoenician city of Mrith or Marathos, and speaks in the strongest terms of admiration of those pyramids of surprising grandeur, constructed of blocks of stone from twenty-six to twenty eight feet long, whose thickness exceeded the stature of a tall man. ("Prehistoric Nations," p. 144.)

"If," says Ferguson, "we still hesitate to pronounce that there was any connection between the builders of the pyramids of Suku and Oajaca, or the temples of Xochialco and Boro Buddor, we must at least allow that the likeness is startling, and difficult to account for on the theory of mere accidental coincidence."

The Egyptian pyramids all stand with their sides to the cardinal points, while many of the Mexican pyramids do likewise. The Egyptian pyramids were penetrated by small passage-ways; so were the Mexican. The Pyramid of Teotihuacan, according to Almarez, has, at a point sixty-nine feet from the base, a gallery large enough to admit a man crawling on hands and knees, which extends, inward, on an incline, a distance of twenty feet, and terminates in two square wells or chambers, each five feet square and one of them fifteen feet deep. Mr. Löwenstern states, according to Mr. Bancroft ("Native Races," vol. iv., p. 533), that "the gallery is one hundred and fifty-seven feet long, increasing in height to over six feet and a half as it penetrates the pyramid; that the well is over six feet square, extending (apparently) down to the base and up to the summit; and that other cross-galleries are blocked up by débris." In the Pyramid of Cheops there is a similar opening or passage-way forty-nine feet above the base; it is three feet eleven inches high, and three feet five and a half inches wide; it leads down a slope to a sepulchral chamber or well, and connects with other passage-ways leading up into the body of the pyramid.

In both the Egyptian the American pyramids the outside of the structures was covered with a thick coating of smooth, shining cement.

Humboldt considered the Pyramid of Cholula of the same type as the Temple of Jupiter Belus, the pyramids of Meidoun Dachhour, and the group of Sakkarah, in Egypt.

In both America and Egypt the pyramids were used as places of sepulture; and it is a remarkable fact that the system of earthworks and mounds, kindred to the pyramids, is found even in England. Silsbury Hill, at Avebury, is an artificial mound one hundred and seventy feet high. It is connected with ramparts, avenues (fourteen hundred and eighty yards long), circular ditches, and stone circles, almost identical with those found in the valley of the Mississippi. In Ireland the dead were buried in vaults of stone, and the earth raised over them in pyramids flattened on the top. They were called "moats" by the people. We have found the stone vaults at the base of similar truncated pyramids in Ohio. There can be no doubt that the pyramid was a developed and perfected mound, and that the parent form of these curious structures is to be found in Silsbury Hill, and in the mounds of earth of Central America and the Mississippi Valley.

We find the emblem of the Cross in pre-Christian times venerated as a holy symbol on both sides of the Atlantic; and we find it explained as a type of the four rivers of the happy island where the civilization of the race originated.

We find everywhere among the European and American nations the memory of an Eden of the race, where the first men dwelt in primeval peace and happiness, and which was afterward destroyed by water.

We find the pyramid on both sides of the Atlantic, with its four sides pointing, like the arms of the Cross, to the four cardinal points—a reminiscence of Olympus; and in the Aztec representation of Olympos (Aztlan) we find the pyramid as the central and typical figure.

Is it possible to suppose all these extraordinary coincidences to be the result of accident? We might just as well say that the similarities between the American and English forms of government were not the result of relationship or descent, but that men placed in similar circumstances had spontaneously and necessarily reached the same results.

CHAPTER VI. GOLD AND SILVER THE SACRED METALS OF ATLANTIS.

Money is the instrumentality by which man is lifted above the limitations of barter. Baron Storch terms it "the marvellous instrument to which we are indebted for our wealth and civilization."

It is interesting to inquire into the various articles which have been used in different countries and ages as money. The following is a table of some of them:

Articles of Utility.

-+ | India | Cakes of tea. | +
-+ | China | Pieces of silk. | +
-+ | Abyssinia | Salt. | +
-+ | Iceland and Newfoundland | Codfish. | +
-+ | Illinois (in early days) | Coon-skins. | +

-+ | Bornoo (Africa) | Cotton shirts. | +
-+ | Ancient Russia | Skins of wild animals. | +
-+ | West India Islands (1500) | Cocoa-nuts. | +
-+ | Massachusetts Indians | Wampum and musket-balls. | +
-+ | Virginia (1700) | Tobacco. | +
-+ | British West India Islands | Pins, snuff, and whiskey. | +
-+ | Central South America | Soap, chocolate, and eggs. | +
-+ | Ancient Romans | Cattle. | +
-+ | Ancient Greece | Nails of copper and iron. | +
-+ | The Lacedemonians | Iron. | +
-+ | The Burman Empire | Lead. | +
-+ | Russia (1828 to 1845) | Platinum. | +
-+ | Rome (under Numa Pompilius) | Wood and leather. | +
-+ | Rome (under the Cæsars) | Land. | +
-+ | Carthaginians | Leather. | +
-+ | Ancient Britons Cattle, | slaves, brass, and iron. | +
-+ | England (under James II.) | Tin, gun-metal, and pewter. | +
-+ | South Sea Islands | Axes and hammers. | +
-+

Articles of Ornament.

+

| Ancient Jews | Jewels. | +
The Indian Islands and Africa | Cowrie shells, | +
Conventional Signs.
+ | Holland (1574) | Pieces of pasteboard. |
+ | China (1200) | Bark of the mulberry-tree. | +
+

It is evident that every primitive people uses as money those articles upon which they set the highest value—as cattle, jewels, slaves, salt, musket-balls, pins, snuff, whiskey, cotton shirts, leather, axes, and hammers; or those articles for which there was a foreign demand, and which they could trade off to the merchants for articles of necessity—as tea, silk, codfish, coonskins, cocoa-nuts, and tobacco. Then there is a later stage, when the stamp of the government is impressed upon paper, wood, pasteboard, or the bark of trees, and these articles are given a legal-tender character.

When a civilized nation comes in contact with a barbarous people they seek to trade with them for those things which they need; a metal-working people, manufacturing weapons of iron or copper, will seek for the useful metals, and hence we find iron, copper, tin, and lead coming into use as a standard of values—as money; for they can always be converted into articles of use and weapons of war. But when we ask how it chanced that gold and silver came to be used as money, and why it is that gold is regarded as so much more valuable than silver, no answer presents itself. It was impossible to make either of them into pots or pans, swords or spears; they were not necessarily more beautiful than glass or the combinations of tin and copper. Nothing astonished the American races more than the extraordinary value set upon gold and silver by the Spaniards; they could not understand it. A West Indian savage traded a handful of gold-dust with one of the sailors accompanying Columbus for some tool, and then ran for his life to the woods lest the sailor should repent his bargain and call him back. The Mexicans had coins of tin shaped like a letter T. We can understand this, for tin was necessary to them in hardening their bronze implements, and it may have been the highest type of metallic value among them. A round copper coin with a serpent stamped on it was found at Palenque, and T-shaped copper coins are very abundant in the ruins of Central America. This too we can understand, for copper was necessary in every work of art or utility.

All these nations were familiar with gold and silver, but they used them as sacred metals for the adornment of the temples of the sun and moon. The color of gold was something of the color of the sun's rays, while the color of silver resembled the pale light of the moon, and hence they were respectively sacred to the gods of the sun and moon. And this is probably the origin of the comparative value of these metals: they became the precious metals because they were the sacred metals, and gold was more valuable than silver—just as the sun-god was the great god of the nations, while the mild moon was simply an attendant upon the sun.

The Peruvians called gold "the tears wept by the sun." It was not used among the people for ornament or money. The great temple of the sun at Cuzco was called the "Place of Gold." It was, as I have shown, literally a mine of gold. Walls, cornices, statuary, plate, ornaments, all were of gold; the very ewers, pipes, and aqueducts—even the agricultural implements used in the garden of the temple—were of gold and silver. The value of the jewels which adorned the temple was equal to one hundred and eighty millions of dollars! The riches of the kingdom can be conceived when we remember that from a pyramid in Chimu a Spanish explorer named Toledo took, in

1577, $4,450,284 in gold and silver. ("New American Cyclopædia," art. American Antiquities.) The gold and silver of Peru largely contributed to form the metallic currency upon which Europe has carried on her commerce during the last three hundred years.

Gold and silver were not valued in Peru for any intrinsic usefulness; they were regarded as sacred because reserved for the two great gods of the nation. As we find gold and silver mined and worked on both sides of the Atlantic at the earliest periods of recorded history, we may fairly conclude that they were known to the Atlanteans; and this view is confirmed by the statements of Plato, who represents a condition of things in Atlantis exactly like that which Pizarro found in Peru. Doubtless the vast accumulations of gold and silver in both countries were due to the fact that these metals were not permitted to be used by the people. In Peru the annual taxes of the people were paid to the Inca in part in gold and silver from the mines, and they were used to ornament the temples; and thus the work of accumulating the sacred metals went on from generation to generation. The same process doubtless led to the vast accumulations in the temples of Atlantis, as described by Plato.

Now, as the Atlanteans carried on an immense commerce with all the countries of Europe and Western Asia, they doubtless inquired and traded for gold and silver for the adornment of their temples, and they thus produced a demand for and gave a value to the two metals otherwise comparatively useless to man—a value higher than any other commodity which the people could offer their civilized customers; and as the reverence for the great burning orb of the sun, master of all the manifestations of nature, was tenfold as great as the veneration for the smaller, weaker, and variable goddess of the night, so was the demand for the metal sacred to the sun ten times as great as for the metal sacred to the moon. This view is confirmed by the fact that the root of the word by which the Celts, the Greeks, and the Romans designated gold was the Sanscrit word karat, which means, "the color of the sun." Among the Assyrians gold and silver were respectively consecrated to the sun and moon precisely as they were in Peru. A pyramid belonging to the palace of Nineveh is referred to repeatedly in the inscriptions. It was composed of seven stages, equal in height, and each one smaller in area than the one beneath it; each stage was covered with stucco of different colors, "a different color representing each of the heavenly bodies, the least important being at the base: white (Venus); black (Saturn); purple (Jupiter); blue (Mercury); vermillion (Mars); silver (the Moon); and gold (the Sun)." (Lenormant's "Ancient History of the East," vol. i., p. 463.) "In England, to this day the new moon is saluted with a bow or a courtesy, as well as the curious practice of 'turning one's silver,' which seems a relic of the offering of the moon's proper metal." (Tylor's "Anthropology", p. 361.) The custom of wishing, when one first sees the new moon, is probably a survival of moon-worship; the wish taking the place of the prayer.

And thus has it come to pass that, precisely as the physicians of Europe, fifty years ago, practised bleeding, because for thousands of years their savage ancestors had used it to draw away the evil spirits out of the man, so the business of our modern civilization is dependent upon the superstition of a past civilization, and the bankers of the world are to-day perpetuating the adoration of "the tears wept by the sun" which was commenced ages since on the island of Atlantis.

And it becomes a grave question—when we remember that the rapidly increasing business of the world, consequent upon an increasing population, and a civilization advancing with giant steps, is measured by the standard of a currency limited by natural laws, decreasing annually in production, and incapable of expanding proportionately to the growth of the world—whether this Atlantean superstition may not yet inflict more incalculable injuries on mankind than those which resulted from the practice of phlebotomy.

PART V. THE COLONIES OF ATLANTIS.

CHAPTER I. THE CENTRAL AMERICAN AND MEXICAN COLONIES.

The western shores of Atlantis were not far distant from the West India Islands; a people possessed of ships could readily pass from island to island until they reached the continent. Columbus found the natives making such voyages in open canoes. If, then, we will suppose that there was no original connection between the inhabitants of the main-land and of Atlantis, the commercial activity of the Atlanteans would soon reveal to them the shores of the Gulf. Commerce implies the plantation of colonies; the trading-post is always the nucleus of a settlement; we have seen this illustrated in modern times in the case of the English East India Company and the Hudson Bay Company. We can therefore readily believe that commercial intercourse between Atlantis and Yucatan, Honduras and Mexico, created colonies along the shores of the Gulf which gradually spread into the interior, and to the high table-lands of Mexico. And, accordingly, we find, as I have already shown, that all the traditions of Central America and Mexico point to some country in the East, and beyond the sea, as the source of their first civilized people; and this region, known among them as "Aztlan," lived in the memory of the people as a beautiful and happy land, where their ancestors had dwelt in peace for many generations.

Dr. Le Plongeon, who spent four years exploring Yucatan, says:

"One-third of this tongue (the Maya) is pure Greek. Who brought the dialect of Homer to America? or who took to Greece that of the Mayas?

Greek is the offspring of the Sanscrit. Is Maya? or are they coeval?... The Maya is not devoid of words from the Assyrian."

That the population of Central America (and in this term I include Mexico) was at one time very dense, and had attained to a high degree of civilization, higher even than that of Europe in the time of Columbus, there can be no question; and it is also probable, as I have shown, that they originally belonged to the white race. Dêsirè Charnay, who is now exploring the ruins of Central America, says (North American Review, January, 1881, p. 48), "The Toltecs were fair, robust, and bearded. I have often seen Indians of pure blood with blue eyes." Quetzalcoatl was represented as large, "with a big head and a heavy beard." The same author speaks (page 44) of "the ocean of ruins all around, not inferior in size to those of Egypt." At Teotihuacan he measured one building two thousand feet wide on each side, and fifteen pyramids, each nearly as large in the base as Cheops. "The city is indeed of vast extent ... the whole ground, over a space of five or six miles in diameter, is covered with heaps of ruins— ruins which at first make no impression, so complete is their dilapidation." He asserts the great antiquity of these ruins, because he found the very highways of the ancient city to be composed of broken bricks and pottery, the débris left by earlier populations. "This continent," he says (page 43), "is the land of mysteries; we here enter an infinity whose limits we cannot estimate.... I shall soon have to quit work in this place. The long avenue on which it stands is lined with ruins of public buildings and palaces, forming continuous lines, as in the streets of modern cities. Still, all these edifices and halls were as nothing compared with the vast substructures which strengthened their foundations."

We find the strongest resemblances to the works of the ancient European races: the masonry is similar; the cement is the same; the sculptures are alike; both peoples used the arch; in both continents we find bricks, glassware, and even porcelain (North American Review, December, 1880, pp. 524, 525), "with blue figures on a white ground;" also bronze composed of the same elements of copper and tin in like proportions; coins made of copper, round and T-shaped, and even metallic candlesticks.

Dêsirè Charnay believes that he has found in the ruins of Tula the bones of swine, sheep, oxen, and horses, in a fossil state, indicating an immense antiquity. The Toltecs possessed a pure and simple religion, like that of Atlantis, as described by Plato, with the same sacrifices of fruits and flowers; they were farmers; they raised and wove cotton; they cultivated fruits; they used the sign of the Cross extensively; they cut and engraved precious stones; among their carvings have been found representations of the elephant and the lion, both animals not known in America. The forms of sepulture were the same as among the ancient races of the Old World; they burnt the bodies of their great men, and enclosed the dust in funeral urns; some of their dead were buried in a sitting position, others reclined at full length, and many were embalmed like the Egyptian mummies.

When we turn to Mexico, the same resemblances present themselves.

The government was an elective monarchy, like that of Poland, the king being selected from the royal family by the votes of the nobles of the kingdom. There was a royal family, an aristocracy, a privileged priesthood, a judiciary, and a common people. Here we have all the several estates into which society in Europe is divided.

There were thirty grand nobles in the kingdom, and the vastness of the realm may be judged by the fact that each of these could muster one hundred thousand vassals from their own estates, or a total of three millions. And we have only to read of the vast hordes brought into the field against Cortez to know that this was not an exaggeration.

They even possessed that which has been considered the crowning feature of European society, the feudal system. The nobles held their lands upon the tenure of military service.

But the most striking feature was the organization of the judiciary. The judges were independent even of the king, and held their offices for life. There were supreme judges for the larger divisions of the kingdom, district judges in each of the provinces, and magistrates chosen by the people throughout the country.

There was also a general legislative assembly, congress, or parliament, held every eighty days, presided over by the king, consisting of all the judges of the realm, to which the last appeal lay

"The rites of marriage," says Prescott, "were celebrated with as much formality as in any Christian country; and the institution was held in such reverence that a tribunal was instituted for the sole purpose of determining questions relating to it. Divorces could not be obtained until authorized by a sentence of the court, after a patient hearing of the parties."

Slavery was tolerated, but the labors of the slave were light, his rights carefully guarded, and his children were free. The slave could own property, and even other slaves.

Their religion possessed so many features similar to those of the Old World, that the Spanish priests declared the devil had given them a bogus imitation of Christianity to destroy their souls. "The devil," said they, "stole all he could."

They had confessions, absolution of sins, and baptism. When their children were named, they sprinkled their lips and bosoms with water, and "the Lord was implored to permit the holy drops to wash away the sin that was given it before the foundation of the world."

The priests were numerous and powerful. They practised fasts, vigils, flagellations, and many of them lived in monastic seclusion.

The Aztecs, like the Egyptians, had progressed through all the three different modes of writing—the picture-writing, the symbolical, and the phonetic. They recorded all their laws, their tribute-rolls specifying the various imposts, their mythology, astronomical calendars, and rituals, their political annals and their chronology. They wrote on cotton-cloth, on skins prepared like parchment, on a composition of silk and gum, and on a species of paper, soft and beautiful, made from the aloe. Their books were about the size and shape of our own, but the leaves were long strips folded together in many folds.

They wrote poetry and cultivated oratory, and paid much attention to rhetoric. They also had a species of theatrical performances.

Their proficiency in astronomy is thus spoken of by Prescott:

"That they should be capable of accurately adjusting their festivals by the movements of the heavenly bodies, and should fix the true length of the tropical year with a precision unknown to the great philosophers of antiquity, could be the result only of a long series of nice and patient observations, evincing no slight progress in civilization."

"Their women," says the same author, "are described by the Spaniards as pretty, though with a serious and rather melancholy cast of countenance. Their long, black hair might generally be seen wreathed with flowers, or, among the richer people, with strings of precious stones and pearls from the Gulf of California. They appear to have been treated with much consideration by their husbands; and passed their time in indolent tranquillity, or in such feminine occupations as spinning, embroidery, and the like; while their maidens beguiled the hours by the rehearsal of traditionary tales and ballads.

"Numerous attendants of both sexes waited at the banquets. The balls were scented with perfumes, and the courts strewed with odoriferous herbs and flowers, which were distributed in profusion among the guests as they arrived. Cotton napkins and ewers of water were placed before them as they took their seats at the board. Tobacco was then offered, in pipes, mixed with aromatic

389

substances, or in the form of cigars inserted in tubes of tortoise-shell or silver. It is a curious fact that the Aztecs also took the dried tobacco leaf in the pulverized form of snuff.

"The table was well supplied with substantial meats, especially game, among which the most conspicuous was the turkey. Also, there were found very delicious vegetables and fruits of every variety native to the continent. Their palate was still further regaled by confections and pastry, for which their maize-flower and sugar furnished them ample materials. The meats were kept warm with chafing-dishes. The table was ornamented with vases of silver and sometimes gold of delicate workmanship. The favorite beverage was chocolatl, flavored with vanilla and different spices. The fermented juice of the maguey, with a mixture of sweets and acids, supplied various agreeable drinks of different degrees of strength."

It is not necessary to describe their great public works, their floating gardens, their aqueducts, bridges, forts, temples, palaces, and gigantic pyramids, all ornamented with wonderful statuary.

We find a strong resemblance between the form of arch used in the architecture of Central America and that of the oldest buildings of Greece. The Palenque arch is made by the gradual overlapping of the strata of the building. It was the custom of these ancient architects to fill in the arch itself with masonry, as shown in the picture of the Arch of Las Monjas, Palenque. If now we look at the representation of the "Treasure-house of Atreus" at Mycenæ,—one of the oldest structures in Greece—we find precisely the same form of arch, filled in in the same way.

Rosengarten ("Architectural Styles," p. 59) says:

"The base of these treasure-houses is circular, and the covering of a dome shape; it does not, however, form an arch, but courses of stone are laid horizontally over one another in such a way that each course projects beyond the one below it, till the space at the highest course becomes so narrow that a single stone covers it. Of all those that have survived to the present day the treasure-house at Atreus is the most venerable."

The same form of arch is found among the ruins of that interesting people, the Etruscans.

"Etruscan vaults are of two kinds. The more curious and probably the most ancient are false arches, formed of horizontal courses of stone, each a little overlapping the other, and carried on until the aperture at the top could be closed by a single superincumbent slab. Such is the construction of the Regulini-Galassi vault, at Cervetere, the ancient Cære." (Rawlinson's "Origin of Nations," p. 117.) It is sufficient to say, in conclusion, that Mexico, under European rule, or under her own leaders, has never again risen to her former standard of refinement, wealth, prosperity, or civilization.

CHAPTER II. THE EGYPTIAN COLONY.

What proofs have we that the Egyptians were a colony from Atlantis?

1. They claimed descent from "the twelve great gods," which must have meant the twelve gods of Atlantis, to wit, Poseidon and Cleito and their ten sons.

2. According to the traditions of the Phoenicians, the Egyptians derived their civilization from them; and as the Egyptians far antedated the rise of the Phoenician nations proper, this must have meant that Egypt derived its civilization from the same country to which the Phoenicians owed their own origin. The Phoenician legends show that Misor, from whom the Egyptians were descended, was the child of the Phoenician gods Amynus and Magus. Misor gave birth to Taaut, the god of letters, the inventor of the alphabet, and Taaut became Thoth, the god of history of the Egyptians. Sanchoniathon tells us that "Chronos (king of Atlantis) visited the South, and gave all Egypt to the god Taaut, that it might be his kingdom." "Misor" is probably the king "Mestor" named by Plato.

3. According to the Bible, the Egyptians were descendants of Ham, who was one of the three sons of Noah who escaped from the Deluge, to wit, the destruction of Atlantis.

4. The great similarity between the Egyptian civilization and that of the American nations.

5. The fact that the Egyptians claimed to be red men.

6. The religion of Egypt was pre-eminently sun-worship, and Ra was the sun-god of Egypt, Rama, the sun of the Hindoos, Rana, a god of the Toltecs, Raymi, the great festival of the sun of the Peruvians, and Rayam, a god of Yemen.

7. The presence of pyramids in Egypt and America.

8. The Egyptians were the only people of antiquity who were well-informed as to the history of Atlantis. The Egyptians were never a maritime people, and the Atlanteans must have brought that knowledge to them. They were not likely to send ships to Atlantis.

9. We find another proof of the descent of the Egyptians from Atlantis in their belief as to the "under-world." This land of the dead was situated in the West—hence the tombs were all placed, whenever possible, on the west bank of the Nile. The constant cry of the mourners as the funeral procession moved forward was, "To the west; to the west." This under-world was beyond the water, hence the funeral procession always crossed a body of water. "Where the tombs were, as in most cases, on the west bank of the Nile, the Nile was crossed; where they were on the eastern shore the procession passed over a sacred lake."

(R. S. Poole, Contemporary Review, August, 1881, p. 17.) In the procession was "a sacred ark of the sun."

All this is very plain: the under-world in the West, the land of the dead, was Atlantis, the drowned world, the world beneath the horizon, beneath the sea, to which the peasants of Brittany looked from Cape Raz, the most western cape projecting into the Atlantic. It was only to be reached from Egypt by crossing the water, and it was associated with the ark, the emblem of Atlantis in all lands.

The soul of the dead man was supposed to journey to the under-world by "a water progress" (Ibid., p. 18), his destination was the Elysian Fields, where mighty corn grew, and where he was expected to cultivate the earth; "this task was of supreme importance." (Ibid., p. 19.) The Elysian Fields were the "Elysion" of the Greeks, the abode of the blessed, which we have seen was an island in the remote west. The Egyptian belief referred to a real country; they described its cities, mountains, and rivers; one of the latter was called Uranes, a name which reminds us of the Atlantean god Uranos. In connection with all this we must not forget that Plato described Atlantis as "that sacred island lying beneath the sun." Everywhere in the ancient world we find the minds of men looking to the west for the land of the dead. Poole says, "How then can we account for this strong conviction? Surely it must be a survival of an ancient belief which flowed in the very veins of the race." (Contemporary Review, 1881, p. 19.) It was based on an universal tradition that under "an immense ocean," in "the far west," there was an "under-world," a world comprising millions of the dead, a mighty race, that had been suddenly swallowed up in the greatest catastrophe known to man since he had inhabited the globe.

10. There is no evidence that the civilization of Egypt was developed in Egypt itself; it must have been transported there from some other country. To use the words of a recent writer in Blackwood,

"Till lately it was believed that the use of the papyrus for writing was introduced about the time of Alexander the Great; then Lepsius found the hieroglyphic sign of the papyrus-roll on monuments of the twelfth dynasty; afterward he found the same sign on monuments of the fourth dynasty, which is getting back pretty close to Menes, the protomonarch; and, indeed, little doubt is entertained that the art of writing on papyrus was understood as early as the days of Menes himself. The fruits of investigation in this, as in many other subjects, are truly most marvellous. Instead of exhibiting the rise and progress of any branches of knowledge, they tend to prove that nothing had any rise or progress, but that everything is referable to the very earliest dates. The experience of the Egyptologist must teach him to reverse the observation of Topsy, and to ''spect that nothing growed,' but that as soon as men were planted on the banks of the Nile they were already the cleverest men that ever lived, endowed with more knowledge and more power than their successors for centuries and centuries could attain to. Their system of writing, also, is found to have been complete from the very first....

"But what are we to think when the antiquary, grubbing in the dust and silt of five thousand years ago to discover some traces of infant effort—some rude specimens of the ages of Magog and Mizraim, in which we may admire the germ that has since developed into a wonderful art—breaks his shins against an article so perfect that it equals if it does not excel the supreme stretch of modern ability? How shall we support the theory if it come to our knowledge that, before Noah was cold in his grave, his descendants were adepts in construction and in the fine arts, and that their achievements were for magnitude such as, if we possess the requisite skill, we never attempt to emulate?...

"As we have not yet discovered any trace of the rude, savage Egypt, but have seen her in her very earliest manifestations already skilful, erudite, and strong, it is impossible to determine the order of her inventions. Light may yet be thrown upon her rise and progress, but our deepest researches have hitherto shown her to us as only the mother of a most accomplished race. How they came by their knowledge is matter for speculation; that they possessed it is matter of fact. We never find them without the ability to organize labor, or shrinking from the very boldest efforts in digging canals and irrigating, in quarrying rock, in building, and in sculpture."

The explanation is simple: the waters of the Atlantic now flow over the country where all this magnificence and power were developed by slow stages from the rude beginnings of barbarism.

And how mighty must have been the parent nation of which this Egypt was a colony!

Egypt was the magnificent, the golden bridge, ten thousand years long, glorious with temples and pyramids, illuminated and illustrated by the most complete and continuous records of human history, along which the civilization of Atlantis, in a great procession of kings and priests, philosophers and astronomers, artists and artisans, streamed forward to Greece, to Rome, to Europe, to America. As far back in the ages as the eye can penetrate, even where the perspective dwindles almost to a point, we can still see the swarming multitudes, possessed of all the arts of the highest civilization, pressing forward from out that other and greater empire of which even this wonderworking Nile-land is but a faint and imperfect copy.

Look at the record of Egyptian greatness as preserved in her works: The pyramids, still in their ruins, are the marvel of mankind. The river Nile was diverted from its course by monstrous embankments to make a place for the city of Memphis. The artificial lake of Moeris was created as a reservoir for the waters of the Nile: it was four hundred and fifty miles in circumference and three hundred and fifty feet deep, with subterranean channels, flood-gates, locks, and dams, by which the wilderness was redeemed from sterility. Look at the magnificent mason-work of this ancient people! Mr. Kenrick, speaking of the casing of the Great Pyramid, says, "The joints are scarcely perceptible, and not wider than the thickness of silver-paper, and the cement so tenacious that fragments of the casing-stones still remain in their original position, notwithstanding the lapse of so many centuries, and the violence by which they were detached." Look at the ruins of the Labyrinth, which aroused the astonishment of Herodotus; it had three thousand chambers, half of them above ground and half below—a combination of courts, chambers, colonnades, statues, and pyramids. Look at the Temple of Karnac, covering a square each side of which is eighteen hundred feet. Says a recent writer, "Travellers one and all appear to have been unable to find words to express the feelings with which these sublime remains inspired them. They have been astounded and overcome by the magnificence and the prodigality of workmanship here to be admired. Courts, halls, gate-ways, pillars, obelisks, monolithic figures, sculptures, rows of sphinxes, are massed in such profusion that the sight is too much for modern comprehension." Denon says, "It is hardly possible to believe, after having seen it, in the reality of the existence of so many buildings collected on a single point—in their dimensions, in the resolute perseverance which their construction required, and in the incalculable expense of so much magnificence." And again, "It is necessary that the reader should fancy what is before him to be a dream, as he who views the objects themselves occasionally yields to the doubt whether he be perfectly awake." There were lakes and mountains within the periphery of the sanctuary. "The cathedral of Notre Dame at Paris could be set inside one of the halls of Karnac, and not touch the walls!... The whole valley and delta of the Nile, from the Catacombs to the sea, was covered with temples, palaces, tombs, pyramids, and pillars." Every stone was covered with inscriptions.

The state of society in the early days of Egypt approximated very closely to our modern civilization. Religion consisted in the worship of one God and the practice of virtue; forty-two commandments prescribed the duties of men to themselves, their neighbors, their country, and the Deity; a heaven awaited the good and a hell the vicious; there was a judgment-day when the hearts of men were weighed:

"He is sifting out the hearts of men
Before his judgment-seat."

Monogamy was the strict rule; not even the kings, in the early days, were allowed to have more than one wife. The wife's rights of separate property and her dower were protected by law; she was "the lady of the house;" she could "buy, sell, and trade on her own account;" in case of divorce her dowry was to be repaid to her, with interest at a high rate. The marriage-ceremony embraced an oath not to contract any other matrimonial alliance. The wife's status was as high in the earliest days of Egypt as it is now in the most civilized nations of Europe or America.

Slavery was permitted, but the slaves were treated with the greatest humanity. In the confessions, buried with the dead, the soul is made to declare that "I have not incriminated the slave to his master," There was also a clause in the commandments "which protected the laboring man against the exaction of more than his day's labor." They were merciful to the captives made in war; no picture represents torture inflicted upon them; while the representation of a sea-fight shows them saving their drowning enemies. Reginald Stuart Poole says (Contemporary Review, August, 1881, p. 43):

"When we consider the high ideal of the Egyptians, as proved by their portrayals of a just life, the principles they laid down as the basis of ethics, the elevation of women among them, their humanity in war, we must admit that their moral place ranks very high among the nations of antiquity.

"The true comparison of Egyptian life is with that of modern nations. This is far too difficult a task to be here undertaken. Enough has been said, however, to show that we need not think that in all respects they were far behind us."

Then look at the proficiency in art of this ancient people.

They were the first mathematicians of the Old World. Those Greeks whom we regard as the fathers of mathematics were simply pupils of Egypt. They were the first land-surveyors. They were the first astronomers, calculating eclipses, and watching the periods of planets and constellations. They knew the rotundity of the earth, which it was supposed Columbus had discovered!

"The signs of the zodiac were certainly in use among the Egyptians 1722 years before Christ. One of the learned men of our day, who for fifty years labored to decipher the hieroglyphics of the ancients, found upon a mummy-case in the British Museum a delineation of the signs of the zodiac, and the position of the planets; the date to which they pointed was the autumnal equinox of the year 1722 B.C. Professor Mitchell, to whom the fact was communicated, employed his assistants to ascertain the exact position of the heavenly bodies belonging to our solar system on the equinox of that year. This was done, and a diagram furnished by parties ignorant of his object, which showed that on the 7th of October, 1722 B.C. the moon and planets occupied the exact point in the heavens marked upon the coffin in the British Museum." (Goodrich's "Columbus," p. 22.)

They had clocks and dials for measuring time. They possessed gold and silver money. They were the first agriculturists of the Old World, raising all the cereals, cattle, horses, sheep, etc. They manufactured linen of so fine a quality that in the days of King Amasis (600 years B.C.) a single thread of a garment was composed of three hundred and sixty-five minor threads. They worked in gold, silver, copper, bronze, and iron; they tempered iron to the hardness of steel. They were the first chemists. The word "chemistry" comes from chemi, and chemi means Egypt. They manufactured glass and all kinds of pottery; they made boats out of earthenware; and, precisely as we are now making railroad car-wheels of paper, they manufactured vessels of paper. Their dentists filled teeth with gold; their farmers hatched poultry by artificial heat. They were the first musicians; they possessed guitars, single and double pipes, cymbals, drums, lyres, harps, flutes, the sambric, ashur, etc.; they had even castanets, such as are now used in Spain. In medicine and surgery they had reached such a degree of perfection that several hundred years B.C. the operation for the removal of cataract from the eye was performed among them; one of the most delicate and difficult feats of surgery, only attempted by us in the most recent times. "The papyrus of Berlin" states that it was discovered, rolled up in a case, under the feet of an Anubis in the town of Sekhem, in the days of Tet (or Thoth), after whose death it was transmitted to King Sent, and was then restored to the feet of the statue. King Sent belonged to the second dynasty, which flourished 4751 B.C., and the papyrus was old in his day. This papyrus is a medical treatise; there are in it no incantations or charms; but it deals in reasonable remedies, draughts, unguents and injections. The later medical papyri contain a great deal of magic and incantations.

"Great and splendid as are the things which we know about oldest Egypt, she is made a thousand times more sublime by our uncertainty as to the limits of her accomplishments. She presents not a great, definite idea, which, though hard to receive, is, when once acquired, comprehensible and clear. Under the soil of the modern country are hid away thousands and thousands of relics which may astonish the world for ages to come, and change continually its conception of what Egypt was. The effect of research seems to be to prove the objects of it to be much older than we thought them to be—some things thought to be wholly modern having been proved to be repetitions of things Egyptian, and other things known to have been Egyptian being by every advance in knowledge carried back more and more toward the very beginning of things. She shakes our most rooted ideas concerning the world's history; she has not ceased to be a puzzle and a lure: there is a spell over her still."

Renan says, "It has no archaic epoch." Osborn says, "It bursts upon us at once in the flower of its highest perfection." Seiss says ("A, Miracle in Stone," p. 40), "It suddenly takes its place in the world in all its matchless magnificence, without father, without mother, and as clean apart from all evolution as if it had dropped from the unknown heavens." It had dropped from Atlantis.

Rawlinson says ("Origin of Nations," p. 13): "Now, in Egypt, it is notorious that there is no indication of any early period of savagery or barbarism. All the authorities agree that, however far back we go, we find in Egypt no rude or uncivilized time out of which civilization is developed. Menes, the first king, changes the course of the Nile, makes a great reservoir, and builds the temple of Phthah at Memphis.... We see no barbarous customs, not even the habit, so slowly abandoned by all people, of wearing arms when not on military service."

Tylor says ("Anthropology," p. 192):

"Among the ancient cultured nations of Egypt and Assyria handicrafts had already come to a stage which could only have been reached by thousands of years of progress. In museums still may be examined the work of their joiners, stone-cutters, goldsmiths, wonderful in skill and finish, and in putting to shame the modern artificer.... To see gold jewellery of the highest order, the student should examine that of the ancients, such as the Egyptian, Greek, and Etruscan."

The carpenters' and masons' tools of the ancient Egyptians were almost identical with those used among us to-day.

There is a plate showing an Aztec priestess in Delafield's "Antiquities of America," p. 61, which presents a head-dress strikingly Egyptian. In the celebrated "tablet of the cross," at Palenque, we see a cross with a bird perched upon it, to which (or to the cross) two priests are offering sacrifice. In Mr. Stephens's representation from the Vocal Memnon we find almost the same thing, the difference being that, instead of an ornamented Latin cross, we have a crux commissa, and instead of one bird there are two, not on the cross, but immediately above it. In both cases the hieroglyphics, though the characters are of course different, are disposed upon the stone in much the same manner. (Bancroft's "Native Races," vol. v., p. 61.)

Even the obelisks of Egypt have their counterpart in America.

Quoting from Molina ("History of Chili," tom. i., p. 169), McCullough writes, "Between the hills of Mendoza and La Punta is a pillar of stone one hundred and fifty feet high, and twelve feet in diameter." ("Researches," pp. 171, 172.) The columns of Copan stand detached and solitary, so do the obelisks of Egypt; both are square or four-sided, and covered with sculpture. (Bancroft's "Native Races," vol. v., p. 60.)

In a letter by Jomard, quoted by Delafield, we read, "I have recognized in your memoir on the division of time among the Mexican nations, compared with those of Asia, some very striking analogies between the Toltec characters and institutions observed on the banks of the Nile. Among these analogies there is one which is worthy of attention—it is the use of the vague year of three hundred and sixty-five days, composed of equal months, and of five complementary days, equally employed at Thebes and Mexico—a distance of three thousand leagues.... In reality, the intercalation of the Mexicans being thirteen days on each cycle of fifty-two years, comes to the same thing as that of the Julian calendar, which is one day in four years; and consequently supposes the duration of the year to be three hundred and sixty-five days six hours. Now such was the length of the year among the Egyptians—they intercalated an entire year of three hundred and seventy-five days every one thousand four hundred and sixty years.... The fact of the intercalation (by the Mexicans) of thirteen days every cycle that is, the use of a year of three hundred and sixty-five days and a quarter—is a proof that it was borrowed from the Egyptians, or that they had a common origin." ("Antiquities of America," pp. 52, 53.)

The Mexican century began on the 26th of February, and the 26th of February was celebrated from the time of Nabonassor, 747 B.C., because the Egyptian priests, conformably to their astronomical observations, had fixed the beginning of the month Toth, and the commencement of their year, at noon on that day. The five intercalated days to make up the three hundred and sixty-five days were called by the Mexicans Nemontemi, or useless, and on them they transacted no business; while the Egyptians, during that epoch, celebrated the festival of the birth of their gods, as attested by Plutarch and others.

It will be conceded that a considerable degree of astronomical knowledge must have been necessary to reach the conclusion that the true year consisted of three hundred and sixty-five days and six hours (modern science has demonstrated that it consists of three hundred and sixty-five days and five hours, less ten seconds); and a high degree of civilization was requisite to insist that the year must be brought around, by the intercalation of a certain number of days in a certain period of time, to its true relation to the seasons. Both were the outgrowth of a vast, ancient civilization of the highest order, which transmitted some part of its astronomical knowledge to its colonies through their respective priesthoods.

Can we, in the presence of such facts, doubt the statements of the Egyptian priests to Solon, as to the glory and greatness of Atlantis, its monuments, its sculpture, its laws, its religion, its civilization?

In Egypt we have the oldest of the Old World children of Atlantis; in her magnificence we have a testimony to the development attained by the parent country; by that country whose kings were the gods of succeeding nations, and whose kingdom extended to the uttermost ends of the earth. The Egyptian historian, Manetho, referred to a period of thirteen thousand nine hundred years as "the reign of the gods," and placed this period at the very beginning of Egyptian history. These thirteen thousand nine hundred years were probably a recollection of Atlantis. Such a lapse of time, vast as it may appear, is but as a day compared with some of our recognized geological epochs.

CHAPTER III. THE COLONIES OF THE MISSISSIPPI VALLEY

If we will suppose a civilized, maritime people to have planted colonies, in the remote past, along the headlands and shores of the Gulf of Mexico, spreading thence, in time, to the tablelands of Mexico and to the plains and mountains of New Mexico and Colorado, what would be more natural than that these adventurous navigators, passing around the shores of the Gulf, should, sooner or later, discover the mouth of the Mississippi River; and what more certain than that they would enter it, explore it, and plant colonies along its shores, wherever they found a fertile soil and a salubrious climate. Their outlying provinces would penetrate even into regions where the severity of the climate would prevent great density of population or development of civilization.

The results we have presupposed are precisely those which we find to have existed at one time in the Mississippi Valley.

The Mound Builders of the United States were pre-eminently a river people. Their densest settlements and greatest works were near the Mississippi and its tributaries. Says Foster ("Prehistoric Races," p. 110), "The navigable streams were the great highways of the Mound Builders."

Mr. Fontaine claims ("How the World was Peopled") that this ancient people constructed "levees" to control and utilize the bayous of the Mississippi for the purpose of agriculture and commerce. The Yazoo River is called Yazoo-okhinnah—the River of Ancient Ruins. "There is no evidence that they had reached the Atlantic coast; no authentic remains of the Mound Builders are found in the New England States, nor even in the State of New York." ("North Americans of Antiquity," p. 28.) This would indicate that the civilization of this people advanced up the Mississippi River and spread out over its tributaries, but did not cross the Alleghany {sic} Mountains. They reached, however, far up the Missouri and Yellowstone rivers, and thence into Oregon. The head-waters of the Missouri became one of their great centres of population; but their chief sites were upon the Mississippi and Ohio rivers. In Wisconsin we find the northern central limit of their work; they seem to have occupied the southern counties of the State, and the western shores of Lake Michigan. Their circular mounds are found in Minnesota and Iowa, and some very large ones in Dakota. Illinois and Indiana were densely populated by them: it is believed that the vital centre of their colonies was near the junction of the Ohio and Mississippi rivers.

The chief characteristic of the Mound Builders was that from which they derived their name—the creation of great structures of earth or stone, not unlike the pyramids of Mexico and Egypt. Between Alton and East St. Louis is the great mound of Cahokia, which may be selected as a type of their works: it rises ninety-seven feet high, while its square sides are 700 and 500 feet respectively. There was a terrace on the south side 160 by 300 feet, reached by a graded way; the summit of the pyramid is flattened, affording a platform 200 by 450 feet. It will thus be seen that the area covered by the mound of Cahokia is about as large as that of the greatest pyramid of Egypt, Cheops, although its height is much less.

The number of monuments left by the Mound Builders is extraordinarily great. In Ohio alone there are more than ten thousand tumuli, and from one thousand to fifteen hundred enclosures. Their mounds were not cones but four-sided pyramids—their sides, like those of the Egyptian pyramids, corresponding with the cardinal points. (Foster's "Prehistoric Races," p. 112.)

The Mound Builders had attained a considerable degree of civilization; they were able to form, in the construction of their works, perfect circles and perfect squares of great accuracy, carried over the varying surface of the country. One large enclosure comprises exactly forty acres. At Hopetown, Ohio, are two walled figures—one a square, the other a circle—each containing precisely twenty acres. They must have possessed regular scales of measurement, and the means of determining angles and of computing the area to be enclosed by the square and the circle, so that the space enclosed by each might exactly correspond.

"The most skilful engineer of this day would find it difficult," says Mr. Squier, "without the aid of instruments, to lay down an accurate square of the great dimensions above represented, measuring, as they do, more than four-fifths of a mile in circumference.... But we not only find accurate squares and perfect circles, but also, as we have seen, octagons of great dimensions."

They also possessed an accurate system of weights; bracelets of copper on the arms of a skeleton have been found to be of uniform size, measuring each two and nine-tenth inches, and each weighing precisely four ounces.

They built great military works surrounded by walls and ditches, with artificial lakes in the centre to supply water. One work, Fort Ancient, on the Little Miami River, Ohio, has a circuit of between four and five miles; the embankment was twenty feet high; the fort could have held a garrison of sixty thousand men with their families and provisions.

Not only do we find pyramidal structures of earth in the Mississippi Valley very much like the pyramids of Egypt, Mexico, and Peru, but a very singular structure is repeated in Ohio and Peru: I refer to the double walls or prolonged pyramids, if I may coin an expression, shown in the cut page 375.

The Mound Builders possessed chains of fortifications reaching from the southern line of New York diagonally across the country, through Central and Northern Ohio to the Wabash. It would appear probable, therefore, that while they advanced from the south it was from the north-east the savage races came who drove them south or exterminated them.

At Marietta, Ohio, we find a combination of the cross and pyramid. At Newark, Ohio, are extensive and intricate works: they occupy an area two miles square, embraced within embankments twelve miles long. One of the mounds is a threefold symbol, like a bird's foot; the central mound is 155 feet long, and the other two each 110 feet it length. Is this curious design a reminiscence of Atlantis and the three-pronged trident of Poseidon?

The Mound Builders made sun-dried brick mixed with rushes, as the Egyptians made sun-dried bricks mixed with straw; they worked in copper, silver, lead, and there are evidences, as we shall see, that they wrought even in iron.

Copper implements are very numerous in the mounds. Copper axes, spear-heads, hollow buttons, bosses for ornaments, bracelets, rings, etc., are found in very many of them strikingly similar to those of the Bronze Age in Europe. In one in Butler County, Ohio, was found a copper fillet around the head of a skeleton, with strange devices marked upon it.

Silver ornaments have also been found, but not in such great numbers. They seem to have attached a high value to silver, and it is often found in thin sheets, no thicker than paper, wrapped over copper or stone ornaments so neatly as almost to escape detection. The great esteem in which they held a metal so intrinsically valueless as silver, is another evidence that they must have drawn their superstitions from the same source as the European nations.

Copper is also often found in this manner plated over stone pipes, presenting an unbroken metallic lustre, the overlapping edges so well polished as to be scarcely discoverable. Beads and stars made of shells have sometimes been found doubly plated, first with copper then with silver.

The Mound Builders also understood the art of casting metals, or they held intercourse with some race who did; a copper axe it "cast" has been found in the State of New York. (See Lubbock's "Prehistoric Times," p. 254, note.) Professor Foster ("Prehistoric Races," p. 259) also proves that the ancient people of the Mississippi Valley possessed this art, and he gives us representations of various articles plainly showing the marks of the mould upon them.

A rude article in the shape of an axe, composed of pure lead, weighing about half a pound, was found in sinking a well within the trench of the ancient works at Circleville. There can be no doubt it was the production of the Mound Builders, as galena has often been found on the altars in the mounds.

It has been generally thought, by Mr. Squier and others, that there were no evidences that the Mound Builders were acquainted with the use of iron, or that their plating was more than a simple overlaying of one metal on another, or on some foreign substance.

Some years since, however, a mound was opened at Marietta, Ohio, which seems to have refuted these opinions. Dr. S. P. Hildreth, in a letter to the American Antiquarian Society, thus speaks of it:

"Lying immediately over or on the forehead of the body were found three large circular bosses, or ornaments for a sword-belt or buckler; they are composed of copper overlaid with a thick plate of silver. The fronts are slightly convex, with a depression like a cup in the centre, and they measure two inches and a quarter across the face of each. On the back side, opposite the depressed portion, is a copper rivet or nail, around which are two separate plates by which they were fastened to the leather. Two small pieces of leather were found lying between the plates of one of the bosses; they resemble the skin of a mummy, and seem to have been preserved by the salts of copper. Near the side of the body was found a plate of silver, which appears to have been the upper part of a sword scabbard; it is six inches in length, two in breadth, and weighs one ounce. It seems to have been fastened to the scabbard by three or four rivets, the holes of which remain in the silver.

"Two or three pieces of copper tube were also found, filled with iron rust. These pieces, from their appearance, composed the lower end of the scabbard, near the point of the sword. No signs of the sword itself were discovered, except the rust above mentioned.

"The mound had every appearance of being as old as any in the neighborhood, and was at the first settlement of Marietta covered with large trees. It seems to have been made for this single personage, as this skeleton alone was discovered. The bones were very much decayed, and many of them crumbled to dust upon exposure to the air."

Mr. Squier says, "These articles have been critically examined, and it is beyond doubt that the copper bosses were absolutely plated, not simply overlaid, with silver. Between the copper and the silver exists a connection such as, it seems to me, could only be produced by heat; and if it is admitted that these are genuine relics of the Mound Builders, it must, at the same time, be admitted that they possessed the difficult art of plating one metal upon another. There is but one alternative, viz., that they had occasional or constant intercourse with a people advanced in the arts, from whom these articles were obtained. Again, if Dr. Hildreth is not mistaken, oxydized iron or steel was also discovered in connection with the above remains, from which also follows the extraordinary conclusion that the Mound Builders were acquainted with the use of iron, the conclusion being, of course, subject to the improbable alternative already mentioned."

In connection with this subject, we would refer to the interesting evidences that the copper mines of the shore of Lake Superior had been at some very remote period worked by the Mound Builders. There were found deep excavations, with rude ladders, huge masses of rock broken off, also numerous stone tools, and all the evidences of extensive and long-continued labor. It is even said that the great Ontonagon mass of pure copper which is now in Washington was excavated by these ancient miners, and that when first found its surface showed numerous marks of their tools.

There seems to be no doubt, then, that the Mound Builders were familiar with the use of copper, silver, and lead, and in all probability of iron. They possessed various mechanical contrivances. They were very probably acquainted with the lathe. Beads of shell have been found looking very much like ivory, and showing the circular striæ, identical with those produced by turning in a lathe.

In a mound on the Scioto River was found around the neck of a skeleton triple rows of beads, made of marine shells and the tusks of some animal. "Several of these," says Squier, "still retain their polish, and bear marks which seem to indicate that they were turned in some machine, instead of being carved or rubbed into shape by hand."

"Not among the least interesting and remarkable relics," continues the same author, "obtained from the mounds are the stone tubes. They are all carved from fine-grained materials, capable of receiving a polish, and being made ornamental as well as useful. The finest specimen yet discovered, and which can scarcely be surpassed in the delicacy of its workmanship, was found in a mound in the immediate vicinity of Chillicothe. It is composed of a compact variety of slate. This stone cuts with great clearness, and receives a fine though not glaring polish. The tube under notice is thirteen inches long by one and one-tenth in diameter; one end swells slightly, and the other terminates in a broad, flattened, triangular mouth-piece of fine proportions, which is carved with mathematical precision. It is drilled throughout; the bore is seven-tenths of an inch in diameter at the cylindrical end of the tube, and retains that calibre until it reaches the point where the cylinder subsides into the mouth-piece, when it contracts gradually to one-tenth of an inch. The inner surface of the tube is perfectly smooth till within a short distance of the point of contraction. For the remaining distance the circular striæ, formed by the drill in boring, are distinctly marked. The carving upon it is very fine."

That they possessed saws is proved by the fact that on some fossil teeth found in one of the mounds the striæ of the teeth of the saw could be distinctly perceived.

When we consider that some of their porphyry carvings will turn the edge of the best-tempered knife, we are forced to conclude that they possessed that singular process, known to the Mexicans and Peruvians of tempering copper to the hardness of steel.

We find in the mounds adzes similar in shape to our own, with the edges bevelled from the inside.

Drills and gravers of copper have also been found, with chisel-shaped edges or sharp points.

"It is not impossible," says Squier, "but, on the contrary, very probable, from a close inspection of the mound pottery, that the ancient people possessed the simple approximation toward the potter's wheel; and the polish which some of the finer vessels possess is due to other causes than vitrification."

Their sculptures show a considerable degree of progress. They consist of figures of birds, animals, reptiles, and the faces of men, carved from various kinds of stones, upon the bowls of pipes, upon toys, upon rings, and in distinct and separate figures. We give the opinions of those who have examined them.

Mr. Squier observes: "Various though not abundant specimens of their skill have been recovered, which in elegance of model, delicacy, and finish, as also in fineness of material, come fully up to the best Peruvian specimens, to which they bear, in many respects, a close resemblance. The bowls of most of the stone pipes are carved in miniature figures of animals, birds, reptiles, etc. All of them are executed with strict fidelity to nature, and with exquisite skill. Not only are the features of the objects faithfully represented, but their peculiarities and habits are in some degree exhibited.... The two heads here presented, intended to represent the eagle, are far superior in point of finish, spirit, and truthfulness, to any miniature carvings, ancient or modern, which have fallen under the notice of the authors. The peculiar defiant expression of the king of birds is admirably preserved in the carving, which in this respect, more than any other, displays the skill of the artist."

Traces of cloth with "doubled and twisted fibre" have been found in the mounds; also matting; also shuttle-like tablets, used in weaving. There have also been found numerous musical pipes, with mouth-pieces and stops; lovers' pipes, curiously and delicately carved, reminding us of Bryant's lines—

"Till twilight came, and lovers walked and wooed

In a forgotten language; and old tunes,

From instruments of unremembered forms,

Gave the soft winds a voice."

There is evidence which goes to prove that the Mound Builders had relations with the people of a semi-tropical region in the direction of Atlantis. Among their sculptures, in Ohio, we find accurate representations of the lamantine, manatee, or sea-cow—found to-day on the shores of Florida, Brazil, and Central America—and of the toucan, a tropical and almost exclusively

South American bird. Sea-shells from the Gulf, pearls from the Atlantic, and obsidian from Mexico, have also been found side by side in their mounds.

The antiquity of their works is now generally conceded. "From the ruins of Nineveh and Babylon," says Mr. Gliddon, "we have bones of at least two thousand five hundred years old; from the pyramids and the catacombs of Egypt both mummied and unmummied crania have been taken, of still higher antiquity, in perfect preservation; nevertheless, the skeletons deposited in our Indian mounds, from the Lakes to the Gulf, are crumbling into dust through age alone."

All the evidence points to the conclusion that civilized or semi-civilized man has dwelt on the western continent from a vast antiquity. Maize, tobacco, quinoa, and the mandico plants have been cultivated so long that their wild originals have quite disappeared.

"The only species of palm cultivated by the South American Indians, that known as the Gulielma speciosa, has lost through that culture its original nut-like seed, and is dependent on the hands of its cultivators for its life. Alluding to the above-named plants Dr. Brinton ("Myths of the New World," p. 37) remarks, 'Several are sure to perish unless fostered by human care. What numberless ages does this suggest? How many centuries elapsed ere man thought of cultivating Indian corn? How many more ere it had spread over nearly a hundred degrees of latitude and lost all resemblance to its original form?' In the animal kingdom certain animals were domesticated by the aborigines from so remote a period that scarcely any of their species, as in the case of the lama of Peru, were to be found in a state of unrestrained freedom at the advent of the Spaniards." (Short's "North Americans of Antiquity," p. 11.)

The most ancient remains of man found in Europe are distinguished by a flattening of the tibia; and this peculiarity is found to be present in an exaggerated form in some of the American mounds. This also points to a high antiquity.

"None of the works, mounds, or enclosures are found on the lowest formed of the river terraces which mark the subsidence of the streams, and as there is no good reason why their builders should have avoided erecting them on that terrace while they raised them promiscuously on all the others, it follows, not unreasonably, that this terrace has been formed since the works were erected." (Baldwin's "Ancient America," p. 47.)

We have given some illustrations showing the similarity between the works of the Mound Builders and those of the Stone and Bronze Age in Europe. (See pp. 251, 260, 261, 262, 265, 266, ante.)

The Mound Builders retreated southward toward Mexico, and probably arrived there some time between A.D. 29 and A.D. 231, under the name of Nahuas. They called the region they left in the Mississippi Valley "Hue Hue

Tlapalan"—the old, old red land—in allusion, probably, to the red-clay soil of part of the country.

In the mounds we find many works of copper but none of bronze. This may indicate one of two things: either the colonies which settled the Mississippi Valley may have left Atlantis prior to the discovery of the art of manufacturing bronze, by mixing one part of tin with nine parts of copper, or, which is more probable, the manufactures of the Mound Builders may have been made on the spot; and as they had no tin within their territory they used copper alone, except, it may be, for such tools as were needed to carve stone, and these, perhaps, were hardened with tin. It is known that the Mexicans possessed the art of manufacturing true bronze; and the intercourse which evidently existed between Mexico and the Mississippi Valley, as proved by the presence of implements of obsidian in the mounds of Ohio, renders it probable that the same commerce which brought them obsidian brought them also small quantities of tin, or tin-hardened copper implements necessary for their sculptures.

The proofs, then, of the connection of the Mound Builders with Atlantis are: 1. Their race identity with the nations of Central America who possessed Flood legends, and whose traditions all point to an eastern, over-sea origin; while the many evidences of their race identity with the ancient Peruvians indicate that they were part of one great movement of the human race, extending from the Andes to Lake Superior, and, as I believe, from Atlantis to India.

2. The similarity of their civilization, and their works of stone and bronze, with the civilization of the Bronze Age in Europe.

3. The presence of great truncated mounds, kindred to the pyramids of Central America, Mexico, Egypt, and India.

4. The representation of tropical animals, which point to an intercourse with the regions around the Gulf of Mexico, where the Atlanteans were colonized.

5. The fact that the settlements of the Mound Builders were confined to the valley of the Mississippi, and were apparently densest at those points where a population advancing up that, stream would first reach high, healthy, and fertile lands.

6. The hostile nations which attacked them came from the north; and when the Mound Builders could no longer hold the country, or when Atlantis sank in the sea, they retreated in the direction whence they came, and fell back upon their kindred races in Central America, as the Roman troops in Gaul and Britain drew southward upon the destruction of Rome.

406

7. The Natchez Indians, who are supposed to have descended from the Mound Builders, kept a perpetual fire burning before an altar, watched by old men who were a sort of priesthood, as in Europe.

8. If the tablet said to have been found in a mound near Davenport, Iowa, is genuine, which appears probable, the Mound Builders must either have possessed an alphabet, or have held intercourse with some people who did. (See "North Americans of Antiquity," p. 38.) This singular relic exhibits what appears to be a sacrificial mound with a fire upon it; over it are the sun, moon, and stars, and above these a mass of hieroglyphics which bear some resemblance to the letters of European alphabets, and especially to that unknown alphabet which appears upon the inscribed bronze celt found near Rome. (See p. 258 of this work.) For instance, one of the letters on the celt is this, ###; on the Davenport tablet we find this sign, ###; on the celt we have ##; on the tablet, ###; on the celt we have ###; on the tablet, ###.

CHAPTER IV. THE IBERIAN COLONIES OF ATLANTIS

At the farthest point in the past to which human knowledge extends a race called Iberian inhabited the entire peninsula of Spain, from the Mediterranean to the Pyrenees. They also extended over the southern part of Gaul as far as the Rhone.

"It is thought that the Iberians from Atlantis and the north-west part of Africa," says Winchell, "settled in the south-west of Europe at a period earlier than the settlement of the Egyptians in the north-east of Africa. The Iberians spread themselves over Spain, Gaul, and the British Islands as early as 4000 or 5000 B.C.... The fourth dynasty (of the Egyptians), according to Brugsch, dates from about 3500 B.C. At this time the Iberians had become sufficiently powerful to attempt the conquest of the known world." ("Preadamites," p. 443.)

"The Libyan-Amazons of Diodorus—that is to say, the Libyans of the Iberian race—must be identified with the Libyans with brown and grizzly skin, of whom Brugsch has already pointed out the representations figured on the Egyptian monuments of the fourth dynasty." (Ibid.)

The Iberians, known as Sicanes, colonized Sicily in the ancient days. They were the original settlers in Italy and Sardinia. They are probably the source of the dark-haired stock in Norway and Sweden. Bodichon claims that the Iberians embraced the Ligurians, Cantabrians, Asturians, and Aquitanians. Strabo says, speaking of the Turduli and Turdetani, "they are the most cultivated of all the Iberians; they employ the art of writing, and have written books containing memorials of ancient times, and also poems and laws set in verse, for which they claim an antiquity of six thousand years." (Strabo, lib. iii., p. 139.)

The Iberians are represented to-day by the Basques.

The Basque are "of middle size, compactly built, robust and agile, of a darker complexion than the Spaniards, with gray eyes and black hair. They are simple but proud, impetuous, merry, and hospitable. The women are beautiful, skilful in performing men's work, and remarkable for their vivacity and grace. The Basques are much attached to dancing, and are very fond of the music of the bagpipe." ("New American Cyclopædia," art. Basques.)

"According to Paul Broca their language stands quite alone, or has mere analogies with the American type. Of all Europeans, we must provisionally hold the Basques to be the oldest inhabitants of our quarter of the world." (Peschel, "Races of Men," p. 501.)

The Basque language—the Euscara—"has some common traits with the Magyar, Osmanli, and other dialects of the Altai family, as, for instance, with the Finnic on the old continent, as well as the Algonquin-Lenape language and some others in America." ("New American Cyclopædia," art. Basques.)

Duponceau says of the Basque tongue: "This language, preserved in a corner of Europe by a few thousand mountaineers, is the sole remaining fragment of, perhaps, a hundred dialects constructed on the same plan, which probably existed and were universally spoken at a remote period in that quarter of the world. Like the bones of the mammoth, it remains a monument of the destruction produced by a succession of ages. It stands single and alone of its kind, surrounded by idioms that have no affinity with it."

We have seen them settling, in the earliest ages, in Ireland. They also formed the base of the dark-haired population of England and Scotland. They seem to have race affinities with the Berbers, on the Mediterranean coast of Africa.

Dr. Bodichon, for fifteen years a surgeon in Algiers, says:

"Persons who have inhabited Brittany, and then go to Algeria, are struck with the resemblance between the ancient Armoricans (the Brètons) and the Cabyles (of Algiers). In fact, the moral and physical character is identical. The Breton of pure blood has a long head, light yellow complexion of bistre tinge, eyes black or brown, stature short, and the black hair of the Cabyle. Like him, he instinctively hates strangers; in both are the same perverseness and obstinacy, same endurance of fatigue, same love of

408

independence, same inflexion of the voice, same expression of feelings. Listen to a Cabyle speaking his native tongue, and you will think you bear a Breton talking Celtic."

The Bretons, he tells us, form a strong contrast to the people around them, who are "Celts of tall stature, with blue eyes, white skins, and blond hair: they are communicative, impetuous, versatile; they pass rapidly from courage to despair. The Bretons are entirely different: they are taciturn, hold strongly to their ideas and usages, are persevering and melancholic; in a word, both in morale and physique they present the type of a southern race—of the Atlanteans."

By Atlanteans Dr. Bodichon refers to the inhabitants of the Barbary States—that being one of the names by which they were known to the Greeks and Romans. He adds:

"The Atlanteans, among the ancients, passed for the favorite children of Neptune; they made known the worship of this god to other nations—to the Egyptians, for example. In other words, the Atlanteans were the first known navigators. Like all navigators, they must have planted colonies at a distance. The Bretons, in our opinion, sprung from one of them."

Neptune was Poseidon, according to Plato, founder of Atlantis.

I could multiply proofs of the close relationship between the people of the Bronze Age of Europe and the ancient inhabitants of Northern Africa, which should be read remembering that "connecting ridge" which, according to the deep-sea soundings, united Africa and Atlantis.

CHAPTER V. THE PERUVIAN COLONY.

If we look at the map of Atlantis, as revealed by the deep sea soundings, we will find that it approaches at one point, by its connecting ridge, quite closely to the shore of South America, above the mouth of the Amazon, and that probably it was originally connected with it.

If the population of Atlantis expanded westwardly, it naturally found its way in its ships up the magnificent valley of the Amazon and its tributaries; and, passing by the low and fever-stricken lands of Brazil, it rested not until it had reached the high, fertile, beautiful, and healthful regions of Bolivia, from which it would eventually cross the mountains into Peru.

Here it would establish its outlying colonies at the terminus of its western line of advance, arrested only by the Pacific Ocean, precisely as we have seen it advancing up the valley of the Mississippi, and carrying on its mining operations on the shores of Lake Superior; precisely as we have seen it going eastward up the Mediterranean, past the Dardanelles, and founding

Aryan, Hamitic, and probably Turanian colonies on the farther shores of the Black Sea and on the Caspian. This is the universal empire over which, the Hindoo books tell us, Deva Nahusha was ruler; this was "the great and aggressive empire" to which Plato alludes; this was the mighty kingdom, embracing the whole of the then known world, from which the Greeks obtained their conception of the universal father of all men in King Zeus. And in this universal empire Señor Lopez must find an explanation of the similarity which, as we shall show, exists between the speech of the South American Pacific coast on the one hand, and the speech of Gaul, Ireland, England, Italy, Greece, Bactria, and Hindostan on the other.

Montesino tells us that at some time near the date of the Deluge, in other words, in the highest antiquity, America was invaded by a people with four leaders, named Ayar-manco-topa, Ayar-chaki, Ayar-aucca, and Ayar-uyssu. "Ayar," says Señor Lopez, "is the Sanscrit Ajar, or aje, and means primitive chief; and manco, chaki, aucca, and uyssu, mean believers, wanderers, soldiers, husbandmen. We have here a tradition of castes like that preserved in the four tribal names of Athens." The laboring class (naturally enough in a new colony) obtained the supremacy, and its leader was named Pirhua-manco, revealer of Pir, light (p[~u]r, Umbrian pir). Do the laws which control the changes of language, by which a labial succeeds a labial, indicate that the Mero or Merou of Theopompus, the name of Atlantis, was carried by the colonists of Atlantis to South America (as the name of old York was transplanted in a later age to New York), and became in time Pérou or Peru? Was not the Nubian "Island of Merou," with its pyramids built by "red men," a similar transplantation? And when the Hindoo priest points to his sacred emblem with five projecting points upon it, and tells us that they typify "Mero and the four quarters of the world," does he not refer to Atlantis and its ancient universal empire?

Manco, in the names of the Peruvian colonists, it has been urged, was the same as Mannus, Mann, and the Santhal Maniko. It reminds us of Menes, Minos, etc., who are found at the beginning of so many of the Old World traditions.

The Quichuas—this invading people—were originally a fair skinned race, with blue eyes and light and even auburn hair; they had regular features, large heads, and large bodies. Their descendants are to this day an olive-skinned people, much lighter in color than the Indian tribes subjugated by them.

They were a great race. Peru, as it was known to the Spaniards, held very much the same relation to the ancient Quichua civilization as England in the sixteenth century held to the civilization of the empire of the Cæsars. The Incas were simply an offshoot, who, descending from the mountains, subdued the rude races of the sea-coast, and imposed their ancient civilization upon them.

The Quichua nation extended at one time over a region of country more than two thousand miles long. This whole region, when the Spaniards arrived, "was a populous and prosperous empire, complete in its civil organization, supported by an efficient system of industry, and presenting a notable development of some of the more important arts of civilized life." (Baldwin's "Ancient America," p. 222.)

The companions of Pizarro found everywhere the evidences of a civilization of vast antiquity. Cieça de Leon mentions "great edifices" that were in ruins at Tiahuanaca, "an artificial hill raised on a groundwork of stone," and "two stone idols, apparently made by skilful artificers," ten or twelve feet high, clothed in long robes. "In this place, also," says De Leon, "there are stones so large and so overgrown that our wonder is excited, it being incomprehensible how the power of man could have placed them where we see them. They are variously wrought, and some of them, having the form of men, must have been idols. Near the walls are many caves and excavations under the earth; but in another place, farther west, are other and greater monuments, such as large gate-ways with hinges, platforms, and porches, each made of a single stone. It surprised me to see these enormous gate-ways, made of great masses of stone, some of which were thirty feet long, fifteen high, and six thick."

The capital of the Chimus of Northern Peru at Gran-Chimu was conquered by the Incas after a long and bloody struggle, and the capital was given up to barbaric ravage and spoliation. But its remains exist to-day, the marvel of the Southern Continent, covering not less than twenty square miles. Tombs, temples, and palaces arise on every hand, ruined but still traceable. Immense pyramidal structures, some of them half a mile in circuit; vast areas shut in by massive walls, each containing its water-tank, its shops, municipal edifices, and the dwellings of its inhabitants, and each a branch of a larger organization; prisons, furnaces for smelting metals, and almost every concomitant of civilization, existed in the ancient Chimu capital. One of the great pyramids, called the "Temple of the Sun," is 812 feet long by 470 wide, and 150 high. These vast structures have been ruined for centuries, but still the work of excavation is going on.

One of the centres of the ancient Quichua civilization was around Lake Titicaca. The buildings here, as throughout Peru, were all constructed of

411

hewn stone, and had doors and windows with posts, sills, and thresholds of stone.

At Cuelap, in Northern Peru, remarkable ruins were found. "They consist of a wall of wrought stones 3600 feet long, 560 broad, and 150 high, constituting a solid mass with a level summit. On this mass was another 600 feet long, 500 broad, and 150 high," making an aggregate height of three hundred feet! In it were rooms and cells which were used as tombs.

Very ancient ruins, showing remains of large and remarkable edifices, were found near Huamanga, and described by Cieça de Leon. The native traditions said this city was built "by bearded white men, who came there long before the time of the Incas, and established a settlement."

"The Peruvians made large use of aqueducts, which they built with notable skill, using hewn stones and cement, and making them very substantial." One extended four hundred and fifty miles across sierras and over rivers. Think of a stone aqueduct reaching from the city of New York to the State of North Carolina!

The public roads of the Peruvians were most remarkable; they were built on masonry. One of these roads ran along the mountains through the whole length of the empire, from Quito to Chili; another, starting from this at Cuzco, went down to the coast, and extended northward to the equator. These roads were from twenty to twenty-five feet wide, were macadamized with pulverized stone mixed with lime and bituminous cement, and were walled in by strong walls "more than a fathom in thickness." In many places these roads were cut for leagues through the rock; great ravines were filled up with solid masonry; rivers were crossed by suspension bridges, used here ages before their introduction into Europe. Says Baldwin, "The builders of our Pacific Railroad, with their superior engineering skill and mechanical appliances, might reasonably shrink from the cost and the difficulties of such a work as this. Extending from one degree north of Quito to Cuzco, and from Cuzco to Chili, it was quite as long as the two Pacific railroads, and its wild route among the mountains was far more difficult." Sarmiento, describing it, said, "It seems to me that if the emperor (Charles V.) should see fit to order the construction of another road like that which leads from Quito to Cuzco, or that which from Cuzco goes toward Chili, I certainly think he would not be able to make it, with all his power." Humboldt said, "This road was marvellous; none of the Roman roads I had seen in Italy, in the south of France, or in Spain, appeared to me more imposing than this work of the ancient Peruvians."

Along these great roads caravansaries were established for the accommodation of travellers.

These roads were ancient in the time of the Incas. They were the work of the white, auburn-haired, bearded men from Atlantis, thousands of years before the time of the Incas. When Huayna Capac marched his army over the main road to invade Quito, it was so old and decayed "that he found great difficulties in the passage," and he immediately ordered the necessary reconstructions.

It is not necessary, in a work of this kind, to give a detailed description of the arts and civilization of the Peruvians. They were simply marvellous. Their works in cotton and wool exceeded in fineness anything known in Europe at that time. They had carried irrigation, agriculture, and the cutting of gems to a point equal to that of the Old World. Their accumulations of the precious metals exceeded anything previously known in the history of the world. In the course of twenty-five years after the Conquest the Spaniards sent from Peru to Spain more than eight hundred millions of dollars of gold, nearly all of it taken from the Peruvians as "booty." In one of their palaces "they had an artificial garden, the soil of which was made of small pieces of fine gold, and this was artificially planted with different kinds of maize, which were of gold, their stems, leaves, and ears. Besides this, they had more than twenty sheep (llamas) with their lambs, attended by shepherds, all made of gold." In a description of one lot of golden articles, sent to Spain in 1534 by Pizarro, there is mention of "four llamas, ten statues of women of full size, and a cistern of gold, so curious that it excited the wonder of all."

Can any one read these details and declare Plato's description of Atlantis to be fabulous, simply because he tells us of the enormous quantities of gold and silver possessed by the people? Atlantis was the older country, the parent country, the more civilized country; and, doubtless, like the Peruvians, its people regarded the precious metals as sacred to their gods; and they had been accumulating them from all parts of the world for countless ages. If the story of Plato is true, there now lies beneath the waters of the Atlantic, covered, doubtless, by hundreds of feet of volcanic débris, an amount of gold and silver exceeding many times that brought to Europe from Peru, Mexico, and Central America since the time of Columbus; a treasure which, if brought to light, would revolutionize the financial values of the world.

I have already shown, in the chapter upon the similarities between the civilizations of the Old and New Worlds, some of the remarkable

413

coincidences which existed between the Peruvians and the ancient European races; I will again briefly, refer to a few of them:

1. They worshipped the sun, moon, and planets.

2. They believed in the immortality of the soul.

3. They believed in the resurrection of the body, and accordingly embalmed their dead.

4. The priest examined the entrails of the animals offered in sacrifice, and, like the Roman augurs, divined the future from their appearance.

5. They had an order of women vowed to celibacy—vestal virgins-nuns; and a violation of their vow was punished, in both continents, by their being buried alive.

6. They divided the year into twelve months.

7. Their enumeration was by tens; the people were divided into decades and hundreds, like the Anglo-Saxons; and the whole nation into bodies of 500, 1000, and 10,000, with a governor over each.

8. They possessed castes; and the trade of the father descended to the son, as in India.

9. They had bards and minstrels, who sung at the great festivals.

10. Their weapons were the same as those of the Old World, and made after the same pattern.

11. They drank toasts and invoked blessings.

12. They built triumphal arches for their returning heroes, and strewed the road before them with leaves and flowers.

13. They used sedan-chairs.

14. They regarded agriculture as the principal interest of the nation, and held great agricultural fairs and festivals for the interchange of the productions of the farmers.

15. The king opened the agricultural season by a great celebration, and, like the kings of Egypt, he put his hand to the plough, and ploughed the first furrow.

16. They had an order of knighthood, in which the candidate knelt before the king; his sandals were put on by a nobleman, very much as the spurs were buckled on the European knight; he was then allowed to use the girdle or sash around the loins, corresponding to the toga virilis of the Romans; he was then crowned with flowers. According to Fernandez, the candidates wore white shirts, like the knights of the Middle Ages, with a cross embroidered in front.

17. There was a striking resemblance between the architecture of the Peruvians and that of some of the nations of the Old World. It is enough for me to quote Mr. Ferguson's words, that the coincidence between the buildings of the Incas and the Cyclopean remains attributed to the Pelasgians in Italy and Greece "is the most remarkable in the history of architecture."

"The sloping jambs, the window cornice, the polygonal masonry, and other forms so closely resemble what is found in the old Pelasgic cities of Greece and Italy, that it is difficult to resist the conclusion that there may be some relation between them."

Even the mode of decorating their palaces and temples finds a parallel in the Old World. A recent writer says:

"We may end by observing, what seems to have escaped Señor Lopez, that the interior of an Inca palace, with its walls covered with gold, as described by Spaniards, with its artificial golden flowers and golden beasts, must have been exactly like the interior of the house of Alkinous or Menelaus—

"'The doors were framed of gold,
Where underneath the brazen floor doth glass
Silver pilasters, which with grace uphold
Lintel of silver framed; the ring was burnished gold,
And dogs on each side of the door there stand,
Silver and golden.'"

"I can personally testify" (says Winchell, "Preadamites," p. 387) "that a study of ancient Peruvian pottery has constantly reminded me of forms with which we are familiar in Egyptian archæology."

Dr. Schliemann, in his excavations of the ruins of Troy, found a number of what he calls "owl-headed idols" and vases.

In Peru we find vases with very much the same style of face.

I might pursue those parallels much farther; but it seems to me that these extraordinary coincidences must have arisen either from identity of origin or long-continued ancient intercourse. There can be little doubt that a fair-skinned, light-haired, bearded race, holding the religion which Plato says prevailed in Atlantis, carried an Atlantean civilization at an early day up the valley of the Amazon to the heights of Bolivia and Peru, precisely as a similar emigration of Aryans went westward to the shores of the Mediterranean and Caspian, and it is very likely that these diverse migrations habitually spoke the same language.

Señor Vincente Lopez, a Spanish gentleman of Montevideo, in 1872 published a work entitled "Les Races Aryennes in Pérou," in which he attempts to prove that the great Quichua language, which the Incas imposed on their subjects over a vast extent of territory, and which is still a living tongue in Peru and Bolivia, is really a branch of the great Aryan or Indo-European speech. I quote Andrew Lang's summary of the proofs on this point:

"Señor Lopez's view, that the Peruvians were Aryans who left the parent stock long before the Teutonic or Hellenic races entered Europe, is supported by arguments drawn from language, from the traces of institutions, from religious beliefs, from legendary records, and artistic remains. The evidence from language is treated scientifically, and not as a kind of ingenious guessing. Señor Lopez first combats the idea that the living dialect of Peru is barbarous and fluctuating. It is not one of the casual and shifting forms of speech produced by nomad races. To which of the stages of language does this belong—the agglutinative, in which one root is fastened on to another, and a word is formed in which the constitutive elements are obviously distinct, or the inflexional, where the auxiliary roots get worn down and are only distinguishable by the philologist? As all known Aryan tongues are inflexional, Señor Lopez may appear to contradict himself when he says that Quichua is an agglutinative Aryan language. But he quotes Mr. Max Müller's opinion that there must have been a time when the germs of Aryan tongues had not yet reached the inflexional stage, and shows that while the form of Quichua is agglutinative, as in Turanian, the roots of words are Aryan. If this be so, Quichua may be a linguistic missing link.

"When we first look at Quichua, with its multitude of words, beginning with hu, and its great preponderance of q's, it seems almost as odd as Mexican. But many of these forms are due to a scanty alphabet, and really express familiar sounds; and many, again, result from the casual spelling of the Spaniards. We must now examine some of the forms which Aryan roots are supposed to take in Quichua. In the first place, Quichua abhors the shock of two consonants. Thus, a word like ple'w in Greek would be unpleasant to the Peruvian's ear, and he says pillui, 'I sail.' The plu, again, in pluma, a feather, is said to be found in pillu, 'to fly.' Quichua has no v, any more than Greek has, and just as the Greeks had to spell Roman words beginning with V with Ou, like Valerius—Ou?ale'rios—so, where Sanscrit has v, Quichua has sometimes hu. Here is a list of words in hu:

+	QUICHUA.	SANSCRIT.
+	Huakia, to call.	Vacc, to speak.
+	Huasi, a house.	Vas, to inhabit.
+	Huayra, air, au?'ra.	Vâ, to breathe.
+	Huasa, the back.	Vas, to be able (pouvoir).
+		

"There is a Sanscrit root, kr, to act, to do: this root is found in more than three hundred names of peoples and places in Southern America. Thus there are the Caribs, whose name may have the same origin as that of our old friends the Carians, and mean the Braves, and their land the home of the Braves, like Kaleva-la, in Finnish. The same root gives kara, the hand, the Greek xei'r, and kkalli, brave, which a person of fancy may connect with kalo's. Again, Quichua has an 'alpha privative'—thus A-stani means 'I change a thing's place;' for ni or mi is the first person singular, and, added to the root of a verb, is the sign of the first person of the present indicative. For instance, can means being, and Can-mi, or Cani, is 'I am.' In the same way Munanmi, or Munani, is 'I love,' and Apanmi, or Apani, 'I carry.' So Lord Strangford was wrong when he supposed that the last verb in mi lived with the last patriot in Lithuania. Peru has stores of a grammatical form which has happily perished in Europe. It is impossible to do more than refer to the supposed Aryan roots contained in the glossary, but it may be noticed that the future of the Quichuan verb is formed in s—I love, Munani; I shall love, Munasa—and that the affixes denoting cases in the noun are curiously like the Greek prepositions."

The resemblance between the Quichua and Mandan words for I or me—mi—will here be observed.

Very recently Dr. Rudolf Falb has announced (Neue Freie Presse, of Vienna) that he has discovered that the relation of the Quichua and Aimara languages to the Aryan and Semitic tongues is very close; that, in fact, they "exhibit the most astounding affinities with the Semitic tongue, and particularly the Arabic," in which tongue Dr. Falb has been skilled from his boyhood. Following up the lines of this discovery, Dr. Falb has found (1) a connecting link with the Aryan roots, and (2) has ultimately arrived face to face with the surprising revelation that "the Semitic roots are universally Aryan." The common stems of all the variants are found in their purest condition in Quichua and Aimara, from which fact Dr. Falb derives the conclusion that the high plains of Peru and Bolivia must be regarded as the point of exit of the present human race.

[Since the above was written I have received a letter from Dr. Falb, dated Leipsic, April 5th, 1881. Scholars will be glad to learn that Dr. Falb's great work on the relationship of the Aryan and Semitic languages to the Quichua and Aimara tongues will be published in a year or two; the manuscript contains over two thousand pages, and Dr. Falb has devoted to it ten years of study. A work from such a source, upon so curious and important a subject, will be looked for with great interest.]

But it is impossible that the Quichuas and Aimaras could have passed across the wide Atlantic to Europe if there had been no stepping-stone in the shape of Atlantis with its bridge-like ridges connecting the two continents.

It is, however, more reasonable to suppose that the Quichuas and Aimaras were a race of emigrants from Plato's island than to think that Atlantis was populated from South America. The very traditions to which we have referred as existing among the Peruvians, that the civilized race were white and bearded, and that they entered or invaded the country, would show that civilization did not originate in Peru, but was a transplantation from abroad, and only in the direction of Atlantis can we look for a white and bearded race.

In fact, kindred races, with the same arts, and speaking the same tongue in an early age of the world, separated in Atlantis and went east and west—the one to repeat the civilization of the mother-country along the shores of the Mediterranean Sea, which, like a great river, may be said to flow out from the Black Sea, with the Nile as one of its tributaries, and along the shores of the Red Sea and the Persian Gulf; while the other emigration advanced up the Amazon, and created mighty nations upon its head-waters in the valleys of the Andes and on the shores of the Pacific.

CHAPTER VI. THE AFRICAN COLONIES.

Africa, like Europe and America, evidences a commingling of different stocks: the blacks are not all black, nor all woolly-haired; the Africans pass through all shades, from that of a light Berber, no darker than the Spaniard, to the deep black of the Iolofs, between Senegal and Gambia.

The traces of red men or copper-colored races are found in many parts of the continent. Prichard divides the true negroes into four classes; his second class is thus described:

"2. Other tribes have forms and features like the European; their complexion is black, or a deep olive, or a copper color approaching to black, while their hair, though often crisp and frizzled, is not in the least woolly.

Such are the Bishari and Danekil and Hazorta, and the darkest of the Abyssinians.

"The complexion and hair of the Abyssinians vary very much, their complexion ranging from almost white to dark brown or black, and their hair from straight to crisp, frizzled, and almost woolly." (Nott and Gliddon, "Types of Mankind," p. 194.)

"Some of the Nubians are copper-colored or black, with a tinge of red." (Ibid., p. 198.)

Speaking of the Barbary States, these authors further say (Ibid., p. 204):

"On the northern coast of Africa, between the Mediterranean and the Great Desert, including Morocco, Algiers, Tunis, Tripoli, and Benzazi, there is a continuous system of highlands, which have been included under the general term Atlas—anciently Atlantis, now the Barbary States.... Throughout Barbary we encounter a peculiar group of races, subdivided into many tribes of various shades, now spread over a vast area, but which formerly had its principal and perhaps aboriginal abode along the mountain slopes of Atlas.... The real name of the Berbers is Mazirgh, with the article prefixed or suffixed—T-amazirgh or Amazirgh-T—meaning free, dominant, or 'noble race.'... We have every reason to believe the Berbers existed in the remotest times, with all their essential moral and physical peculiarities.... They existed in the time of Menes in the same condition in which they were discovered by Phoenician navigators previously to the foundation of Carthage. They are an indomitable, nomadic people, who, since the introduction of camels, have penetrated in considerable numbers into the Desert, and even as far as Nigritia.... Some of these clans are white, others black, with woolly hair."

Speaking of the Barbary Moors, Prichard says:

"Their figure and stature are nearly the same as those of the southern Europeans, and their complexion, if darker, is only so in proportion to the higher temperature of the country. It displays great varieties."

Jackson says: "The men of Temsena and Showiah are of a strong, robust make, and of a copper color; the women are beautiful. The women of Fez are fair as the Europeans, but hair and eyes always dark. The women of Mequinas are very beautiful, and have the red-and-white complexion of English women."

Spix and Martins, the German travellers, depict the Moors as follows:

"A high forehead, an oval countenance, large, speaking, black eyes, shaded by arched and strong eyebrows, a thin, rather long, but not too pointed nose, rather broad lips, meeting in an acute angle, brownish-yellow complexion, thick, smooth, and black hair, and a stature greater than the middle height."

Hodgson states:

"The Tuarycks are a white people, of the Berber race; the Mozabiaks are a remarkably white people, and mixed with the Bedouin Arabs. The Wadreagans and Wurgelans are of a dark bronze, with woolly hair."

The Foolahs, Fulbe (sing. Pullo), Fellani, or Fellatah, are a people of West and Central Africa. It is the opinion of modern travellers that the Foolahs are destined to become the dominant people of Negro-land. In language, appearance, and history they present striking differences from the neighboring tribes, to whom they are superior in intelligence, but inferior, according to Garth, in physical development. Golbery describes them as "robust and courageous, of a reddish-black color, with regular features, hair longer and less woolly than that of the common negroes, and high mental capacity." Dr. Barth found great local differences in their physical characteristics, as Bowen describes the Foolahs of Bomba as being some black, some almost white, and many of a mulatto color, varying from dark to very bright. Their features and skulls were cast in the European mould. They have a tradition that their ancestors were whites, and certain tribes call themselves white men. They came from Timbuctoo, which lies to the north of their present location.

The Nubians and Foolahs are classed as Mediterraneans. They are not black, but yellowish-brown, or red-brown. The hair is not woolly but curly, and sometimes quite straight; it is either dark-brown or black, with a fuller growth of beard than the negroes. The oval face gives them a Mediterranean type. Their noses are prominent, their lips not puffy, and their languages have no connection with the tongues of the negroes proper. ("American Cyclopædia," art. Ethnology, p. 759.)

"The Cromlechs (dolmens) of Algeria" was the subject of an address made by General Faidherbe at the Brussels International Congress. He considers these structures to be simply sepulchral monuments, and, after examining five or six thousand of them, maintains that the dolmens of Africa and of Europe were all constructed by the same race, during their emigration from the shores of the Baltic to the southern coast of the Mediterranean. The author does not, however, attempt to explain the existence of these monuments in other countries—Hindostan, for instance, and America. "In Africa," he says, "cromlechs are called tombs of the idolaters"—the idolaters being neither Romans, nor Christians, nor Phoenicians, but some antique race. He regards the Berbers as the descendants of the primitive dolmen-builders. Certain Egyptian monuments tell of invasions of Lower Egypt one thousand five hundred years before our era by blond tribes from the West. The bones found in the cromlechs are those of a large and dolichocephalous race. General Faidherbe gives the average stature (including the women) at 1.65 or 1.74 metre, while the average stature of French carabineers is only 1.65 metre. He did not find a single brachycephalous skull. The profiles indicated great intelligence. The Egyptian documents already referred to call the invaders Tamahu, which must have come from the invaders' own language, as it is not Egyptian. The Tuaregs of the present day may be regarded as the best representatives of the Tamahus. They are of lofty stature, have blue eyes, and cling to the custom of bearing long swords, to be wielded by both hands. In Soudan, on the banks of the Niger, dwells a negro tribe ruled by a royal family (Masas), who are of rather fair complexion, and claim descent from white men. Masas is perhaps the same as Mashash, which occurs in the Egyptian documents applied to the Tamahus. The Masas wear the hair in the same fashion as the Tamahus, and General Faidherbe is inclined to think that they too are the descendants of the dolmen-builders.

These people, according to my theory, were colonists from Atlantis—colonists of three different races—white, yellow, and sunburnt or red.

CHAPTER VII. THE IRISH COLONIES FROM ATLANTIS.

We have seen that beyond question Spain and France owed a great part of their population to Atlantis. Let us turn now to Ireland.

We would naturally expect, in view of the geographical position of the country, to find Ireland colonized at an early day by the overflowing population of Atlantis. And, in fact, the Irish annals tell us that their island was settled prior to the Flood. In their oldest legends an account is given of three Spanish fishermen who were driven by contrary winds on the coast of Ireland before the Deluge. After these came the Formorians, who were led into the country prior to the Deluge by the Lady Banbha, or Kesair; her maiden name was h'Erni, or Berba; she was accompanied by fifty maidens and three men—Bith, Ladhra, and Fintain. Ladhra was their conductor, who was the first buried in Hibernia. That ancient book, the "Cin of Drom-Snechta," is quoted in the "Book of Ballymote" as authority for this legend.

The Irish annals speak of the Formorians as a warlike race, who, according to the "Annals of Clonmacnois," "were a sept descended from

Cham, the son of Noeh, and lived by pyracie and spoile of other nations, and were in those days very troublesome to the whole world."

Were not these the inhabitants of Atlantis, who, according to Plato, carried their arms to Egypt and Athens, and whose subsequent destruction has been attributed to divine vengeance invoked by their arrogance and oppressions?

The Formorians were from Atlantis. They were called Fomhoraicc, F'omoraig Afraic, and Formoragh, which has been rendered into English as Formorians. They possessed ships, and the uniform representation is that they came, as the name F'omoraig Afraic indicated, from Africa. But in that day Africa did not mean the continent of Africa, as we now understand it. Major Wilford, in the eighth volume of the "Asiatic Researches," has pointed out that Africa comes from Apar, Aphar, Apara, or Aparica, terms used to signify "the West," just as we now speak of the Asiatic world as "the East." When, therefore, the Formorians claimed to come from Africa, they simply meant that they came from the West—in other words, from Atlantis—for there was no other country except America west of them.

They possessed Ireland from so early a period that by some of the historians they are spoken of as the aborigines of the country.

The first invasion of Ireland, subsequent to the coming of the Formorians, was led by a chief called Partholan: his people are known in the Irish annals as "Partholan's people." They were also probably Atlanteans. They were from Spain. A British prince, Gulguntius, or Gurmund, encountered off the Hebrides a fleet of thirty ships, filled with men and women, led by one Partholyan, who told him they were from Spain, and seeking some place to colonize. The British prince directed him to Ireland. ("De Antiq. et Orig. Cantab.")

Spain in that day was the land of the Iberians, the Basques; that is to say, the Atlanteans.

The Formorians defeated Partholan's people, killed Partholan, and drove the invaders out of the country.

The Formorians were a civilized race; they had "a fleet of sixty ships and a strong army."

The next invader of their dominions was Neimhidh; he captured one of their fortifications, but it was retaken by the Formorians under "Morc." Neimhidh was driven out of the country, and the Atlanteans continued in undisturbed possession of the island for four hundred years more. Then came the Fir-Bolgs. They conquered the whole island, and divided it into five provinces. They held possession of the country for only thirty-seven years, when they were overthrown by the Tuatha-de-Dananns, a people more advanced in civilization; so much so that when their king, Nuadha, lost his hand in battle, "Creidne, the artificer," we are told, "put a silver hand upon him, the fingers of which were capable of motion." This great race ruled the country for one hundred and ninety-seven years: they were overthrown by an immigration from Spain, probably of Basques, or Iberians, or Atlanteans, "the sons of Milidh," or Milesius, who "possessed a large fleet and a strong army." This last invasion took place about the year 1700 B.C.; so that the invasion of Neimhidh must have occurred about the year 2334 B.C.; while we will have to assign a still earlier date for the coming of Partholan's people, and an earlier still for the occupation of the country by the Formorians from the West.

In the Irish historic tales called "Catha; or Battles," as given by the learned O'Curry, a record is preserved of a real battle which was fought between the Tuatha-de-Dananns and the Fir Bolgs, from which it appears that these two races spoke the same language, and that they were intimately connected with the Formorians. As the armies drew near together the Fir-Bolgs sent out Breas, one of their great chiefs, to reconnoitre the camp of the strangers; the Tuatha-de-Dananns appointed one of their champions, named Sreng, to meet the emissary of the enemy; the two warriors met and talked to one another over the tops of their shields, and each was delighted to find that the other spoke the same language. A battle followed, in which Nunda, king of the Fir-Bolgs, was slain; Breas succeeded him; he encountered the hostility of the bards, and was compelled to resign the crown. He went to the court of his father-in-law, Elathe, a Formorian sea-king or pirate; not being well received, he repaired to the camp of Balor of the Evil Eye, a Formorian chief. The Formorian head-quarters seem to have been in the Hebrides. Breas and Balor collected a vast army and navy and invaded Ireland, but were defeated in a great battle by the Tuatha-de-Dananns.

These particulars would show the race-identity of the Fir-Bolg and Tuatha-de-Dananns; and also their intimate connection, if not identity with, the Formorians.

The Tuatha-de-Dananns seem to have been a civilized people; besides possessing ships and armies and working in the metals, they had an organized body of surgeons, whose duty it was to attend upon the wounded in battle; and they had also a bardic or Druid class, to preserve the history of the country and the deeds of kings and heroes.

According to the ancient books of Ireland the race known as "Partholan's people," the Nemedians, the Fir-Bolgs, the Tuatha-de-Dananns, and the Milesians were all descended from two brothers, sons of Magog, son of Japheth, son of Noah, who escaped from the catastrophe which destroyed his country. Thus all these races were Atlantean. They were connected with the African colonies of Atlantis, the Berbers, and with the Egyptians. The Milesians lived in Egypt: they were expelled thence; they stopped a while in Crete, then in Scythia, then they settled in Africa (See MacGeoghegan's "History of Ireland," p. 57), at a place called Gæthulighe or Getulia, and lived there during eight generations, say two hundred and fifty years; "then they entered Spain, where they built Brigantia, or Briganza, named after their king Breogan: they dwelt in Spain a considerable time. Milesius, a descendant of Breogan, went on an expedition to Egypt, took part in a war against the Ethiopians, married the king's daughter, Scota: he died in Spain, but his people soon after conquered Ireland. On landing on the coast they offered sacrifices to Neptune or Poseidon"—the god of Atlantis. (Ibid., p. 58.)

The Book of Genesis (chap. x.) gives us the descendants of Noah's three sons, Shem, Ham, and Japheth. We are told that the sons of Japheth were Gomer, and Magog, and Madai, and Javan, and Tubal, and Meshech, and Tiras. We are then given the names of the descendants of Gomer and Javan, but not of Magog. Josephus says the sons of Magog were the Scythians. The Irish annals take up the genealogy of Magog's family where the Bible leaves it. The Book of Invasions, the "Cin of Drom-Snechta," claims that these Scythians were the Phoenicians; and we are told that a branch of this family were driven out of Egypt in the time of Moses: "He wandered through Africa for forty-two years, and passed by the lake of Salivæ to the altars of the Philistines, and between Rusicada and the mountains Azure, and he came by the river Monlon, and by the sea to the Pillars of Hercules, and through the Tuscan sea, and he made for Spain, and dwelt there many years, and he increased and multiplied, and his people were multiplied."

From all these facts it appears that the population of Ireland came from the West, and not from Asia—that it was one of the many waves of population flowing out from the Island of Atlantis—and herein we find the explanation of that problem which has puzzled the Aryan scholars. As Ireland is farther from the Punjab than Persia, Greece, Rome, or Scandinavia, it would follow that the Celtic wave of migration must have been the earliest sent out from the Sanscrit centre; but it is now asserted by Professor Schleicher and others that the Celtic tongue shows that it separated from the Sanscrit original tongue later than the others, and that it is more closely allied to the Latin than any other Aryan tongue. This is entirely inexplicable upon any theory of an Eastern origin of the Indo-European races, but very easily understood if we recognize the Aryan and Celtic migrations as going out about the same time from the Atlantean fountain-head.

There are many points confirmatory of this belief. In the first place, the civilization of the Irish dates back to a vast antiquity. We have seen their annals laying claim to an immigration from the direction of Atlantis prior to the Deluge, with no record that the people of Ireland were subsequently destroyed by the Deluge. From the Formorians, who came before the Deluge, to the Milesians, who came from Spain in the Historic Period, the island was continuously inhabited. This demonstrates (1) that these legends did not come from Christian sources, as the Bible record was understood in the old time to imply a destruction of all who lived before the Flood except Noah and his family; (2) it confirms our view that the Deluge was a local catastrophe, and did not drown the whole human family; (3) that the coming of the Formorians having been before the Deluge, that great cataclysm was of comparatively recent date, to wit, since the settlement of Ireland; and (4) that as the Deluge was a local catastrophe, it must have occurred somewhere not far from Ireland to have come to their knowledge. A rude people could scarcely have heard in that day of a local catastrophe occurring in the heart of Asia.

There are many evidences that the Old World recognized Ireland as possessing a very ancient civilization. In the Sanscrit books it is referred to as Hiranya, the "Island of the Sun," to wit, of sun-worship; in other words, as pre-eminently the centre of that religion which was shared by all the ancient races of Europe, Asia, Africa, and America. It is believed that Ireland was the "Garden of Phoebus" of the Western mythologists.

The Greeks called Ireland the "Sacred Isle" and "Ogygia."

"Nor can any one," says Camden, "conceive why they should call it Ogygia, unless, perhaps, from its antiquity; for the Greeks called nothing Ogygia unless what was extremely ancient." We have seen that Ogyges was connected by the Greek legends with a first deluge, and that Ogyges was "a quite mythical personage, lost in the night of ages."

It appears, as another confirmation of the theory of the Atlantis origin of these colonies, that their original religion was sun-worship; this, as was the case in other countries, became subsequently overlaid with idol-worship. In the reign of King Tighernmas the worship of idols was introduced. The priests constituted the Order of Druids. Naturally many analogies have been found to exist between the beliefs and customs of the Druids and the other religions which were drawn from Atlantis. We have seen in the chapter on sun-worship how extensive this form of religion was in the Atlantean days, both in Europe and America.

It would appear probable that the religion of the Druids passed from Ireland to England and France. The metempsychosis or transmigration of souls was one of the articles of their belief long before the time of Pythagoras; it had probably been drawn from the storehouse of Atlantis, whence it passed to the Druids, the Greeks, and the Hindoos. The Druids had a pontifex maximus to whom they yielded entire obedience. Here again we see a practice which extended to the Phoenicians, Egyptians, Hindoos, Peruvians, and Mexicans.

The Druids of Gaul and Britain offered human sacrifices, while it is claimed that the Irish Druids did not. This would appear to have been a corrupt after-growth imposed upon the earlier and purer sacrifice of fruits and flowers known in Atlantis, and due in part to greater cruelty and barbarism in their descendants. Hence we find it practised in degenerate ages on both sides of the Atlantic.

The Irish Druidical rites manifested themselves principally in sun worship. Their chief god was Bel or Baal—the same worshipped by the Phoenicians—the god of the sun. The Irish name for the sun, Grian, is, according to Virgil, one of the names of Apollo—another sun-god, Gryneus. Sun-worship continued in Ireland down to the time of St. Patrick, and some of its customs exist among the peasantry of that country to this day. We have seen that among the Peruvians, Romans, and other nations, on a certain day all fires were extinguished throughout the kingdom, and a new fire kindled at the chief temple by the sun's rays, from which the people obtained their fire for the coming year. In Ireland the same practice was found to exist. A piece of land was set apart, where the four provinces met, in the present county of Meath; here, at a palace called Tlachta, the divine fire was kindled. Upon the night of what is now All-Saints-day the Druids assembled at this place to offer sacrifice, and it was established, under heavy penalties, that no fire should be kindled except from this source. On the first of May a convocation of Druids was held in the royal palace of the King of Connaught, and two fires were lit, between which cattle were driven, as a preventive of murrain and other pestilential disorders. This was called Beltinne, or the day of Bel's fire. And unto this day the Irish call the first day of May "Lha-Beul-tinne," which signifies "the day of Bel's fire." The celebration in Ireland of St. John's-eve by watch-fires is a relic of the ancient sun-worship of Atlantis. The practice of driving cattle through the fire continued for a longtime, and Kelly mentions in his "Folk-lore" that in Northamptonshire, in England, a calf was sacrificed in one of these fires to "stop the murrain" during the present century. Fires are still lighted in England and Scotland as well as Ireland for superstitious purposes; so that the people of Great Britain, it may be said, are still in some sense in the midst of the ancient sun-worship of Atlantis.

We find among the Irish of to-day many Oriental customs. The game of "jacks," or throwing up five pebbles and catching them on the back of the hand, was known in Rome. "The Irish keen (caoine), or the lament over the dead, may still be heard in Algeria and Upper Egypt, even as Herodotus heard it chanted by the Libyan women." The same practice existed among the Egyptians, Etruscans, and Romans. The Irish wakes are identical with the funeral feasts of the Greeks, Etruscans, and Romans. (Cusack's "History of Ireland," p. 141.) The Irish custom of saying "God bless you!" when one sneezes, is a very ancient practice; it was known to the Romans, and referred, it is said, to a plague in the remote past, whose first symptom was sneezing.

We find many points of resemblance between the customs of the Irish and those of the Hindoo. The practice of the creditor fasting at the door-step of his debtor until he is paid, is known to both countries; the kindly "God save you!" is the same as the Eastern "God be gracious to you, my son!" The reverence for the wren in Ireland and Scotland reminds us of the Oriental and Greek respect for that bird. The practice of pilgrimages, fasting, bodily macerations, and devotion to holy wells and particular places, extends from Ireland to India.

All these things speak of a common origin; this fact has been generally recognized, but it has always been interpreted that the Irish came from the East, and were in fact a migration of Hindoos. There is not the slightest evidence to sustain this theory. The Hindoos have never within the knowledge of man sent out colonies or fleets for exploration; but there is abundant evidence, on the other hand, of migrations from Atlantis eastward. And how could the Sanscrit writings have preserved maps of Ireland, England, and Spain, giving the shape and outline of their coasts, and their very names, and yet have preserved no memory of the expeditions or colonizations by which they acquired that knowledge?

Another proof of our theory is found in "the round-towers" of Ireland. Attempts have been made to show, by Dr. Petrie and others, that these extraordinary structures are of modern origin, and were built by the Christian priests, in which to keep their church-plate. But it is shown that the "Annals of Ulster" mention the destruction of fifty-seven of them by an earthquake in A.D. 448; and Giraldus Cambrensis shows that Lough Neagh was created by an inundation, or sinking of the land, in A.D. 65, and that in his day the fishermen could

"See the round-towers of other days

In the waves beneath them shining."

Moreover, we find Diodorus Siculus, in a well-known passage, referring to Ireland, and describing it as "an island in the ocean over against Gaul, to the north, and not inferior in size to Sicily, the soil of which is so fruitful that they mow there twice in the year." He mentions the skill of their harpers, their sacred groves, and their singular temples of round form.

We find similar structures in America, Sardinia, and India. The remains of similar round-towers are very abundant in the Orkneys and Shetlands. "They have been supposed by some," says Sir John Lubbock, "to be Scandinavian, but no similar buildings exist in Norway, Sweden, or Denmark, so that this style of architecture is no doubt anterior to the arrival of the Northmen." I give above a picture of the Burgh or Broch of the little island of Moussa, in the Shetlands. It is circular in form, forty-one feet in height. Open at the top; the central space is twenty feet in diameter, the walls about fourteen feet thick at the base, and eight feet at the top. They contain a staircase, which leads to the top of the building. Similar structures are found in the Island of Sardinia.

In New Mexico and Colorado the remains of round-towers are very abundant. The illustration below represents one of these in the valley of the Mancos, in the south-western corner of Colorado. A model of it is to be found in the Smithsonian collection at Washington. The tower stands at present, in its ruined condition, twenty feet high. It will be seen that it resembles the towers of Ireland, not only in its circular form but also in the fact that its door-way is situated at some distance from the ground.

It will not do to say that the resemblance between these prehistoric and singular towers, in countries so far apart as Sardinia, Ireland, Colorado, and India, is due to an accidental coincidence. It might as well be argued that the resemblance between the roots of the various Indo-European languages was also due to accidental coincidence, and did not establish any similarity of origin. In fact, we might just as well go back to the theory of the philosophers of one hundred and fifty years ago, and say that the resemblance between the fossil forms in the rocks and the living forms upon them did not indicate relationship, or prove that the fossils were the remains of creatures that had once lived, but that it was simply a way nature had of working out extraordinary coincidences in a kind of joke; a sort of "plastic power in nature," as it was called.

We find another proof that Ireland was settled by the people of Atlantis in the fact that traditions long existed among the Irish peasantry of a land in the "Far West," and that this belief was especially found among the posterity of the Tuatha-de-Dananns, whose connection with the Formorians we have shown.

The Abbé Brasseur de Bourbourg, in a note to his translation of the "Popol Vuh," says:

"There is an abundance of legends and traditions concerning the passage of the Irish into America, and their habitual communication with that continent many centuries before the time of Columbus. We should bear in mind that Ireland was colonized by the Phoenicians (or by people of that race). An Irish Saint named Vigile, who lived in the eighth century, was accused to Pope Zachary of having taught heresies on the subject of the antipodes. At first he wrote to the pope in reply to the charge, but afterward he went to Rome in person to justify himself, and there he proved to the pope that the Irish had been accustomed to communicate with a transatlantic world."

"This fact," says Baldwin, "seems to have been preserved in the records of the Vatican."

The Irish annals preserve the memory of St. Brendan of Clonfert, and his remarkable voyage to a land in the West, made A.D. 545. His early youth was passed under the care of St. Ita, a lady of the princely family of the Desii. When he was five years old he was placed under the care of Bishop Ercus. Kerry was his native home; the blue waves of the Atlantic washed its shores; the coast was full of traditions of a wonderful land in the West. He went to see the venerable St. Enda, the first abbot of Arran, for counsel. He was probably encouraged in the plan he had formed of carrying the Gospel to this distant land. "He proceeded along the coast of Mayo, inquiring as he went for traditions of the Western continent. On his return to Kerry he decided to set out on the important expedition. St. Brendan's Hill still bears his name; and from the bay at the foot of this lofty eminence be sailed for the 'Far West.' Directing his course toward the southwest, with a few faithful companions, in a well-provisioned bark, he came, after some rough and dangerous navigation, to calm seas, where, without aid of oar or sail, he was borne along for many weeks." He had probably entered upon the same great current which Columbus travelled nearly one thousand years later, and which extends from the shores of Africa and Europe to America.

He finally reached land; he proceeded inland until he came to a large river flowing from east to west, supposed by some to be the Ohio. "After an absence of seven years he returned to Ireland, and lived not only to tell of the marvels he had seen, but to found a college of three thousand monks at Clonfert." There are eleven Latin MSS. in the Bibliothèque Impériale at Paris of this legend, the dates of which vary from the eleventh to the fourteenth century, but all of them anterior to the time of Columbus.

The fact that St. Brendan sailed in search of a country in the west cannot be doubted; and the legends which guided him were probably the traditions of Atlantis among a people whose ancestors had been derived directly or at second-hand from that country.

This land was associated in the minds of the peasantry with traditions of Edenic happiness and beauty. Miss Eleanor C. Donnelly, of Philadelphia, has referred to it in her poem, "The Sleeper's Sail," where the starving boy dreams of the pleasant and plentiful land:

"'Mother, I've been on the cliffs out yonder,
Straining my eyes o'er the breakers free
To the lovely spot where the sun was setting,
Setting and sinking into the sea.
"'The sky was full of the fairest colors
Pink and purple and paly green,
With great soft masses of gray and amber,
And great bright rifts of gold between.
"'And all the birds that way were flying,
Heron and curlew overhead,
With a mighty eagle westward floating,
Every plume in their pinions red.
"'And then I saw it, the fairy city,
Far away o'er the waters deep;
Towers and castles and chapels glowing
Like blessèd dreams that we see in sleep.
"'What is its name?' 'Be still, acushla
(Thy hair is wet with the mists, my boy);
Thou hast looked perchance on the Tir-na-n'oge,
Land of eternal youth and joy!
"'Out of the sea, when the sun is setting,
It rises, golden and fair to view;

No trace of ruin, or change of sorrow,

No sign of age where all is new.

"'Forever sunny, forever blooming,

Nor cloud nor frost can touch that spot,

Where the happy people are ever roaming,

The bitter pangs of the past forgot.'

This is the Greek story of Elysion; these are the Elysian Fields of the Egyptians; these are the Gardens of the Hesperides; this is the region in the West to which the peasant of Brittany looks from the shores of Cape Raz; this is Atlantis.

The starving child seeks to reach this blessed land in a boat and is drowned.

"High on the cliffs the light-house keeper

Caught the sound of a piercing scream;

Low in her hut the lonely widow

Moaned in the maze of a troubled dream;

"And saw in her sleep a seaman ghostly,

With sea-weeds clinging in his hair,

Into her room, all wet and dripping,

A drownéd boy on his bosom bear.

"Over Death Sea on a bridge of silver

The child to his Father's arms had passed!

Heaven was nearer than Tir-na-n'oge,

And the golden city was reached at last."

CHAPTER VIII. THE OLDEST SON OF NOAH.

That eminent authority, Dr. Max Müller, says, in his *"Lectures on the Science of Religion":* "If we confine ourselves to the Asiatic continent, with its important peninsula of Europe, we find that in the vast desert of drifting human speech three, and only three, oases have been formed in which, before the beginning of all history, language became permanent and traditional—assumed, in fact, a new character, a character totally different from the original character of the floating and constantly varying speech of human beings. These three oases of language are known by the name of Turanian, Aryan, and Semitic. In these three centres, more particularly in the Aryan and Semitic, language ceased to be natural; its growth was arrested, and it became permanent, solid, petrified, or, if you like, historical speech. I have always maintained that this centralization and traditional conservation of language could only have been the result of religious and political influences, and I now mean to show that we really have clear evidence of three independent settlements of religion—the Turanian, the Aryan, and the Semitic—concomitantly with the three great settlements of language."

There can be no doubt that the Aryan and another branch, which Müller calls Semitic, but which may more properly be called Hamitic, radiated from Noah; it is a question yet to be decided whether the Turanian or Mongolian is also a branch of the Noachic or Atlantean stock.

To quote again from Max Müller: "If it can only be proved that the religions of the Aryan nations are united by the same bonds of a real relationship which have enabled us to treat their languages as so many varieties of the same type—and so also of the Semitic—the field thus opened is vast enough, and its careful clearing, and cultivation will occupy several generations of scholars. And this original relationship, I believe, can be proved. Names of the principal deities, words also expressive of the most essential elements of religion, such as prayer, sacrifice, altar, spirit, law, and faith, have been preserved among the Aryan and among the Semitic nations, and these relics admit of one explanation only. After that, a comparative study of the Turanian religions may be approached with better hope of success; for that there was not only a primitive Aryan and a primitive Semitic religion, but likewise a primitive Turanian religion, before each of these primeval races was broken up and became separated in language, worship and national sentiment, admits, I believe, of little doubt.... There was a period during which the ancestors of the Semitic family had not yet been divided, whether in language or in religion. That period transcends the recollection of every one of the Semitic races, in the same way as neither Hindoos, Greeks, nor Romans have any recollection of the time when they spoke a common language, and worshipped their Father in heaven by a name that was as yet neither Sanscrit, nor Greek, nor Latin. But I do not hesitate to call this Prehistoric Period historical in the best sense of the word. It was a real period, because, unless it was real, all the realities of the Semitic languages and the Semitic religions, such as we find them after their separation, would be unintelligible. Hebrew, Syriac, and Arabic point to a common source as much as Sanscrit, Greek, and Latin; and unless we can bring ourselves to doubt that the Hindoos, the Greeks, the Romans, and the Teutons derived the worship of their principal deity from their common Aryan sanctuary, we shall not be able to deny that there was likewise a primitive religion of the whole Semitic race, and that El, the

Strong One in heaven, was invoked by the ancestors of all the Semitic races before there were Babylonians in Babylon, Phoenicians in Sidon and Tyrus—before there were Jews in Mesopotamia or Jerusalem. The evidence of the Semitic is the same as that of the Aryan languages: the conclusion cannot be different....

"These three classes of religion are not to be mistaken—as little as the three classes of language, the Turanian, the Semitic, and the Aryan. They mark three events in the most ancient history of the world, events which have determined the whole fate of the human race, and of which we ourselves still feel the consequences in our language, in our thoughts, and in our religion."

We have seen that all the evidence points to the fact that this original seat of the Phoenician-Hebrew family was in Atlantis.

The great god of the so-called Semites was El, the Strong One, from whose name comes the Biblical names Beth-el, the house of God; Ha-el, the strong one; El-ohim, the gods; El-oah, God; and from the same name is derived the Arabian name of God, Al-lah.

Another evidence of the connection between the Greeks, Phoenicians, Hebrews, and Atlanteans is shown in the name of Adonis.

The Greeks tell us that Adonis was the lover of Aphrodite, or Venus, who was the offspring of Uranus—"she came out of the sea;" Uranus was the father of Chronos, and the grandfather of Poseidon, king of Atlantis.

Now we find Adonâi in the Old Testament used exclusively as the name of Jehovah, while among the Phoenicians Adonâi was the supreme deity. In both cases the root Ad is probably a reminiscence of Ad-lantis.

There seem to exist similar connections between the Egyptian and the Turanian mythology. The great god of Egypt was Neph or Num; the chief god of the Samoyedes is Num; and Max Müller established an identity between the Num of the Samoyedes and the god Yum-ala of the Finns, and probably with the name of the god Nam of the Thibetians.

That mysterious people, the Etruscans, who inhabited part of Italy, and whose bronze implements agreed exactly in style and workmanship with those which we think were derived from Atlantis, were, it is now claimed, a branch of the Turanian family.

"At a recent meeting of the English Philological Society great interest was excited by a paper on Etruscan Numerals, by the Rev. Isaac Taylor. He stated that the long-sought key to the Etruscan language had at last been discovered. Two dice had been found in a tomb, with their six faces marked with words instead of pips. He showed that these words were identical with the first six digits in the Altaic branch of the Turanian family of speech. Guided by this clew, it was easy to prove that the grammar and vocabulary of the 3000 Etruscan inscriptions were also Altaic. The words denoting kindred, the pronouns, the conjugations, and the declensions, corresponded closely to those of the Tartar tribes of Siberia. The Etruscan mythology proved to be essentially the same as that of the Kalevala, the great Finnic epic."

According to Lenormant ("Ancient History of the East," vol. i., p. 62; vol. ii., p. 23), the early contests between the Aryans and the Turanians are represented in the Iranian traditions as "contests between hostile brothers ... the Ugro-Finnish races must, according to all appearances, be looked upon as a branch, earlier detached than the others from the Japhetic stem."

If it be true that the first branch originating from Atlantis was the Turanian, which includes the Chinese and Japanese, then we have derived from Atlantis all the building and metalworking races of men who have proved themselves capable of civilization; and we may, therefore, divide mankind into two great classes: those capable of civilization, derived from Atlantis, and those essentially and at all times barbarian, who hold no blood relationship with the people of Atlantis.

Humboldt is sure "that some connection existed between ancient Ethiopia and the elevated plain of Central Asia." There were invasions which reached from the shores of Arabia into China. "An Arabian sovereign, Schamar-Iarasch (Abou Karib), is described by Hamza, Nuwayri, and others as a powerful ruler and conqueror, who carried his arms successfully far into Central Asia; he occupied Samarcand and invaded China. He erected an edifice at Samarcand, bearing an inscription, in Himyarite or Cushite characters, 'In the name of God, Schamar-Iarasch has erected this edifice to the sun, his Lord." (Baldwin's "Prehistoric Nations," p. 110.) These invasions must have been prior to 1518 B.C.

Charles Walcott Brooks read a paper before the California Academy of Sciences, in which he says:

"According to Chinese annals, Tai-Ko-Fokee, the great stranger king, ruled the kingdom of China. In pictures he is represented with two small horns, like those associated with the representations of Moses. He and his successor are said to have introduced into China 'picture-writing,' like that in use in Central America at the time of the Spanish conquest. He taught the motions of the heavenly bodies, and divided time into years and months; he also introduced many other useful arts and sciences.

"Now, there has been found at Copan, in Central America, a figure strikingly like the Chinese symbol of Fokee, with his two horns; and, in like manner, there is a close resemblance between the Central American and the Chinese figures representing earth and heaven. Either one people learned from the other, or both acquired these forms from a common source. Many physico-geographical facts favor the hypothesis that they were derived in very remote ages from America, and that from China they passed to Egypt. Chinese records say that the progenitors of the Chinese race came from across the sea."

The two small horns of Tai-Ko-Fokee and Moses are probably a reminiscence of Baal. We find the horns of Baal represented in the remains of the Bronze Age of Europe. Bel sometimes wore a tiara with his bull's horns; the tiara was the crown subsequently worn by the Persian kings, and it became, in time, the symbol of Papal authority. The Atlanteans having domesticated cattle, and discovered their vast importance to humanity, associated the bull and cow with religious ideas, as revealed in the oldest hymns of the Aryans and the cow-headed idols of Troy, a representation of one of which is shown on the preceding page. Upon the head of their great god Baal they placed the horns of the bull; and these have descended in popular imagination to the spirit of evil of our day. Burns says:

"O thou! whatever title suit thee,

Auld Hornie, Satan, Nick, or Clootie."

"Clootie" is derived from the cleft hoof of a cow; while the Scotch name for a bull is Bill, a corruption, probably, of Bel. Less than two hundred years ago it was customary to sacrifice a bull on the 25th of August to the "God Mowrie" and "his devilans" on the island of Inis Maree, Scotland. ("The Past in the Present," p. 165.) The trident of Poseidon has degenerated into the pitchfork of Beelzebub!

And when we cross the Atlantic, we find in America the horns of Baal reappearing in a singular manner. The first cut on page 429 represents an idol of the Moquis of New Mexico: the head is very bull-like. In the next figure we have a representation of the war-god of the Dakotas, with something like a trident in his hand; while the next illustration is taken from Zarate's "Peru," and depicts "the god of a degrading worship." He is very much like the traditional conception of the European devil-horns, pointed ears, wings, and poker. Compare this last figure, from Peru, with the representation on page 430 of a Greek siren, one of those cruel monsters who, according to Grecian mythology, sat in the midst of bones and blood,

435

tempting men to ruin by their sweet music. Here we have the same bird-like legs and claws as in the Peruvian demon.

Heeren shows that a great overland commerce extended in ancient times between the Black Sea and "Great Mongolia;" he mentions a "Temple of the Sun," and a great caravansary in the desert of Gobi. Arminius Vámbéry, in his "Travels in Central Asia," describes very important ruins near the eastern shore of the Caspian Sea, at a place called Gömüshtepe; and connected with these are the remains of a great wall which he followed "ten geographical miles." He found a vast aqueduct one hundred and fifty miles long, extending to the Persian mountains. He reports abundant ruins in all that country, extending even to China.

The early history of China indicates contact with a superior race. "Fuh-hi, who is regarded as a demi-god, founded the Chinese Empire 2852 B.C. He introduced cattle, taught the people how to raise them, and taught the art of writing." ("American Cyclopædia," art. China.) He might have invented his alphabet, but he did not invent the cattle; he must have got them from some nation who, during many centuries of civilization, had domesticated them; and from what nation was he more likely to have obtained them than from the Atlanteans, whose colonies we have seen reached his borders, and whose armies invaded his territory! "He instituted the ceremony of marriage." (Ibid.) This also was an importation from a civilized land. "His successor, Shin-nung, during a reign of one hundred and forty years, introduced agriculture and medical science. The next emperor, Hwang-ti, is believed to have invented weapons, wagons, ships, clocks, and musical instruments, and to have introduced coins, weights, and measures." (Ibid.) As these various inventions in all other countries have been the result of slow development, running through many centuries, or are borrowed from some other more civilized people, it is certain that no emperor of China ever invented them all during a period of one hundred and sixty-four years. These, then, were also importations from the West. In fact, the Chinese themselves claim to have invaded China in the early days from the north-west; and their first location is placed by Winchell near Lake Balkat, a short distance east of the Caspian, where we have already seen Aryan Atlantean colonies planted at an early day. "The third successor of Fuh-hi, Ti-ku, established schools, and was the first to practise polygamy. In 2357 his son Yau ascended the throne, and it is from his reign that the regular historical records begin. A great flood, which occurred in his reign, has been considered synchronous and identical with the Noachic Deluge, and to Yau is attributed the merit of having successfully battled against the waters."

436

There can be no question that the Chinese themselves, in their early legends, connected their origin with a people who were destroyed by water in a tremendous convulsion of the earth. Associated with this event was a divine personage called Niu-va (Noah?).

Sir William Jones says: "The Chinese believe the earth to have been wholly covered with water, which, in works of undisputed authenticity, they describe as flowing abundantly, then subsiding and separating the higher from the lower ages of mankind; that this division of time, from which their poetical history begins, just preceded the appearance of Fo-hi on the mountains of Chin." ("Discourse on the Chinese; Asiatic Researches," v.ii., p. 376.)

The following history of this destruction of their ancestors vividly recalls to us the convulsion depicted in the Chaldean and American legends: "The pillars of heaven were broken; the earth shook to its very foundations; the heavens sunk lower toward the north; the sun, the moon, and the stars changed their motions; the earth fell to pieces, and the waters enclosed within its bosom burst forth with violence and overflowed it. Man having rebelled against Heaven, the system of the universe was totally disordered. The sun was eclipsed, the planets altered their course, and the grand harmony of nature was disturbed."

A learned Frenchman, M. Terrien de la Couperie, member of the Asiatic Society of Paris, has just published a work (1880) in which he demonstrates the astonishing fact that the Chinese language is clearly related to the Chaldean, and that both the Chinese characters and the cuneiform alphabet are degenerate descendants of an original hieroglyphical alphabet. The same signs exist for many words, while numerous words are very much alike. M. de la Couperie gives a table of some of these similarities, from which I quote as follows:

English. | Chinese. | Chaldee. |

+ | To shine | Mut | Mul. |
+ | To die | Mut | Mit. |
+ | Book | King | Kin. |
+ | Cloth | Sik | Sik. |
+ | Right hand | Dzek | Zag. |
+ | Hero | Tan | Dun. |
+ | Earth | Kien-kai | Kiengi. |
+ | Cow | Lub | Lu, lup. |
+ | Brick | Ku | Ku. |

This surprising discovery brings the Chinese civilization still nearer to the Mediterranean head-quarters of the races, and increases the probability that the arts of China were of Atlantean origin; and that the name of Nai Hoang-ti, or Nai Korti, the founder of Chinese civilization, may be a reminiscence of Nakhunta, the chief of the gods, as recorded in the Susian texts, and this, in turn, a recollection of the Deva-Nahusha of the Hindoos, the Dionysos of the Greeks, the king of Atlantis, whose great empire reached to the "farther parts of India," and embraced, according to Plato, "parts of the continent of America."

Linguistic science achieved a great discovery when it established the fact that there was a continuous belt of languages from Iceland to Ceylon which were the variant forms of one mother-tongue, the Indo-European; but it must prepare itself for a still wider generalization. There is abundant proof—proof with which pages might be filled—that there was a still older mother-tongue, from which Aryan, Semitic, and Hamitic were all derived—the language of Noah, the language of Atlantis, the language of the great "aggressive empire" of Plato, the language of the empire of the Titans.

The Arabic word bin, within, becomes, when it means interval, space, binnon; this is the German and Dutch binnen and Saxon binnon, signifying within. The Ethiopian word aorf, to fall asleep, is the root of the word Morpheus, the god of sleep. The Hebrew word chanah, to dwell, is the parent of the Anglo-Saxon inne and Icelandic inni, a house, and of our word inn, a hotel. The Hebrew word naval or nafal signifies to fall; from it is derived our word fall and fool (one who falls); the Chaldee word is nabal, to make foul, and the Arabic word nabala means to die, that is, to fall. From the last syllable of the Chaldee nasar, to saw, we can derive the Latin serra, the High German sagen, the Danish sauga, and our word to saw. The Arabic nafida, to fade, is the same as the Italian fado, the Latin fatuus (foolish, tasteless), the Dutch vadden, and our to fade. The Ethiopic word gaber, to make, to do, and the Arabic word jabara, to make strong, becomes the Welsh word goberu, to work, to operate, the Latin operor, and the English operate. The Arabic word abara signifies to prick, to sting; we see this root in the Welsh bar, a summit, and pâr, a spear, and per, a spit; whence our word spear. In the Chaldee, Syriac, and Arabic zug means to join, to couple; from this the Greeks obtained zugos, the Romans jugum, and we the word yoke; while the Germans obtained jok or jog, the Dutch juk, the Swedes ok. The Sanscrit is juga. The Arabic sanna, to be old, reappears in the Latin senex, the Welsh hen, and our senile. The Hebrew banah, to build, is the Irish bun, foundation, and the Latin fundo, fundare, to found. The Arabic baraka, to bend the knee, to fall on the breast, is probably the Saxon brecau,

438

the Danish bräkke, the Swedish bräcka, Welsh bregu, and our word to break. The Arabic baraka also signifies to rain violently; and from this we get the Saxon roegn, to rain, Dutch regen, to rain, Cimbric roekia, rain, Welsh rheg, rain. The Chaldee word braic, a branch, is the Irish braic or raigh, an arm, the Welsh braic, the Latin brachium, and the English brace, something which supports like an arm. The Chaldee frak, to rub, to tread out grain, is the same as the Latin frico, frio, and our word rake. The Arabic word to rub is fraka. The Chaldee rag, ragag, means to desire, to long for; it is the same as the Greek oregw, the Latin porrigere, the Saxon roeccan, the Icelandic rakna, the German reichen, and our to reach, to rage. The Arabic rauka, to strain or purify, as wine, is precisely our English word rack, to rack wine. The Hebrew word bara, to create, is our word to bear, as to bear children: a great number of words in all the European languages contain this root in its various modifications. The Hebrew word kafar, to cover, is our word to cover, and coffer, something which covers, and covert, a secret place; from this root also comes the Latin cooperio and the French couvrir, to cover. The Arabic word shakala, to bind under the belly, is our word to shackle. From the Arabic walada and Ethiopian walad, to beget, to bring forth, we get the Welsh llawd, a shooting out; and hence our word lad. Our word matter, or pus, is from the Arabic madda; our word mature is originally from the Chaldee mita. The Arabic word amida signifies to end, and from this comes the noun, a limit, a termination, Latin meta, and our words meet and mete.

I might continue this list, but I have given enough to show that all the Atlantean races once spoke the same language, and that the dispersion on the plains of Shinar signifies that breaking up of the tongues of one people under the operation of vast spaces of time. Philology is yet in its infancy, and the time is not far distant when the identity of the languages of all the Noachic races will be as clearly established and as universally acknowledged as is now the identity of the languages of the Aryan family of nations.

And precisely as recent research has demonstrated the relationship between Pekin and Babylon, so investigation in Central America has proved that there is a mysterious bond of union connecting the Chinese and one of the races of Mexico. The resemblances are so great that Mr. Short ("North Americans of Antiquity," p. 494) says, "There is no doubt that strong analogies exist between the Otomi and the Chinese." Señor Najera ("Dissertacion Sobre la lingua Othomi, Mexico," pp. 87, 88) gives a list of words from which I quote the following:

|Chinese. | Othomi. | English. | Chinese. | Othomi | English. |

—+	Cho	To	The, that.	Pa	Da	To give.	
—+	Y	N-y	A wound.	Tsun	Nsu	Honor.	
—+	Ten	Gu, mu	Head.	Hu	Hmu	Sir, Lord.	
—+	Siao	Sui	Night	Na	Na	That.	
—+	Tien	Tsi	Tooth	Hu	He	Cold.	
—+	Ye	Yo	Shining	Ye	He	And.	
—+	Ky	Hy (ji)	Happiness.	Hoa	Hia	Word.	
—+	Ku	Du	Death	Nugo	Nga	I	
—+	Po	Yo	No	Ni	Nuy	Thou.	
—+	Na	Ta	Man	Hao	Nho	The good.	
—+	Nin	Nsu	Female	Ta	Da	The great.	
—+	Tseu	Tsi, ti	Son	Li	Ti	Gain.	
—+	Tso	Tsa	To perfect	Ho	To	Who.	
—+	Kuan	Khuani	True	Pa	Pa	To leave.	
—+	Siao	Sa	To mock	Mu, mo	Me	Mother.	

Recently Herr Forchhammer, of Leipsic, has published a truly scientific comparison of the grammatical structure of the Choctaw, Chickasaw, Muscogee, and Seminole languages with the Ural-Altaic tongues, in which he has developed many interesting points of resemblance.

It has been the custom to ascribe the recognized similarities between the Indians of America and the Chinese and Japanese to a migration by way of Behring's Strait from Asia into America; but when we find that the Chinese themselves only reached the Pacific coast within the Historical Period, and that they came to it from the direction of the Mediterranean and Atlantis, and when we find so many and such distinct recollections of the destruction of Atlantis in the Flood legends of the American races, it seems more reasonable to conclude that the resemblances between the Othomi and the Chinese are to be accounted for by intercourse through Atlantis.

We find a confirmation in all these facts of the order in which Genesis names the sons of Noah:

"Now these are the generations of the sons of Noah: Shem, Ham, and Japheth, and unto them were sons born after the flood."

Can we not suppose that those three sons represent three great races in the order of their precedence?

The record of Genesis claims that the Phoenicians were descended from Ham, while the Hebrews were descended from Shem; yet we find the Hebrews and Phoenicians united by the ties of a common language, common traditions, and common race characteristics. The Jews are the great merchants of the world eighteen centuries after Christ, just as the Phoenicians were the great merchants of the world fifteen centuries before Christ.

Moreover, the Arabians, who are popularly classed as Semites, or sons of Shem, admit in their traditions that they are descended from "Ad, the son of Ham;" and the tenth chapter of Genesis classes them among the descendants of Ham, calling them Seba, Havilah, Raamah, etc. If the two great so-called Semitic stocks—the Phoenicians and Arabians—are Hamites, surely the third member of the group belongs to the same "sunburnt" race.

If we concede that the Jews were also a branch of the Hamitic stock, then we have, firstly, a Semitic stock, the Turanian, embracing the Etruscans, the Finns, the Tartars, the Mongols, the Chinese, and Japanese; secondly, a Hamitic family, "the sunburnt" race—a red race—including the Cushites, Phoenicians, Egyptians, Hebrews, Berbers, etc.; and, thirdly, a Japhetic or whiter stock, embracing the Greeks, Italians, Celts, Goths, and the men who wrote Sanscrit—in other words, the entire Aryan family.

If we add to these three races the negro race—which cannot be traced back to Atlantis, and is not included, according to Genesis, among the descendants of Noah—we have the four races, the white, red, yellow, and black, recognized by the Egyptians as embracing all the people known to them.

There seems to be some confusion in Genesis as to the Semitic stock. It classes different races as both Semites and Hamites; as, for instance, Sheba and Havilah; while the race of Mash, or Meshech, is classed among the sons of Shem and the sons of Japheth. In fact, there seems to be a confusion of Hamitic and Semitic stocks. "This is shown in the blending of Hamitic and Semitic in some of the most ancient inscriptions; in the facility of intercourse between the Semites of Asia and the Hamites of Egypt; in the peaceful and unobserved absorption of all the Asiatic Hamites, and the Semitic adoption of the Hamitic gods and religious system. It is manifest that, at a period not long previous, the two families had dwelt together and spoken the same language." (Winchell's "Pre-Adamites," p. 36.) Is it not more reasonable to suppose that the so-called Semitic races of Genesis were a mere division of the Hamitic stock, and that we are to look for the third great division of the sons of Noah among the Turanians?

Francis Lenormant, high authority, is of the opinion that the Turanian races are descended from Magog, the son of Japheth. He regards the Turanians as intermediate between the white and yellow races, graduating insensibly into each. "The Uzbecs, the Osmanli Turks, and the Hungarians are not to be distinguished in appearance from the most perfect branches of the white race; on the other hand, the Tchondes almost exactly resemble the Tongouses, who belong to the yellow race.

The Turanian languages are marked by the same agglutinative character found in the American races.

The Mongolian and the Indian are alike in the absence of a heavy beard. The royal color of the Incas was yellow; yellow is the color of the imperial family in China. The religion of the Peruvians was sun-worship; "the sun was the peculiar god of the Mongols from the earliest times." The Peruvians regarded Pachacamac as the sovereign creator. Camac-Hya was the name of a Hindoo goddess. Haylli was the burden of every verse of the song composed in praise of the sun and the Incas. Mr. John Ranking derives the word Allah from the word Haylli, also the word Halle-lujah. In the city of Cuzco was a portion of land which none were permitted to cultivate except those of the royal blood. At certain seasons the Incas turned up the sod here, amid much rejoicing, and many ceremonies. A similar custom prevails in China: The emperor ploughs a few furrows, and twelve illustrious persons attend the plough after him. (Du Halde, "Empire of China," vol. i., p. 275.) The cycle of sixty years was in use among most of the nations of Eastern Asia, and among the Muyscas of the elevated plains of Bogota. The "quipu," a knotted reckoning-cord, was in use in Peru and in China. (Bancroft's "Native Races," vol. v., p. 48.) In Peru and China "both use hieroglyphics, which are read from above downward." (Ibid.)

"It appears most evident to me," says Humboldt, "that the monuments, methods of computing time, systems of cosmogony, and many myths of America, offer striking analogies with the ideas of Eastern Asia—analogies which indicate an ancient communication, and are not simply the result of that uniform condition in which all nations are found in the dawn of civilization." ("Exam. Crit.," tom. ii., p. 68.)

"In the ruined cities of Cambodia, which lies farther to the east of Burmah, recent research has discovered teocallis like those in Mexico, and the remains of temples of the same type and pattern as those of Yucatan. And when we reach the sea we encounter at Suku, in Java, a teocalli which is absolutely identical with that of Tehuantepec. Mr. Ferguson said, 'as we advance eastward from the valley of the Euphrates, at every step we meet with forms of art becoming more and more like those of Central America.'" ("Builders of Babel," p. 88.)

Prescott says:

"The coincidences are sufficiently strong to authorize a belief that the civilization of Anahuac was in some degree influenced by that of Eastern Asia; and, secondly, that the discrepancies are such as to carry back the communication to a very remote period." ("Mexico," vol. iii., p. 418.)

"All appearances," continues Lenormant ("Ancient History of the East," vol. i., p. 64), "would lead us to regard the Turanian race as the first branch of the family of Japheth which went forth into the world; and by that premature separation, by an isolated and antagonistic existence, took, or rather preserved, a completely distinct physiognomy.... It is a type of the white race imperfectly developed."

We may regard this yellow race as the first and oldest wave from Atlantis, and, therefore, reaching farthest away from the common source; then came the Hamitic race; then the Japhetic.

CHAPTER IX. THE ANTIQUITY OF SOME OF OUR GREAT INVENTIONS.

It may seem like a flight of the imagination to suppose that the mariner's compass was known to the inhabitants of Atlantis. And yet, if my readers are satisfied that the Atlantean were a highly civilized maritime people, carrying on commerce with regions as far apart as Peru and Syria, we must conclude that they possessed some means of tracing their course in the great seas they traversed; and accordingly, when we proceed to investigate this subject, we find that as far back as we may go in the study of the ancient races of the world, we find them possessed of a knowledge of the virtues of the magnetic stone, and in the habit of utilizing it. The people of Europe, rising a few centuries since out of a state of semi-barbarism, have been in the habit of claiming the invention of many things which they simply borrowed from the older nations. This was the case with the mariner's compass. It was believed for many years that it was first invented by an Italian named Amalfi, A.D. 1302. In that interesting work, Goodrich's "Life of Columbus," we find a curious history of the magnetic compass prior to that time, from which we collate the following points:

"In A.D. 868 it was employed by the Northmen." ("The Landnamabok," vol. i., chap. 2.) An Italian poem of A.D. 1190 refers to it as in use among the

Italian sailors at that date. In the ancient language of the Hindoos, the Sanscrit—which has been a dead language for twenty-two hundred years—the magnet was called "the precious stone beloved of Iron." The Talmud speaks of it as "the stone of attraction;" and it is alluded to in the early Hebrew prayers as Kalamitah, the same name given it by the Greeks, from the reed upon which the compass floated. The Phoenicians were familiar with the use of the magnet. At the prow of their vessels stood the figure of a woman (Astarte) holding a cross in one hand and pointing the way with the other; the cross represented the compass, which was a magnetized needle, floating in water crosswise upon a piece of reed or wood. The cross became the coat of arms of the Phoenicians—not only, possibly, as we have shown, as a recollection of the four rivers of Atlantis, but because it represented the secret of their great sea-voyages, to which they owed their national greatness. The hyperborean magician, Abaras, carried "a guiding arrow," which Pythagoras gave him, "in order that it may be useful to him in all difficulties in his long journey." ("Herodotus," vol. iv., p. 36.)

The magnet was called the "Stone of Hercules." Hercules was the patron divinity of the Phoenicians. He was, as we have shown elsewhere, one of the gods of Atlantis—probably one of its great kings and navigators. The Atlanteans were, as Plato tells us, a maritime, commercial people, trading up the Mediterranean as far as Egypt and Syria, and across the Atlantic to "the whole opposite continent that surrounds the sea;" the Phoenicians, as their successors and descendants, and colonized on the shores of the Mediterranean, inherited their civilization and their maritime habits, and with these that invention without which their great voyages were impossible. From them the magnet passed to the Hindoos, and from them to the Chinese, who certainly possessed it at an early date. In the year 2700 B.C. the Emperor Wang-ti placed a magnetic figure with an extended arm, like the Astarte of the Phoenicians, on the front of carriages, the arm always turning and pointing to the south, which the Chinese regarded as the principal pole. (See Goodrich's "Columbus," p. 31, etc.) This illustration represents one of these chariots:

In the seventh century it was used by the navigators of the Baltic Sea and the German Ocean.

The ancient Egyptians called the loadstone the bone of Haroeri, and iron the bone of Typhon. Haroeri was the son of Osiris and grandson of Rhea, a goddess of the earth, a queen of Atlantis, and mother of Poseidon; Typhon was a wind-god and an evil genius, but also a son of Rhea, the earth goddess. Do we find in this curious designation of iron and loadstone as "bones of the descendants of the earth," an explanation of that otherwise

444

inexplicable Greek legend about Deucalion "throwing the bones of the earth behind him, when instantly men rose from the ground, and the world was repeopled?" Does it mean that by means of the magnet he sailed, after the Flood, to the European colonies of Atlantis, already thickly inhabited?

A late writer, speaking upon the subject of the loadstone, tells us:

"Hercules, it was said, being once overpowered by the heat of the sun, drew his bow against that luminary; whereupon the god Phoebus, admiring his intrepidity, gave him a golden cup, with which he sailed over the ocean. This cup was the compass, which old writers have called Lapis Heracleus. Pisander says Oceanus lent him the cup, and Lucian says it was a sea-shell. Tradition affirms that the magnet originally was not on a pivot, but set to float on water in a cup. The old antiquarian is wildly theoretical on this point, and sees a compass in the Golden Fleece of Argos, in the oracular needle which Nero worshipped, and in everything else. Yet undoubtedly there are some curious facts connected with the matter. Osonius says that Gama and the Portuguese got the compass from some pirates at the Cape of Good Hope, A.D. 1260. M. Fauchet, the French antiquarian, finds it plainly alluded to in some old poem of Brittany belonging to the year A.D. 1180. Paulo Venetus brought it in the thirteenth century from China, where it was regarded as oracular. Genebrand says Melvius, a Neapolitan, brought it to Europe in A.D. 1303. Costa says Gama got it from Mohammedan seamen. But all nations with whom it was found associate it with regions where Heraclean myths prevailed. And one of the most curious facts is that the ancient Britons, as the Welsh do to-day, call a pilot llywydd (lode). Lodemanage, in Skinner's 'Etymology,' is the word for the price paid to a pilot. But whether this famous, and afterward deified, mariner (Hercules) had a compass or not, we can hardly regard the association of his name with so many Western monuments as accidental."

Hercules was, as we know, a god of Atlantis, and Oceanos, who lent the magnetic cup to Hercules, was the name by which the Greeks designated the Atlantic Ocean. And this may be the explanation of the recurrence of a cup in many antique paintings and statues. Hercules is often represented with a cup in his hand; we even find the cup upon the handle of the bronze dagger found in Denmark, and represented in the chapter on the Bronze Age, in this work. (See p. 254 ante.)

So "oracular" an object as this self-moving needle, always pointing to the north, would doubtless affect vividly the minds of the people, and appear in their works of art. When Hercules left the coast of Europe to sail to the island of Erythea in the Atlantic, in the remote west, we are told, in

Greek mythology (Murray, p. 257), that he borrowed "the cup" of Helios, in (with) which "he was accustomed to sail every night." Here we seem to have a reference to the magnetic cup used in night sailing; and this is another proof that the use of the magnetic needle in sea-voyages was associated with the Atlantean gods.

Lucian tells us that a sea-shell often took the place of the cup, as a vessel in which to hold the water where the needle floated, and hence upon the ancient coins of Tyre we find a sea-shell represented.

Here, too, we have the Pillars of Hercules, supposed to have been placed at the mouth of the Mediterranean, and the tree of life or knowledge, with the serpent twined around it, which appears in Genesis; and in the combination of the two pillars and the serpent we have, it is said, the original source of our dollar mark [$].

Compare these Phoenician coins with the following representation of a copper coin, two inches in diameter and three lines thick, found nearly a century ago by Ordonez, at the city of Guatemala. "M. Dupaix noticed an indication of the use of the compass in the centre of one of the sides, the figures on the same side representing a kneeling, bearded, turbaned man between two fierce heads, perhaps of crocodiles, which appear to defend the entrance to a mountainous and wooded country. The reverse presents a serpent coiled around a fruit-tree, and an eagle on a hill." (Bancroft's "Native Races," vol. iv., p. 118.) The mountain leans to one side: it is a "culhuacan," or crooked mountain.

We find in Sanchoniathon's "Legends of the Phoenicians" that Ouranus, the first god of the people of Atlantis, "devised Bætulia, contriving stones that moved as having life, which were supposed to fall from heaven." These stones were probably magnetic loadstones; in other words, Ouranus, the first god of Atlantis, devised the mariner's compass.

I find in the "Report of United States Explorations for a Route for a Pacific Railroad" a description of a New Mexican Indian priest, who foretells the result of a proposed war by placing a piece of wood in a bowl of water, and causing it to turn to the right or left, or sink or rise, as he directs it. This is incomprehensible, unless the wood, like the ancient Chinese compass, contained a piece of magnetic iron hidden in it, which would be attracted or repulsed, or even drawn downward, by a piece of iron held in the hand of the priest, on the outside of the bowl. If so, this trick was a remembrance of the mariner's compass transmitted from age to age by the medicine men. The reclining statue of Chac-Mol, of Central America, holds a bowl or dish upon its breast.

Divination was the ars Etrusca. The Etruscans set their temples squarely with the cardinal points of the compass; so did the Egyptians, the Mexicans, and the Mound Builders of America. Could they have done this without the magnetic compass?

The Romans and the Persians called the line of the axis of the globe cardo, and it was to cardo the needle pointed. Now "Cardo was the name of the mountain on which the human race took refuge from the Deluge... the primitive geographic point for the countries which were the cradle of the human race." (Urquhart's "Pillars of Hercules," vol. i., p. 145.) From this comes our word "cardinal," as the cardinal points.

Navigation.—Navigation was not by any means in a rude state in the earliest times:

"In the wanderings of the heroes returning from Troy, Aristoricus makes Menelaus circumnavigate Africa more than 500 years before Neco sailed from Gadeira to India." ("Cosmos," vol. ii., p. 144.)

"In the tomb of Rameses the Great is a representation of a naval combat between the Egyptians and some other people, supposed to be the Phoenicians, whose huge ships are propelled by sails." (Goodrich's "Columbus," p. 29.)

The proportions of the fastest sailing-vessels of the present day are about 300 feet long to 50 wide and 30 high; these were precisely the proportions of Noah's ark—300 cubits long, 50 broad, and 30 high.

"Hiero of Syracuse built, under the superintendence of Archimedes, a vessel which consumed in its construction the material for fifty galleys; it contained galleries, gardens, stables, fish-ponds, mills, baths, a temple of Venus, and an engine to throw stones three hundred pounds in weight, and arrows thirty-six feet long. The floors of this monstrous vessel were inlaid with scenes from Homer's 'Iliad.'" (Ibid., p. 30.)

The fleet of Sesostris consisted of four hundred ships; and when

Semiramis invaded India she was opposed by four thousand vessels.

It is probable that in the earliest times the vessels were sheeted with metal. A Roman ship of the time of Trajan has been recovered from Lake Ricciole after 1300 years. The outside was covered with sheets of lead fastened with small copper nails. Even the use of iron chains in place of ropes for the anchors was known at an early period. Julius Cæsar tells us that the galleys of the Veneti were thus equipped. (Goodrich's "Columbus," p. 31.)

Gunpowder.—It is not impossible that even the invention of gunpowder may date back to Atlantis. It was certainly known in Europe long before the

447

time of the German monk, Berthold Schwarz, who is commonly credited with the invention of it. It was employed in 1257 at the siege of Niebla, in Spain. It was described in an Arab treatise of the thirteenth century. In A.D. 811 the Emperor Leo employed fire-arms. "Greek-fire" is supposed to have been gunpowder mixed with resin or petroleum, and thrown in the form of fuses and explosive shells. It was introduced from Egypt A.D. 668. In A.D. 690 the Arabs used fire-arms against Mecca, bringing the knowledge of them from India. In A.D. 80 the Chinese obtained from India a knowledge of gunpowder. There is reason to believe that the Carthaginian (Phoenician) general, Hannibal, used gunpowder in breaking a way for his army over the Alps. The Romans, who were ignorant of its use, said that Hannibal made his way by making fires against the rocks, and pouring vinegar and water over the ashes. It is evident that fire and vinegar would have no effect on masses of the Alps great enough to arrest the march of an army. Dr. William Maginn has suggested that the wood was probably burnt by Hannibal to obtain charcoal; and the word which has been translated "vinegar" probably signified some preparation of nitre and sulphur, and that Hannibal made gunpowder and blew up the rocks. The same author suggests that the story of Hannibal breaking loose from the mountains where he was surrounded on all sides by the Romans, and in danger of starvation, by fastening firebrands to the horns of two thousand oxen, and sending them rushing at night among the terrified Romans, simply refers to the use of rockets. As Maginn well asks, how could Hannibal be in danger of starvation when he had two thousand oxen to spare for such an experiment? And why should the veteran Roman troops have been so terrified and panic-stricken by a lot of cattle with firebrands on their horns? At the battle of Lake Trasymene, between Hannibal and Flaminius, we have another curious piece of information which goes far to confirm the belief that Hannibal was familiar with the use of gunpowder. In the midst of the battle there was, say the Roman historians, an "earthquake;" the earth reeled under the feet of the soldiers, a tremendous crash was heard, a fog or smoke covered the scene, the earth broke open, and the rocks fell upon the heads of the Romans. This reads very much as if the Carthaginians had decoyed the Romans into a pass where they had already planted a mine, and had exploded it at the proper moment to throw them into a panic. Earthquakes do not cast rocks up in the air to fall on men's heads!

And that this is not all surmise is shown by the fact that a city of India, in the time of Alexander the Great, defended itself by the use of gunpowder: it was said to be a favorite of the gods, because thunder and lightning came from its walls to resist the attacks of its assailants.

As the Hebrews were a branch of the Phoenician race, it is not surprising that we find some things in their history which look very much like legends of gunpowder.

When Korah, Dathan, and Abiram led a rebellion against Moses, Moses separated the faithful from the unfaithful, and thereupon "the ground clave asunder that was under them: and the earth opened her mouth, and swallowed them up, and their houses, and all the men that appertained unto Korah, and all their goods.... And there came out a fire from the Lord, and consumed the two hundred and fifty men that offered incense.... But on the morrow all the congregation of the children of Israel murmured against Moses and against Aaron, saying, Ye have killed the people of the Lord." (Numb. xvi., 31-41.)

This looks very much as if Moses had blown up the rebels with gunpowder.

Roger Bacon, who himself rediscovered gunpowder, was of opinion that the event described in Judges vii., where Gideon captured the camp of the Midianites with the roar of trumpets, the crash caused by the breaking of innumerable pitchers, and the flash of a multitude of lanterns, had reference to the use of gunpowder; that the noise made by the breaking of the pitchers represented the detonation of an explosion, the flame of the lights the blaze, and the noise of the trumpets the thunder of the gunpowder. We can understand, in this wise, the results that followed; but we cannot otherwise understand how the breaking of pitchers, the flashing of lamps, and the clangor of trumpets would throw an army into panic, until "every man's sword was set against his fellow, and the host fled to Beth-shittah;" and this, too, without any attack upon the part of the Israelites, for "they stood every man in his place around the camp; and all the host ran and cried and fled."

If it was a miraculous interposition in behalf of the Jews, the Lord could have scared the Midianites out of their wits without the smashed pitchers and lanterns; and certain it is the pitchers and lanterns would not have done the work with out a miraculous interposition.

Having traced the knowledge of gunpowder back to the most remote times, and to the different races which were descended from Atlantis, we are not surprised to find in the legends of Greek mythology events described which are only explicable by supposing that the Atlanteans possessed the secret of this powerful explosive.

A rebellion sprang up in Atlantis (see Murray's "Mannal of Mythology," p. 30) against Zeus; it is known in mythology as the "War of the Titans:"

449

"The struggle lasted many years, all the might which the Olympians could bring to bear being useless, until, on the advice of Gæa, Zeus set free the Kyklopes and the Hekatoncheires" (that is, brought the ships into play), "of whom the former fashioned thunder-bolts for him, while the latter advanced on his side with force equal to the shock of an earthquake. The earth trembled down to lowest Tartarus as Zeus now appeared with his terrible weapon and new allies. Old Chaos thought his hour had come, as from a continuous blaze of thunder-bolts the earth took fire, and the waters seethed in the sea. The rebels were partly slain or consumed, and partly hurled into deep chasms, with rocks and hills reeling after them."

Do not these words picture the explosion of a mine with a "force equal to the shock of an earthquake?"

We have already shown that the Kyklopes and Hekatoncheires were probably great war-ships, armed with some explosive material in the nature of gunpowder.

Zeus, the king of Atlantis, was known as "the thunderer," and was represented armed with thunder-bolts.

Some ancient nation must, in the most remote ages, have invented gunpowder; and is it unreasonable to attribute it to that "great original race" rather than to any one people of their posterity, who seem to have borrowed all the other arts from them; and who, during many thousands of years, did not add a single new invention to the list they received from Atlantis?

Iron.—have seen that the Greek mythological legends asserted that before the submergence of the great race over whom their gods reigned there had been not only an Age of Bronze but an Age of Iron. This metal was known to the Egyptians in the earliest ages; fragments of iron have been found in the oldest pyramids. The Iron Age in Northern Europe far antedated intercourse with the Greeks or Romans. In the mounds of the Mississippi Valley, as I have shown, the remains of iron implements have been found. In the "Mercurio Peruano" (tom. i., p. 201, 1791) it is stated that "anciently the Peruvian sovereigns worked magnificent iron mines at Ancoriames, on the west shore of Lake Titicaca." "It is remarkable," says Molina, "that iron, which has been thought unknown to the ancient Americans, had particular names in some of their tongues." In official Peruvian it was called quillay, and in Chilian panilic. The Mound Builders fashioned implements out of meteoric iron. (Foster's "Prehistoric Races," p. 333.)

As we find this metal known to man in the earliest ages on both sides of the Atlantic, the presumption is very strong that it was borrowed by the nations, east and west, from Atlantis.

Paper.—The same argument holds good as to paper. The oldest Egyptian monuments contain pictures of the papyrus roll; while in Mexico, as I have shown, a beautiful paper was manufactured and formed into books shaped like our own. In Peru a paper was made of plantain leaves, and books were common in the earlier ages. Humboldt mentions books of hieroglyphical writings among the Panoes, which were "bundles of their paper resembling our volumes in quarto."

Silk Mannfacture.—The manufacture of a woven fabric of great beauty out of the delicate fibre of the egg-cocoon of a worm could only have originated among a people who had attained the highest degree of civilization; it implies the art of weaving by delicate instruments, a dense population, a patient, skilful, artistic people, a sense of the beautiful, and a wealthy and luxurious class to purchase such costly fabrics.

We trace it back to the most remote ages. In the introduction to the "History of Hindostan," or rather of the Mohammedan Dynasties, by Mohammed Cassim, it is stated that in the year 3870 B.C. an Indian king sent various silk stuffs as a present to the King of Persia. The art of making silk was known in China more than two thousand six hundred years before the Christian era, at the time when we find them first possessed of civilization. The Phoenicians dealt in silks in the most remote past; they imported them from India and sold them along the shores of the Mediterranean. It is probable that the Egyptians understood and practised the art of manufacturing silk. It was woven in the island of Cos in the time of Aristotle. The "Babylonish garment" referred to in Joshua (chap. vii., 21), and for secreting which Achan lost his life, was probably a garment of silk; it was rated above silver and gold in value.

It is not a violent presumption to suppose that an art known to the Hindoos 3870 B.C., and to the Chinese and Phoenicians at the very beginning of their history—an art so curious, so extraordinary—may have dated back to Atlantean times.

Civil Government.—Mr. Baldwin shows ("Prehistoric Nations," p. 114) that the Cushites, the successors of the Atlanteans, whose very ancient empire extended from Spain to Syria, were the first to establish independent municipal republics, with the right of the people to govern themselves; and that this system was perpetuated in the great Phoenician communities; in "the fierce democracies" of ancient Greece; in the "village republics" of the African Berbers and the Hindoos; in the "free cities" of the Middle Ages in Europe; and in the independent governments of the Basques, which continued down to our own day. The Cushite state was an aggregation of municipalities, each possessing the right of self-government, but subject within prescribed limits to a general authority; in other words, it was precisely the form of government possessed to-day by the United States. It is a surprising thought that the perfection of modern government may be another perpetuation of Atlantean civilization.

Agriculture.—The Greek traditions of "the golden apples of the Hesperides" and "the golden fleece" point to Atlantis. The allusions to the golden apples indicate that tradition regarded the "Islands of the Blessed" in the Atlantic Ocean as a place of orchards. And when we turn to Egypt we find that in the remotest times many of our modern garden and field plants were there cultivated. When the Israelites murmured in the wilderness against Moses, they cried out (Numb., chap. xi., 4, 5), "Who shall give us flesh to eat? We remember the fish which we did eat in Egypt freely; the cucumbers, and the melons, and the leeks, and the onions, and the garlic." The Egyptians also cultivated wheat, barley, oats, flax, hemp, etc. In fact, if we were to take away from civilized man the domestic animals, the cereals, and the field and garden vegetables possessed by the Egyptians at the very dawn of history, there would be very little left for the granaries or the tables of the world.

Astronomy.—The knowledge of the ancients as to astronomy was great and accurate. Callisthenes, who accompanied Alexander the Great to Babylon, sent to Aristotle a series of Chaldean astronomical observations which he found preserved there, recorded on tablets of baked clay, and extending back as far as 2234 B.C. Humboldt says, "The Chaldeans knew the mean motions of the moon with an exactness which induced the Greek astronomers to use their calculations for the foundation of a lunar theory." The Chaldeans knew the true nature of comets, and could foretell their reappearance. "A lens of considerable power was found in the ruins of Babylon; it was an inch and a half in diameter and nine-tenths of an inch thick." (Layard's "Nineveh and Babylon," pp. 16, 17.) Nero used optical glasses when he watched the fights of the gladiators; they are supposed to have come from Egypt and the East. Plutarch speaks of optical instruments used by Archimedes "to manifest to the eye the largeness of the sun." "There are actual astronomical calculations in existence, with calendars formed upon them, which eminent astronomers of England and France admit to be genuine and true, and which carry back the antiquity of the science of astronomy, together with the constellations, to within a few years of the

Deluge, even on the longer chronology of the Septuagint." ("The Miracle in Stone," p. 142.) Josephus attributes the invention of the constellations to the family of the antediluvian Seth, the son of Adam, while Origen affirms that it was asserted in the Book of Enoch that in the time of that patriarch the constellations were already divided and named. The Greeks associated the origin of astronomy with Atlas and Hercules, Atlantean kings or heroes. The Egyptians regarded Taut (At?) or Thoth, or At-hotes, as the originator of both astronomy and the alphabet; doubtless he represented a civilized people, by whom their country was originally colonized. Bailly and others assert that astronomy "must have been established when the summer solstice was in the first degree of Virgo, and that the solar and lunar zodiacs were of similar antiquity, which would be about four thousand years before the Christian era. They suppose the originators to have lived in about the fortieth degree of north latitude, and to have been a highly-civilized people." It will be remembered that the fortieth degree of north latitude passed through Atlantis. Plato knew ("Dialogues, Phædo," 108) that the earth "is a body in the centre of the heavens" held in equipoise. He speaks of it as a "round body," a "globe;" he even understood that it revolved on its axis, and that these revolutions produced day and night. He says—"Dialogues, Timæus"—"The earth circling around the pole (which is extended through the universe) be made to be the artificer of night and day." All this Greek learning was probably drawn from the Egyptians.

Only among the Atlanteans in Europe and America do we find traditions preserved as to the origin of all the principal inventions which have raised man from a savage to a civilized condition. We can give in part the very names of the inventors.

Starting with the Chippeway legends, and following with the Bible and Phoenician records, we make a table like the appended:

The Invention or Discovery.	The Race.	The Inventors.
Fire	Atlantean	Phos, Phur, and Phlox.
The bow and arrow	**Chippeway**	Manaboshu.
The use of flint	"	"	+
The use of copper	"	"	
The manufacture of bricks	**Atlantean**	Autochthon and Technites.
Agriculture and hunting	"	Argos and Agrotes.

453

| Village life, and the | " | Amynos and Magos. | | rearing of flocks
| The use of salt | " | Misor and Sydyk.
| The use of letters | " | Taautos, or Taut.
| Navigation | " | The Cabiri, or Corybantes.
| The art of music | **Hebrew** | Jubal.
| Metallurgy, and the use of | " | Tubal-cain. | | iron
| The syrinx | **Greek** | Pan.
| The lyre | " | Hermes.

We cannot consider all these evidences of the vast antiquity of the great inventions upon which our civilization mainly rests, including the art of writing, which, as I have shown, dates back far beyond the beginning of history; we cannot remember that the origin of all the great food-plants, such as wheat, oats, barley, rye, and maize, is lost in the remote past; and that all the domesticated animals, the horse, the ass, the ox, the sheep, the goat, and the hog had been reduced to subjection to man in ages long previous to written history, without having the conclusion forced upon us irresistibly that beyond Egypt and Greece, beyond Chaldea and China, there existed a mighty civilization, of which these states were but the broken fragments.

CHAPTER X. THE ARYAN COLONIES FROM ATLANTIS.

We come now to another question: "Did the Aryan or Japhetic race come from Atlantis?"

If the Aryans are the Japhetic race, and if Japheth was one of the sons of the patriarch who escaped from the Deluge, then assuredly, if the tradition of Genesis be true, the Aryans came from the drowned land, to wit, Atlantis. According to Genesis, the descendants of the Japheth who escaped out of the Flood with Noah are the Ionians, the inhabitants of the Morea, the dwellers on the Cilician coast of Asia Minor, the Cyprians, the Dodoneans of Macedonia, the Iberians, and the Thracians. These are all now recognized as Aryans, except the Iberians.

"From non-Biblical sources," says Winchell, "we obtain further information respecting the early dispersion of the Japhethites or Indo-Europeans—called also Aryans. All determinations confirm the Biblical account of their primitive residence in the same country with the Hamites and Semites. Rawlinson informs us that even Aryan roots are mingled with Presemitic in some of the old inscriptions of Assyria. The precise region where these three families dwelt in a common home has not been pointed out." ("Preadamites," p. 43.)

I have shown in the chapter in relation to Peru that all the languages of the Hamites, Semites, and Japhethites are varieties of one aboriginal speech.

The centre of the Aryan migrations (according to popular opinion) within the Historical Period was Armenia. Here too is Mount Ararat, where it is said the ark rested—another identification with the Flood regions, as it represents the usual transfer of the Atlantis legend by an Atlantean people to a high mountain in their new home.

Now turn to a map: Suppose the ships of Atlantis to have reached the shores of Syria, at the eastern end of the Mediterranean, where dwelt a people who, as we have seen, used the Central American Maya alphabet; the Atlantis ships are then but two hundred miles distant from Armenia. But these ships need not stop at Syria, they can go by the Dardanelles and the Black Sea, by uninterrupted water communication, to the shores of Armenia itself. If we admit, then, that it was from Armenia the Aryans stocked Europe and India, there is no reason why the original population of Armenia should not have been themselves colonists from Atlantis.

But we have seen that in the earliest ages, before the first Armenian migration of the historical Aryans, a people went from Iberian Spain and settled in Ireland, and the language of this people, it is now admitted, is Aryan. And these Iberians were originally, according to tradition, from the West.

The Mediterranean Aryans are known to have been in Southeastern Europe, along the shores of the Mediterranean, 2000 B.C. They at that early date possessed the plough; also wheat, rye, barley, gold, silver, and bronze. Aryan faces are found depicted upon the monuments of Egypt, painted four thousand years before the time of Christ. "The conflicts between the Kelts (an Aryan race) and the Iberians were far anterior in date to the settlements of the Phoenicians, Greeks, Carthaginians, and Noachites on the coasts of the Mediterranean Sea." ("American Cyclopædia," art. Basques.) There is reason to believe that these Kelts were originally part of the population and Empire of Atlantis. We are told (Rees's "British Encyclopædia," art. Titans) that "Mercury, one of the Atlantean gods, was placed as ruler over the Celtæ, and became their great divinity." F. Pezron, in his "Antiquity of the Celtæ," makes out that the Celtæ were the same as the Titans, the giant race who rebelled in Atlantis, and "that their princes were the same with the giants of Scripture." He adds that the word Titan "is perfect Celtic, and comes from tit, the earth, and ten or den, man, and hence the Greeks very properly also called them terriginæ, or earth-born." And it will be remembered that Plato uses the same phrase when he speaks of the race into which Poseidon intermarried as "the earth-born primeval men of that country."

The Greeks, who are Aryans, traced their descent from the people who were destroyed by the Flood, as did other races clearly Aryan.

"The nations who are comprehended under the common appellation of Indo-European," says Max Müller—"the Hindoos, the Persians, the Celts, Germans, Romans, Greeks, and Slavs—do not only share the same words and the same grammar, slightly modified in each country, but they seem to have likewise preserved a mass of popular traditions which had grown up before they left their common home."

"Bonfey, L. Geiger, and other students of the ancient Indo-European languages, have recently advanced the opinion that the original home of the Indo-European races must be sought in Europe, because their stock of words is rich in the names of plants and animals, and contains names of seasons that are not found in tropical countries or anywhere in Asia." ("American Cyclopædia," art. Ethnology.)

By the study of comparative philology, or the seeking out of the words common to the various branches of the Aryan race before they separated, we are able to reconstruct an outline of the civilization of that ancient people. Max Müller has given this subject great study, and availing ourselves of his researches we can determine the following facts as to the progenitors of the Aryan stock: They were a civilized race; they possessed the institution of marriage; they recognized the relationship of father, mother, son, daughter, grandson, brother, sister, mother-in-law, father-in-law, son-in-law, daughter-in-law, brother-in-law, and sister-in-law, and had separate words for each of these relationships, which we are only able to express by adding the words "in-law." They recognized also the condition of widows, or "the husbandless." They lived in an organized society, governed by a king. They possessed houses with doors and solid walls. They had wagons and carriages. They possessed family names. They dwelt in towns and cities, on highways. They were not hunters or nomads. They were a peaceful people; the warlike words in the different Aryan languages cannot be traced back to this original race. They lived in a country having few wild beasts; the only wild animals whose names can be assigned to this parent stock being the bear, the wolf, and the serpent. The name of the elephant, "the beast with a hand," occurs only twice in the "Rig-Veda;" a singular omission if the Aryans were from time immemorial an Asiatic race;

and "when it does occur, it is in such a way as to show that he was still an object of wonder and terror to them." (Whitney's "Oriental and Linguistic Studies," p. 26.) They possessed nearly all the domestic animals we now have—the ox and the cow, the horse, the dog, the sheep, the goat, the hog, the donkey, and the goose. They divided the year into twelve months. They were farmers; they used the plough; their name as a race (Aryan) was derived from it; they were, par excellence, ploughmen; they raised various kinds of grain, including flax, barley, hemp, and wheat; they had mills and millers, and ground their corn. The presence of millers shows that they had proceeded beyond the primitive condition where each family ground its corn in its own mill. They used fire, and cooked and baked their food; they wove cloth and wore clothing; they spun wool; they possessed the different metals, even iron: they had gold. The word for "water" also meant "salt made from water," from which it might be inferred that the water with which they were familiar was saltwater. It is evident they manufactured salt by evaporating salt water. They possessed boats and ships. They had progressed so far as to perfect "a decimal system of enumeration, in itself," says Max Müller, "one of the most marvellous achievements of the human mind, based on an abstract conception of quantity, regulated by a philosophical classification, and yet conceived, nurtured, and finished before the soil of Europe was trodden by Greek, Roman, Slav, or Teuton."

And herein we find another evidence of relationship between the Aryans and the people of Atlantis. Although Plato does not tell us that the Atlanteans possessed the decimal system of numeration, nevertheless there are many things in his narrative which point to that conclusion "There were ten kings ruling over ten provinces; the whole country was divided into military districts or squares ten stadia each way; the total force of chariots was ten thousand; the great ditch or canal was one hundred feet deep and ten thousand stadia long; there were one hundred Nereids," etc. In the Peruvian colony the decimal system clearly obtained: "The army had heads of ten, fifty, a hundred, five hundred, a thousand, ten thousand.... The community at large was registered in groups, under the control of officers over tens, fifties, hundreds, and so on." (Herbert Spencer, "Development of Political Institutions," chap. x.) The same division into tens and hundreds obtained among the Anglo-Saxons.

Where, we ask, could this ancient nation, which existed before Greek was Greek, Celt was Celt, Hindoo was Hindoo, or Goth was Goth, have been located! The common opinion says, in Armenia or Bactria, in Asia. But where in Asia could they have found a country so peaceful as to know no terms for war or bloodshed—a country so civilized as to possess no wild beasts save the bear, wolf, and serpent? No people could have been developed in Asia without bearing in its language traces of century-long battles for life with the rude and barbarous races around them; no nation could have fought for ages for existence against "man-eating" tigers, lions, elephants, and hyenas, without bearing the memory of these things in their tongue. A tiger, identical with that of Bengal, still exists around Lake Aral, in Asia; from time to time it is seen in Siberia. "The last tiger killed in 1828 was on the Lena, in latitude fifty-two degrees thirty minutes, in a climate colder than that of St. Petersburg and Stockholm."

The fathers of the Aryan race must have dwelt for many thousand years so completely protected from barbarians and wild beasts that they at last lost all memory of them, and all words descriptive of them; and where could this have been possible save in some great, long-civilized land, surrounded by the sea, and isolated from the attack of the savage tribes that occupied the rest of the world? And if such a great civilized nation had dwelt for centuries in Asia, Europe, or Africa, why have not their monuments long ago been discovered and identified? Where is the race who are their natural successors, and who must have continued to live after them in that sheltered and happy land, where they knew no human and scarcely any animal enemies? Why would any people have altogether left such a home? Why, when their civilization had spread to the ends of the earth, did it cease to exist in the peaceful region where it originated?

Savage nations cannot usually count beyond five. This people had names for the numerals up to one hundred, and the power, doubtless, of combining these to still higher powers, as three hundred, five hundred, ten hundred, etc. Says a high authority, "If any more proof were wanted as to the reality of that period which must have preceded the dispersion of the Aryan race, we might appeal to the Aryan numerals as irrefragable evidence of that long-continued intellectual life which characterizes that period." Such a degree of progress implies necessarily an alphabet, writing, commerce, and trade, even as the existence of words for boats and ships has already implied navigation.

In what have we added to the civilization of this ancient people? Their domestic animals were the same as our own, except one fowl adopted from America. In the past ten thousand years we have added one bird to their list of domesticated animals! They raised wheat and wool, and spun and wove as we do, except that we have added some mechanical contrivances to produce the same results. Their metals are ours. Even iron, the triumph, as we had supposed, of more modern times, they had already discovered. And it must not be forgotten that Greek mythology tells us that the god-like race

458

who dwelt on Olympus, that great island "in the midst of the Atlantic," in the remote west, wrought in iron; and we find the remains of an iron sword and meteoric iron weapons in the mounds of the Mississippi Valley, while the name of the metal is found in the ancient languages of Peru and Chili, and the Incas worked in iron on the shores of Lake Titicaca.

A still further evidence of the civilization of this ancient race is found in the fact that, before the dispersion from their original home, the Aryans had reached such a degree of development that they possessed a regularly organized religion: they worshipped God, they believed in an evil spirit, they believed in a heaven for the just. All this presupposes temples, priests, sacrifices, and an orderly state of society.

We have seen that Greek mythology is really a history of the kings and queens of Atlantis.

When we turn to that other branch of the great Aryan family, the Hindoos, we find that their gods are also the kings of Atlantis. The Hindoo god Varuna is conceded to be the Greek god Uranos, who was the founder of the royal family of Atlantis.

In the Veda we find a hymn to "King Varuna," in which occurs this passage:

"This earth, too, belongs to Varuna, the king, and this wide sky, with its ends far apart. The two seas are Varuna's loins; he is contained also in this drop of water."

Again in the Veda we find another hymn to King Varuna:

"He who knows the place of the birds that fly through the sky; who on the waters knows the ships. He, the upholder of order, who knows the twelve months with the offspring of each, and knows the month that is engendered afterward."

This verse would seem to furnish additional proof that the Vedas were written by a maritime people; and in the allusion to the twelve months we are reminded of the Peruvians, who also divided the year into twelve parts of thirty days each, and afterward added six days to complete the year. The Egyptians and Mexicans also had intercalary days for the same purpose.

But, above all, it must be remembered that the Greeks, an Aryan race, in their mythological traditions, show the closest relationship to Atlantis. At-tika and At-hens are reminiscences of Ad, and we are told that Poseidon, god and founder of Atlantis, founded Athens. We find in the "Eleusinian mysteries" an Atlantean institution; their influence during the whole period of Greek history down to the coming of Christianity was extraordinary; and even then this masonry of Pre-Christian days, in which kings and emperors begged to be initiated, was, it is claimed, continued to our own times in our own Freemasons, who trace their descent back to "a Dionysiac fraternity which originated in Attika." And just as we have seen the Saturnalian festivities of Italy descending from Atlantean harvest-feasts, so these Eleusinian mysteries can be traced back to Plato's island. Poseidon was at the base of them; the first hierophant, Eumolpus, was "a son of Poseidon," and all the ceremonies were associated with seed-time and harvest, and with Demeter or Ceres, an Atlantean goddess, daughter of Chronos, who first taught the Greeks to use the plough and to plant barley. And, as the "Carnival" is a survival of the "Saturnalia," so Masonry is a survival of the Eleusinian mysteries. The roots of the institutions of to-day reach back to the Miocene Age.

We have seen that Zeus, the king of Atlantis, whose tomb was shown at Crete, was transformed into the Greek god Zeus; and in like manner we find him reappearing among the Hindoos as Dyaus. He is called "Dyaus-pitar," or God the Father, as among the Greeks we have "Zeus-pater," which became among the Romans "Jupiter."

The strongest connection, however, with the Atlantean system is shown in the case of the Hindoo god Deva-Nahusha.

We have seen in the chapter on Greek mythology that Dionysos was a son of Zeus and grandson of Poseidon, being thus identified with Atlantis. "When he arrived at manhood," said the Greeks, "he set out on a journey through all known countries, even into the remotest parts of India, instructing the people, as he proceeded, how to tend the vine, and how to practise many other arts of peace, besides teaching them the value of just and honorable dealings. He was praised everywhere as the greatest benefactor of mankind." (Murray's "Mythology," p. 119.)

In other words, he represented the great Atlantean civilization, reaching into "the remotest parts of India," and "to all parts of the known world," from America to Asia. In consequence of the connection of this king with the vine, he was converted in later times into the dissolute god Bacchus. But everywhere the traditions concerning him refer us back to Atlantis. "All the legends of Egypt, India, Asia Minor, and the older Greeks describe him as a king very great during his life, and deified after death.... Amon, king of Arabia or Ethiopia, married Rhea, sister of Chronos, who reigned over Italy, Sicily, and certain countries of Northern Africa." Dionysos, according to the Egyptians, was the son of Amon by the beautiful Amalthea. Chronos and Amon had a prolonged war; Dionysos defeated Chronos and captured his capital, dethroned him, and put his son Zeus in his place; Zeus reigned

460

nobly, and won a great fame. Dionysos succeeded his father Amon, and "became the greatest of sovereigns. He extended his sway in all the neighboring countries, and completed the conquest of India.... He gave much attention to the Cushite colonies in Egypt, greatly increasing their strength, intelligence, and prosperity." (Baldwin's "Prehistoric Nations," p. 283.)

When we turn to the Hindoo we still find this Atlantean king.

In the Sanscrit books we find reference to a god called Deva-Nahusha, who has been identified by scholars with Dionysos. He is connected "with the oldest history and mythology in the world." He is said to have been a contemporary with Indra, king of Meru, who was also deified, and who appears in the Veda as a principal form of representation of the Supreme Being.

"The warmest colors of imagination are used in portraying the greatness of Deva-Nahusha. For a time he had sovereign control of affairs in Meru; he conquered the seven dwipas, and led his armies through all the known countries of the world; by means of matchless wisdom and miraculous heroism he made his empire universal." (Ibid., p. 287.)

Here we see that the great god Indra, chief god of the Hindoos, was formerly king of Meru, and that Deva-Nahusha (De(va)nushas—De-onyshas) had also been king of Meru; and we must remember that Theopompus tells us that the island of Atlantis was inhabited by the "Meropes;" and Lenormant has reached the conclusion that the first people of the ancient world were "the men of Mero."

We can well believe, when we see traces of the same civilization extending from Peru and Lake Superior to Armenia and the frontiers of China, that this Atlantean kingdom was indeed "universal," and extended through all the "known countries of the world."

"We can see in the legends that Pururavas, Nahusha, and others had no connection with Sanscrit history. They are referred to ages very long anterior to the Sanscrit immigration, and must have been great personages celebrated in the traditions of the natives or Dasyus.... Pururavas was a king of great renown, who ruled over thirteen islands of the ocean, altogether surrounded by inhuman (or superhuman) personages; he engaged in a contest with Brahmans, and perished. Nahusha, mentioned by Maull, and in many legends, as famous for hostility to the Brahmans, lived at the time when Indra ruled on earth. He was a very great king, who ruled with justice a mighty empire, and attained the sovereignty of three worlds." (Europe, Africa, and America?) "Being intoxicated with pride, he was arrogant to

461

Brahmans, compelled them to bear his palanquin, and even dared to touch one of them with his foot" (kicked him?), "whereupon he was transformed into a serpent." (Baldwin's "Prehistoric Nations," p. 291.)

The Egyptians placed Dionysos (Osiris) at the close of the period of their history which was assigned to the gods, that is, toward the close of the great empire of Atlantis.

When we remember that the hymns of the "Rig-Veda" are admitted to date back to a vast antiquity, and are written in a language that had ceased to be a living tongue thousands of years ago, we can almost fancy those hymns preserve some part of the songs of praise uttered of old upon the island of Atlantis. Many of them seem to belong to sun-worship, and might have been sung with propriety upon the high places of Peru:

"In the beginning there arose the golden child. He was the one born Lord of all that is. He established the earth and the sky. Who is the god to whom we shall offer sacrifice?

"He who gives life; He who gives strength; whose command all the bright gods" (the stars?) "revere; whose light is immortality; whose shadow is death.... He who through his power is the one God of the breathing and awakening world. He who governs all, man and beast. He whose greatness these snowy mountains, whose greatness the sea proclaims, with the distant river. He through whom the sky is bright and the earth firm.... He who measured out the light in the air... Wherever the mighty water-clouds went, where they placed the seed and lit the fire, thence arose He who is the sole life of the bright gods.... He to whom heaven and earth, standing firm by His will, look up, trembling inwardly.... May he not destroy us; He, the creator of the earth; He, the righteous, who created heaven. He also created the bright and mighty waters."

This is plainly a hymn to the sun, or to a god whose most glorious representative was the sun. It is the hymn of a people near the sea; it was not written by a people living in the heart of Asia. It was the hymn of a people living in a volcanic country, who call upon their god to keep the earth "firm" and not to destroy them. It was sung at daybreak, as the sun rolled up the sky over an "awakening world."

The fire (Agni) upon the altar was regarded as a messenger rising from the earth to the sun:

"Youngest of the gods, their messenger, their invoker.... For thou, O sage, goest wisely between these two creations (heaven and earth, God and man) like a friendly messenger between two hamlets."

The dawn of the day (Ushas), part of the sun-worship, became also a god:

"She shines upon us like a young wife, rousing every living being to go to his work. When the fire had to be kindled by man, she made the light by striking down the darkness."

As the Egyptians and the Greeks looked to a happy abode (an underworld) in the west, beyond the waters, so the Aryan's paradise was the other side of some body of water. In the Veda (vii. 56, 24) we find a prayer to the Maruts, the storm-gods: "O, Maruts, may there be to us a strong son, who is a living ruler of men; through whom we may cross the waters on our way to the happy abode." This happy abode is described as "where King Vaivasvata reigns; where the secret place of heaven is; where the mighty waters are ... where there is food and rejoicing ... where there is happiness and delight; where joy and pleasure reside." (Rig-Veda ix. 113, 7.) This is the paradise beyond the seas; the Elysion; the Elysian Fields of the Greek and the Egyptian, located upon an island in the Atlantic which was destroyed by water. One great chain of tradition binds together these widely separated races.

"The religion of the Veda knows no idols," says Max Müller; "the worship of idols in India is a secondary formation, a degradation of the more primitive worship of ideal gods."

It was pure sun-worship, such as prevailed in Peru on the arrival of the Spaniards. It accords with Plato's description of the religion of Atlantis.

"The Dolphin's Ridge," at the bottom of the Atlantic, or the high land revealed by the soundings taken by the ship Challenger, is, as will be seen, of a three-pronged form—one prong pointing toward the west coast of Ireland, another connecting with the north-east coast of South America, and a third near or on the west coast of Africa. It does not follow that the island of Atlantis, at any time while inhabited by civilized people, actually reached these coasts; there is a strong probability that races of men may have found their way there from the three continents of Europe, America, and Africa; or the great continent which once filled the whole bed of the present Atlantic Ocean, and from whose débris geology tells us the Old and New Worlds were constructed, may have been the scene of the development, during immense periods of time, of diverse races of men, occupying different zones of climate.

There are many indications that there were three races of men dwelling on Atlantis. Noah, according to Genesis, had three sons—Shem, Ham, and Japheth—who represented three different races of men of different colors.

The Greek legends tell us of the rebellions inaugurated at different times in Olympus. One of these was a rebellion of the Giants, "a race of beings sprung from the blood of Uranos," the great original progenitor of the stock. "Their king or leader was Porphyrion, their most powerful champion Alkyoneus." Their mother was the earth: this probably meant that they represented the common people of a darker line. They made a desperate struggle for supremacy, but were conquered by Zeus. There were also two rebellions of the Titans. The Titans seem to have had a government of their own, and the names of twelve of their kings are given in the Greek mythology (see Murray, p. 27). They also were of "the blood of Uranos," the Adam of the people. We read, in fact, that Uranos married Gæa (the earth), and had three families: 1, the Titans; 2, the Hekatoncheires; and 3, the Kyklopes. We should conclude that the last two were maritime peoples, and I have shown that their mythical characteristics were probably derived from the appearance of their ships. Here we have, I think, a reference to the three races: 1, the red or sunburnt men, like the Egyptians, the Phoenicians, the Basques, and the Berber and Cushite stocks; 2, the sons of Shem, possibly the yellow or Turanian race; and 3, the whiter men, the Aryans, the Greeks, Kelts, Goths, Slavs, etc. If this view is correct, then we may suppose that colonies of the pale-faced stock may have been sent out from Atlantis to the northern coasts of Europe at different and perhaps widely separated periods of time, from some of which the Aryan families of Europe proceeded; hence the legend, which is found among them, that they were once forced to dwell in a country where the summers were only two months long.

From the earliest times two grand divisions are recognized in the Aryan family: "to the east those who specially called themselves Arians, whose descendants inhabited Persia, India, etc.; to the west, the Yavana, or the Young Ones, who first emigrated westward, and from whom have descended the various nations that have populated Europe. This is the name (Javan) found in the tenth chapter of Genesis." (Lenormant and Chevallier, "Ancient History of the East," vol. ii., p. 2.) But surely those who "first emigrated westward," the earliest to leave the parent stock, could not be the "Young Ones;" they would be rather the elder brothers. But if we can suppose the Bactrian population to have left Atlantis at an early date, and the Greeks, Latins, and Celts to have left it at a later period, then they would indeed be the "Young Ones" of the family, following on the heels of the earlier migrations, and herein we would find the explanation of the resemblance between the Latin and Celtic tongues. Lenormant says the name of Erin (Ireland) is derived from Aryan; and yet we have seen this island populated and named Erin by races distinctly connected with Spain, Iberia, Africa, and Atlantis.

There is another reason for supposing that the Aryan nations came from Atlantis.

We find all Europe, except a small corner of Spain and a strip along the Arctic Circle, occupied by nations recognized as Aryan; but when we turn to Asia, there is but a corner of it, and that corner in the part nearest Europe, occupied by the Aryans. All the rest of that great continent has been filled from immemorial ages by non-Aryan races. There are seven branches of the Aryan family: 1. Germanic or Teutonic; 2. Slavo-Lithuanic; 3. Celtic; 4. Italic; 5. Greek; 6. Iranian or Persian; 7. Sanscritic or Indian; and of these seven branches five dwell on the soil of Europe, and the other two are intrusive races in Asia from the direction of Europe. The Aryans in Europe have dwelt there apparently since the close of the Stone Age, if not before it, while the movements of the Aryans in Asia are within the Historical Period, and they appear as intrusive stocks, forming a high caste amid a vast population of a different race. The Vedas are supposed to date back to 2000 B.C., while there is every reason to believe that the Celt inhabited Western Europe 5000 B.C. If the Aryan race had originated in the heart of Asia, why would not its ramifications have extended into Siberia, China, and Japan, and all over Asia? And if the Aryans moved at a comparatively recent date into Europe from Bactria, where are the populations that then inhabited Europe—the men of the ages of stone and bronze? We should expect to find the western coasts of Europe filled with them, just as the eastern coasts of Asia and India are filled with Turanian populations. On the contrary, we know that the Aryans descended upon India from the Punjab, which lies to the north-west of that region; and that their traditions represent that they came there from the west, to wit, from the direction of Europe and Atlantis.

CHAPTER XI. ATLANTIS RECONSTRUCTED.

The farther we go back in time toward the era of Atlantis, the more the evidences multiply that we are approaching the presence of a great, wise, civilized race. For instance, we find the Egyptians, Ethiopians, and Israelites, from the earliest ages, refusing to eat the flesh of swine. The Western nations departed from this rule, and in these modern days we are beginning to realize the dangers of this article of food, on account of the trichina contained in it; and when we turn to the Talmud, we are told that it was forbidden to the Jews, "because of a small insect which infests it."

The Egyptians, the Ethiopians, the Phoenicians, the Hebrews, and others of the ancient races, practised circumcision. It was probably resorted to in Atlantean days, and imposed as a religious duty, to arrest one of the most dreadful scourges of the human race—a scourge which continued to decimate the people of America, arrested their growth, and paralyzed their civilization. Circumcision stamped out the disease in Atlantis; we read of one Atlantean king, the Greek god Ouranos, who, in a time of plague, compelled his whole army and the armies of his allies to undergo the rite. The colonies that went out to Europe carried the practice but not the disease out of which it originated with them; and it was not until Columbus reopened communication with the infected people of the West India Islands that the scourge crossed the Atlantic and "turned Europe," as one has expressed it, "into a charnal-house."

Life-insurance statistics show, nowadays, that the average life and health of the Hebrew is much greater than that of other men; and he owes this to the retention of practices and beliefs imposed ten thousand years ago by the great, wise race of Atlantis.

Let us now, with all the facts before us, gleaned from various sources, reconstruct, as near as may be, the condition of the antediluvians.

They dwelt upon a great island, near which were other smaller islands, probably east and west of them, forming stepping-stones, as it were, toward Europe and Africa in one direction, and the West India Islands and America in the other. There were volcanic mountains upon the main island, rising to a height of fifteen hundred feet, with their tops covered with perpetual snow. Below these were elevated table-lands, upon which were the royal establishments. Below these, again, was "the great plain of Atlantis." There were four rivers flowing north, south, east, and west from a central point. The climate was like that of the Azores, mild and pleasant; the soil volcanic and fertile, and suitable at its different elevations for the growth of the productions of the tropical and temperate zones.

The people represented at least two different races: a dark brown reddish race, akin to the Central Americans, the Berbers and the Egyptians; and a white race, like the Greeks, Goths, Celts, and Scandinavians. Various battles and struggles followed between the different peoples for supremacy. The darker race seems to have been, physically, a smaller race, with small hands; the lighter-colored race was much larger—hence the legends of the Titans and Giants. The Guanches of the Canary Islands were men of very great stature. As the works of the Bronze Age represent a small-handed race, and as the races who possessed the ships and gunpowder joined in the war against the Giants, we might conclude that the dark races were the more civilized, that they were the metal-workers and navigators.

The fact that the same opinions and customs exist on both sides of the ocean implies identity of origin; it might be argued that the fact that the explanation of many customs existing on both hemispheres is to be found only in America, implies that the primeval stock existed in America, the emigrating portion of the population carrying away the custom, but forgetting the reason for it. The fact that domestic cattle and the great cereals, wheat, oats, barley, and rye, are found in Europe and not in America, would imply that after the population moved to Atlantis from America civilization was developed in Atlantis, and that in the later ages communication was closer and more constant between Atlantis and Europe than between Atlantis and America. In the case of the bulky domestic animals, it would be more difficult to transport them, in the open vessels of that day, from Atlantis across the wider expanse of sea to America, than it would be to carry them by way of the now submerged islands in front of the Mediterranean Sea to the coast of Spain. It may be, too, that the climate of Spain and Italy was better adapted to the growth of wheat, barley, oats and rye, than maize; while the drier atmosphere of America was better suited to the latter plant. Even now comparatively little wheat or barley is raised in Central America, Mexico, or Peru, and none on the low coasts of those countries; while a smaller quantity of maize, proportionately, is grown in Italy, Spain, and the rest of Western Europe, the rainy climate being unsuited to it. We have seen (p. 60, ante) that there is reason to believe that maize was known in a remote period in the drier regions of the Egyptians and Chinese.

As science has been able to reconstruct the history of the migrations of the Aryan race, by the words that exist or fail to appear in the kindred branches of that tongue, so the time will come when a careful comparison of words, customs, opinions, arts existing on the opposite sides of the Atlantic will furnish an approximate sketch of Atlantean history.

The people had attained a high position as agriculturists. The presence of the plough in Egypt and Peru implies that they possessed that implement. And as the horns and ox-head of Baal show the esteem in which cattle were held among them, we may suppose that they had passed the stage in which the plough was drawn by men, as in Peru and Egypt in ancient times, and in Sweden during the Historical Period, and that it was drawn by oxen or horses. They first domesticated the horse, hence the association of Poseidon or Neptune, a sea-god, with horses; hence the race-courses for horses described by Plato. They possessed sheep, and

467

manufactured woollen goods; they also had goats, dogs, and swine. They raised cotton and made cotton goods; they probably cultivated maize, wheat, oats, barley, rye, tobacco, hemp, and flax, and possibly potatoes; they built aqueducts and practised irrigation; they were architects, sculptors, and engravers; they possessed an alphabet; they worked in tin, copper, bronze, silver, gold, and iron.

During the vast period of their duration, as peace and agriculture caused their population to increase to overflowing, they spread out in colonies east and west to the ends of the earth. This was not the work of a few years, but of many centuries; and the relations between these colonies may have been something like the relation between the different colonies that in a later age were established by the Phoenicians, the Greeks, and the Romans; there was an intermingling with the more ancient races, the autochthones of the different lands where they settled; and the same crossing of stocks, which we know to have been continued all through the Historical Period, must have been going on for thousands of years, whereby new races and new dialects were formed; and the result of all this has been that the smaller races of antiquity have grown larger, while all the complexions shade into each other, so that we can pass from the whitest to the darkest by insensible degrees.

In some respects the Atlanteans exhibited conditions similar to those of the British Islands: there were the same, and even greater, race differences in the population; the same plantation of colonies in Europe, Asia, and America; the same carrying of civilization to the ends of the earth. We have seen colonies from Great Britain going out in the third and fifth centuries to settle on the shores of France, in Brittany, representing one of the nationalities and languages of the mother-country—a race Atlantean in origin. In the same way we may suppose Hamitic emigrations to have gone out from Atlantis to Syria, Egypt, and the Barbary States. If we could imagine Highland Scotch, Welsh, Cornish, and Irish populations emigrating en masse from England in later times, and carrying to their new lands the civilization of England, with peculiar languages not English, we would have a state of things probably more like the migrations which took place from Atlantis. England, with a civilization Atlantean in origin, peopled by races from the same source, is repeating in these modern times the empire of Zeus and Chronos; and, just as we have seen Troy, Egypt, and Greece warring against the parent race, so in later days we have seen Brittany and the United States separating themselves from England, the race characteristics remaining after the governmental connection had ceased.

In religion the Atlanteans had reached all the great thoughts which underlie our modern creeds. They had attained to the conception of one universal, omnipotent, great First Cause. We find the worship of this One God in Peru and in early Egypt. They looked upon the sun as the mighty emblem, type, and instrumentality of this One God. Such a conception could only have come with civilization. It is not until these later days that science has realized the utter dependence of all earthly life upon the sun's rays:

"All applications of animal power may be regarded as derived directly or indirectly from the static chemical power of the vegetable substance by which the various organisms and their capabilities are sustained; and this power, in turn, from the kinetic action of the sun's rays.

"Winds and ocean currents, hailstorms and rain, sliding glaciers, flowing rivers, and falling cascades are the direct offspring of solar heat. All our machinery, therefore, whether driven by the windmill or the water-wheel, by horse-power or by steam—all the results of electrical and electro-magnetic changes—our telegraphs, our clocks, and our watches, all are wound up primarily by the sun.

"The sun is the great source of energy in almost all terrestrial phenomena. From the meteorological to the geographical, from the geological to the biological, in the expenditure and conversion of molecular movements, derived from the sun's rays, must be sought the motive power of all this infinitely varied phantasmagoria."

But the people of Atlantis had gone farther; they believed that the soul of man was immortal, and that he would live again in his material body; in other words, they believed in "the resurrection of the body and the life everlasting." They accordingly embalmed their dead.

The Duke of Argyll ("The Unity of Nature") says:

"We have found in the most ancient records of the Aryan language proof that the indications of religious thought are higher, simpler, and purer as we go back in time, until at last, in the very oldest compositions of human speech which have come down to us, we find the Divine Being spoken of in the sublime language which forms the opening of the Lord's Prayer. The date in absolute chronology of the oldest Vedic literature does not seem to be known. Professor Max Müller, however, considers that it may possibly take us back 5000 years.... All we can see with certainty is that the earliest inventions of mankind are the most wonderful that the race has ever made.... The first use of fire, and the discovery of the methods by which it can be kindled; the domestication of wild animals; and, above all, the processes by which the various cereals were first developed out of some wild grasses—these are all discoveries with which, in ingenuity and in importance, no subsequent discoveries may compare. They are all unknown to history—all lost in the light of an effulgent dawn."

The Atlanteans possessed an established order of priests; their religious worship was pure and simple. They lived under a kingly government; they had their courts, their judges, their records, their monuments covered with inscriptions, their mines, their founderies, their workshops, their looms, their grist-mills, their boats and sailing-vessels, their highways, aqueducts, wharves, docks, and canals. They had processions, banners, and triumphal arches for their kings and heroes; they built pyramids, temples, round-towers, and obelisks; they practised religious ablutions; they knew the use of the magnet and of gunpowder. In short, they were in the enjoyment of a civilization nearly as high as our own, lacking only the printing-press, and those inventions in which steam, electricity, and magnetism are used. We are told that Deva-Nahusha visited his colonies in Farther India. An empire which reached from the Andes to Hindostan, if not to China, must have been magnificent indeed. In its markets must have met the maize of the Mississippi Valley, the copper of Lake Superior, the gold and silver of Peru and Mexico, the spices of India, the tin of Wales and Cornwall, the bronze of Iberia, the amber of the Baltic, the wheat and barley of Greece, Italy, and Switzerland.

It is not surprising that when this mighty nation sank beneath the waves, in the midst of terrible convulsions, with all its millions of people, the event left an everlasting impression upon the imagination of mankind. Let us suppose that Great Britain should to-morrow meet with a similar fate. What a wild consternation would fall upon her colonies and upon the whole human family! The world might relapse into barbarism, deep and almost universal. William the Conqueror, Richard Coeur de Lion, Alfred the Great, Cromwell, and Victoria might survive only as the gods or demons of later races; but the memory of the cataclysm in which the centre of a universal empire instantaneously went down to death would never be forgotten; it would survive in fragments, more or less complete, in every land on earth; it would outlive the memory of a thousand lesser convulsions of nature; it would survive dynasties, nations, creeds, and languages; it would never be forgotten while man continued to inhabit the face of the globe.

Science has but commenced its work of reconstructing the past and rehabilitating the ancient peoples, and surely there is no study which appeals more strongly to the imagination than that of this drowned nation, the true antediluvians. They were the founders of nearly all our arts and sciences; they were the parents of our fundamental beliefs; they were the first civilizers, the first navigators, the first merchants, the first colonizers of the earth; their civilization was old when Egypt was young, and they had passed away thousands of years before Babylon, Rome, or London were dreamed of. This lost people were our ancestors, their blood flows in our veins; the words we use every day were heard, in their primitive form, in their cities, courts, and temples. Every line of race and thought, of blood and belief, leads back to them.

Nor is it impossible that the nations of the earth may yet employ their idle navies in bringing to the light of day some of the relics of this buried people. Portions of the island lie but a few hundred fathoms beneath the sea; and if expeditions have been sent out from time to time in the past, to resurrect from the depths of the ocean sunken treasure-ships with a few thousand doubloons hidden in their cabins, why should not an attempt be made to reach the buried wonders of Atlantis? A single engraved tablet dredged up from Plato's island would be worth more to science, would more strike the imagination of mankind, than all the gold of Peru, all the monuments of Egypt, and all the terra-cotta fragments gathered from the great libraries of Chaldea.

May not the so-called "Phoenician coins" found on Corvo, one of the Azores, be of Atlantean origin? Is it probable that that great race, pre-eminent as a founder of colonies, could have visited those islands within the Historical Period, and have left them unpeopled, as they were when discovered by the Portuguese?

We are but beginning to understand the past: one hundred years ago the world knew nothing of Pompeii or Herculaneum; nothing of the lingual tie that binds together the Indo-European nations; nothing of the significance of the vast volume of inscriptions upon the tombs and temples of Egypt; nothing of the meaning of the arrow-headed inscriptions of Babylon; nothing of the marvellous civilizations revealed in the remains of Yucatan, Mexico, and Peru. We are on the threshold. Scientific investigation is advancing with giant strides. Who shall say that one hundred years from now the great museums of the world may not be adorned with gems, statues, arms, and implements from Atlantis, while the libraries of the world shall contain translations of its inscriptions, throwing new light upon all the past history of the human race, and all the great problems which now perplex the thinkers of our day?

THE END.

BOOK FOUR.
THE NEW ATLANTIS

SIR FRANCIS BACON

INTRODUCTORY NOTE

Bacon's literary executor, Dr. Rowley, published "The New Atlantis" in 1627, the year after the author's death. It seems to have been written about 1623, during that period of literary activity which followed Bacon's political fall. None of Bacon's writings gives in short apace so vivid a picture of his tastes and aspirations as this fragment of the plan of an ideal commonwealth. The generosity and enlightenment, the dignity and splendor, the piety and public spirit, of the inhabitants of Bensalem represent the ideal qualities which Bacon the statesman desired rather than hoped to see characteristic of his own country; and in Solomon's House we have Bacon the scientist indulging without restriction his prophetic vision of the future of human knowledge. No reader acquainted in any degree with the processes and results of modern scientific inquiry can fail to be struck by the numerous approximations made by Bacon's imagination to the actual achievements of modern times. The plan and organization of his great college lay down the main lines of the modern research university; and both in pure and applied science he anticipates a strikingly large number of recent inventions and discoveries. In still another way is "The New Atlantis" typical of Bacon's attitude. In spite of the enthusiastic and broad-minded schemes he laid down for the pursuit of truth, Bacon always had an eye to utility. The advancement of science which he sought was conceived by him as a means to a practical end the increase of man's control over nature, and the comfort and convenience of humanity. For pure metaphysics, or any form of abstract thinking that yielded no "fruit," he had little interest; and this leaning to the useful is shown in the practical applications of the discoveries made by the scholars of Solomon's House. Nor does the interest of the work stop here. It contains much, both in its political and in its scientific ideals, that we have as yet by no means achieved, but which contain valuable elements of suggestion and stimulus for the future.

THE NEW ATLANTIS

We sailed from Peru, (where we had continued for the space of one whole year) for China and Japan, by the South Sea; taking with us victuals for twelve months; and had good winds from the east, though soft and weak, for five months space, and more. But the wind came about, and settled in the west for many days, so as we could make little or no way, and were sometime in purpose to turn back. But then again there arose strong and great winds from the south, with a point east, which carried us up (for all that we could do) towards the north; by which time our victuals failed us, though we had made good spare of them. So that finding ourselves, in the midst of the greatest wilderness of waters in the world, without victuals, we gave ourselves for lost men and prepared for death. Yet we did lift up our hearts and voices to God above, who showeth his wonders in the deep, beseeching him of his mercy, that as in the beginning he discovered the face of the deep, and brought forth dry land, so he would now discover land to us, that we might not perish.

And it came to pass that the next day about evening we saw within a kenning before us, towards the north, as it were thick clouds, which did put us in some hope of land; knowing how that part of the South Sea was utterly unknown; and might have islands, or continents, that hitherto were not come to light. Wherefore we bent our course thither, where we saw the appearance of land, all that night; and in the dawning of the next day, we might plainly discern that it was a land; flat to our sight, and full of boscage; which made it show the more dark. And after an hour and a half's sailing, we entered into a good haven, being the port of a fair city; not great indeed, but well built, and that gave a pleasant view from the sea: and we thinking every minute long, till we were on land, came close to the shore, and offered to land. But straightways we saw divers of the people, with bastons in their hands (as it were) forbidding us to land; yet without any cries of fierceness, but only as warning us off, by signs that they made. Whereupon being not a little discomforted, we were advising with ourselves, what we should do.

During which time, there made forth to us a small boat, with about eight persons in it; whereof one of them had in his hand a tipstaff of a yellow cane, tipped at both ends with blue, who came aboard our ship, without any show of distrust at all. And when he saw one of our number, present himself somewhat before the rest, he drew forth a little scroll of parchment (somewhat yellower than our parchment, and shining like the leaves of writing tables, but otherwise soft and flexible,) and delivered it to our foremost man. In which scroll were written in ancient Hebrew, and in ancient Greek, and in good Latin of the school, and in Spanish, these words: Land ye not, none of you; and provide to be gone from this coast, within sixteen days, except you have further time given you. Meanwhile, if you want fresh water or victuals, or help for your sick, or that your ship needeth repairs, write down your wants, and you shall have that, which belongeth to mercy. This scroll was signed with a stamp of cherubim: wings, not spread, but hanging downwards; and by them a cross. This being delivered, the officer returned, and left only a servant with us to receive our answer.

Consulting hereupon amongst ourselves, we were much perplexed. The denial of landing and hasty warning us away troubled us much; on the other side, to find that the people had languages, and were so full of humanity, did comfort us not a little. And above all, the sign of the cross to that instrument was to us a great rejoicing, and as it were a certain presage of good. Our answer was in the Spanish tongue; that for our ship, it was well; for we had rather met with calms and contrary winds than any tempests. For our sick, they were many, and in very ill case; so that if they were not permitted to land, they ran danger of their lives. Our other wants we set down in particular; adding, That we had some little store of merchandise, which if it pleased them to deal for, it might supply our wants, without being chargeable unto them. We offered some reward in pistolets unto the servant, and a piece of crimson velvet to be presented to the officer; but the servant took them not, nor would scarce look upon them; and so left us, and went back in another little boat, which was sent for him.

About three hours after we had dispatched our answer, there came towards us a person (as it seemed) of place. He had on him a gown with wide sleeves, of a kind of water chamolet, of an excellent azure colour, fair more glossy than ours; his under apparel was green; and so was his hat, being in the form of a turban, daintily made, and not so huge as the Turkish turbans; and the locks of his hair came down below the brims of it. A reverend man was he to behold. He came in a boat, gilt in some part of it, with four persons more only in that boat; and was followed by another boat, wherein were some twenty. When he was come within a flightshot of our ship, signs were made to us, that we should send forth some to meet him upon the water; which we presently did in our ship-boat, sending the principal man amongst us save one, and four of our number with him.

When we were come within six yards of their boat, they called to us to stay, and not to approach farther; which we did. And thereupon the man, whom I before described, stood up, and with a loud voice, in Spanish, asked, "Are ye Christians?" We answered, "We were;" fearing the less, because of the cross we had seen in the subscription. At which answer the said person lifted up his right hand towards Heaven, and drew it softly to his mouth (which is the gesture they use, when they thank God;) and then said: "If ye will swear (all of you) by the merits of the Saviour, that ye are no pirates, nor have shed blood, lawfully, nor unlawfully within forty days past, you may have licence to come on land." We said, "We were all ready to take that oath." Whereupon one of those that were with him, being (as it seemed) a notary, made an entry of this act. Which done, another of the attendants of the great person which was with him in the same boat, after his Lord had spoken a little to him, said aloud: "My Lord would have you know, that it is not of pride, or greatness, that he cometh not aboard your ship; but for that in your answer you declare that you have many sick amongst you, he was warned by the Conservator of Health of the city that he should keep a distance." We bowed ourselves towards him, and answered, "We were his humble servants; and accounted for great honour, and singular humanity towards us, that which was already done; but hoped well, that the nature of the sickness of our men was not infectious." So he returned; and a while after came the Notary to us aboard our ship; holding in his hand a fruit of that country, like an orange, but of color between orange-tawney and scarlet; which cast a most excellent odour. He used it (as it seemeth) for a preservative against infection. He gave us our oath; "By the name of Jesus, and his merits:" and after told us, that the next day, by six of the Clock, in the Morning, we should be sent to, and brought to the Strangers' House, (so he called it,) where we should be accommodated of things, both for our whole, and for our sick. So he left us; and when we offered him some pistolets, he smiling said, "He must not be twice paid for one labour:" meaning (as I take it) that he had salary sufficient of the State for his service. For (as I after learned) they call an officer that taketh rewards, "twice paid."

The next morning early, there came to us the same officer that came to us at first with his cane, and told us, He came to conduct us to the Strangers' House; and that he had prevented the hour, because we might have the whole day before us, for our business. "For," said he, "if you will follow my advice, there shall first go with me some few of you, and see the place, and how it may be made convenient for you; and then you may send for your sick, and the rest of your number, which ye will bring on land." We thanked him, and said, "That this care, which he took of desolate strangers, God would reward." And so six of us went on land with him: and when we were on land, he went before us, and turned to us, and said, "He was but our servant, and our guide." He led us through three fair streets; and all the way we went, there were gathered some people on both sides, standing in a row; but in so civil a fashion, as if it had been, not to wonder at us, but to welcome us: and divers of them, as we passed by them, put their arms a little abroad; which is their gesture, when they did bid any welcome.

The Strangers' House is a fair and spacious house, built of brick, of somewhat a bluer colour than our brick; and with handsome windows, some of glass, some of a kind of cambric oiled. He brought us first into a fair parlour above stairs, and then asked us, "What number of persons we were? And how many sick?" We answered, "We were in all, (sick and whole,) one and fifty persons, whereof our sick were seventeen." He desired us to have patience a little, and to stay till he came back to us; which was about an hour after; and then he led us to see the chambers which were provided for us, being in number nineteen: they having cast it (as it seemeth) that four of those chambers, which were better than the rest, might receive four of the principal men of our company; and lodge them alone by themselves; and the other fifteen chambers were to lodge us two and two together. The chambers were handsome and cheerful chambers, and furnished civilly. Then he led us to a long gallery, like a dorture, where he showed us all along the one side (for the other side was but wall and window), seventeen cells, very neat ones, having partitions of cedar wood. Which gallery and cells, being in all forty, many more than we needed, were instituted as an infirmary for sick persons. And he told us withal, that as any of our sick waxed well, he might be removed from his cell, to a chamber; for which purpose there were set forth ten spare chambers, besides the number we spake of before. This done, he brought us back to the parlour, and lifting up his cane a little, (as they do when they give any charge or command) said to us, "Ye are to know, that the custom of the land requireth, that after this day and to-morrow, (which we give you for removing of your people from your ship,) you are to keep within doors for three days. But let it not trouble you, nor do not think yourselves restrained, but rather left to your rest and ease. You shall want nothing, and there are six of our people appointed to attend you, for any business you may have abroad." We gave him thanks, with all affection and respect, and said, "God surely is manifested in this land." We offered him also twenty pistolets; but he smiled, and only said; "What? twice paid!" And so he left us.

Soon after our dinner was served in; which was right good viands, both for bread and treat: better than any collegiate diet, that I have known in Europe. We had also drink of three sorts, all wholesome and good; wine of the grape; a drink of grain, such as is with us our ale, but more clear: And a kind of cider made of a fruit of that country; a wonderful pleasing and refreshing drink. Besides, there were brought in to us, great store of those scarlet oranges, for our sick; which (they said) were an assured remedy for sickness taken at sea. There was given us also, a box of small gray, or whitish pills, which they wished our sick should take, one of the pills, every night before sleep; which (they said) would hasten their recovery.

The next day, after that our trouble of carriage and removing of our men and goods out of our ship, was somewhat settled and quiet, I thought good to call our company together; and when they were assembled, said unto them; "My dear friends, let us know ourselves, and how it standeth with us. We are men cast on land, as Jonas was, out of the whale's belly, when we were as buried in the deep: and now we are on land, we are but between death and life; for we are beyond, both the old world, and the new; and whether ever we shall see

Europe, God only knoweth. It is a kind of miracle bath brought us hither: and it must be little less, that shall bring us hence. Therefore in regard of our deliverance past, and our danger present, and to come, let us look up to God, and every man reform his own ways. Besides we are come here amongst a Christian people, full of piety and humanity: let us not bring that confusion of face upon ourselves, as to show our vices, or unworthiness before them. Yet there is more. For they have by commandment, (though in form of courtesy) cloistered us within these wall, for three days: who knoweth, whether it be not, to take some taste of our manners and conditions? And if they find them bad, to banish us straightways; if good, to give us further time. For these men that they have given us for attendance, may withal have an eye upon us. Therefore for God's love, and as we love the weal of our souls and bodies, let us so behave ourselves, as we may be at peace with God, and may find grace in the eyes of this people." Our company with one voice thanked me for my good admonition, and promised me to live soberly and civilly, and without giving any the least occasion of offence. So we spent our three days joyfully, and without care, in expectation what would be done with us, when they were expired. During which time, we had every hour joy of the amendment of our sick; who thought themselves cast into some divine pool of healing; they mended so kindly, and so fast.

The morrow after our three days were past, there came to us a new man, that we had not seen before, clothed in blue as the former was, save that his turban was white, with a small red cross on the top. He had also a tippet of fine linen. At his coming in, he did bend to us a little, and put his arms abroad. We of our parts saluted him in a very lowly and submissive manner; as looking that from him, we should receive sentence of life, or death: he desired to speak with some few of us: whereupon six of us only staid, and the rest avoided the room. He said, "I am by office governor of this House of Strangers, and by vocation I am a Christian priest: and therefore am come to you to offer you my service, both as strangers and chiefly as Christians. Some things I may tell you, which I think you will not be unwilling to hear. The State hath given you license to stay on land, for the space of six weeks; and let it not trouble you, if your occasions ask further time, for the law in this point is not precise; and I do not doubt, but my self shall be able, to obtain for you such further time, as may be convenient. Ye shall also understand, that the Strangers' House is at this time rich, and much aforehand; for it hath laid up revenue these thirty-seven years; for so long it is since any stranger arrived in this part: and therefore take ye no care; the State will defray you all the time you stay; neither shall you stay one day the less for that. As for any merchandise ye have brought, ye shall be well used, and have your return, either in merchandise, or in gold and silver: for to us it is all one. And if you have any other request to make, hide it not. For ye shall find we will not make your countenance to fall by the answer ye shall receive. Only this

I must tell you, that none of you must go above a karan," (that is with them a mile and an half) "from the walls of the city, without especial leave."

We answered, after we had looked awhile one upon another, admiring this gracious and parent-like usage; "That we could not tell what to say: for we wanted words to express our thanks; and his noble free offers left us nothing to ask. It seemed to us, that we had before us a picture of our salvation in Heaven; for we that were a while since in the jaws of death, were now brought into a place, where we found nothing but consolations. For the commandment laid upon us, we would not fail to obey it, though it was impossible but our hearts should be enflamed to tread further upon this happy and holy ground." We added, "That our tongues should first cleave to the roofs of our mouths, ere we should forget, either his reverend person, or this whole nation, in our prayers." We also most humbly besought him, to accept of us as his true servants; by as just a right as ever men on earth were bounden; laying and presenting, both our persons, and all we had, at his feet. He said; "He was a priest, and looked for a priest's reward; which was our brotherly love, and the good of our souls and bodies." So he went from us, not without tears of tenderness in his eyes; and left us also confused with joy and kindness, saying amongst ourselves; "That we were come into a land of angels, which did appear to us daily, and prevent us with comforts, which we thought not of, much less expected."

The next day about ten of the clock, the Governor came to us again, and after salutations, said familiarly; "That he was come to visit us;" and called for a chair, and sat him down: and we, being some ten of us, (the rest were of the meaner sort, or else gone abroad,) sat down with him, And when we were set, he began thus: "We of this island of Bensalem," (for so they call it in their language,) "have this; that by means of our solitary situation; and of the laws of secrecy, which we have for our travellers, and our rare admission of strangers; we know well most part of the habitable world, and are ourselves unknown. Therefore because he that knoweth least is fittest to ask questions, it is more reason, for the entertainment of the time, that ye ask me questions, than that I ask you."

We answered; "That we humbly thanked him that he would give us leave so to do: and that we conceived by the taste we had already, that there was no worldly thing on earth, more worthy to be known than the state of that happy land. But above all," (we said,) "since that we were met from the several ends of the world, and hoped assuredly that we should meet one day in the kingdom of Heaven, (for that we were both parts Christians,) we desired to know, (in respect that land was so remote, and so divided by vast and unknown seas, from the land where our Saviour walked on earth,) who was the apostle of that nation, and how it was converted to the faith?" It appeared in his face that he took great contentment in this our question: he said; "Ye knit my heart to you, by asking this question in the first place; for it sheweth that you first seek the kingdom of heaven; and I shall gladly, and briefly, satisfy your demand.

"About twenty years after the ascension of our Saviour, it came to pass, that there was seen by the people of Renfusa, (a city upon the eastern coast of our island,) within night, (the night was cloudy, and calm,) as it might be some mile into the sea, a great pillar of light; not sharp, but in form of a column, or cylinder, rising from the sea a great way up towards heaven; and on the top of it was seen a large cross of light, more bright and resplendent than the body of the pillar. Upon which so strange a spectacle, the people of the city gathered apace together upon the sands, to wonder; and so after put themselves into a number of small boats, to go nearer to this marvellous sight. But when the boats were come within (about) sixty yards of the pillar, they found themselves all bound, and could go no further; yet so as they might move to go about, but might not approach nearer: so as the boats stood all as in a theatre, beholding this light as an heavenly sign. It so fell out, that there was in one of the boats one of the wise men, of the society of Salomon's House; which house, or college (my good brethren) is the very eye of this kingdom; who having awhile attentively and devoutly viewed and contemplated this pillar and cross, fell down upon his face; and then raised himself upon his knees, and lifting up his hands to heaven, made his prayers in this manner.

"'LORD God of heaven and earth, thou hast vouchsafed of thy grace to those of our order, to know thy works of Creation, and the secrets of them: and to discern (as far as appertaineth to the generations of men) between divine miracles, works of nature, works of art, and impostures and illusions of all sorts. I do here acknowledge and testify before this people, that the thing which we now see before our eyes is thy Finger and a true Miracle. And forasmuch as we learn in our books that thou never workest miracles, but to divine and excellent end, (for the laws of nature are thine own laws, and thou exceedest them not but upon great cause,) we most humbly beseech thee to prosper this great sign, and to give us the interpretation and use of it in mercy; which thou dost in some part secretly promise by sending it unto us.'

"When he had made his prayer, he presently found the boat he was in, moveable and unbound; whereas all the rest remained still fast; and taking that for an assurance of leave to approach, he caused the boat to be softly and with silence rowed towards the pillar. But ere he came near it, the pillar and cross of light brake up, and cast itself abroad, as it were, into a firmament of many stars; which also vanished soon after, and there was nothing left to be seen, but a small ark, or chest of cedar, dry, and not wet at all with water, though it swam. And in the fore-end of it, which was towards him, grew a small green branch of palm; and when the wise man had taken it, with all reverence, into his boat, it opened of itself, and there were found in it a Book and a Letter; both written in fine parchment, and wrapped in sindons of linen. The Book contained all the canonical books of the Old and New Testament, according as you have them; (for we know well what the churches with you receive); and the Apocalypse itself, and some other books of the New Testament, which were not at that time written, were nevertheless in the Book. And for the Letter, it was in these words:

"'I, Bartholomew, a servant of the Highest, and Apostle of Jesus Christ, was warned by an angel that appeareth to me, in a vision of glory, that I should commit this ark to the floods of the sea. Therefore I do testify and declare unto that people where God shall ordain this ark to come to land, that in the same day is come unto them salvation and peace and good-will, from the Father, and from the Lord Jesus.'

"There was also in both these writings, as well the Book, as the Letter, wrought a great miracle, conform to that of the Apostles, in the original Gift of Tongues. For there being at that time in this land Hebrews, Persians, and Indians, besides the natives, every one read upon the Book, and Letter, as if they had been written in his own language. And thus was this land saved from infidelity (as the remainder of the old world was from water) by an ark, through the apostolical and miraculous evangelism of Saint Bartholomew." And here he paused, and a messenger came, and called him from us. So this was all that passed in that conference.

The next day, the same governor came again to us, immediately after dinner, and excused himself, saying; "That the day before he was called from us, somewhat abruptly, but now he would make us amends, and spend time with us if we held his company and conference agreeable." We answered, "That we held it so agreeable and pleasing to us, as we forgot both dangers past and fears to come, for the time we hear him speak; and that we thought an hour spent with him, was worth years of our former life." He bowed himself a little to us, and after we were set again, he said; "Well, the questions are on your part."

One of our number said, after a little pause; that there was a matter, we were no less desirous to know, than fearful to ask, lest we might presume too far. But encouraged by his rare humanity towards us, (that could scarce think ourselves strangers, being his vowed and professed servants,) we would take the hardiness to propound it: humbly beseeching him, if he thought it not fit to be answered, that he would pardon it, though he rejected it. We said; "We well observed those his words, which he formerly spake, that this happy island, where we now stood, was known to few, and yet knew most of the nations of the world; which we found to be true, considering they had the languages of Europe, and knew much of our state and business; and yet we in Europe, (notwithstanding all the remote discoveries and navigations of this last age), never heard of the least inkling or glimpse of this island. This we found wonderful strange; for that all nations have inter-knowledge one of another, either by voyage into foreign parts, or by strangers that come to them: and though the traveller into a foreign country, doth commonly know more by the eye, than he that stayeth at home can by relation of the traveller; yet both ways suffice to make a mutual knowledge, in some degree, on both parts. But for this island, we never heard tell of any ship of theirs that had been seen to arrive upon any shore of Europe; nor of either the East or West Indies; nor yet of any ship of any other part of the world, that had made return from them. And yet the marvel rested not in this. For the situation of it (as his lordship said) in the secret conclave' of such a vast sea might cause it. But then, that they should have knowledge of the languages, books, affairs, of those that lie such a distance from them, it was a thing we could not tell what to make of; for that it seemed to us a conditioner and propriety of divine powers and beings, to be hidden and unseen to others, and yet to have others open and as in a light to them."

At this speech the Governor gave a gracious smile, and said; "That we did well to ask pardon for this question we now asked: for that it imported, as if we thought this land, a land of magicians, that sent forth spirits of the air into all parts, to bring them news and intelligence of other countries." It was answered by us all, in all possible humbleness, but yet with a countenance taking knowledge, that we knew that he spake it but merrily, "That we were apt enough to think there was somewhat supernatural in this island; but yet rather as angelical than magical. But to let his lordship know truly what it was that made us tender and doubtful to ask this question, it was not any such conceit, but because we remembered, he had given a touch in his former speech, that this land had laws of secrecy touching strangers." To this he said; "You remember it aright and therefore in that I shall say to you, I must reserve some particulars, which it is not lawful for me to reveal; but there will be enough left, to give you satisfaction."

"You shall understand (that which perhaps you will scarce think credible) that about three thousand years ago, or somewhat more, the navigation of the world, (especially for remote voyages,) was greater than at this day. Do not think with yourselves, that I know not how much it is increased with you, within these six-score years: I know it well: and yet I say greater then than now; whether it was, that the example of the ark, that saved the remnant of men from the universal deluge, gave men confidence to adventure upon the waters; or what it was; but such is the truth. The Phoenicians, and especially the Tyrians, had great fleets. So had the Carthaginians their colony, which is yet further west. Toward the east the shipping of Egypt and of Palestine was likewise great. China also, and the great Atlantis, (that you call America,) which have now but junks and canoes, abounded then in tall ships. This island, (as appeareth by faithful registers of those times,) had then fifteen hundred strong ships, of great content. Of all this, there is with you sparing memory, or none; but we have large knowledge thereof.

"At that time, this land was known and frequented by the ships and vessels of all the nations before named. And (as it cometh to pass) they had many times men of other countries, that were no sailors, that came with them; as Persians, Chaldeans, Arabians; so as almost all nations of might and fame resorted hither; of whom we have some stirps, and little tribes with us at this day. And for our own ships, they went sundry voyages, as well to your straits, which you call the Pillars of Hercules, as to other parts in the Atlantic and Mediterrane Seas; as to Paguin, (which is the same with Cambaline,) and Quinzy, upon the Oriental Seas, as far as to the borders of the East Tartary.

"At the same time, and an age after, or more, the inhabitants of the great Atlantis did flourish. For though the narration and description, which is made by a great man with you; that the descendants of Neptune planted there; and of the magnificent temple, palace, city, and hill; and the manifold streams of goodly navigable rivers, (which as so many chains environed the same site and temple); and the several degrees of ascent, whereby men did climb up to the same, as if it had been a scala coeli, be all poetical and fabulous: yet so much is true, that the said country of Atlantis, as well that of Peru, then called Coya, as that of Mexico, then named Tyrambel, were mighty and proud kingdoms in arms, shipping and riches: so mighty, as at one time (or at least within the space of ten years) they both made two great expeditions; they of Tyrambel through the Atlantic to the Mediterrane Sea; and they of Coya through the South Sea upon this our island: and for the former of these, which was into Europe, the same author amongst you (as it seemeth) had some relation from the Egyptian priest whom he cited. For assuredly such a thing there was. But whether it were the ancient Athenians that had the glory of the repulse and resistance of those forces, I can say nothing: but certain it is, there never came back either ship or man from that voyage. Neither had the other voyage of those of Coya upon us had better fortune, if they had not met with enemies of greater clemency. For the king of this island, (by name Altabin,) a wise man and a great warrior, knowing well both his own strength and that of his enemies, handled the matter so, as he cut off their land-forces from their ships; and entoiled both their navy and their tamp with a greater power than theirs, both by sea and land: arid compelled them to render themselves without striking stroke and after they were at his mercy, contenting himself only with their oath that they should no more bear arms against him, dismissed them all in safety.

"But the divine revenge overtook not long after those proud enterprises. For within less than the space of one hundred years, the great Atlantis was utterly lost and destroyed: not by a great earthquake, as your man saith; (for that whole tract is little subject to earthquakes;) but by a particular' deluge or inundation; those countries having, at this day, far greater rivers and far higher mountains to pour down waters, than any part of the old world. But it is true that the same inundation was not deep; not past forty foot, in most places, from the ground; so that although it destroyed man and beast generally, yet some few wild inhabitants of the wood escaped. Birds also were saved by flying to the high trees and woods. For as for men, although they had buildings in many places, higher than the depth of the water, yet that inundation, though it were shallow, had a long continuance; whereby they of the vale that were not drowned, perished for want of food and other things necessary.

"So as marvel you not at the thin population of America, nor at the rudeness and ignorance of the people; for you must account your inhabitants of America as a young people; younger a thousand years, at the least, than the rest of the world: for that there was so much time between the universal flood and their particular inundation. For the poor remnant of human seed, which remained in their mountains, peopled the country again slowly, by little and little; and being simple and savage people, (not like Noah and his sons, which was the chief family of the earth;) they were not able to leave letters, arts, and civility to their posterity; and having likewise in their mountainous habitations been used (in respect of the extreme cold of those regions) to clothe themselves with the skins of tigers, bears, and great hairy goats, that they have in those parts; when after they came down into the valley, and found the intolerable heats which are there, and knew no means of lighter apparel, they were forced to begin the custom of going naked, which continueth at this day. Only they take great pride and delight in the feathers of birds; and this also they took from those their ancestors of the mountains, who were invited unto it by the infinite flights of birds that came up to the high grounds, while the waters stood below. So you see, by this main accident of time, we lost our traffic with the Americans, with whom of, all others, in regard they lay nearest to us, we had most commerce.

"As for the other parts of the world, it is most manifest that in the ages following (whether it were in respect of wars, or by a natural revolution of time,) navigation did every where greatly decay; and specially far voyages (the rather by the use of galleys, and such vessels as could hardly brook the ocean,) were altogether left and omitted. So then, that part of intercourse which could be from other nations to sail to us, you see how it hath long since ceased; except it were by some rare accident, as this of yours. But now of the cessation of that other part of intercourse, which might be by our sailing to other nations, I must yield you some other cause. For I cannot say (if I shall say truly,) but our shipping, for number, strength, mariners, pilots, and all things that appertain to navigation, is as great as ever; and therefore why we should sit at home, I shall now give you an account by itself: and it will draw nearer to give you satisfaction to your principal question.

483

"There reigned in this land, about nineteen hundred years ago, a king, whose memory of all others we most adore; not superstitiously, but as a divine instrument, though a mortal man; his name was Solamona: and we esteem him as the lawgiver of our nation. This king had a large heart, inscrutable for good; and was wholly bent to make his kingdom and people happy. He therefore, taking into consideration how sufficient and substantive this land was to maintain itself without any aid (at all) of the foreigner; being five thousand six hundred miles in circuit, and of rare fertility of soil in the greatest part thereof; and finding also the shipping of this country might be plentifully set on work, both by fishing and by transportations from port to port, and likewise by sailing unto some small islands that are not far from us, and are under the crown and laws of this state; and, recalling into his memory the happy and flourishing estate wherein this land then was; so as it might be a thousand ways altered to the worse, but scarce any one way to the better; thought nothing wanted to his noble and heroical intentions, but only (as far as human foresight might reach) to give perpetuity to that which was in his time so happily established. Therefore amongst his other fundamental laws of this kingdom, he did ordain the interdicts and prohibitions which we have touching entrance of strangers; which at that time (though it was after the calamity of America) was frequent; doubting novelties, and commixture of manners. It is true, the like law against the admission of strangers without licence is an ancient law in the kingdom of China, and yet continued in use. But there it is a poor thing; and hath made them a curious, ignorant, fearful, foolish nation. But our lawgiver made his law of another temper. For first, he hath preserved all points of humanity, in taking order and making provision for the relief of strangers distressed; whereof you have tasted."

At which speech (as reason was) we all rose up and bowed ourselves. He went on.

"That king also, still desiring to join humanity and policy together; and thinking it against humanity, to detain strangers here against their wills, and against policy that they should return and discover their knowledge of this estate, he took this course: he did ordain that of the strangers that should be permitted to land, as many (at all times) might depart as would; but as many as would stay should have very good conditions and means to live from the state. Wherein he saw so far, that now in so many ages since the prohibition, we have memory not of one ship that ever returned, and but of thirteen persons only, at several times, that chose to return in our bottoms. What those few that returned may have reported abroad I know not. But you must think, whatsoever they have said could be taken where they came but for a dream. Now for our travelling from henna into parts abroad, our Lawgiver thought fit altogether to restrain it. So is it not in China. For the Chinese sail where they will or can; which sheweth that their law of keeping out strangers is a law of

484

pusillanimity and fear. But this restraint of ours hath one only exception, which is admirable; preserving the good which cometh by communicating with strangers, and avoiding the hurt; and I will now open it to you. And here I shall seem a little to digress, but you will by and by find it pertinent.

"Ye shall understand (my dear friends) that amongst the excellent acts of that king, one above all hath the pre-eminence. It was the erection and institution of an Order or Society, which we call Salomon's House; the noblest foundation (as we think) that ever was upon the earth; and the lanthorn of this kingdom. It is dedicated to the study of the works and creatures of God. Some think it beareth the founder's name a little corrupted, as if it should be Solamona's House. But the records write it as it is spoken. So as I take it to be denominate of the king of the Hebrews, which is famous with you, and no stranger to us. For we have some parts of his works, which with you are lost; namely, that natural history, which he wrote, of all plants, from the cedar of Libanus to the moss that groweth out of the wall, and of all things that have life and motion. This maketh me think that our king, finding himself to symbolize in many things with that king of the Hebrews (which lived many years before him), honored him with the title of this foundation. And I am rather induced to be of this opinion, for that I find in ancient records this Order or Society is sometimes called Salomon's House, and sometimes the College of the Six Days Works; whereby I am satisfied that our excellent king had learned from the Hebrews that God had created the world and all that therein is within six days: and therefore he instituting that House for the finding out of the true nature of all things, (whereby God might have the more glory in the workmanship of them, and insert the more fruit in the use of them), did give it also that second name.

"But now to come to our present purpose. When the king had forbidden to all his people navigation into any part that was not under his crown, he made nevertheless this ordinance; that every twelve years there should be set forth, out of this kingdom two ships, appointed to several voyages; That in either of these ships there should be a mission of three of the Fellows or Brethren of Salomon's House; whose errand was only to give us knowledge of the affairs and state of those countries to which they were designed, and especially of the sciences, arts, manufactures, and inventions of all the world; and withal to bring unto us books, instruments, and patterns in every kind: That the ships, after they had landed the brethren, should return; and that the brethren should stay abroad till the new mission. These ships are not otherwise fraught, than with store of victuals, and good quantity of treasure to remain with the brethren, for the buying of such things and rewarding of such persons as they should think fit. Now for me to tell you how the vulgar sort of mariners are contained from being discovered at land; and how they that must be put on shore for any time, color themselves under the names of other nations; and to

485

what places these voyages have been designed; and what places of rendezvous are appointed for the new missions; and the like circumstances of the practique; I may not do it: neither is it much to your desire. But thus you see we maintain a trade not for gold, silver, or jewels; nor for silks; nor for spices; nor any other commodity of matter; but only for God's first creature, which was Light: to have light (I say) of the growth of all parts of the world."

And when he had said this, he was silent; and so were we all. For indeed we were all astonished to hear so strange things so probably told. And he, perceiving that we were willing to say somewhat but had it not ready in great courtesy took us off, and descended to ask us questions of our voyage and fortunes and in the end concluded, that we might do well to think with ourselves what time of stay we would demand of the state; and bade us not to scant ourselves; for he would procure such time as we desired: Whereupon we all rose up, and presented ourselves to kiss the skirt of his tippet; but he would not suffer us; and so took his leave. But when it came once amongst our people that the state used to offer conditions to strangers that would stay, we had work enough to get any of our men to look to our ship; and to keep them from going presently to the governor to crave conditions. But with much ado we refrained them, till we might agree what course to take.

We took ourselves now for free men, seeing there was no danger of our utter perdition; and lived most joyfully, going abroad and seeing what was to be seen in the city and places adjacent within our tedder; and obtaining acquaintance with many of the city, not of the meanest quality; at whose hands we found such humanity, and such a freedom and desire to take strangers as it were into their bosom, as was enough to make us forget all that was dear to us in our own countries: and continually we met with many things right worthy of observation and relation: as indeed, if there be a mirror in the world worthy to hold men's eyes, it is that country.

One day there were two of our company bidden to a Feast of the Family, as they call it. A most natural, pious, and reverend custom it is, shewing that nation to be compounded of all goodness. This is the manner of it. It is granted to any man that shall live to see thirty persons descended of his body alive together, and all above three years old, to make this feast which is done at the cost of the state. The Father of the Family, whom they call the Tirsan, two days before the feast, taketh to him three of such friends as he liketh to choose; and is assisted also by the governor of the city or place where the feast is celebrated; and all the persons of the family, of both sexes, are summoned to attend him. These two days the Tirsan sitteth in consultation concerning the good estate of the family. There, if there be any discord or suits between any of the family, they are compounded and appeased. There, if any of the family be distressed or decayed, order is taken for their relief and competent means to live. There, if any be subject to vice, or take ill courses, they are reproved and censured. So likewise direction is given touching marriages, and the courses of life, which any of them should take, with divers other the like orders and advices. The governor assisteth, to the end to put in execution by his public authority the decrees and orders of the Tirsan, if they should be disobeyed; though that seldom needeth; such reverence and obedience they give to the order of nature. The Tirsan doth also then ever choose one man from among his sons, to live in house with him; who is called ever after the Son of the Vine. The reason will hereafter appear.

On the feast day, the father or Tirsan cometh forth after divine service into a large room where the feast is celebrated; which room hath an half-pace at the upper end. Against the wall, in the middle of the half-pace, is a chair placed for him, with a table and carpet before it. Over the chair is a state, made round or oval, and it is of ivy; an ivy somewhat whiter than ours, like the leaf of a silver asp; but more shining; for it is green all winter. And the state is curiously wrought with silver and silk of divers colors, broiding or binding in the ivy; and is ever of the work of some of the daughters of the family; and veiled over at the top with a fine net of silk and silver. But the substance of it is true ivy; whereof, after it is taken down, the friends of the family are desirous to have some leaf or sprig to keep.

The Tirsan cometh forth with all his generation or linage, the males before him, and the females following him; and if there be a mother from whose body the whole linage is descended, there is a traverse placed in a loft above on the right hand of the chair, with a privy door, and a carved window of glass, leaded with gold and blue; where she sitteth, but is not seen. When the Tirsan is come forth, he sitteth down in the chair; and all the linage place themselves against the wall, both at his back and upon the return of the half-pace, in order of their years without difference of sex; and stand upon their feet. When he is set; the room being always full of company, but well kept and without disorder; after some pause, there cometh in from the lower end of the room, a taratan (which is as much as an herald) and on either side of him two young lads; whereof one carrieth a scroll of their shining yellow parchment; and the other a cluster of grapes of gold, with a long foot or stalk. The herald and children are clothed with mantles of sea-water green satin; but the herald's mantle is streamed with gold, and hath a train.

Then the herald with three curtesies, or rather inclinations, cometh up as far as the half-pace; and there first taketh into his hand the scroll. This scroll is the king's charter, containing gifts of revenew, and many privileges, exemptions, and points of honour, granted to the Father of the Family; and is ever styled and directed, To such do one our well beloved friend and creditor: which is a title proper only to this case. For they say the king is debtor to no man, but for propagation of his subjects. The seal set to the king's charter is the king's image, imbossed or moulded in gold; and though such charters be expedited of course, and as of right, yet they are varied by discretion, according to the number and dignity of the family. This charter the herald readeth aloud; and while it is read, the father or Tirsan standeth up supported by two of his sons, such as he chooseth. Then the herald mounteth the half-pace and delivereth the charter into his hand: and with that there is an acclamation by all that are present in their language, which is thus much: Happy are the people of Bensalem.

Then the herald taketh into his hand from the other child the cluster of grapes, which is of gold, both the stalk and the grapes. But the grapes are daintily enamelled; and if the males of the family be the greater number, the grapes are enamelled purple, with a little sun set on the top; if the females, then they are enamelled into a greenish yellow, with a crescent on the top. The grapes are in number as many as there are descendants of the family. This golden cluster the herald delivereth also to the Tirsan; who presently delivereth it over to that son that he had formerly chosen to be in house with him: who beareth it before his father as an ensign of honour when he goeth in public, ever after; and is thereupon called the Son of the Vine.

After the ceremony endeth the father or Tirsan retireth; and after some time cometh forth again to dinner, where he sitteth alone under the state, as before; and none of his descendants sit with him, of what degree or dignity soever, except he hap to be of Salomon's House. He is served only by his own children, such as are male; who perform unto him all service of the table upon the knee; and the women only stand about him, leaning against the wall. The room below the half-pace hath tables on the sides for the guests that are bidden; who are served with great and comely order; and towards the end of dinner (which in the greatest feasts with them lasteth never above an hour and an half) there is an hymn sung, varied according to the invention of him that composeth it (for they have excellent posy) but the subject of it is (always) the praises of Adam and Noah and Abraham; whereof the former two peopled the world, and the last was the Father of the Faithful: concluding ever with a thanksgiving for the nativity of our Saviour, in whose birth the births of all are only blessed.

Dinner being done, the Tirsan retireth again; and having withdrawn himself alone into a place, where he makes some private prayers, he cometh forth the third time, to give the blessing with all his descendants, who stand about him as at the first. Then he calleth them forth by one and by one, by name, as he pleaseth, though seldom the order of age be inverted. The person that is called (the table being before removed) kneeleth down before the chair, and the father layeth his hand upon his head, or her head, and giveth the blessing in these words: Son of Bensalem, (or daughter of Bensalem,) thy father with it: the man by whom thou hast breath and life speaketh the word: the blessing of the everlasting Father, the Prince of Peace, and the Holy Dove, be upon thee, and make the days of thy pilgrimage good and many. This he saith to every of them; and that done, if there be any of his sons of eminent merit and virtue, (so they be not above two,) he calleth for them again; and saith, laying his arm over their shoulders, they standing; Sons, it is well ye are born, give God the praise, and persevere to the end. And withall delivereth to either of them a jewel, made in the figure of an ear of wheat, which they ever after wear in the front of their turban or hat. This done, they fall to music and dances, and other recreations, after their manner, for the rest of the day. This is the full order of that feast.

By that time six or seven days were spent, I was fallen into straight acquaintance with a merchant of that city, whose name was Joabin. He was a Jew and circumcised: for they have some few stirps of Jews yet remaining among them, whom they leave to their own religion. Which they may the better do, because they are of a far differing disposition from the Jews in other parts. For whereas they hate the name of Christ; and have a secret inbred rancour against the people among whom they live: these (contrariwise) give unto our Saviour many high attributes, and love the nation of Bensalem extremely. Surely this man of whom I speak would ever acknowledge that Christ was born of a virgin and that he was more than a man; and he would tell how God made him ruler of the seraphims which guard his throne; and they call him also the Milken Way, and the Eliah of the Messiah; and many other high names; which though they be inferior to his divine majesty, yet they are far from the language of other Jews.

And for the country of Bensalem, this man would make no end of commending it; being desirous, by tradition among the Jews there, to have it believed that the people thereof were of the generations of Abraham, by another son, whom they call Nachoran; and that Moses by a secret Cabala ordained the Laws of Bensalem which they now use; and that when the Messiah should come, and sit in his throne at Hierusalem, the king of Bensalem should sit at his feet, whereas other kings should keep a great distance. But yet setting aside these Jewish dreams, the man was a wise man, and learned, and of great policy, and excellently seen in the laws and customs of that nation.

Amongst other discourses, one day I told him I was much affected with the relation I had, from some of the company, of their custom, in holding the Feast of the Family; for that (methought) I had never heard of a solemnity wherein nature did so much preside. And because propagation of families proceedeth from the nuptial copulation, I desired to know of him what laws and customs they had concerning marriage; and whether they kept marriage well and whether they were tied to one wife; for that where population is so much

489

affected,' and such as with them it seemed to be, there is commonly permission of plurality of wives.

To this he said, "You have reason for to commend that excellent institution of the Feast of the Family. And indeed we have experience that those families that are partakers of the blessing of that feast do flourish and prosper ever after in an extraordinary manner. But hear me now, and I will tell you what I know. You shall understand that there is not under the heavens so chaste a nation as this of Bensalem; nor so free from all pollution or foulness. It is the virgin of the world. I remember I have read in one of your European books, of an holy hermit amongst you that desired to see the Spirit of Fornication; and there appeared to him a little foul ugly Aethiop. But if he had desired to see the Spirit of Chastity of Bensalem, it would have appeared to him in the likeness of a fair beautiful Cherubim. For there is nothing amongst mortal men more fair and admirable, than the chaste minds of this people. Know therefore, that with them there are no stews, no dissolute houses, no courtesans, nor anything of that kind. Nay they wonder (with detestation) at you in Europe, which permit such things. They say ye have put marriage out of office: for marriage is ordained a remedy for unlawful concupiscence; and natural concupiscence seemeth as a spar to marriage. But when men have at hand a remedy more agreeable to their corrupt will, marriage is almost expulsed. And therefore there are with you seen infinite men that marry not, but chose rather a libertine and impure single life, than to be yoked in marriage; and many that do marry, marry late, when the prime and strength of their years is past. And when they do marry, what is marriage to them but a very bargain; wherein is sought alliance, or portion, or reputation, with some desire (almost indifferent) of issue; and not the faithful nuptial union of man and wife, that was first instituted. Neither is it possible that those that have cast away so basely so much of their strength, should greatly esteem children, (being of the same matter,) as chaste men do. So likewise during marriage, is the case much amended, as it ought to be if those things were tolerated only for necessity? No, but they remain still as a very affront to marriage. The haunting of those dissolute places, or resort to courtesans, are no more punished in married men than in bachelors. And the depraved custom of change, and the delight in meretricious embracements, (where sin is turned into art,) maketh marriage a dull thing, and a kind of imposition or tax. They hear you defend these things, as done to avoid greater evils; as advoutries, deflowering of virgins, unnatural lust, and the like. But they say this is a preposterous wisdom; and they call it Lot's offer, who to save his guests from abusing, offered his daughters: nay they say farther that there is little gained in this; for that the same vices and appetites do still remain and abound; unlawful lust being like a furnace, that if you stop the flames altogether, it will quench; but if you give it any vent, it will rage. As for masculine love, they have no touch of it; and yet there are not so faithful and inviolate friendships in the world again as are there; and to speak generally, (as I said before,) I have not read of any such chastity, in any people as theirs. And their usual saying is, That whosoever is unchaste cannot reverence himself; and they say, That the reverence of a man's self, is, next to religion, the chiefest bridle of all vices."

And when he had said this, the good Jew paused a little; whereupon I, far more willing to hear him speak on than to speak myself, yet thinking it decent that upon his pause of speech I should not be altogether silent, said only this; "That I would say to him, as the widow of Sarepta said to Elias; that he was come to bring to memory our sins; and that I confess the righteousness of Bensalem was greater than the righteousness of Europe." At which speech he bowed his head, and went on in this manner:

"They have also many wise and excellent laws touching marriage. They allow no polygamy. They have ordained that none do intermarry or contract, until a month be past from their first interview. Marriage without consent of parents they do not make void, but they mulct it in the inheritors: for the children of such marriages are not admitted to inherit above a third part of their parents' inheritance. I have read in a book of one of your men, of a Feigned Commonwealth, where the married couple are permitted, before they contract, to see one another naked. This they dislike; for they think it a scorn to give a refusal after so familiar knowledge: but because of many hidden defects in men and women's bodies, they have a more civil way; for they have near every town a couple of pools, (which they call Adam and Eve's pools,) where it is permitted to one of the friends of the men, and another of the friends of the woman, to see them severally bathe naked."

And as we were thus in conference, there came one that seemed to be a messenger, in a rich huke, that spake with the Jew: whereupon he turned to me and said; "You will pardon me, for I am commanded away in haste." The next morning he came to me again, joyful as it seemed, and said; "There is word come to the Governor of the city, that one of the Fathers of Salomon's House will be here this day seven-night: we have seen none of them this dozen years. His coming is in state; but the cause of his coming is secret. I will provide you and your fellows of a good standing to see his entry." I thanked him, and told him, I was most glad of the news.

The day being come, he made his entry. He was a man of middle stature and age, comely of person, and had an aspect as if he pitied men. He was clothed in a robe of fine black cloth, with wide sleeves and a cape. His under garment was of excellent white linen down to the foot, girt with a girdle of the same; and a sindon or tippet of the same about his neck. He had gloves, that were curious," and set with stone; and shoes of peach-coloured velvet. His neck was bare to the shoulders. His hat was like a helmet, or Spanish montera; and

491

his locks curled below it decently: they were of colour brown. His beard was cut round, and of the same colour with his hair, somewhat lighter. He was carried in a rich chariot without wheels, litter-wise; with two horses at either end, richly trapped in blue velvet embroidered; and two footmen on each side in the like attire. The chariot was all of cedar, gilt, and adorned with crystal; save that the fore-end had panels of sapphires, set in borders of gold; and the hinder-end the like of emeralds of the Peru colour. There was also a sun of gold, radiant, upon the top, in the midst; and on the top before, a small cherub of gold, with wings displayed. The chariot was covered with cloth of gold tissued upon blue. He had before him fifty attendants, young men all, in white satin loose coats to the mid leg; and stockings of white silk; and shoes of blue velvet; and hats of blue velvet; with fine plumes of diverse colours, set round like hat-bands. Next before the chariot, went two men, bare-headed, in linen garments down the foot, girt, and shoes of blue velvet; who carried, the one a crosier, the other a pastoral staff like a sheep-hook; neither of them of metal, but the crosier of balm-wood, the pastoral staff of cedar. Horsemen he had none, neither before nor behind his chariot: as it seemeth, to avoid all tumult and trouble. Behind his chariot went all the officers and principals of the companies of the city. He sat alone, upon cushions of a kind of excellent plush, blue; and under his foot curious carpets of silk of diverse colours, like the Persian, but far finer. He held up his bare hand as he went, as blessing the people, but in silence. The street was wonderfully well kept: so that there was never any army had their men stand in better battle-array than the people stood. The windows likewise were not crowded, but every one stood in them as if they had been placed.

When the shew was past, the Jew said to me; "I shall not be able to attend you as I would, in regard of some charge the city hath laid upon me, for the entertaining of this great person." Three days after the Jew came to me again, and said; "Ye are happy men; for the Father of Salomon's House taketh knowledge of your being here, and commanded me to tell you that he will admit all your company to his presence, and have private conference with one of you, that ye shall choose: and for this hath appointed the next day after to-morrow. And because he meaneth to give you his blessing, he hath appointed it in the forenoon."

We came at our day and hour, and I was chosen by my fellows for the private access. We found him in a fair chamber, richly hanged, and carpeted under foot without any degrees to the state. He was set upon a low Throne richly adorned, and a rich cloth of state over his head, of blue satin embroidered. He was alone, save that he had two pages of honour, on either hand one, finely attired in white. His under garments were the like that we saw him wear in the chariot; but instead of his gown, he had on him a mantle with a cape, of the same fine black, fastened about him. When we came in, as we were taught, we bowed low at our first entrance; and when we were come near his chair, he stood up, holding forth his hand ungloved, and in posture of blessing; and we every one of us stooped down, and kissed the hem of his tippet. That done, the rest departed, and I remained. Then he warned the pages forth of the room, and caused me to sit down beside him, and spake to me thus in the Spanish tongue.

"God bless thee, my son; I will give thee the greatest jewel I have. For I will impart unto thee, for the love of God and men, a relation of the true state of Salomon's House. Son, to make you know the true state of Salomon's House, I will keep this order. First, I will set forth unto you the end of our foundation. Secondly, the preparations and instruments we have for our works. Thirdly, the several employments and functions whereto our fellows are assigned. And fourthly, the ordinances and rites which we observe.

"The end of our foundation is the knowledge of causes, and secret motions of things; and the enlarging of the bounds of human empire, to the effecting of all things possible.

"The Preparations and Instruments are these. We have large and deep caves of several depths: the deepest are sunk six hundred fathom: and some of them are digged and made under great hills and mountains: so that if you reckon together the depth of the hill and the depth of the cave, they are (some of them) above three miles deep. For we find, that the depth of a hill, and the depth of a cave from the flat, is the same thing; both remote alike, from the sun and heaven's beams, and from the open air. These caves we call the Lower Region; and we use them for all coagulations, indurations, refrigerations, and conservations of bodies. We use them likewise for the imitation of natural mines; and the producing also of new artificial metals, by compositions and materials which we use, and lay there for many years. We use them also sometimes, (which may seem strange,) for curing of some diseases, and for prolongation of life in some hermits that choose to live there, well accommodated of all things necessary, and indeed live very long; by whom also we learn many things.

"We have burials in several earths, where we put diverse cements, as the Chineses do their porcellain. But we have them in greater variety, and some of them more fine. We have also great variety of composts and soils, for the making of the earth fruitful.

"We have high towers; the highest about half a mile in height; and some of them likewise set upon high mountains; so that the vantage of the hill with the tower is in the highest of them three miles at least. And these places we call the Upper Region; accounting the air between the high places and the low, as a Middle Region. We use these towers, according to their several heights, and situations, for insolation, refrigeration, conservation; and for the view of divers meteors; as winds, rain, snow, hail; and some of the fiery meteors also. And upon them, in some places, are dwellings of hermits, whom we visit sometimes, and instruct what to observe.

"We have great lakes, both salt, and fresh; whereof we have use for the fish and fowl. We use them also for burials of some natural bodies: for we find a difference in things buried in earth or in air below the earth, and things buried in water. We have also pools, of which some do strain fresh water out of salt; and others by art do turn fresh water into salt. We have also some rocks in the midst of the sea, and some bays upon the shore for some works, wherein is required the air and vapor of the sea. We have likewise violent streams and cataracts, which serve us for many motions: and likewise engines for multiplying and enforcing of winds, to set also on going diverse motions.

"We have also a number of artificial wells and fountains, made in imitation of the natural sources and baths; as tincted upon vitriol, sulphur, steel, brass, lead, nitre, and other minerals. And again we have little wells for infusions of many things, where the waters take the virtue quicker and better, than in vessels or basins. And amongst them we have a water which we call Water of Paradise, being, by that we do to it made very sovereign for health, and prolongation of life.

"We have also great and spacious houses where we imitate and demonstrate meteors; as snow, hail, rain, some artificial rains of bodies and not of water, thunders, lightnings; also generations of bodies in air; as frogs, flies, and divers others.

"We have also certain chambers, which we call Chambers of Health, where we qualify the air as we think good and proper for the cure of divers diseases, and preservation of health.

"We have also fair and large baths, of several mixtures, for the cure of diseases, and the restoring of man's body from arefaction: and others for the confirming of it in strength of sinewes, vital parts, and the very juice and substance of the body.

"We have also large and various orchards and gardens; wherein we do not so much respect beauty, as variety of ground and soil, proper for divers trees and herbs: and some very spacious, where trees and berries are set whereof we make divers kinds of drinks, besides the vineyards. In these we practise likewise all conclusions of grafting, and inoculating as well of wild-trees as fruit-trees, which produceth many effects. And we make (by art) in the same orchards and gardens, trees and flowers to come earlier or later than their seasons; and to come up and bear more speedily than by their natural course they do. We make them also by art greater much than their nature; and their fruit greater and sweeter and of differing taste, smell, colour, and figure, from their nature. And many of them we so order, as they become of medicinal use.

"We have also means to make divers plants rise by mixtures of earths without seeds; and likewise to make divers new plants, differing from the vulgar; and to make one tree or plant turn into another.

"We have also parks and enclosures of all sorts of beasts and birds which we use not only for view or rareness, but likewise for dissections and trials; that thereby we may take light what may be wrought upon the body of man. Wherein we find many strange effects; as continuing life in them, though divers parts, which you account vital, be perished and taken forth; resuscitating of some that seem dead in appearance; and the like. We try also all poisons and other medicines upon them, as well of chirurgery, as physic. By art likewise, we make them greater or taller than their kind is; and contrariwise dwarf them, and stay their growth: we make them more fruitful and bearing than their kind is; and contrariwise barren and not generative. Also we make them differ in colour, shape, activity, many ways. We find means to make commixtures and copulations of different kinds; which have produced many new kinds, and them not barren, as the general opinion is. We make a number of kinds of serpents, worms, flies, fishes, of putrefaction; whereof some are advanced (in effect) to be perfect creatures, like bests or birds; and have sexes, and do propagate. Neither do we this by chance, but we know beforehand, of what matter and commixture what kind of those creatures will arise.

"We have also particular pools, where we make trials upon fishes, as we have said before of beasts and birds.

"We have also places for breed and generation of those kinds of worms and flies which are of special use; such as are with you your silk-worms and bees.

"I will not hold you long with recounting of our brewhouses, bake-houses, and kitchens, where are made divers drinks, breads, and meats, rare and of special effects. Wines we have of grapes; and drinks of other juice of fruits, of grains, and of roots; and of mixtures with honey, sugar, manna, and fruits dried, and decocted; Also of the tears or woundings of trees; and of the pulp of canes. And these drinks are of several ages, some to the age or last of forty years. We have drinks also brewed with several herbs, and roots, and spices; yea with several fleshes, and white-meats; whereof some of the drinks are such, as they are in effect meat and drink both: so that divers, especially in age, do desire to live with them, with little or no meat or bread. And above all, we strive to have drink of extreme thin parts, to insinuate into the body, and yet without all biting, sharpness, or fretting; insomuch as some of them put upon the back of your hand will, with a little stay, pass through to the palm, and yet taste mild to the mouth. We have also waters which we ripen in that fashion, as they become nourishing; so that they are indeed excellent drink; and many will use no other. Breads we have of several grains, roots, and kernels; yea and some of flesh and fish dried; with divers kinds of leavenings and seasonings: so that

495

some do extremely move appetites; some do nourish so, as divers do live of them, without any other meat; who live very long. So for meats, we have some of them so beaten and made tender and mortified,' yet without all corrupting, as a weak heat of the stomach will turn them into good chylus; as well as a strong heat would meat otherwise prepared. We have some meats also and breads and drinks, which taken by men enable them to fast long after; and some other, that used make the very flesh of men's bodies sensibly' more hard and tough and their strength far greater than otherwise it would be.

"We have dispensatories, or shops of medicines. Wherein you may easily think, if we have such variety of plants and living creatures more than you have in Europe, (for we know what you have,) the simples, drugs, and ingredients of medicines, must likewise be in so much the greater variety. We have them likewise of divers ages, and long fermentations. And for their preparations, we have not only all manner of exquisite distillations and separations, and especially by gentle heats and percolations through divers strainers, yea and substances; but also exact forms of composition, whereby they incorporate almost, as they were natural simples.

"We have also divers mechanical arts, which you have not; and stuffs made by them; as papers, linen, silks, tissues; dainty works of feathers of wonderful lustre; excellent dies, and, many others; and shops likewise, as well for such as are not brought into vulgar use amongst us as for those that are. For you must know that of the things before recited, many of them are grown into use throughout the kingdom; but yet, if they did flow from our invention, we have of them also for patterns and principals.

"We have also furnaces of great diversities, and that keep great diversity of heats; fierce and quick; strong and constant; soft and mild; blown, quiet; dry, moist; and the like. But above all, we have heats, in imitation of the Sun's and heavenly bodies' heats, that pass divers inequalities, and (as it were) orbs, progresses, and returns, whereby we produce admirable effects. Besides, we have heats of dungs; and of bellies and maws of living creatures, and of their bloods and bodies; and of hays and herbs laid up moist; of lime unquenched; and such like. Instruments also which generate heat only by motion. And farther, places for strong insulations; and again, places under the earth, which by nature, or art, yield heat. These divers heats we use, as the nature of the operation, which we intend, requireth.

"We have also perspective-houses, where we make demonstrations of all lights and radiations; and of all colours: and out of things uncoloured and transparent, we can represent unto you all several colours; not in rain-bows, (as it is in gems, and prisms,) but of themselves single. We represent also all multiplications of light, which we carry to great distance, and make so sharp as to discern small points and lines. Also all colourations of light; all delusions and deceits of the sight, in figures, magnitudes, motions, colours all demonstrations of shadows. We find also divers means, yet unknown to you, of producing of light originally from divers bodies. We procure means of seeing objects afar off; as in the heaven and remote places; and represent things near as afar off; and things afar off as near; making feigned distances. We have also helps for the sight, far above spectacles and glasses in use. We have also glasses and means to see small and minute bodies perfectly and distinctly; as the shapes and colours of small flies and worms, grains and flaws in gems, which cannot otherwise be seen, observations in urine and blood not otherwise to be seen. We make artificial rain-bows, halo's, and circles about light. We represent also all manner of reflexions, refractions, and multiplications of visual beams of objects.

"We have also precious stones of all kinds, many of them of great beauty, and to you unknown; crystals likewise; and glasses of divers kinds; and amongst them some of metals vitrificated, and other materials besides those of which you make glass. Also a number of fossils, and imperfect minerals, which you have not. Likewise loadstones of prodigious virtue; and other rare stones, both natural and artificial.

"We have also sound-houses, where we practise and demonstrate all sounds, and their generation. We have harmonies which you have not, of quarter-sounds, and lesser slides of sounds. Divers instruments of music likewise to you unknown, some sweeter than any you have, together with bells and rings that are dainty and sweet. We represent small sounds as great and deep; likewise great sounds extenuate and sharp; we make divers tremblings and warblings of sounds, which in their original are entire. We represent and imitate all articulate sounds and letters, and the voices and notes of beasts and birds. We have certain helps which set to the ear do further the hearing greatly. We have also divers strange and artificial echoes, reflecting the voice many times, and as it were tossing it: and some that give back the voice louder than it came, some shriller, and some deeper; yea, some rendering the voice differing in the letters or articulate sound from that they receive. We have also means to convey sounds in trunks and pipes, in strange lines and distances.

"We have also perfume-houses; wherewith we join also practices of taste. We multiply smells, which may seem strange. We imitate smells, making all smells to breathe outs of other mixtures than those that give them. We make divers imitations of taste likewise, so that they will deceive any man's taste. And in this house we contain also a confiture-house; where we make all sweet-meats, dry and moist; and divers pleasant wines, milks, broths, and sallets; in far greater variety than you have.

"We have also engine-houses, where are prepared engines and instruments for all sorts of motions. There we imitate and practise to make swifter motions than any you have, either out of your muskets or any engine that you have: and to make them and multiply them more easily, and with small force, by wheels and other means: and to make them stronger and more violent than yours are; exceeding your greatest cannons and basilisks. We represent also ordnance and instruments of war, and engines of all kinds: and likewise new mixtures and compositions of gun-powder, wild-fires burning in water, and unquenchable. Also fireworks of all variety both for pleasure and use. We imitate also flights of birds; we have some degrees of flying in the air. We have ships and boats for going under water, and brooking of seas; also swimming-girdles and supporters. We have divers curious clocks, and other like motions of return: and some perpetual motions. We imitate also motions of living creatures, by images, of men, beasts, birds, fishes, and serpents. We have also a great number of other various motions, strange for equality, fineness, and subtilty.

"We have also a mathematical house, where are represented all instruments, as well of geometry as astronomy, exquisitely made.

"We have also houses of deceits of the senses; where we represent all manner of feats of juggling, false apparitions, impostures, and illusions; and their fallacies. And surely you will easily believe that we that have so many things truly natural which induce admiration, could in a world of particulars deceive the senses, if we would disguise those things and labour to make them seem more miraculous. But we do hate all impostures, and lies; insomuch as we have severely forbidden it to all our fellows, under pain of ignominy and fines, that they do not show any natural work or thing, adorned or swelling; but only pure as it is, and without all affectation of strangeness.

"These are (my son) the riches of Salomon's House.

"For the several employments and offices of our fellows; we have twelve that sail into foreign countries, under the names of other nations, (for our own we conceal); who bring us the books, and abstracts, and patterns of experiments of all other parts. These we call Merchants of Light.

"We have three that collect the experiments which are in all books. These we call Depredators.

"We have three that collect the experiments of all mechanical arts; and also of liberal sciences; and also of practices which are not brought into arts. These we call Mystery-men.

"We have three that try new experiments, such as themselves think good. These we call Pioneers or Miners.

"We have three that draw the experiments of the former four into titles and tables, to give the better light for the drawing of observations and axioms out of them. These we call Compilers.

"We have three that bend themselves, looking into the experiments of their fellows, and cast about how to draw out of them things of use and practise for man's life, and knowledge, as well for works as for plain demonstration of causes, means of natural divinations, and the easy and clear discovery of the virtues and parts of bodies. These we call Dowry-men or Benefactors.

"Then after divers meetings and consults of our whole number, to consider of the former labours and collections, we have three that take care, out of them, to direct new experiments, of a higher light, more penetrating into nature than the former. These we call Lamps.

"We have three others that do execute the experiments so directed, and report them. These we call Inoculators.

"Lastly, we have three that raise the former discoveries by experiments into greater observations, axioms, and aphorisms. These we call Interpreters of Nature.

"We have also, as you must think, novices and apprentices, that the succession of the former employed men do not fail; besides, a great number of servants and attendants, men and women. And this we do also: we have consultations, which of the inventions and experiences which we have discovered shall be published, and which not: and take all an oath of secrecy, for the concealing of those which we think fit to keep secret: though some of those we do reveal sometimes to the state and some not.

"For our ordinances and rites: we have two very long and fair galleries: in one of these we place patterns and samples of all manner of the more rare and excellent inventions in the other we place the statues of all principal inventors. There we have the statue of your Columbus, that discovered the West Indies: also the inventor of ships: your monk that was the inventor of ordnance and of gunpowder: the inventor of music: the inventor of letters: the inventor of printing: the inventor of observations of astronomy: the inventor of works in metal: the inventor of glass: the inventor of silk of the worm: the inventor of wine: the inventor of corn and bread: the inventor of sugars: and all these, by more certain tradition than you have. Then have we divers inventors of our own, of excellent works; which since you have not seen, it were too long to make descriptions of them; and besides, in the right understanding of those descriptions you might easily err. For upon every invention of value, we erect a statue to the inventor, and give him a liberal and honourable reward. These statues are some of brass; some of marble and touch-stone; some of cedar and other special woods gilt and adorned; some of iron; some of silver; some of gold.

"We have certain hymns and services, which we say daily, of Lord and thanks to God for his marvellous works: and forms of prayers, imploring his aid and blessing for the illumination of our labours, and the turning of them into good and holy uses.

"Lastly, we have circuits or visits of divers principal cities of the kingdom; where, as it cometh to pass, we do publish such new profitable inventions as we think good. And we do also declare natural divinations of diseases, plagues, swarms-of hurtful creatures, scarcity, tempests, earthquakes, great inundations, comets, temperature of the year, and divers other things; and we give counsel thereupon, what the people shall do for the prevention and remedy of them."

And when he had said this, he stood up; and I, as I had been taught, kneeled down, and he laid his right hand upon my head, and said; "God bless thee, my son; and God bless this relation, which I have made. I give thee leave to publish it for the good of other nations; for we here are in God's bosom, a land unknown." And so he left me; having assigned a value of about two thousand ducats, for a bounty to me and my fellows. For they give great largesses where they come upon all occasions.

[The rest was not perfected.]

Made in the USA
Las Vegas, NV
06 November 2023

80324184R00275